PENGUIN CLASSICS

THE EGYPTIAN BOOK OF THE DEAD

ERNEST ALFRED THOMPSON WALLIS BUDGE (1857–1934) was Keeper of the Department of Egyptian and Assyrian Antiquities at the British Museum for thirty years. Knighted for services to the Museum, Budge travelled widely on its behalf throughout the Middle East, collecting an enormous number of antiquities and excavating at many sites in Egypt, the Sudan and in Iraq. Born of a poor Cornish family and something of a child prodigy, Budge had earlier worked as a runner at a London stationers for eight years, deciphering Assyrian cuneiform texts in his spare time, before finally obtaining a scholarship to Cambridge University and his long-dreamt-of employment at the British Museum. Working with an astonishing variety of ancient languages, Budge eventually published an unmatched 140 major works, many of them pioneering translations, dealing with texts and objects in the British Museum's collections that he himself had found. Although his manner raised the ire of many of his colleagues, Budge was a vivid writer and a great popularizer – a man who, it was later said, had done 'more than anyone to arouse an interest in the language and writings of ancient Egypt'.

JOHN ROMER graduated from the Royal College of Art in 1966 and began his work in Middle Eastern archaeology shortly thereafter, serving on American and German expeditions in Egyptian Thebes and acting as Field Director of the Brooklyn Museum Theban Expedition, conducting the first physical survey and conservation studies in the Valley of the Kings, and excavating the tomb of Ramesses XI. Romer has also dedicated a great part of his time to archaeological conservation and, as an aid to raising public awareness of the importance and fragility of the past, has made many TV and radio documentaries, to international critical acclaim. Besides numerous specialist articles and reports, his books have included *Valley of the Kings*, *Ancient Lives: The Story of the Pharaohs' Tombmakers*, *Testament: The Bible and History* and *The Seven Wonders of the World: A History of the Modern Imagination* (with Elizabeth Romer). His latest book is *The Great Pyramid: Ancient Egypt Revisited* (2007).

John and Elizabeth Romer live and work around the Mediterranean and the Middle East, and share a house in Tuscany.

E. A. WALLIS BUDGE

The Egyptian Book of the Dead

With a new Introduction by JOHN ROMER

PENGUIN BOOKS

PENGUIN CLASSICS

Published by the Penguin Group
Penguin Books Ltd, 80 Strand, London WC2R 0RL, England
Penguin Group (USA) Inc., 375 Hudson Street, New York, New York 10014, USA
Penguin Group (Canada), 90 Eglinton Avenue East, Suite 700, Toronto, Ontario, Canada M4P 2Y3
(a division of Pearson Penguin Canada Inc.)
Penguin Ireland, 25 St Stephen's Green, Dublin 2, Ireland (a division of Penguin Books Ltd)
Penguin Group (Australia), 250 Camberwell Road, Camberwell, Victoria 3124, Australia
(a division of Pearson Australia Group Pty Ltd)
Penguin Books India Pvt Ltd, 11 Community Centre, Panchsheel Park, New Delhi – 110 017, India
Penguin Group (NZ), 67 Apollo Drive, Rosedale, North Shore 0632, New Zealand
(a division of Pearson New Zealand Ltd)
Penguin Books (South Africa) (Pty) Ltd, 24 Sturdee Avenue,
Rosebank, Johannesburg 2196, South Africa

Penguin Books Ltd, Registered Offices: 80 Strand, London WC2R 0RL, England
www.penguin.com

First published in Great Britain as *The Book of the Dead* by Kegan Paul, Trench, Trubner 1899
One-volume revised edition published 1923
This edition first published in Penguin Classics 2008
013

Printed in England by Clays Ltd, St Ives plc

ISBN: 978-0-140-45550-2

www.greenpenguin.co.uk

CONTENTS

THE EGYPTIAN BOOK OF THE DEAD

PART I.

PART II.

PART III.

INTRODUCTION
to this Edition by John Romer

This book is part of our intellectual history. Just as John Bull is British, the Eiffel Tower is French, and God often speaks in King James English, so this particular Book of the Dead is an integral part of what we now call 'ancient Egypt'. Apart from the sacred texts of the great religions, it is also the bestselling edition of any ancient text. And its influence extends beyond the realms of ancient history.

The remarkable celebrity of these ancient funerary texts is due to their translator, Sir Ernest Alfred Thompson Wallis Budge. His was the first edition of the Book of the Dead to have been produced in English in a convenient and inexpensive format. Published in 1899 and re-issued in 1909 in an enlarged and revised three-volume edition – the version given here – it has remained continuously in print. From T. S. Eliot, Ezra Pound and William Faulkner to J. R. R. Tolkien and Norman Mailer, everyone read and absorbed the contents of Budge's compact book with its yellow dust-jacket, its light brown buckram binding and its inky illustrations.

The book's greatest influence flowed through the meticulous pen of Sir James Frazer, Budge's near-contemporary at Cambridge and, arguably, the world's most influential anthropologist. Frazer's famed Osiris, one of the 'dying and resurrecting gods' on whom he lavished several bestselling volumes, is largely drawn from Budge's Book of the Dead – a borrowing that Budge reciprocated in his last work, which was, in turn, partly based on Frazer's *Golden Bough*. It is unlikely, though, that either Budge or Frazer were happy with the uses to which Sigmund Freud and Carl Jung put their joint researches, and to such vast effect.

Curiously enough, when Jean-François Champollion, the decipherer of hieroglyphs, first read some of ancient Egypt's funerary scrolls in the 1820s, the West was disappointed. Though studious antiquaries had long maintained that they held forgotten wisdoms, Champollion declared that their diffuse and difficult calligraphy appeared to record nothing but the rites of ancient funerals. A few years later, a closer study by Dr Richard Lepsius, a Berlin professor and Champollion's successor, established that some of these scrolls also appeared to contain words spoken by the dead themselves. Yet later, Lepsius came to understand that they also held an even wider diversity of themes within them – prayers, incantations, hymns, dialogues, confessionals, lamentations and rituals – each one divided from its neighbour by pretty illustrations.

In 1842 Lepsius published the first modern edition of one of these funerary scrolls, setting its ancient text into 165 separate chapters, and rendering the abbreviate forms of its cursive script into long lines of formal hieroglyphics that could easily be read by egyptologists. Entitling his work

Das Todtenbuch der Aegypter, derived from the Arabic phrase *Kitab al Mayyitun* – 'dead people's books' – that had long been used by Egyptian villagers to describe the scrolls they occasionally found beside the mummies of the ancient dead, Lepsius perpetuated the generic name that Champollion had first given the scrolls. And, when in 1867 Dr Samuel Birch of the British Museum published an English translation of Lepsius' hieroglyphics, he re-confirmed this designation in his direct translation into English as 'The Book of the Dead'.

After Lepsius, all that was required to constitute the Book of the Dead that Budge would later use was the compilation of a broad anthology of texts taken from a range of ancient sources. This work began in 1874, at a Congress of Orientalists, when Lepsius proposed that a Book of the Dead should be assembled in the manner of European classical scholars – who, for centuries past, had devoted a great part of their time to distilling masses of contradictory, damaged and even garbled versions of surviving Greek and Roman manuscripts into perfected texts that, in the opinion of their compilers, were as close to their supposed lost originals as possible.

And so it was, some twelve years later, that a three-volume edition of the Book of the Dead – compiled by that 'most competent scholar' Henri Édouard Naville of Geneva – was published in Berlin. Comparing and correcting the texts of seventy-seven different papyri, some written during the period when the ancient Greeks had ruled in Egypt and others that were older by a thousand years, Naville's hieroglyphics were separated out both by Lepsius' chapter divisions and, also, by copies of the papyri's ancient illustrations – these being the so-called 'vignettes' – drawn by Madame Naville. This, with additions, alterations and emendations, is the standard hieroglyphic version of the Book of the Dead that is still used today.

Like so much to do with 'ancient Egypt', the Book of the Dead is a scholarly illusion conjured from the randomly surviving relics of a distant past. No 'genuine' ancient version of it has ever been discovered and, considering that it was compiled from a wide variety of sources, nor is such a find remotely likely.

Such abstract scholarship, however, can be very useful: 'perfected' texts make handy primers that enable the remains of otherwise unintelligible ancient documents to be understood. Yet at the same time, they can also blind us to reality. Imagine, for example, that seventy-seven versions of the New Testament and its related literature were combined into a similar 'perfected' version. The individual qualities of each source text would be entirely lost, as would all traces of the documents' development through time and space. Inevitably, as well, such 'perfected' compilations must reflect the attitudes and beliefs of their compilers. And so it is with Naville's Book of the Dead: whilst it has helped to shape our modern vision of ancient Egypt and unscramble many damaged documents, it has also served to give the relics of that intelligent and most inventive culture a fixed identity in which millions of its people have been posed in set religious attitudes for millennia upon millennia.

However, it is undeniable that Naville's Book of the Dead holds the constant themes of ancient Egypt's funerary literature within its hieroglyphs. Just as John Bull and the Eiffel Tower represent something of the essential character of their respective cultures, so Naville's Book of the Dead contains much of the funerary literature that literate Egyptians living in the latter half of their ancient history would have recognized as an essential ingredient of a proper burial.

Let a document be written for me, (for) inside the coffin of Aleppo-pinewood in which it will be placed. Let the papyrus-roll be placed within my mummy. (In the) writing (of) Nesmin.

Scribbled in the late fourth century BC, this rare short text was composed by a man ordering a funerary papyrus; some of his texts would be destined to appear in a 'perfected' form in Naville's Book of the Dead. Written out in various combinations and on a variety of media, such funerary texts were common enough from around 1500 BC for a period of some 2,000 years. Generally, they are a kind of passport to the afterlife. They usually provide descriptions of the journey on which each individual will embark at death, and they offer advice and aid. As with Egypt's other funerary texts, they describe aspects of the ancient Egyptian universe. Following the elaborate rites of funeral, the dead are enabled to travel once again on desert roads, within the green flat fields beside the Nile's bank, and in boats upon it; they travel as well through the agricultural year, and with the daily passage of the sun and the moon; through guarded gateways to a Hall of Judgement where one's fate was sealed in the manner of the Christian Book of the Apocalypse. It is a journey from death and burial to the darkest caverns and to the eternal stars, and on the way the dead enter fiery pits, confront snakes and flesh-eaters; they meet ferrymen and gods and kings.

Unlike the smooth calm of the ancient tombs, these funerary texts display a fear of death and an anxiety to partially revive the dead so that they can communicate again. Thus, they also show a care towards the living. They deal in universal human experiences, and therefore they are of universal interest.

The extraordinary success of Budge's translation, however, is due to its specific qualities and, also, to the circumstances of its publication. Widely read throughout a bloody century, at a time when many people were preoccupied with notions of the survival of the spirit after death, the Book of the Dead dealt at length with something that receives but scant attention in the Christian Bible. Half-blind and worrying about darkness, death and resurrection, James Joyce, for one, was fascinated. As one might expect, he collected up and scribbled down such Budgian phrases as the 'great cackler' as he thumbed through Budge's tome, along with such lovely confabulations of scholarly jargon as 'Heliotropolis', 'Horuscoups' and 'Mastabatooms'. Yet Joyce also responded to the lilt and span of Budge's prose, as this speech from *Finnegans Wake* (1939) quite clearly shows:

So may the priest of seven worms and scalding tayboil, Papa Vestray, come never anear you as your hair grows wheater beside the Liffey that's in Heaven! Hep, hep, hurrah there! Hero! Seven times thereto we salute you! . . . Your heart is in the system of the Shewolf and your crested head is in the tropic of Copricapron. Your feet are in the cloister of Virgo. Your olala is in the region of sahuls.

Most obvious, in this masterly parody, is the use of Biblicalese; fifty years on, Philip Glass's opera *Akhnaten* also employed Budge's elliptical and rhythmic text to good effect; even Jim Morrison, indeed, nodded, on occasion, towards Sir Ernest's antique scansions.

Yet Budge's prose is founded on a wider range of sources than Jacobean English. Coming to ancient Egyptian after years of working with other Middle Eastern languages, his Book of the Dead also holds something of the exoticism and the rhythms of ancient Ethiopian and early Coptic liturgy, and of Assyrian and Aramaic, too. And Budge, of course, was a master storyteller with a quick eye for a literary image, as his memoirs show. It is hardly surprising, then, that this exotic translation entered so completely into the imagination of the early twentieth century, with its fascination with primitivism, spiritualism and the occult.

What is most surprising, though, is that the author of this influential book, Sir Ernest Alfred Thompson Wallis Budge, MA and Litt.D. Cantab, MA and D.Litt. Oxon, D.Lit. Durham, Fellow of the Society of Antiquaries, Keeper of Egyptian and Assyrian Antiquities at the British Museum for thirty years and knighted for his devotion to those same collections during the First World War, has all but been disowned by his own profession. Budge, indeed, is something of an embarrassment to it, and that, in turn, accords this celebrated book a certain notoriety.

The story is still difficult to fathom. Beside his papers at the British Museum, not much is left of Budge beyond a book of tales of his early life and travels, some blurred photographs of a portly civil servant and a knighted courtier, and two generous university scholarships, named for Lady Wallis Budge, his wife. And a truly enormous shelf of books, for Budge wrote more than 140 finished works, many of which are in several separate volumes, an output unmatched by any other Orientalist.

Budge, as you may have gathered, was something of a prodigy. Born in 1857, the illegitimate son of a Cornishwoman and brought to London as a child, he spent his youth working as a runner in W. H. Smith's bookshop on the Strand where, he said, he passed the time by translating Assyrian texts and dreaming of a post at the British Museum. Whilst still at Smith's, he also corresponded with William Gladstone, the Prime Minister, successfully convincing him to establish a subscription list to support him during three years of study for a degree in ancient languages at Cambridge University. Small wonder that this unlikely happenstance later provoked the rumour that Budge was the illegitimate son of royalty! The truth, however, is probably less romantic. It would appear that Gladstone, who was passionately interested in the relics of the ancient East, had realized that the British Museum required an enlarged bureaucracy to continue cataloguing and translating its ever growing collections. For more than forty years, a great part of this enormous task had been performed by Dr Samuel Birch, a Keeper of Antiquities: after his graduation from Cambridge University, Budge was well equipped to assist in this work. And that, indeed, is how he spent his life; the better part of Budge's books have direct connections to the Museum's vast collections.

Being fatherless, Budge seems to have become particularly attached to some of the people and institutions that figured in his early life – from W. H. Smith, who gave him £150 and time off to prepare for his entrance exam to Cambridge, to the British Museum itself (he even published a small volume in his old age entitled *Mike, the Museum Cat*). Above all, however, Budge followed the hardworking routines of Dr Birch, whose broad-brimmed black silk stove-pipe hat, he later remembered, had been 'quite the worst in the Museum' and so thick with dust that 'with the help of a little water, peas might be planted in it and they would grow'. It had been the dusty Dr Birch, though, who in 1883 began to teach the young admiring Budge to read Egyptian hieroglyphics, when he joined the staff of the museum.

Samuel Birch, who had known the great Champollion himself, was a prodigious pioneering scholar. Budge, on the other hand, was never much interested in grammar or lexicography for their own sakes; he used them as a tool in his life's work of translating and cataloguing the museum's collections, and teaching the public about them. So the reforms and discoveries of the so-called Berlin School, which from the 1890s dominated and transformed the study of the ancient Egyptian language, had little influence upon Budge, either on his publications or indeed on the labels or the catalogues of the British Museum which, by the turn of the twentieth century, were scandalously out of date. Not that Budge seems to have cared. Up until he retired in 1924, by which time his contemporaries were travelling to the British Museum by the London Underground and not on horseback as many of his earlier colleagues had done, he would not even use a typewriter.

Not surprisingly, both Birch and Budge in turn were hostile to the emerging professions of archaeology and egyptology. Both of them were used to working with aristocratic amateurs – clever individuals who spent time in Egypt and Iraq and who, on their return to England, graciously presented their collections to the nation and expected, in return, the nation's civil servants to translate, conserve and label them. Neither Birch nor Budge had much time or patience for the cool and careful scholarship of middle-class professionals who, by the 1880s, were transforming egyptology into a modern academic subject. When the forerunner to the modern Egypt Exploration Society was founded to enable the scientific excavation of Egypt by professional egyptologists, both were implacably opposed – and they, of course – civil servants at the British Museum – were the public face of egyptology. Thirty years later, long after Birch had died, Budge was still employing the irascible manners of his youth to hold back this same inevitable tide, on one occasion in the public galleries loudly informing an eminent American egyptologist, who had travelled from Egypt to London expressly to examine a royal coffin, that 'it was a damn fool request' and that he was 'trying to paint the lily'. Though he had simply walked away, the visiting archaeologist recalled that he had felt like hitting this vulgar ill-bred boor right in his puffy face.

By that time, old Budge had alienated virtually all of the younger generations of his profession. In that same year, 1920, and, again, to their acute embarrassment, he published – to popular acclaim – a rollicking two-volume account of his early travels through the East collecting for the British Museum. One of its many scandalous stories describes his participation in the theft of a funerary papyrus from an Egyptian government storeroom, and how he had arranged with officers of the British Administration to have it posted to the museum where, after Budge had published it in fine facsimile as the 'Papyrus of Ani', it became one of the most celebrated Books of the Dead in all the world. No wonder that Budge's nickname among the profession was 'Bugbear'. That such a fellow could have compiled such an informative and influential work as the Book of the Dead must have been doubly vexing.

So how, then, does the old Bugbear's translation stand up today? Here, for direct comparison, set below Budge's earlier version, are fragments of two modern versions of Chapter 30 of the Book of the Dead. Both were published in the 1970s, one by an English scholar, Raymond Faulkner – the most respected contemporary translator of ancient Egyptian religious texts – the other by Miriam Lichtheim – an American Egyptologist, widely regarded as one of the very finest translators of ancient Egyptian literature.

First, then, Budge's version (from page 150):

THE CHAPTER OF NOT LETTING THE HEART OF OSIRIS, THE SCRIBE OF THE HOLY OFFERINGS OF ALL THE GODS, ANI, TRIUMPHANT, BE DRIVEN FROM HIM IN THE UNDERWORLD. He saith:-

'My heart, my mother; my heart, my mother! My heart whereby I came into being! May naught stand up to oppose me at [my] judgment; may there be no opposition to me in the presence of the sovereign princes (*Tchatcha*); may there be no parting of thee from me in the presence of him that keepeth the Balance!'

Next, Faulkner's:

Spell for not letting N's heart create opposition against him in the realm of the dead

O my heart which I had from my mother, O my heart which I had upon earth, do not rise up against me as a witness in the presence of the Lord of Things; do not speak against me concerning what I have done, do not bring up anything against me in the presence of the Great God, Lord of the West.

Finally, Lichtheim's:

The heart as witness

Formula for not letting the heart of N oppose him in the necropolis. He shall say:

O my heart of my mother,
O my heart of my mother,
O my heart of my being! Do not rise up against me as witness,
Do not oppose me in the tribunal,
Do not rebel against me before the guardian of the scales!

The first thing to be noticed – and, given Budge's reputation, this is extraordinary – is how little the burden of his text differs from the two modern ones. There is as much divergence between the two modern translations themselves as there is between these two and that of Budge.

Both modern versions, though, are easier to read. Budge's *thee*s and *eth*s have been cast aside, along with the rhythms of his prose, the explanatory commentaries, and the elaborate and lengthy apparatus of Victorian scholarship. To a modern reader, the immediate effect is that both modern versions appear more accurate and 'closer' to the ancient original than Budge's.

Yet the differences between the two modern translations show that their authors are still exercising a considerable degree of personal choice. Faulkner, indeed, tells us directly that once the rules of grammar and the dictionary have been met, significant margins of doubt as to the meaning of such ancient texts still remain; that ultimately their translators' final choice of words depends upon 'an intuitive appreciation of the trend of the ancient writer's mind'. How, then, does such intuition work? Sometimes the translators offer us clues. Lichtheim, as her introduction shows, believes the papyri's ancient authors may well have been naive or even primitive, for as she notes they yoke magic and morality together, though 'they remain incompatible'. Faulkner, unfortunately, never tells us how he made his choices.

Budge, on the other hand, most surely does. A man of confident transparency, with views typical of the late nineteenth-century West, his expansive notes and commentaries to his Book of the Dead display his attitudes for all to see. Above all – and this is really surprising for a time when most of his contemporaries held ancient religion to be little more than savage superstition – he is concerned to show us that a subtle living faith is held within these ancient texts. His commentaries describe a morality in the Book of the Dead, the discovery of which is usually credited to scholars of succeeding generations.

It is interesting that Dr Birch's much earlier translation of Lepsius' *Todtenbuch* had been written in language close to the English of the day. Budge, however, took up the tone of the King James Bible, in an attempt, it would appear, to grasp something of the religiosity he sensed behind the hieroglyphs, to implant humility into his translation. In contrast, the two modern versions stand together like Osbert Lancaster's description of a modern building set up beside a baroque palace: 'No attempt was made to achieve any unconvincing pastiche and the result was immediately recognized as a forthright and welcome expression of twentieth-century ideals in a contemporary idiom.'

Budge's version displays other virtues too. Unlike most translators who work from the synthetic forms of Naville's redaction, Budge, although following Lepsius' chapter order, acknowledges the integrity of every individual ancient papyrus by translating one document at a time. And by placing different versions of the same text side by side, he lets us see the different facets of the text. So whilst other versions can only give a generic 'N', for 'Name', and so lose all touch with time and individuality, Budge names the individual for whom the specific text was written – in the instance given above, this is the 'Osiris' – that is, the dead form – of the long-suffering Ani, of the purloined papyrus.

Budge's Book of the Dead also provides generous numbers of 'vignettes', each one drawn from individual ancient papyri. Like the hieroglyphic pictograms whose images define the meaning of the words spelled out beside them, these little drawings show the stage on which the accompanying texts are set. So, for example, Budge's vignettes (on pages 149 and 150) that illuminate the translation that I quote above, show that the accompanying text is concerned with an event in which the heart of the dead person is weighed upon a balance. Although Lichteim does not tell us the source of her information, she also uses this pictorial material in the last line of her translation when she alludes to 'the scales': Faulkner, a grammarian, utterly ignores it. Budge, though, as well as providing two vignettes, also adds two lively commentaries on this remarkable event (pages cxl–cxli and pages 21–34), which, as he alone points out, is a description in both words and pictures of the oldest recorded Last Judgement scene in human history!

And yet, despite such obvious advantages, Budge's text still presents a major problem to modern students. As workmanlike, as instinctive and as idiosyncratic as a nineteenth-century bridge, his translation is also, like a nineteenth-century bridge, quite out of date. Even at the time of its first publication his understanding of the ancient grammar was old-fashioned, as were his renderings of ancient names and places.

However, the other modern versions of the Book of the Dead are out of date as well. A vast mass of scholarly research has been undertaken in the years since they were made. And in 1984, a computerized database was established in the Universities of Cologne and Bonn; this currently holds some 1,500 records and exemplars of funerary texts that contain chapters of the Book of the Dead. Scholars need no longer work from Naville's synthesis at all. Those with a good command of ancient Egyptian can read most of the variant texts themselves, plot their changes through both time and space and even, on occasion, identify the individual hands of the ancient scribes who wrote them. For such scholars the 'Book of the Dead' itself may be said to have disappeared.

Yet the burden, theologies and underlying significance of these ancient texts still seem elusive. And nowadays, many of the most modern commentaries on them have taken to quoting Budge's Book of the Dead as a prime source of information and opinion. Being 'out of date', it seems, is relative. And Budge's book is the only one to comment upon the texts in such a way as to allow us to see both the ancient scribes and their translator side by side, and sitting at their work.

How, then, should one read this extraordinary book? It is best, I would suggest, to slide through its texts as one might read *Finnegans Wake*, marvelling all the while at the expansive scholarship, and at the lilt and span of its exotic prose. Better not to begin, as might a modern literary student, with the ambition to understand each and every word. For this you would require the use of a substantial egyptological library, and access to the database in Bonn and Cologne. And even then, right from the early lines of Budge's translation – 'The chapter of making the Sahu to enter into the Tuat (i.e. Underworld)' – the questions that most readily arise are not really to be answered by the information that modern egyptologists now call the 'Tuat', the 'Duat', nor, even, by Budge's generous footnote discussing the meaning of the term 'Sahu'. Like the major part of the text that follows, a full explanation of these ancient lines is still a long way off.

Ultimately, the 'full explanation' will depend upon cracking the code that once filled the ancient words of our Book of the Dead with real meaning. A code such as this is held in the spare words of the Lord's Prayer that Christians have imbued with meanings far beyond the information given in the text itself, which tells us that it is a prayer addressed to a common father who is the king of heaven and who may or may not provide supplicants with a daily bread ration. The same Christian code, of course, ratifies the apparently contradictory texts that tell us that this same God had but a single son, and that he is at the same time three in one – a deeply coded concept that the *Oxford Dictionary of the Christian Church* informs us 'is held to be a mystery in the strict sense, in that it can neither be known by unaided human reason . . . nor demonstrated by reason after it has been revealed'.

And so it was, perhaps, for those millennial Egyptians who, like Nesmin, took funerary papyri into the grave – papyri whose texts and pictures were filled with meanings and significance that had changed so much through the ages so that neither Nesmin nor the scribes who wrote out the words understood them in the way that we today would wish to understand them. What is left for us are kaleidoscopic hints of meaning, and prose that shimmers off the page.

Headed towards death, language turns back upon itself: it encounters something like a mirror, and to stop this death which would stop it, it possesses but a single power; that of giving birth to its own image in a play of mirrors that has no limits. (Michel Foucault)

John Romer, 2008

HISTORICAL OUTLINE

In the decades after Henri Édouard Naville's publication of the Book of the Dead in 1886, two similar compilations of ancient Egyptian religious texts were undertaken – work that is still ongoing. The first of these was based upon a mass of funerary texts that were discovered on the walls of previously unexcavated pyramids. The second collection was founded on a body of inscriptions on a series of massive wooden coffins exhibited in the Cairo Museum.

Each of these three scholarly compilations – which Budge calls 'recensions' – are based on groups of texts that were created one after the other during the three phases of ancient Egyptian history, the three 'kingdoms', when the state was centralized and monuments of stone were made. Thus, the so-called 'Pyramid Texts' that contain the oldest known religious literature are dated to the Old Kingdom, which began about 3000 BC and lasted for eight centuries. (More precisely the first known examples of the Pyramid Texts, and a near-perfectly preserved corpus in their own right, were engraved *c.* 2257–2237 BC on the interior chambers and corridors of the Pyramid of Unis.)

The second compilation, dubbed the 'Coffin Texts', is dated to the so-called Middle Kingdom, which began about

2150 BC and lasted for 400 years. The third compilation, the Book of the Dead, is dated to the five-century-long New Kingdom, which began about 1550 BC, though a few chapters are known that are half a century older. Many other religious texts, some of them elaborate and integrated compositions, also appear to have been composed during that period of time.

Extensive collections of chapters that appear in the Book of the Dead also continued to be used in burials throughout the Late Period (from around 700 BC) and down into Ptolemaic and Roman times, just as did some of the chapters – sometimes known as 'spells' – from the Pyramid Texts and the Coffin Texts until, eventually, the pagan faith was banned by order of the Christian Roman emperors.

Erik Hornung's *Ancient Egyptian Books of the Afterlife* (Ithaca, 1999) sets the Book of the Dead into this broader ancient context, and provides an overview of modern scholarship upon the subject.

FURTHER READING AND SOURCES

The Literary Influence of Budge's Book of the Dead

No one, to my knowledge, has catalogued the effect of Budge's Book of the Dead upon modern culture. Its influence on James Frazer's *The Golden Bough*, however, is briefly outlined in Robert Ackerman's *J. G. Frazer* (Cambridge, 1987). The book by Budge that in turn was influenced by Frazer's writings was his *Osiris and the Egyptian Resurrection* (London, 1911).

As for James Joyce, the very structure of his final novel – *Finnegans Wake* (1939) – owes so much to Budge's Book of the Dead that a recent commentary, (John Bishop, 1986), is entitled *Joyce's Book of the Dark: Finnegans Wake. Notebook* VI B 52, pp. 11–14, of *The 'Finnegans Wake' Notebooks at Buffalo* (Turnhout, Belgium, 2004) details Joyce's use of one of Budge's Museum pamphlets, *The Book of the Dead* (London, 1922), outlining the contents of the ancient texts.

In the *Sunday Times* of 5 June 1983, Norman Mailer says, 'I read A. Wallis-Bridge [sic] – a great British egyptologist – the Book of the Dead – and I was a goner. Egypt it was, for eleven years.' The product was his *Ancient Evenings* (New York, 1983). Hana Navratilova (*Acta Orientalia* 71.4, 2003) reports J. R. R. Tolkien as describing the inhabitants of Middle Earth as 'best pictured in Egyptian terms'; that Tolkien's Egypt was largely drawn from Budge's Book of the Dead is underlined by Tolkien's sketches of his protagonists' helmets, which are derived from the Book's vignettes.

Budge's book has also had long and lasting influence upon Hollywood's vision of ancient Egypt – witness, for example, the three *Mummy* films of 1933, 1999 and 2001. In many modern esoteric faiths, as well, born of Theosophy and Rosicrucianism, Budge's translation has become the language of the ancient gods, and the division of its chapters marks the order of their worship.

Translations of the Book of the Dead, and books on ancient Egypt

The latest edition of R. O. Faulkner's translation, *The Book of the Dead*, was published in 1985 (London & Texas). His comments upon translation are in the Introduction to his *Ancient Egyptian Pyramid Texts* (Oxford, 1969). Miriam Lichtheim's partial translations from the Book of the Dead are found in Volume 2 of her *Ancient Egyptian Literature* (Berkeley, CA, 1976). A useful third alternative is T. G. Allen's *The Book of the Dead or Going Forth By Day* (Chicago, 1974), which contains tables showing how some chapters are related to much older texts.

Samuel Birch's English translation of Richard Lepsius' *Todtenbuch* first appeared in Volume 5 of Christian Bunsen's *Egypt's Place in Universal History* (London, 1867).

The Introduction to Erik Hornung's German translation *Das Todtenbuch der Ägypter* (Zurich, 1979) holds the best account of the scholarship that grew up around the Book of the Dead; his text also provides extensive references to studies on its individual chapters, and lists the tombs and other artefacts where some of its individual chapters are also inscribed.

Information on the ongoing Book of the Dead project at

the Universities of Bonn and Cologne may be found at: www.uni-bonn.de/en/www/Book_of_the_Dead_Project/

Intended for the general reader, Barry Kemp's *The Egyptian Book of the Dead* (Oxford, 2007), provides a thoughtful commentary on the ancient text; the same author's *Ancient Egypt* (2nd edn, London, 2005) is the best modern overview of ancient Egyptian culture.

The Oxford History of Ancient Egypt (ed. I. Shaw, Oxford, 2000) offers an excellent contemporary account of ancient Egyptian history, whilst Jan Assmann's *The Search for God in Ancient Egypt* (Ithaca, 2001) and *The Mind of Egypt* (New York, 2002) provide masterly descriptions of the mentalities that shaped ancient Egyptian religious and social life throughout its history.

Nesmin's order for the writing of his funerary papyrus is translated by Cary J. Martin and Kim Ryholt in *The Journal of Egyptian Archaeology* 92, 2006.

Sir E. A. Wallis Budge

No full biography of Wallis Budge has yet been published. Though frequently traduced, his lively autobiographic memoir *By Nile and Tigris* (London, 1920) gives a flavour of the man in his heyday; Robert Morrell's '*Budgie*' (privately printed, 2002) somewhat innocently rises to his defence, and presents fresh evidence concerning Budge's private life.

The account of Budge's row with the American archaeologist can be found, along with a discussion of other of his misdemeanours, in Julie Hankey's *A Passion for Egypt* (London, 2001). A more friendly picture of the Keeper in his prime emerges from I. E. S. Edwards's *From the Pyramids to Tutankhamun* (Oxford, 2000). Birch's opposition to the newborn Egypt

Excavation Fund is outlined in Margaret Drower's essay in *Excavating in Egypt* (London, 1982); this same author provides further information about Wallis Budge in *Flinders Petrie* (London, 1985).

The quotation from Osbert Lancaster was taken from *Scene Changes* (London, 1978); that from Michel Foucault, from an essay in *Self and Form in Modern Narrative* by Vincent Pecora (Baltimore, 1989).

PREFACE

THE translations of the Egyptian hymns and religious texts printed in this and the two following volumes form a representative collection of the various compositions which the Egyptians inscribed upon the walls of tombs and sarcophagi, coffins and funeral stelae, papyri and amulets, etc., in order to ensure the well-being of their dead in the world beyond the grave. They have been translated from papyri and other documents which were found chiefly at Thebes, and, taken together, they are generally known as the Theban Recension of the Book of the Dead, that is to say, the Recension of the great national funeral work which was copied by the scribes for themselves and for Egyptian kings and queens, princes and nobles, gentle and simple, rich and poor, from about B.C. 1600 to B.C. 900. These translations first appeared in the third volume of my work on the Book of the Dead, which was published under the title of "The Chapters of Coming Forth by Day," at the end of the year 1897, where they seemed to be a necessary accompaniment to the edition of the hieroglyphic texts of the Theban Recension and the hieroglyphic vocabulary thereto. The demand for that bulky and comparatively expensive work proved that it filled a want, but soon after its appearance frequent requests were made that the English translation might be issued in a smaller and handier form. In answer to these requests, Messrs. Kegan Paul, Trench, Trübner, and Co. decided to publish the complete English translation of the Book of the Dead in their series of books on Egypt and Chaldaea, together with such introductory matter, index, etc., as are necessary to make this edition of use to the general reader.

The translation given in the present series is, however, no mere reprint, for it has been carefully revised and compared with the original texts, and many brief explanatory notes have been added; and, with the view of placing in the hands of the reader as complete an edition as possible, more than four hundred vignettes, taken from the best papyri, have been reproduced in the volumes of the present edition at the heads of the Chapters, the general contents of which the ancient Egyptian scribes and artists intended them to illustrate. The greater number of these have been specially drawn or traced for this purpose, and they faithfully represent the originals in form and outline; to reproduce the colours of the originals was out of the question, for the cost of coloured illustrations would have placed this book beyond the reach of the general public.

Many of the ideas and beliefs embodied in the texts here translated are coeval with Egyptian civilization, and the actual forms of some of the most interesting of these are identical with those which we now know to have existed in the Vth and VIth Dynasties, about B.C. 3500. On the other hand, many of them date from the predynastic period, and, in the chapter on the History of the Book of the Dead, which forms part of the Introduction to the present edition, an attempt has been made to show how some of the religious views of the north-east African race, which formed the main indigenous substratum of the dynastic Egyptians, found their way into the Book of the Dead and maintained their position there.

The greater number of the translations here given belong to the group to which the Egyptians gave the name, "Chapters of Coming Forth by Day," and the remainder are introductory hymns, supplementary extracts from ancient cognate works, rubrics, etc., which were intended to be used as words of power by the deceased in the underworld. The papyri and other originals which have been selected as authorities are the best now known, and they have been chosen with the view of illustrating the development of the Theban Recension and the changes which took place in it during the various periods of its history. Since no papyrus contains all the Chapters and Vignettes of this Recension, and no two papyri agree either in respect of contents or arrangement of the Chapters, and the critical value of every text in a papyrus is not always the same, it follows that a complete edition of all the known Chapters of the Theban Recension would be impossible unless recourse were had to several papyri. Since the year 1886, in which M. Naville's *Das Todtenbuch der Aegypter* appeared, several extremely important papyri of the Book of the Dead have been discovered, and it is now possible to add considerably to the number of Chapters of the Theban Recension which he published. Thus the Papyrus of Ani supplies us with Introductions to Chapters XVIII. and CXXV., and hymns to Rā and Osiris, and texts referring to the Judgment Scene, and all of these are new; besides, we gain a complete, though short, version of Chapter CLXXV. And from the Papyrus of Nu, which is the oldest of the illuminated papyri known, we have obtained about twenty Chapters of the Theban Recension, which were unknown until 1897, and several which have, up to the present, been only known to exist in single manuscripts. Use has therefore been made of several papyri, and as a result translations of about one hundred and sixty Chapters, not including different versions, Hymns, and Rubrics, are given in the present edition. Translation of sixteen Chapters of the Saïte Recension have also been added, both because they form good specimens of the religious compositions of the later period of Egyptian history, and illustrate some curious beliefs, and because, having adopted the numbering of the Chapters employed by Lepsius, they were needed to make the numbering of the Chapters in this edition consecutive.

The translation has been made as literal as possible, my aim being to let the reader judge the contents of the Theban Recension of the Book of the Dead for himself; the notes are short, and it was thought to be unnecessary to encumber the pages of a book which is intended for popular use with voluminous disquisitions and references. The reader who needs to consult other works on the subject will find a tolerably full Bibliography to the printed literature of the Book of the Dead in my *Papyrus of Ani*, London, 1895, pp. 371 ff.

It has been the fashion during the last few years among certain writers on Egyptology to decry the Book of the Dead, and to announce as a great discovery that the hieroglyphic and hieratic texts thereof are corrupt; but that several passages of the work are hopelessly corrupt has been well known to Egyptolgists for the last fifty years, and they have never concealed the fact that they could not translate them. Moreover, the Egyptian scribes informed their readers by the frequent use of the words "ki tchet," i.e., "otherwise said," that they themselves did not know which variants represented the correct readings, and recent investigations have proved that the scribes and sages of the XIXth Dynasty had as much difficulty as we have in reading certain hieratic signs which were written during the Early Empire, and were as undecided as we are about the true transcription of them. The text of every great national religious composition which is handed down first by oral tradition, and secondly by copies which are multiplied by professional scribes and others, is bound to become corrupt in places; this result is due partly to carelessness of the copyists, and partly to their inability to understand the allusions and the obscure words which occur in them. But the history of the religious literatures of the world shows that when a series of compositions has once attained to the position of a recognized national religious work, the corruptions in the text thereof do not in any way affect the minds of their orthodox readers in the general credibility of the passages in which they occur. And the Book of the Dead forms no exception to this rule, for the work, which was very old even in the reign of Semti, a king of the First Dynasty, and was, moreover, so long at that time as to need abbreviation, was copied and re-copied, and added to by one generation after another for a period of nearly 5000 years; and the pious Egyptian, whether king or ploughman, queen or maid-servant, lived with the teaching of the Book of the Dead before his eyes, and he was buried according to its directions, and he based his hope of everlasting life and happiness upon the efficacy of its hymns and prayers, and words of power. By him its Chapters were not regarded as materials for grammatical exercises, but as all-powerful guides along the road which, passing through death and the grave, led into the realms of light and life, and into the presence of the divine being Osiris, the conqueror of death, who made men and women "to be born again." The more the Book of the Dead is read and examined, the better chance there is of its difficult allusions being explained, and its dark passages made clear, and this much to be desired result can only be brought about by the study, and not by the neglect, of its texts.

In the introduction to the present translation Chapters are added on the literary history of the Book of the Dead, on the doctrines of Osiris, and of the Judgment and Resurrection, and on the Object and Contents of the Book of the Dead. The limits, however, of this work make it impossible to include within it the chapter on the Magic of the Book of the Dead which appeared in the edition of 1897. The renderings of the funeral texts written for Nesi-Khensu, Ḳerāsher, and Takhert-p-uru-ȧbt, and the Book of Breathings, the Book of Traversing Eternity, &c., appended to the third volume will, it is hoped, enable the reader to make a comparison of the beliefs of the Egyptians in the early and later periods of their history.

E. A. Wallis Budge.

British Museum,
August 6th, 1909.

INTRODUCTION

THE HISTORY OF THE BOOK OF THE DEAD

THE early history of the great collection of religious texts which has now become well known throughout the world by the names "Das Todtenbuch," "Das Aegyptische Todtenbuch," "Le Livre des Morts," "Rituel Funéraire," "Il Libro dei funerali degli antichi Egiziani," and "The Book of the Dead," is shrouded in the mists of remote antiquity, and up to the present no evidence has been forthcoming which will enable us to formulate it in an accurate manner. The very title "Book of the Dead" is unsatisfactory, for it does not in any way describe the contents of the mass of religious texts, hymns, litanies, etc., which are now best known by that name, and it is no rendering whatever of their ancient Egyptian title REU NU PERT EM HRU , i.e., "Chapters of Coming Forth by Day." The name "Book of the Dead" is, however, more satisfactory than that of "Ritual of the Dead," or "Funeral Ritual," for only a very small section of it can be rightly described as of a ritual character, whilst the whole collection of compositions does certainly refer to the dead and to what happens to the dead in the world beyond the grave.

Of the home and origin also of the Book of the Dead but little can be said. Now that so many of the pre-dynastic graves of Egypt have been excavated, and their contents have been so fully described and discussed, we find no evidence forthcoming that would justify us in assuming that the aboriginal inhabitants of the country possessed any collection of religious texts which might be regarded as the original work from which, by interpolations and additions, the Recensions of the Book of the Dead now known could have descended, or even that they made use of any collection of religious texts at the burial of the dead. That there are references in the various Recensions to the funeral customs of the aborigines of Egypt is fairly certain, and it is evident from the uniform manner in which the dead were laid in their graves in the earliest pre-dynastic times that the aborigines possessed tolerably well defined general ideas about the future life, but we cannot regard them as the authors even of the earliest Recension of the Book of the Dead, because that work presupposes the existence of ideas which the aborigines did not possess, and refers to an elaborate system of sepulture which they never practised. Whether we regard the aborigines of Egypt as of Libyan origin or not it is certain that they employed a system of sepulture which, in its earliest forms, was quite different from that in use among their latest pre-dynastic and their earliest dynastic descendants. If the known facts be examined it is difficult not to arrive at the conclusion that many of the *beliefs* found in the Book of the Dead were either voluntarily borrowed from some nation without, or were introduced into Egypt by some conquering immigrants who made their way into the country from Asia, either by way of the Red Sea or across the Arabian peninsula; that they were brought into Egypt by new-comers seems most probable. Who those new-comers were or where they came from cannot be definitely said at present, but there are good grounds for thinking that they first adopted certain of the general customs which they found in use among the dwellers on the Nile, and then modified them, either to suit the religious texts with which they were acquainted, or their own individual views which they evolved after they had arrived in Egypt. The excavation of pre-dynastic cemeteries in Egypt has revealed the fact that its aboriginal or pre-dynastic inhabitants disposed of their dead by burial and by burning; the bodies which were buried were either dismembered or cut up into a considerable number of pieces, or buried whole. Bodies buried whole were laid on their left sides with their heads to the south, and were sometimes laid in the skins of gazelles and sometimes in grass mats; no attempt was made to mummify them in the strict sense of the term. This seems to be the oldest method of burial in the Nile Valley. The dismembering or cutting up of the body into a number of pieces was due probably both to a wish to economize space, and to prevent the spirit of the deceased from returning to his old village; in such cases the head is separated from the body, and the limbs are laid close together. Chronologically, the disposal of the dead by burning comes next; usually the bodies were only partially burnt, and afterwards the skull and the bones were thrown into a comparatively shallow pit, care being, however, taken to keep those of the hands and feet together. Speaking generally, these two classes of burials are well defined, and the cemeteries in which each class is found are usually quite separate and distinct, lying ordinarily some distance apart. Whether we are to distinguish two distinct peoples in those who buried the bodies of their dead whole, and in those who burnt them first and buried their remains, it is almost too early to decide, but there is abundant evidence to show that both of these classes of the inhabitants of Egypt had many funeral customs in common. They both used covered pits for tombs, both buried their dead in the valleys, both oriented the dead in the same direction, and both made funeral offerings to the dead. The offerings prove beyond all doubt that both those who buried and those who burnt their dead held definite views about the future life, and these can hardly have existed in their minds without some perception, however dim, of a divine power being there also. It is idle to speculate on the nature of such a perception with our present limited knowledge, but it must not be forgotten that the widespread custom of burying the dead with the head to the south, and the presence of funeral offerings, indicate the existence of religious convictions which are not of a low order, and are not common among savage or semi-barbarous tribes.

It has been said above that the people who buried their dead whole made no attempt to mummify the bodies in the strict sense of the term, still, as Dr. Fouquet found traces of bitumen in some of the skeletons to which he devoted an exhaustive examination, and as many bodies have been found wrapped in skins of animals, and grass mats, and even rough cloths, we may rightly assume that they would have taken far more elaborate precautions to preserve their dead had they possessed the necessary knowledge. These early inhabitants of Egypt embalmed their dead either because they wished to keep their material bodies with them upon earth, or because they believed that the future welfare of the departed depended in some way upon the preservation of the bodies which they had left behind them upon earth. Whatever the motive, it is quite certain that it must have been a very powerful one, for the custom of preserving the dead by one means or another lasted in Egypt without a break from the earliest pre-dynastic times almost down to the conquest of the country by the Arabs, about A.D. 640.

Meanwhile, however, we may note that the graves of those who were buried whole, and of those who were burnt, or dismembered, contain no inscriptions, and it is evident that the habit of writing religious texts upon the objects laid in the tombs, a habit which became universal in the times of the historical Egyptians, was not yet in existence. Still, it is impossible to think that people who evidently believed in a future life, and who tried to preserve the bodies of their dead from religious motives, would bury their beloved friends and relatives without uttering some pious wish for their welfare in the world beyond the grave, or causing the priest of the community to recite some magical charm or formula, or repeat certain incantations, which had been composed for such occasions, on their behalf. It is more than probable that, if prayers or formulae were recited at the time of burial, the recital was accompanied by the performance of certain ceremonies, which must have partaken of a magical character; both prayers and ceremonies must have been traditional, and were, no doubt, primarily designed to protect the dead from the attacks of wild animals, damp-rot, dry-rot, and decay. Now although we may not regard a collection of such funeral prayers, however large, as the earliest Recension of the Book of the Dead, there is little doubt that many of the formulae found in the Heliopolitan Recension of the Book of the Dead, which was in use during the IVth and Vth Dynasties, date from a very early pre-dynastic period, and that they are as old as, or older than, the civilization of the historic Egyptians and their immediate predecessors. Such formulæ are directed against snakes and scorpions, and other noxious reptiles, and the forms in which they were written by the scribes about B.C. 3500, and the mistakes which occur in them, prove that the copyists were dealing with texts that were at that remote time so old as to be unintelligible in many passages, and that they copied many of them without understanding them. In any case such formulae date from a period when the banks of the Nile were overrun by wild beasts, and when they formed the home of creatures of all kinds which were hostile to man, and which the early dwellers on the Nile sought to cajole or frighten away from their dead; indeed, there is little doubt that before the forests which lined the river banks were cut down for fuel Egypt must have resembled in many respects certain sections of the Nile Valley much further south, and that river monsters of all kinds, and amphibious beasts which are only now to be found on the upper reaches of the Blue Nile and near the Great Lakes, lived happily in the neighbourhood of Memphis, and even farther to the north.

Towards the close of the period when the bodies of the dead were burnt, or dismembered, the objects found in the graves vary in character considerably from those which occur in the graves wherein the bodies are buried whole, and whereas in the older graves weapons of flint occur in abundance, and stone jars and vases are rare, in the later flint weapons are the exceptions, the hard stone vases become more numerous, and objects in metal are found in comparative abundance. To what cause these-changes are due cannot exactly be said, but the presence of bronze and other metal objects most probably indicates the appearance of some foreign influence in the Valley of the Nile, and that that influence proceeded from immigrants is tolerably certain. Whether these immigrants belonged remotely to a Semitic stock, or whether they were descendants of a people akin to the nation which is now by common consent called Sumerian, are questions impossible to answer at present; for, while the presence in the earliest hieroglyphic inscriptions of grammatical usages, and verbal forms, and idioms, and pronouns which are certainly identical with many of those in use in all the Semitic dialects indicates Semitic influence, or kinship with Semitic peoples to a considerable degree, the religious beliefs of the pre-dynastic and early dynastic Egyptians have few parallels with those of the Semitic peoples of antiquity known to us. But, whether the immigrants were of Semitic origin or not, they seem to have come originally from the East, and, whether by force of arms or otherwise, they certainly effected a permanent settlement in the Nile Valley; a people armed with metal weapons conquered those who relied upon weapons of flint and stone, and having made themselves masters of the country these men ruled it according to their own ideas and methods, as far as its climate and natural conditions permitted. Conquest was followed by intermarriage, which was an absolute necessity if the immigrants came from the East and wished their descendants to abide in the land, and thus it comes to pass that the historic Egyptians are the descendants of an indigenous north-east African people, and of immigrants from the East, who having settled in Egypt were gradually absorbed into the native populations. It is easy to see that the debt which the indigenous peoples of Egypt owed to the new-comers from the East is very considerable, for they learned from them the art of working in metals (although they continued to make use of flint weapons, i.e., knives, axe-heads, spear-heads, arrow-heads, scrapers, etc., without a break down to the time of the dynastic Egyptians), and the art of writing. M. de Morgan declares that the knowledge of [working in] bronze is of Asiatic origin, and he thinks that the art of brick-making was introduced into Egypt from Mesopotamia, where it was, as we learn from the ruins of early Sumerian cities, extensively practised, with many other things which he duly specifies.[1]

With the art of writing the new-comers in Egypt undoubtedly brought certain religious beliefs, and funeral customs, and literature, and gradually the system of burial which was universal in Egypt up to the time of their arrival in the country became completely changed.

[1] *Ethnographie Préhistorique*, p. 21 ff.

The covered pits and troughs which served for graves, and which were dug almost anywhere on the banks of the river, were replaced by crude brick buildings containing one or more chambers; graves were no longer dug in the valley but in the hill sides; dead bodies were neither burnt nor dismembered, and the head was not separated from the body; bandages systematically wound round the body took the place of skins of animals and grass mats and rough cloth wrappings; and dead bodies were laid on their backs in coffins, instead of being bent up and laid on their side on the ground. The change in the character of the offerings and other objects found in the graves at this period was no less marked, for pottery made on a wheel took the place of that made by hand, and maces and more formidable weapons appeared, together with a large number of various kinds of amulets of a new class. It is, unfortunately, impossible to assign a date to this period of change, and it cannot be said how long it lasted, but it is certain that at this time both the indigenous peoples and the new-comers modified their burial customs, and that the foundations of the sepulchral customs and of the system of mummification which were universal among the historical Egyptians were then laid. The indigenous peoples readily saw the advantage of brick-built tombs and of the other improvements which were introduced by the new-comers, and gradually adopted them, especially as they tended to the preservation of the natural body, and were beneficial for the welfare of the soul; but the changes introduced by the new-comers were of a radical character, and the adoption of them by the indigenous peoples of Egypt indicates a complete change in what may be described as the fundamentals of their belief. In fact they abandoned not only the custom of dismembering and burning the body, but the half savage views and beliefs which led them to do such things also, and little by little they put in their place the doctrine of the resurrection of man, which was in turn based upon the belief that the god-man and king Osiris had suffered death and mutilation, and had been embalmed, and that his sisters Isis and Nephthys had provided him with a series of amulets which protected him from all harm in the world beyond the grave, and had recited a series of magical formulae which gave him everlasting life; in other words, they embraced the most important of all the beliefs which are found in the Book of the Dead. The period of this change is, in the writer's opinion, the period of the introduction into Egypt of many of the religious and funeral compositions which are now known by the name of "Book of the Dead." Whether the primitive form of the doctrine of Osiris included the view that his body was hacked to pieces after death and his head severed from it is not known, but it is quite certain that many influential people in Egypt objected to the decapitation of the dead, and their objection found expression in the XLIIIrd Chapter of the Book of the Dead, which, according to its title, provides expressly that "the head of a man shall not be cut off in the underworld." The text of this remarkable Chapter is of great interest; and reads, "I am the Great One, the "son of the Great One; I am Fire, the son of "Fire, to whom was given his head after it had been "cut off. The head of Osiris was not taken away from "him, let not the head of (*here follows the name of the "deceased, who is also called Osiris*) be taken away "from him. I have knit myself together; I have "made myself whole and complete; I have renewed "my youth; I am Osiris, the lord of eternity." The title of this Chapter is definite enough, but the text seems to indicate that for a man to be certain of possession of his head in the next world it was necessary to have it first removed from his body after death, and then rejoined to it. The historic Egyptians seem to have abandoned any such belief, however, and there is no doubt that they viewed with dismay any mutilation of the body, although they preserved in their religious texts frequent allusions to the collecting of the members of the body, and the gathering together of the bones. The LXIIIrd Chapter, which existed in two versions in the XVIIIth Dynasty, also seems to allude to certain funeral practices of the pre-dynastic Egyptians, for one version was written to protect a man from being burnt in the underworld, and the other to prevent him from being scalded or boiled. In historic times the Egyptians neither burned nor scalded nor boiled their dead, but we have seen above that the pre-dynastic Egyptians partly burned their dead, and it is probable that they often removed the flesh from the bones of the dead by boiling as well as by scraping them. There are numerous passages in the various Chapters of the Book of the Dead which seem to contain allusions to pre-dynastic funeral customs, and many of the Chapters refer to natural conditions of the country which can only have obtained during the period that preceded the advent of the immigrants from the East. It is clear that those who introduced the Book of the Dead into Egypt claimed to be able to protect the dead body from calamities of every kind, either by means of magical names, or words, or ceremonies, and that the indigenous peoples of the country accepted their professions and adopted many of their funeral customs, together with the beliefs which had produced them. They never succeeded wholly in inducing them to give up many of their crude notions and fantastic beliefs and imageries, and more and more we see in all ages the ideas and notions of the semi-barbarous, North African, element in the Book of the Dead contending for recognition with the superior and highly moral and spiritual beliefs which it owed to the presence of the Asiatic element in Egypt. The Chapters of the Book of the Dead are a mirror in which are reflected most of the beliefs of the various races which went to build up the Egyptian of history, and to this fact is due the difficultv of framing a connected and logical account of what the Egyptians believed at any given period in their history. But there is reason for hoping that, as the texts become more studied, and more information and facts concerning the pre-dynastic peoples of Egypt become available, it will be possible to sift such beliefs and to classify them according to their source.

To assign a date to the period when the Book of the Dead was introduced into Egypt is impossible, but it is certain that it was well known in that country before the kings of the Ist Dynasty began to rule over the country. In the first instance the prayers and petitions, which in later days were grouped and classified into Chapters, were comparatively simple, and probably few in number, and their subject matter was in keeping with the conditions under which the dead were buried in the home of those who brought them into Egypt. At first also they were recited from memory, and not from written copies, and they were, no doubt, preserved by oral tradition for a very long time. Meanwhile the prayers, and petitions, and formulae increased in number and in length, and were in other particulars made applicable to the conditions under which men were buried in Egypt, and at length they were done into writing; but this only took place when the priests began to be in doubt about the meaning of their contents, and when they found that certain of them were becoming forgotten. It is scarcely likely that at that remote period any effective supervision of the accuracy of the written copies by a central authority was attempted, and though the copyists in their copies adhered in the main to the versions of the prayers, etc., which they had received, variations, additions, and mistakes, that were often due to the misreading of the characters, soon crept into them. Experience has shown that it is extremely difficult to preserve, even in these days of printing and stereotype, the text of a work in an accurate and genuine state, and when copies of a text have to be multiplied by hand the difficulty is increased a thousand-fold. For, besides the mistakes due to the carelessness and ignorance, and to the fatigue of the eye and the hand of the copyist, there remain to be considered the additions and interpolations which are always made by the scribe who wishes the text he is copying to represent his own views. It was such tendencies as these on the part of scribes and copyists which made it necessary for Talmudic sages to resort to the means of "casuistic exegesis" for the preservation not of the original text of the Hebrew Bible but even of that text which had become authoritative in their time; and it is a well known fact that, within a few years after the death of Muḥammad the Prophet the notables of the Muḥammadan world were alarmed at the variations which had already crept into the Suras of the Ḳur'ân, and that one of them warned[1] his master to "stop the

[1] See Muir, *The Life of Mahomet*, pp. xx., xxi.

people, before they should differ regarding their Scripture, as did the Jews and Christians!" In this case the variant readings of a national religious book, which was held to be of divine origin, were disposed of in a most effectual manner, for, as soon as the four authorities who had been appointed to make a final recension of the Arabic text began work, they collected copies of the Ḳur'ân from all parts of the Muḥammadan dominions, and having decided what readings were to be retained, they burnt all the manuscripts containing those which they rejected. It seems almost a pity that some such drastic method was not employed in the formation of a *textus receptus* of the Book of the Dead.

The graves of the pre-dynastic dwellers in Egypt contain no religious inscriptions, and it is not until we come to the time of the dynastic Egyptians that the tombs afford much evidence of the existence of the Book of the Dead; it is, however, certain that parts of the Book of the Dead were in general use before the period of the rule of the kings of the Ist Dynasty. The numerous tombs of priestly officials, and the inscriptions in them, testify that the men for whom they were made performed during their lifetime offices in connexion with the burial of the dead, such as the reading of texts and the performance of ceremonies, which we know from the rubrics of the recensions of the Book of the Dead of a later period were regarded by the Egyptians as essential for salvation; now if the official lived and read the texts and performed the ceremonies of the Book of the Dead, that work must certainly have existed in one form or another, for priests were not appointed to read religious books which did not exist. The Egyptians themselves have not left behind any very definite statement as to their belief about the existence of the Book of the Dead in pre-dynastic times, but they had no hesitation in asserting that certain parts of it were as old as the Ist Dynasty, as we may see from the following facts. The oldest copy of the Book of the Dead now known to exist on papyrus is that which was written for Nu, the son of "the overseer of the house of the overseer of the seal, Àmen-ḥetep, and of the lady of the house, Senseneb;" this extremely valuable document cannot be of later date than the early part of the XVIIIth Dynasty.[1] Of the Sixty-fourth Chapter it gives two versions, one much longer than the other, and to each version is appended a rubric which assigns a date to the text which it follows; the rubric of the shorter version declares that the "Chapter was found in the "foundations of the shrine of Ḥennu by the chief "mason during the reign of his Majesty, the king of "the South and North, Semti" (or, Hesepti), and that of the longer version that it "was found in the city of "Khemennu (Hermopolis, the city of Thoth) upon a "block of iron of the south, which had been inlaid [with

[1] The complete text, edited by myself, is published in *Facsimiles of the Papyri of Hunefer, Anhai, Ḳerāsher, and Netchemet, with supplementary text from the Papyrus of Nu.* Published by order of the Trustees of the British Museum, London, fol. 1899.

"letters] of real lapis-lazuli, under the feet of the god "(i.e. Thoth) during the reign of his Majesty, the king "of the South and North, Men-kau-Rā (i.e. Mycerinus), "by the royal son Ḥeru-ṭā-ṭā-f." Here then we have two statements, one of which ascribes the "finding" of the Chapter to the time of the Ist Dynasty, and the other to the IVth Dynasty; and it is probable that both statements are correct, for it is clear that the longer version, which is ascribed to the IVth Dynasty, is much longer than that which is ascribed to the Ist Dynasty, and it is evident that it is an amplified version of the shorter form of the Chapter. The meaning of the word "found" in connexion with the Chapter is not quite clear, but it is probable that it does not mean "discovery" only, and that the performance of some literary work on the text, such as revision or editing, is intended. The mention of king Semti in the rubric to the shorter version of the Chapter is of interest, especially when we consider the representations which are found upon the ebony tablet of the royal chancellor Ḥemaka;[1] this tablet appears to have been dedicated to the honour of Semti, for his Horus name Ṭen appears upon it side by side with that of his royal chancellor Ḥemaka. To the right of the name is a scene in which we see the god Osiris, wearing the white crown, and seated in a shrine set

Ṭen, the Horus name of Semti.

[1] See Third Egyptian Room, British Museum, Table-case L,

upon the top of a short flight of steps; before him is a figure of king Semti, who is dancing away out of the presence of the god, and he wears the crowns of the South and North on his head, and holds in one hand the object , and in the other a staff or paddle. That the god in the shrine is Osiris is beyond doubt, for he occupies the position at the top of the staircase which in later days gained for Osiris the title of "the "god at the top of the staircase;"[1] on sarcophagi and elsewhere pictures are sometimes given of the god sitting on the top of the staircase.[2] Other examples are known of kings dancing before their god with a view of pleasing him, e.g., Usertsen danced before the god Ȧmsu or Min, and Seti I. danced before Sekhet, and the reference in the text of Pepi I.[3] to the king dancing before the god, i.e., Osiris, like the reference to the pigmy, proves that the custom was common in Egypt in early dynastic times; that the custom was not confined to Egypt is certain from the passage in the Bible (2 Samuel vi. 14, ff.), where we are told that David danced before the ark of the Lord. Below the dancing scene on the tablet are a number of hieroglyphics, the meaning of which is very doubtful, but in the left hand corner is one which must represent the boat of Ḥennu, and as we are told that the earliest

[1] Compare "May I, Osiris the scribe Ani, triumphant, have a portion with him who is on the top of the staircase," Book of the Dead, xxii. 6, 7.
[2] See my *Egyptian Heaven and Hell*, vol. ii., p. 159.
[3] See *Recueil de Travaux*. vii. 162, 163.

form of the LXIVth Chapter was found in the foundations of the shrine of Ḥennu, it seems as if king Semti was in some way specially attached to the service of this god, or to the performance of ceremonies in which the boat of Ḥennu was a prominent feature; it must also be noted that the figure of Osiris seated in his shrine on the top of a short staircase is the oldest representation of the god which we have. From the fact that the chancellor Ḥemaka depicts the dancing scene on the tablet, and also the boat of Ḥennu, we may assume that the king's connexion both with the god and with the boat was of such a special nature that the loyal servant, regarding it as one of the most important features of the king's life, determined to keep it in remembrance. There remains another point to notice about the LXIVth Chapter. The version of it to which the name of Semti is attached is entitled, "The Chapter of Knowing the Chapters of Coming Forth [by Day] in a single Chapter." Now, we have said above that the Egyptians called the Chapters of the Book of the Dead the "Chapters of Coming Forth by Day," and judging from the title it would seem that as early as Semti's time these Chapters had become so numerous that it was all-important to compose, or edit one of the Chapters which then existed, in such a way that it should contain all the knowledge necessary to the dead for their salvation; if this view be correct, and there is no reason to doubt it, we have here an extraordinary proof of the antiquity of certain parts of the Book of the Dead. The contents of the LXIVth Chapter are of a remarkable nature, and there is no doubt that in all periods of Egyptian history it was believed to contain the essence of the Book of the Dead, and to be equal in value to all its other Chapters, and to have a protective power over the dead which was not less than that of all the other Chapters taken together. That some important event in the history of the Book of the Dead happened during the reign of Semti is certain, and that this event had a connexion with the doctrine and worship of Osiris is certain from the representation of the god and of the boat of Ḥennu, which are given on the contemporaneous tablet of Semti's chancellor Ḥemaka.

Of the history of the Book of the Dead during the IInd, IIIrd, and IVth Dynasties we know nothing, and no copy of any part of the Recension of it then in use has come down to us. During the reign of Men-kau-Rā (Mycerinus), a king of the IVth Dynasty, it is said that Chapters XXXB., LXIV., and CXLVIII. were "found" by Ḥeru-ṭā-ṭā-f, the son of Khufu, a man to whom in later ages the possession of great learning was ascribed, and it is very probable that, like King Semti, he revised or edited the Chapters to which his name is attached in rubrics; for the numerous funeral inscriptions of the period prove that at that time a Recension of the Book of the Dead was in general use.

During the period of the Vth and VIth Dynasties a great development took place in the funeral ceremonies that were performed for Egyptian Kings, and Unȧs, Tetȧ, Pepi I., and others covered the greater part of the chambers, corridors, etc., of their pyramid tombs with series of texts selected from the Book of the Dead in the earliest Recension of that work known to us.[1] We possess five selections of texts from this Recension, to which, on account of its containing the views held by the priests of the colleges of Ȧnnu, or Heliopolis, the name Heliopolitan has been given, but we have no reason for assuming that the Chapters supplied by the five selections constitute the entire work. It is impossible at present to indicate exactly all the changes, modifications, and additions which the priests of Ȧnnu made in the work, but scattered throughout their Recension there is abundant evidence to show that the Recension upon which they worked was based upon two, or perhaps three, earlier Recensions. In their Recension also will be found religious ideas and beliefs which belong to entirely different strata of civilization and religious thought, and it is clear that some of them came down from the North African section of their ancestors, who at the time when they formulated them must have stood but little higher on the ladder of civilization than the semi-barbarous tribes of Western Africa and the Sûdân.

Between the VIth and the XIth Dynasties we know

[1] See Maspero, *Les Inscriptions des Pyramides de Saqqarah*, Paris, 1894; this work appeared in sections in *Recueil de Travaux*, tom. iii. ff.

nothing of the history of the Book of the Dead, and it is not until we come to some period in the XIth Dynasty that we find other selections from the work. But little is known of the events which happened in the interval between the VIth and the XIth Dynasties, and although in Upper Egypt tombs of considerable size and beauty were built, yet no striking development in funeral ceremonies took place, and we may assume in consequence that no new Recension of the Book of the Dead was made; if it was, we certainly have no record of it. Belonging to the XIth and XIIth Dynasties, however, we have a number of coffins and tombs which are inscribed with selections of texts from the so-called Heliopolitan Recension; such texts differ in extent only and not in character or contents from those of the royal pyramids of Ṣaḳḳâra of the Vth and VIth Dynasties. Coffins at this period were made to represent the main funeral chamber or hall of a tomb of an older period, and are covered inside with lengthy texts traced in hieratic characters in black ink upon the wood, while the outside is plain except for a few short inscriptions, which record the name and titles of the deceased, and short prayers. Above the perpendicular lines of text on all four sides inside the coffin are painted pictures of the objects which it was customary in those days to present as funeral offerings, and above these is a horizontal line of hieroglyphics which contains the name of the deceased and usually a prayer that funeral offerings may be made to him for ever. The texts in such coffins are rarely identical, and they have no fixed order, and it seems as if individual fancy either of the deceased or of the funeral scribe dictated the selection. As no pyramids were inscribed with extracts from the Book of the Dead at this period it is clear that economy prescribed the custom of burying the dead in inscribed wooden coffins, which were far cheaper than stone pyramids.

Between the XIIth and XVIIIth Dynasties there comes another break in the history of the Book of the Dead, and with the beginning of the XVIIIth Dynasty that work enters a new phase of its existence; from pyramids the transition was to coffins, and now the transition is from coffins to papyri. And here again economy probably played an important part. Inscribed pyramids, and sarcophagi, and coffins would, necessarily, be only made for royal personages and for great and wealthy folk, but a roll of papyrus was, in comparison with these, an inexpensive thing, especially if the services of an ordinary scribe were employed in transcribing it, or if a man wrote his own copy of the Book of the Dead. The greater number of the papyri inscribed with selections of texts from the Book of the Dead have been found in the tombs of Thebes, where they were copied chiefly for the priests and their wives and families, the majority of whom were attached to the service of "Åmen-Rā, the king of the gods, the lord of the thrones of the world," the seat of whose worship was at Thebes; and for this reason the Recension of the Book of the Dead which we find in common use from the XVIIIth to the XXIInd Dynasty is generally called the Theban Recension. The texts which the priests of Ȧmen copied were, of course, those of Ȧnnu, or Heliopolis, and during the earlier centuries of the existence of the great brotherhood of the priests of Ȧmen they did little more than adopt the religious views and doctrines of the sages of that place. As time went on, however, and the brotherhood obtained greater power, they slowly but surely made their god Ȧmen to usurp the attribute of the oldest gods of Egypt, and at length, as we may see from Chapter CLXXI. (infra, p. 580), his name is included among theirs. Fine copies of papyri of the Theban Recension vary in length from 15 to 90 feet, and in width from 12 to 18 inches. In the early part of the XVIIIth Dynasty the text is always written in black ink in vertical columns of hieroglyphics, which are separated from each other by black lines; the titles and initial words of the Chapters, and the rubrics and catch-words are written in red ink. At this period the scribes began to ornament their papyri with designs traced in black outline, but such designs, or "vignettes," were not wholly invented by the priests of Ȧmen, for on some of the finest coffins of the XIth Dynasty we find painted a number of vignettes which illustrate the texts, and in the case of such a vignette as that which represents the Elysian Fields we find that the scribe of the XVIIIth Dynasty copied the design of the scribe of the XIth Dynasty in all essentials. It is possible that the scribe of the earlier period possessed an archetype which was their ultimate authority for their vignettes, but if they did, no remains of it have up to the present been found. In the XIXth Dynasty the vignettes were painted in very bright colours, and the texts were, little by little, driven into the subordinate position which the vignettes occupied at the beginning of the XVIIIth Dynasty, when they were traced in black outline. In the Papyrus of Hunefer (Brit. Mus. No. 9901) almost everything has been sacrificed to the beautifully coloured vignettes which it contains, and as a result its text of the XVIIth Chapter is so full of mistakes that many parts of it have no meaning at all. At first the "setting out" of a papyrus was done by the scribe, and the artist, if one was employed, filled in his vignettes in the spaces which had been left blank by the scribe; but subsequently the artist seems to have painted his vignettes first and the scribe had to be content with the spaces which had been allotted to him by the artist. Long copies of the Theban Recension were made in sections, which were afterwards joined together, and sometimes several scribes and artists, who seem to have been ignorant or careless of what each other was doing, were employed upon them. Thus fine papyri which have been made in sections contain duplicates, and even triplicates of some Chapters, and in some cases where duplicates occur the arrangement, both of texts and vignettes, is quite different in each. One of the finest illustrated papyri in existence, the Papyrus of Ani, omits a large section of the text of the XVIIth Chapter, a result which is probably due to the scribe, who omitted to copy what seems to be the contents of a whole sheet ot the text. Vignettes, however, have at times a peculiar value, for they often supply descriptions of mythological scenes, names of gods, etc., which occur nowhere in the texts; of special importance in this connexion are the Judgment Scenes and its accompanying texts, and the long vignette to the XVIIth Chapter. In the XXIst and XXIInd Dynasties we note a gradual falling off in the skill exhibited in the artistic work on the papyri of the Book of the Dead, and many changes take place in respect of the form as well as their contents. In the first place they are shorter and narrower, especially those which were made for the priests of Åmen, and texts are inserted in them which belong to a great funeral composition entitled "The Book of that which is in the Underworld." Some papyri, however, preserve many of the characteristics of those of the best period, but it almost seems as if the work of both scribes and artists had greatly deteriorated, and it is certain that the views of the priests of Åmen with reference to the Book of the Dead had changed. Thus in the Papyrus of Ånhai, of the XXIInd Dynasty (Brit. Mus. No. 10,472), we find a vignette representing the Creation, and others which have no connexion with the Book of the Dead in the strict sense of the term; the artist's work is good of its kind, and the use of gold in it for purposes of illumination is instructive. The texts are fragmentary and incomplete, and often have no connexion whatsoever with the vignettes which accompany them. About this period texts are copied in which the scribe has read from the *end* of the composition instead of the beginning; omissions of whole sections of texts are frequent; vignettes are frequently assigned to Chapters with which they have no connexion; and what appears at first sight to be a Chapter frequently consists of nothing but a series of fragments of sentences, copied without break merely to fill up the space which the artist had left blank for the text. In short, showy papyri with inaccurate texts are common at this period. It is interesting too to note how great had become the influence of the priests of Åmen in the XXIInd Dynasty, and how they gradually made their god to usurp the attributes of the older gods of Egypt. In the Papyrus of the Princess Nesi Khensu which is preserved in the Cairo Museum, the hieratic text opens with a long detailed list of the titles of Åmen-Rā, and instead of a selection of Chapters from the Theban Recension we find a series of statements, couched apparently in legal language, in which Åmen-Rā swears that he will confer every possible favour upon the deceased lady. About the same period it became customary to write copies of the Book of the Dead in hieratic, and to illustrate them with vignettes traced in outline in black ink; some of these papyri measure about 50ft. by 1ft. 6in., but in others the dimensions are considerably less. As in the old days, the scribes who wrote such papyri observed no rule in the order of the Chapters, to which, however, they gave special titles; these were, of course, like the texts which followed them, copied from the Theban Recension.

Of the history of the Book of the Dead in the period which lies between the end of the XXIInd and the beginning of the XXVIth Dynasty we know nothing, but this is not much to be wondered at when we consider that the period was one of trouble and tumult. The priests of Àmen-Rā, having made their god to usurp the position of Rā and the other gods in the religious system of Egypt, next usurped the kingdom on behalf of themselves; but they were unable to maintain the authority of Egypt in the countries which had been conquered by the great kings of the XVIIIth and XIXth Dynasties, and as an inevitable result the subject nations and tribes refused to pay the tribute which had been imposed upon them. The failure in tribute spelt failure in offerings to the temples, and consequently loss of temporal power by the priests, and when the people of Egypt realized that they were losing their position among the nations they brought the rule of the priests of Àmen to an end. The loss of income of both priests and people resulted promptly in the curtailment of expense in connexion with funeral ceremonies, and thus it happens that the burials of the priests were attended with less pomp, and the custom of making copies of the Book of the Dead fell into abeyance; indeed, a time came, about B.C. 700, when no copies at all were made, and it seems as if this time corresponded with the period of the final failure of the priests of Amen to rule the country.

With the rise to power of the kings of the XXVIth Dynasty, a general revival of ancient religious and funeral customs took place, and the temples were cleansed and repaired, and ancient and long-forgotten texts were unearthed and copies of them taken, and artists and sculptors took the models for their work from the best productions of the masters of the Early Empire. In such a revival the Book of the Dead was not forgotten, and there is no doubt that those who were the principal authors of the movement became fully aware of the fact that the texts which formed their old national and religious work sorely needed re-editing and re-arranging, and measures were accordingly taken to put some system into them. How and when exactly this was done cannot be said, but it is probable that it was carried out by an assembly or college of priests, and the result of their labours was the Saïte Recension of the Book of the Dead. The papyri extant which may be rightly assigned to this period show that in this Recension the Chapters have a fixed order, and that although some selections of texts may be smaller than others, the Chapters common to all papyri have always the same relative order. Each of the early Recensions of the Book of the Dead exhibits peculiarities which reflect the religious views of the time when it was written, and the Saïte Recension is no exception to the rule, for included in it are four Chapters (CLXII.-CLXV.) which have no counterparts in the papyri of the older period. These Chapters contain many foreign words and unusual ideas, and it is much to be wished that the circumstances under which they were introduced into the Book of the Dead were known. The characteristics of the papyri containing the Saïte Recension are:—I. The text is written in long, vertical columns of hieroglyphics of purely conventional form, separated by black lines; 2. The vignettes are traced in outline in black, and generally occupy small spaces at the top of the text to which they refer, the usual exceptions being those which represent the Sunrise or Sunset, the Judgment Scene, the Elysian Fields, and the Seven Cows and their Bull which illustrates the text of Chapter CXLVIII.

The Recension of the Book of the Dead in use in Ptolemaïc times was the Saïte, but before the rule of the Ptolemies had come to an end a number of short religious works intended to be written upon funeral papyri had been composed, and it became customary to make copies of these for the benefit of the dead, and to lay them in the coffin or tomb, rather than selections from the older work. It appears as if an attempt was made by the scribes to extract from the texts of a bygone time only such parts as were believed to be absolutely necessary for the salvation of the deceased, and they omitted the hymns of praise and the addresses to the gods, and the compositions which were the outcome of beliefs and of a mythology which had long been forgotten. Many things in papyri of the period show that the scribes were quite ignorant of the meaning of the texts which they were copying, and also of the correct arrangement of the vignettes which they added. Of special interest among the works which were popular in the Ptolemaïc and Græco-Roman periods, and probably later, is the "Shai en Sensen," or "Book of Breathings." In this composition we find ideas and beliefs which were derived from the Book of the Dead, and which show that the fundamental conceptions of the future life were the same as ever in the minds of the people; as a summary of all the ideas and beliefs that appertain to the immortality and happiness of the soul of the deceased and of his dead body it is remarkable, and considered from this point of view contains scarcely an unnecessary word.[1] In the Roman period small rolls of papyrus were inscribed with series of asseverations concerning the piety of life of deceased persons and their happiness in the world beyond the grave, and were buried with them, the writers' aim being not so much to glorify the gods of Egypt as to secure for the dead the happiness and

[1] A rendering of it will be found in the Appendix (Vol. III., p. 657).

blessings of immortality in the next world at the least possible expense in this. But the knowledge of the old Recensions of the Book of the Dead was not quite dead in the early centuries of the Christian era, for on a coffin in Paris, which probably dates from the second century after Christ, are written a number of texts which are certainly as old as the Pyramids at Ṣaḳḳâra, a fact which proves that, when such were needed, originals from which to copy them could be found, even at that late period. The various Recensions of the Book of the Dead may be thus summarized:—

1. The Heliopolitan Recension: (*a*) That which was used in the Vth and VIth Dynasties, and is found inscribed in hieroglyphics upon the walls and chambers of the Pyramids at Ṣaḳḳâra; (*b*) That which was written in cursive hieroglyphics upon coffins in the XIth and XIIth Dynasties.
2. The Theban Recension: (*a*) That which was written upon papyri and painted upon coffins in hieroglyphics from the XVIIIth to the XXIInd Dynasties; (*b*) That which was written in the hieratic character upon papyri in the XXIst and XXIInd Dynasties.
3. The Saïte Recension, which was written upon papyri, coffins, etc., in the hieroglyphic, hieratic, and demotic characters during the XXVIth and following Dynasties; this was the Recension

which was much used in the Ptolemaic period, and which may be regarded as the last form of the Book of the Dead.

In the Graeco-Roman and Roman periods extracts from the last Recension were written upon papyri a few inches square and buried with the dead, and we see that the great religious work of the ancient Egyptians, which had been in existence for at least 5000 years, and mere selections from which would fill the walls of the chambers and passages of a pyramid, or which would fill several scores of feet of papyrus, or would cover a whole coffin, ended its existence in almost illegible scrawls hastily traced upon scraps of papyrus only a few inches square.

From first to last throughout the Book of the Dead, with the exceptions of Kings Semti and Men-kau-Rā, and Heru-ṭā-ṭā-f, the son of Khufu, the name of no man is mentioned as the author or reviser of any part of it. Certain Chapters may show the influence of the cult of a certain city or cities, but the Book of the Dead cannot be regarded as the work of any one man or body of men, and it does not represent the religious views and beliefs of any one part only of Egypt; on the contrary, the beliefs of many peoples and periods are gathered together in it. As a whole, the Book of the Dead was regarded as the work of the god Thoth, the scribe of the gods, and thus was believed to be of divine origin; it was Thoth who spoke the words at the Creation which were carried into effect by Ptaḥ and Khnemu, and as advocate and helper of the god Osiris, and therefore of every believer in Osiris, the ascription of the authorship to him is most fitting This view was held down to a late period, for in the Book of Breathings,[1] in an address to the deceased it is said, "Thoth, the most mighty god, the lord of "Khemennu (Hermopolis), cometh to thee, and he "writeth for thee the Book of Breathings with his own "fingers." Copies of the Book of the Dead, and works of a similar nature, were placed either in the coffin with the deceased, or in some part of the hall of the tomb, or of the mummy chamber, generally in a niche which was cut for the purpose. Sometimes the papyrus was laid loosely in the coffin, but more frequently it was placed between the legs of the deceased, either just above the ankles or near the upper part of the thighs, before the swathing of the mummy took place. In the XXIst Dynasty the custom grew up of placing funeral papyri in hollow wooden figures of the god Osiris, which were placed in the tombs, but in later times, when funeral papyri were much smaller, they were laid in rectangular cavities sunk either in the tops or sides of the pedestals to which such figures were attached. At first the figure was that of the god Osiris, in his character of god of the dead and judge of the underworld, but the attributes of the triune god Ptah-

[1] See page 657 ff.

Seker-Ásár, the god of the resurrection, were subsequently added to it, and suitable variations in the texts written on the papyri which were placed in or beneath them were made accordingly.

OSIRIS, THE GOD OF JUDGMENT, THE RESURRECTION, IMMORTALITY, THE ELYSIAN FIELDS, ETC.

In the oldest religious texts known the absolute identity of the deceased with Osiris is always assumed by the writer, and in later times the deceased is actually called by the name of the god; moreover, in every detail of the funeral ceremonies the friends and relatives of the dead sought to imitate the ceremonies which were declared by tradition to have been performed for the god, believing that thereby only could everlasting life and happiness be assured to the departed. The history of Osiris is shrouded in the mists of remote antiquity, and as the ancient Egyptian writers supply us with no information concerning their theories about the god there are small grounds for hoping that we shall ever possess any authentic history of him. It is, however, quite certain that even in the earliest dynastic times in Egypt the history of Osiris was legendary, and that all the main features of the story which Plutarch gave in *De Iside et Osiride* were then current; the scene on the plaque of Semti (see British Museum, No. 32,650), a king of the Ist Dynasty, proves that the "god on the top of the staircase" occupied a most prominent position in the religion of the country. The texts of the Heliopolitan Recension of the Book of Dead assume throughout that Osiris occupied the position of chief of the cycle of the gods of the dead, and down to the earliest centuries of the Christian era the fundamental ideas expressed in every text which was written for the benefit of the dead rest on this assumption. It was universally believed that Osiris was of divine origin, that he lived upon earth in a material body, that he was treacherously murdered and cut in pieces, that his sister Isis collected the limbs of his body, and, by means of magical words which had been specially provided by the god Thoth, reconstituted it, that the god came to life again by these means, that he became immortal, and entered into the underworld, where he became both the judge and king of the dead. The dismembering of the body of Osiris rather calls to mind the practice of the predynastic Egyptians who, at one period, cut the bodies of their dead into pieces before burial, and removed the head from the body, to which, however, they showed special honour by placing it in a raised position in the grave. Thus one portion of the legend of Osiris may be of indigenous or North African origin; at all events the ceremonies connected with the raising up of the Ṭeṭ which were performed in early dynastic times at Abydos, where the head of the god was believed to be buried, suggest the commemoration of funeral rites which can hardly have been introduced by the conquerors from the East. In the XVIIIth Dynasty it is expressly stated in Chapter CLIV. of the Book of the Dead (*infra*, p. 517) that Osiris neither decayed, nor putrefied, nor rotted away, nor became worms, nor perished, and that he enjoyed existence, being in the full possession of all the members of his body. Thus the deceased King Thothmes III. is made to say, "I "shall live, I shall live. I shall grow, I shall grow, I "shall grow. I shall wake up in peace; I shall not "putrefy; my intestines shall not perish; I shall not "suffer from any defect; mine eye shall not decay, "the form of my visage shall not disappear; mine "ear shall not become deaf; my head shall not be "separated from my neck; my tongue shall not be "carried away; my hair shall not be cut off; mine "eyebrows shall not be shaved off; and no baleful "injury shall come upon me. My body shall be "stablished (i.e., constituted), and it shall neither "fall into decay nor be destroyed upon this earth." And the king, and every other follower of Osiris, believed that he would enjoy everlasting life and happiness in a perfectly constituted body *because* Osiris had conquered death, and had risen from the dead, and was living in a body which was perfect in all its members; moreover, for countless generations Osiris was the type and emblem of the resurrection, and relying upon his power to give immortality to man untold generations lived and died. In the hymns which are addressed to him he is called the "king of eternity, the "lord of the everlasting, who passeth through millions "of years in his existence" (see p. 18); and again it is said (see p. 67), "The dead rise up to see thee, they "breathe the air and they look upon thy face when the "Disk riseth on its horizon; their hearts are at peace "inasmuch as they behold thee, O thou who art "Eternity and Everlastingness." Still more remarkable are the words which were addressed to him by the god Thoth and which are found in the Papyrus of Hu-nefer (see p. 623); the scribe of the gods having enumerated all the titles of Osiris in a series of paragraphs, and shown how love for him permeates every god, says, "Homage to thee, O Governor of those who are "in Amentet, who dost make men and women to "be born again," ,

mes temem u em uḥem

the new birth being the birth into the new life of the world which is beyond the grave, and is everlasting.

All the pictures of the god Osiris known to us in funeral texts represent him as a being swathed in mummied form, and wearing on his head the white crown, and holding in his hands the emblems of sovereignty and dominion; but those which represent the deceased make him to appear in the ordinary garb of a man who is dressed in ceremonial attire, and he is seen in the Judgment Hall and other places in heaven in the form wherein he went about upon earth. There is reason for thinking that pre-dynastic man believed that his dead would live again in the identical bodies which they had upon earth, i.e., in a material resurrection, and there is no doubt that the funeral offerings which they placed in their graves and tombs were intended to be their food in the next world whilst they were accommodating themselves to their new circumstances. In later times, although the funeral offerings were made as before, the belief in a material resurrection was given up by educated Egyptians, and in texts, both of the earliest and latest periods of Egyptian history, it is distinctly stated that the material part of man rests in the earth whilst the immaterial part has its abode in heaven. Thus in a text of the Vth Dynasty[1] we read, "Rā receiveth thee, soul in heaven, body in earth;" and in one of the VIth Dynasty[2] it is said to the deceased, "Thine essence is in heaven, thy body is in the "earth"; and in a text of the Ptolemaic period[3] it is declared to the deceased, "Heaven hath thy soul, "earth hath thy body." In another text, also of a late date,[4] the deceased is addressed in these words, "Thy "soul is in heaven before Rā, thy double hath that "which should be given unto it with the gods, thy "spiritual body is glorious among the spirits of fire,

[1] Pyramid of Unȧs, line 582.

[2] Pyramid of Tetȧ, line 304.

[3] See J. de Horrack, *Lamentations d'Isis et de Nephthys*, Paris, 1866, p. 6.

[4] See Lieblein, *Que mon nom fleurisse*, p. 2, l. 2 ff., and p. 17, l. 2 ff.

"and thy material body is stablished in the under-"world (i.e., grave)." All the available evidence shows that the Egyptians of dynastic times mummified the dead body because they believed that a spiritual body would "germinate" or develop itself in it. We know that an ancient belief held that the head of Osiris was buried at Abydos, and many cities of Egypt claimed that limbs of Osiris were buried in them, and one tradition affirmed that the whole body of the god rested in Ȧnnu or Heliopolis. The texts show that the Egyptians believed that, if the prescribed prayers were said and the appropriate ceremonies were properly performed over the dead body by duly appointed priests, it acquired the power of developing from out of itself an immaterial body called *sāḥu*, which was able to ascend to heaven and to dwell with the gods there. The *sāḥu* took the form of the body from which it sprang and was immortal, and in it lived the soul. The god Osiris possessed a *sāḥu* in the Egyptian heaven, and in Chapter CXXX. of the Book of the the Dead (line 36) the deceased Nu is declared to have received this *sāḥu* from the god; in other words, Osiris rewarded the beatified dead by bestowing upon them his own spiritual form; and elsewhere (see p. 349) the deceased says, "Behold, verily I have said unto "thee, O Osiris, 'I am a *sāḥu* of the god,'" i.e., of Osiris. The proof that the soul dwelt in the *sāḥu* is furnished by a passage in the LXXXIXth Chapter, wherein the deceased addresses the "gods who make "souls to enter into their *sāḥu*" (see p. 280), and the distinct difference between the material and spiritual body is well illustrated by the following petition, which comes at the end of the same Chapter:—"And behold, "grant ye that the soul of Osiris Ani, triumphant, may "come forth before the gods and that it may be triumphant along with you in the eastern part of the sky "to follow unto the place where it (i.e., the 'boat of "millions of years') was yesterday [and that my soul "may have] peace, peace in Ȧmentet. May it look "upon its material body, may it rest upon its spiritual "body; and may its body neither perish nor suffer "corruption for ever." It now remains to enumerate briefly the constituent parts of man physically, mentally, and spiritually.

1. The physical body, which was called *khat* , i.e., that which was liable to decay, and could only be preserved by mummification.

2. The *ka* 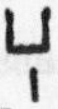, a word which by general consent is translated "double"; the Coptic equivalent is κω, and it can in most cases be accurately rendered by one of the meanings of *εἴδωλον*. The *ka* was an abstract individuality or personality which possessed the form and attributes of the man to whom it belonged, and, though its normal dwelling place was in the tomb with the body, it could wander about at will; it was independent of the man and could go and dwell in any statue of him. It was supposed to eat and drink, and

the greatest care was usually taken to lay abundant supplies of offerings in the tombs lest the *kas* of those who were buried in them should be reduced to the necessity of leaving their tombs and of wandering about and eating offal and drinking filthy water.

3. The *ba* 𓅽, or heart-soul, was in some way connected with the *ka*, in whom or with whom it was supposed to dwell in the tomb, and to partake of the funeral offerings, although in many texts it is made to live with Rā or Osiris in heaven. It seems to have been able to assume a material or immaterial form at will, and in the former character it is depicted as a human-headed hawk; in the Papyrus of Nebqet at Paris (ed. Devéria and Pierret, pl. 3) it is seen in this form flying down the funeral pit, bearing air and food to the mummified body to which it belongs. The soul could visit the body whensoever it pleased.

4. The *ab* 𓄣, or heart, was closely associated with the soul, and it was held to be the source both of the animal life and of good and evil in man. The preservation of the heart of a man was held to be of the greatest importance, and in the Judgment it is the one member of the body which is singled out for special examination; here, however, the heart is regarded as having been the centre of the spiritual and thinking life, and as the organ through which the manifestations of virtue and vice revealed themselves, and it typifies

everything which the word "conscience" signifies to us. The necessity of preserving the material heart was very great, and four Chapters of the Book of the Dead (XXVII.—XXXB.) were composed to prevent the heart of a man from being carried off or driven away from him in the underworld by the "stealers of hearts." The most favourite of these Chapters was XXXB., which is found inscribed on large numbers of green basalt amulets, which date from the period of the XIIth Dynasty to that of the Romans. The heart amulet is made in the form of a scarab or beetle, and both it and the Chapter which is associated with it are connected, in the Papyrus of Nu (see p. 221), with that version of the LXIVth Chapter which is there declared to be as old as the time of Men-kau-Rā, a king of the IVth Dynasty.

5. The *khaibit* 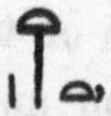, or shadow, was closely associated with the *ba* or soul, and was certainly regarded as an integral portion of the human economy; it, like the *ka*, seems to have been nourished by the offerings which were made in the tomb of the person to whom it belonged. Like the *ka* also it had an existence apart from the body, and it had the power of going whereso-ever it pleased. As far back as the time of King Unȧs[1] we find that souls and spirits and shadows are mentioned together, and in the XCIInd Chapter of the Book of the Dead (see p. 286) the deceased is made to

[1] *La Pyramide du roi Ounas*, line 523.

say, "O keep not captive my soul, O keep not ward "over my shadow, but let a way be opened for my soul "and for my shadow, and let them see the Great God "in the shrine on the day of the judgment of souls, "and let them recite the utterances of Osiris, whose "habitations are hidden, to those who guard the "members of Osiris, and who keep ward over the "spirits, and who hold captive the shadows of the dead "who would work evil against me."

6. The *khu* , or spiritual soul, is often mentioned in connexion with the *ba* or heart-soul, and it seems to have been regarded as an ethereal being, in fact the SOUL which under no circumstances could die; it dwelt in the *sāḥu* or spiritual body.

7. The *sekhem* , or power, which we may look upon as the incorporeal personification of the vital force of a man; the *sekhem* dwelt in heaven among the *khus* or spirits, and in the texts it is usually mentioned in connexion with the soul and the spirit.

8. The *ren* , or name, to preserve which the Egyptians took the most extraordinary precautions, for the belief was widespread that unless the name of a man was preserved he ceased to exist. Already in the time of King Pepi the name was regarded as a most important portion of a man's economy, and in the following passage[1] it ranks equally with the *ka* :—

[1] *La Pyramide du Roi Pepi Ier*, line 169.

"The iron which is the ceiling of heaven openeth "itself before Pepi, and he passeth through it with his 'panther skin upon him, and his staff and whip in his "hand; Pepi passeth with his flesh, and he is happy "with his name, and he liveth with his double." Already in the Pyramid Texts[1] we find the deceased making supplication that his name may "grow" or

[1] *La Pyramide du Roi Pepi* II., line 669 ff. The extract reads:—
"Hail, Great Company of the gods who are in Ȧnnu, grant that "Pepi Nefer-ka-Rā may flourish, and grant that his pyramid, his "everlasting building, may flourish, even as the name of Temu, "the Governor of the Great Company of the gods, flourisheth. If "the name of Shu, the lord of the upper shrine in Ȧnnu, flourisheth, "Pepi Nefer-ka-Rā shall flourish, and this his pyramid, his ever-"lasting building, shall flourish. If the name of Tefnut, the lady "of the lower shrine in Ȧnnu, is stablished, the name of this Pepi "Nefer-ka-Rā shall be stablished, and this pyramid shall be "stablished for ever. If the name of Seb, the soul of the earth (?), "flourisheth, the name of Pepi Nefer-ka-Rā shall flourish, and this "his pyramid shall flourish, and his everlasting building shall "flourish. If the name of Nut flourisheth in Ḥet-Shenth in Ȧnnu, "the name of this Pepi Nefer-ka-Rā shall flourish, and this his "pyramid shall flourish, and this his building shall flourish for "ever. If the name of Osiris flourisheth in the nome Teni, the "name of this Pepi Nefer-ka-Rā shall flourish, and this his pyramid "shall flourish, and this his building shall flourish for ever. If the "name of Osiris, Governor of Ȧmenti, flourisheth, the name of "this Pepi Nefer-ka-Rā shall flourish, and this his pyramid shall "flourish, and this his building shall flourish for ever. If the "name of Set in Nubt (Ombos) flourisheth, the name of Pepi "Nefer-ka-Rā shall flourish, and this his pyramid shall flourish, "and this his building shall flourish for ever. If the name of "Horus of Beḥuṭet flourisheth, the name of this Pepi Nefer-ka-Rā "shall flourish, and this his pyramid shall flourish, and this his "building shall flourish for ever. If the name of Rā flourisheth in "the horizon, the name of this Pepi Nefer-ka-Rā shall flourish, "and this his building shall flourish for ever. If the name of "Khent-Merti in Sekhem is stablished, the name of this Pepi "Nefer-ka-Rā shall flourish, and this his Pyramid shall flourish, "and this his building shall flourish for ever. If the name of "Uatchit who dwelleth in Ṭep flourisheth, the name of this Pepi "Nefer-ka-Rā shall flourish, and this his pyramid shall flourish, "and this his building shall flourish for ever."

"shoot forth" and endure as long as the names of Tem, Shu, Seb, and other gods, and, with modifications, the prayer written for Pepi II. in the VIth Dynasty was in common use at the Graeco-Roman period in Egypt. To preserve the name of his parents was the bounden duty of every pious son, and every offering which was made in a man's tomb, however small, provided it was coupled with the mention of the deceased's name, helped to keep in existence the person whose name was mentioned.[1]

9. The *sāḥu* , or spiritual body, which formed the habitation of the soul. It sprang from the material body, through the prayers which were said, and the ceremonies which were performed at the tomb or elsewhere by duly appointed and properly qualified priests, and was lasting and incorruptible. In it all the mental and spiritual attributes of the natural body were united to the new powers of its own nature.

There is little doubt that the beliefs in the existence of these various members of the spiritual and material bodies are not all of the same age, and they probably

[1] The idea is pithily expressed in the text of Pepi I. (l. 20)

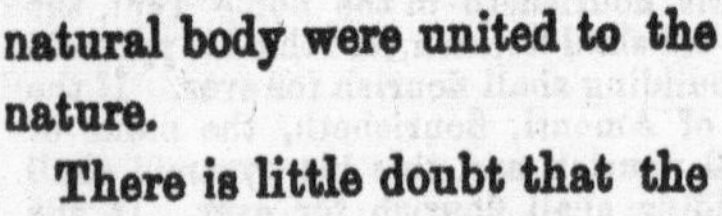. "Thy name shall live upon earth; thy name shall endure upon earth; thou shalt never perish, thou shalt never, never come to an end."

represent several stages of intellectual development on the part of the Egyptians; their origin and development it is now impossible to trace, and the contradictions in the texts prove that the Egyptians themselves had not always definite ideas about the functions of each.

The judgment of the dead took place in the Judgment Hall of Osiris, the exact position of which is unknown; the Judge was Osiris, who was supported by the gods which formed his *paut*  or company. The judgment of each individual seems to have taken place soon after death; those who were condemned in the judgment were devoured straightway by the Eater of the Dead, and ceased to exist, and those who were not condemned entered into the domains of Osiris, where they found everlasting life and happiness. There are no grounds for thinking that the Egyptians believed either in a general resurrection or in protracted punishment. The deceased whose heart or conscience had been weighed in the balance, and not found wanting, was declared to be "maā kheru" 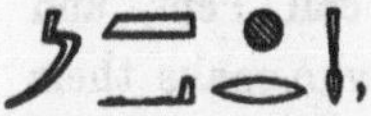, and in papyri these words always follow the names of the persons for whom they were written. They are commonly rendered "triumphant," or "victorious," "disant la vérité," "véridique," "juste," "justifié," "vainqueur," "waltend des Wortes," "mächtig der Rede," "vrai de voix," "juste de voix," etc., but their true meaning seems to be "he whose word is right and true," *i.e.*, he whose word is held to be right and true by those to whom it is addressed, and as a result, whatsoever is ordered or commanded by the person who is declared in the Judgment Hall to be *maā kheru* is straightway performed by the beings or things who are commanded or ordered. Thus before the person who possessed the "right word," the doors of the halls of the underworld were opened, and the beings who had power therein became his servants; he had power to go wheresoever he pleased, and to do whatsoever he pleased, and he became the equal of the gods. The ideas which attached to the words *maā kheru* are well illustrated by the following passage from the text of Pepi I. (l. 171 ff.):—"O enter into the verdant stream of "the Lake of Kha, O fill with water the Fields of "Åaru, and let Pepi set sail for the eastern half "of heaven towards that place where the gods are "brought forth, wherein Pepi himself may be borne "along with them as Ḥeru-khuti, for Pepi is *maā* "*kheru*, and Pepi acclaimeth, and the *ka* of Pepi "acclaimeth [the gods]. And they call Pepi, and "they bring to him these four [gods] who make their "way over the tresses of Horus, and who stand with "their sceptres in the eastern half of heaven; and "they declare to Rā the excellent name of Pepi, and "they exalt the excellent name of Pepi before Neḥeb-"kau, for Pepi is *maā kheru*, and Pepi acclaimeth, and "his *ka* acclaimeth [the gods]. The sister of Pepi is

"Sothis, and the birth of Pepi is the morning star, "and it is he who is under the body of heaven before "Rā. Pepi is *maā kheru*, and he acclaimeth and his "*ka* acclaimeth [the gods]."

The allusion to the "Fields of Åaru" in the above extract leads naturally to a brief mention of the "Sekhet-ḥetepet," or Elysian Fields, wherein the beatified were believed to lead a life of celestial happiness. At a very early period in their history the Egyptians believed in the existence of a place wherein the blessed dead led a life of happiness, the characteristics of which much resemble those of the life which he had led upon earth; these characteristics are so similar that it is hard to believe that in the early times the one life was not held to be a mere continuation of the other. At all events, the delights and pleasures of this world were believed to be forthcoming in the next, and a life there in a state of happiness which depended absolutely upon material things was contemplated. Such ideas date from the time when the Egyptians were in a semi-savage state, and the preservation of them is probably due to their extreme conservatism in all matters connected with religion; the remarkable point about them is their persistence, for they occur in texts which belong to periods when it was impossible for the Egyptians to have attached any serious importance to them, and some of the coarsest ideas are in places mingled with the expression of lofty spiritual conceptions. In a passage in the text of Unȧs it is said of this king (l. 623), "Unȧs hath come to his pools which are on "both sides of the stream of the goddess Meḥt-urt, and "to the place of verdant offerings, and to the fields "which are on the horizon; he hath made his fields "on both sides of the horizon to be verdant. He hath "brought the crystal to the Great Eye which is in the "field, he hath taken his seat in the horizon, he "riseth like Sebek the son of Neith, he eateth with his "mouth, he voideth water, he enjoyeth the pleasures of "love, and he is the begetter who carrieth away women "from their husbands whenever it pleaseth him so to "do." And in the text of Tetȧ (l. 286 f.) we read, "Hail, Osiris Tetȧ, Horus hath granted that Thoth "shall bring thine enemy unto thee. He hath placed "thee behind him that he may not harm thee and that "thou mayest make thy seat upon him, and that when "coming forth thou mayest sit upon him so that he "may not be able to force intercourse upon thee." Such passages give a very clear idea of the state of Egyptian morals when they were written, and they indicate the indignities to which those vanquished in war, both male and female, were exposed at the hands of the conquerors.

The texts of the early period supply much information about the pleasures of the deceased in the world beyond the grave, but no attempt to *illustrate* the employments of the blessed dead is given until the XVIIIth Dynasty, when the vignette to the CXth

Chapter of the Book of the Dead was inserted in papyri.[1] Here we have an idea given of the conception which the Egyptian formed of the place wherein he was to dwell after death. A large homestead or farm, intersected with canals, is at once his paradise and the home of the blessed dead, and the abode of the god of his city. This place is called Sekhet-Åaru or "Field of Reeds," and the name certainly indicates that at one time the Egyptian placed his paradise in the north of Egypt, probably in some part of the Delta, near Ṭaṭṭu, or Busiris, the capital of the Busirite or ninth nome of Lower Egypt. It was here that the reconstitution of the dismembered body of Osiris took place, and it was here that the solemn ceremony of setting up the 𓊽, or backbone of Osiris, was performed each year. The Field of Reeds, however, was but a portion of the district called "Sekhet-Ḥetep" or "Sekhet-Ḥetepet," or "Fields of Peace," over which there presided a number of gods, and here the deceased led a life which suggests that the idea of the whole place originated with a nation of agriculturists. In the vignettes we see the deceased sailing in a boat laden with offerings which he is bearing to the hawk-god. In another place he is reaping wheat and driving the oxen which tread out the corn, and beyond that he is kneeling before two heaps of grain, one red and one white. In the next

[1] The earliest form of this vignette known to me occurs inside one of the Al-Barshah coffins, and is as old as the XIth or XIIth Dynasty.

division he is ploughing the land of Sekhet-Ånru or Sekhet-Åaru, by the side of a stream of vast length and unknown breadth, which contains neither worm nor fish. In the fourth division is the abode of the god Osiris, and here are the places where dwell those who are nourished upon divine food, and the spiritual bodies of the dead. In one section of this division the deceased placed the god of his city, so that even in respect of his religious observances his life might be as perfect as it was upon earth. His wishes in the matter of the future life are represented by the following prayer :—"Let me be rewarded with thy fields, O god "Ḥetep; that which is thy wish shalt thou do, O "lord of the winds. May I become a spirit therein, "may I eat therein, may I drink therein, may I plough "therein, may I reap therein, may I fight therein, may "I make love therein, may my words be mighty therein, "may I never be in a state of servitude therein, but "may I have authority therein." Elsewhere in the same Chapter the deceased addresses the gods of the various lakes and sections of the Elysian Fields, and he states that he has bathed in the holy lake, that all uncleanness has departed from him, and that he has arrayed himself in the apparel of Rā; in his new life even amusements are provided (but they are the amusements of earth), for he snares feathered fowl and sails about in his boat catching worms and serpents.

In the texts of all periods we read often that the deceased lives with Rā, that he stands among the company of the gods, and that he is one like unto the divine beings who dwell with them; but little is told us concerning his intercourse with those whom he has known upon earth, and if it were not for some two or three passages in the Theban Recension of the Book of the Dead we should be obliged to assume that the power to recognize the friends of earth in the next world was not enjoyed by the deceased. But that he really possessed this power, at least so far as his parents were concerned, we learn from the CXth Chapter, where the deceased, addressing a pool or lake situated in the first section of the Elysian Fields, says, "O "Qenqentet, I have entered into thee, and I have seen "the Osiris [my father], and I have recognized my "mother," a delight, however, which he brackets with the pleasures of making love and of catching worms and serpents! In the papyrus of the priestess Anhai (see p. 325) we actually see the deceased lady in converse with two figures, one of whom is probably her father and the other certainly her mother, for above the head of the latter are written the words "her mother" (*mut-s*) followed by the name. A supplementary proof of this is afforded by a passage in the LIInd Chapter, where the deceased says:—"The gods "shall say unto me: 'What manner of food wouldst "'thou have given unto thee?' [And I reply:] 'Let me "'eat my food under the sycamore tree of my lady, the "'goddess Hathor, and let my times be among the "'divine beings who have alighted thereon. Let me "'have the power to order my own fields in Ṭaṭṭu "'and my own growing crops in Ȧnnu. Let me live "'upon bread made of white barley, and let my ale be "'[made] from red grain, and may the persons of my "'father and my mother be given unto me as guardians "'of my door and for the ordering of my territory.'" The same idea is also expressed in the CLXXXIXth Chapter (l. 7). Thus the deceased hoped to have in the next world an abundance of the material comforts which he enjoyed in this world, and to meet again his own god, and his father and mother; as we see him frequently accompanied by his wife in several vignettes to other Chapters we may assume that he would meet her again along with the children whom she bore him.

It will be noticed that little is said throughout the Book of the Dead about the spiritual occupations of the blessed dead, and we are told nothing of the choirs of angels who hymn the Deity everlastingly in the religious works of later Western nations. The dead who attained to everlasting life became in every respect like the divine inhabitants of heaven, and they ate the same meat, and drank the same drink, and wore the same apparel, and lived as they lived. No classification of angels is mentioned, and grades of them like Cherubim, and Seraphim, Thrones, Powers, Dominions, etc., such as are found in the celestial hierarchy of Semitic nations, are unknown; a celestial city constructed on the model described in the Apocalypse is also unknown.

We have seen that the Elysian Fields much resembled the flat, fertile lands intersected by large canals and streams of running water, such as must always have existed and may still be seen in certain parts of the Delta; of the distance to be traversed by the dead before they were reached nothing whatever is said. As the Egyptian made his future world a counterpart of the Egypt which he knew and loved, and gave to it heavenly counterparts of all the sacred cities thereof, he must have conceived the existence of a water way like the Nile, with tributaries and branches, whereon he might sail and perform his journeys. According to some texts the abode of the dead was away beyond Egypt to the north, but according to others it might be either above or below the earth. The oldest tradition of all placed it above the earth, and the sky was the large flat or vaulted iron surface which formed its floor; this iron surface was supported upon four pillars; one at each of the cardinal points, and its edges were some height above the earth. To reach this iron ceiling of the earth and floor of heaven a ladder was thought to be necessary, as we may see from the following passage, in which Pepi the king says, "Homage to thee, O "ladder[1] of the god, homage to thee, O ladder of Set. "Set thyself up, O ladder of the god, set thyself up, "O ladder of Set, set thyself up, O ladder of Horus, "whereby Osiris appeared in heaven when he wrought

[1] 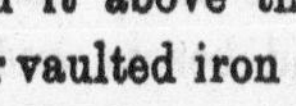 *maqet* (Pepi I., l. 192).

"protection for Rā . . . . . For it is thy son Pepi, and "this Pepi is Horus, and thou hast given birth to this "Pepi even as thou hast given birth to the god who is "the lord of the ladder. Thou hast given unto him "the ladder of the god, and thou hast given unto him "the ladder of Set, whereby this Pepi hath appeared in "heaven, when he wrought protection for Rā."

A later belief placed the abode of the departed away to the west or north-west of Egypt, and the souls of the dead made their way thither through a gap in the mountains on the western bank of the Nile near Abydos. A still later belief made out that the abode of the departed was a long, mountainous, narrow valley with a river running along it; starting from the east, it made its way to the north, and then taking a circular direction it came back to the east. In this valley there lived all manner of fearful monsters and beasts, and here was the country through which the sun passed during the twelve hours of night.[1] It is impossible to reconcile all the conflicting statements concerning the abode of the dead, and the Egyptians themselves held different views about it at different periods.

The Egyptians, from the earliest to the latest period of their history, were addicted to the use of magical formulae which were thought to be able to effect results usually beyond the power of man, and they accompanied the recital of such formulae by the performance of certain ceremonies. The formulae consisted of the

[1] See my *Egyptian Heaven and Hell*, vol. i.

repetition of the names of gods and supernatural beings, benevolent or hostile to man as the case might be, and of entreaties or curses; the ceremonies were of various kinds.[1]

The Egyptian believed that every word spoken under certain circumstances must be followed by some effect, good or bad; a prayer uttered by a properly qualified person, or by a man ceremonially pure, in the proper place, and in the proper manner, must necessarily be answered favourably; and similarly the curses which were pronounced upon a man, or beast, or thing, in the name of a hostile supernatural being were bound to result in harm to the object cursed. This idea had its origin in the belief that the world and all that therein is came into being immediately after Thoth had interpreted in words the will of the deity, in respect of the creation of the world, and that creation was the result of the god's command. In very early times the Egyptian called in the professional religious man to utter words of good omen over the dead body of his relative or friend, and later the same words written upon some substance and buried with him were believed to be effectual in procuring for him the good things of the life beyond the grave. In the text on the pyramid of Unȧs (l. 583) is a reference to something written which the deceased was supposed to possess, in the following words:—"The bone and flesh which have no writing[2] are

See my *Egyptian Magic*, London, 1899. [2] 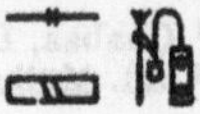 *sesh*.

"wretched, but, behold, the writing of Unás is under "the great seal, and behold, it is not under the little "seal." And in the text on the pyramid of Pepi I. we find the words, "The uraeus of this Pepi is upon his "head, there is a writing on each side of him, and he "hath words of magical power at his two feet"; thus equipped the king enters heaven.

A common way to effect certain results, good or evil, was to employ figures made of various substances, chiefly wax, or amulets made of precious stones and metals in various forms; both figures and amulets were inscribed with words which gave them the power to carry out the work assigned to them by those who caused them to be made. It is well known that the Egyptians believed that the qualities and much else, including the *ka*, of a living original could be transferred to an image thereof by means of the repetition over it of certain formulae, and a good or evil act done to a statue or figure resulted in good or evil to the person whom it represented.

About the time of the XVIIIth Dynasty, we learn from a papyrus[1] that a man was prosecuted in Egypt for having made figures of men and women in wax, by which he caused sundry and divers pains and sicknesses to the living beings whom they represented. And, according to Pseudo-Callisthenes,[2] Nectanebus wrought magic by means of a bowl of water, some

[1] Chabas, *Le Papyrus Magique Harris*, p. 170 ff.
[2] Ed. Müller, lib. 1, cap. 1 ff.

waxen figures, and an ebony rod. The waxen figures were made in the forms of the soldiers of the enemy who were coming against him by sea or by land, and were placed upon the water in the basin by him. Nectanebus then arrayed himself in suitable apparel, and, having taken the rod in his hand, began to recite certain formulae and the names of divine powers known unto him, whereupon the waxen figures became animated, and straightway sank to the bottom of the bowl; at the same moment the hosts of the enemy were destroyed. If the foe was coming by sea he placed the waxen soldiers in waxen ships, and at the sound of the words of power both ships and men sank into the waves as the waxen models sank to the bottom of the bowl. The same informant tells us that when Nectanebus wished Olympias, the mother of Alexander the Great, to believe that the god Ammon had visited her during the night, he went forth from her presence into the plain and gathered a number of herbs which had the power of causing dreams, and pressed out the juice from them. He then fashioned a female figure in the form of Olympias, and inscribed the Queen's name upon it, and having made the model of a bed he laid the figure thereon. Nectanebus next lit a lamp, and reciting the words of power which would compel the demons to send Olympias a dream, he poured out the juice of the herbs over the waxen figure; and at the moment of the performance of these acts Olympias dreamed that she was in the arms of the god Ammon.

The most important mention of figures in the Book of the Dead occurs in the VIth Chapter. When the Egyptian, in very early days, conceived the existence of the Elysian Fields it occurred to him that the agricultural labours which would have to be carried out there might entail upon himself toil and fatigue. To avoid this a short Chapter (V.) was drawn up, the recital of which was believed to free the deceased from doing any work in the underworld. But it was felt that the work must be done by some person or thing, and eventually it became the custom to bury a figure or figures of the deceased with him in his tomb so that it or they might perform whatever work fell to his share. To these figures the Egyptian gave the name *ushabtiu*, a word which is commonly rendered by "respondents" or "answerers," and they are often described in modern times as the "working figures of Hades."

Several of the Chapters of the Book of the Dead are followed by Rubrics which give directions for the performance of certain magical ceremonies, and among them may be specially mentioned the following:—

Chap. XIII. This Chapter was to be recited over two rings made of *ānkhām* flowers; one was to be laid on the right ear of the deceased, and the other was to be wrapped up in a piece of byssus whereon the name of the deceased was inscribed.

Chap. XIX. This Chapter was to be recited over the divine chaplet which was laid upon the face of the deceased while incense was burnt on his behalf.

Chap. C. This Chapter was to be recited over a picture of the boat of the Sun painted with a special ink upon a piece of new papyrus, which was to be laid on the breast of the deceased, who would then have power to embark in the boat of Rā and to journey with the god.

Chap. CXXV. The Judgment Scene was to be painted upon a tile made of earth upon which neither the pig nor any other animal had trodden; and if the text of the Chapter was also written upon it, the deceased and his children would flourish for ever, his name would never be forgotten, and his place would henceforth be with the followers of Osiris.

Chap. CXXX. This Chapter was to be recited over a picture of the god Rā wherein a figure of the deceased sitting in the bows was drawn; this done, the soul of the deceased would live for ever.

Chap. CXXXIII. This Chapter was to be recited over a *faïence* model of the boat of Rā, four cubits in length, whereon the figures of the divine chiefs were painted; painted figures of Rā and of the *Khu* of the deceased were to be placed in the boat. A model of the starry heavens was also to be made and upon it the model of the boat of Rā was to be moved about, in imitation of the motion of the boat of the god in heaven; this ceremony would cause the deceased to be received by the gods in heaven as one of themselves.

Chap. CXXXIV. This Chapter was to be recited over figures of a hawk (Rā), Tem, Shu, Tefnut, Seb,

Nut, Osiris, Isis, Suti, and Nephthys painted on a plaque, which was to be placed in a model of the boat of Rā wherein the deceased was seated; this ceremony would cause the deceased to travel with Rā in the sky.

Chap. CXXXVIA. This Chapter was to be recited over a figure of the deceased seated in the boat of Rā.

Chap. CXXXVIIA. This Chapter was to be recited over four fires, fed by a special kind of cloth anointed with unguent, which were to be placed in the hands of four men who had the names of the pillars of Horus written upon their shoulders. Four clay troughs, whereon incense had been sprinkled, were to be filled with the milk of a white cow, and the milk was to be employed in extinguishing the four fires. If this Chapter were recited daily (?) for the deceased he would become like unto Osiris in every respect. The Rubric supplies a series of texts which were to be recited:—(1) over a Ṭeṭ of crystal set in a plinth, which was to be placed in the west wall of the tomb; (2) over a figure of Anubis set in a plinth, which was to be placed in the east wall; (3) over a brick smeared with pitch which was set on fire, and then placed in the south wall; and (4) over a brick inscribed with the figure of a palm tree, which was set in the north wall.

Chap. CXL. This Chapter was to be recited over an *utchat*, or figure of the Eye of Horus, made either of lapis-lazuli or *Maḳ* stone, and over another made of jasper. During the recital of the Chapter four altars were to be lighted for Rā-Tem, and four for the *Utchat*, and four for the gods who were mentioned therein.

Chap. CXLIV. The seven sections of this Chapter were to be recited over a drawing of the Seven Ārits, at each of which three gods were seated; by these means the deceased was prevented from being turned back at the door of any one of the seven mansions of Osiris.

Chap. CLXII. This Chapter was to be recited over the figure of a cow made of fine gold which was to be placed at the neck of the deceased; during the performance of this ceremony the priest is ordered to say, "O Åmen, O Åmen, who art in heaven, turn "thy face upon the dead body of thy son and make "him sound and strong in the underworld."

Chap. CLXIII. This Chapter was to be recited over a serpent having legs and wearing a disk and two horns, and over two *utchats* having both eyes and wings.

Chap. CLXIV. This Chapter was to be recited over a three-headed, ithyphallic figure of Mut painted upon a piece of linen, and over the figures of two dwarfs painted one on each side of the goddess.

Chap. CLXV. This Chapter was to be recited over the figure of the "god of the litted hand," who had a body in the form of that of a beetle.

Besides these a number of Chapters have Rubrics,

varying in length from two to twenty lines, which declare that if the deceased be acquainted with their contents or if they be inscribed upon his coffin, they will enable him to attain great happiness and freedom in the world beyond the grave. Seven other Chapters consist of texts which were written upon the amulets that were usually laid upon the mummy, namely, Nos. XXXB., LXXXIX., CLV., CLVI., CLVII., CLVIII., and CLIX.

Finally, mention must be made here of the great importance attached by the Egyptians to the knowledge of the names of gods, supernatural beings, etc., and it seems that the deceased who was ignorant of them must have fared badly in the underworld. Thus in Chapter IB. it is said that the deceased knoweth Osiris and his names; in Chapter XCIX. the deceased is obliged to tell the names of every portion of the boat wherein he wishes to cross the great river in the underworld; in Chapter CXXV. Anubis makes him declare the names of the two leaves of the door of the Hall of Osiris before he will let him in, and even the bolts, and bolt-sockets, and lintels, and planks will not allow him to enter until the deceased has satisfied them that he knows their names. Entrance into the seven Ârits or mansions could not be obtained without a knowledge of the names of the doorkeeper, watcher, and herald who belonged to each; and similarly, the pylons of the domains of Osiris could not be passed through by the deceased without a declaration by him of the name of each. The idea underlying all such statements is that the man who knows the name of a god could invoke and obtain help from him by calling upon him, and that the hostility of a fiend could be successfully opposed by the repetition of his name. The knowledge of the names of fiends and demons constituted the chief power of the magicians of olden times, and the amulets of the Gnostics which were inscribed with numbers of names of supernatural powers are the practical expression of the belief in the efficacy of the knowledge of names which existed in Egypt from time immemorial.

THE OBJECT AND CONTENTS OF THE THEBAN RECENSION OF THE BOOK OF THE DEAD.

THOUGH the Chapters of the Book of the Dead represent beliefs belonging to various periods of the long life of the Egyptian nation, from the Pre-dynastic Period downwards, and opinions held by several schools of thought in Egypt, the object of them all was to benefit the deceased. They were intended to give him the power to have and to enjoy life everlasting, to give him everything which he required in the Other World, to ensure his victory over his foes, to procure for him the power of ingratiating himself with friendly beings in the Other World, and of going whithersoever he pleased and when and how he pleased, to preserve his mummified remains intact and uninjured, and finally to enable his soul to reach the Kingdom of Osiris, or to enter into the "Boat of Millions of Years," or into any and every abode of felicity which had been conceived of by him.

The various sections of the Book of the Dead, to which the name of "Chapters" was given by the scribes of the XIIth and following dynasties, were originally independent compositions, the greater number of which were written long before the Canon of the Book of the Dead was formed. Of the exact purpose of many of them the ancient scribes were as ignorant as we are, and the titles which now stand above them in papyri contain many proofs of this fact. In the oldest Recension of the Book of the Dead, i.e., the Heliopolitan, the fullest copies of which are found on the walls of the Pyramids of Unȧs, Tetȧ, Pepi I., &c.. at Ṣaḳḳârah, the sections rarely have titles, and the greater number of them follow each other in unbroken succession, the reader being supposed to know for himself where one section ends and the next begins. We may assume that in the early days of dynastic civilization the number of such compositions was very large, and that a certain number, probably selected without much thought by the scribes, or priests, were copied and recited for the benefit of each king and member of the royal family, and of persons of high rank. From the sarcophagi and coffins of the XIth or XIIth Dynasty we learn that the custom of calling such funerary compositions "Chapters" was in use when they were made, but it is not always clear from the actual compositions that their titles have very much connection with their contents. The names of the learned men who composed the sections of the Book of the Dead are never given. The brief descriptions of the contents of the "Chapters" here given will, it is hoped, make clearer the general meaning of the translations printed in the following pages.

In the best papyri of the first half of the XVIIIth Dynasty, e.g., the Papyrus of Nebseni and the Papyrus of Nu, the Chapters are preceded by a large Vignette, in which we see a figure of the great god Osiris seated upon his throne. He is in the form of a mummy, wears the White Crown, and holds a crook and a flail or whip in his hands. Before him is a table loaded with offerings of all kinds, and, in cases where this end of the papyrus is complete, a figure of the person for whom the papyrus was written is seen standing in adoration before the god. Immediately following this Vignette comes the text of the Chapters, whether with or without Vignettes. In the papyri which belong to the period of the end of the XVIIIth Dynasty and the beginning of the XIXth Dynasty, the Chapters are preceded by two or more Hymns and by a large Judgment Scene. Thus in the Papyrus of Ani we have a Hymn to Rā at sunrise and a Hymn to Osiris; in the Papyrus of Qenna we have two Hymns to Rā at sunrise, but in the Papyrus of Hu-Nefer there is one Hymn only. In all three papyri the Hymns, or Hymn, to Rā are followed by elaborately-painted Judgment Scenes. Now, strictly speaking, the Judgment Scene belongs to Chapter CXXV., where it actually occurs, though in a very simple form. In the Papyrus of Ani (see Negative Confession, Chapter CXXV.) the heart of the deceased is being weighed against the feather of Maāt by Anubis, who scrutinizes the tongue of the balance with great care; close to the pillar of the scales is the monster Åm-mit, who is ready to devour the heart in the event of its being found light.

At the beginning of the Papyrus of Ani the Judgment Scene is much developed. The scales are represented as before, with the heart in one pan and the feather in the other, and Anubis conducts the operation of weighing. Ām-mit is also present, but he now appears to be associated with Thoth, the Scribe of the Gods, who is noting on his writing palette with a long reed pen the result of the weighing of the heart. The heart of Ani is now accompanied by his soul, and by Shai, the god of destiny, or perhaps his own destiny, or luck, and by the two goddesses Renenet and Meskhenet. Moreover, twelve deities are seated near the scales, and these await the report of Thoth, their righteous scribe. Ani himself is also present, with his wife, and he addresses to his heart the words of Chapter XXXB. In some papyri two Companies of Gods, the Great and the Little, are represented as being present at the weighing of the heart of the deceased, and in others Maāt, the goddess of Truth, superintends the operation instead of Anubis. Altogether the scales appear in three places in the Book of the Dead, i.e., in the Vignettes of Chapters XXXB. and CXXV., and in the introductory Vignette to the whole work described above.

CHAPTER I.

This is the first of the Chapters of PERT EM HRU, , i.e., of "The Coming Forth by

Day," or perhaps "into the Day," as some authorities would render the words , the allusion being to the well-known belief of the ancient Egyptians that the journey to the Other World occupied the deceased the whole night of the day of his death, and that he did not emerge into the realms of the blessed until the following morning at sunrise. This Chapter was recited by the priest who accompanied the funeral procession to the tomb, and as he walked at its head he declared to the dead man that he was Thoth, and the Great God, and that he had the power to do on his behalf all that he and Horus did for Osiris, to slaughter all his enemies in the Other World, to perform all the symbolic ceremonies which were performed for Osiris at his burial, and to obtain for him a regular and never-failing supply of offerings in the tomb.

CHAPTER I.B.

The object of this Chapter was to enable the *Sāḥu*, or spiritual form of the deceased, which appears to have consisted of one or more of his souls, his intelligence, and his vital power, to enter into the Ṭuat, or Other World, immediately after his body was laid in its tomb. It contains a prayer to the dweller in the Holy Mountain for deliverance from the "worms which are in Re-stau," i.e., the serpents which guarded the corridors in the kingdom of the god Seker, situated near the modern district called Ṣaḳḳârah, "which lived upon the bodies of men and of women, and fed upon their blood," and the "Lord of light" is entreated to swallow them up. In the Papyrus of Iuâu, which was recently discovered by Mr. Theodore M. Davis at Thebes, we find a form of this Chapter in which the names of the "worms" are given, and a Vignette wherein they are depicted.[1] They are nine in number, and are called:—

1. Nārti-ānkh-em-sen-f, 

2. Ḥer-f-em-qeb-f, 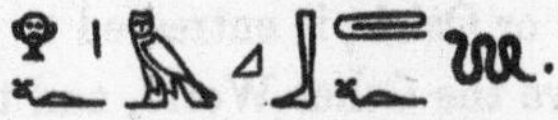

3. Ānkh-em-fentu, 

4. Sām-em-qesu, 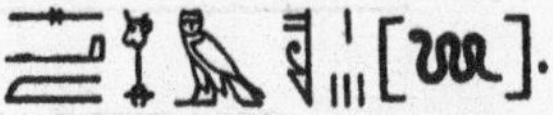

5. Ha-huti-âm-sau, 
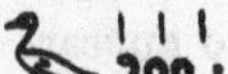

6. Shep-thmesu, 

7. Âm-sāḥu, 

8. Sām-em-snef, 

[1] *Funeral Papyrus of Iouiya*, ed. Naville, pl. xix.

9. Ânkh-em-betu-mit, .

According to the Rubric this Chapter established the deceased in the Other World, and ensured his admission into the Boat of Râ.

CHAPTER II.

In this Chapter he who shines from the Moon, i.e., Horus or Osiris, is entreated to give the deceased power to leave the Other World, and to appear upon the earth again to do his will among the living.

CHAPTER III.

Of similar import to the preceding. Temu, the primeval god of the night sun, who appears in the form of his children the Twin-gods, i.e., Shu and Tefnut, is entreated to let the deceased enter into the assembly of the gods. For he is re-born day after day, like Râ, the Sun-god, he lives again, and the gods shall rejoice in his appearances on earth just as they rejoice when Ptaḥ appears in Ḥet-Ser, the great temple of Heliopolis.

CHAPTER IV.

This Chapter contains the words of power which enabled the deceased to pass through that portion of the sky wherein the Two Combatants, i.e., Horus and Set, contended for victory. They were separated by Thoth, who gave to the former power over the Day, and to the latter power over the Night.

CHAPTER V.

This Chapter is a formula which enabled the deceased to "lift up the hand of the inert one," and to make him do work for him.

CHAPTER VI.

Throughout a large portion of Africa it was, and still is, the custom to bury alive with dead kings a number of slaves, whose souls were intended to go into the Other World, and to wait upon the soul of their king as they waited upon his body in this world. In dynastic times the Egyptians dropped this barbarous custom, and substituted figures (*ushabtiu*) of men and women made of stone, wood, faïence, &c., on which they at first only cut the names of the persons for whom they were made. Subsequently they cut on the figures a formula, in which they called upon them to do any work which might require to be done in the Other World, especially in connection with agriculture. When called upon by the deceased the figures inscribed with his name turned into full-grown men or women, who followed their master, and did all that he commanded them to do. The number of *ushabtiu* figures found in a tomb is sometimes very large; some 700 were taken from the tomb of Seti I. In another tomb 365 were found, and from the inscriptions on some of these it is clear that each figure was intended to do all the work required on one day in the year. The word *shabti* is probably derived from a primitive African word for a funerary human sacrifice.

CHAPTER VII.

The path of Rā and of all good spirits on their way from darkness into light, or from night to day, was obstructed by several monster serpents; the chief of these was Āpep, 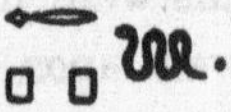. This Chapter contains a spell which, when recited properly by the deceased, made Āpep powerless to block his progress, and enabled him to use the body of Āpep as a road whereby he could reach his destination. In the text Āpep is addressed as a "creature of wax," and these words contain an allusion to the wax figures of the monster which were burned at regular intervals in a fire of *khesau* grass by a priest, who recited appropriate spells whilst the figures were being consumed (see my *Egyptian Magic*, pp. 81 ff.).

CHAPTER VIII.

This Chapter enabled the deceased to obtain the power of Thoth and Horus, to identify himself with Osiris, and to pass through Åmentet as did that god, and to renew his life like the Moon.

CHAPTER IX.

This Chapter enabled the deceased to pass through Åmentet and to enter the light of day, having seen Osiris his father, and having stabbed Set. He then addressed the great Soul-god, who had the form of a ram, and having become a spiritual being (*sāḥu*) and a *khu*-soul, he was in a fit state to greet every god and every fellow *khu*.

CHAPTER X.

This Chapter caused the deceased to be taken in charge by the great Khu-soul of the Other World, and to be identified with him. He was thereby enabled to cleave the horizon and the heavens, to pass through the earth, and to eat food again. In the Papyrus of Ani the Vignette shows us the deceased in the act of spearing a serpent, the typical form of the enemies of the dead, but in the Papyrus of Iuáu (pl. xi.) the deceased is seen driving a short spear into the back of the neck of a human foe, who is kneeling before him and has his hands tied at the elbows behind his back.

CHAPTER XI.

In this Chapter the deceased declares himself to be Rā, and by means of it he obtained the power of walking and talking; being endued with the attributes of Horus and Ptaḥ, and the might of Thoth and the strength of Tem, he was able to destroy all his enemies.

CHAPTER XII.

This Chapter assisted the deceased to go into and out of the Other World, and to pass through the secret gates which stood between the Åmentet and this world. The gates stood hard by the Balance of Rā in which Truth was used as the testing weight daily. The previous Chapters gave the deceased new life and the full use of his limbs, and this Chapter gave him the power to prolong his life into old age.

CHAPTER XIII.

Through this Chapter the deceased identifies himself with the hawk of Horus and the *Bennu* bird, which later Greek tradition pronounced to be the fabulous bird the Phœnix. He was henceforth able to go to the estate of Horus and hunt with his greyhounds, and so enjoy the pleasures of the chase. The Rubric associates this Chapter with two rings, which were to be fastened to the right ear of the deceased on the day of his burial.

CHAPTER XIV.

This Chapter contains a prayer that the god who dwells among mysteries may remove from him sin, wickedness, and transgressions, so that he may be at peace with him, and feel no shame of him in his heart.

CHAPTER XV

This section of the Book of the Dead contains Hymns and Praisings to the Sun-god, some of which were sung in the morning and some in the evening. The Papyrus of Ani includes in it a very interesting Litany to Osiris of nine verses, each of which is addressed to one of the forms of the god; this is found in no other papyrus.

The Vignettes are interesting, for they represent the solar disk, supported on "life," rising on the Mountain of Sunrise out of the Ṭeṭ, 𓊽, the symbol of Osiris, and descending in the form of a hawk into the Mountain of the Sunset. With him are the holy apes who sing praises to him, and represent the spirits who were created daily to praise the god at his rising. Isis, a spirit of dawn, and Nephthys, a spirit of twilight, and the Lion-gods of the Morning and Evening are also represented. In these Hymns the glory and power and majesty of the Sun-god are dwelt upon at length, and the words employed make it certain that the Egyptians fully realized the might of the great luminary of day. The Hymns to the Sun-god were written by the priests of Heliopolis, where the cult of the Sun in Egypt originated. African peoples in general do not worship the sun, and it is probable that they have never paid the same degree of homage to it as to the moon. Many African tribes view sunrise with horror, and take pains to hide themselves from the heat of the sun.

CHAPTER XVI.

This Chapter is, strictly speaking, no Chapter, for the section contains only the Vignettes which illustrate the Hymns that form Chapter XV.

CHAPTER XVII.

This is one of the most valuable and important Chapters of the Book of the Dead, for it contains a statement of the doctrines which the beatified spirit of the deceased was expected to know. Like many other sections of the Book of the Dead this Chapter was composed by the priests of Heliopolis, and it represented their views about the nature of the gods. The earliest copies of the Chapter date from the XIth Dynasty, but they are much shorter than those which appear in the Theban papyri; the Chapter is the only known example of an ancient Egyptian exegetical work, and it proves that various opinions as to the meaning of passages in it existed among the learned. A note in the title declares that the knowledge of its contents was most beneficial to a man even whilst still upon the earth. The opening passage is: "I am Tem in rising "I am the only One. I came into being in Nu. I am "Rā who rose in the beginning, the ruler of what he "made."

On this comes the question: "Who is this?" i.e., "What does this mean?"

The answer is: "It is Rā who rose in the city of "Suten-Ḥenen in primeval time crowned like a king. "He was on the height of the Dweller in Khemennu "before the pillars of Shu (i.e., the pillars of neaven) "were made."

This passage was intended to show that Rā was the oldest of the gods, and that he was identical with Temu, an indigenous solar god of Egypt. Other examples are:—

I. "I am purified in my great double nest which is "in Suten-ḥenen on the day of the offerings of the "followers of the great god who is therein."

Question: "What is this?"

Answer: "The name of one nest is 1. 'Millions of "years,' and of the other, 'Great Green Lake,' "or,

2. "'Traverser of Millions of years,' and "'Great Green Lake,' or,

3. "'Begetter of Millions of years,' and "'Great Green Lake.'"

"The god who dwelleth therein is Rā him-"self."

II. "I am the divine Soul which dwelleth in the divine Twin-gods."

Question: "Who is this?"

Answer: "It is Osiris. He goeth to Ṭaṭṭu, and "findeth there the Soul of Rā, each god em-"braceth the other, and the divine Souls "spring into being within the divine Twin-"gods."

The Twin-gods are:—

Ḥeru-netch-ḥrà-tef-f and Ḥeru-khent-àn-maati.

The double divine Soul is:—

1. The Soul of Rā and the Soul of Osiris,

or,

2. The Soul of Shu and the Soul of Tefnut.

III. "Hail, Kheperȧ in thy boat! Deliver thou the "Osiris from the Watchers who give judgment. . . . . "I have never done the things which the gods hate, for "I am pure in the Mesqet. Cakes and saffron have "been brought unto him in Tanenet."

Question: "Who is this?"

Answer: "It is Kheperȧ in his boat. It is Rā "himself.

"The Watchers are Isis and Nephthys.

"The things which the gods hate are wickedness "and falsehood.

"He to whom cakes are brought is Osiris.

"The saffron cakes are:—

1. "Heaven and earth, or,
2. "Shu, or,
3. "The Eye of Horus.

"Tanenet is the burial-place of Osiris."

CHAPTER XVIII.

In the Introduction to this Chapter in the Papyrus of Ani the deceased is presented to the gods of the great cities of Egypt by the priest Ȧn-mut-f, and by a priest who assumes the character of the Sa-mer-f, or the "son who loveth him." The former states that Ani has committed no sin, and the latter asks that water, air, and an estate in the Field of Peace (or of Offerings) may be given to him. Each priest wears a leopard-skin, the tail of which hangs down between his legs. The title Ȧn-mut-f, , means "pillar of his mother," but this may be a later corruption of the older title "Ȧn-kenemet," , the "pillar of *kenemet*," i.e., the "pillar of the ape." It is interesting to note that in one place[1] the priestly title *Ȧn-mut-f*, , has for its determinative the figure of a priest wearing a leopard-skin and holding one of the forepaws of an ape, which stands on its hind legs. Through a similarity in sound between *kenemet*, "ape," and *mut*, "mother," the latter word in later times took the place of the former, and had reference to the ape referred to in the earlier title. What exactly is to be understood by the words "pillar of his mother," or what part the ape played in connection with the priest, cannot at present be said.

The Chapter proper contains ten addresses to Thoth, in which that god is entreated to make the deceased victorious over his enemies as he made Osiris to be victorious over his enemies in the presence of the groups of gods of the ten chief mythological localities

[1] Griffith, *Beni Hasan*, III. 27.

in Egypt, on ten important occasions in the history of Osiris. The ten localities are:—

1. Ånnu (Heliopolis).	6. Åbṭu (Abydos).
2. Ṭaṭṭu (Busiris).	7. The place of judgment.
3. Sekhem (Latopolis).	8. Ṭaṭṭu (Mendes).
4. Pe-Ṭep (Buto).	9. Ån-ruṭ-f.
5. The Rekhti lands.	10. Re-stau.

The gods of these localities are:—

1. Tem, Shu, Tefnut.
2. Osiris, Isis, Nephthys, Ḥeru-netch-ḥrå-tef-f.
3. Ḥeru-khenti-ån-maati, Thoth.
4. Horus, Isis, Ḳesthå,[1] Ḥāpi.
5. Horus, Isis, Ḳesthå.
6. Osiris, Isis, Åp-uat.
7. Thoth, Osiris, Anubis, Åsṭennu
8. Three gods unnamed.
9. Rā, Osiris, Shu, Bebi.
10. Horus, Osiris, Isis.

CHAPTER XIX.

In late times this Chapter, which is a repetition of the preceding with a few additions, was recited twice at dawn, whilst the priest laid a "beautiful crown of victory which was woven by Tem" upon the brow of the deceased, and whilst incense was cast into the fire

[1] Formerly read *Mesthå*.

on his behalf. The Chapter was regarded as a spell of great and never-failing power, and it was declared that when Horus recited it four times, "all his enemies fell headlong, and were overthrown and cut to pieces."

CHAPTER XX.

This Chapter is a shortened form of Chapter XVIII. arranged as a Litany, and its recital by a man who had cleansed himself in water wherein natron had been dissolved, enabled him to take any form he pleased, and to escape injury by fire.

CHAPTER XXI.

The recital of this Chapter gave to the "pure spirit" the use of his mouth and the power to speak with his lips, and brought back to him his heart.

CHAPTER XXII.

The object of this Chapter is the same as the preceding, i.e., to give back to the deceased his mouth that he might speak therewith in the presence of the Great God (Osiris). Its Vignette is of considerable interest, for in it the "guardian of the Scales," , is represented in the act of touching the lips of the deceased with the fingers of his right hand, instead of with the instrument Ur-ḥeka. The god on the top of the steps is, no doubt, Osiris. The earliest representation of the god on the top of the steps is found on a wooden plaque in the British Museum (Fourth Egyptian Room, Table-case L, No. 124), which belongs to the period of the reign of king Ṭen (Semti-Ḥesepti). The god is also figured on the sarcophagus of Seti I.[1]

CHAPTER XXIII.

This Chapter also deals with the "opening of the mouth" of the deceased, who is supposed to be in the state of a mummy with swathings around his head, which press upon and cover up his mouth. These hindrances to speech are attributed to the operation of Set, the foe of Horus and Osiris, and the deceased beseeches Thoth, the arch-magician, to unloose the swathings, and entreats Tem to hurl them in the faces of those who would fetter him with them. Ancient legends asserted that Ptaḥ untied the swathings which fettered the mouths of the gods, and that Shu opened their mouths with an iron knife. The ceremonies connected with the "opening the mouth" are very ancient, and were certainly performed for the benefit of the dead under the Vth Dynasty. At first they were

[1] See my *Egyptian Heaven and Hell*, vol. ii., p. 159.

performed on the dead body, but subsequently a statue of the deceased was substituted for it. In the Vignette in the Papyrus of Ani a priest is seen performing the ceremonies on a statue of Ani. The Book of Opening the Mouth was discovered by Schiaparelli, who was the first to call the attention of scholars to it.[1]

CHAPTER XXIV.

The object of this Chapter was to provide the deceased with *ḥekau* **, "words of power," that is to say, with magical formulae, the recital of which will enable him to carry out all his wishes and supply all his needs. The deceased demands the words of power which Osiris knew and used, because he has become identified with Tem-Kheperà, the self-produced god.**

CHAPTER XXV.

The recital of this Chapter gave back to the deceased his memory and the faculty of remembering not only his own name, but the name of any god whom he met. It was associated with a ceremony in which a priest held up before the face of the deceased a figure of him

[1] See his *Il Libro dei Funerali*, 2 vols., with volume of texts. The principal texts, with English translations, have also been published in my *Opening of the Mouth*, 2 vols., London, 1909.

so that he might give it his name. The soul without a name was in a terrible plight in the Other World, for its name was an integral part of its being, and if it had forgotten its name, and there was no one there to remind it what it was, it could not be presented to the Great God. No greater harm could be done to the deceased than the erasing of his name from his monuments, for the destruction of his name was equivalent to the destruction of his individuality.

CHAPTER XXVI.

With the opening of the mouth and the restoration of the memory was closely associated the "giving of a heart" to the deceased. The heart was one of the most important organs of the body, not only from a physical point of view, but because it was the seat of one of the members of the dual soul which the Egyptian believed he possessed. The relation between the heart and the soul is well illustrated by the Vignettes to this Chapter, for in one the god Anubis is seen giving a heart to the deceased, and in the other the deceased is addressing a human-headed hawk, which was the corporeal form taken by the heart-soul. Hundreds of passages in the texts prove that it was the heart-soul which partook of offerings placed in the tomb, and in the text of this Chapter it is said, "May my heart be with me, and "may it rest there, [or] I shall not eat of the cakes of

"Osiris on the eastern side of the Lake of Flowers." So soon as the heart was restored to his body, the deceased recovered the use of all his limbs, and the heart-soul was free to leave the body at the gates of the Other World.

CHAPTER XXVII.

This Chapter was written to give the deceased the means of preventing his heart from being stolen from him in the Other World. It is a common belief all through Equatorial Africa and the Sûdân that the heart-soul of a man can be bewitched out of him by magical ceremonies, and that once this soul has left him the heart itself will quickly die, and his body also. It is said that every medicine man is acquainted with means by which these disastrous results can be effected, and the belief in the possibility of human beings being injured in this way is so widespread in the Sûdân that we are justified in assuming that the practice of bewitching the heart is one of very great antiquity. In this Chapter the deceased beseeches the "stealers and crushers of hearts" not to take into account in their dealing with his heart the things which he did, and the "lords of eternity" are entreated not to let evil words rise up against it. In the older Vignette the deceased stands by the side of his heart, which is placed on a pedestal, , in the presence of four gods, who are seated on the symbol of Truth; in the later Vignette from the Turin Papyrus these four gods are identified with the Four Sons of Horus. The heart being restored to him, the deceased becomes master of his own body and of its members.

CHAPTER XXVIII.

This chapter is addressed to a monster in human form, with a tail, who grasps a large knife in his right hand, and holds his tail by its root in his left; the deceased is seated before him in a deprecating attitude, and clasps his heart to his breast with his left hand. The monster has a shaggy mane and whiskers round his face, and his general appearance suggests that he was intended to represent a gorilla or chimpanzee *with a tail,* though the deceased addresses him as the "Lion-god." The beings who the deceased fears will carry off his heart are the "fighting gods in Ȧnnu (Heliopolis)," and Set, the god of evil.

CHAPTER XXIX., XXIX.A AND B.

This chapter, which is extant in three forms, contains other formulae for preventing the heart of the deceased from being carried away from him, and in the longest form he identifies himself with the "Lord of "hearts, the slayer of the heart," and with Horus, the dweller in hearts. The third form was associated with an amulet of the heart made of carnelian, and in it the deceased identifies himself with the Bennu bird, who, like Thoth, was believed to be the heart of Rā. The mention of the *kau*, or doubles, of the gods proves that the heart was believed to be closely connected with the *ka* as well as with one of the souls of man.

CHAPTER XXX., XXX.A AND XXX.B.

This Chapter is one of the most important in the Book of the Dead, and it is unquestionably one of the oldest. It is found in all great papyri which have not been mutilated, and is cut upon hundreds of hard green stone scarabs; the commonest form is that which is called XXXB. The text consists of an address by the deceased to his heart, in which he entreats that :—

1. No one may oppose him in the Judgment before the *Tchatcha*, or Divine Taskmasters.
2. His heart may not leave him.
3. The *Sheniu*, or chief gods of Osiris, may not cause his name to stink.
4. False witness may not be borne against him.
5. A verdict of righteous may be entered for him after his heart has been weighed.

In the course of his petition he says to the heart,

"Thou art my KA, the dweller in me, Khnemu who "knitteth together and strengtheneth my limbs," and he asks it to go with him into felicity. This is an important passage, for it proves how intimate was the connection of the heart with the KA. The rubrics to this Chapter are very interesting. They order that the words shall be said over a green stone scarab mounted in silver-gold, and suspended by a ring from the neck of the deceased. This scarab, one side of which was frequently made in the shape of a heart, was placed either inside the body where the heart was before it was removed during the process of mummification, or over the place of the heart on the breast, after the ceremony of "Opening the Mouth" had been performed. As to the origin of the Chapter there are two traditions: according to the one it was "found" cut upon a stone (?) slab under the feet of a statue of the god Thoth in the reign of Semti-Ḥesepti, a king of the Ist Dynasty, and according to the other it was "found" by Prince Ḥeruṭāṭāf, the son of King Khufu. The older tradition states that it had been cut on the slab by Thoth himself. Here, then, is a proof that the text of this Chapter was believed to be of divine origin, and it is certain that the formulae in it were thought to possess very great power. The Vignettes in several papyri connect them with the weighing of the heart in the presence of Osiris, and in the large pictures of the Judgment Scene they are always assumed to be recited by the deceased whilst his heart is actually in the

Scales. Now the pictures of the Judgment Scene illustrate beliefs which were universal in Egypt some two thousand years before it became the custom to illustrate the sacred texts, and it is clear that during the whole Dynastic Period, i.e., for a period of about four thousand years, the Egyptian entered the Judgment Hall of Osiris believing implicitly that the words which he was about to utter would secure for him a verdict of righteousness, and, in consequence, everlasting life in felicity.

CHAPTER XXXI.

By the recital of this Chapter the deceased was able to frustrate the designs of the monster Sui, which came in the forms of three or four crocodiles to carry off from him the words of power which he had obtained, or the heart-amulet on which they were cut. Only by stealing such words of power could Sui live. The recital of this Chapter made the incisor teeth of the deceased like flints, and his molars like the name of Anubis. In the later version of the Chapter the deceased describes the offices which the words of power enabled him to fill. He was the scribe of the offerings of Osiris and priest in the regions above. Moreover, he was born with Osiris, and he opened the mouth of the gods with the Meskhet (i.e., Thigh) instrument. He was perfect, and strong, and able to avenge wrongs done to him, and he was master of the four quarters of heaven and earth.

CHAPTER XXXII.

This Chapter enabled the deceased to repulse the four crocodiles of the West, East, South and North, and to assume the attributes of the gods Set, Osiris, Sept, and Uatch-Merti, who presided over the four quarters of the earth respectively. Curiously enough, the opening paragraph mentions the "Eight Crocodiles," the names of which are known to the deceased, who is therefore able to repulse them, or to render them powerless to do him harm by casting spells on them.

CHAPTER XXXIII.

Among the foes of the deceased in the Other World serpents formed an important class. This Chapter was directed against the monster serpent Rerek, who was only rendered powerless when the deceased pronounced the names of Seb and Shu. The deceased orders Rerek to stand, promising to give him to eat the "mouse,[1] the abomination of Rā," and the bones of the "filthy cat."[2]

[1] 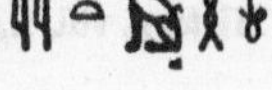 *penu*, the Coptic ⲡⲓⲛ.

[2]

It is difficult to explain the allusion to the "filthy cat," for usually the cat is connected with Rā, the Sun-god.

CHAPTER XXXIV.

This Chapter is also directed against snakes and snake-bites, and by the recital of it the deceased identifies himself with the animal *maftet* . Whether the word *maftet* means "lynx" or not, it is certain that some animal which was inimical to snakes, and was very skilful in destroying them, is referred to. The true lynx is not a native of Africa,[1] and it is probable, as the determinative  suggests, that the *maftet* was a species of wild or hunting cat, perhaps the *felis cerval*. The *maftet* is frequently mentioned in the texts of the Ancient Empire, with allusions to its terrible claws. The kind of serpent mentioned in the text is the *ārārt*, , or cobra, the *οὐραῖος* of the Greeks.

CHAPTER XXXV.

This Chapter was directed against the monster serpent called Seksek, and the other serpents of his class. The allusions in it are hard to understand, and

[1] Lyddeker, *Royal Natural History*, vol. i., p. 486.

suggest that the text was so old when it was copied by the scribes of the XVIIIth Dynasty that parts of it had no meaning for them. This is precisely the case with the formulae against snakes which are found in the Pyramid of Unås (Vth Dynasty).

CHAPTER XXXVI.

This Chapter contains a spell for keeping away from the dead the insect *Āpshait*, , which is figured correctly in the Vignette to the Chapter in the Papyrus of Nekht. In the Papyrus of Nekhtu-Åmen the *āpshait* is depicted in the form of the *scarabaeus sacer*, but it is clearly an incorrect identification. The creature is undoubtedly a kind of beetle, and I believe it to be the weevil, which is often found crushed between the bandages of mummies, and to belong to the *genus Brachycerus.* Figures of it are often found in a more or less conventionalized form on the objects made by the Bakuba of the Kasai District in the Congo Free State. According to Mr. T. A. Joyce, of the British Museum, the insect which occurs in a most naturalistic form on a carved wooden cup published by him is called *Mutu Jambi*, or "the head "of God."[1] A specimen is exhibited in the Department of Ethnography in the British Museum (Table-

[1] See *Man*, vol. ix., No. 1, p. 8

case 194). It is quite clear that the scribes of the XVIIIth and XIXth Dynasties did not know what the *āpshait* was, for whilst one of them thought it was the ordinary *scarabaeus sacer*, another thought it was a *pig*, and wrote *shaȧ*, and the artist who drew the Vignette actually drew a pig!

CHAPTER XXXVII.

The recital of this Chapter enabled the deceased to ward off the attacks of two terrible sister-serpents called Merti, . In the Vignettes the deceased is seen either spearing a serpent or threatening two serpents with a knife, but he relied most of all upon the spell which he cast upon them to render them powerless.

CHAPTER XXXVIII.A AND B.

The formulae of this Chapter were, according to the title, intended to give air to the deceased in the Other World. In form A he identifies himself with Tem, the god of wind and the giver of air, and in form B with the Twin-gods Shu and Tefnut, the gods of the atmosphere. In one Vignette he holds a sail, symbolic of "air," or "wind," and in the other a sail and a knife;

the presence of the three serpents in the second Vignette is difficult to explain. The allusion to the "lily of green felspar," , which blossomed at sunrise under the influence of the cool wind of dawn is peculiarly appropriate to the appearance of the deceased at daybreak in the Other World.

CHAPTER XXXIX.

The recital of this Chapter was intended to free the deceased from the opposition or attack of the monster serpent Rerek, who lived in the darkest part of the Other World and endeavoured to obstruct the passage of Rā the Sun-god, and of the souls who were with him, into the kingdom of day. He had many forms and many names, but the most terrible of all his forms was that which was called Āpep, . He was endowed with immortality, for, although each day the Mafṭet tore his breast open, and the beams of the sun stabbed him with myriads of darts, and Serqet fettered him, and Ḥertit bound him in chains, and the gods held him with ropes, and Rekes overthrew him, and Rā clove his head in twain, and he was dismembered and his bones crushed, he came to life again daily and continued his nefarious efforts. His master was Set, the god of evil, and it is interesting to note that the

deceased identifies himself with Set, the lord of the storm and thunder in the heavens.

CHAPTER XL.

This Chapter is a formula directed against another monster serpent, which is called "Eater of the Ass," , in the title, and Hai, 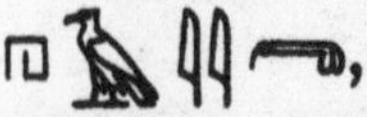, in the text. He attacked the Neshmet Boat, and Thoth cut off his head. In the Vignette he is seen in the form of a serpent which has seized an ass by the middle of his back. Now the "Ass" was associated with the Sun-god, and the Eater of the Ass was probably a local form of Āpep which was destroyed daily. He is said to be an abomination to the god Aḥu, ,[1] but for what reason is unknown; Aḥu appears to have been a "fighting god," and his original home was probably Syria.

CHAPTER XLI.

The recital of this Chapter enabled the deceased to avoid slaughter in the Other World, and to obtain air

[1] I.e., the of the text of Pepi II., l. 849.

therein at eventide, when he had the power to go and converse with the divine crew who worked the Boat of Râ across the sky day by day. The contents of the Chapter have very little connection with its title, a fact which shows that titles were given by the scribes to ancient formulae, often without proper regard for their accuracy or suitability.

CHAPTER XLII.

This Chapter was also intended to enable the deceased to avoid the slaughter which took place in the Other World. It seems clear from the text that a great slaughter of the souls of the dead took place from time to time in Suten-ḥenen, and the deceased feared that violent hands might be laid on him, and that he might be dragged back by his arms. His only way of escaping any such treatment was to identify each member of his body with or transform it into the similar member of a god. The names of the gods are duly enumerated in a remarkable passage which is a modification of a text found in the Pyramid of Pepi I. (l. 565 ff.). Thus we read:—

"My hair is [the hair of] Nu.

"My face is [the face of] Âten.

"My eyes are [the eyes of] Hathor," &c.

In the older text the form is somewhat different, and we read:—

"The head of Pepi is the [head of a] hawk (Horus);[1]
"he cometh forth and raiseth himself to
"heaven.

"The skull of Pepi is the [skull of the] *Khas* bird
"of the god; he cometh forth and raiseth
"himself to heaven," &c.

The members and the gods in the Pyramid of Pepi I. are as follows:—

1.		head.	Horus (?).
2.		skull.	Khas bird.
3.		[neck].	Nu.
4.		face.	Åp-uatu.
5.		two eyes.	Great Ones of Ånnu.
6.		nose.	Thoth.
7.		mouth.	Khens-ur.
8.	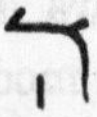	tongue.	The maå beam of the Maåt Boat.
9.	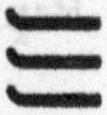	teeth.	Souls of Ånnu.
10.		lips.	. . . . . .
11.		chin.	Khert-Khent-Sekhem

[1] Or, "The head of Pepi is as the hawk," &c.

12.		backbone.	Sma.
13.	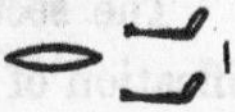	shoulders.	Set.
14.		[breast].	Baäbu, .
15.		heart.	Bastet, .
16.		belly.	Nut.
17.		[reins].	Two Companies of gods
18.		lower part of back.	Ḥeqet.
19.		buttocks.	The boats Semktet and Māt.
20.		phallus.	Ḥāpi.
21.		thighs.	Net and Serqet.
22.		legs.	The two Tcherti (?).
23.		soles.	The double Maāt Boat
24.		heel (?).	Souls of Ȧnnu.

The transformations of his members having been effected the deceased says, "there is no member of my "body which is not the member of a god," or, as the text of Pepi I. reads, "Pepi is a god, the son of a god." The text next identifies the deceased with Rā, and

Horus, and Osiris Un-nefer, and he becomes the "only "One who proceedeth from an only One." The section of this Chapter which provides for the deification of the members was a very favourite one with the Egyptians, and, in a tabular form, it was copied on papyri down to the Ptolemaïc and Roman Periods.

CHAPTER XLIII.

This Chapter refers to the dismemberment of the bodies of the dead which took place in ancient times, and its recital prevented the head of the deceased from being cut off in the Other World. The excavations which have been made in recent years on pre-dynastic sites in Egypt prove beyond all doubt that in primitive times the bodies of the dead were cut into pieces before burial, no doubt in accordance with the religious beliefs which were then current. Osiris himself suffered dismemberment, but we learn from the texts in the royal Pyramids at Ṣaḳḳârah that the goddess Mut gave him back his head, and presented his bones to him, and collected the flesh which had been sliced off him, and brought back his heart and placed it in his body.[1] The reconstituting

[1] 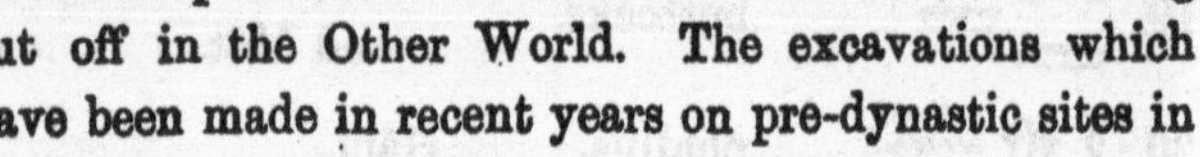
Pepi I., l. 110.

of the body of Osiris was commemorated annually at Abydos by a solemn festival, during which, in a sort of miracle play, every step in the process was acted by priests and their assistants. The crowning scene was the erection of the backbone of Osiris and the placing of the head of the god upon it. The formulae of this Chapter identified the deceased with Osiris, and assured him therefore of the possession of his head. As the cult of Osiris grew and spread in Egypt in early dynastic times the practice of dismembering the body gradually fell into disuse, and at length the only portions of the body which were removed from it during the process of embalming were the viscera, and these were mummified separately.

CHAPTER XLIV.

This Chapter proves the existence of a very curious belief among the Egyptians, i.e., that it was possible for a being in the Other World to die a second time. The animal soul of the deceased in the Other World lived on the souls of the offerings which were made at regular intervals in the tomb wherein his body was laid, and if for any reason the supply of offerings failed that soul suffered greatly. It was driven by hunger to wander about in the deserts seeking food, and for a time it might prolong its existence by devouring offal and drinking dirty water, but unless the supply of offerings was renewed it certainly starved to death. It seems also that the soul might suffer death in the Other World if it incurred the displeasure of the Tchatcha and Sheniu chiefs who administered the kingdom of Osiris, and that in such a case it was destroyed along with the souls of the wicked. The only beings who were superior to this possibility were Rā and Osiris, and this Chapter enabled the deceased to identify himself with them; this effected, he declares boldly, "I am "crowned king of the gods, I shall not die a second "time in the Other World."

CHAPTER XLV.

The object of this Chapter is made quite clear by the Rubric: if it be known by the deceased he shall not suffer corruption in the Other World. The formula is supposed to be addressed to the god Anubis, and in it the deceased entreats that god to fashion his mummy as if he were fashioning that of Osiris himself. Anubis is often called "Åm-ut," i.e., "he who is in the place of "embalmment." To Anubis was attributed the knowledge of the art of embalming, and he was skilled in the use of balms, balsams, unguents and medicaments, and was an expert in the swathing of mummies. It was he who mummified the body of Osiris, and he did his work so well that the body of the god did not crumble away, or decay, or fall to pieces.

CHAPTER XLVI.

The recital of this Chapter gave to the deceased the power to rise up like the Ḥenmemet, , or , a class of beings who are frequently mentioned in religious texts of all periods. Their place of abode was heaven, but some portion of their period of existence may have been passed on earth. The recital of this Chapter also set at liberty the BA, , or heart-soul of the deceased, which, as we have already seen, could die a second time, and the soul, here represented in the form of a BENNU bird, , which was immortal.

CHAPTER XLVII.

The recital of this Chapter prevented the seat and throne of the deceased from being taken away from him in the Other World. In the Vignette we see the heart-soul and the soul in the same forms as in the preceding Chapter, one on each side of a funerary building, from which they appear to have emerged.

The text suggests that each soul desired to have reserved for it an abode wherein it might seek shelter if necessary. In the second version of the Chapter the deceased asserts that he is a *sāḥ*, , i.e., that he has attained to spiritual existence, and that he is the son of Maāti, 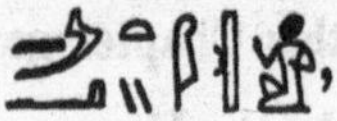, who hates lies.

CHAPTERS XLVIII. AND XLIX.

These Chapters have already been discussed as Chapters X. and XI.

CHAPTER L.A AND L.B.

The recital of this Chapter enabled the deceased to avoid the terrible block of slaughter of the god Osiris, a figure of which is given in the Vignette. From the Book Åm-Ṭuat and the Book of Gates, as well as from the Book of the Dead, we learn that to certain gods was assigned the duty of destroying the dead and consuming their bodies. Some were cast into a lake of liquid fire or boiling water, and others were first cut in pieces and then burnt.[1] Each of the gods who cut the dead in pieces was provided with a block, and they performed their terrible work under the direction of

[1] See my *Egyptian Heaven and Hell*, vol. iii., p. 187.

the headsman of Osiris, whose name was Shesmu , or , as the name is written in the Pyramid Texts. The slaughter of the wicked and the cutting up of their bodies were performed nightly, soon after Osiris had completed the judging of those who had entered the Hall of Maāti.

CHAPTER LI.

The connection of the title with this Chapter is not clear. In the text the deceased declares that he will not eat what is an abomination to him, and prays that he may not be forced to eat filth in place of the sepulchral cakes which are usually offered to the Kau, or Doubles, in their tombs, or to touch it, or even to walk on it in his sandals.

CHAPTER LII.

This Chapter is an amplification of the preceding, and in the latter part of it we are told exactly what food the deceased wishes to eat in the Other World, and under what conditions he wishes to live there. He would partake of the seven loaves which Horus eats and of the bread which Thoth eats, seated under the branches of the Sycamore Tree of Hathor (or Nut), at

the time when the souls of the beatified have alighted thereon. His bread must be made from white grain, and his beer (the modern *marissa*) from red grain, he would have the ancestors[1] of his father and mother to attend to his domestic affairs, he would watch his crops growing, and enjoy health and strength, and would have plenty of space in which to move about, and be able to dwell where he pleased. A much fuller version of this Chapter will be found in the second edition of the Egyptian text, p. 160 ff., where it is called Chapter LII.B. In the first edition it stood as No. CLXXXIX. For the translation see p. 639.

CHAPTER LIII.

The recital of this Chapter prevented the deceased from being tripped up during his journeyings in the Other World, and from the necessity of eating filth and drinking urine. The beginning and end of the Chapter are not found in the other Chapters which were written with the same object as this. In this text the deceased states that he will live upon the heavenly food of Rā and the earthly food of Seb, and that his loaves shall be brought to him by the Sektet and Āṭet Boats in

[1] *Abtu* 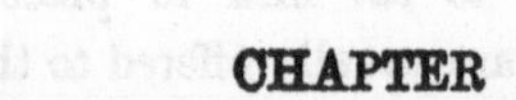, literally, "fathers"; compare אבות.

which Rā sails across the heavens from sunrise to sunset.

CHAPTER LIV

The recital of this Chapter brought to the deceased the "sweet breath which" dwelt in the nostrils of Tem. He identifies himself with the great Egg, which was created by the earth-god Seb and thrust through the earth in the city of the Great Cackler. As the Egg lives he lives, and as it grows old he grows old.

CHAPTER LV.

By the recital of this Chapter the deceased identified himself with the "Jackal of jackals," and with Shu, the god of the atmosphere, and thus was able to roam with the fleetness of the jackal from one end of heaven to the other. and to the ends of the earth, and to the limit of the flight of the Nebeḥ goose, .

CHAPTER LVI.

In this Chapter, as in Chapter LIV., the deceased identifies his life with that of the Egg of the Great

Cackler; his birth is its birth, his life is its life, and his breath is its breath.

CHAPTER LVII.

The recital of this Chapter gave the deceased "dominion over the water," that is, enabled him to obtain a full and constant supply from Ḥāp-ur, "the Great "Nile," and air from every quarter of the earth. By it also he gained the power to breathe freely in Mendes or Busiris, and a settled abode in the celestial Ȧnnu (Heliopolis), where he had his house. The plan of the house was made by the goddess , whose name is read Sesheta or Sefkhet-ābut, and its walls were built by the god Khnemu.

CHAPTER LVIII.

This Chapter is also connected, according to the title, with the dominion of the deceased over the water and the air. The text, however, suggests that the deceased is trying to obtain admission into a portion of the Other World, and that he has with him the two Merti goddesses. A being, name unknown, asks him his name, &c., and apparently provides him with a magical boat, which he is allowed to use provided he knows its name and the names of the oars, rudder, rudder-post, &c.

CHAPTER LIX.

The recital of this Chapter secured for the deceased the air and water which were in the gift of the goddess Nut, who, according to the Vignette, lived in the Sycamore Tree of heaven. The text mentions the Egg of the Great Cackler already noticed, and the first part of the Chapter undoubtedly has reference to the worship of certain trees, which at one time was common in the Sûdân. Such trees were supposed to be the abodes of spirits who, when placated by offerings, bestowed gifts upon those who prayed at their feet.

CHAPTER LX.

The recital of this Chapter caused the gods Thoth and Ḥāp (Nile) to open the gates of heaven and let the deceased into the "Land of cool water," where he was able to drink to his heart's content.

CHAPTER LXI.

The connection of the title of this Chapter with the text is not clear. The deceased identifies himself with the god of the celestial water, which appears on this earth in the form of the Nile, and there is no allusion to any attempt being made to snatch away his heart-soul from him. Its departure from him in quest of water may, however, be referred to; this might be a serious matter for the deceased, for the heart-soul might not return, and then his body would die.

CHAPTER LXII.

The contents of this Chapter resemble those of Chapter LII. In the Vignette we see the deceased washing his hands in a stream preparatory to drinking water out of them, and the allusions to Râ, the Lion-god, and the Bull suggest that the recital of the Chapter gave him the power to wander about in Sekhet-Åaru, and drink from every stream there at will.

CHAPTER LXIII.A AND B.

In version A of this Chapter the deceased prays not to be burned or destroyed by fire, but it is not clear whether by fire he refers to material fire or boiling water, or to burning thirst, or to scalding by boiling water. The Vignette suggests that the recital of the Chapter was intended to secure for him a regular supply of the cool, fresh water of heaven, which he would drink from a bowl as he sat by the side of a lake. The title of version B, "Of not being scalded," is more definite than that of A, and it is clear that the Chapter was written to prevent the possibility of the deceased's drinking boiling water in the Other World. The Book of Gates mentions a "boiling lake," , the waters of which were cool and pleasant to the gods who lived on its shores, but which were veritable fire to the wicked when they attempted to drink them, and which destroyed their bodies.[1] The idea of this boiling lake was derived from the hot springs of bituminous water which are found in certain places in the Western Desert.

CHAPTER LXIV.

This very remarkable Chapter occurs in two versions, one long and one short; it is one of the oldest texts in the Book of the Dead, and the two traditions about its antiquity assign it to the Ist and IVth Dynasties. The title of the longer version is "Chapter of Coming "Forth by Day in the Other World," and the shorter, "Chapter of knowing the Chapters of Coming Forth "by Day in a single Chapter." Thus it seems that this Chapter was supposed to contain in it the essence of the whole Book of the Dead, and according to the Rubrics it constituted a "great and divine protection"

[1] See my *Book of Gates*, p. 109.

to the deceased. If he knew it he was victorious both upon earth and in heaven, he passed through every gate of the Other World without let or hindrance, he performed successfully every transformation he wished to make, and he obtained everlasting life. The formulae which constitute the Chapter are of a highly mystical character, and the recital of them gave to the deceased the power to identify himself with all the great gods, and to make use of all their attributes as he pleased for his own benefit. It was all-important that the man who recited this Chapter should be ceremonially clean and pure, and the Rubric orders that for some time previous to its recital he was to abstain from the use of meats, and fish, and women; but there is no reason for assuming that he was to observe a strict fast. In connection with this Chapter it is further ordered that the formulae which are now generally known as Chapter XXX.B be recited over a green stone scarab, set in a gold mount and anointed with myrrh, and placed in the breast of a man to perform for him the "Opening of the Mouth." It is clear from the above that the recital of the LXIVth Chapter was a very solemn matter.

CHAPTER LXV.

The recital of this Chapter gave the deceased dominion over all his enemies, and enabled him to triumph over Set and his friends and infernal watchers, who lay in wait nightly to destroy Rā as he was emerging from the Ṭuat and the souls of the blessed which were in his train. The deceased also declares that if he is not permitted to emerge from the Other World, the Nile shall never rise again, and Rā shall never again enter its water, and day shall never more appear [on the earth] at its appointed time. In the Saïte Recension of this Chapter the deceased describes his glorious state in the Other World, and says that his enemies shall be led in before him in a state of misery, that his mother's KA, or double, shall rest because of this, and that he will inflict cuts on their legs with a staff of gold!

CHAPTER LXVI.

By reciting this Chapter the deceased identified himself with the son of Sekhet and Neith, and with Horus and the goddess Uatchet, and was able to perch on the brow of Rā in his boat.

CHAPTER LXVII.

The recital of this Chapter caused passages to be opened for the deceased in heaven and in the air, and enabled him to advance to his throne in the Boat of Rā, and to sit there securely.

CHAPTER LXVIII.

In this Chapter the deceased describes the joy and freedom of his life in the Other World. Heaven and earth are open to him, he has gained possession of his members and whole body, he is master of water, air, canal, river, land, furrows, and male and female slaves. He has white bread to eat, beer made from red grain to drink, he sits in a clean place under a date palm and wheresoever he pleases, he stands up or sits down at pleasure, and stands "like a well equipped guide," free in the air. He has "come forth by day," and he goes about among the living.

CHAPTER LXIX.

The title of this composition is merely "Another Chapter," and the ancient scribes appear to have regarded it as a continuation of Chapter LXVIII., which it undoubtedly is. The deceased identifies himself in it with the Fire-god Aseb, 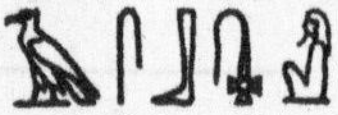, with Osiris ithyphallic, Orion, Anubis, Osiris, Horus and Tem. He opens the mouth of the gods, he is a companion of Thoth, and he offers up sacrifices to Ån-ḥeri-ertitsa, 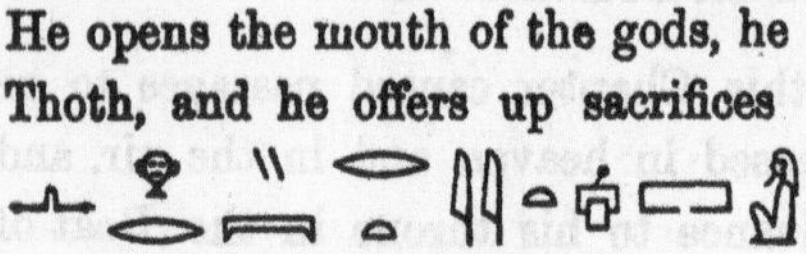, of whose special attributes nothing is known.

CHAPTER LXX.

This Chapter is a further continuation of Chapter LXVIII., and the effect of its recital appears to have been to give the deceased the power of seizing the east and north winds by their hair, the west wind by its body, and the south wind by its eye, and travelling about all four sides of heaven.

CHAPTER LXXI.

This Chapter opens with an address to Nekhen, the lord of the ancient Sky-goddess Meḥ-urt, who is depicted in the Vignette in the form of a cow with the deceased kneeling in adoration before her. Following this comes a paragraph beginning, "Behold, Neb-ḥrâ-"uâ, 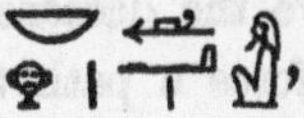, is with me," which was addressed, with modifications, to each of the **Seven Spirits**, whose names were :—

1. Netcheḥ-netcheḥ.
2. Aatqeṭqeṭ.
3. Ânerṭânefbesfkhentihehf.
4. Âq-ḥer-âmi-unnut-f.
5. Ṭeshenmaatiamiḥetânes.
6. Ubesḥrâperemkhetkhet.
7. Maaemḳerḥânnefemhru.

Or,

1. Ḳosthȧ.
2. Ḥāpi.
3. Ṭuamutef.
4. Qebḥsennuf.
5. Maaȧteff.
6. Kheribeqf.
7. Ḥerukhentiȧnmaati.

The knowledge of the names of these terrible beings was of vital importance to the deceased, for it was they who cut off the heads of men, and broke their necks and seized their hearts, and performed slaughters at the Lake of Fire, and it enabled him to come forth from the Other World and shine upon his statue, and gave him a "beautiful tomb" (or, burial) with Osiris. This Chapter was, in fact, a mighty protection for him in the Other World.

CHAPTER LXXII.

The recital of this Chapter gave the deceased the power to leave his tomb and to force a path to the place where the gods lived. It supplied him with the name of the god TEKEM, , and it enabled him to travel through Sekhet-Ȧaru, and eventually to reach Seket-ḥetep, i.e., the Field of Peace, or, the Field of Offerings. According to the Rubric, the writing of this Chapter on the coffin of the deceased produced the same effect as the recital of it by him. In line 8 there is an allusion to the Mesqet, 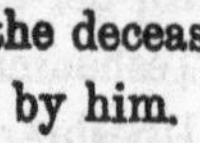, or chamber in which the deceased was reborn, or perhaps annihilated. The Mesqet was originally the skin of a bull in which the deceased was placed, but in later times the word was applied to the Ṭuat, or Other World, in general. Tradition asserted that Osiris was assisted in preserving his life on one occasion by taking refuge in a bull's skin, and the skin of this bull is usually seen hanging to a pole before Osiris in his shrine in pictures of the Judgment.

CHAPTER LXXIII.

See Chapter IX.

CHAPTER LXXIV.

This Chapter contains formulae addressed to Seker, a very ancient god of the dead whose kingdom formed the Other World of the people of Memphis, and is represented to-day by the great necropolis of Ṣaḳḳârah. It is possible that the name "Ṣaḳḳârah" may be derived from the name of the god Seker, . The Vignette contains a picture of Ḥennu, the sacred boat on which the shrine containing the god was placed. The recital of this Chapter gave the deceased the power to emerge from his tomb, and to stand on his feet like Seker in his hidden and mysterious abode.

CHAPTER LXXV.

This Chapter is connected with the preceding, and its recital gave the deceased the power to pass from Ṣaḳḳârah, on the left bank of the Nile, over, or under, the river to Ȧnnu (Heliopolis), on the right bank, and to take up his abode in the sanctuary of the great Sun-god, whose home was in that ancient city. On his way thither he passed through the region where reposed the souls of the blessed dead who are referred to in the later sections of the Book Ȧm-Ṭuat and the Book of Gates, and the gods of that region, Ȧkhsesef, , and Remrem, , or Kemkem, , afforded him their protection. The magical buckle, , which carried with it the mystical power of the blood of Isis, caused the goddesses Khebent, , and Sekseket, , to be gracious to him, and it placed him in the eastern part of the sky where Rā rose daily.

CHAPTER LXXVI.

The recital of this Chapter secured for the deceased the service of the insect *abit* 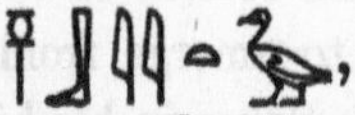, which, on account of the assistance that it rendered to him, may be identified with the mantis. He says, "I have come "into the house of the King through the *abit* which led "me hither." It is a common belief in many parts of Central and South Africa that the mantis acts as guide to the traveller who has lost his way, and the Hottentots say that the insect leads children who have lost themselves in the bush back to their villages and houses. We find that the mantis, the Goliath beetle, and the bee all play a prominent part in the Book of Opening the Mouth, and when we remember the unknown and difficult roads which the deceased had to travel over in the Other World, it is easy to see how important it was for him to be able to take the form of the mantis at pleasure, and find his way back to a place he knew. According to the title this Chapter enabled the deceased to make any transformation, i.e., take any form he pleased.

CHAPTER LXXVII.

The recital of this Chapter enabled the deceased to take the form of a golden hawk, with wings which were like felspar, and had a spread of four cubits. In this form he could fly to the Boat of Rā and visit any and every part of Sekhet-ḥetep.

CHAPTER LXXVIII.

The recital of this Chapter enabled the deceased to take the form of the divine hawk, i.e., the hawk which possessed the powers of Rā himself, and to fly from one end of Egypt to another, and to visit all the great sanctuaries of Rā and Osiris. In this form all the gods of heaven, earth, and the Ṭuat regarded him with awe, for he possessed the soul of Horus, the Hawk-god *par excellence*. All the mysteries of the gods were laid bare before him, for, the soul of Horus being in him, he became the son of Osiris, the King of the Other World.

CHAPTER LXXIX.

In this Chapter the deceased identifies himself with the "great god who created himself," the lord of life and maker of the gods, and becomes therefore the Ruler of the Tchatcha, or chief administrators of the Kingdom of Osiris. The Tchatcha kept the registers of Osiris and the lists of all who were in his kingdom, and they had the power to give rewards to those who performed their appointed tasks and to punish those who did not. They were, in fact, the celestial judges and magistrates under the direct supervision of Osiris, and their power was absolute and their decrees were final.

CHAPTER LXXX.

By the recital of this Chapter the deceased became the "girdle of the robe of Nu," and the great luminary of heaven who was able to lighten not only the darkness about himself, but also the darkness of all those who were in the Other World, and to lead away the darkness captive. When storms or eclipse overtook the Eye, i.e., the Sun, he rescued the Sun-god from destruction, he weighed Set in the scales against the Aged One, i.e., Rā, and sent him to his doom, and he provided Thoth with all that he needed to make the Moon-god shine in the full moon on his fifteenth day. In short, this Chapter enabled the deceased to transform himself into Light.

CHAPTER LXXXI.A AND B.

In this Chapter the deceased identifies himself with the "pure lily" in the waters of the celestial Ocean out of which Rā, under the name of Nefer-Tem, rose daily. The lily, or lotus, was the symbol, or image, of Nefer-Tem, who, according to Memphite theology, was the son of Ptaḥ and the goddess Sekhet.

CHAPTER LXXXII.

In the preceding Chapter the deceased identifies himself with the son of Ptaḥ, and in this he identifies himself with Ptaḥ, the Blacksmith-god of Thebes, thereby obtaining funerary offerings in abundance, and the power to become a living being in Ȧnnu (Heliopolis), and a partaker of the existence of Temu, the chief god of that city. Many passages in the Chapter relating to offerings of food and drink are already familiar from Chapter LII., &c.

CHAPTER LXXXIII.

The text of this Chapter does not make clear exactly what advantage would be gained by the deceased from its recital. The Bennu bird, as we have already seen, was regarded as the soul of Rā, and it no doubt possessed faculties and attributes of a remarkable nature, but what these were is not known. The deceased, by the recital of the words of this Chapter, identifies himself with Khensu, an ancient Moon-god, who was regarded as the "great strider" through the night sky. The words, "I have clothed myself like "the tortoise (or, turtle)," suggest that the deceased wished to clothe himself in apparel as thick and strong as the shell of the tortoise, so that he might be able to withstand the attacks which birds of the Bennu class might make upon him. The existence of the Rubric seems to show that the ancient editors of the Book of the Dead did not know the exact import of this Chapter.

CHAPTER LXXXIV.

This Chapter appears to have some connection with funerary sacrifices and offerings, and its recital probably enabled the deceased to supply himself with such necessary things. The connection of the heron in the Vignette with the formulae to be recited is not clear.

CHAPTER LXXXV.

By the recital of this Chapter the deceased identified himself with the Soul of Rā, the Soul which is God, or is Divine, the Soul of the everlasting gods, and with the body of that Soul, which is eternity itself. As the possessor of that Soul the deceased became the counterpart of Nu and Kheperȧ and the lord of light, i.e., Rā, and the substance of his being was identical with that of the gods. Now the eternal Soul of Rā was also the Soul of Osiris, whose living symbol on earth was the famous Ram-god of Mendes. From the XVIIth Chapter we learn that the Soul of Rā and the Soul of Osiris met in Ṭaṭṭu, and, having joined themselves together in that sacred city, they became the Twin-souls which were known as the TCHAFUI, . Thus the great god of Ṭaṭṭu possessed a dual soul, one member performing functions which resembled those of the heart-soul (*ba*) in man, and the other having the characteristics of the spiritual soul (*khu*) in man. In the Vignettes we see an allusion to a play upon words, for the word ram is *ba*, and the word for the heart-soul is *ba*.

CHAPTER LXXXVI.

The recital of this Chapter gave to the deceased some power possessed by the bird, probably the swallow, which is represented in the Vignette. This bird is said to have rendered service to Isis when she was in trouble, by carrying the news of the calamity which had befallen her to the gods, who straightway went to her aid. It is possible that the deceased expected this Chapter to make him to be received everywhere in the Other World with the same cordial welcome which was given to the swallow on this earth as the harbinger of good tidings. For he says, "Let me advance with my "message, for I have come with words to tell. Open "the doors to me and I will declare the things which "have been seen by me." The news he had to tell was that Horus had risen as the successor of Osiris, and that Set, the god of evil, was bound in the fetters which he had made for the deceased. The connection between the Scorpion, the daughter of Rā, and the swallow is not clear, but to identify himself with the Scorpion-goddess Serqet seems to have been all-important to the deceased.

CHAPTER LXXXVII.

By transforming himself into the Sata serpent the deceased obtained the power of gliding unharmed through the remote parts of the earth, just as by taking the form of the golden hawk he was able to fly to the uttermost parts of heaven in every direction at will.

CHAPTER LXXXVIII.

By the recital of this Chapter the deceased was enabled to take the form of the crocodile, and to traverse the Nile from one end to the other, and to penetrate all the great canals which ran from the river to the hills on its east and west banks. The terror which accompanied the appearance of the crocodile among men now became the attribute of the deceased, and he was able to seize his prey when and where he pleased. The crocodile is one of the oldest objects of veneration in Egypt, and until quite recently it was worshipped in some of the islands in Lake Victoria. At the end of the XVIIIth century of our era the king of the crocodiles was believed to live at Armant in Upper Egypt, and a gigantic crocodile was held in veneration at Kharṭûm during the reign of Muḥammad 'Alî![1] In certain districts on the Blue Nile the natives believed that by the use of magic men were

[1] See my *Egyptian Sûdân*, II., p. 414.

able to enter crocodiles and to cross the river in them, and to the present day the belief exists in the Sûdân that the eating of a portion of the genitals of a crocodile increases in a man the power of begetting children

CHAPTER LXXXIX.

The Egyptians of all periods believed that the souls of the blessed would meet again and recognize in the Other World the souls which they had known and loved upon earth, and several spells and prayers were written with the object of bringing about the reunion of families. By the recital of this Chapter over a golden soul, inlaid with precious stones, placed on the breast of his mummy, the deceased believed he would be able to compel his heart-soul (*Ba*) to come from any and every place and unite itself to his body. Once the heart-soul had returned it was impossible for the body to crumble away and perish. In the text (l. 4) the deceased prays that he may have possession of his heart-soul (*Ba*) and his spiritual soul (*Khu*), and the last line of this very important Chapter proves that the *Ba* joined itself to the material body (*khat* 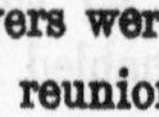), and the *Khu* to its spiritual body (*sāḥ* 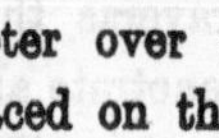). The reunion of souls took place at Ȧnnu (Heliopolis).

CHAPTER XC.

The recital of this Chapter enabled the deceased to spit out of his mouth the "recollection" (or, taste) of foul or evil things. In the formulae he adjures the "cutter off of heads and the splitter of skulls" not to cut off his head or split his skull, and not to prevent him from uttering the words of power which he knows by closing his mouth. This evil being attacked Osiris on one occasion, being urged to do so by Set, but Isis cast spells upon him, and frustrated his nefarious design. As the monster retreated before Osiris so, the deceased believed, he would retreat before him when armed with the words of power contained in this Chapter.

CHAPTER XCI.

This interesting Chapter introduces us to another of the constituent elements of man, namely his shadow, *khaibit*, which was depicted in the form of a parasol or umbrella, . In the text it is mentioned in connection with the heart-soul and the spiritual soul, and, in the light of the beliefs current on the subject of the shadow in Central and West Africa at the present day, we may assume that the shadow is to be regarded as a third soul. At all events, the soul and the shadow are so intimately connected that many tribes use only one word for both soul and shadow,[1] and it is generally thought that the shadow is one of the four souls of man. A man will take infinite pains in the daytime to avoid losing his shadow, even for a short time; at night he is less careful, for then all shadows lie down in the shadow of the Great God and renew their strength.[2] A man may be murdered by the secret stabbing of his shadow, and the man who has lost his shadow necessarily dies. The recital of this Chapter prevented the souls of the deceased from being shut in the tomb or any part of the Other World, and transformed him into a spiritual soul who possessed his heart-soul and his shadow.

CHAPTER XCII.

This Chapter is one of great importance, for it proves that the heart-soul was intimately connected with the Ka, or double of a man. Its recital enabled the Ka and the Ba to leave the tomb at pleasure, and in one Vignette we see the deceased on one side of the tomb door and his Ka and Ba on the other, having passed through the door. From this and the preceding Chapter it seems clear that the Ka and the Ba and the Khaibit were closely associated in the minds of the

[1] Nassau, *Fetichism*, p. 64.
[2] Kingsley, *West African Studies*, p. 207.

Egyptians, and that in early times they represented three phases of that soul in man which could not die.

CHAPTER XCIII.

This Chapter presents some difficulty. The meaning of the text is on the whole clear, and by its recital the deceased was enabled to avoid going to the East, or being carried there against his will. It is possible that the Egyptians thought that the souls of the dead, when setting out on their journey from the earth to the Other World, might take the wrong turning, and so travel to disaster and annihilation. The being seated in the boat with his face turned round behind him, as seen in the Vignette, is a very old god, and his name, Ḥrȧ-f-ḥa-f, , occurs in the Pyramid Texts; his functions are unknown. The allusion to the phallus of Rā is not clear. We may note the threat on the part of the deceased that the Eye of the Sun shall become obscured through the suppuration which shall take place in it if he be kept in restraint, or carried off forcibly to the East.

CHAPTER XCIV.

By the recital of this Chapter the deceased identified himself with Thoth, the righteous scribe of all the gods, and the heart of Râ, and in this character he became the secretary of Osiris, and understood all the mysteries which were written in the Books of God. As Thoth he knew all the words of power which that god had invented, the secrets of all hearts were open to him, and he became the chief recording angel.

CHAPTER XCV.

The object of this Chapter is not quite clear, but the text seems to imply that the deceased by reciting it obtained the power of stilling storms and putting an end to strife among the gods who caused rain and thunder, just as Thoth stopped the fight between Horus and Set, and Râ and Âpep, and Osiris and Set, when the champions of light and order fought against the powers of darkness, wickedness, and chaos. According to a papyrus in the British Museum (No. 10,009) this Chapter is entitled, "Of making the transformation "into a goose," and in the Vignette is a picture of a goose.

CHAPTER XCVI.

The recital of this Chapter placed the deceased near Thoth, and caused him to be identified with Râ, the "god who dwelt in his eye." Armed with the intelligence of Thoth and the power of Rā, he made Set to be at peace with him, and made offerings to the ancient Earth-god Aker and to the Red Devils in the fiery clouds at sunrise and sunset, and did homage to Seb, or Ḳeb.

CHAPTER XCVII.

By the recital of this Chapter the deceased propitiated the Four Khu, viz., Maa-åtef-f, Kheribeqf, Ḥerukhenti[ån]maati, and Ånpu, and was enabled to take up his position in the Boat of Rā, to whom he presented an offering of Maāt, , having purified himself in the sacred lakes, and in the well of the Eye of the God "which is under the holy Sycamore Tree of "heaven," in Heliopolis. This has been a holy well from time immemorial, and it is probably the same well as that which the Muslims called "'Ayn-ash-shems," i.e., "Eye of the Sun," and in the waters of which, according to an ancient tradition, the Virgin Mary washed the raiment of Christ. The traditional well is carefully guarded at the present day in a garden at Maṭarîyah, a few miles from Cairo, and a short distance from the obelisk of Usertsen I., which marks the site of the ancient city of Heliopolis.

CHAPTER XCVIII.

By the recital of this Chapter the deceased obtained the use of a boat in the Other World, and the services of a god who understood how and where to sail it. From the facts that he addresses the Meskhet, or the constellation of the Great Bear, and that the "stars "which never set," i.e., the circumpolar stars, put him on his way, it may be assumed that he wished to have the power to sail over the northern heaven. In line 5 there is an allusion to a Ladder, and in the Papyrus of Ani a picture of it is given. This Ladder is referred to in the Pyramid Texts (Unȧs, l. 579, Pepi, ll. 200 and 471); it was made originally for Osiris, who by means of it ascended into heaven. It was set up by Horus and Set, each of whom held one side, and they assisted the god to mount it; in the tombs of the Ancient and Middle Empires several models of ladders have been found, and in later times, as we have seen, pictures of the Ladder of Heaven were drawn on papyri. This Chapter is of Heliopolitan origin.

CHAPTER XCIX.

The object of this Chapter was to enable the deceased to work and sail a boat, that is to say, a magical boat, over the canals and lakes of the Sekhet-Ȧaru, in one portion of which were placed the Sekhet-ḥetep, or

Elysian Fields, where Osiris and the souls of the blessed lived in everlasting felicity. Every part of this boat (*mākhent* ) possessed a name which identified it with some god or goddess, and the deceased was obliged to declare to each part its name before he was allowed to enter it. This Chapter contained the names of each part, and the knowledge of them made the deceased master of the boat, and enabled him to sail from the east to the west of heaven as Rā did each day.

CHAPTER C.

In the preceding Chapter we have seen that the deceased obtained a boat in which to sail over heaven like Rā, and in this we find that provision was made to enable him to enter into the Boat of Rā himself, wherein were the great gods in his following. This Chapter was, like the preceding, of Heliopolitan origin, and it is possible that the idea of the solar boat, with the shrine of the god placed in it, was derived from some Asiatic people. The Chapter was to be recited over a picture of a boat, drawn upon a piece of new papyrus with a special kind of ink made of sulphate of copper mixed with a solution of myrrh; the picture was placed on the breast of the deceased. The words and the picture secured for him the entry into the Boat of Rā, and prevented Thoth, who kept a list of all those who entered the boat, from omitting to inscribe his name on it.

CHAPTER CI.

This Chapter is a spell which was written upon a strip of fine byssus and placed round the neck of the deceased on the day of his funeral. It contains an address to Rā, in which is mentioned the sacred Eye of magical powers, which was seven cubits long and had a pupil three cubits in diameter; the recital of this Chapter strengthened the power of Rā, and enabled him to resist the attacks of Āpep and the fiends of darkness. In fact, Rā himself needed the protection of spells; if Rā were strong the deceased was strong, and if Rā lost his strength the deceased perished. The formulae of this Chapter transformed the deceased into a "follower of Horus," and made him like Sepṭ (Sothis), and gave him the company of his kinsfolk, and the goddess Menqet caused plants (i.e., grain) to spring up from his body, and Thoth made light to shine on him.

CHAPTER CII.

By the recital of this Chapter the deceased caused Rā to bring his boat to him, and to allow him to enter it, and to sail about with the god among the region of the stars which never set, i.e., the circumpolar stars of the northern sky. He states that he has lived upon the pure food which the solar boats Sektet and Ātet (or Māṭet) have brought to him, and, having eaten of the food of Rā, he is pure like Rā, and of like substance. In line 8 appears to be mentioned the curious custom of spitting, as a sign of healing and blessing, which is common among several peoples of Africa at the present day. Thus Mr. Thomson says, "Little "bits of paper were next dipped in the water, and after "I had spat upon them the ceremony was over, and "the pieces were handed round as an infallible cure "warranted not to fail."[1] Among the Masai spitting "expresses the greatest good-will, and the best of "wishes. It takes the place of the compliments of the "season, and you had better spit upon a damsel than "kiss her. You spit when you meet, and you do the "same on leaving. You seal your bargain in a similar "manner."[2] Among the Egyptians spitting was a creative act, for the god Tem spat, and Tefnut came into being.

CHAPTER CIII.

The recital of this Chapter placed the deceased among the company who followed the goddess Hathor. This goddess was the personification of the sky, and especially of that part of it which was the "house of

[1] *Through Masai Land*, p. 381. [2] *Ibid.*, p. 290.

"Horus"; hence her name, . Her symbol was in the earliest times a cow, and she represented the great mother of the world and the female power of nature which was perpetually conceiving, creating, bringing forth, and rearing and maintaining all things, both great and small. The Greeks identified her with Aphrodite, and she represented what was true, and good, and all that is best in wife, mother, and daughter.

CHAPTER CIV.

By the recital of this Chapter the deceased was able to avail himself of the services of the *abit*[1] or mantis, and to pass through the house of the Seḥăptet Boat, 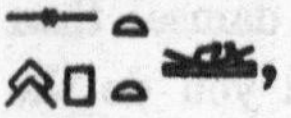, and to take his place among the great gods.

CHAPTER CV.

It has already been said that the KA, or double, and the heart-soul, existed on the offerings which were made in the tombs by the relatives of the deceased, and it was, naturally, one of the first duties of a man whilst upon earth to provide, as far as possible, an endowment to be expended in supplying the statutory offerings.

[1] In this Chapter written *bebait* .

The recital of this Chapter secured food for the KA similar to that on which the KAU of the gods lived, it enabled the deceased to identify himself with the Uatch Amulet, , which was on the neck of Rā, and it prevented his heart from falling away from him.

CHAPTER CVI.

Among the places which the deceased expected to visit in the Other World was the celestial Memphis, the abode of the spirit of Ptaḥ. By the recital of this Chapter the deceased would avoid the possibility of being in that place without food, and would secure a supply of bread, &c., which would be brought to him by the boat of the Other World.

CHAPTER CVII.

The recital of this Chapter gave to the deceased the power to go in and come out from the gate of the gods of the West, and to know these gods in person.

CHAPTER CVIII.

This Chapter also deals with the knowing of the Souls of the West; these were Temu, Sebek, and

Hathor. The place where these Souls lived was the Mountain of Bakhau, or the Mountain of Sunrise, which was 30,000 cubits long and 15,000 cubits broad; its principal god, or "soul," was Sebek. On this mountain lived a serpent 30 cubits long, and his fore-part, for a distance of 8 cubits, was covered with flints and bright metal plates; his name was ÅMI-HEMF, . When Rā came to the mountain in his boat, he attacked the serpent with an iron harpoon, and made him vomit, and thus the power of Suti was broken, and he was turned back. The recital of this Chapter enabled the deceased to do what Rā had done, and to walk boldly over the back of the serpent.

CHAPTER CIX.

The recital of this Chapter gave to the deceased the knowledge of the Souls of the East, i.e., Ḥeru-khuti, the Sucking Calf, and the Morning Star, and of the position of the Gate of the East in the sky, and the Two Sycamores between which Rā appeared daily. It also enabled him to reach that portion of the Sekhet-Åaru where grew wheat with ears two cubits long, and barley with ears three cubits long, which were reaped by the Souls of the Blessed who were nine cubits in height!

CHAPTER CX.

This is a remarkable Chapter, with a large Vignette wherein are depicted the Elysian Fields of the Egyptians. They were surrounded on all sides by water, and were intersected by numerous canals, like many fertile districts in the Delta at the present time. The god of the region was called Ḥetep, whose city was also called Ḥetep, and the soul who had once learned the secret name of the god was able to lead there a life which closely resembled the life he had led upon earth. He sailed at will on the canals, he found there his parents and kinsfolk, he passed from place to place at will, he ploughed, sowed, reaped, ate, drank, married, held converse with the gods, arrayed himself in beautiful apparel, and lived a life of endless happiness. The various Vignettes are explained in detail on pp. 319—323.

CHAPTERS CXI. AND CXII.

By the recital of these Chapters the deceased became acquainted in person with the Souls of the city of Pe in the Delta, whose names were Horus, Ḳesthȧ and Ḥāpi, and learned how to profit by his knowledge of an interesting legend concerning Horus. It seems that in very early times Set, the god of evil, took the form of a black pig, 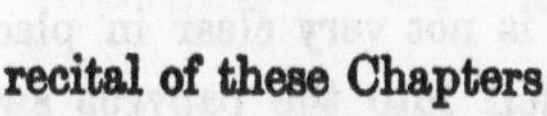, which came into the presence of Horus, who looked on the animal. Soon after this Horus found that a serious injury had been done to his eye through looking at the black pig, and he felt as if he had received a blow in it. Rā ordered him to be placed in a chamber in the city of Pe, and at his request appointed Ḳesthȧ and Ḥāpi to keep watch over him. The legend refers, no doubt, to a great storm which swept over Pe, when the whole heaven was obscured by clouds, and thunders roared, and lightnings flashed, and torrents of rain fell. During the storm Horus was struck in the eye by lightning, or smitten by a thunderbolt, and when the storm had passed Rā appointed two of the sons of Horus to "make the earth blossom," and destroy the thunder-clouds and rain which threatened the city.

CHAPTER CXIII.

This Chapter contains a legend of Horus when he was in the city of Nekhen, in Upper Egypt The meaning of the text is not very clear in places, but it seems that Horus fell into the papyrus swamp, and Isis ordered Sebek, the god of the papyrus swamp, to find him. Sebek took a net and succeeded in recovering the hands and arms of Horus, and by the orders of Rā they were placed in the city of Nekhen, and at the request of Horus, Ṭuamutef and Qebḥsennuf were appointed to watch over them. By the recital of this

Chapter the deceased was enabled to avoid the disaster which fell upon Horus, and to obtain the protection of those who watched over this god.

CHAPTER CXIV.

The city of Khemennu, i.e., the city of the Eight Gods, or Hermopolis, was the seat of the god Thoth, the head of the oldest company of gods in Egypt. This company consisted of four gods and four goddesses, viz. :—

Nu, . Nut, .

Ḥeḥu, . Ḥeḥut, .

Kekiu, . Kekiut, .

Ḳerḥ, . Ḳerḥet, .

These were forms of Thoth and were regarded as his Souls. By the recital of this Chapter the deceased obtained the wisdom, and knowledge, and learning of Thoth and his Souls, and the power to use them to his advantage.

CHAPTER CXV.

By the recital of this Chapter the deceased obtained the power of passing unharmed through the Ȧmmeḥet,

, or Ȧmȧḥet, , and the knowledge of the Souls of Heliopolis, Rā, Shu and Tefnut in person. The Ȧmmeḥet was a division or chamber in the kingdom[1] of the god Seker, wherein certain souls were kept in restraint at the pleasure of the lord of the region, and it seems that at intervals they were tortured by fire. In the text mention is made of the high-priest of Ȧnnu, whose official title was "Urmau," , and there is an allusion to the origin of a beard or tress of hair, , in connection with the god Ȧmi-haf,  , but the exact meaning is not clear.

CHAPTER CXVI.

The purpose for which this Chapter was recited is explained in the Rubric; it prevented the deceased from being obliged to eat offal and drink dirty water. There is probably a mistake in the title which mentions the Souls of Khemennu, whilst the text speaks of the Souls of Ȧnnu who are here said to be Thoth, Sheta-Saa and Rekh-Tem.

[1] It was the fifth Division of the Tuat and was called ȦMENT.

CHAPTER CXVII.

The recital of this Chapter provided the deceased with a staff and a belt, or girdle, and gave him the knowledge of the paths whereon he would travel in Re-stau, a portion of the Other World, and enabled him to pass safely through the funeral valley and reach the Great Lake.

CHAPTER CXVIII.

The recital of this Chapter enabled him to pass through Re-stau, and to emerge safely from it in the company of the Ṣāhu who lived near the abode of Osiris.

CHAPTER CXIX.

This is an interesting Chapter, for it shows how the Egyptians associated the kingdom of Osiris at Abydos with Re-stau, which was in the Other World of Seker near Memphis. Its recital enabled the deceased to identify himself with the Sāḥu (spiritual body) of Osiris, and to enter the presence of Rā in its company.

CHAPTERS CXX. AND CXXI.

These have already been described as Chapters XII. and XIII.

CHAPTER CXXII.

The recital of this Chapter enabled the deceased to re-enter Åmenti at pleasure, and to go in like the hawk and come forth like the *Bennu* bird. The text suggests that he is asking some god to admit him into Åmenti, and in reply to the question "Who art thou?" he recites the names of various parts of the boat in which he is sailing. It seems as if the Chapter represents the belief that the deceased was obliged to return to Åmenti in order to partake of milk, cakes, bread, ale and meat in the Temple of Anubis.

CHAPTER CXXIII.

In this Chapter the deceased identifies himself with Thoth, who made the Two Combatants, Horus and Set, to cease from fighting and to be at peace; being Thoth, he possesses the knowledge of the words of power which are necessary to make the old gods to perform his commands, and the young gods to follow him. The allusion to the Ȧṭu fish, , is not clear, and little is known about the god Nem-ḥrȧ, or Uḥem-ḥrȧ, .

CHAPTER CXXIV.

According to one papyrus the formulae of this Chapter were recited to enable the deceased to transform himself into a *Bennu* bird, and according to another the Chapter contains the speech which he was supposed to make when he entered into the presence of the TCHATCHA, , or chief ministers of Osiris (i.e., the four sons of Horus), or into the presence of Osiris himself.

CHAPTER CXXV.

This Chapter is one of the most interesting and remarkable in the Book of the Dead, and it illustrates the lofty moral and spiritual conceptions of the Egyptians in the XVIIIth Dynasty. In the opening section the deceased is supposed to be standing before the doors of the Judgment Hall of Osiris, which are guarded by Anubis, and he describes to this god the journey which he has made from the Delta to Elephantine, and enumerates the shrines and holy places which he has visited. He has conversed with Set, and visited Mendes, the sacred Acacia Tree, Elephantine, the seat of the goddess Sati, Qem-ur, Busiris, the temple of Anubis, Re-stau in the kingdom of Seker, and Ȧn-ruṭ-f the kingdom of Ḥeru-shefi at Herakleopolis. Having told Anubis the magical names of the Hall of Maāti, the god gave him permission to enter. On his arrival in the Hall the deceased then solemnly declared that he knew the name of Osiris, and the names of Forty-two gods who sat there with him to assist him in examining the souls of those who came in before him for judgment, and that he had not committed the sins which he mentioned one by one. According to this confession he 1. had harmed no man; 2. had not injured his family; 3. had committed no evil in a holy place; 4. had not kept evil companions; 5. had done no evil; 6. had not overworked his men; 7. had not sought for honours; 8. or ill-treated his servants; 9. or scorned God; 10. or seized any man's property; 11. or done what the gods hate; 12. or vilified a servant to his master; 13. or caused pain to any; 14. or let any man go hungry; 15. or made any one weep; 16. or committed murder; 17. or caused murder to be committed; 18. or inflicted pain; 19. had not stolen the offerings in the temple; 20. or the sacred bread; 21. or bread offered to the spirits; 22. had not committed fornication; 23 or polluted himself in the sanctuary of the city god; 24. had not given short measure; 25. or filched land; 26. or encroached on land not his own; 27. had not cheated the seller; 28. or buyer by means of false weights; 29. had not stolen the milk of children; 30. had not raided cattle; 31. or snared sacred birds; 32. or caught fish with bait made of fish of the same kind; 33. had not stopped the flow of water; 34. or cut the bank of a canal; 35. or extinguished a fire which ought to burn; 36. had not defrauded the gods of their meat offerings; 37. or raided sacred cattle; 38. and did not repulse God in his manifestations.

In the second form of the Confession the deceased addresses each negative statement to a god, whose duty it appears to have been to punish all those who committed the particular sin mentioned in connection with his name. The names of the Forty-two gods are:—

1. Usekh-nemmåt.	13. Åm-senf.
2. Ḥept-shet.	14. Åm-besku.
3. Fenṭi.	15. Neb-Maāti.
4. Ām-Khaibitu.	16. Thenemi.
5. Neḥa-ḥāu.	17. Āaṭi.
6. Ruruti (Twin-gods Shu and Tefnut).	18. Ṭuṭuf.
7. Merti-f-em-ṭes.	19. Uamemti.
8. Nebå.	20. Maa-ånu-f.
9. Seṭ-qesu.	21. Ḥeri-seru.
10. Uatch-nes.	22. Khemi.
11. Qerti.	23. Sheṭ-kheru.
12. Ḥetch-åbeḥu.	24. Nekhen.
	25. Ser-kheru.

26. Basti.	35. Tem-sep.
27. Ḥrâf-ḥaf.	36. Maa(?)-em-âb-f.
28. Ta-reṭ.	37. Ḥi.
29. Kenemti.	38. Utu-rekhit.
30. Âm-ḥetep-f.	39. Neḥeb-nefert.
31. Neb-ḥrâu.	40. Neḥeb-kau.
32. Serkhi.	41. Tcheser-ṭep-f.
33. Neb-ābui.	42. Ân-â-f.
34. Nefer-Tem.	

The order of the names is not always the same, and there are a few variants in the lists given by the different papyri. It will be noticed that the names of very few of the great gods are contained in the list, and it seems as if the Forty-two gods of the Judgment Hall of Osiris were merely divine ministers of that god whose sole duty was to help the god to examine souls nightly.

The last section of this Chapter contains an address to the gods of the Other World which was spoken after the deceased had passed successfully through the ordeal of the Judgment. The Rubric to the Chapter is also of great interest, and in it the deceased is ordered to make a picture of the Judgment Scene in colour upon a new tile made of earth upon which no pig or any other animal has trodden. If he did this it would have the effect of making him and his family to flourish, his name would never be forgotten, and he would be able to satisfy the hearts of the king and his princes. He lived on the food of the gods, went wherever he pleased in the Other World, and followed in the train of Osiris continually.

CHAPTER CXXVI.

In this Chapter the deceased entreats the Four Apes who sat each at a corner of the Lake of Fire, or of boiling water, in the Ȧmmeḥet chamber in the kingdom of Seker, to put away his "evil deeds and sin "which deserved stripes upon earth, and to destroy any "evil which clung to him," and to let him enter Re-stau, and to grant him sepulchral meals. To this petition the Apes reply that they have granted his prayer.

CHAPTER CXXVII.A AND B.

The two versions of Chapter CXXVII. contain hymns of praise to the gods of the QERTI, , i.e., the "Circles" of the Other World, which the deceased sang before he entered into the Great Temple of the Other World.

CHAPTER CXXVIII.

This Chapter contains a hymn to Osiris, the lord of souls, , which the deceased sang to the god as he presented his offerings to him. It belongs to a late period, and contains nothing which is not found in older texts.

CHAPTER CXXIX.

This Chapter has already been described as Chapter C.

CHAPTER CXXX.

This Chapter was recited on the birthday of Osiris, and the object of its recital by the deceased was to "make perfect his spiritual soul." The Rubric directs that it shall be recited over a picture of the Boat of Rā, and that a figure of the deceased be placed in it, with a Sektet Boat on one side and an Āṭet Boat on the other. In the Vignette the deceased is seen standing between the two boats. The object of the Chapter is clear. The recital of it enabled the deceased to identify himself with Rā-Osiris, that is to say, with the Day-sun and the Night-sun, and it provided him either with a passage in both boats of Rā-Osiris, or with two boats in which to follow the god across heaven by day and through the Ṭuat by night. This Chapter is probably of Heliopolitan origin. In the Saïte Recension the Rubric contains an interesting statement to the effect that this Chapter was "found" in the large hall of the temple during the reign of the Majesty of Semti-Ḥesepti, , having been "found" in a cave in a hill which Horus made for his father Osiris Un-nefer,  . Thus it is clear that in the Ptolemaic Period the Chapter was believed to have been in existence under the Ist Dynasty.

CHAPTER CXXXI.

By the recital of this Chapter the deceased identified himself with Rā, and attained the object of his prayer, i.e., permission to enter the boat of the god and to be in the company of Thoth, who was the heart of Rā. The deceased refers to the deity Meḥen, under whose protection Rā sailed, and to her everlasting existence, and to the Lake of a Million Years, and he declares that through all these years Rā is the Lord, and that his path is in the fire. This Chapter also is probably of Heliopolitan origin.

CHAPTER CXXXII.

The recital of this Chapter enabled the deceased to return to earth and to visit his old house, or perhaps tomb. In one of the Vignettes the form of the deceased is standing at the door, and in the other his heart-soul is alighting on the roof of the building.

CHAPTER CXXXIII.

This Chapter is to all intents and purposes a hymn to Rā, and is, no doubt, of Heliopolitan origin. It was intended to be said or sung over a model of the Boat of Rā, four (or seven) cubits long, made of green porcelain, in which were a figure of Rā and a figure of the deceased. No one was to look upon the boat except the father, or son, of the man for whose benefit it was made. If these things were done they would cause Rā to look upon the soul of the deceased as perfect, and the gods would consider him to be an equal, and men and the dead would fall on their faces when they saw him, and in the Other World he would appear as the radiance of Rā.

CHAPTER CXXXIV.

This Chapter resembles the preceding, and is also of Heliopolitan origin. It was to be recited over a model of the Boat of Rā, in which, painted on a plaque, were figures of the deceased, a hawk, Tem, Shu, Tefnut, Seb,

Nut, Osiris, Isis, Suti, Nephthys, and the solar disk; this done the deceased enjoyed existence with Rā daily, and helped to overthrow his enemies.

CHAPTER CXXXV.

This Chapter was to be recited by the deceased on the day when the new moon appeared in the sky, and its recital helped him to become a perfect soul in the Other World, and to escape a second death. The new moon was the symbol of Osiris risen from the dead, and the Egyptians believed that the knowledge of this Chapter would enable the deceased to pass unharmed through the Other World, and to emerge, unfettered by storm and darkness, into the clear vault of heaven. He would then, like Rā, enter his boat and sail over the sky. This and the following Chapter were also of Heliopolitan origin.

CHAPTER CXXXVI.A AND B.

This Chapter is in character similar to the preceding, and was recited with the object of making perfect the soul of the deceased and of securing for it a seat in the Boats of Rā, where it would live for ever and ever.

CHAPTER CXXXVIIA.

This Chapter was recited during the performance in the tomb of some interesting ceremonies which are described in the Vignette. Four men assumed the character of the four pillars of Horus, and each had the name of one of the pillars, i.e., sons of Horus, on his shoulder. Each took in his hand a torch made of strips of *àṭmà* cloth, which had been dipped in the finest Theḥennu unguent, and set fire to it, and after it had been burning some time, that is, during the recital of certain portions of the Chapter, they extinguished them in four earthen vessels containing the milk of a white cow. This ceremony was to be performed daily, with very great secrecy, for it was regarded as a great mystery. If the instructions given in the Rubric were carried out faithfully, the deceased became a "living "soul for ever," and enjoyed all the powers and attributes of Osiris himself. The formulae are said to have been composed by Thoth in very early times, and copies of them are said to have been "found" by Prince Ḥeruṭāṭāf, the son of King Khufu, in a hidden chest in Hermopolis. After the lighting of the torches, a crystal Ṭeṭ, , set on a block of crude Nile mud, was inserted in a cavity in the west wall of the tomb; and a figure of Anubis, set on a similar block, was inserted in a cavity in the east wall; another block of crude Nile mud, containing a hollow filled with lighted incense, was inserted in a cavity in the south wall; and another block, with a figure of a palm-tree set in it, was inserted in the cavity in the north wall. On each block was inscribed a formula which was recited by the deceased, and which prevented the approach of any enemy to the wall of the tomb in which was placed the amulet referred to in the formula. Like certain other Chapters this Chapter was to be recited by a man who had eaten neither fish nor meat, and who had not had intercourse with women. A set of mud blocks with the amulets upon them from a tomb of a priestess of Åmen-Rā at Thebes may be seen in Wall-case No. 73 in the Second Egyptian Room in the British Museum.

In the Vignette of the second and shorter form of the Chapter the Hippopotamus-goddess "Åpit, lady of "amulets," is seen kindling a lamp set on a stand, and the text makes it clear that the flame is a type of the Eye of Horus, or the Sun-god, the "Pillar of his "mother," . It is possible that the ape-goddess mentioned in connection with Ån-mut-f (see above, p. c, Chap. XVIII.) may be a hippopotamus-goddess.

CHAPTER CXXXVIII.

The recital of this Chapter by the deceased gave him the power to enter into the kingdom of Osiris at

Abydos, to become one of the followers of the god, and to identify himself with Horus, the son of Osiris, on the day of the great ceremony when the reconstitution of the body of Osiris was commemorated by setting up the Ṭeṭ, 𓊽, and placing the head of the god on the top of it. The Vignette represents the setting up of the Ṭeṭ by Horus and Isis, and grouped about it are the Souls of Pe and Nekhen, the Ram-gods (i.e., Soul-gods), the Lions of Sunrise and Sunset, the Four Utchats of heaven, the Two Fly-flappers, &c.

CHAPTER CXXXIX.

This Chapter has already been described as Chapter CXXIII.

CHAPTER CXL.

This Chapter was to be recited on the day of the full moon of the sixth month of the Egyptian year over two Utchat amulets, 𓂀, one made of lapis-lazuli and one made of jasper, which were to be placed on the body of the deceased. At the same time four altars were to be dedicated to Rā-Tem, and four to the full moon, and four to the gods whose names are mentioned in the Chapter, and each altar was to be supplied with offerings, according to the list given in the Rubric.

CHAPTERS CXLI. AND CXLII.

These Chapters originally formed one composition, which contained the names of all the gods of heaven, earth, and the Other World, to whom on the ninth day of the festival it was meet and right that the deceased should make offerings on behalf of his father or his son. These names were followed by a list of the forms of Osiris, to which also offerings were to be made. In the Saïte Recension the list of the forms of Osiris comes first, and is fuller than that given in the Theban Recension.

CHAPTER CXLIII.

This Chapter consists of a series of five Vignettes only.

CHAPTER CXLIV.

This Chapter was to be recited during the performance of a number of ceremonies which are described in the long Rubric. The first portion of it, which is arranged in tabular form, contains a representation of the SEVEN ĀRITS, i.e., Halls, which formed the abode of

Osiris in the Other World. Before each Ārit stood three beings: one of these guarded the door, another kept a look-out to see when any one was approaching, and the third acted as herald, and announced the name of the comer to the god. No one could gain admission into the Ārits unless he was able to recite the names of the doorkeepers, watchmen, and heralds. The second portion of the Chapter contains a long address to the Ārits and their keepers, which the deceased was supposed to recite. The Rubric ordered that figures of the gods of the Ārits were to be painted with their Ārits, and that a figure of the deceased was to be made to approach each Ārit in turn. At each Ārit the Chapter was to be recited, and certain offerings made, among them being four vessels of blood.

CHAPTER CXLV.

In the preceding Chapter we have seen that the Hall-gates of the Kingdom of Osiris were seven in number, but in this Chapter the Pylons of the Sekhet-Āaru, or Elysian Fields, which also formed a part of the domain of Osiris, were twenty-one in number. Each Pylon was under the care of two gods, whose names had to be proclaimed by the deceased before he was permitted to pass through it. As he came to each Pylon he uttered the names of the gods and told them what acts of purification he had performed. This done he was allowed to proceed. The speech recited before the XXIst Pylon is the longest of all, and in it the deceased enumerates the shrines which he has visited, and the pious acts which he has performed.

CHAPTER CXLVI.

This Chapter is a version of Chapter CXLV.

CHAPTER CXLVII.

This Chapter is a version of Chapter CXLIV.

CHAPTER CXLVIII.

The recital of this Chapter by the deceased enabled him to supply himself with animal food, milk, cream, &c., and gave him the names of the seven divine cows and their bull, the figures of which are seen in the Vignette. In the text he addresses the god of the kine and their bull, and also the animals themselves. Following the prayer for offerings are pictures of the Rudders of the four quarters of heaven, and of the gods who preside over them, and these also are entreated to give food to the deceased. This Chapter is described

in the Rubric as the "Book of Un-Nefer," 
, and it is ordered that it be recited by the deceased only when he is quite alone. If the instructions in the Rubric be faithfully carried out, Rā himself will be the Rudder of the deceased and his protecting power.

CHAPTER CXLIX.

This Chapter was originally the last of the Chapters of the Book of the Dead, for the words "Here endeth "[the book] in peace," , come at the end of it. It contains pictures of the Fourteen Āats, , of Sekhet-Āaru, or the Elysian Fields, and a series of texts which gives the names of many of the gods who live in them, and descriptions of the Āats. In the Pyramid Texts frequent allusions to the Āats, or Domains, of Horus and Set are met with, but the Āats of Sekhet-Āaru were under the rule of Osiris. The Āats and their gods, according to two lists, were:—

Āat.	God.
I. Ament	. . . .
II. Sekhet-Āaru	Rā-Ḥeru-khuti.
III. Khu	. . . .
IV. Ṭui-qaui-āāui	. . . .

V.	Khu	. . . .
VI.	Åmmeḥet	Sekher-remu.
VII.	Åses	Rerek or Mafṭet (?).
VIII.	Ha-ḥetep	Qa-ha-ḥetep.
IX.	Åksi	. . . .
X.	Nut-ent-qaḥu	. . . .
XI.	Nut-åmt-neter-khert	. . . .
XII.	Åstcheṭet	. . . .
XIII.	Uārt-ent-mu	. . . .
XIV.	Kher-āḥa	. . . .

	ÅAT.	GOD.
I.	Sekhet-Åaru	Rā-Ḥeru-Khuti.
II.	Åpt-ent-shet	Fa-ākhu.
III.	Ṭu-qa-āat	. . . .
IV.	Åat of the Souls	. . . .
V.	Åmmeḥet	Sekher-remu.
VI.	Åsset	. . . .
VII.	Ha-sert	Åkh-pet.
VIII.	Åpt-ent-Qaḥu	. . . .
IX.	Åṭu	Sepṭ.
X.	Unt	Ḥetemet-baiu.
XI.	Åpt-ent-mu	Åa-sekhemu.
XII.	Kher-āḥa	Ḥāp (Nile).
XIII.	Åtru-en-nes-f-shet	. . . .
XIV.	Åksi	Maa-thet-f.
XV.	Åment-nefert	. . . .

CHAPTER CL.

This Chapter contains a list of Fifteen Áats, with a picture of each; it is practically a summary of Chapter CXLIX. in a tabular form.

CHAPTER CLI.A AND B.

The Vignette of this Chapter is of great interest, for in it are represented the form and decoration of the mummy chamber of a tomb, according to the views of those who were learned in matters concerning the Other World. This chamber was rectangular in shape, and in the centre of it the deceased is seen lying on a bier, with his feet to the south, and with the jars containing his viscera beneath it; by his feet stands Anubis, and Nephthys and Isis kneel at the head and foot of the bier respectively. In each corner is a figure of one of the sons of Horus; these figures may have been painted on the walls. Each wall had in it a cavity. In the cavities of the north and south walls were placed bowls of incense, which is here represented as burning, in the cavity of the east wall is a figure of Anubis, and in that of the west wall a Ṭeṭ. A shabti figure stands at the north-east and south-east corners, and a figure of the heart-soul in the north-west and south-west corners. The texts which accompany the gods, amulets, &c., are magical formulae intended to protect the mummy. The text of Chapter CLI.B contains a speech of the god Anubis, in which the beatified state of the deceased is described.

CHAPTER CLII.

The recital of this Chapter secured for the deceased the possession of a house in this world which he could visit daily. The goddess Sesheta, the mistress of architectural knowledge, drew the plan, and its foundations were laid in Heliopolis, the city of Rā. To this house beasts for slaughter were brought by the south wind, and grain by the north wind, and his barley came from the ends of the earth.

CHAPTER CLIII.A AND B.

By the recital of this Chapter the deceased was enabled to avoid capture in the net of "the fowler "whose fingers are hidden," whether the net were cast on land or in the waters. The net itself, and its ropes, and the instruments with which it was fastened to the ground and worked, had each a magical name, and by the knowledge of all these names the deceased not only avoided capture himself but was enabled to use the net and capture fowl and fish for his own needs. Nets are used for catching game to this day by many African tribes, and the Fân tie them on to trees in two long lines which converge to an acute angle, the bottom part of the net lying on the ground. Then a party of men and women accompanied by their trained dogs, which have bells hung round their necks, beat the surrounding bushes, and the frightened small game rush into the nets, and become entangled.[1] The Bible contains several allusions to the net, both as a weapon of evil men and as a hunting instrument. Thus we read of the "wild bull in a net" (Isaiah li. 20), "they "have prepared a net for my steps" (Psalm lvii. 6), and see Psalms ix. 15, x. 9, xxv. 15, xxxi. 4, xxxv. 7; Proverbs xxix. 5; Micah vii. 2, &c. Anthony the Great also spoke of the net of the Enemy.[2]

CHAPTER CLIV.

This is a remarkable Chapter, and is one of the most important in the Book of the Dead. It consists of an address to the god Osiris wherein the deceased prays to his "divine father" not to let his body decay or perish. He appeals to Osiris because, like Tem and Kheperà, he was one who never saw corruption, and entreats him to deliver him from decay even as he delivered his

[1] Kingsley, *Travels in West Africa*, p. 322.
[2] See my *Paradise of the Fathers*, I., p. 11.

own body from the worms and corruption which seize upon the bodies of "every god, and every goddess, and "every animal, and every reptile, as soon as the breath "hath departed from them." The recital of this Chapter enabled the deceased to identify himself with Kheperà, and at the end of the text he says, "My "members shall have an everlasting existence. I shall "neither decay, nor rot, nor putrefy, nor turn into "worms, nor see corruption. I shall have my being, I "shall live, I shall flourish, I shall wake up in peace." A version of the text of this Chapter was written upon one of the linen sheets in which the mummy of Thothmes III. was wrapped.

CHAPTER CLV.

The recital of this Chapter over a Ṭeṭ, 𓊽, of gold, which was placed on the neck of the deceased on the day of the funeral, gave him the power to rise up like Ȯsiris with strength in his back, shoulders, and neck.

CHAPTER CLVI.

The recital of this Chapter over a buckle of carnelian, which was placed on the neck of the deceased on the day of the funeral, gave him the protection of the blood of Isis, and the strength of the goddess and the knowledge of her words of power. It caused Horus to rejoice when he saw him, and one hand of the deceased would be towards heaven, and the other towards earth, regularly and continually.

CHAPTER CLVII.

This Chapter is ordered by the Rubric to be cut upon a figure of a vulture made of gold, which was to be placed on the neck of the deceased on the day of the funeral. This figure and the formula cut on it secured for him the protection and motherly love which Isis lavished upon her son Horus, whom she brought forth in the papyrus swamps of the Delta. According to the legend, Horus who had been left by Isis sleeping in safety was, during her absence, stung to death by a scorpion. Isis, in the form of a vulture, flew about over the swamps, uttering cries as she went, until at length she found the body of her son. Her sister Nephthys cried out to Thoth, who was in the Boat of Râ, and who stopped the solar boat, and came to earth and gave Isis the words of power which enabled her to restore Horus to life. By the recital of this Chapter the deceased identified himself with Horus who was raised up from the dead.

CHAPTER CLVIII.

The words of this Chapter were cut upon a pectoral of gold, which was placed on the neck of the deceased on the day of the funeral, and they secured for him the protection of Isis, whom he calls "my father, my "brother, my mother."

CHAPTER CLIX.

The words of this Chapter were cut upon an amulet of felspar, made in the form of a papyrus column, which was placed on the neck of the deceased on the day of the funeral. They secured for him the protection of Isis and the strength of Horus.

CHAPTER CLX.

By the recital of this Chapter the deceased obtained possession of the health and strength which were in the Eye of Horus, and of the Uatch amulet, , which was bestowed upon the righteous by Thoth.

CHAPTER CLXI.

By the recital of this Chapter the deceased was enabled to enter each of the four quarters of heaven at will, and to breathe the air in them. Osiris gave him the north wind, Rā the south wind, Isis the west wind, and Nephthys the east wind. This Chapter was a "great "mystery," and it was only to be recited in the presence of the father or son of the deceased.

CHAPTER CLXII.

This Chapter was the last of a series which was not originally connected with the Book of the Dead. It was to be recited over a gold figure of a cow, which was to be placed on the neck of the deceased, and to be written on a strip of new papyrus which was to be placed under his head. The object of the Chapter was to keep heat in the body of the deceased until his resurrection, and it is said to have been composed by the Cow-goddess of heaven for the benefit of her son Rā when he was surrounded by beings of fire. It contains the magic names of the Cow and of the Divine Body in Heliopolis, and is one of the few Chapters which mentions Åmen. Of the god PAR, or PAL, 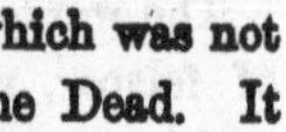 (l. 1), nothing is known.

CHAPTER CLXIII.

By the recital of this Chapter the deceased identified himself with the Divine Soul in Åthabu and with the Divine Soul in Saïs, and became the emanations of the eyes of Åmen, the divine Bull-Scarab, the Lord of the Utchats, and the very essence of the pupils of the eyes of the god. By the knowledge of this Chapter he prevented his body from decaying, by it he avoided the devourers of souls and the things which he hated on earth, and vanquished all the "worms" in the Other World. The Rubric is unusually interesting, and illustrates the magical ceremonies which were performed in connection with the Chapters of the Book of the Dead in the late period.

CHAPTER CLXIV.

This Chapter contains an address to the goddess Sekhet-Bast-Rā, which was to be recited over a three-headed figure of the goddess Mut and two figures of two-headed dwarfs, and it gives the name by which she was known among the dwellers in the Sûdân, viz., Tekaharesapusaremkakaremet, 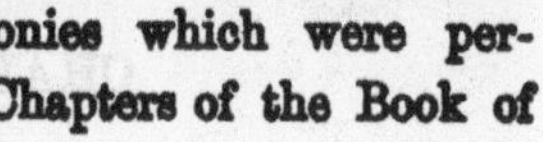

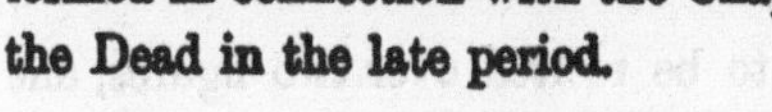. Her father's name

was Ḥarpuḳakasharushabaiu, 

, and the names of the two dwarf-gods were Åtaruåmtcherqemturenu-parsheta,  , and Panemmå,  . If the instructions given in the Rubric were followed, the flesh and bones of the deceased became like those of one who had never been dead.

CHAPTER CLXV.

This Chapter was to be recited over two figures, one of which represented the "god of the lifted arm," and the other a man with a ram's head above each shoulder. The god of the lifted arm was a form of Åmen, and he had the head, arms, hands, and legs of a man, the body of a beetle, and the tail of an animal; he is ithyphallic. The deceased addresses Åmen by various names, several of which appear to be of Sûdânî origin, and entreats the god to let him comprehend him; by the recital of this Chapter the deceased obtained water in the Other World, and shone like the stars of heaven. The attributes of the god Sukati, 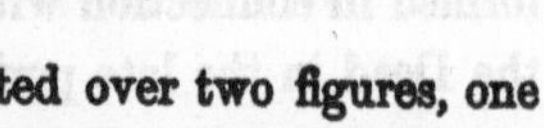, are unknown.

CHAPTER CLXVI.

By the recital of this Chapter the head of the deceased was lifted up in heaven by the gods and preserved for ever. He was enabled by it to avoid slaughter in the Other World, and his head was never carried away from him.

CHAPTER CLXVII.

The recital of this Chapter gave to the deceased the strength which was in the Eye (*Utchat*) of Horus. Making a play on the words *utchat*, "eye," and *utcha*, "strength," he says, "I am sound, and it is sound." The mention of Thoth bringing the Utchat is an allusion to the legend which states that on one occasion Set stole the Eye of Horus and carried it off, whereupon Horus became sick. Thoth went in pursuit of Set, and having found him he took away the Eye of Horus and carried it back to the god; in the struggle between Thoth and Set the latter received a wound in the thigh. On another occasion Set was wandering through the sky on the evening of the new moon, and finding the little crescent there he swallowed it, but Thoth made him vomit, and the moon was restored to the sky. According to another view Set bit a piece off the moon each night after the full moon, and thus the waning of the moon was accounted for.

CHAPTER CLXVIII.

This section contains a series of prayers to the gods of the Eighth, Tenth, Eleventh, and Twelfth Circles of the Other World, who are entreated to grant to the deceased favours and benefits, in return for which offerings on his behalf are to be made to them. The prayers form a sort of Litany of the Gods.

CHAPTER CLXIX.

In this Chapter we have a detailed statement of the various benefits which have been conferred on the deceased by the gods, and its recital secured for the deceased everlasting felicity in the Other World. In the text it is assumed that he has performed all ceremonial obligations, he has passed through the Hall of Judgment with credit to himself, none has obstructed his passage or kept him under restraint, he does as the gods do, he eats what they eat, drinks what they drink, lives with them, holds converse with them, rests happily in the haven of the Gap at Abydos, where he is sheltered from the whirlwind and the storm, and death cannot again approach him. The Great God ordered him to be brought to this place of felicity, and he dwells within Rā.

CHAPTER CLXX.

This Chapter is a continuation of Chapter CLXIX.; the recital of either was equally beneficial for the deceased. Among the favours which the gods bestowed upon him was the gift of books, written in hieroglyphics, which the god Thoth himself brought to him. Shesmu, the headsman of Osiris, also snared and killed the fowl of heaven, which he brought to him, and thus saved him the trouble of working the net for himself.

CHAPTER CLXXI.

This Chapter contains a prayer to all the great gods and goddesses, and to all the divine beings who are in heaven and earth, that when the deceased arrayeth himself in the *ābu* apparel, , he may at the same time be freed from every taint of evil, and may put on all the strength and purity which are the peculiar attributes of all the gods who are mentioned in the text, and may be a pure and undefiled soul for evermore. Among the names of the gods we find the name of Åmen, a fact which suggests that the Chapter is not older than the XVIIIth Dynasty.

CHAPTER CLXXII.

This Chapter consists of an introductory paragraph, and Nine Houses or Stanzas, wherein the triumph, and beauty, and happiness of the deceased are described in picturesque and highly poetical language. He is wholly identified with every power of heaven, and every god and every goddess share their natures and attributes with him. As bearing upon the question of the efficacy of funerary offerings and sacrifices and ceremonies, it is important to note the words, "Hail, "thou who hast been raised up, thou art raised up by "means of the ceremonies which have been performed "for thee."

CHAPTER CLXXIII.

By the recital of this Chapter the deceased identified himself with Horus, the son of Osiris, who came from the Åbt chamber to see Rā in the form of Un-Nefer, i.e., Osiris, the Lord of the Holy Land. When Horus met his father Osiris each god embraced the other, and Horus enumerated in forty short statements the things which he had done on his father's behalf. Each statement opens with the words "I have come," and it will be remembered that in the famous inscription of Thothmes III., which contains a series of addresses to the king by Åmen-Rā, Lord of Karnak, and which enumerates all the great things which the god had performed for him, each address opens with the words "I have come." The recital of this Chapter by the deceased before Osiris caused the god to regard him as his son Horus.

CHAPTER CLXXIV.

The text forming this Chapter was originally a section of the Heliopolitan Recension of the Book of the Dead which was in use under the Vth and VIth Dynasties; it is found in the Pyramid of Unås, ll. 379—399. The title is a later addition, and the Vignette merely illustrates the title. The "great door" alluded to in both is probably the door of the star-god Sept (Sothis), 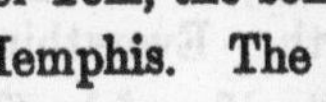, at which the deceased was brought forth by the goddess Sekhet. The Heliopolitan or Memphite origin of the Chapter is proved by the fact that in the text the deceased identifies himself with Nefer-Tem, the son of Ptaḥ and Sekhet, the great gods of Memphis. The symbol of Nefer-Tem was the lily, or lotus, *seshen* , and with this the deceased identifies himself.

CHAPTER CLXXV.

This Chapter is of very great interest, but is full of difficulties. The text as it stands in the Papyrus of Ani shows that the deceased is supposed to have become dissatisfied with the actions of the divine children of Nut, who have brought wickedness and trouble into everything. In his difficulty he appeals to Thoth, the righteous scribe of Osiris. Next, the deceased is supposed to find himself in a region of unfathomable depth and darker than the darkest night, where there is neither air nor water. Allusions are made to Horus, and the throne of the Dweller in the Lake of Fire, the Boat of Millions of Years, &c., but it is impossible to fit these together in a connected fashion with the prayers of the deceased. Immortality is assured to the deceased, for in answer to his question, "How long have I to live?" he is told, "Thou shalt "live for millions of millions of years, a life of millions "of years." In the longer but sadly mutilated version of the Chapter given in a papyrus at Leyden, M. Naville sees the remains of a Heracleopolitan legend of the Flood. The great god Tem informs the deceased that he is about to destroy all that he has made by a flood which he will bring on the earth. Everything will be destroyed except Osiris and himself, and he (Tem) will take the form of a very small serpent which no man shall know of and no god shall see. Osiris will then be left in possession of the earth, and in due time he shall transfer his rule and his throne to his successor Horus.

CHAPTER CLXXVI.

By the recital of this Chapter the deceased became a "perfect soul" in the Other World, and he passed through the Mesqet Chamber and avoided the place where the slaughtering of the enemies of Rā and Osiris was carried out. And he attained to such a state of perfection that he could never die again.

CHAPTER CLXXVII.

By the recital of this Chapter the deceased's soul was raised up, and his heart-soul was made to live in the Other World. This Chapter was originally a section of the text in the Heliopolitan Recension of the Book of the Dead, and its ancient form is found in the Pyramid of Unȧs, l. 361 ff. It mentions some of the gods of the older mythology, e.g., the four Uaipu cow-goddesses, 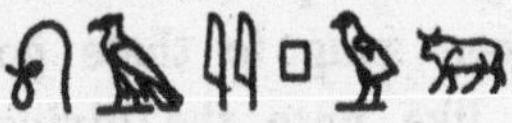, and the blue-eyed Horus, , and the red-eyed Horus, .

CHAPTER CLXXVIII.

By the recital of this Chapter the head of the deceased was established, he gained the sight of his eyes, the hearing of his ears, and protection for his face. The Chapter consists chiefly of extracts from the Heliopolitan Recension of the Book of the Dead; their original forms are found in the Pyramid of Unȧs, ll. 166 ff., 199, 200, and 399 ff.

CHAPTER CLXXIX.

By the recital of this Chapter the deceased advanced from yesterday, and came forth by day, and obtained food in the Other World. His enemy was delivered into his hands, and the God of the Red Eye gave him the shadow and form of the living gods.

CHAPTER CLXXX.

This Chapter is a hymn of praise to Rā and Osiris, and when it had been sung to these gods by the deceased he became like unto the divine and holy Soul-god who is in the Other World. He was thus enabled to travel through heaven with long strides, to go where he pleased, and to perform all his transformations.

CHAPTER CLXXXI.

This Chapter is also a hymn of praise to Osiris, Governor of Åmentet, and to his counterpart, Rā.

CHAPTER CLXXXII.

By the recital of this Chapter the deceased identified himself with Thoth; it contains eight paragraphs in which he describes all the things which he has done for Osiris as Thoth, and a hymn to Osiris, Prince and Governor of Åmentet.

CHAPTER CLXXXIII.

This Chapter is a really fine Hymn to Osiris, in which the deceased, who identifies himself with Thoth, declares all the things which he has done to vivify the Still-Heart, i.e., Osiris. In the form in which it is here given it belongs to the reign of Seti I., B.C. 1370.

CHAPTER CLXXXIV.

By the recital of this Chapter the deceased obtained the power of being near Osiris, and in the Vignette he is seen standing near the god. The text of this Chapter is much mutilated, and from the remains of it, which are found in one papyrus only, it is impossible to make a connected translation.

CHAPTER CLXXXV.

This Chapter is a short hymn to Osiris.

CHAPTER CLXXXVI.

This Chapter contains a short hymn to Hathor, the Lady of Ȧmentet, and a prayer to her by the deceased that he may join those who follow in her train, and may receive funerary offerings in Ȧmentet.

CHAPTER CLXXXVII.

This Chapter contains a short prayer addressed by the deceased to the company of the gods of Rā, and by its recital he was enabled to join that company, and to make his way among them.

CHAPTER CLXXXVIII.

This is an interesting Chapter. The deceased is supposed to have entered into the Utchat, i.e., the Eye of Horus, and to have gained possession of his soul, and heart-soul, and shadow; but according to the title he longed for his heart-soul to have the power to build habitations for itself upon earth, and to come forth by day on earth among men.

CHAPTER CLXXXIX.

This Chapter appears to be an amplification of Chapter LII., many passages in the texts of both being identical; it appears to represent an attempt on the part of a scribe to collect under one heading all the important formulae, the recital of which enabled the deceased to avoid eating filth and drinking urine in the Other World. In the first paragraph the deceased prays for an allowance of seven cakes [daily ?], four cakes of Horus and three of Thoth; these he would eat under the Sycamore of Hathor, and would have his maternal and paternal ancestors to look after his estate and house. In the second paragraph he holds a conversation with the god Pen-ḥeseb (?), , concerning his supply of food, and he tells the Ȧukhemu beings, , his wishes in respect of those who are to bring him his food, to watch over his estate, to plough his fields, and to reap his harvest.

The last-named work shall be done by Suti, or Set, the god of evil.

CHAPTER CXC.

This section, although it has a long title stating that the text, or "Book," has the power of making perfect the soul of the deceased before Rā, Tem, and Osiris, and of making it mighty before the gods, is practically only a Rubric, which may really belong to Chapter CLXXXIX. or Chapter CXLVIII. The recital of the Chapter to which it belonged gave the deceased the power to pass through the Other World in safety, it destroyed the "deafness of his face," and made "a way "for his face with the god." The formula was held to be most solemn and holy, and the Rubric orders it to be said by a man in the strict privacy of a cloth tent decorated with stars. It was also a "great mystery," and none of the dwellers in the papyrus swamps of the Delta was to be allowed to look upon it.

From the above brief analysis of the Chapters which I have included in the Theban Recension of the Book of the Dead, the reader will see that there is in many of them much over-lapping of subject-matter, and may think that the Egyptian revelled in texts full of repetitions both of words and ideas. It must, however, be remembered that the Chapters and formulae do not all belong to the same period, and that collectively they cover a period of some two thousand years. These formulae represent a number of different and, in some cases, diametrically opposite opinions, and the influences of many schools of thought are manifest in them. The oldest formulae were composed, no doubt, by the priests of Heliopolis, and in their original forms were very different from those in which we find them in the Theban Papyri. This is fully proved by Chapters CLXXIV., CLXXVII., and CLXXVIII., where it is clear that, owing to the want of an adequate number of determinatives, the scribes wholly misunderstood the meaning of certain passages, and that they altered and modified the texts of several passages to suit modern views, or to make them mean what they thought they ought to mean. And sometimes passages of a coarse nature were omitted, probably because they offended the susceptibilities of the men of a more refined time. Thus in the passage from the text of Unás (l. 166 ff.; see *infra*, p. 603) we have a reference to the love-making[1] of the deceased which is entirely omitted from

[1] M. Maspero's rendering of the passage (see *Les Inscriptions des Pyramides de Saqqarah*, p. 21) runs:—"O Râ, sois bon pour lui en ce jour dès hier; car Ounas a connu la déesse Mâouît, Ounas a respiré la flamme d'Isi. Ounas s'est uni au lotus, Ounas a connu une jeune femme, mais sa force manquait de grains et de liqueurs réconfortantes: lorsque la force d'Ounas a attaqué la jeune femme, elle a donné du pain à Ounas, puis elle lui a servi de femme en ce jour."

the later copy of it given in the Papyrus of Nebseni; and it seems as if the ideas expressed in it found no favour with the cultured mind of Nebseni, the great designer, draughtsman, and artist, who was attached to the Temple of Ptaḥ at Memphis. In a similar manner most of the coarse expressions and ideas which are found in the religious books of the old period have no counterparts in the Theban Recension of the Book of the Dead. Moreover, as the balance of power moved southwards after the fall of the VIth Dynasty, the beliefs of the Heracleopolitans were grafted on to those of Memphis and Heliopolis, and they found expression in many interpolated passages. The doctrines also of the priests of Abydos were duly incorporated, those of the priests of Heliopolis were made to harmonize with them, and still later the priests of Åmen-Rā at Thebes succeeded in obtaining recognition of the power of their god in a few Chapters. Over and above all this the natural evolution and development of religious thought must be taken into account, and, if it did not overthrow the old religious literature entirely, it must certainly have influenced priests and others in making the selection of texts which were written on their funerary papyri. The Egyptian masses were intensely conservative, and they clung to precedent and tradition to a remarkable degree; the older the text the more they reverenced it, and though they were tolerant enough to accept new settings of old thoughts, or new versions of old legends, they did not allow themselves to give up the old, but kept both the old *and* the new. The Book of the Dead contains beliefs of all periods gathered together from every part of Egypt and the Sûdân, and its gods, though perhaps under different names, were well known throughout the country. The forms of the beliefs and the attributes of the gods changed from time to time, but the principal doctrine which the Book of the Dead, as a whole, was intended to teach, i.e., the belief in immortality, never changed. The fundamentals of the Egyptian religion were:—

I. Belief in the immortality of the soul, and the recognition of relatives and friends after death.

II. Belief in the resurrection of a spiritual body, in which the soul lived after death.

III. Belief in the continued existence of the heart-soul, the ka (the double), and the shadow.

IV. Belief in the transmutation of offerings, and the efficacy of funerary sacrifices and gifts.

V. Belief in the efficacy of words of power, including names, magical and religious formulae, &c.

VI. Belief in the Judgment, the good being rewarded with everlasting life and happiness, and the wicked with annihilation.

All the above appear to be indigenous African beliefs, which existed in the Predynastic Period, and are current under various forms at the present day among most of the tribes of the Sûdân who have any religious belief at all.

Early in the Dynastic Period the cult of Osiris was introduced, and this god, whose mutilated body, tradition asserted, was reconstituted, became the centre round which all the beliefs enumerated above grouped themselves. During the whole Dynastic Period the cult of Osiris was the dominant feature of the Egyptian religion, and the same funerary rites were performed, and the same religious formulae were recited at Memphis during the early centuries of the Christian Era as under the dynasties of the Ancient Empire, in precisely the same way and with precisely the same object. The worship of ancestral spirits in the Predynastic Period gave way to the cult of the deified man Osiris who had risen from the dead, but the ancient beliefs about the dead and their future state remained unchanged. With these morality had nothing to do, for breaches of morals, private or public, were only regarded as offences against Moral Law, which could be atoned for by gifts and offerings.

THE BOOK OF THE DEAD

PART I

HYMNS INTRODUCTORY TO THE BOOK OF THE DEAD.

Hymn to Rā when he riseth.

[From the Papyrus of Ani (Brit. Mus. No. 10,470, sheet 1).]

Vignette: The scribe Ani standing, with hands raised in adoration, before a table of offerings consisting of haunches of beef, loaves of bread, and cakes, vases of wine and oil, fruits, and flowers. He wears a fringed linen garment and has a wig, necklace, bracelets, &c. Behind him stands his wife Thuthu, a member of the College of Ȧmen-Rā at Thebes; she is similarly robed and holds a sistrum, a vine branch, and a *menȧt*, or emblem of pleasure, in her hands.[1]

Text: (1) A HYMN OF PRAISE TO RĀ WHEN HE RISETH IN THE EASTERN PART OF HEAVEN. Behold

[1] The vignette which accompanies the hymn in the papyrus is broken in places; a more perfect one from another section of the papyrus is therefore substituted.

Osiris,[1] Ani the scribe of the holy offerings of all the gods, (2) who saith :—

"Homage to thee, O thou who hast come as Kheperȧ, "Kheperȧ[2] the creator of the gods. Thou risest, thou "shinest, (3) thou makest light [in] thy mother [the "goddess Nut[3]]; thou art crowned king of the gods. "[Thy] mother Nut doeth an act of homage unto thee "with both her hands. (4) The land of Manu[4] re-"ceiveth thee with satisfaction, and the goddess Maāt[5] "embraceth thee both at morn and at eve. May he "(*i.e.* Rā) give glory, and power, and triumph, (5) and "a coming forth as a living soul to see Ḥeru-khuti[6] "(*i.e.*, Horus of the two horizons) to the double (*ka*)[7]

[1] The god who after death and mutilation upon earth rose again and became the king of the underworld and judge of the dead; he was the type of eternal existence, and the symbol of immortality. The deceased pleads the resurrection of this god as the reason for his own resurrection, and he always identifies himself with Osiris in funereal texts.

[2] He is a form of the rising sun, and his seat is in the boat of the Sun-god. He is the god of matter which is on the point of passing from inertness into life, and also of the dead body from which a spiritual and glorified body is about to burst forth. His emblem is a beetle.

[3] The feminine principle of Nu, *i.e.*, the watery mass out of which all the gods were evolved; she is the goddess of the sky, across which sailed the boat of the Sun-god.

[4] *Manu* was the name of the mountain where the sun set in the west.

[5] The wife of Thoth, and daughter of Rā; she assisted at the work of creation. She is the goddess of absolute regularity and order, and of moral rectitude, and of right and truth. Her emblem is the feather .

[6] He is a form of the Sun-god; the words "two horizons" refer to the mountains of Bakhatet and Manu, the most easterly and westerly points of the sun's course, and the places where he rose and set.

[7] The life of the *ka*  was sustained by the funeral offerings; its abiding place was the tomb.

"of Osiris, the scribe Ani, victorious before Osiris, (6) "who saith:—Hail, all ye gods of the Temple of the "Soul,[1] who weigh heaven and earth in the balance, "and who provide sepulchral meals[2] in abundance. "Hail, Tatunen,[3] thou One, (7) thou Creator of man-"kind and Maker of the substance of the gods of the "south and of the north, of the west and of the east. "O come and acclaim ye Rā, the lord of heaven, "(8) the Prince (Life, Health, Strength!), the Creator "of the gods, and adore ye him in his beautiful form "at his rising in the *Āṭet*[4] boat. (9) They who dwell "in the heights and they who dwell in the depths[5] "worship thee. The god Thoth[6] and the goddess "Maāt have written down [thy course] for thee daily "and every day. Thine enemy the serpent hath been "given over to (10) the fire, the serpent-fiend Sebàu "hath fallen down headlong; his arms have been "bound in chains, and his legs hath Rā hacked off "from him. The children of (11) impotent revolt shall "never more rise up. The Temple of the Aged One[7]

[1] The name of a part of the sky where the gods lived; a place which had a counterpart upon earth, probably at Annu (On, Heliopolis) and at Tattu (Mendes).

[2] *Tchefau* was the name given to the food upon which the gods lived.

[3] The god of the earth, and one of the oldest gods of Egypt; he is sometimes identified with Seb.

[4] A name for the boat of the morning sun.

[5] *I.e.*, the gods who live in the heights and depths of heaven, or celestial and terrestrial beings.

[6] The divine intelligence which at the creation uttered the words which resulted in the formation of the world. He was self-produced, and was lord of earth, air, sea, and sky; he was the scribe of the gods, and the inventor of all arts and sciences.

[7] *I.e.*, the Temple of Rā at Ànnu (*i.e.*, On or Heliopolis).

"keepeth festival, and the voice of those who rejoice is "in the mighty dwelling. (12) The gods exult when "they see Rā as he riseth, and when his beams flood "the world with light. The Majesty (13) of the holy "god goeth forth and advanceth even unto the land of "Manu; he maketh brilliant the earth at his birth "each day: he journeyeth on to the place where he "was yesterday. (14) O be thou at peace with me, "and let me behold thy beauties;[1] may I journey forth "upon earth, may I smite the Ass;[2] may I crush "(15) the serpent-fiend Sebȧu;[3] may I destroy Ȧpep[4] "in his hour; may I see the *Ȧbṭu*[5] fish at his season, "and the *Ȧnt*[5] fish [piloting] (16) the *Ȧnt* boat in its "lake. May I see Horus acting as steersman, with "the god Thoth and the goddess Maāt, one on each "side of him; may I grasp the bows of the (17) *Sektet* "boat,[6] and the stern of the *Āṭet* boat. May he (*i.e.*, "Rā) grant unto the double (*ka*) of Osiris Ani to behold "the disk of the Sun and to see the Moon-god without "ceasing, each and every day; and (18) may my soul

[1] Or, "thy beautiful form."

[2] We should probably read, "May I smite the eater of the Ass," and consider the word "eater" to refer to the serpent who is seen attacking the Ass in the vignette of Chapter XL. Otherwise "Ass" must be the name of a fiend of darkness; but then again, it must be remembered that "Ass" is one of the names of the Sun-god.

[3] Sebȧu is, in reality, the name of a legion of devils.

[4] The great antagonist of the Sun-god, of which many types are known.

[5] The name of a mythological fish which, on coffins, &c., is seen swimming at the bows of the boat of the Sun-god.

[6] A name for the boat of the setting sun.

"come forth and walk hither and thither (19) and "whithersoever it pleaseth. (20) May my name be "proclaimed (21), and may it be found upon the board "(22) of the table of offerings; may offerings (23) be "made unto me in my presence, even as [they are made "unto] the followers (24) of Horus; may there be made "ready for me (25) a seat in the boat of the Sun on the "day when (26) the god goeth forth; and may I be "received (27) into the presence of Osiris in the land of "victory."

Hymn to Rā when he riseth.

[From the Papyrus of Qenna (see Leemans, *Papyrus Égyptiens*, T. 2, Plate 2).]

Vignette: Qenna and his wife standing with hands raised in adoration.

Text: (1) A HYMN OF PRAISE TO RĀ WHEN HE RISETH IN THE EASTERN PART OF HEAVEN. Behold Osiris, Qenna the merchant, (2) who saith:—

"Homage to thee, O Rā, when thou risest [and to "thee], O Temu,[1] in thy risings of beauty. Thou risest, "thou risest, thou shinest, (3) thou shinest, at dawn of "day. Thou art crowned king of the gods, and the "goddesses Maāti[2] perform an act of homage unto "thee. The company (4) of the gods praise thee from

[1] A form of Rā, and the type of the night sun; he was self-created, and was declared to be the creator of gods and men.

[2] The goddesses Isis and Nephthys are probably referred to here.

"the places of sunrise and sunset. Thou passest over "the height of heaven and thy heart is filled with "gladness. The *Sektet* boat draweth on, and [Rā] "advanceth (5) in the *Āṭet* boat with fair winds. Rā "rejoiceth, Rā rejoiceth. Thy father is Nu, thy "mother is Nut, O (6) thou who art crowned as "Rā-Ḥeru-khuti[1] (Rā-Harmachis), thy divine boat "advanceth in peace. [Thine enemy] hath been given "over [to the flame, and he] hath fallen; his head hath "been cut off. (7) The heart of the Lady of Life "(*i.e.*, Isis) is glad [because] the foe[2] of her lord hath "fallen headlong. The mariners of Rā have content of "heart and Annu (Heliopolis) exulteth." (8)

The merchant Qenna, victorious, saith:—

"I have come to thee, O Lord of the gods, Temu-"Ḥeru-khuti[3] (Temu-Harmachis) whom Maāt directeth "(9) . . . . I know that whereby thou dost live.[4] "Grant thou that I may be like unto one of those who "are thy favoured ones (10) [among] the followers of "the Great God; may my name be proclaimed, may it "be found, may it be set (11) with their [names?]. "The oar[s] have been taken into the *Sektet* boat, and "the boat of the Sun advanceth in peace. (12) May I "see Rā when he appeareth in the sky at dawn and "when his Enemy hath fallen at the block. (13) May

[1] A form of the rising sun.
[2] *I.e.*, Āpep (see p. 6, note 4).
[3] *I.e.*, the forms of the Sun-god in the evening and morning.
[4] The gods live by *maāt*, *i.e.*, never-failing and unalterable regularity and order.

"I see Horus working the rudder on each side and "bringing along the boat. May I see the *Ȧbṭu* fish at "[its] time of (14) coming into being (?); may I see "the *Ȧnt* fish as it becometh the pilot of the *Ȧnt* boat "in its waters. O thou only One, O thou Perfect One, "O thou (15) who dost endure, who sufferest never an "evil moment, who canst not be smitten down by him "that doeth deeds of might, none other shall have "power and might over the things which belong to "thee. (16) None shall obtain by fraud possession of "the things which belong to the divine Father, who "hath need of abundance, the tongue (?) of veneration, "(17) the lord of Ȧbṭu (Abydos)."

The merchant Qenna, victorious, saith: "Homage "to thee, O Ḥeru-khuti-Temu Ḥeru (18) Kheperȧ,[1] "thou mighty hawk, who makest glad the body [of "man], thou beautiful of face by reason of thy two "great plumes! Awake, (19) O lord of beauty, at "dawn when the company of the gods and mortals say "unto thee, 'Hail!' They (20) sing hymns of praise "unto thee at eventide, and the starry deities also "adore thee. O thou firstborn, who dost lie motionless "(21), thy mother sheweth loving-kindness unto thee "daily. Rā liveth, and the serpent-fiend Nȧk[2] is dead; "thou art in good case, for thine enemy (22) hath fallen "headlong. Thou sailest over heaven with life and

[1] *I.e.*, Harmachis-Tem-Horus-Kheperȧ, or four forms of the Sun-god.

[2] An active opponent of the Sun-god.

"strength. The goddess Neḥebka[1] is in the *Āṭet* boat, "and thy boat rejoiceth; (23) thy heart is glad, and "the two uraei goddesses rise upon thy brow."

Hymn to Rā when he riseth.

[From the Papyrus of Qenna (see Leemans, *Papyrus Égyptiens*, T. 2, Plate 4).]

Vignette: Qenna and his wife standing with hands raised in adoration.

Text: (1) A HYMN OF PRAISE TO RĀ WHEN HE RISETH IN THE EASTERN PART OF HEAVEN. Behold Osiris, Qenna the merchant, victorious,[2] (2) who saith:—

"Homage to thee, O thou who risest in Nu, and "who at thy manifestation dost make the world bright "with light; the whole company of gods sing hymns "of praise unto thee after thou hast come forth. "(3) The divine Merti[3] who minister unto thee

[1] The goddess of matter revivified.

[2] The words rendered "victorious" are *maā kheru*, and mean, literally, "right" (*maā*) and "word," *or*, "voice" (*kheru*). They indicate a belief on the part of the writer that the deceased by means of the ceremonies which have been performed, and the words which have been said, on his behalf, has satisfactorily passed the ordeal of judgment, and has attained to a state of knowledge which will enable him to utter commands, whatever they may be, in such a manner as will cause them to be carried out by those to whom they are addressed, whether gods or devils.

[3] *I.e.*, the "Two Eyes," a name given to the goddesses Isis and Nephthys who, in the form of two serpents, have their places on the head of the Sun-god.

"cherish thee as King of the North and South, thou "beautiful and beloved Man-child. When thou risest, "men and women live. (4) The nations rejoice in "thee, and the Souls of Ȧnnu (Heliopolis) sing unto "thee songs of joy. (5) The souls of the cities of "Pe[1] and Nekhen[2] exalt thee, the apes of dawn adore "thee, and (6) all beasts and cattle praise thee with "one accord. The goddess Sebȧ overthroweth thine "enemies, therefore rejoice thou within (7) thy boat; "thy mariners are content thereat. Thou hast attained "unto the Ȧṭet boat, and thy heart swelleth with joy. "O lord of the gods, when thou didst create (8) them "they ascribed unto thee praises. The azure goddess "Nut doth compass thee on every side, and the god "Nu[3] (9) floodeth thee with his rays of light. O cast "thou thy light upon me and let me see thy beauties, "me the Osiris (10) Qenna the merchant, victorious, "and when thou goest forth over the earth I will sing "praises unto thy fair face. Thou risest in heaven's "horizon, (11) and [thy] disk is adored [when] it "resteth upon the mountain to give life unto the "world."

Saith Qenna the merchant, victorious: (12) "Thou "risest, thou risest, and thou comest forth from the "god Nu. Thou dost renew thy youth and thou dost "set thyself in the place where thou wast yesterday.

[1] *I.e.*, Buto, a city in the Delta.
[2] A very ancient city in Upper Egypt, supposed to be near Eileithyiapolis.
[3] Nu is here regarded as the god of the sky.

"O divine youth who hast created thyself, (13) I am "not able [to describe] thee. Thou hast come with "thy diadems,[1] and thou hast made heaven and earth "bright with thy rays of pure emerald light. (14) The "land of Punt[2] is stablished [to give] the perfumes "which thou smellest with thy nostrils. Thou risest, "O marvellous Being,[3] (15) in heaven, the two serpent-"goddesses Merti are stablished upon thy brow, and "thou art the giver of laws, O lord of the world and of "the inhabitants thereof; (16) all the gods and Qenna "the merchant, victorious, adore thee."

Hymn to Rā when he riseth.

[From the Papyrus of Hu-nefer (Brit. Mus. No. 9901, sheet 1).]

Text: (1) A HYMN OF PRAISE TO RĀ WHEN HE RISETH IN THE (2) EASTERN PART OF HEAVEN. Behold Osiris, Hu-nefer, (3) victorious, who saith:—

"Homage to thee, O thou who art Rā when thou "risest (4) and Temu when thou settest. Thou risest, "thou risest, thou shinest, thou shinest, (5) thou who

[1] Or, "in thy rising."

[2] A district situated near the most easterly part of Somali land, which was famous in antiquity as the home of the spice and incense trees.

[3] Or, "Being of iron." According to one view, the floor of heaven consisted of an iron plate through holes in which the lamps of the stars were hung out.

"art crowned king of the gods. Thou art the lord of "heaven, [thou art] the lord of earth; [thou art] the "creator of those who dwell (6) in the heights and of "those who dwell in the depths.[1] [Thou art] the God "One who came into being (7) in the beginning of "time. Thou didst create the earth, thou didst fashion "man, (8) thou didst make the watery abyss of the "sky, thou didst form Ḥāpi,[2] thou didst create the "watery abyss, (9) and thou dost give life unto all that "therein is. Thou hast knit together the mountains, "thou hast made (10) mankind and the beasts of the "field to come into being, thou hast made the heavens "and the earth. Worshipped be thou whom the "goddess Maāt embraceth at morn and at eve. Thou "dost travel across the sky with heart swelling with "joy; the Lake of Testes[3] (11) becometh contented "thereat. The serpent-fiend Nȧk hath fallen and his "two arms are cut off. The *Sektet* boat receiveth fair "winds, and the heart of him that is in the shrine "thereof rejoiceth. Thou art crowned (12) Prince of "heaven, thou art the One dowered [with all sove-"reignty] who comest forth from the sky. Rā is "victorious! O thou divine youth, thou heir of "everlastingness, thou self-begotten one, O thou who

[1] Or, "creator of the starry gods in heaven above and of the dwellers upon earth below."

[2] *I.e.*, the god of the Nile, who was worshipped under two forms, Ḥāpi of the South, and Ḥāpi of the North; he is represented as a man having the breasts of a woman, which indicate fertility, and crowned with lotus and papyrus flowers.

[3] A name of heaven (?).

"didst give thyself birth! O One (13), mighty [one], "of myriad forms and aspects, king of the world, "Prince of Ȧnnu (Heliopolis), lord of eternity and "ruler of everlastingness,[1] the company of the gods "rejoice when thou risest and when thou sailest "(14) across the sky, O thou who art exalted in the "*Sektet* boat."

"Homage to thee, O Ȧmen-Rā, who dost rest upon "Maāt,[2] and who passest over the heaven, every face "seeth thee. Thou dost wax great (15) as thy Majesty "doth advance, and thy rays are upon all faces. Thou "art unknown and no tongue is worthy (?) to declare "thy likeness; only thou thyself [canst do this]. Thou "art One, even as is he (16) that bringeth the *ṭena* "basket. Men praise thee in thy name [Rā], and they "swear by thee, for thou art lord over them. Thou "hearest with thine ears and thou seest with thine "eyes. (17) Millions of years have gone over the "world; I cannot tell the number of those through "which thou hast passed. Thy heart hath decreed a "day of happiness in thy name of 'Traveller.' Thou "dost pass over (18) and dost travel through untold "spaces [requiring] millions and hundreds of thousands "of years [to pass over]; thou passest through them in "peace, and thou steerest thy way across the watery "abyss to the place which thou lovest; this thou doest

[1] Or, "who endurest through everlastingness."

[2] *I.e.*, "thou whose existence and whose risings and settings are ordered and defined by fixed, unchanging, and unalterable laws."

"in one (19) little moment of time, and then thou dost "sink down and dost make an end of the hours."

Behold Osiris, the governor of the palace of the lord of the two lands,[1] Hu-nefer, victorious, saith: (20) "Hail, my lord, thou who passest through eternity, "whose being is everlasting. Hail, thou Disk, lord of "beams of light, thou risest and thou makest all man-"kind to live. Grant thou that I may behold thee at "dawn each day."

Hymn to Rā when he riseth.

[From the Papyrus of Nekht (Brit. Mus. No. 10,471, sheet 21).]

Text: A Hymn of Praise to Rā by Nekht, the royal scribe, the captain of soldiers, who saith :—

"Homage to thee, O thou glorious Being, thou who "art dowered [with all sovereignty]. O Tem Ḥeru-khuti "(Tem-Harmachis), when thou risest in the horizon of "heaven, a cry of joy cometh forth to thee from the "mouth of all peoples. O thou beautiful Being, thou "dost renew thyself in thy season in the form of the "Disk within thy mother Hathor;[2] therefore in every "place every heart swelleth with joy at thy rising, for

[1] The king here referred to is Seti I., who began to reign about B.C. 1370.

[2] The goddess of those portions of the sky in which the sun rose and set.

"ever. The regions of the North and South come to "thee with homage, and send forth acclamations at thy "rising in the horizon of heaven; thou illuminest the "two lands with rays of turquoise light. O Rā, thou "who art Ḥeru-khuti (Harmachis), the divine man-"child, the heir of eternity, self-begotten and self-born, "king of earth, prince of the Ṭuat,[1] governor of the "regions of Åuḳert;[2] thou comest forth from the "water, thou hast sprung from the god Nu, who "cherisheth thee and ordereth thy members. O thou "god of life, thou lord of love, all men live when thou "shinest; thou art crowned king of the gods. The "goddess Nut doeth homage unto thee, and the goddess "Maāt embraceth thee at all times. Those who are in "thy following sing unto thee with joy and bow down "their foreheads to the earth when they meet thee, "thou lord of heaven, thou lord of earth, thou king of "Right and Truth, thou lord of eternity, thou prince "of everlastingness, thou sovereign of all the gods, "thou god of life, thou creator of eternity, thou maker "of heaven wherein thou art firmly established! The "company of the gods rejoice at thy rising, the earth is "glad when it beholdeth thy rays; the peoples that "have been long dead come forth with cries of joy to "see thy beauties every day. Thou goest forth each "day over heaven and earth and art made strong each

[1] The name of a district or region, neither in heaven nor upon earth, where the dead dwelt, and through which the sun passed during the night.

[2] A name of the underworld.

"day by thy mother Nut. Thou passest through the "heights of heaven, thy heart swelleth with joy; and "the Lake of Testes[1] is content thereat. The Serpent-"fiend hath fallen, his arms are hewn off, the knife "hath cut asunder his joints. Rā liveth by *Maāt*[2] the "beautiful. The *Sektet* boat draweth on and cometh "into port; the South and the North, the West and "the East turn to praise thee, O thou primeval "substance of the earth who didst come into being of "thine own accord. Isis[3] and Nephthys[4] salute thee, "they sing unto thee songs of joy at thy rising in the "boat, they protect thee with their hands. The souls "of the East follow thee, the souls of the West praise "thee. Thou art the ruler of all the gods and thou "hast joy of heart within thy shrine; for the serpent-"fiend Nȧk hath been condemned to the fire, and thy "heart shall be joyful for ever. Thy mother Nut is "adjudged to thy father Nu."

[1] A name of heaven (?).

[2] *I.e.*, "Rā liveth by unchanging and eternal law and order."

[3] The daughter of Seb and Nut, the wife of Osiris, and the mother of Horus.

[4] The daughter of Seb and Nut, the wife of Set, the sister of Isis and Osiris, and the mother of Anubis.

Hymn to Osiris Un-nefer.

[From the Papyrus of Ani (Brit. Mus. No. 10,470, sheet 2).]

Vignette: The scribe Ani standing, with both hands raised in adoration, before a table of offerings consisting of haunches of beef, loaves of bread and cakes, vases of wine and oil, fruits and flowers, &c. He wears a double linen garment and a wig, bracelets, &c. Behind him stands his wife Thuthu, a member of the College of Ȧmen-Rā at Thebes; she is similarly robed and holds a sistrum, a vine branch, and a *menȧt* in her hands.

Text: (1) "Glory be to Osiris Un-nefer, the great "god within Ȧbṭu (Abydos), king of eternity, lord of "everlastingness, who passeth through millions of years "in his existence. Eldest son of the (2) womb of Nut, "engendered by Seb[1] the Erpāt,[2] lord of the crowns of

[1] He was the son of Shu and Tefnut, husband of Nut, and father by her of Osiris, Isis, Set, Nephthys, and Horus dwelling in darkness.
[2] *I.e.*, the great ancestor of the tribe of the gods.

"the North and South, lord of the lofty white crown: "as prince of gods and of men (3) he hath received the "crook, and the whip, and the dignity of his divine "fathers. Let thy heart, which is in the Mountain of "Åment,[1] be content, for thy son Horus is established "upon thy throne. (4) Thou art crowned lord of "Ṭaṭṭu[2] and ruler in Abṭu (Abydos). Through thee "the world waxeth green in (5) triumph before the might "of Neb-er-tcher.[3] He leadeth in his train that which "is, and that which is not yet, in his name of 'Ta-ḥer- "(6) sta-nef';[4] he toweth along the earth by Maāt in "his name of 'Seker';[5] he is exceedingly mighty (7) "and most terrible in his name 'Osiris';[6] he endureth "for ever and for ever[7] in his name of 'Un-nefer.'"

(8) "Homage to thee, King of kings, Lord of lords, "Prince of princes, who from the womb of Nut hast "ruled (9) the world and Aḳert.[8] Thy body is of "bright and shining metal, thy head is of azure blue, "and the brilliance of the turquoise encircleth thee.

[1] The "hidden" place, or abode of the dead, which was usually situated on the left or western bank of the Nile.

[2] Two cities in Egypt bore the name "Tattu," viz., Busiris and Mendes.

[3] *I.e.*, the "lord of all." In the Book of the Dead Osiris is frequently called by this name, the allusion being to the complete reconstruction of his body after it had been hacked to pieces by Set.

[4] A name meaning something like "he leadeth the earth."

[5] A play on the sounds of the words *sek*, "to pull along," and *seker*, "he who is coffined," is here intended.

[6] A play on the sounds of the words *user*, "strong," and *Ausår*, "Osiris," is here intended.

[7] A play on the words *un*, "to exist," and *un* in the proper name "Un-nefer" is here intended.

[8] A name of the underworld.

"O god An[1] of millions of years, (10) all-pervading with "thy body and beautiful in countenance in Ta-tchesert,[2] "grant thou to the *Ka* (*i.e.*, double) of Osiris, the scribe "Ani, splendour in heaven, and might upon earth, and "triumph in the underworld; and grant that I may "sail down (11) to Ṭaṭṭu like a (12) living soul and up "to (13) Ȧbṭu (Abydos) like a *Bennu*[3] bird; and that "I may go in and come out (14) without repulse at the "pylons[4] (15) of the lords of the underworld. May "there be given unto me (16) loaves of bread in the "house of coolness, and (17) offerings of food in Annu "(Heliopolis), and a homestead (18) for ever in "Sekhet-Ȧru[5] with wheat and barley therefor."

[1] A form of the Sun-god; he is mentioned again in Chapter XV.
[2] A name of the underworld.
[3] The *Bennu* is commonly identified with the phoenix.
[4] For the twenty-one pylons of the House of Osiris see Chapter CXLV.
[5] A division of the Sekhet-Ḥetepu or "Elysian Fields," for which see Chapter CX.

THE JUDGMENT.

THE Judgment Scene, of which a description is here given, forms a very important section of the Book of the Dead as contained in papyri of the XVIIIth, XIXth, and following Dynasties. It follows the two or more hymns with which a large papyrus opens, and seems to occupy a suitable place, and to form a fitting introduction to the selections of the chapters of Coming Forth by Day which follow it. These chapters refer to and deal with the events which took place in the life of the deceased, who has succeeded in entering the realm of Osiris, the god of the dead, but they, of necessity, were absolutely useless to any one who had not passed the judgment and been permitted by this god to enter his dominions. Those who were condemned in the judgment were devoured straightway by the Eater of the Dead, and ceased to exist. The Judgment Scene, as given in the large papyri, seems to have been developed from the vignette which illustrates one of the Chapters of the Heart (XXXB.), in which special reference is made to the weighing of the heart, or from one which, properly speaking, belonged to the CXXVth Chapter. Where and when the judgment took place is unknown, but the original idea seems to have been that the broad heavens, or a certain portion of them, formed the Judgment Hall, and that the judgment took place in the presence of the three Companies of the gods; as the head of the funereal Company Osiris occupied a very prominent position, and he eventually became the sole judge of the dead. The judgment of each individual seems to have taken place soon after death, and annihilation or everlasting life and bliss to have been decreed at once for the souls of the dead; there are no sufficient grounds for assuming that the Egyptians believed either in a general resurrection, or in protracted punishment. How far they thought that the prayers of the living for the dead were efficacious in arresting or modifying the decree of doom cannot be said, but very considerable importance was attached by them to funeral prayers and ceremonies in all ages, and there is no doubt that they were the outcome of the firm belief that they would result in the salvation and well-being of the souls of the dead.

The Scene of the Weighing of the Heart of the Dead.

[From the Papyrus of Ani (Brit. Mus. No. 10,470, plates 3 and 4).]

Vignette: The scribe Ani and his wife Thuthu enter the Hall of Double Maāt, wherein the heart, symbolic of the conscience, is to be weighed in the balance against the feather, emblematical of Right and Truth. In the upper register are the gods who sit in judgment, whose names are "Harmachis, the great god in his boat, Temu, Shu, Tefnut the lady of heaven,

THE JUDGMENT.

Hu and Sa. Hathor. Horus. Isis. Nephthys. Nut. Seb. Tefnut. Shu. Temu. Harmachis.

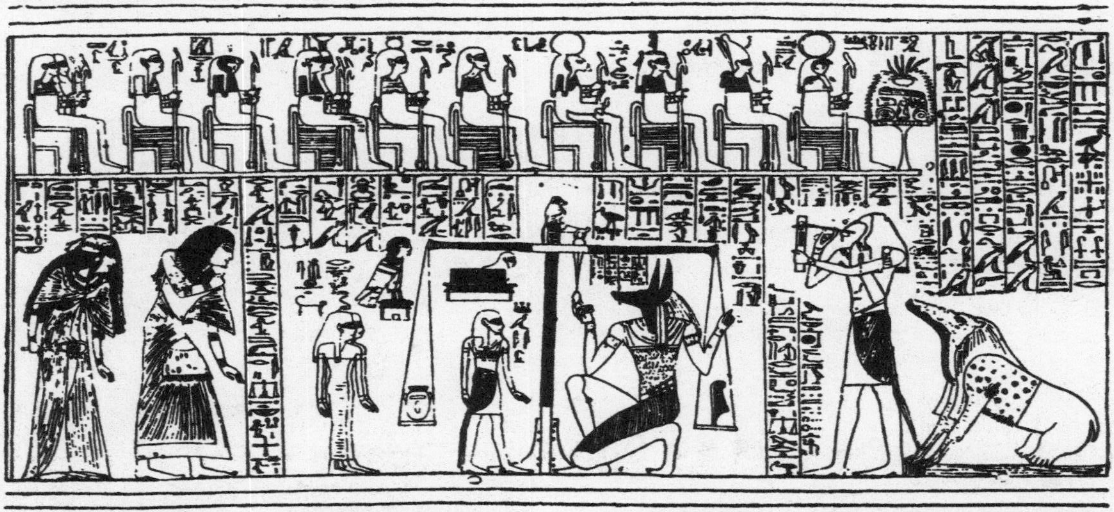

Ani and his wife Thuthu. Meskhenet. Renenet. Ani's heart. The Luck. Anubis. The feather of Maāt. Thoth. The "Eater of the Dead."

Seb, Nut the lady of heaven, Isis, Nephthys, Horus the great god, Hathor the lady of Amenta, Ḥu and Sa." On the standard of the scales sits the dog-headed ape, the companion of Thoth, the scribe of the gods; and the god Anubis, jackal-headed, tests the tongue of the balance. On the left of the balance, facing Anubis are:—(1) Ani's "Luck"; (2) the *Meskhen* or "cubit with human head," thought by some to be connected with the place of birth; (3) the goddesses Meskhenet and Renenet who presided over the birth, birth-place, and early education of children; and (4) the soul of Ani in the form of a human-headed bird standing on a pylon. On the right of the balance, behind Anubis, stands Thoth, the scribe of the gods, who holds in his hands his reed-pen and palette with which to record the result of the trial. Behind Thoth stands the monster called either Ămām, the "Devourer," or Ām-mit, the "Eater of the Dead."

Text: Osiris, the scribe Ani, saith:—

"My[1] heart my mother, my heart my mother, my "heart my coming into being. May there be nothing "to resist me at [my] judgment; may there be no "opposition to me from the *Tchatcha*;[2] may there be "no parting of thee from me in the presence of him "that keepeth the scales. Thou art my *Ka* (*i.e.*, double) "within my body [which] knitteth together and "strengtheneth my limbs. Mayest thou come forth "to the place of happiness to which I am advancing. "May the *Shenit*[3] not cause my name to stink, "and may no lies be spoken against me in the

[1] This speech of Ani is actually Chapter XXXB. (*q.v.*), but the last line has been omitted by the scribe for want of room.

[2] *I.e.*, the "Heads" or "Chiefs." The *Tchatcha* of Osiris were Mesthȧ, Ḥāpi, Ṭuamāutef and Qebḥsennuf.

[3] *I.e.*, divine officials.

"presence of the god. Good, good is it for thee to "hear" . . . .

Thoth, the judge of Right and Truth of the great company of the gods who are in the presence of Osiris, saith:—"Hear ye this judgment. The heart of "Osiris hath in very truth been weighed, and his soul "hath stood as a witness for him; it hath been found "true by trial in the Great Balance. There hath not "been found any wickedness in him; he hath not "wasted the offerings in the temples; he hath not "done harm by his deeds; and he hath uttered no evil "reports while he was upon earth."

The great company of the gods reply to Thoth who dwelleth in Khemennu (Hermopolis):—"That which "cometh forth from thy mouth shall be declared true. "Osiris, the scribe Ani victorious, is holy and righteous. "He hath not sinned, neither hath he done evil against "us. It shall not be allowed to the devourer Amemet "to prevail over him. Meat-offerings and entrance "into the presence of the god Osiris shall be granted "unto him, together with a homestead for ever in "Sekhet-ḥetepu,[1] as unto the followers of Horus."

Vignette: The scribe Ani is led by Horus, the son of Isis, into the presence of Osiris who is enthroned within a shrine in the form of a funeral chest. Osiris has upon his head the *Atef* crown, and he holds in his hands the crook, the sceptre and the whip, emblematic of authority, dominion, and sovereignty; from his neck hangs the *menất*. His title here is "Osiris, the

[1] See Chapter CX.

THE JUDGMENT.

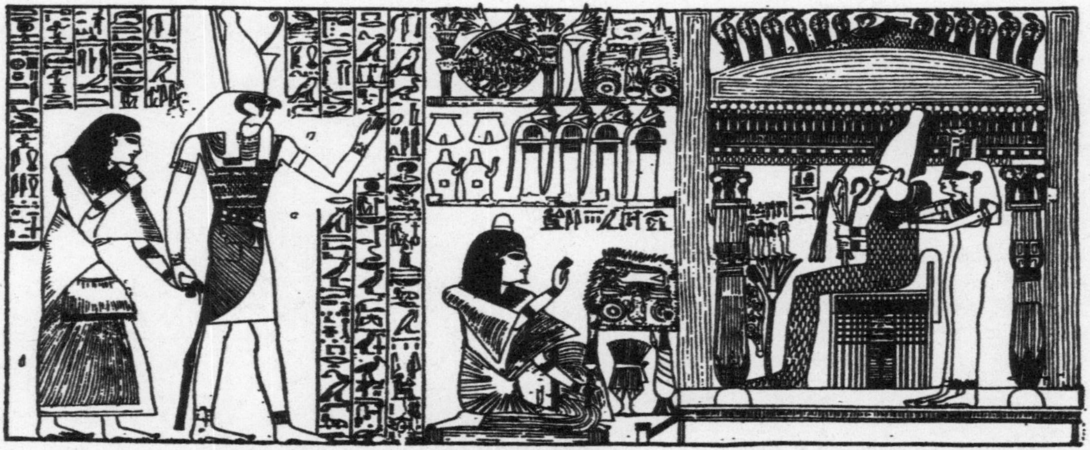

Ani. — Horus, the Son of Isis. — Ani kneeling in adoration before Osiris. — Osiris in his shrine, with Isis, Nephthys, and the four children of Horus.

lord of everlastingness." Behind him stand Nephthys, his sister, on his right hand and Isis, his sister and wife, on his left. Before him, standing on a lotus flower, are the gods of the cardinal points or, as they are sometimes called, "the Children of Horus" and "Children of Osiris." The first, Mestha, has the head of a man; the second, Ḥāpi, the head of an ape; the third, Ṭuamāutef, the head of a jackal; and the fourth, Qebḥsennuf, the head of a hawk. Near the lotus hangs the skin of an animal. The side of the throne of Osiris is painted to resemble that of a funeral chest. The roof of the shrine is supported on pillars with lotus capitals, and is surmounted by a figure of Horus-Sept or Horus-Seker, and by rows of uraei. The pedestal on which the shrine rests is in the form of the hieroglyphic which is emblematic of *Maāt* or "Right and Truth." Before the shrine is a table of offerings by which, on a reed mat, kneels Ani with his right hand raised in adoration; in the left hand he holds the *Kherp* sceptre. He wears on his head a whitened wig and the so-called "cone," the signification of which is unknown.

Text: (1) Saith Horus the son of Isis: "I have "come to thee, O Un-nefer, and I have brought unto "thee the Osiris Ani. His heart is [found] righteous, "(2) and it hath come forth from the balance; it hath "not sinned against any god or any goddess. Thoth "hath weighed it according to the decree pronounced "(3) unto him by the company of the gods; and it is "most true and righteous. Grant that cakes and ale "may be given unto him, and let him appear in the "presence of the god Osiris; (4) and let him be like "unto the followers of Horus for ever and for ever."

(1) And Osiris Ani (2) saith: "Behold, I am in thy "presence, O lord of (3) Ȧmentet. There is no sin in "my (4) body. I have not spoken that which is not

"true (5) knowingly, nor have I done aught with a "false heart. Grant thou that I may be like unto "those favoured ones who are in thy following, (6) and "that I may be an Osiris greatly favoured of the "beautiful god, and beloved of the lord of the world. "[I] who am, indeed, a royal scribe who loveth thee, "Ani, victorious before the god Osiris."

The details of the Judgment Scene vary considerably in the papyri of different periods, and it seems as if every scribe or artist felt himself free to follow out his own ideas of its treatment. First, as regards the Great Balance. The beam is always exactly horizontal, a fact which proves that the Egyptian was only asked to make his heart or conscience to just counterbalance, and *not* outweigh the feather of Maāt. The pillar of the Balance is at times (see pp. 23 and 32) surmounted by the ape of Thoth, at others by the head of Maāṭ (see p. 31), at others by the head of Anubis (see p. 31), and at others by the head of Thoth himself. The feather of Maāt, 𓆄, which is in one pan of the scales, is often exchanged for the figure of the goddess herself 𓁦 (see p. 32). The actúal weighing of the heart is performed sometimes by Anubis (see pp. 31, 32), and sometimes by Maāt (see p. 31); usually the deceased enters the Hall of Judgment alone or accompanied by his wife, but sometimes he is led in by Anubis, and sometimes by a dog-headed god who carries a knife in his left hand. The Eater of the Dead sometimes sits,

The Weighing of the Heart. (From the Papyrus of Hu-nefer.)

The Weighing of the Heart. (From the Papyrus of Qenna.)

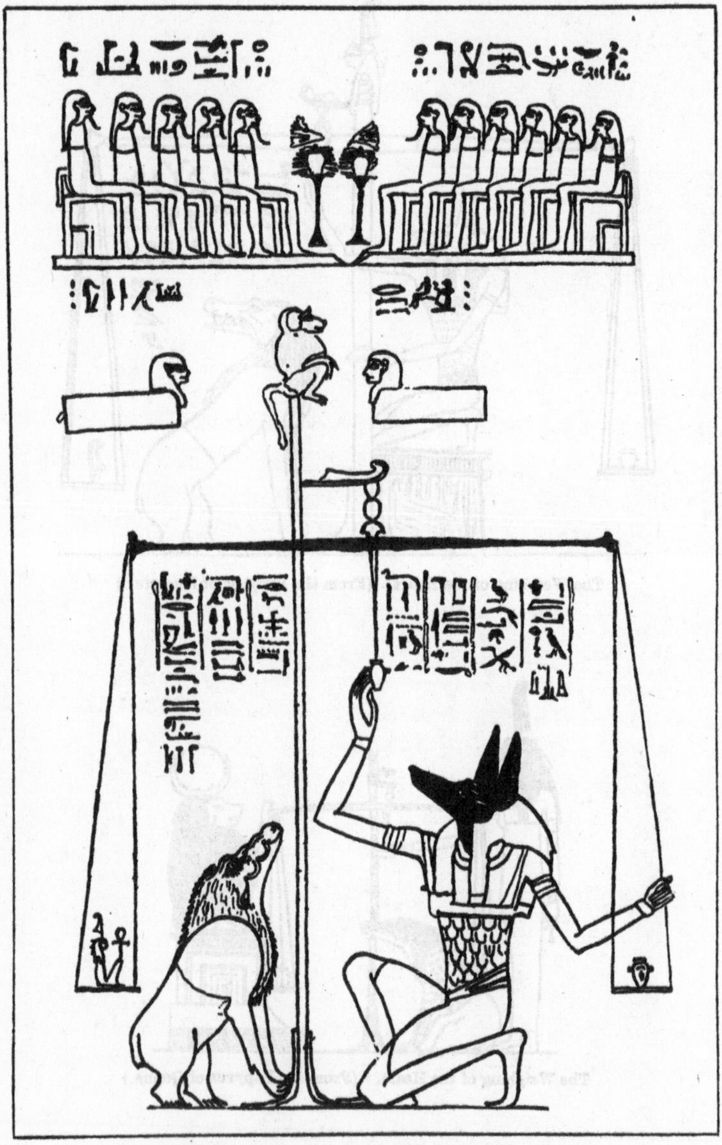

The Weighing of the Heart (from the Papyrus of Ánhai).

and sometimes stands by the side of the pillar of the Balance; in the Papyrus of Hu-nefer (see p. 31) a description of her appears above her head, thus:—"Åm-mit, her forepart [is that of] crocodiles, her hind-"part [is that of a] hippopotamus, and her middle [is "that of a] lion." In details the Judgment Scene as given in the Papyrus of Ani is very full (see p. 23), and very few papyri contain the "Luck" and the nursing goddesses Meskhenet and Renenet in human form. The arrangement of one part of the Scene in the Papyrus of Anhai (see p. 32) is most unusual. In the upper register we have the Great and Little Companies of the gods arranged facing each other; the former contains five gods and the latter six. Now a *paut*, or Company of gods, rarely contained less than nine gods, though often more. Each Company is seated before a meagre table of offerings. Below these gods are two human-headed objects which are called respectively Shai and Renenet; each has the head of a woman, but one, Shai, should have had that of a man, and a beard. It is noteworthy that the Eater of the Dead is not seated by Anubis, and that the god Anubis grasps one of the cords by which the pan of the Balance that contains the heart is suspended, as if to steady the beam. The text above the head of Anubis is unusual (see also the Scene from the Papyrus of Ani, p. 23), and contains an exhortation addressed to the ape of Thoth seated on the top of the pillar, that this god will give his careful attention to the correct weighing of the heart of the deceased in the Balance. The text above the Eater of the Dead is a prayer by the deceased, who entreats the god, saying, "Set my heart upon the throne of right in the presence of the Great God." The result of the weighing of the heart is always noted by Thoth, who records it upon his palette. The deceased is sometimes led into the presence of Osiris by Horus, the son of Isis, and sometimes by Anubis. In papyri wherein the the vignettes are not very elaborate, Osiris stands or sits in his shrine alone, but in fully illustrated papyri he is accompanied by Isis and Nephthys, and by the four children of Horus, who stand on a lotus flower (see pp. 27, 35). The stem of this flower springs from out of the waters of a lake, whereon the throne of Osiris is placed (see the following illustration from the Papyrus of Hu-nefer); this lake was fed by the celestial Nile, or by one of its branches, and was the source whence the beatified, as well as the gods, drank. This scene is of considerable interest from the point of view of comparative mythology, for many Semitic writers held the opinion that the throne of the deity was placed, or rested upon, a stream of water, or a river. Even in the Book of Revelation we have a reference to a "pure river of water, clear as crystal, proceeding out of the throne of God" (see chapter xxii. 1).

The god Osiris seated in his shrine in the Hall of Judgment.
(From the Papyrus of Hu-nefer.)

THE CHAPTERS

OF

COMING FORTH BY DAY

THE FUNERAL PROCESSION.

The bier being drawn to the tomb preceded by a priest burning incense, and followed by attendants bearing funeral furniture.

Men bearing offerings. Weeping women. Animals for sacrifice. Priests reading the funeral service and performing ceremonies before the mummy in front of the tomb.

CHAPTER I.

[From the Papyrus of Ani (Brit. Mus. No. 10,470, sheets 5 and 6).]

Vignettes : The funeral procession to the tomb, and the ceremony thereat, are here depicted. The mummy of the deceased, lying in a funeral chest placed in a boat, is being drawn along by oxen: figures of the goddesses Nephthys and Isis stand at the head and foot respectively. By the side kneels the wife of the deceased. In front of the boat stands the *Sem* priest, dressed in a panther's skin, burning incense and sprinkling water, and behind follow eight male mourners; in the rear are servants drawing a small funeral chest surmounted by a figure of Anubis, and carrying vases of unguents along with the couch, staff, chair, palette, &c., of the deceased. Preceding the oxen drawing the funeral boat are men carrying on yokes boxes of flowers, vases of unguents, &c., and a group of wailing women with uncovered heads and breasts, who smite their heads and faces in token of grief. Close by stand a cow and her calf, intended to be slaughtered for the funeral feast, and tables loaded with offerings of herbs, fruits, &c. At the door of the tomb stands the god of the dead, Anubis, clasping the mummy of the deceased, before which kneels the weeping wife. At a table of funeral offerings stand two priests. One, the *Sem* priest, wears a panther's skin and holds in his hand a libation vase and censer; the other holds in his right hand the instrument UR ḤEKA[1] in the form of a ram-headed serpent, the head of which is surmounted by an uraeus, and in his left hand an instrument in the shape of an adze . With the former he is about to touch the mouth

[1] *I.e.*, the "mighty one of enchantments."

and eyes of the mummy, and with the latter the mouth. On the ground, by their side, lie the instruments which are to be employed in the ceremony of opening the mouth, *i.e.*, the ceremony which will give the deceased the power to eat, and to drink, and to talk in the next world, namely the *Meskhet* 𓍑, the group of instruments in the form of adzes 𓌻, the *Pesh-en-kef* 𓋹, the libation vases, the boxes of purification, the bandlet, the feather, &c. Behind them stands the "Reader," who recites the funeral service from a papyrus roll, and to the rear is a ministrant who holds the haunch of beef which is to be used in the ceremony at the door of the tomb.

FUNERAL CEREMONIES AT THE TOMB.

In the upper register we see the tomb in the Theban hills, with a sepulchral stele inscribed with prayers by the deceased. Annbis supports the mummy, before which kneel Hu-nefer's wife, and, probably, his daughter. Two priests performing ceremonies connected with "opening the mouth," and the "Reader" burning incense and sprinkling water. In the lower register are the instruments used in the ceremonies, priests, and animals for sacrifice.

Text: (1) HERE BEGIN THE CHAPTERS OF "COMING FORTH BY DAY," AND OF THE SONGS OF PRAISE AND GLORIFYING, (2) AND OF COMING FORTH FROM, AND OF GOING INTO THE GLORIOUS NETER-KHERT[1] IN THE BEAUTIFUL ÅMENTET, WHICH ARE TO BE RECITED ON (3) THE DAY OF THE BURIAL [WHEREBY THE DECEASED] SHALL GO IN AFTER COMING FORTH.

Saith Osiris Ani, (4) Osiris the scribe Ani:—

"Homage to thee, O Bull of Åmentet,[2] the god "Thoth, (5) the king of eternity, is with me. I am "the Great God near the divine boat, I have fought "(6) for thee. I am one of the gods, those divine "chiefs, who make (7) Osiris to be victorious over his "enemies on the day of the weighing of words. (8) I "am thy mediator (?), O Osiris. I am [one] of the "gods (9) born of the goddess Nut, who slay the foes "of Osiris and who hold in bondage (10) for him the "fiend Sebåu. I am thy mediator (?), O Horus. (11) I "have fought for thee, and I have put to flight the "enemy for thy name's sake. I am Thoth, who made "Osiris to be victorious[3] (12) over his enemies on the "day of the weighing of words[4] (13) in the great House "of the Aged One (*i.e.*, Rā) who dwelleth in Ånnu

[1] *I.e.*, the "divine lower region," or the underworld.
[2] *I.e.*, the "hidden" place, or the underworld. The Bull is Osiris.
[3] *I.e.*, Thoth provided him with certain words, and with instructions as to their utterance, which enabled Osiris, and therefore every just man, to pass the ordeal of judgment, and to gain everlasting life, and to make every being to perform what he ordered him to do.
[4] *I.e.*, the dry of judgment.

"(Heliopolis). I am Ṭeṭṭeṭi, the son of Ṭeṭṭeṭi; (14) I "was begotten in Ṭaṭṭu, I was born in (15) Ṭaṭṭu.[1] I "am with those who weep and with the women who "bewail (16) Osiris in the two lands of the Rekht,[2] and "I make Osiris to be victorious over his enemies. "(17) Rā commanded Thoth to make Osiris victorious "over his enemies; and that which was decreed [for "Osiris] (18) Thoth did for me. I am with Horus on "the day of the clothing of (19) Teshtesh[3] and of the "opening of the wells of water for the purification of "the divine being whose heart moveth not,[4] (20) and "of the drawing the bolt of the door of the concealed "things in Re-stau.[5] I am with Horus who [acteth] "(21) as the guardian of the left shoulder of Osiris in "Sekhem (Letopolis),[6] (22) and I go in and I come forth "from among the divine flames on the day of the "destruction of the (23) Sebàu fiends in Sekhem. I "am with Horus on the days (24) of the festivals of "Osiris, and of the making of offerings on the Sixth "day festival,[7] and on the Tenàt festival[8] [which is "celebrated] in (25) Ànnu.

[1] *I.e.*, Mendes.

[2] *I.e.*, the goddesses Isis and Nephthys.

[3] *I.e.*, the figure of Osiris upon which the funeral ceremonies were performed at Abydos, Mendes, &c.

[4] *Urṭ-àb*, *i.e.*, "Still-Heart," a name of Osiris.

[5] *I.e.*, the "door of the passages" of the tomb. For the picture of Re-stau see p. 96.

[6] The shrine at Sekhem boasted the possession of the shoulder of Osiris.

[7] *I.e.*, the day of the festival of Osiris.

[8] *I.e.*, the festival which took place on the seventh day of the month.

"I am the *āb*[1] priest who poureth out libations in "Ṭaṭṭu [for] Rere (?) the dweller in the Temple of "Osiris,[2] [on the day of] (26) casting up the earth. I "see the things which are concealed in Re-stau, (27) I "read from the book of the festival of the divine Ram[3] "[which is] in Ṭaṭṭu. I am the *Sem*[4] priest (28) [and "I perform] his course. I [perform the duties of] the "Great Chief of the Work[5] on the day of placing the "*Ḥennu*[6] boat (29) of the god Seker[7] upon its sledge. "I have grasped the spade (30) on the day of digging "the ground in Suten-ḥenen (Heracleopolis Magna)."

"O ye who make perfected souls (31) to enter into "the Temple of Osiris, may ye cause the perfected soul "of Osiris, the (32) scribe Ani, to be victorious with "you in the Temple of Osiris. May he hear as ye "hear; may he see (33) as ye see; may he stand as ye "stand; may he sit as ye (34) sit [therein]."

"O ye who give cakes and ale to perfected souls in "the Temple (35) of Osiris, give ye cakes and ale at "the two seasons (*i.e.*, at morn and at eve, or sunrise "and sunset) to the soul of Osiris Ani, who is

[1] *I.e.*, the priest who performs ceremonial purification with water.

[2] Per-Ȧusȧr, *i.e.*, "House of Osiris" = the Greek Busiris, or capital of the ninth nome of Lower Egypt.

[3] *I.e.*, Osiris as Ba-neb-Taṭṭu, the "Ram, lord of Mendes."

[4] The functions of this priest in funeral ceremonies were very important.

[5] The official title of the chief priest of Ptaḥ, the great god of Memphis.

[6] The Ḥennu boat was placed upon its sledge and drawn round the sanctuary at dawn, probably in imitation of the sun's course.

[7] A name given to Osiris, having reference to the god being shut up in his coffin.

"(36) victorious before all the gods of Ȧbṭu (Abydos), "and who is victorious with you."

"O ye who open the way (37) and lay open the paths "to perfected souls in the Temple (38) of Osiris, open "ye the way and lay open the paths (39) to the soul of "Osiris, the scribe and steward of all the divine "offerings, Ani [who is victorious] (40) with you. "May he enter in confidence, and may he come forth in "peace from the Temple of Osiris. May he not (41) be "rejected, may he not be turned back, may he enter "in [as he] pleaseth, may he come forth [as he] "(42) desireth, and may he be victorious. May the "things which he commandeth be performed in the "Temple of Osiris; may he walk (43) and may he talk "with you, and may he become a glorious being along "with you. He hath not been found to rise up "(44) there,[1] and the Balance [having weighed him] is "now empty."

In the Turin papyrus this Chapter ends with the following lines, for which no equivalent occurs in the earlier texts:—(16) "Let not the decree of judgment "passed upon me be placed," or, according to another "reading, "made known in the mouths of the multitude. "May my soul lift itself up before (17) [Osiris], having "been found to have been pure when on earth. May I "come before thee, O lord of the gods; may I arrive at

[1] *I.e.*, in the Balance. The meaning is that the heart, or conscience, of the deceased has not been outweighed by the emblem of right and truth.

"the nome of Double Right and Truth; may I be "crowned[1] like a god endowed with life; may I give "forth light like the company of the gods who dwell in "heaven; may I become (18) like one of you, lifting "up [my] feet in the city of Kher-āḥaut;[2] may I see "the *Sekṭet* boat of the sacred Saḥu[3] passing forth "over the sky; may I not be driven away from the "sight of the lords of the Ṭuat"[4] (19) or, according to another reading, "the company of the gods; may I "smell the sweet savour of the food of the company of "the gods, and may I sit down with them. May the "Kher-ḥeb (*i.e.*, the Reader)[5] make invocation at [my] "coffin, and may I hear the prayers which are recited "[when] the offerings [are made]. May I draw nigh "(20) unto the *Neshem*[6] boat and may neither my "soul nor its lord be turned back."

"Homage to thee, O thou who art at the head of "Ȧmentet, thou Osiris who dwellest in the city of "Nifu-ur.[7] Grant thou that I may arrive in peace in "Ȧmentet and that the lords of Ta-tchesertet[8] may "receive me and may (21) say unto me, 'Hail! Hail,

[1] Or, "may I rise."

[2] A city near Memphis.

[3] *I.e.*, Orion.

[4] The three divisions ═══ ═══ ⊗ *pet ta ṭuat* into which the Egyptians divided the world correspond roughly to the words, "heaven, earth, and hell."

[5] Literally, "he that hath the book."

[6] A name given to the sacred boat of the Sun-God; the word *neshem* means "light green," and is commonly applied to green felspar.

[7] The metropolis of the nome of Ȧbṭu (Abydos).

[8] *I.e.*, the "holy land," a name of the underworld.

"[thou that comest] in peace!' May they prepare for "me a place by the side of the Chief in the presence of "divine chiefs; may Isis and Nephthys, the two divine "nursing goddesses, receive me at the seasons, and "may I come forth (22) into the presence of Un-nefer "(*i.e.*, Osiris) in triumph. May I follow after Horus "through Re statet, and after Osiris in Ṭaṭṭu; and "may I perform all the transformations according to "my heart's desire in every place wheresoever my *ka* "(double) pleaseth so to do."

RUBRIC: If this text be known [by the deceased] upon earth, (23) or if he causeth it to be done in writing upon [his] coffin, then will he be able to come forth on any day that he pleaseth, and to enter into his habitation without being driven back. The cakes, and ale, and haunches of meat (24) which are upon the altar of Rā shall be given unto him, and his homestead shall be among the fields in the Sekhet-Áanru, and to him shall be given wheat and barley therein, for he shall be vigorous there even as he was upon earth.

CHAPTER IB.

[From the Papyrus of Nekhtu-Åmen (Naville, *Todtenbuch*, Bd. I. Bl. 5).]

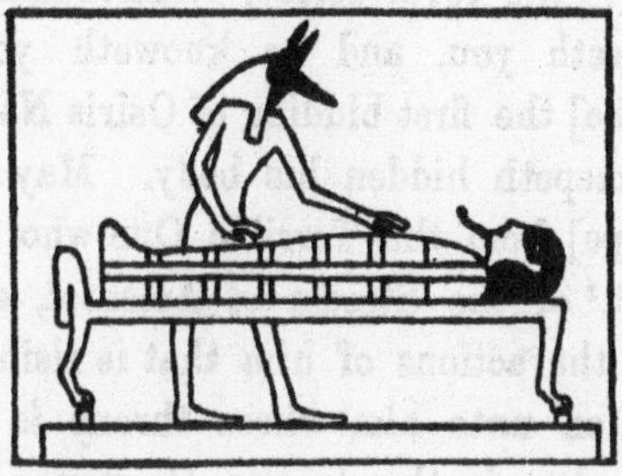

Vignette: The god Anubis, jackal-headed, standing by the side of the bier on which lies the mummy.

Text: (1) THE CHAPTER OF MAKING THE SĀḤU [1] TO ENTER INTO THE ṬUAT (*i.e.*, UNDERWORLD) ON THE DAY OF THE FUNERAL (2) WHEN THESE WORDS ARE TO BE SAID:—

"Homage to thee, O thou that dwellest in Set-"Tchesert [2] of Åmentet: (3) Osiris, the royal scribe

[1] Sāḥu  means a body which has attained to a degree of knowledge and power and glory, whereby it becomes henceforth lasting and incorruptible. It could hold converse with the soul, and could ascend into heaven and dwell with the beatified. The Sāḥu, or spiritual body, sprang from the material body through the prayers which were said, and the ceremonies which were performed at the tomb, or elsewhere, by duly appointed and properly qualified priests.

[2] *I.e.*, the Holy Mountain.

"Nekhtu-Åmen, victorious, knoweth thee, (4) and he "knoweth thy name. Deliver thou him from the "worms (5) which are in Re-stau, which live upon the "bodies of men and women and (6) which feed upon "their blood, for Osiris, the favoured one of the god of "his city, (7) the royal scribe, Nekhtu-Åmen, victori-"ous, knoweth you, and he knoweth your names. "[Let this be] the first bidding of Osiris Neb-er-tcher [1] "(8) who keepeth hidden his body. May he give air "[and escape] from the Terrible One who dwelleth in "the Bight [2] of the Stream of Åmentet, and may he "decree (9) the actions of him that is rising up. Let "him pass on unto him whose throne is within the "darkness, who giveth glory in Re-stau. (10) O lord "of light, come thou and swallow up the worms "which are in Åmentet. The great god who dwelleth "in Ṭaṭṭu, (11) and who is unseen, heareth his prayers, "but those who are in affliction fear him as he cometh "forth (12) with the sentence to the divine block. I "Osiris, the royal scribe, Nekhtu-Åmen, have come "bearing the decree of (13) Neb-er-tcher, and Horus "hath taken possession of his throne for him. His "father, the lord of those who are (14) in the boat of "father Horus, hath ascribed praise unto him. He "cometh with tidings . . . and may he see (15) Ånnu "(Heliopolis). Their chief standeth upon the earth

[1] *I.e.*, Osiris, reconstructed and complete, the "lord of wholeness."

[2] According to Chapter XVII., line 46, the Terrible One is the "heart of Osiris, which is the devourer of all slaughtered things."

"before him, and the scribes magnify him at the door "of their assemblies, (16) and they bind his swathings "in Ȧnnu. He hath led captive heaven, and he hath "seized the earth in [his] grasp. Neither the heavens "nor the earth (17) can be taken away from him, for "behold, he is Rā, the first-born of the gods. His "mother suckleth him and she giveth [to him] her "breast (18) in the horizon."

RUBRIC: The words of this chapter are to be recited after [the deceased] is laid to rest in Ȧmentet, whereby the region Tanenet is made to be content with her lord. Then shall Osiris, the royal scribe, Nekhtu-Ȧmen, triumphant, come forth, (19) and he shall embark in the boat of Rā, and [his] body upon its bier shall be counted [with those therein], and he shall be stablished in the Ṭuat (underworld).

CHAPTER II.

[From the Papyrus of Ani (Brit. Mus. No. 10,470, sheet 18).]

Vignette: A man, standing upright, holding a staff.

Text: (1) THE CHAPTER OF COMING FORTH BY DAY AND OF LIVING AFTER DEATH. Saith Osiris Ani, victorious:—

"Hail, One, shining from the Moon! (2) Hail, One, "shining from the Moon! Grant that this Osiris Ani "may come forth among those multitudes which are

"(3) outside; and let him be established as a dweller "(*or* let him go about) among the denizens of heaven; "and let the underworld be opened unto him. And "behold, Osiris, (4) Osiris Ani, shall come forth by day "to do whatsoever he pleaseth upon the earth among "the living ones."

CHAPTER III.

[From the Papyrus of Nu (Brit. Mus. No. 10,477, sheet 13).]

Vignette: This Chapter has no vignette.

Text: (1) ANOTHER CHAPTER LIKE UNTO THE PRECEDING. The overseer of the house of the overseer of the seal, Nu, triumphant, saith:— (2)

"Hail, thou god Tem, who comest forth from the "Great Deep,[1] and who shinest with glory under the "form of the double Lion-god,[2] send out with might "thy words unto those who are in thy presence, (3) and "let the overseer of the house of the overseer of the "seal, Nu, triumphant, enter into their assembly. He "hath performed the decree which hath been spoken to "the mariners of Rā at eventide, (4) and the Osiris "Nu, triumphant, liveth after he hath died, even as

[1] *I.e.*, the celestial Nile.
[2] *I.e.*, the god Shu and the goddess Tefnut.

"doth Rā day by day . . . . . . As Rā is born from "(5) yesterday even so shall the Osiris Nu be born "[from yesterday], and every god shall rejoice at the "life of the Osiris Nu, even as they rejoice at (6) the "life of Ptaḥ when he maketh his appearance from the "great Temple[1] of the Aged One which is in Ȧnnu."

CHAPTER IV.

[From the Papyrus of Nu (Brit. Mus. No. 10,477, sheet 19).]

Vignette: This Chapter has no vignette.

Text: (1) THE CHAPTER OF PASSING OVER THE CELESTIAL ROAD (2) OF RE-STAU. The overseer of the house of the overseer of the seal, the Osiris Nu, triumphant, saith:—

"I open out a way over the watery abyss which "formeth a path between the two Combatants[2] and I "have come; may the fields of Osiris be given over "into my power."

[1] *I.e.*, the temple of Rā at Heliopolis.

[2] *I.e.*, Horus and Set. Horus engaged in battle with Set, his father's murderer, and after a prolonged fight which lasted three days, vanquished his opponent. Set threw filth at Horus, but Horus destroyed the members of Set; see Chapter XVII., ll. 67-69. As nature powers Horus and Set typified Light and Darkness respectively.

CHAPTER V.

[From the Papyrus of Nebseni (Brit. Mus. No. 9900, sheet 11).]

Vignette: A seated man (see Papyrus of Sutimes, plate 1.)

Text: (1) THE CHAPTER OF NOT LETTING WORK BE DONE IN THE UNDERWORLD by Nebseni, the scribe and draughtsman in the Temple of Ptaḥ, who saith:—

"I lift up the hand of the man who is inactive. I "have come from the city of Unnu (Hermopolis). I "am the divine Soul which liveth, and I lead with me "the hearts of the apes."[1]

[1] *I.e.*, the six apes which are seen adoring the Sun-god Râ when he rises; in the Papyrus of Hu-nefer (see the vignette on p. 77) the apes (*àmhetet*) are *seven* in number.

CHAPTER VI.

[From the Papyrus of Nebseni (Brit. Mus. No. 9900, sheet 10).]

Vignette: A standing, bearded male figure, or a man stretching out his hands to a god.

Text: (1) THE CHAPTER OF MAKING THE SHABTI[1] FIGURE TO DO WORK FOR A MAN IN THE UNDERWORLD. The scribe Nebseni, the draughtsman in the Temples (2) of the North and South, the man highly venerated in the Temple of Ptaḥ, saith:—

"O thou *shabti* figure (3) of the scribe Nebseni, the "son of the scribe Thena, victorious, and of the lady of

[1] The original meaning of the word *shabti* is unknown, but at a comparatively late period the word was connected with the word *usheb* 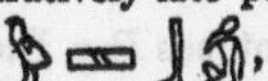, "to answer," probably because the figure is supposed to *answer* the address of the deceased. Several forms of the Chapter are known, and the oldest seems to date from the VIth Dynasty; they are found on figures made of stone, wood, porcelain, &c., and all great collections of Egyptian antiquities contain hundreds of examples of them.

"the house Mutrestha, victorious, (4) if I be called, or "if I be adjudged to do any work whatsoever of the "labours which are to be done in the underworld— "behold, [for thee] opposition will there be (5) set "aside—by a man in his turn, let the judgment fall "upon thee instead of upon me always, in the matter "of sowing the fields, of filling (6) the water-courses "with water, and of bringing the sands of this east [to] "the west."

[The *shabti* figure answereth], "Verily I am here "[and will come] whithersoever thou biddest me."

CHAPTER VII.

[From the Papyrus of Nu (Brit. Mus. No. 10,477, sheet 22).]

Vignette: **The deceased spearing a serpent (see *Pap. Funéraire de Nebset*, ed. Pierret and Devéria, pl. 5).**

Text: (1) THE CHAPTER OF PASSING OVER THE ABOMINABLE BACK OF (2) APEP. The overseer of the house of the overseer of the seal, Nu, triumphant, saith :—

"Hail, thou creature of wax,[1] who leadest away "[victims] and destroyest them, and who livest upon "the weak and helpless, may I never become weak and "helpless (3) [before] thee, may I never suffer collapse "[before] thee. And thy poison shall never enter into "my members, for my members are [as] the members of "the god Tem; and since thou thyself dost not suffer "collapse [I shall not suffer collapse]. O let not the "pains of death (4) which come upon thee enter into "my members. I am the god Tem, and I am in the "foremost part of Nu (*i.e.*, the sky), and the power "which protecteth me is that which is with all the "gods for ever. I am he whose name is hidden, and "whose habitation is holy for millions of years. I am "he who dwelleth therein (?) and I come forth along "with the god Tem. I am he who shall not be "condemned (?); I am strong, I am strong."

[1] This address shows that the Chapter was said over a wax figure of a fiend, which was burnt in a fire during its recital; the fiend addressed is Âpep, and a figure of him was burnt to "prevent the coming on of storms." See my *Egyptian Magic*, p. 81 ff.

CHAPTER VIII.

[From the Papyrus of Ani (Brit. Mus. No. 10,470, sheet 18).]

Vignette: The emblem of Ȧmenta, towards which Ani, clad in white and holding a staff in his left hand and a bandlet in the right, is walking.

Text: (1) THE CHAPTER OF PASSING THROUGH ȦMENTET [AND COMING FORTH] BY DAY. Saith Osiris Ani:—

"The city of Unnu (Hermopolis) is opened. My "head (2) is sealed up, O Thoth, and strong is the Eye "of Horus. I have delivered the Eye of Horus which "shineth with splendours on the forehead of Rā, "(3) the father of the gods. I am the same Osiris, "the dweller in Ȧmentet. Osiris knoweth his day, and "that he shall live through his period of life; and "shall not I do likewise? (4) I am the Moon-god, "who dwelleth among the gods, I shall not perish. "Stand up, therefore, O Horus, for [Osiris] hath "reckoned thee among the gods."

CHAPTER IX.

[From the Papyrus of Ani (Brit. Mus. No. 10,470, sheet 18).]

Vignette : A ram having upon his head the *Atef* crown standing upon a pylon-shaped pedestal, which rests on a green reed-mat; before him is an altar upon which stand a libation vase and a lotus flower. The scribe Ani, clothed in white, stands with both hands raised in adoration.

Text : (1) THE CHAPTER OF COMING FORTH BY DAY AFTER HAVING MADE THE PASSAGE THROUGH THE TOMB. Saith Osiris Ani :—

"Hail Soul, thou mighty one of strength! (2) Verily "I am here, I have come, I behold thee. I have "passed through the Ṭuat (underworld), I have seen "(3) [my] divine father Osiris, I have scattered the "gloom of night. I am his beloved one. I have "come; I have seen my divine father Osiris. I have "stabbed the heart of Suti.[1] [I] have performed [all]

[1] Suti or Set, the personification of darkness, and the mighty antagonist of Horus, by whom he was slain.

"the ceremonies for my divine father Osiris, (5) I have "opened every way in heaven and in earth. I am the "son who loveth his father Osiris. (6) I have become "a *sāḥu*,[1] I have become a *khu*,[2] I am furnished [with "what I need]. Hail, every god, hail every *khu!* I "have made a path [for myself, I] Osiris, the scribe "Ani, victorious."

CHAPTER X.[3]

[From the Papyrus of Ani (Brit. Mus. No. 10,470, sheet 18).]

Vignette : Ani, clad in white, spearing a serpent.

[1] *I.e.*, the spiritual form of a man which has come into being through the prayers which have been said and the ceremonies which have been performed over his dead body.

[2] A shining or translucent, intangible casing or covering which the deceased possesses in the underworld; it is frequently depicted in the form of a mummy.

[3] In the Saïte Recension this Chapter is found twice, viz., as Chapters X. and XLVIII.; as there is no good reason why it should be Chapter XLVIII., it has been placed here.

Text: (1) ANOTHER CHAPTER [TO BE SAID] BY A MAN WHO COMETH FORTH BY DAY AGAINST HIS ENEMIES IN THE UNDERWORLD. [Saith Osiris Ani :—]

"I have divided the heavens, (2) I have cleft the "horizon, I have traversed the earth, [following] upon "his footsteps. The Mighty KHU taketh possession of "me and carrieth me away, because, behold, (3) I am "provided with his magical words for millions of years. "I eat with my mouth, I crush my food with my "jawbones. (4) Behold, I am the god who is the lord "of the Ṭuat (underworld); may there be given unto "me, Osiris Ani, these things in perpetuity without fail "or lessening."

CHAPTER XI.[1]

[From the Papyrus of Nu (Brit. Mus. No. 10,477, sheet 21).]

Vignette: This Chapter is without a vignette in both the Theban and Saïte Recensions.

Text: (1) THE CHAPTER OF [A MAN] COMING FORTH AGAINST HIS ENEMIES IN THE UNDERWORLD. The overseer of the house of the overseer of the seal, Nu, triumphant, saith:— (2)

"O thou god who eatest thine arm,[2] I have departed "from thy road. I am Rā, and I have come forth

[1] In the Saïte Recension this Chapter is found twice, viz., as Chapters XI. and XLIX.; as there is no good reason why it should be Chapter XLIX., it has been placed here.

[2] This Chapter is addressed either to Āpep, or to one of his fiends.

"from the horizon against my enemies, and he hath "granted to me that they shall not escape (3) from me. "I have made an offering, and my hand is like that of "the lord of the *Ureret* crown. I have lifted up my "feet even as the uraei goddesses rise up. My over-"throw shall not be accomplished, (4) and as for mine "enemy he hath been given over into my power and he "shall not be delivered from me. I shall stand up like "Horus, and I shall sit down like Ptaḥ, and I shall be "mighty like Thoth, (5) and I shall be strong like "Tem. I shall, therefore, walk with my legs, I shall "speak with my mouth, I shall go round about in "quest of mine enemy, and [as] he hath been delivered "over to me he shall not escape from me."

CHAPTER XII.[1]

[From the Papyrus of Nu (Brit. Mus. No. 10,477, sheet 9).]

Vignette: This Chapter is without a vignette in both the Theban and Saïte Recensions.

Text: (1) THE CHAPTER OF GOING INTO AND OF COMING FORTH FROM [THE UNDERWORLD]. The Osiris Nu, triumphant, saith:—

"Hymns of praise to thee, O Râ! thou keeper (?) of "secret (2) gates which are on the brow of the god

[1] In the Saïte Recension this Chapter is found twice, viz., as Chapters XII. and CXX.; as there is no good reason why it should be Chapter CXX., it has been placed here.

"Seb,[1] by the side of the Balance of Rā, wherein he lifteth "up Right and Truth (Maāt) (3) day by day. In very "truth I have burst through the earth,[2] grant [thou] "unto me that I may go forward and arrive at the "state of old age."

CHAPTER XIII.[3]

[From the Papyrus of Nebseni (Brit. Mus. No. 9900, sheet 12).]

Vignette: This Chapter is without a vignette in both the Theban and Saïte Recensions.

Text: [THE CHAPTER OF ENTERING INTO AND OF COMING FORTH FROM ÅMENTET].

[Osiris, the scribe Nebseni, victorious, saith:—]

"...... mortals .... I go in like the "Hawk and I come forth like the *Bennu* bird, the "morning star (?) of Rā. May a path be made for me "whereby I may enter in peace into the beautiful "Åmentet; and may I be by the Lake of Horus; [and "may I lead the greyhounds of Horus]; and may a path

[1] *I.e.*, the Earth-god, in whose domain the body of the deceased was laid after death.

[2] The allusion is to the freedom to come and to go in the underworld which the deceased enjoys through the religious texts which he knows.

[3] In the Saïte Recension this Chapter is found twice, viz., as Chapters XIII. and CXXI.; as there is no good reason why it should be Chapter CXXI., it has been placed here.

"be made for me whereby I may enter in and adore "[Osiris, the lord of Life]."

In the Theban Recension this Chapter appears without a rubric, but in the Saïte Recension as given in the Turin Papyrus (Lepsius, *Todtenbuch*, Bll. 4 and 45) we have the following:—

RUBRIC: [This Chapter] is to be recited over a ring [made] of *ānkham* flowers, which shall be laid on the right ear of the *khu*, together with another ring wrapped up in a strip of byssus cloth, whereon the name of Osiris, Åuf-ānkh, victorious, born of the Lady Shert-åmsu, victorious, shall be done [in writing] on the day of sepulture.

CHAPTER XIV.

[From the Papyrus of Mes-em-neter (Naville, *Todtenbuch*, Bd. I. Bl. 13).]

Vignette: This Chapter has no vignette either in the Theban or in the Saïte Recension.

Text: (1) THE CHAPTER OF PUTTING AN END TO ANY SHAME THAT MAY BE IN THE HEART OF THE GOD for the chief deputy of Åmen, [the scribe] Mes-em-neter, victorious, [who saith:—]

"Hymns of praise to thee, O thou god who makest "the moment to advance, (2) thou dweller among "mysteries of every kind, thou guardian of the word "which I speak. Behold, the god hath shame of me, "but let my faults be washed away and let them fall "(3) upon both hands of the god of Right and Truth.

"Do away utterly with the transgression which is in "me, together with [my] wickedness and sinfulness, O "god of Right and Truth. May this god be at peace "with me! Do away utterly with the (4) obstacles "which are between thee and me. O thou to whom "offerings are made in the divine [city] of Ḳenur,[1] grant "thou that I may bring to thee the offerings which will "make peace [between thee and men] whereon thou "livest, and that I also may live thereon. Be thou at "peace (5) with me and do away utterly with all the "shame of me which thou hast in thy heart because "of me."

CHAPTER XV.

[From the Papyrus of Ani (Brit. Mus. No. 10,470, sheets 18 and 19).]

Vignette: Ani standing, with both hands raised in adoration, before Rā, hawk-headed, and seated in a boat floating upon

[1] The variants of this name are "Ḳemur" and "Ḳer-ur" (see Naville, *op. cit.*, Bd. II. p. 21).

the sky. On a platform in the bows sits the god Ḥeru-pa-khrat[1] with his right hand raised to his mouth, which he touches with one finger; the side of the boat is ornamented with feathers of Maāt and with an *Utchat*.[2] The handles of the oars and the tops of the rowlocks are in the form of hawks' heads, and on the blades of the oars are *Utchats*.

Text: (1) A HYMN OF PRAISE TO RĀ WHEN HE RISETH UPON THE HORIZON, AND WHEN HE SETTETH IN THE LAND OF LIFE. Osiris, the scribe Ani, saith:—

"Homage to thee, (2) O Rā, when thou risest [as] "Tem-Ḥeru-khuti.[3] Thou art adored [by me when] "thy beauties are before mine eyes, and [when thy] "(3) radiance [falleth] upon [my] body. Thou goest "forth to thy setting in the *Sektet* boat with [fair] "winds, and thy heart is glad; the (4) heart of the "*Māṭet*[4] boat rejoiceth. Thou stridest over the heavens "in peace, and all thy foes are cast down; the never "resting stars (5) sing hymns of praise unto thee, and "the stars which rest, and the stars which never fail "glorify thee as thou (6) sinkest to rest in the horizon "of Manu,[5] O thou who art beautiful at morn and at "eve, O thou lord who livest and art established, O "my lord!

"Homage to thee, O thou who art Rā when thou

[1] *I.e.*, "Horus the Child," the Harpocrates of the Greeks.

[2] The two *Utchats*, 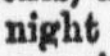, represent the Sun and the Moon, and also the two halves of the Sun's orbit.

[3] *I.e.*, Tem-Harmachis, a double god who united within himself the attributes of the night and the early morning suns.

[4] The name of the morning boat of the sun.

[5] *I.e.*, the mountain of sunset.

"risest, and (7) Tem when thou settest [in] beauty. "Thou risest and shinest on the back of thy mother "[Nut], O thou who art crowned king (8) of the gods! "Nut doeth homage unto thee, and everlasting and "never-changing order[1] embraceth thee at morn and at "eve. Thou stridest over the heaven, being glad of "heart, and the Lake of Testes[2] (9) is content [thereat]. "The Sebáu Fiend hath fallen to the ground; his arms "and his hands have been hacked off, and the knife hath "severed the joints of his body. Rā hath a fair wind "(10); the *Sektet* boat goeth forth and sailing along it "cometh into port. The gods of the south and of the "north, of the west and of the east, praise (11) thee, O "thou divine substance, from whom all forms of life "come into being. Thou sendest forth the word, and "the earth is flooded with silence, O thou only One, "who didst dwell in heaven before ever the earth and "the mountains came into existence. (12) O Runner, "O Lord, O only One, thou maker of things which are, "thou hast fashioned the tongue of the company of the "gods, thou hast produced whatsoever cometh forth "from the waters, and thou springest up from them "over the flooded land of the Lake of Horus. (13) Let "me snuff the air which cometh forth from thy nostrils, "and the north wind which cometh forth from thy "mother [Nut]. O make thou to be glorious my "shining form (*khu*), O Osiris, (14) make thou to be

[1] *I.e.*, Maāt. [2] A name of heaven, or of a part of it.

"divine my soul (*ba*)! Thou art worshipped [in] peace "(*or* [in] setting), O lord of the gods, thou art exalted "by reason of thy wondrous works. Shine thou with "thy rays of light upon my body day by day (15) [upon "me], Osiris the scribe, the teller of the divine offerings "of all the gods, the overseer of the granary of the "lords of Ȧbṭu (Abydos), the royal scribe in truth who "loveth thee; Ani, victorious in peace."

CHAPTER XV.

Hymn and Litany to Osiris.

[From the Papyrus of Ani (Brit. Mus. No. 10,470, sheet 19).]

Vignette: "Osiris Ani, the royal scribe in truth, who loveth "him, the scribe and teller of the divine offerings of all the "gods," and "Osiris Thuthu, the lady of the house, the singing

"woman of Amen," with hands raised in adoration presumably before the god Osiris who, accompanied by the goddess Isis, stands in a shrine made in the form of a funeral chest.[1]

Text: "Praise be unto thee, O Osiris, lord of "eternity, Un-nefer, Ḥeru-Khuti (Harmachis), whose "forms are manifold, and whose attributes are majestic, "(2) Ptaḥ-Seker-Tem[2] in Ȧnnu (Heliopolis), the lord "of the hidden place, and the creator of Ḥet-ka-Ptaḥ[3] "and of the gods [therein], the guide of the underworld, "(3) whom [the gods] glorify when thou settest in Nut. "Isis embraceth thee in peace, and she driveth away "the fiends from the (4) mouth of thy paths. Thou "turnest thy face upon Ȧmentet, and thou makest the "earth to shine as with refined copper. Those who "have lain down (*i.e.*, the dead) rise up to see thee, "they (5) breathe the air and they look upon thy face "when the disk riseth on its horizon; their hearts are "at peace inasmuch as they behold thee, O thou who "art Eternity and Everlastingness!"

Litany.

(1) *Petition.*—"Homage to thee, [O lord of] starry "deities in Ȧnnu, and of heavenly beings in Kher-āḥa;

[1] The shrine of Osiris is separated from the figures of Ani and his wife by the Litany and several lines of a hymn to Rā; this portion of the vignette is given on p. 71.

[2] A triad composed of forms of the morning, evening, and night suns.

[3] *I.e.*, the House of the *ka* of Ptaḥ, a name of Memphis.

"thou god Unti,[1] who art more glorious than the gods "who are hidden in Ȧnnu."

Response.—(10) "O grant[2] thou unto me a path "whereon I may pass in peace, for I am just and true; "I have not spoken lies wittingly, nor have I done "aught with deceit."

(2) *Petition.*—"Homage to thee, O Ȧn in Ȧntes (?), "Ḥeru-khuti (Harmachis), with long strides thou "stridest over heaven, O Ḥeru-khuti."

Response.—(10) "O grant thou unto me a path "whereon I may pass in peace, for I am just and true; "I have not spoken lies wittingly, nor have I done "aught with deceit."

(3) *Petition.*—"Homage to thee, O Soul of everlast-"ingness, thou Soul that dwellest in Ṭaṭṭu, Un-nefer, "son of Nut; thou art lord of Ȧḳert."

Response.—(10) "O grant thou unto me a path "whereon I may pass in peace, for I am just and true; "I have not spoken lies wittingly, nor have I done "aught with deceit."

(4) *Petition.*—"Homage to thee in thy dominion "over Ṭaṭṭu; the *Ureret* crown is established upon thy "head; thou art the One who maketh the strength

[1] A god who is represented holding a star in each hand, and walking before a solar bark.

[2] The following petition, "O grant thou unto me a path," &c., is written once only, and at the end of the Litany, but it was clearly intended to be repeated after each of the nine addresses. This is proved by the Saïte Recension (see Lepsius, *op. cit.*, Bl. 5), where the words, "Grant thou the sweet breath of the north wind to the Osiris Ȧuf-ānkh" are written in two places, and are intended to be said after each of the ten addresses above them.

"which protecteth himself, and thou dwellest in peace "in Ṭaṭṭu."

Response.—(10) "O grant thou unto me a path "whereon I may pass in peace, for I am just and true; "I have not spoken lies wittingly, nor have I done "aught with deceit."

(5) *Petition.*—"Homage to thee, O lord of the Acacia "Tree, the *Seker* boat is set upon its sledge; thou "turnest back the Fiend, the worker of evil, and thou "causest the *Utchat* to rest upon its seat."

Response.—(10) "O grant thou unto me a path "whereon I may pass in peace, for I am just and true; "I have not spoken lies wittingly, nor have I done "aught with deceit."

(6) *Petition.*—"Homage to thee, O thou who art "mighty in thine hour, thou great and mighty Prince, "dweller in Ȧn-ruṭ-f,[1] lord of eternity and creator of ever-"lastingness, thou art the lord of Suten-ḥenen."[2]

Response.—(10) "O grant thou unto me a path "whereon I may pass in peace, for I am just and true; "I have not spoken lies wittingly, nor have I done "aught with deceit."

(7) *Petition.*—"Homage to thee, O thou who restest

[1] *I.e.*, "the place where nothing groweth," the name of a district in the underworld.

[2] *I.e.*, Heracleopolis Magna, the capital of the Heracleopolites nome. Egyptian mythology declares that here Osiris was first crowned, that here Horus succeeded to the rank and dignity of his father, that here the sky was first separated from the earth, and that from this place Sekhet set out on her mission to destroy mankind because they had rebelled against Rā, who, they declared, had become old and incapable of ruling them rightly.

"upon Right and Truth, thou art the lord of Ȧbṭu "(Abydos), and thy limbs are joined unto Ta-tchesertet; "thou art he to whom fraud and guile are hateful."

Response.—(10) "O grant thou unto me a path "whereon I may pass in peace, for I am just and true; "I have not spoken lies wittingly, nor have I done "aught with deceit."

(8) *Petition.*—"Homage to thee, O thou who art "within thy boat, thou bringest Ḥāpi (*i.e.*, the Nile) "forth from his source; the light shineth upon thy body "and thou art the dweller in Nekhen."[1]

Response.—(10) "O grant thou unto me a path "whereon I may pass in peace, for I am just and true; "I have not spoken lies wittingly, nor have I done "aught with deceit."

(9) *Petition.*—"Homage to thee, O creator of the "gods, thou King of the North and of the South, O "Osiris, victorious one, ruler of the world in thy "gracious seasons; thou art the lord of the celestial "world."[2]

Response.—(10) "O grant thou unto me a path "whereon I may pass in peace, for I am just and true; "I have not spoken lies wittingly, nor have I done "aught with deceit."

[1] The name of the sanctuary of the goddess Nekhebet in Upper Egypt, the Eileithyiapolis of the Greeks.

[2] *I.e.*, the two lands *Ȧṭebui* which were situated one on each side of the celestial Nile.

Hymn to Rā.

[From the Papyrus of Ani (Brit. Mus. No. 10,470, sheet 20).]

Vignette : Osiris, wearing the white crown and holding the crook, whip, and sceptre, standing in a shrine; behind him is the goddess Isis in the character of the Divine Mother.

Text : (1) A HYMN OF PRAISE TO RĀ WHEN HE RISETH IN THE EASTERN PART OF HEAVEN. Those who are in his train (2) rejoice, and lo! Osiris Ani victorious, saith :—

"Hail, thou Disk, "thou lord of rays, "(3) who risest on "the horizon day by "day! Shine thou "with thy beams "of light upon the "face of Osiris Ani, "who is victorious; "for he singeth "hymns of praise "unto thee at (4) "dawn, and he "maketh thee to set "at eventide with "words of adora-"tion. May the "soul of Osiris Ani, the triumphant one, come forth

"(5) with thee into heaven, may he go forth in the *Māṭet* "boat. May he come into port in the *Sektet* boat, and "may he cleave his path among the never (6) resting "stars in the heavens."

Osiris Ani, being in peace and in triumph, adoreth his lord, (7) the lord of eternity, saying: "Homage to thee, "O Ḥeru-khuti (Harmachis), who art the god Kheperá, "the self-created; when thou risest on the (8) horizon "and sheddest thy beams of light upon the lands of "the North and of the South, thou art beautiful, yea "beautiful, and all the gods rejoice when they behold "thee, (9) the King of heaven. The goddess Nebt-"Unnut[1] is stablished upon thy head; and her uraei "of the South and of the North are upon thy brow; "(10) she taketh up her place before thee. The god "Thoth is stablished in the bows of thy boat to destroy "utterly all thy foes. (11) Those who are in the Ṭuat "(underworld) come forth to meet thee, and they bow "in homage as they come towards thee, to behold [thy] "(12) beautiful Image. And I have come before thee "that I may be with thee to behold thy Disk every "day. May I not be shut up in [the tomb], may I not "be (13) turned back, may the limbs of my body be "made new again when I view thy beauties, even as "[are those of] all thy favoured ones, (14) because I "am one of those who worshipped thee [whilst I lived] "upon earth. May I come in unto the land of eternity,

[1] A name meaning something like the "lady of the hour."

"may I come even (15) unto the everlasting land, for "behold, O my lord, this hast thou ordained for me."

And lo, Osiris Ani triumphant in peace, the triumphant one, saith: (16) "Homage to thee, O thou who "risest in thy horizon as Rā, thou reposest upon law

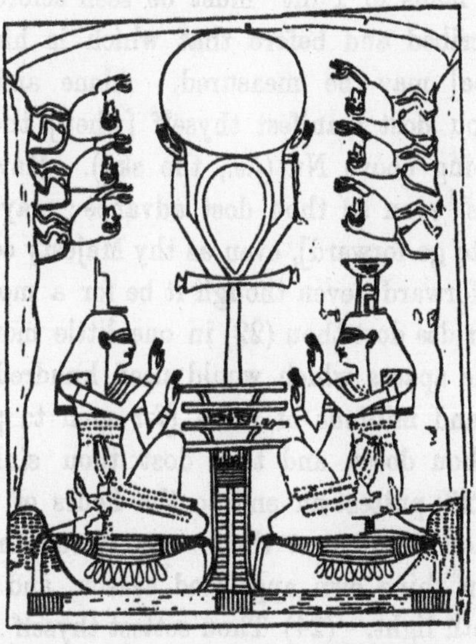

THE SUNRISE. The Ṭeṭ, [Ṭeṭ sign], or tree-trunk which held the body of Osiris, standing between Isis and Nephthys, who kneel in adoration, one on each side of it. From the Ṭeṭ proceeds the emblem of life, which has arms that support the Disk of the Sun. The six apes represent the spirits of the dawn. (This scene is from the Papyrus of Ani, plate 2.)

"[which changeth not nor can it be altered]. Thou "passest over the sky, and every face watcheth thee "(17) and thy course, for thou hast been hidden from "their gaze. Thou dost shew thyself at dawn and at "eventide day by day. (18) The *Sektet* boat, wherein "is thy Majesty, goeth forth with might; thy beams "[shine] upon [all] faces; [the number] of thy red and "yellow rays cannot be known, nor can thy bright (19) "beams be depicted. The lands of the gods, and the "eastern lands of Punt[1] must be seen before they can "be described and before that which is hidden (20) "[in thee] may be measured. Alone and by thy-"self thou dost manifest thyself [when] thou comest "into being above Nu (*i.e.*, the sky). May Ani (21) "advance, even as thou dost advance; may he never "cease [to go forward], even as thy Majesty ceaseth not "[to go forward], even though it be for a moment; for "with strides dost thou (22) in one little moment pass "over the spaces which would need hundreds of thou-"sands and millions of years [for man to pass over; "this] thou doest, and then dost thou sink to rest. "Thou (23) puttest an end to the hours of the night, "and thou dost count them, even thou; thou endest "them in thine own appointed season, and the earth "becometh light. (24) Thou settest thyself before thy "handiwork in the likeness of Rā; thou risest in the "horizon."

Osiris, the scribe Ani, victorious, declareth (25) his praise of thee when thou shinest, and when thou risest at dawn he crieth in his joy at thy birth: (26) "Thou "art crowned with the majesty of thy beauties; thou

[1] *I.e.*, the spice-producing land near the most easterly part of Somali land.

"mouldest thy limbs as thou dost advance, and thou "bringest them forth without birth-pangs in the form "of (27) Rā, as thou dost rise up into the upper air. "Grant thou that I may come unto the heaven which "is everlasting, and unto the mountain where dwell "thy favoured ones. May I be joined (28) unto those "shining beings, holy and perfect, who are in the "underworld; and may I come forth with them to

THE SUNRISE. (From the Papyrus of Qenna, plate 1.)

"behold thy beauties when thou shinest (29) at even-"tide and goest to thy mother Nut.[1] Thou dost place "thyself in the west, and my two hands are [raised] in "adoration [of thee] (30) when thou settest as a living "being. Behold, thou art the maker of eternity, and

[1] *I.e.*, Nut, , the night sky, as opposed to , the day sky.

"thou art adored [when] thou settest in the heavens. "I have given my heart unto thee (31) without wavering, O thou who art mightier than the gods."

Osiris Ani, triumphant, saith: "A hymn of praise to "thee, O thou who risest (32) like unto gold, and who "dost flood the world with light on the day of thy birth. "Thy mother giveth thee birth upon [her] hand, and "thou dost give light unto the course of the Disk (33). "O thou great Light who shinest in the heavens, thou "dost strengthen the generations of men with the Nile-"flood, and thou dost cause gladness in all lands, and "in all cities (34), and in all the temples. Thou art "glorious by reason of thy splendours, and thou makest "strong thy KA (*i.e.*, Double), with *ḥu* and *tchefau* "foods.[1] O thou who art the mighty one of victories, "(35) thou who art the power of [all] Powers, who "dost make strong thy throne against evil fiends; who "art glorious in majesty in the *Sektet* boat, and who "art exceeding mighty (36) in the *Āṭet* boat, make "thou glorious Osiris Ani with victory in the under-"world; grant thou that in the netherworld he may be "(37) without evil. I pray thee to put away [his] "faults behind thee: grant thou that he may be one of "thy venerable servants (38) who are with the shining "ones; may he be joined unto the souls which are in Ta-"tchesertet; and may he journey into the Sekhet-Åaru[2]

[1] *Ḥu* and *tchefau* are the celestial foods upon which the gods and the beatified live.

[2] The Field of lilies, reeds, and water plants, which formed one of the sections of the Sekhet-Ḥetepet, or "Elysian Fields."

"(39) by a prosperous and happy decree, he the Osiris, "the scribe, Ani, triumphant."

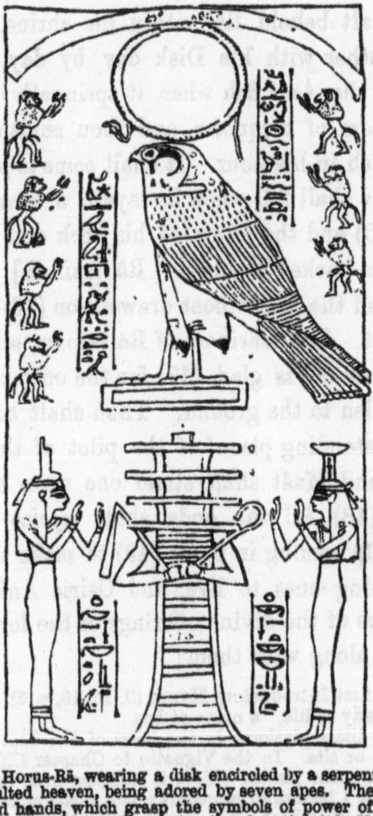

THE SUNRISE. Horus-Rā, wearing a disk encircled by a serpent, and standing beneath the vaulted heaven, being adored by seven apes. The Tet below has human arms and hands, which grasp the symbols of power of Osiris; on the left stands Isis, the "divine mother," and on the right Nephthys.
(From the Papyrus of Hu-nefer, plate 1.)

(And the god saith :—)

(40) "Thou shalt come forth into heaven, thou shalt

"pass over the sky, thou shalt be joined unto the starry "deities. Praises shall be offered (41) unto thee in "thy boat, thou shalt be hymned in the *Āṭet* boat, (42) "thou shalt behold Rā within his shrine, thou shalt "set together with his Disk day by day, thou shalt "see (43) the *Ȧnt*[1] fish when it springeth into being in "the waters of turquoise, and thou shalt see (44) the "*Ȧbṭu*[1] fish in his hour. It shall come to pass that the "Evil One shall fall when he layeth a snare to destroy "thee, (45) and the joints of his neck and of his back "shall be hacked asunder. Rā [saileth] with a fair "wind, and the *Sektet* boat draweth on (46) and cometh "into port. The mariners of Rā rejoice, and the heart "of Nebt-ānkh[2] is glad, (47) for the enemy of her lord "hath fallen to the ground. Thou shalt behold Horus "on the standing place[3] of the pilot of the boat, and "Thoth and Maāt shall stand one upon each side of "him. (48) All the gods shall rejoice when they "behold Rā coming in peace (49) to make the hearts of "the shining ones to live, and Osiris Ani, victorious, "the scribe of the divine offerings of the lord of Thebes, "shall be along with them!"

[1] See the first Introductory Hymn (ll. 15, 16, p. 6).

[2] *I.e.*, "Lady of life," a name of Isis.

[3] *I.e.*, the little platform in the bows of the boat on which the pilot stands or sits. In the Vignette to Chapter CXXXIII. it will be seen that some plaited object is hanging over the prow of the boat, and this I believe to represent a mat made of reeds and grass. The pilot of a Nile boat often has to sound the depth of the water under his boat, and this he does by means of a pole. As he lifts the pole out of the water, some drops fall on the place where he is standing, which eventually becomes wet and slippery; to secure a good foothold a reed-mat or layer of grass is thrown down, and I have seen a layer of sugar-canes also used as a mat.

THE BOOK OF THE DEAD

PART II

THE BOOK OF THE DEAD

CHAPTER XV. (*continued*).

A Hymn to the Setting Sun.

[From the Papyrus of Mut-ḥetep (Brit. Mus. No. 10,010, sheet 5).]

Vignette : In this papyrus this Chapter is without a vignette

Text : I. (1) [ANOTHER CHAPTER OF] THE MYSTERY OF THE ṬUAT (UNDERWORLD) AND OF PASSING THROUGH THE UNSEEN NETHERWORLD, and of seeing the Disk when he setteth in Amentet, [when] he is adored by the gods and by the *Khus* in the underworld, and [when] the Soul (2) which dwelleth in Rā is made perfect. He is made mighty before Tem ; he is made great before Osiris ; he setteth his terror before the company of the gods who are the guides of the netherworld ; he maketh long (?) (3) his steps and he maketh his face to enter (?) [with that of] the great god. Now every *Khu*, for whom these words shall have been said, shall come forth by day in any form which he is pleased to take ; (4) he shall gain power among the gods of the Ṭuat (underworld), and they shall recognize him as one of themselves ; and he shall enter in at the hidden gate with power.

The lady (5) Mut-ḥetep, victorious, singeth hymns of praise to thee, [saying] : "O Rā-Tem, in thy splendid

"progress thou risest, and thou settest as a living being "in the glories (6) of the western horizon; thou settest "in thy territory which is in Manu.[1] Thy uraeus is "behind thee, thy uraeus is behind thee. Homage to "thee, O thou who art in peace, homage to thee, O "thou who art in peace. Thou art joined unto the "Eye of Tem,[2] and it chooseth (7) its powers of protec-"tion [to place] behind thy members. Thou goest forth "through heaven, thou travellest over the earth, and "thou journeyest onward. O Luminary, the northern "and southern halves of heaven come to thee and they "bow low in adoration, (8) and they pay homage unto "thee, day by day. The gods of Àmentet rejoice in "thy beauties and the unseen places sing hymns of "praise unto thee. Those who dwell in the *Sektet* "boat (9) go round about thee, and the Souls of the "East[3] pay homage to thee, and when they meet thy "Majesty they cry: 'Come, come in peace!' There is "a shout of welcome to thee (10), O lord of heaven and "governor of Àmentet! Thou art acknowledged by "Isis who seeth her son in thee, the lord of fear, the "mighty one of terror. Thou settest as a living being in "(11) the hidden place. Thy father [Ta-]tunen raiseth "thee up and he placeth both his hands behind thee; "thou becomest endowed with divine attributes in [thy]

[1] *I.e.*, the mountain of the sunset.

[2] Like "Eye of Horus" and "Eye of Rā," a name for a form of the Sun-god.

[3] *I.e.*, the Souls or Spirits who take the forms of apes immediately the sun has risen; see the vignettes on pp. 73—77.

"members of earth; thou wakest in peace and thou "settest (12) in Manu.[1] Grant thou that I may become "a being honoured before Osiris, and that I may come "to thee, O Rā-Tem! I have adored thee, therefore "do thou for me that which I wish. Grant thou (13)

THE SUNSET. The Sun-god in the form of a hawk wearing a disk about to set in the West. The three hawk-headed figures on the right are called Horus, Mesthà, and Ḥāpi, and the three jackal-headed figures, Horus, Ṭuamāutef, and Qebḥ-sennuf. Below are seen Isis and Nephthys adoring the two Lion-gods, who represent the Evening Sun and the Morning Sun respectively. (From the Papyrus of Qenna, plate 3.)

"that I may be victorious in the presence of the com-"pany of the gods. Thou art beautiful, O Rā, in thy "western horizon of Àmentet, thou lord of Maāt, thou

[1] *I.e.*, the mountain of the sunset.

"mighty one of fear, thou whose attributes are majestic, "O thou who art greatly (14) beloved by those who "dwell in the Ṭuat (underworld); thou shinest with "thy beams upon the beings that are therein per-"petually, and thou sendest forth thy light upon the "path of Re-stau. Thou openest up the path of the "double Lion-god,[1] thou settest the (15) gods upon "[their] thrones, and the *Khus* in their abiding places. "The heart of Naȧrerf[2] is glad [when] Rā setteth, the "heart of Naȧrerf is glad when Rā setteth."

"Hail, O ye gods of the land of Ȧmentet who make "offerings and oblations unto (16) Rā-Tem, ascribe "ye glory [unto him when] ye meet him. Grasp ye "your weapons and overthrow ye the fiend Sebȧ on "behalf of Rā, and (17) repulse the fiend Nebṭ on behalf "of Osiris. The gods of the land of Ȧmentet rejoice "and lay hold upon the cords of the *Sektet* boat, and "they come in peace; (18) the gods of the hidden place "who dwell in Ȧmentet triumph."

"Hail, Thoth, who didst make Osiris to triumph over "his enemies, make thou Mut-ḥetep, victorious, to "triumph over her enemies (19) in the presence of the "great divine sovereign chiefs who live with Osiris, the "lord of life. The great god who dwelleth in his Disk "cometh forth, that is, Horus the avenger of his father, "Unnefer-Rā. (20) Osiris setteth, and the *Khu*[*s*] who

[1] See the accompanying vignette, and that of Chapter XVII., p. 94.
[2] *I.e.*, *An-ruṭ-f*, the place where nothing groweth.

"are in the Ṭuat (underworld) say: Homage to thee, O "thou who comest as Tem, and who comest into being "as the creator of the gods. Homage to thee, O thou "who comest as the holy Soul of souls, who dwellest in "the horizon. Homage to thee who art more glorious "than [all] the gods and who illuminest the Ṭuat with "thine Eye. Homage to thee who sailest in thy glory "and who goest round about in thy Disk."

A Hymn to the Setting Sun.

[From the Papyrus of Nekhtu-Amen (Naville, *op. cit.*, Bd. II. p. 23).]

Vignette I.: The deceased standing in adoration before the Sun-god, who is spearing a serpent.

Vignette II.: The deceased spearing a serpent; compare the vignette to Chapter XXXIX. The following vignette, in which the deceased is seen kneeling in adoration before Ra in company with certain gods, is taken from the Papyrus of Qenna (plate 17).

Text: ANOTHER CHAPTER OF THE MYSTERY OF THE ṬUAT (UNDERWORLD) AND OF TRAVERSING THE UNSEEN

PLACES OF THE UNDERWORLD, of seeing the Disk when he setteth in Amentet, [when] he is adored by the gods and by the *Khus* of the Tuat (underworld), and [when] the divine *Khu* which dwelleth within Rā is made perfect. He setteth his might before Rā, he setteth his power before Tem, [he setteth his strength] before Khenti-Ȧmentet, and he setteth his terror before the company of the gods. The Osiris of the gods goeth as leader through the Ṭuat (underworld), he crasheth through mountains, he bursteth through rocks, he maketh glad (?) the heart of every *Khu*. This composition shall be recited by the deceased when he cometh forth and when he goeth in with the gods, among whom he findeth no opposition; then shall he come forth by day in all the manifold and exceedingly numerous forms which he may be pleased to take. [The Osiris . . . . . saith :—]

"A hymn of praise to Rā at eventide [when] he "setteth as a living being in Baȧkha.[1] The great god "who dwelleth in his Disk riseth in his Two Eyes[2] and "all the *Khus* of the underworld receive him in his "horizon of Ȧmentet; they shout praises unto Ḥeru-"khuti (Harmachis) in his form of Tem, and they sing "hymns of joy to Rā when they have received him at "the head of his beautiful path of Ȧmentet."

[1] *I.e.*, The mountain of sunrise, but the scribe appears to have written Baȧkha, instead of Manu.

[2] *I.e.*, the Sun and the Moon.

He (*i.e.*, the deceased) saith: "Praise be unto thee, "O Rā, praise be unto thee, O Tem, in thy splendid "progress. Thou hast risen and thou hast put on "strength, and thou settest like a living being amid thy "glories in the horizon of Àmentet, in thy domain which "is in Manu. Thy uraeus-goddess is behind thee; thy "uraeus-goddess is behind thee. Hail to thee, in peace; "hail to thee, in peace. Thou joinest thyself unto the "Eye of Horus, and thou hidest thyself within its secret "place; it destroyeth for thee all the convulsions of thy "face, it maketh thee strong with life, and thou livest. "It bindeth its protecting amulets behind thy members. "Thou sailest forth over heaven, and thou makest the "earth to be stablished; thou joinest thyself unto the "upper heaven, O Luminary. The two regions of the "East and West make adoration unto thee, bowing "low and paying homage unto thee and they praise "thee day by day; the gods of Àmentet rejoice in thy "splendid beauties. The hidden places adore thee, the "aged ones make offerings unto thee, and they create "for thee protecting powers. The divine beings who "dwell in the eastern and western horizons transport "thee, and those who are in the *Sektet* boat convey "thee round and about. The Souls of Àmentet cry "out unto thee and say unto thee when they meet thy "majesty (Life, Health, Strength!) 'All hail, all hail!' "When thou comest forth in peace there arise shouts "of delight to thee, O thou lord of heaven, thou Prince "of Àmentet. Thy mother Isis embraceth thee, and in "thee she recognizeth her son, the lord of fear, the "mighty one of terror. Thou settest as a living being "within the dark portal. Thy father Tatunen lifteth "thee up and he stretcheth out his two hands behind "thee; thou becomest a divine being in the earth. "Thou wakest as thou settest, and thy habitation is in "Manu. Grant thou that I may be venerated before "Osiris, and come thou [to me], O Rā-Tem. Since "thou hast been adored [by me] that which I wish "thou shalt do for me day by day. Grant thou victory "[unto me] before the great company of the gods, O Rā "who art doubly beautiful in thy horizon of Åmentet, "thou lord of Maāt who dwellest in the horizon. The "fear of thee is great, thy forms are majestic, and the "love of thee is great among those who dwell in the "underworld."

A Hymn to the Setting Sun.

[From a Papyrus of the XIXth Dynasty preserved at Dublin (see Naville, *Todtenbuch*, Bd. I. Bl. 19).]

Vignette: The deceased and his wife[1] standing with both hands raised in adoration before a table of offerings, upon which are a libation vase and lotus flowers.

Text: (1) A Hymn of Praise to Rā-Ḥeru-(2) Khuti (Rā-Harmachis) when he setteth in (3)

[1] The general treatment of the figures resembles that followed by the artist in the Papyrus Hu-nefer; the man, however, has a fillet round his head.

THE WESTERN PART OF HEAVEN. He (*i.e.*, the deceased) saith :—

"Homage to thee, (4) O Rā [who] in thy setting art "(5) Tem-Ḥeru-khuti (Tem-Harmachis) (6) thou divine "god, thou self-created (7) being, thou primeval matter "[from which all things were made]. When [thou] "appearest (8) in the bows of [thy] bark men shout for "joy at (9) thee, O maker of the gods! (10) Thou didst "stretch out the heavens wherein thy two eyes[1] might "travel, thou didst make the earth to be a vast chamber "for thy *Khus*,[2] so that (11) every man might know his "fellow. The *Sektet* boat is glad, and the *Māṭet* boat "rejoiceth; (12) and they greet thee with exultation "as thou journeyest along. The god Nu is content "and thy (13) mariners are satisfied; the uraeus-"goddess hath overthrown thine enemies, and thou "hast carried off the legs of Apep. Thou art beautiful, "(14) O Rā, each day, and thy mother Nut embraceth "thee; thou settest in beauty, and thy heart is glad "(15) in the horizon of Manu, and the holy beings "therein rejoice. (16) Thou shinest there with thy "beams, O thou great god, Osiris, the everlasting "Prince. The lords of (17) the zones of the Ṭuat in "their caverns stretch out their hands in adoration "before (18) thy *Ka* (double), and they cry out to thee, "and they all come forth in the train of thy form "shining brilliantly. (19) The hearts of the lords of

[1] *I.e.*, the Sun and Moon.
[2] *I.e.*, the beatified dead and the gods of heaven.

"the Ṭuat (underworld) are glad when thou (20) "sendest forth thy glorious light in Åmentet; their "two eyes are directed towards thee, (21) and they "press forward to see thee, and their hearts rejoice "when they do see thee. Thou hearkenest unto (22) "the acclamations of those that are in the funeral "chest,[1] thou doest away with their helplessness and "drivest away the evils which are about (23) them. "Thou givest breath to their nostrils and they take "hold of the bows of thy bark (24) in the horizon of "Manu. Thou art beautiful each day, O Rā, and may "thy mother Nut embrace Osiris . . . . . .[2], victorious."

CHAPTER XVI.

The scene to which Lepsius inadvertently gave the number XVI. and which he regarded as a Chapter of the Book of the Dead is, strictly speaking, only a vignette intended to accompany the hymn to the rising Sun that forms part of the introductory matter to the Chapters of the Book of the Dead which we find in some of the oldest papyri of the Theban period. In the Papyrus of Ani[3] we see the Sun's disk supported by a pair of arms which emerge from the sign of life;

[1] *I.e.*, the dead.
[2] The name of the deceased is wanting.
[3] See above, page 73.

this, in its turn, is supported by the pillar which symbolizes the tree-trunk which contained the dead body of Osiris. This pillar rests upon the horizon. On each side of it are three apes typical of the Spirits of the Dawn, adoring the disk; on the right is the goddess Nephthys and on the left is the goddess Isis, Nephthys kneels upon the symbol of the sunset, and Isis upon the symbol of the dawn. Above the whole scene is the vaulted sky. In the Papyrus of Hu-nefer [1] the pillar is endowed with human arms and hands, which grasp the crook and flail, emblematic of Osiris' reign and rule, and the two goddesses are standing upright; one says: "I am thy sister Nephthys," and the other: "I am thy sister Isis, the divine mother." The sun is typified by a hawk having a disk, encircled by an uraeus, upon his head. The apes are here seven in number, four stand in front and three behind; above the whole scene is the vaulted sky.

Certain papyri have also vignettes which illustrate the hymns to the setting sun.[2] In this case the hawk usually stands upon the emblem of the West, while apes and gods adore him. In the Papyrus of Qenna on the right three hawk-headed gods kneel in adoration with their left arms raised, and on the left three jackal-headed gods, with their right arms raised in adoration. Below, two lion-headed gods, with disks on their heads, are seated back to back in a cluster of

[1] See above, page 77. [2] See above, pages 81, 83.

lotus flowers; these typify dawn and eventide. The goddess Isis kneels in adoration before the lion of the dawn, and the goddess Nephthys before the lion of eventide.

CHAPTER XVII.—VIGNETTES.

[From the Papyrus of Ani (Brit. Mus. No. 10,470, sheets 7—10).]

I. II. III.

Vignette: Plate 7. I. Ani and his wife seated in a hall; he is moving a piece on a draught-board (see lines 3 and 4 of the text).

II. The souls of Ani and his wife, in the form of human-headed hawks standing upon a pylon-shaped building; the bearded soul is described as "the soul of Osiris."

III. A table of offerings upon which are lotus flowers, a libation vase, &c.

IV. Two lions seated back to back and supporting the horizon with the sun's disk, over which extends the sky; the lion on the right is called *Sef*, *i.e.*, "Yesterday," and that on the left *Ṭuau*, *i.e.*, "To-day" (see lines 13—16 of the text).

V. The *Bennu* bird and a table of offerings (see lines 26—30 of the text).

VI. The mummy of Ani on a bier within a funeral shrine; at the head and foot are Nephthys and Isis in the form of hawks. Beneath the bier are Ani's palette, variegated marble or glass vessels, &c.

Plate 8. I. The god of "Millions of years"; on his head and in his right hand is the emblem of "years." His left hand is stretched out over a pool containing the Eye of Horus (see line 45 of the text).

II. The god Uatchet-urȧ (*i.e.*, "Great Green Water"), with each hand extended over a pool; that under his right hand is called "Lake of Natron," and that under his left hand, "Lake of Nitre" (see lines 46—50 of the text).

III. A pylon with doors, called Re-stau, *i.e.*, the "Gate of the passages of the tomb" (see lines 56—58 of the text).

IV. The *Utchat*, facing to the left, above a pylon (see line 73 of the text).

V. The cow "Meḥ-urt the eye of Rā," with disk and horns, collar and *menȧt* and whip (see lines 75—79 of the text).

VI. A funeral chest from which emerge the head of Rā and his two arms and hands, each holding the emblem of life. The chest, which is called "the district of Ȧbṭu (Abydos)," or "the burial-place of the East," has upon its sides figures of the four children of Horus, who protect the intestines of Osiris or the deceased. On the right stand Ṭuamȧutef and Qebḥsennuf, and on the left Mesthȧ and Ḥāpi (see lines 82 and 83 of the text).

Plate 9. I. Figures of three gods who, together with Mesthȧ, Ḥāpi, Ṭuamȧutef and Qebḥsennuf are the "seven *Khus*" referred to in line 99 of the text. Their names are:—Maa-ȧtef-f,[1] Kheri-beq-f,[2] and Ḥeru-kḥenti[ȧn-]maati (*or* merti).[3]

II. The god Ȧnpu (Anubis) jackal-headed.

III. Figures of seven gods, whose names are: Netchehnet-cheh, Ȧaqeṭ-qeṭ,[4] Khenti-heh-f,[5] Ȧmi-unnut-f,[6] Ṭesher-maa,[7] Bes-maa-em-ḳerḥ,[8] and Ȧn-em-hru[9] (see lines 99—106 of the text).

[1] *I.e.*, "He who looketh upon his father."
[2] *I.e.*, "He who is under his olive tree."
[3] *I.e.*, "Horus in blindness."
[4] *I.e.*, "He who is mighty in revolving."
[5] *I.e.*, "He dwelleth in his flame."
[6] *I.e.*, "He who is in his hour."
[7] *I.e.*, "Red of both eyes."
[8] *I.e.*, "Flame seeing in the night."
[9] *I.e.*, "Bringing by day."

IV. The soul of Rā, in the form of a hawk with a disk on his head, conversing in Ṭaṭṭu with the soul of Osiris in the form of a human-headed bird wearing the white crown; this scene is of the rarest occurrence (see lines 111 and 112 of the text).

Plate 10. I. The Cat, emblematic of the Sun, cutting off the head of the serpent Āpep or Āpepi, typical of darkness.

II. Ani and his wife Thuthu, kneeling in adoration before the god Kheperȧ, beetle-headed, who is seated in the boat of the rising sun (see lines 116 ff. of the text).

III. Two apes, emblematic of the goddesses Isis and Nephthys (see lines 124 and 125 of the text).

IV. The god Tem, seated within the Sun-disk in the boat of the setting sun.

V. The god Reḥu, in the form of a lion (see line 133 of the text).

VI. The serpent Uatchet, the lady of flame, a symbol of the Eye of Rā, coiled round a lotus flower. Above is the emblem of fire.

CHAPTER XVII.—Texts.

[From the Papyrus of Ani (Brit. Mus. No. 10,470, sheets 7—10), and from the Papyrus of Nebseni (Brit. Mus. No, 9,900, sheet 14, l. 16 ff.).]

Text : (1) HERE BEGIN THE PRAISES AND GLORIFYINGS OF COMING OUT FROM AND OF GOING INTO THE GLORIOUS UNDERWORLD WHICH IS IN THE BEAUTIFUL ȦMENTET, OF COMING OUT (2) BY DAY IN ALL THE FORMS OF EXISTENCE WHICH PLEASE HIM (*i.e.*, THE DECEASED), OF PLAYING AT DRAUGHTS AND SITTING IN THE HALL, AND OF COMING FORTH (3) AS A LIVING SOUL.

Saith Osiris, the scribe Ani, (4) after he hath come to his haven of rest—it is good for [a man] to recite [this work whilst he is] upon earth, for [then] all the words of (5) Tem come to pass :—

"I am the god Tem in rising ; I am the only One.
"I came into existence in (6) Nu. I am Rā who rose
"in the beginning, the ruler of . . . . this."[1] (7)

Who then is this ?

It is Rā when at the beginning he rose in (8) the city of Suten-ḥenen (Heracleopolis Magna), crowned like a king in [his] rising. The pillars[2] of the god Shu[3] were not as yet created, when he was (9) upon the high ground[4] of him that dwelleth in Khemennu (Hermopolis Magna).

"I am the great god who gave birth to himself, even
"Nu, (10) who made his name[s to become] the company
"of the gods as god."

Who then (11) is this ?

It is Rā, the creator of the name[s] of his limbs, which came into being (12) in the form of the gods who are in the train of Rā.

"I am he who is not driven back among the gods." (13)

Who then is this ?

[1] Var. "the ruler of what he hath made" (Papyrus of Nebseni).
[2] *I e.*, the cardinal points.
[3] Shu was the first-born son of Rā, by the goddess Hathor, the sky ; he typified the light, and lifted up the sky (Nut) from the earth (Seb), and placed it upon the steps which were in Khemennu (Hermopolis).
[4] Or "stair-case."

It is Tem the dweller in his disk, or (as others say), (14) It is Rā in his rising in the eastern horizon of heaven.

The gods of Yesterday and To-day. The *Bennu*.

"I am Yesterday; I know (15) To-day."

Who then is this?

Yesterday is Osiris, (16) and To-day is Rā on the day when he shall destroy the enemies of Neb-er-tcher,[1] (17) and when he shall establish as prince and ruler his son (18) Horus, or (as others say), on the day when we commemorate the festival (19) of the meeting of the dead Osiris with his father Rā, and when the battle of the (20) gods was fought in which Osiris, the lord of Ȧmentet, was the leader.

What then is this? (21)

It is Ȧmentet, [that is to say] the creation of the souls of the gods when Osiris was leader in Set-Ȧmentet;[2] or (22) (as others say), It is Ȧmentet which Rā hath given unto me; when any god cometh, he doth arise and (23) doeth battle for it.

"I know the god who dwelleth therein." (24)

[1] *I.e.*, Osiris.

[2] *I.e.*, the "Mountain of Ȧmentet," or the "Mountain of the Underworld."

Who then is this?

It is Osiris; or (as others say), Rā is his name, (or) It is the (25) phallus of Rā wherewith he was united to himself.

"I am the *Bennu* bird (26) which is in Ȧnnu (Helio- "polis), and I am the keeper of the volume of the book "of things which are and of things which shall be."

Who then (27) is this?

The dead body of Osiris on his bier.

It is Osiris; or (as others say), It is his dead body, or (as others say), (28) It is his filth. The things which are and the things which shall be are his dead body; or (as others say), (29) They are eternity and everlastingness. Eternity is the day, and everlastingness is the (30) night.

"I am the god Ȧmsu in his coming forth; may his "two plumes (31) be set upon my head for me."

Who then is this?

Ȧmsu is Horus, the avenger (32) of his father, and his coming forth is his birth. The plumes (33) upon his head are Isis and Nephthys when they go forth to set themselves (34) there, even as his protectors, and they provide that which his head (35) lacketh, or (as others say), They are the two exceeding great uraei which are upon the head of their father (36) Tem, or (as others say), His two eyes are the two plumes which are upon his head.

"Osiris Ani, (37) the scribe of all the holy offerings, "riseth up in his place in triumph, he cometh into (38) "his city."

What then is this?

It is the horizon of his father Tem. (39)

"I have made an end of my short-comings, and I "have put away my faults."

What then (40) is this?

"It is the cutting off of the corruptible in the body "of Osiris, the scribe Ani, (41) victorious before all the "gods; and all his faults are driven out."

What (42) then is this?

It is the purification [of Osiris] on the day of his birth. (43)

"I am purified in my great double nest which is in "Suten-ḥenen (Heracleopolis Magna), (44) on the day "of the offerings of the followers of the great god who "is (45) therein."

The god of Millions of Years. Great Green Lake. Re-stau. The *Utchat*.

What then is this?

"Millions of years" is the name of the one [nest], "Great Green Lake" (46) is the name of the other; a pool of natron, and a pool of nitre (47); or (as others say), "The Traverser of millions of years" is the name of one, "Great Green Lake" (48) is the name of the other; or (as others say), "The Begetter of millions of years" is the name of one, "Great Green Lake" (49) is the name of the other. Now as concerning the great god who dwelleth therein, it is Rā (50) himself.

"I pass over the way, I know the head of the Pool of Maāti." (51)

What then is this?

It is Re-stau; that is to say, it is the underworld on the (52) south of Na-áruṭ-f,[1] and it is the northern door of the tomb.

Now as concerning (53) the Pool of Maāti, it is Ȧbṭu (Abydos); or (as others say), It is the way by which his father (54) Tem travelleth when he goeth forth to Sekhet-Ȧaru, (55) which bringeth forth the food and nourishment of the gods who are behind [their] shrines. (56) Now the gate of Tchesert is the gate of the pillars of Shu, (57) the northern gate of the Ṭuat (underworld); or (as others say), It is the two leaves of the door (58) through which the god Tem passeth when he goeth forth to the eastern horizon of heaven. (59)

"O ye gods who are in the presence [of Osiris], grant

[1] Or Ȧn-ruṭ-f, the "place where nothing groweth."

"me your arms, for I am the god who (60) shall come "into being among you."

Who then are these?

They are the drops of blood which (61) came forth from the phallus of Rā when he went forth to perform mutilation (62) upon himself. They sprang into being as the gods Ḥu and Sa, who are in the following (63) of Rā, and who accompany (64) the god Tem daily and every day.

"I, Osiris, the scribe Ani, triumphant, (65) have "filled for thee the *Utchat* after it had suffered failure "(66) on the day of the combat of the two Fighters" (*i.e.*, Horus and Set).

What then (67) is this?

It is the day on which Horus fought with Ṣet, (68) who cast filth in the face of Horus, and when Horus destroyed the members (69) of Set. Now this Thoth did with his own fingers.

"I lift up the (70) hair[-cloud] when there are "storms and quakings in the sky."

What then is this? (71)

It is the right Eye of Rā, which raged against [Set] when (72) he sent it forth.

Thoth raised up the hair[-cloud], and brought the Eye (73) alive, and whole, and sound, and without defect to [its] lord; or (as others say), It is the Eye of Rā when it is sick and when it (74) weepeth for its fellow-eye; then Thoth standeth up to cleanse it. (75)

"I behold Rā who was born yesterday from the

"buttocks of (76) the goddess Meḥ-urt; his strength "is my strength, and my strength is his strength."

Meḥ-urt. The gods in the train of Horus.

What then is this? (77)

It is the watery abyss of heaven, or (as others say), It is the image (78) of the Eye of Rā in the morning at his daily birth. (79) Meḥ-urt is the Eye (*Utchat*) of Rā. Therefore Osiris, (80) the scribe Ani, triumphant, is a great one among the gods who are in the train of (81) Horus. The words are spoken for him that loveth his lord.

What (82) then is this?

[The gods who are in the train of Horus are] Mesthȧ, Ḥāpi, Ṭuamāutef, and Qebḥsennuf.[1]

(83) "Homage to you, O ye lords of right and truth, "ye sovereign princes who [stand] behind Osiris, who "utterly do away with (84) sins and crimes and who "are in the following of the goddess Ḥetep-sekhus, (85) "grant [ye] that I may come unto you. Destroy ye "[all] the faults which (86) are within me, even as ye

[1] These four are the gods of the cardinal points, and each watched over a portion of the intestines of the deceased.

"did for the Seven Spirits[1] (87) who are among the "followers of their lord Sepa.[2] Anubis appointed (88) "their place on the day [when was said], 'Come therefore "thither.'"

The Three Spirits and Anubis.

What then (89) is this?

These lords of right and truth are Thoth and (90) Åsṭes,[3] the lord of Åmentet. The sovereign princes [who stand] behind Osiris, even Mesthȧ, (91) Ḥāpi, Ṭuamāutef, and Qebḥsennuf, are they who are (92) behind the Thigh in the northern sky.

Now those who do utterly away with (93) sins and crimes and who are in the following of Ḥetep-sekhus (94) are the god Sebek [and his company] who dwell in the water.

The goddess Ḥetep-sekhus is the Eye of (95) Rā; or (as others say), It is the flame which followeth after Osiris to burn up (96) the souls of his enemies.

As concerning all the faults which are in (97) Osiris, the scribe of the offerings of all the gods, Ani, trium-

[1] The Seven *Khus* have been identified with the seven stars of the constellation of the Great Bear.

[2] A name of Osiris.

[3] This god was an associate of Osiris and Anubis.

phant, [this is all that he hath done against the lords of eternity] since he came forth from (98) his mother's womb.

The Seven Spirits.

As concerning the Seven Spirits (99), even Mestha, Ḥāpi, Ṭuamāutef, Qebḥsennuf, (100) Maa-ȧtef-f, Kheri-beq-f, and Ḥerukhenti-[ȧn]maati, (101) Anubis appointed them to be protectors of the dead body of Osiris, or (as others say), [set them] (102) behind the place of purification of Osiris; or (as others say), those Seven Spirits are (103) Netcheh-netcheh, Ȧatqeṭqeṭ,[1] Ȧnerṭā-nef-bes-f-khenti-heh-(104)f,[2] Ȧq-ḥer-ȧmi-unnut-f,[3] Ṭesh-ermaati-ȧmi-(105)ḥet-Ȧnes,[4] Ubes-ḥrȧ-per-em-khet-khet,[5] and (106) Maa-em-ķerḥ-ȧn-nef-em-hru.[6] The chief of the sovereign princes (107) who are in Naȧruṭ-f is Horus, the avenger of his father.

As concerning (108) the day [upon which was said], "Come therefore thither," it referreth to the words,

[1] *I.e.*, "He who is mighty in revolving."
[2] *I.e.*, "The dweller in his flame giveth not his flame."
[3] *I.e.*, "He entereth in his hour."
[4] *I.e.*, "The Red-eyed one in the house of Anes."
[5] *I.e.*, "The Fiery-face who cometh onwards and retreateth."
[6] *I.e.*, "He seeth in the dark and bringeth in the day."

"Come (109) then thither," which Rā spake unto Osiris. Lo, may this be said unto me in Àmentet!

"I am the divine Soul which dwelleth in the divine Twin-Gods." (110)

The Souls of Rā and Osiris in Ṭaṭṭu.

What then is this?

It is Osiris [when] he goeth into Ṭaṭṭu (111) and findeth there the Soul of Rā; there the one god embraceth (112) the other, and divine souls spring into being within the divine Twin-Gods.

[The following lines are from the Papyrus of Nebseni (Brit. Mus. No. 9900, sheet 14, l. 16 ff.).]

(16) As concerning the divine Twin-Gods they are Ḥeru-netch-ḥrà-tef-f[1] (17) and Ḥeru-khent-àn-maati;[2] or (as others say), the double divine Soul which dwelleth in the divine Twin-Gods is the Soul of Rā and the Soul of Osiris; [or (as others say),] It is the

[1] *I.e.*, "Horus, the avenger of his father (Osiris)."
[2] *I.e.*, "Horus, the dweller in darkness," *i.e.*, Blind Horus.

Soul (18) which dwelleth in Shu, [and] the Soul which dwelleth in Tefnut,[1] and these are the double divine Soul which dwelleth in Ṭaṭṭu.

"I am the Cat which fought (?) hard by the Persea "tree (19) in Ȧnnu (Heliopolis), on the night when the "foes of Neb-er-tcher were destroyed."

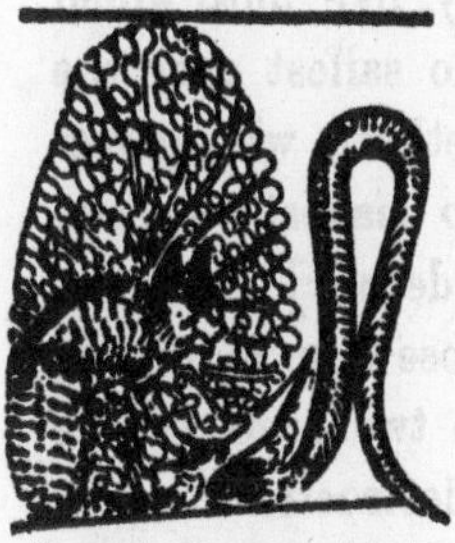

From the Papyrus of Ani.

From the Papyrus of Hu-nefer.

Who then is this?

The male Cat is Rā (20) himself, and he is called 'Màu' by reason of the speech of the god Sa, [who said] concerning him: "He is like (*màu*) unto that which he hath made"; thus his name became 'Màu';[2] or (as others say), it is the god (21) Shu who maketh over the possessions of Seb to Osiris.

As concerning the fight (?) hard by the Persea tree in Ȧnnu, it concerneth the children of impotent revolt when (22) justice is wrought on them for what they have done.

[1] *I.e.*, the feminine counterpart of Shu.

[2] This is a very ancient pun on the words *màu* "cat" and *màu* "like."

As concerning the night of the battle [these words refer to] the inroad [of the children of impotent revolt] into the eastern part of heaven, whereupon there arose a battle in heaven and in all the earth.

"O thou who art in thine egg (23) (*i.e.*, Rā), who "shinest from thy Disk and risest in thy horizon, and "dost shine like gold above the sky, like unto whom "there is none among the gods, who sailest over the "pillars (24) of Shu (*i.e.*, in the ether), who givest "blasts of fire from thy mouth, [who makest the two "lands bright with thy radiance, deliver] thou the "pious Nebseni from the god (25) whose form is hidden, "whose eyebrows are like unto the two arms of the "Balance on the night of reckoning destruction."

Who then is this?

It is Ȧn-ā-f (*i.e.*,[1] the god who bringeth his arm). (26)

As concerning "the night of reckoning destruction," it is the night of the burning of the damned, and of the overthrow of the wicked at the block, (27) and of the slaughter of souls.

Who then is this?

It is Nemu, the headsman of Osiris, or (as others say), It is Ȧpep when he riseth up with one head bearing Maāt (*i.e.*, right and truth) [upon it]; (28) or (as others say), It is Horus when he riseth up with a double head, whereof the one beareth right and truth and the other wickedness. (29) He bestoweth wicked-

[1] A name of Ȧmsu, the god of generating power and fertility.

ness on him that worketh wickedness, and right and truth upon him that followeth righteousness and truth; or (as others say), It is Horus the Great who (30) dwelleth in Sekhem (Letopolis); or (as others say), It is Thoth; or (as others say), It is Nefer-Tem; [or (as others say),] It is Sept who doth thwart the acts of the foes of Neb-er-tcher.

"Deliver thou the scribe Nebseni, victorious, from "the Watchers who bear slaughtering knives, and who "have cruel fingers, and who slay those who are in the "following of Osiris. (31) May they never gain the "mastery over me, may I never fall under their knives."

What then is this?

It is Anubis, and it is Horus in the form of Khent-(32)ȧn-maati; or (as others say), It is the sovereign princes who thwart the works of their weapons; or (as others say), It is the chiefs of the *Sheniu*[1] chamber.

"May (33) their knives never gain the mastery over "me, may I never fall under their instruments of "cruelty, for (34) I know their names, and I know the "being Mātcheṭ who is among them in the House of "Osiris, shooting rays of light from [his] eye, but who "himself is unseen. (35) He goeth round about "heaven robed in the flame of his mouth, commanding "Ḥāpi, but remaining himself unseen. May I be "strong upon earth before Rā, may I come happily "into haven (36) in the presence of Osiris. Let not

[1] A place where tortures were inflicted on the enemies of Rā.

"your offerings be wanting to me, O ye who preside "over your altars, for I am among those who follow "after Neb-er-tcher according to the writings (37) of "Kheperà. I fly as a hawk, I cackle as a goose; I "ever slay, even as the serpent goddess Neḥeb-ka."

What then is this? (38)

Those who preside over their altars are the similitude of the Eye of Rā and the similitude of the Eye of Horus.

"O Rā- (39) Tem, thou lord of the Great House,[1] "thou Sovereign (Life, Strength and Health!) of all "the gods, deliver thou the scribe Nebseni, victorious, "from the god whose face (40) is like unto that of a "greyhound, whose brows are as those of a man, and "who feedeth upon the dead, who watcheth at the "Bight of the Lake (41) of Fire, and who devoureth "the bodies of the dead and swalloweth hearts, and "who shooteth forth filth, but he himself remaineth "unseen."

Who then is (42) this?

"Devourer for millions of years" is his name, and he liveth in the Àat.[2] As concerning the Àat of flame, it is that which is in Ànruṭ-f, hard by (43) the *Sheniu* chamber. The unclean man who would walk thereover doth fall down among the knives; or (as others say), His name is "Māṭes,"[3] (44) and he is the Watcher of

[1] *I.e.*, the great temple of Rā in Heliopolis.
[2] Var. "and he dwelleth in the Lake of Unt."
[3] *I.e.*, "he who hath the flint knife."

the door of Ȧmentet; or (as others say), His name is "Beba," and it is he who watcheth the Bight of Ȧmentet; or (as others say), "Ḥeri-sep-f" is his name.

"Hail, Lord of terror, chief of the lands of the North "and South, thou lord of the red glow (or red lands), "(45) who preparest the slaughter-block, and who dost "feed upon the inward parts!"

Who then is this?

The guardian of the Bight of Ȧmentet. (46)

What then is this?

It is the heart of Osiris, which is the devourer of all slaughtered things. The *Urerct* crown hath been given unto him with gladness of heart as lord of Suten-ḥenen (Heracleopolis Magna).

What then (47) is this?

He to whom hath been given the *Ureret* crown with gladness of heart as lord of Suten-ḥenen is Osiris. He was bidden to rule among the gods on the day of the union of earth (48) in the presence of Neb-er-tcher.

What then is this?

He that was bidden to rule among the gods is [Horus] the son of Isis, who was appointed to rule in the place of his father (49) Osiris. As concerning the "day of the union of earth with earth," it is the mingling of earth with earth in the coffin of Osiris, the Soul that liveth in Suten-ḥenen, the giver of meat and drink, the destroyer of wrong, and the guide of the everlasting paths.

Who then is this?

It is Rā himself.

"Deliver thou the Osiris Nebseni, victorious,"

[The following lines are from the Papyrus of Ani (Brit. Mus. No. 10,470, sheet 10, l. 7 ff.).]

"(113) from the great god who carrieth away the soul, "who eateth hearts, and who feedeth upon (114) offal, "the guardian of the darkness, the dweller in the *Seker* "boat; those who live in crime (115) fear him."

Who then is this?

It is Suti, or (as others say), It is Smam-ur, (116) the soul of Seb.

The deceased and his wife adoring Kheperȧ. The Two Apes.

"Hail, Kheperȧ in thy boat, the two-fold company of "the gods is thy body! Deliver thou Osiris (117) Ani, "victorious, from the Watchers who give judgment, "who have been appointed by the god Neb-er-tcher "(118) to protect him and to fasten the fetters on his "foes, and who slaughter in the (119) shambles; there "is no escape from their grasp. May they never stab "me with their knives, (120) may I never fall helpless "into their chambers of torture. (121) Never have the "things which the gods hate been done by me, for I "am pure within the *Mesqet*.[1] (122) Cakes of saffron "have been brought unto him in Tanenet."

Who then is this? (123)

It is Kheperȧ in his boat. It is Rā himself. As concerning the Watchers (124) who give judgment, they are the apes Isis and Nephthys. As concerning the things which are abominated by the gods they are wickedness (125) and falsehood; and he who passeth through the place of purification within the *Mesqet* is Ȧnpu (Anubis), who is behind the chest (126) which containeth the inward parts of Osiris. He to whom saffron cakes have been brought (127) in Tanenet is Osiris; or (as others say), The saffron cakes (128) in Tanenet are heaven and earth; or (as others say), They are Shu, strengthener of the two lands in (129) Suten-ḥenen (Heracleopolis Magna). The saffron cakes are the Eye of Horus; and Tanenet (130) is the burial-place of Osiris. Tem hath built thy house, and the double Lion-god hath founded thy habitation; (131) lo! drugs are brought, and Horus purifieth and Set strengtheneth, and Set purifieth and Horus strengtheneth. (132)

"The Osiris, the scribe Ani, victorious before Osiris, "hath come into the land, and he hath taken possession "thereof with his two feet. He is Tem, and he is in "thy city."

[1] A chamber where tortures are inflicted on the enemies of Rā.

(133) "Turn thou back, O Reḥu, whose mouth "shineth, whose head moveth, turn thou back from "before his strength," or (as others say), "Turn thou

Temu in his boat. Reḥu and Uatchit.

"back from him who keepeth (134) watch and is un-"seen." The Osiris Ani is safely guarded. He is "Isis, and he is found (135) with [her] hair spread over "him, I shake it out over his brow. He was conceived "in Isis and begotten (136) in Nephthys; and they cut "off from him the things which should be cut off."

"Fear followeth after thee, terror is upon (137) thine "arms. Thou hast been embraced for millions of years "by the arms [of the nations]; mortals go round about "thee. Thou smitest down the mediators (138) of thy "foes, and thou seizest the arms of the powers of dark-"ness. The two sisters (*i.e.*, Isis and Nephthys) are "given to thee for thy delight. (139) Thou hast "created that which is in Kher-āḥa and that which is "in Ȧnnu (Heliopolis). Every god feareth thee, for "thou art exceeding great and terrible: thou [avengest] "every (140) god on the man that curseth him, and thou "shootest out arrows . . . . . Thou livest according to "thy will; thou art Uatchit, the Lady of Flame. "Evil cometh (141) among those who set themselves up "against thee."

What then is this?

"Hidden in form, granted of (142) Menḥu," is the name of the tomb. "He seeth what is on his hand" is the name of Qerâu; or (as others say), (143) the name of the block.

Now he whose mouth shineth and whose head moveth is the member of Osiris, or (as others say) (144) of Rā. "Thou spreadest thy hair and I shake it out over his brow" is spoken concerning Isis, who hideth in her hair (145) and draweth her hair over her. Uatchit, the Lady of Flames, is the eye of Rā.

CHAPTER XVIII.—Introduction.

[From the Papyrus of Ani (Brit. Mus. No. 10,470, sheet 12).]

Vignette : (Upper register): Ani and his wife with hands raised in adoration; the priest Ȧn-māut-f, who wears a leopard's skin, and has on the right side of his head the lock of hair of Ḥeru-pa-khrat (Harpocrates), introducing them to the gods.

I. Text : The Speech of Ȧn-māut-f: (1) "I have "come unto you, O great and godlike sovereign rulers "who dwell in heaven, and in earth, and (2) in the "underworld, and I have brought unto you Osiris Ani. "He hath not sinned against any of the gods. Grant "ye that he may be with you for all time."

II. [Ani's Speech] :—

(1) The adoration of Osiris, the lord of Re-

STAU, AND OF THE GREAT COMPANY OF THE GODS WHO DWELL IN THE UNDERWORLD, BY OSIRIS THE SCRIBE ANI (2) who saith :—

"Homage to thee, O thou ruler of Àmentet, Un-"nefer in Àbṭu (Abydos)! I have come unto thee, and "my heart holdeth right and truth. There is no (3) "sin in my body; nor have I lied wittingly, nor have "I done aught with a false heart. Grant thou to me "food in the tomb, (4) and that I may come forth into "[thy] presence at the altar of the lords of right and "truth, and that I may enter into and come forth from "the underworld, and that my soul be not turned back, "and that I may behold the face of the Sun, and that I "may behold the (5) Moon for ever and for ever."

Vignette: (Lower register: Ani and his wife with hands

raised in adoration; the priest Sa-mer-f, who wears a leopard's skin, and has on the right side of his head the lock of hair of Ḥeru-pa-khrat (Harpocrates), introducing them to the gods.

III. Text: (1) The Speech of Sa-mer-f:—"I have "come unto you, O sovereign princes who dwell in "Re-stau, and I have brought unto you Osiris (2) Ani. "Grant ye [to him], as to the followers of Horus, cakes, "and water, and air, and a homestead in Sekhet-ḥetep."

[ANI'S SPEECH]:—

IV. (1) THE ADORATION OF OSIRIS, LORD OF EVERLASTINGNESS, AND OF THE SOVEREIGN PRINCES, THE LORDS OF RE-STAU, BY OSIRIS [THE SCRIBE ANI], (2) who saith:—

"Homage to thee, O king of the underworld, thou "governor of Åḳert, I have come unto thee. I know "thy ways, (3) and I am furnished with the forms "which thou takest in the underworld. Grant thou to "me a place in the underworld near unto the lords of "(4) right and truth. May my homestead be abiding "in Sekhet-ḥetep, and may I receive cakes in thy "presence."

CHAPTER XVIII.

[From the Papyrus of Nebseni (Brit. Mus. No. 9,900, sheet 15); and from the Papyrus of Ani (Brit. Mus. No. 10,470, sheets 13—14).]

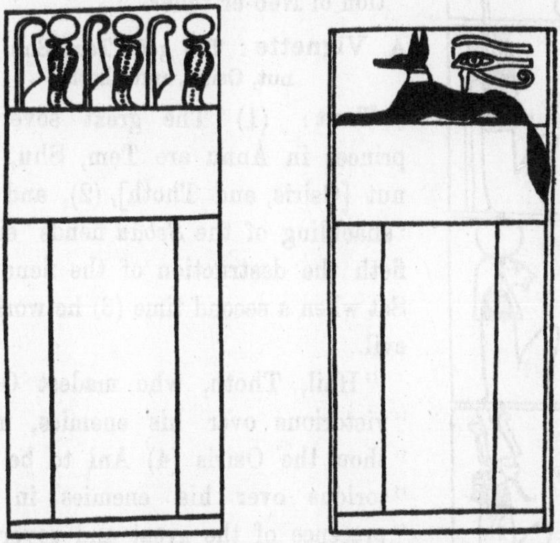

Vignettes : A pylon surmounted by feathers typical of Maāt and by uraei wearing disks, and a pylon surmounted by Ȧnpu (Anubis) or Ȧp-uat and by an *Utchat*.

Text : (1) "Hail, Thoth, who madest Osiris "victorious (2) over his enemies, make thou the scribe "Nebseni to be victorious over his enemies, as thou "didst make Osiris victorious over his enemies in

A.

"the presence of the (3) sovereign "princes who are with Rā and Osiris "in Ȧnnu (Heliopolis), on the night of "the 'things of the night,' and on the "night of the battle, (4) and on the "night of the shackling of the *Sebȧu* "fiends, and on the day of the destruc-"tion of Neb-er-tcher."[1]

A. **Vignette**: The gods Tem, Shu, Tefnut, Osiris, and Thoth.

Text: (1) The great sovereign princes in Ȧnnu are Tem, Shu, Tefnut [Osiris, and Thoth], (2), and the 'shackling of the *Sebȧu* fiends' signifieth the destruction of the fiends of Set when a second time (3) he worketh evil.

"Hail, Thoth, who madest Osiris "victorious over his enemies, make "thou the Osiris (4) Ani to be vic-"torious over his enemies in the "presence of the great and sovereign "princes who are in Ṭaṭṭu, on the "night of making the *Ṭeṭ* to stand up "in Ṭaṭṭu."[2]

[1] *I.e.*, the day of the mutilation of Osiris.

[2] In the ceremony which took place annually at Mendes, a Ṭeṭ was "set up" with great reverence in memory of the resurrection of the body of Osiris.

B. Vignette: The gods Osiris, Isis, Nephthys, and Horus.

B.

Text: (1) The great sovereign princes in Ṭaṭṭu are Osiris, Isis, Nephthys, and Ḥeru-netch-ḥrȧ-tef.[1] Now the [night of] of making the Ṭeṭ to stand up (2) in Ṭaṭṭu signifieth [the lifting up of] the arm and shoulder of Horus who dwelleth in Sekhem (Letopolis); and these gods stand behind Osiris [to protect him] even as do the swathings which clothe him (3).

"Hail, Thoth, who madest Osiris "victorious over his enemies, make "thou Osiris Ani triumphant over his "enemies in the presence of (4) the "sovereign princes who are in Sek-"hem (Letopolis), on the night of the "'things of the night [festival] in "'Sekhem.'"

C. Vignette: The gods Osiris and Horus, the two *Utchats* upon pylons, and the god Thoth.

Text: (1) The great sovereign princes who are in Sekhem are Ḥeru-khenti-ȧn maati,[2] and Thoth who is

[1] *I.e.*, "Horus, the avenger of his father."
[2] *I.e.*, "Horus dwelling without eyes."

C.

with the sovereign princes in Narerut-f[1] (2). Now the night of the "things of the night [festival] in Sekhem" signifieth the light of the rising sun on the coffin of Osiris.

"Hail, Thoth, who madest Osiris "victorious (3) over his enemies, make "thou the Osiris Ani triumphant over "his enemies in the presence of the "great sovereign princes who are in "Pet and in Țept,[2] on the (4) night of "setting up the columns of Horus, and "of making him to be established as "heir of the things which belonged to "his father Osiris."

D. Vignette: The gods Horus, Isis, Mesthȧ, and Hāpi.

Text: (1) The great sovereign princes who are in Pet and Țept are Horus, Isis, Mesthȧ, and Ḥāpi. Now "setting up the columns of (2) Horus" signifieth the command given by Set unto his followers: "Set up columns "upon it."

"Hail, Thoth, who madest Osiris

[1] *I.e.*, Ȧn-rutț-f.

[2] Pet and Țept were the two halves of the city Per-Uatchet, or the metropolis of the XIXth nome of Lower Egypt.

"victorious over (3) his enemies, make "thou the Osiris Ani, triumphant in "peace, victorious over his enemies in "the presence of the great sovereign "princes who are in the lands of "Rekhti, (?) on the (4) night when "Isis lay down to keep watch in order "to make lamentation for her brother "Osiris."

D.

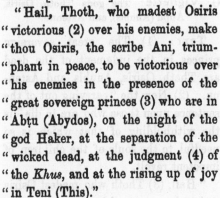

E. **Vignette**: **The gods Isis, Horus,[1] Ànpu (Anubis), Mesthȧ, and Thoth.**

Text: (1) The great sovereign princes who are in the lands of Rekhti (?) are Horus, Isis [Anubis], Mesthȧ [and Thoth].

"Hail, Thoth, who madest Osiris "victorious (2) over his enemies, make "thou Osiris, the scribe Ani, triumphant in peace, to be victorious over "his enemies in the presence of the "great sovereign princes (3) who are in "Àbṭu (Abydos), on the night of the "god Haker, at the separation of the "wicked dead, at the judgment (4) of "the *Khus*, and at the rising up of joy "in Teni (This)."

[1] The artist has actually given a figure of Osiris.

E.

F. Vignette: **The gods Osiris, Isis, and Ȧp-uat, and the Ṭeṭ.**

Text: (1) The great sovereign princes who are in Ȧbṭu are Osiris, Isis, and Ȧp-uat.

"Hail, Thoth, who madest Osiris "victorious (2) over his enemies, make "thou Osiris Ani, the scribe and teller "of the sacred offerings of all the gods, "(3) to be victorious over his enemies "in the presence of the sovereign "princes who judge the dead, on the "night (4) of the carrying out of the "sentence upon those who are to die."

G. Vignette: **The gods Thoth, Osiris, Ȧnpu (Anubis), and Ȧsṭennu.**[1]

Text: (1) The great sovereign princes in the judgment of the dead are Thoth, Osiris, Anubis, and Ȧsṭennu. (2) Now the "carrying out of the sentence upon those who are to die" is the withholding of that which is so needful to the souls of the children of impotent revolt.

"Hail, (3) Thoth who madest Osiris "victorious over his enemies, make

[1] A form of the god Thoth.

"thou Osiris, the scribe Ani, to be "victorious over his enemies in the "presence of the great (4) sovereign "princes, on the festival of the break-"ing and turning up of the earth in "Ṭaṭṭu, on the night of the breaking "and turning up of the earth in their "blood, and of making Osiris to be "victorious over his enemies."

F.

H. **Vignette**: The three gods of the festival of breaking up the earth in Ṭaṭṭu.

Text: (1) When the fiends of Set come and change themselves into beasts, the great sovereign princes, on the festival of the breaking and turning up of the earth in Taṭṭu, (2) slay them in the presence of the gods therein, and their blood floweth among them as they are smitten down. (3) These things are allowed to be done by them by the judgment of those who are in Ṭaṭṭu.

"Hail, Thoth, who madest Osiris to "triumph over his enemies, make thou "the Osiris Ani (4) to be victorious "over his enemies in the presence of "the great sovereign princes who are "in Na-àrerut-f,[1] on the night of him

[1] *I.e.*, Àn-ruṭ-f.

G.

"who concealeth him-
"self in divers forms,
"even Osiris."

I. **Vignette**: The gods Rā, Osiris, Shu, and Bebi, who is dog-headed.

Text: (1) The great sovereign princes who are in Na-ȧrerut-f are Rā, Osiris, Shu, and Bebi. Now the "night of him who (2) concealeth himself in divers forms, even Osiris," is when the thigh, [and the head] and the heel, and the leg, are brought nigh unto the coffin of Osiris Un-nefer.

"Hail, Thoth, who
"madest Osiris (3) to
"triumph over his
"enemies, make thou
"Osiris Ani to be
"victorious over his
"enemies in the pre-
"sence of the great
"sovereign princes in

H.

I.

"(4) Re-stau, on the "night when Anubis "lay with his arms "and his hands over "the things behind "Osiris, and when "Horus was made to "triumph over his "enemies."

J. **Vignette**: The gods Horus, Osiris, Isis, and . . . . .[1]

Text: (1) The great sovereign princes in Re-stau are Horus, Osiris, and Isis. The heart of Osiris rejoiceth, and the heart of (2) Horus; and therefore are the northern and southern parts of heaven at peace.

"Hail, Thoth, who

J.

[1] The artist seems to have painted one god too many, and the third deity has not the usual form of Isis.

"madest Osiris victorious over his enemies, make thou "(3) Osiris Ani, the scribe and teller of the divine "offerings of all the gods, to triumph over his enemies "in the presence of the ten companies of great (4) "sovereign princes who are with Rā, and with Osiris, "and with every god and goddess in the presence of Neb-"er-tcher. He hath destroyed his enemies, and (5) he "hath destroyed every evil thing belonging unto him."

RUBRIC: This chapter being recited, the deceased shall come forth by day, purified after death, (6) and [he shall make all] the transformations which his heart shall dictate. Now, if this chapter be recited over him, he shall come forth upon earth, he shall escape from every fire; and none of the foul things which appertain unto him shall encompass him for eternity or for ever and ever.

CHAPTER XIX.

[From Lepsius, *Todtenbuch*, Bl. 13.]

Vignette: This Chapter is without a vignette.

Text: THE CHAPTER OF THE CHAPLET OF VICTORY. (1) Osiris, Åuf-ānkh, victorious, born of Sheret-Åmsu, victorious, saith:—

"Thy father Tem hath woven for thee a beautiful "chaplet of victory [to be placed] on [thy] living brow, "O thou who lovest the gods, (2) and thou shalt live "for ever. Osiris-khent-Àmentet[1] hath made thee to "triumph over thine enemies, and thy father Seb hath "decreed for thee all his inheritance. Come, therefore, "O Horus, son of Isis, for thou, O son of Osiris, sittest "upon the throne of thy (3) father Rā to overthrow "thine enemies, for he hath ordained for thee the two "lands to their utmost limits. Àtem[2] hath [also] "ordained this, and the company of the gods hath "confirmed the splendid power of the victory of Horus "the son of Isis and the son of Osiris for ever and (4) "for ever. And Osiris Àuf-ānkh shall be victorious "for ever and ever. O Osiris-khent-Àmentet, the whole "of the northern and southern parts of the heavens, "and every god and every goddess, who are in heaven "and who are upon earth [will] the victory of Horus, "the son of Isis and the son of Osiris, over his enemies "in the presence of (5) Osiris-khent-Àmentet who will "make Osiris Àuf-ānkh, victorious, to triumph over his "enemies in the presence of Osiris-khent-Àmentet, Un-"nefer, the son of Nut, on the day of making him to "triumph over Set and his fiends (6) in the presence of "the great sovereign chiefs who are in Ànnu (Helio-"polis); on the night of the battle and overthrow of "the Sebà-fiend in the presence of the great sovereign "princes who are in Àbṭu; on the night of making "Osiris to triumph over his enemies (7) make thou "Osiris Àuf-ānkh, victorious, to triumph over his

[1] *I.e.*, "Osiris, Governor of Àmentet."
[2] *I.e.*, Tem or Temu, the Night Sun.

"enemies in the presence of the great sovereign princes, "who are in the horizon of Åmentet; on the day of the "festival of Haker in the presence of the great sovereign "princes who are in Ṭaṭṭu; on the night (8) of the "setting up of the Ṭeṭ in Ṭaṭṭu in the presence of the "great sovereign princes who are in the ways of the "damned; on the night of the judgment of those who "shall be annihilated in the presence of the great "sovereign princes who are in Sekhem (Letopolis); (9) "on the night of the 'things of the altars in Sekhem' "in the presence of the great sovereign princes who are "in Pet and Ṭept; on the night of the stablishing of "the inheriting by Horus of the things of his father "Osiris in the presence of the great sovereign princes "(10) who are at the great festival of the ploughing "and turning up of the earth in Ṭaṭṭu, or (as others "say), [in] Åbṭu; on the night of the weighing of "words," or (as others say), "weighing of locks in the "presence of the great sovereign princes who are in "Ån-ruṭ-f on its place; on the night when Horus "receiveth the birth-chamber of the gods (11) in the "presence of the great sovereign princes who are in the "lands of Rekhti; on the night when Isis lieth down "to watch [and] to make lamentation for her brother in "the presence of the great sovereign princes who are in "Re-stau; on the night of making Osiris to triumph "over all his enemies" (12).

"Horus repeated [these] words four times, and all his "enemies fell headlong and were overthrown and were "cut to pieces; and Osiris Åuf-ānkh, triumphant, "repeated [these] words four times, therefore let all his "enemies fall headlong, and be (13) overthrown and cut "to pieces. Horus the son of Isis and son of Osiris "celebrated in turn millions of festivals, and all his "enemies fell headlong, and were overthrown and cut "to pieces. Their habitation hath gone forth to the "block of the East, their heads have been cut off; (14) "their necks have been destroyed; their thighs have "been cut off; they have been given over to the Great "Destroyer who dwelleth in the valley of the grave; "and they shall never come forth from under the "restraint of the god Seb."

RUBRIC: This chapter shall be recited over the divine chaplet (15) which is laid upon the face of the deceased, and thou shalt cast incense into the fire on behalf of Osiris Åuf-ānkh, triumphant, born of Sheret-åmsu, triumphant; thus shalt thou cause him to triumph over his enemies, (16) dead or alive, and he shall be among the followers of Osiris; and a hand shall be stretched out to him with meat and drink in the presence of the god. [This chapter] shall be said by thee twice at dawn—now it is a never-failing charm—regularly and continually.

CHAPTER XX.

[From the Papyrus of Nebseni (Brit. Mus. No. 9,900, sheet 12).]

Vignette: This Chapter, in the Theban Version, has neither vignette nor title.

Text: (1) "Hail, Thoth, who didst make Osiris (2) "to triumph over his enemies, snare thou the enemies "of Osiris, the scribe Nebseni, the lord of piety, in the "presence of the great sovereign princes of every god "and goddess; (3) in the presence of the great "sovereign princes who are in Ȧnnu (Heliopolis) on "the night of the battle and of the overthrow of the "Sebȧu-fiend in Ṭaṭṭu; on (4) the night of making to "stand up the double Ṭeṭ in Sekhem (Letopolis); on "the night of the things of the night in Sekhem, in Pet, "(5) and in Ṭepu;[1] on the night of the stablishing of "Horus in the heritage of the things of his father in "the double land of Rekhti; (6) on the night when "Isis maketh lamentation at the side of her brother "Osiris in Ȧbṭu (Abydos); on the night of the Haker "festival (7) of the distinguishing [between] the dead "(*i.e.*, the damned) and the Spirits on the path of the "dead (*i.e.*, the damned); on the night of the judgment "of those who are to be annihilated at the great [festival

[1] Pet and Ṭepu were the two halves of the city Per-Uatchet, or the metropolis of the XIXth nome of Lower Egypt.

"of] the ploughing and the turning up of the earth (8) "great in Náarerut-f in Re-stau; and on the night of "making Horus to triumph over his enemies. Horus is "mighty, the northern and southern halves of heaven "rejoice, (9) Osiris is content thereat and his heart is "glad. Hail, Thoth, make thou to triumph Osiris, the "scribe Nebseni, over his enemies (10) in the presence "of the sovereign princes of every god and every goddess, "and in the presence of you, ye sovereign princes who "passed judgment on Osiris behind the shrine."

In the Saïte Recension this Chapter has no vignette, but it has the title, "Another Chapter of the Chaplet "of victory," and is arranged in tabular form. The words "Hail, Thoth, make Osiris Ȧuf-ānkh, trium-"phant, to triumph over his enemies even as thou "didst make Osiris to triumph over his enemies," which are written in two horizontal lines, are to be repeated before each column of text. The "great sovereign princes" invoked are those of:—(1) Ȧnnu (Heliopolis), (2) Ṭaṭṭu, (3) Sekhem (Letopolis), (4) Pe and Ṭep, (5) Ȧn-ȧruṭ-f, (6) the double land of Rekhti, (7) Re-stau, (8) Ȧbṭu, (9) the Paths of the Dead, (10) the Ploughing festival in Ṭaṭṭu, (11) Kher-āḥa, (12) Osiris, (13) heaven and earth, (14) every god and every goddess. The rubric reads:—

If this chapter be recited regularly and always by a man who hath purified himself in water of natron, he shall come forth by day after he hath come into port (*i.e.*, is dead), and he shall perform all the transformations which his heart shall dictate, and he shall come forth from the fire.

CHAPTER XXI.

[From the Papyrus of Nu (Brit. Mus. No. 10,477, sheet 9).]

In the Papyrus of Ani the XXIst Chapter follows the XXIInd, but it is there given without title and without vignette; in the Turin papyrus published by Lepsius (*Todtenbuch*, Bl. 14) the XXIst and XXIInd Chapters are quite distinct, and each has its own title, while a single vignette stands over both.

Vignette: The deceased standing in the presence of a beatified person, who holds the symbol of life in one hand, and a staff in the other. A priest is holding in his right hand the UR-ḤEKAU instrument, and is about to touch the mouth of the deceased; in his left hand he holds a vase of ointment. (From Lepsius, *Todtenbuch*, Bl. 14.) The UR-ḤEKAU instrument, *i.e.*, "the Mighty one of Enchantments," was made in the form of a ram-headed serpent, and it was believed to possess magical powers.

Text: (1) THE CHAPTER OF GIVING A MOUTH TO THE OVERSEER OF THE HOUSE OF THE OVERSEER OF

THE SEAL, NU, TRIUMPHANT, (2) IN THE UNDERWORLD. He saith:—

"Homage to thee, O thou lord of brightness, thou "who art at the head of the Great House, prince of the "night and of thick darkness! I have come unto thee "being a pure (3) *khu*. Thy two hands are behind "thee, and thou hast thy lot with [thy] ancestors. O "grant thou unto me my mouth that I may speak "therewith; and guide thou to me my heart at the "season when there is (4) cloud and darkness."

CHAPTER XXII.

[From the Papyrus of Ani (Brit. Mus. No. 10,470, sheet 6).]

From the Papyrus of Nebseni.

Vignette: In the Papyrus of Nebseni (sheet 5), the "Guardian of the Balance" is seen with his right hand stretched out to touch the mouth of the deceased who stands before him. In other papyri the deceased himself is seen standing with either his right or his left hand raised to his mouth, as if to perform the ceremony of "opening the mouth" for himself.

Text: (1) THE CHAPTER OF GIVING A MOUTH (2) TO OSIRIS ANI, THE SCRIBE AND TELLER OF THE HOLY OFFERINGS OF ALL THE GODS, VICTORIOUS, IN THE UNDERWORLD. He saith :—

"I rise (3) out of the egg in the hidden land. May "my mouth be given (4) unto me that I may speak "therewith in the presence of the great god, the lord of "the (5) Ṭuat (underworld). May my hand and my "arm not be forced back in the presence of the sovereign "princes of any god. I am Osiris, the lord of Re-stau, "(6); may I, Osiris the scribe Ani, victorious, have a "portion with him who is (7) on the top of the Steps "(*i.e.*, Osiris). According to the desire of my heart, I "have come from the Pool of Fire, and I have quenched "the fire."

CHAPTER XXIII.

[From the Papyrus of Ani (Brit. Mus. No. 10,470, sheet 15).]

From the Papyrus of Ani.

From the Turin Papyrus.

Vignette: The statue of Ani, the scribe, seated upon a pedestal in the form of the emblem of *Maāt* (*i.e.*, right and truth). Before it stands the *Sem* priest clad in a panther's skin and holding in his right hand the ram-headed, serpent-like instrument "Ur-ḥekau," with which he is about to touch the lips of the statue and so perform the ceremony of "Opening the Mouth." At his feet are a sepulchral box for holding unguents, &c.; three instruments called respectively "Seb-ur," "Ṭun-tet," and "Ṭemānu"; and the object called "Pesh-en-kef." In the Papyrus of Nebseni the scene is described as "the *Sem* priest performing [the ceremony] of the 'Opening of the Mouth'" (sheet 5). In the Saïte Recension a priest is seen offering a vase of ointment only to the deceased.

Text: (1) THE CHAPTER OF OPENING THE MOUTH OF OSIRIS. THE SCRIBE ANI, TRIUMPHANT, saith:—

"May the god Ptaḥ open my mouth, and may the god "of my city loose the swathings, even the swathings "which are over my mouth. (2) Moreover, may Thoth,[1] "being filled and furnished with charms, come and loose "the bandages, even the bandages of Set[2] which fetter "my mouth (3); and may the god Tem hurl them at "those who would fetter [me] with them, and drive "them back. May my mouth be opened, may my mouth "be unclosed by Shu[3] (4) with his iron knife wherewith "he opened the mouth of the gods. I am the goddess

[1] The allusion here is to the belief that Thoth was the great master of the use of magical names and formulae. He gave the word which resulted in the creation of the world; he supplied Isis with words of magical power which enabled her to effect the resurrection of Osiris, and also of her son Horus after he had been stung to death by a scorpion.

[2] The great antagonist of Horus, and god both of darkness and of dark deeds.

[3] Some texts call the god Ptaḥ.

"Sekhet,[1] and I sit upon [my] place in the great (5) "wind (?) of heaven. I am the great goddess Saḥ who "dwelleth among the Souls of Ȧnnu (Heliopolis).[2] "Now as concerning every charm and all the words "which may be spoken against me, (6) may the gods "resist them, and may each and every one of the "company of the gods withstand them."

CHAPTER XXIV.

[From the Papyrus of Ani (Brit. Mus. No. 10,470, sheet 15).]

Vignette: This Chapter has no vignette in the Theban papyri. The above vignette is from the Turin Papyrus, and represents a priest addressing the deceased.

Text: (1) THE CHAPTER OF BRINGING CHARMS UNTO OSIRIS ANI [IN THE UNDERWORLD]; he saith:—(2)

"I am Tem-Kheperȧ, who brought himself into being "upon the thigh of his divine mother. Those who are

[1] The goddess of the heat of the sun as a power of destruction.

[2] The Souls of Ȧnnu are Rā, Shu, and Tefnut; see the vignette to Chapter CXV.

"in Nu (*i.e.*, the sky) are made wolves, (3) and those "who are among the sovereign princes are become "hyenas. Behold, I gather together the charm [from "every place where] it is, and from every man with "whom it is, swifter than greyhounds and quicker than "light. (4) Hail, thou who towest along the *Mākhent* "boat of Rā, the stays of thy sails and of thy rudder are "taut in the wind as thou sailest up the Pool of Fire in "the underworld. Behold, thou gatherest together the "charm (5) from every place where it is, and from every "man with whom it is, swifter than greyhounds and "quicker than light, [the charm] which created the "forms of being from the .... (6) mother, and which "either createth the gods or maketh them to be silent, "and which giveth the heat of fire unto the gods. "Behold, the charm is given unto me, from wherever it "is [and from him with whom it is], (7) swifter than "greyhounds and quicker than light," or (as others say), "quicker than a shadow."

CHAPTER XXV.

[From the Papyrus of Nu (Brit. Mus. No. 10,477, sheet 5).]

Vignette: In the greater number of the Theban papyri this Chapter is without vignette. In the Brocklehurst papyrus, however (see Naville, *Todtenbuch*, Bd. I. Bl. 36), the *Sem* priest, wearing a panther's skin, is seen holding up before the face of the deceased, who stands before him, a small bearded figure like an *ushabti*. In the Turin papyrus (Lepsius, *Todtenbuch*, Bl. 15), the priest and the deceased are standing facing each other, and no ceremony is being performed.

Text: (1) THE CHAPTER OF MAKING A MAN TO POSSESS MEMORY IN THE UNDERWORLD. The overseer of the house of the overseer of the seal, Nu, triumphant, the son of the overseer of the house of the overseer of the seal, Ȧmen-ḥetep, saith:—

(2) "May my name be given to me in the Great "House, and may I remember my name in the House of "Fire on the night (3) of counting the years and of "telling the number of the months. I am with the "Divine One, [and I sit on the eastern side of heaven]. "If any god whatsoever should advance unto me (4), "let me be able to proclaim his name forthwith."

CHAPTER XXVI.

[From the Papyrus of Ani (Brit. Mus. No. 10,470, sheet 15).]

From the Papyrus of Ani.

Vignette: The scribe Ani, clothed in white, and with his heart in his right hand, addressing the god Ånpu (Anubis), jackal-headed. In his left hand, which is outstretched, Ani holds a necklace of several rows of coloured beads; the clasp is made in the form of a pylon or gateway, and on the side of the pendant, which is in the same form, is a representation of a scarab or beetle in a boat to typify the Sun-god Rā-Kheperȧ in his boat. From the pendant hang lotus flowers. In other Theban papyri the vignettes are different. In the Papyrus of Nebseni (sheet 5) the god "Anubis who dwelleth in the city of embalmment" gives a heart to the deceased; and in others (see Naville, *Todtenbuch,* Bd. I. Bl. 37) the deceased is seen either being embraced by Anubis or addressing his heart which rests upon a standard before him. In the Turin papyrus (Lepsius, *Todtenbuch,* Bl. 15) the deceased is seen kneeling before his own soul, which is in the form of a human-headed hawk, and clasping his heart to his breast with his left hand.

From the Papyrus of Nebseni.

From the Turin Papyrus.

Text: (1) THE CHAPTER OF GIVING A HEART TO OSIRIS (2) IN THE UNDERWORLD. He saith:—

"May my heart (*àb*)[1] be with me in the House of "Hearts! May my heart (*ḥāt*) be with me in the "House of Hearts! May my heart be with me, and "may it rest there, [or] I shall not eat of the cakes of "Osiris on the eastern side of the Lake (3) of Flowers, "neither shall I have a boat wherein to go down the "Nile, nor another wherein to go up, nor shall I be able "to sail down the Nile with thee. May my mouth [be "given] to me that I may (4) speak therewith, and my "two legs to walk therewith, and my two hands and "arms to overthrow my foe. May the doors of heaven "be opened unto me (5); may Seb, the Prince[2] of the "gods, open wide his two jaws unto me; may he open "my two eyes which are blindfolded; may he cause me "to stretch apart (6) my two legs which are bound "together; and may Ànpu (Anubis) make my thighs

[1] *Àb* is undoubtedly the "heart," and *ḥāt* is the region wherein is the heart; the word may be fairly well rendered by "breast," though the *pericardium* is probably intended.

[2] *Erpāt*, *i.e.*, "hereditary tribal chief."

"firm so that I may stand upon them. May the goddess "Sekhet make me to rise (7) so that I may ascend unto "heaven, and that that may be done which I command "in the House of the *ka* (double) of Ptaḥ (*i.e.*, Mem-"phis). I understand with my heart. I have gained "the mastery over my (8) heart, I have gained the "mastery over my two hands, I have gained the "mastery over my legs, I have gained the power to "do whatsoever my *ka* (double) pleaseth. (9) My soul "shall not be fettered to my body at the gates of the "underworld; but I shall enter in peace and I shall "come forth in peace."

CHAPTER XXVII.

[From the Papyrus of Ani (Brit. Mus. No. 10,470, sheets 15 and 16).]

Vignette: The scribe Ani, with hands raised in adoration, and his heart, which is set upon a pedestal, in the presence of four gods who are seated upon a pedestal in the form of the emblem of *Maāt*. In the Turin Papyrus (Lepsius, *Todtenbuch*, Bl. 15) the deceased is shown kneeling before the four children of Horus.

Text: (1) THE CHAPTER OF NOT LETTING THE HEART (ḤĀTI) OF A MAN BE TAKEN FROM HIM IN THE UNDERWORLD.[1] Saith Osiris Ani:—

" Hail, ye who carry away hearts! [Hail], ye who steal " and crush hearts, and who make [the heart of a man to " go through its transformations according to his deeds, " let not what he hath done harm him before you].[2] (2) " Homage to you, O ye lords of eternity, ye possessors " of everlastingness, take ye not this heart of Osiris Ani " into (3) your grasp, this heart of Osiris, and cause ye " not words of evil to spring up against it; because this " is the heart of (4) Osiris Ani, victorious, and it be- " longeth unto him of many names (*i.e.*, Thoth), the " mighty one whose words are his limbs, and who " sendeth forth his heart to dwell (5) in his body. The

[1] The Papyrus of Mes-em-neter (Naville, *Todtenbuch*, Bd. II. p. 92) adds:—" His heart goeth forth to take up its abode in his body, his heart is renewed before the gods, and he hath gained the mastery over it."

[2] The words within brackets are from the Papyrus of Mes-em-neter.

"heart of Osiris Ani is victorious, it is made new "before the gods, he hath gained power over it, he hath "not been spoken to [according to] what he hath done. "He hath gotten power over (6) his own members. "His heart obeyeth him, he is the lord thereof, it is in "his body, and it shall never fall away therefrom. I, "Osiris, the scribe Ani, victorious in peace, and trium-"phant in the beautiful Àmenta and on the mountain "of eternity, bid thee to be obedient unto me in the "underworld."

CHAPTER XXVIII.

[From the Papyrus of Nu (Brit. Mus. No. 10,477, sheet 5).]

Vignette: In some papyri containing the Theban Recension of the Book of the Dead (*e.g.*, those of Nu and Àmen-neb (Brit. Mus. No. 9964), this Chapter has no vignette. In the Papyrus of Nefer-uben-f the deceased is seen holding his heart upon his breast with his left hand, and kneeling before a monster in human form who holds a knife in his right hand, and grasps his tail with the left. Another papyrus shows the deceased offering incense to Osiris, who, standing on a pedestal in the form of *Maāt*, holds the flail and sceptre in his hands; in the Brocklehurst papyrus the deceased is kneeling and holding his heart in his left hand, which is outstretched (see Naville, *Todtenbuch*, Bd. I. Bl. 39). In the Turin Papyrus the deceased is adoring his heart, which is placed on a pedestal, before a seated deity (Lepsius, *Todtenbuch*, Bl. 15).

Text: (1) THE CHAPTER OF NOT LETTING THE HEART OF THE OVERSEER OF THE HOUSE OF THE OVERSEER OF THE SEAL, NU, TRIUMPHANT, BE CARRIED AWAY (2) FROM HIM IN THE UNDERWORLD. He saith:—

"Hail, thou Lion-god! I am the Flower Bush (*Unb*). "That which is an abomination unto me is the divine "block. Let not this my heart (*ḥāti*) be carried away "from me by (3) the fighting gods in Ȧnnu. Hail, "thou who dost wind bandages round Osiris and who "hast seen Set! Hail, thou who returnest after "smiting and destroying him before the mighty ones! "(4) This my heart (*ȧb*) [sitteth] and weepeth for itself "before Osiris; it hath made supplication for me. I "have given unto him and I have decreed unto him the "thoughts (5) of the heart in the House of the god "Usekh-ḥrȧ[1] and I have brought to him sand (*sic*) at "the entry to Khemennu (Hermopolis Magna). Let "not this my heart (*ḥāti*) be carried away from me! I "make thee to (6) dwell (?) upon his throne, O thou who "joinest together hearts (*ḥātu*) [in Sekhet-ḥetep (with)

[1] *I.e.*, the god of the "Large Face."

"years] of strength against all things that are an "abomination unto thee, and to carry off (7) food from "among the things which belong unto thee, and are in "thy grasp by reason of thy two-fold strength. And "this my heart (*ḥāti*) is devoted to the decrees of the "god Tem who leadeth me into the (8) dens of Suti, but "let not this my heart, which hath done its desire "before the sovereign princes who are in the under-"world, be given unto him. When they find the leg "and the swathings (9) they bury them."

CHAPTER XXIXA.

[From the Papyrus of Ani (Brit. Mus. No. 10,470, sheet 15).]

Vignette: Ani standing, with a staff in his hand. In the Turin Papyrus (Lepsius, *Todtenbuch*, Bl. 15) this Chapter has no vignette.

Text: (1) THE CHAPTER OF NOT LETTING THE HEART OF A MAN BE TAKEN AWAY FROM HIM IN THE UNDERWORLD. Osiris Ani, victorious, saith:—

"Turn thou back, O messenger of every god! (2) Is "it that thou art come [to carry away] this my heart "which liveth? But my heart which liveth shall not "be given unto thee. (3) [As I] advance, the gods "hearken unto my offerings, and they all fall down "upon their faces in their own places."

CHAPTER XXIXB.

[From the Papyrus of Ȧmen-ḥetep (Naville, *Todtenbuch*, Bd. I. Bl. 40).]

Vignette: This Chapter has no vignette.

Text: (1) THE CHAPTER OF NOT ALLOWING THE HEART OF ȦMEN-ḤETEP, VICTORIOUS, TO BE CARRIED AWAY DEAD IN THE UNDERWORLD. The deceased saith:—

"My heart is with me, (2) and it shall never come to "pass that it shall be carried away. I am the lord of "hearts, the slayer of the heart. (3) I live in right "and truth (*Maāt*) and I have my being therein. I "am Horus, the dweller in hearts, (4) who is within "the dweller in the body. I live in my word, and my "heart hath being. Let not my heart be taken away "(5) from me, let it not be wounded, and may neither "wounds nor gashes be dealt upon me because it hath "been taken away from me. (6) Let me have my being "in the body of [my] father Seb, [and in the body of my] "mother Nut. I have not done that which is held in "abomination by the gods; let me not suffer defeat "there, [but let me be] triumphant."

CHAPTER XXIXc.

[From the Papyrus of Ani (Brit. Mus. No. 10,470, sheet 33).]

Vignette : A heart.

Text : (1) THE CHAPTER OF A HEART OF CARNELIAN. Osiris Ani, triumphant, saith :—

"I am the *Bennu*, the soul of Rā, and the guide of "the gods (2) in the Ṭuat (underworld). Their divine "souls come forth upon earth to do the will of their "*kas*, let therefore the soul of Osiris Ani come forth to "do the will of his *ka*."

CHAPTER XXX.

[From Lepsius, *Todtenbuch*, Bl. 16.]

Vignette: The deceased, with hands raised in adoration, standing before a beetle placed on a pedestal.

Text: THE CHAPTER OF NOT LETTING THE HEART OF A MAN BE DRIVEN AWAY FROM HIM IN THE UNDERWORLD. (1) Osiris Åuf-ānkh, triumphant, born of Sheret-Åmsu, triumphant, saith:—

"My heart, my mother; my heart, my mother! My "heart of my existence upon earth. May naught stand "up to oppose me in judgment; may there be no "opposition to me in the presence of the sovereign "princes; (2) may [no evil] be wrought against me in "the presence of the gods; may there be no parting [of "thee] from me in the presence of the great god, the "lord of Åmentet. Homage to thee, O thou heart of "Osiris-khent-Åmentet! Homage to you, O my reins! "Homage to you, O ye gods (3) who dwell in the divine "clouds, and who are exalted (*or* holy) by reason of your "sceptres! Speak ye fair words for the Osiris Åuf-"ānkh, and make ye him to prosper before Neḥebka. "And behold, though I be joined unto the (4) earth, "and am in the mighty innermost part of heaven, let me "remain on the earth and not die in Åmentet, and let "me be a *khu* therein for ever and ever."

RUBRIC: This [chapter] shall be recited over a basalt scarab, which shall be set in a gold setting, and it shall be placed inside the heart of the man[1] for whom the ceremonies of "opening the mouth" and of anointing with unguent have been performed. And there shall be recited by way of a magical charm the words:—"My heart, my mother; my heart, my mother! My heart of transformations."

CHAPTER XXXA.

[From the Papyrus of Nu (Brit. Mus. No. 10,477, sheet 5).]

Vignette: In many of the papyri containing the Theban Recension this Chapter has no vignette; in one, however, the vignette is a heart standing above a vase, in another the

[1] *I.e.*, the deceased.

deceased is seen adoring his heart, and in another the deceased is standing before four gods, one of whom is offering a heart to him (see Naville, *Todtenbuch*, Bd. I. Bl. 42).

Text: (1) The Chapter of not letting the heart of the overseer of the house of the overseer of the seal, Nu, triumphant, be driven away from him in the underworld. He saith:—(2) "O my heart, my mother; O my heart, my mother! "O my heart of my existence upon earth. May naught "stand up to oppose me in judgment in the presence of "the lords of the trial (3); let it not be said of me and "of that which I have done, 'He hath done deeds "'against that which is right and true'; may naught "be against me in the presence of the great god, the "lord of Åmentet. Homage to thee, O my heart! (4) "Homage to thee, O my heart! Homage to you, O my "reins! Homage to you, O ye gods who dwell in the "divine clouds, and who are (5) exalted (*or* holy) by "reason of your sceptres! Speak ye [for me] fair "things to Rā, and make ye me to prosper before "Neḥebka.[1] And behold me, even though I be joined "to the earth in the mighty innermost parts thereof, "let me remain upon the earth and let me not die in "Åmentet, but become a *Khu* therein."

[1] One of the forty-two judges in the Hall of Osiris.

CHAPTER XXXB.

[From the Papyrus of Ani (Brit. Mus. No. 10,470, sheet 15).]

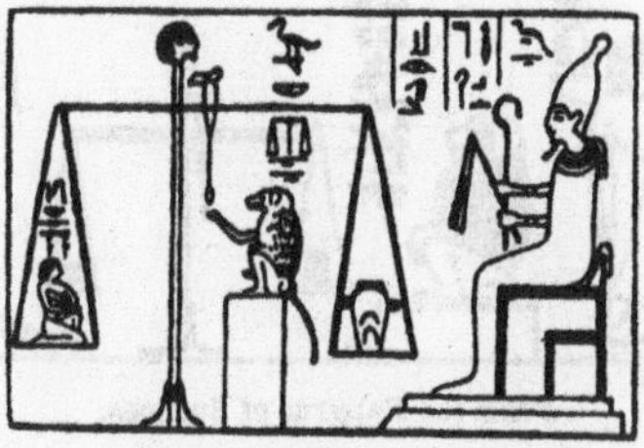

From the Papyrus of Nebseni.

Vignette : (1) Some papyri containing the Theban Recension give this Chapter without any vignette, and it is probable that this arises from the fact that it often appears as one of the texts which occur in the great Judgment Scene, where it forms the prayer put into the mouth of the deceased; see the Papyrus of Ani, sheet 3, and the Papyrus of Hu-nefer, sheet 3. In the Papyrus of Nebseni, sheet 4, the deceased kneels in one pan of the Balance, and he is being weighed against his heart which rests in the other in the presence of "Osiris, the great god, the Governor of Everlastingness." The support of the beam is surmounted by a human head, and the tongue of the Balance is being scrutinized by a dog-headed ape, seated on a pedestal, who is called "Thoth, the lord of the Balance." Elsewhere this ape is seated on a pedestal with steps, and is called "The lord of Khemennu (Hermopolis Magna), the righteous weigher" (see Naville, *Todtenbuch*, Bd. I. Bl. 43). In the Papyrus of Ȧmen-neb (Brit. Mus. No. 9964), the deceased stands by the Balance while a figure of himself is being weighed against his heart; in this example of the scene the support of the beam is surmounted by the head of a jackal. Elsewhere the vignette is simply a heart, or a scarab, or the deceased seated adoring his heart, or the deceased standing in adoration before a beetle, which is the symbol of the god Kheperȧ, the self-created god and the type of the Resurrection (see Lepsius, *Todtenbuch*, Bl. 16).

From the Papyrus of Sutimes.

Text: (1) The Chapter of not (2) letting the heart of Osiris, the scribe of the holy offerings of all the gods, Ani, triumphant, be driven from him in the underworld. He saith:—

"My heart, my mother; (3) my heart, my mother! "My heart whereby I came into being! May naught "stand up to oppose me at [my] judgment; may there "be no opposition to me in the presence of the sovereign "princes (*Tchatcha*); may there be no parting of thee "from me in the presence of him that keepeth the "Balance! Thou art my *ka*, the dweller in (4) my "body; the god Khnemu[1] who knitteth and strength-"eneth my limbs. Mayest thou come forth into the

[1] Khnemu was the fellow-worker with Ptaḥ in carrying out the mandate for creation which was uttered by Thoth. He is depicted at Philae in the act of fashioning a man on a potter's wheel. The name Khnemu means "moulder," "fashioner," and the like.

"place of happiness whither we go. May the *Shenit* "(*i.e.*, the divine officers of the court of Osiris), who "form the conditions of the lives of men, not cause my "name to stink. [Let it be satisfactory unto us, and "let the listening be satisfactory unto us, and let there "be joy of heart unto us at the weighing of words. "Let not that which is false be uttered against me "before the great god, the lord of Åmentet. Verily "how great shalt thou be when thou risest in "triumph!] [1]"

RUBRIC.

[From the Papyrus of Åmen-ḥetep (see Naville, *Todtenbuch*, Bd. II. p. 99).]

(1) These words are to be said over a scarab of green stone encircled with a band of refined copper and [having] a ring of silver, (2) which shall be placed on the neck of the *khu*.

This chapter was found in the city of Khemennu (Hermopolis Magna) under the feet of [the statue of] (3) this god. [It was inscribed] upon a slab of iron of the south, in the writing of the god himself, in the time of (4) the majesty of the king of the north and of the south, (Men-kau-Rā), [2] triumphant, by the royal son Ḥeru-ṭā-ṭā-f, who discovered it whilst he was on his journey (5) to make an inspection of the temples and of their estates.

In some ancient papyri the text of this chapter is made to follow the Rubric of Chapter LXIV., with which it had some close connexion, and in others it follows the Rubric of Chapter CXLVIII. The Rubrical

[1] The words within brackets are translated from the Papyrus of Nebseni (sheet 4).

[2] *I.e.*, Mycerinus, a king of the IVth Dynasty.

direction concerning Chapter LXIV. reads :—"Behold, "make a scarab of green stone, wash it with gold and "place it in the heart of a man (*i.e.*, the deceased), and "it will perform for him the 'opening of the mouth'; "anoint it with *āntu* unguent, and recite over it as a "charm the following words :—'My heart, my mother; "my heart, my mother!'" etc. In the Turin Papyrus (Lepsius, *Todtenbuch*, Bl. 16) it follows Chapter XXX. which contains parts of Chapters XXXA. and XXXB.

CHAPTER XXXI.

[From the Papyrus of Nu (Brit. Mus. No. 10,477, sheet 5).]

Vignette: In the Papyrus of Nekht the vignette of this Chapter represents the deceased attacking three crocodiles, but in the Saite Recension he is attacking four (see Lepsius, *Todtenbuch* Bl. 16).

Text: (1) THE CHAPTER OF BEATING BACK THE CROCODILE THAT COMETH TO CARRY AWAY THE CHARM FROM NU, THE OVERSEER OF THE HOUSE OF THE OVERSEER OF THE SEAL, TRIUMPHANT, THE SON OF THE OVERSEER OF THE HOUSE, ÅMEN-ḤETEP, TRIUMPHANT, IN THE UNDERWORLD. He saith:—(2)

"Get thee back, return, get thee back, thou crocodile-"fiend Sui; thou shalt not advance to me, for I live by "reason of the magical words which I have by me. I "do not utter that name of thine to the great god (3) "who will cause thee to come to the two divine envoys; "the name of the one is Betti,[1] and the name of the "other is 'Ḥrà-k-en-Maāt.'[2] Heaven hath power over "its seasons, (4) and the magical word hath power over "that which is in its possession, let therefore my mouth "have power over the magical word which is therein. "My front teeth are like unto flint knives, and my back "teeth are like unto the Nome of Ṭutef.[3] Hail thou "that sittest with thine eyeball upon these my magical "words! Thou shalt not carry them away, O thou "crocodile that livest by means of magical words!"

In the Turin Papyrus (Lepsius, *op. cit.*, Bl. 16) the following lines are added to this Chapter:—

"I am the Prince in the field. I, even I, am Osiris, "who hath shut in his father Seb together with his

[1] *I.e.*, "He of two teeth" (*or* two horns); the Saïte Recension (Lepsius, *op. cit.*, Bl. 16) reads *Bent*, *i.e.*, "ape."
[2] *I.e.*, "Thy face is of right and truth."
[3] We should probably add the word *ṭep* and read *Ṭep ṭu-f*, "He that is upon his hill," *i.e.*, Anubis.

"mother Nut (5) on the day of the great slaughter. "My father is Seb and my mother is Nut. I am Horus, "the first-born of Rā, who is crowned. I am Ȧnpu "(Anubis) on the day of reckoning. I, even I, am "Osiris, (6) the prince who goeth in and declareth the "offerings which are written down, I am the guardian "of the door of Osiris, even I. I have come, I have "become glorious (*or* a *Khu*), I have been reckoned up, "I am strong, I have come and I avenge mine own self. "(7) I have sat in the birth chamber of Osiris, and I "was born with him, and I renew my youth along with "him. I have laid hold upon the Thigh which was by "Osiris, (8) and I have opened the mouth of the gods "therewith. I sit upon the place where he sitteth, and "I write down the number [of the things] which make "strong (?) the heart, thousands of loaves of bread, "thousands of vases of beer, which are upon the altars "of his father Osiris, [numbers of] jackals, wolves, (9) "oxen, red fowl, geese and ducks. Horus hath done "away with the sacrifices of Thoth. I fill the office of "priest in the regions above, and I write down there "[the things] which make strong the heart. I make "offerings (*or* offerings are made to me) (10) at the "altars of the Prince of Ṭaṭṭu, and I have my being "through the oblations [made to] him. I snuff the "wind of the East by his head, and I lay hold "upon the breezes of the West thereby, (11) . . . . . I "go round about heaven in the four quarters thereof, "I stretch out my hand and grasp the breezes of the "south [which] are upon its hair. Grant unto me air "among the venerable beings and among those who "eat bread."

RUBRIC: If this chapter be known by [the deceased] he shall come forth by day, he shall rise up to walk upon the earth among the living, and he shall never fail and come to an end, never, never, never.

CHAPTER XXXII.

[From Lepsius, *Todtenbuch*, Bll. 16 and 17.]

Vignette: Four crocodiles advancing against the deceased who is spearing one of them.

Text:[1] THE CHAPTER OF BEATING BACK THE CROCODILE THAT COMETH TO CARRY AWAY THE MAGICAL WORDS FROM THE KHU IN THE UNDERWORLD. (1) Osiris Åuf-ānkh, triumphant, saith:—

"The Mighty One fell down upon the place where he "is, or (as others say), upon his belly, but the company

[1] From no Papyrus containing the Theban Recension can a connected translation of this Chapter be made; it has, therefore, been thought best to give a rendering of it from the text as found in the Saïte Recension.

"of the gods caught him and set him up again. [My] "soul cometh and it speaketh with its father, and the "Mighty One delivereth it (2) from these eight[1] croco-"diles. I know them by their names and [what] they "live upon, and I am he who hath delivered his father "from them."

"Get thee back, O Crocodile that dwellest in the "West, thou that livest upon the stars which never "rest, (3) for that which is an abomination unto thee "is in my belly, O thou that hast eaten the forehead of "Osiris, I am Set."

"Get thee back, O Crocodile that dwelleth in the "West, for the serpent-fiend Nāāu is in my belly, and "I will give him unto thee; let not thy flame be "against me."

"Get thee back, O (4) Crocodile that dwellest in the "East, who feedest upon those who eat their own "filth, for that which is an abomination unto thee is "in my belly; I advance, I am Osiris."

"Get thee back, O Crocodile that dwellest in the "East, the serpent-fiend Nāāu is in (5) my belly, and I "will give [him] unto thee; let not thy flame come "against me."

"Get thee back, O Crocodile that dwellest in the "South, who feedest upon filth, and waste, and dirt, "for that which is an abomination unto thee is in my "belly; shall not the flame be on thy hand? I am "Sept." (6)

[1] The Theban texts mention *four* crocodiles only.

"Get thee back, O Crocodile that dwellest in the "South, for I am safe by reason of my charm; my fist "is among the flowers and I will not give it unto thee."

"Get thee back, O Crocodile that dwellest in the "North, who feedest upon what is offered (?) within "the hours, (7) for that which thou abominatest is in "my belly; let [not] thy venom be upon my head, for "I am Tem."

"Get thee back, O Crocodile that dwellest in the "North, for the goddess Serqet is in my belly and I "have not yet brought her forth (8). I am Uatch-"Maati (*or* Merti)."

"The things which are created are in the hollow of "my hand, and those which have not yet come into "being are in my body. I am clothed and wholly "provided with thy magical words, O Rā, the which "are in heaven above me and in the earth beneath me. "(9) I have gained power, and exaltation, and a full-"breathing throat in the abode of my father Ur (*i.e.*, "the Mighty One), and he hath delivered unto me the "beautiful Åmentet which destroyeth living men and "women; but strong is its divine lord, who suffereth "from weakness," (10) or (as others say) "exhaustion "two-fold, therein day by day. My face is open, my "heart is upon its seat, and the crown with the serpent "is upon me day by day. I am Rā, who is his own "protector, and nothing shall ever cast me to the "ground."

CHAPTER XXXIII.

[From the Papyrus of Nu (Brit. Mus. No. 10,477, sheet 6).]

Vignette: This Chapter is without a vignette in the Papyrus of Nu, but in one MS. the deceased, with a knife in each hand, is seen attacking four serpents, and in another four serpents only are given; see Naville, *op. cit.*, Bd. I. Bl. 46. In the Turin Papyrus (Lepsius, *op. cit.*, Bl. 17) the deceased is spearing a single serpent.

Text: (1) THE CHAPTER OF REPULSING SERPENTS (*or* WORMS) Nu, the overseer of the house of the overseer of the seal, triumphant, saith:—(2)

"Hail, thou serpent Rerek, advance not hither. "Behold Seb and Shu. Stand still now, and thou "shalt eat the rat which is an abominable thing unto "Rā, and (3) thou shalt crunch the bones of the filthy "cat."

CHAPTER XXXIV.

[From the Papyrus of Nu (Brit. Mus. No. 10,477, sheet 6).]

Vignette : This Chapter is without a vignette in the Theban and Saïte Recensions.

Text : (1) THE CHAPTER OF NOT [LETTING] OSIRIS NU, TRIUMPHANT, BE BITTEN BY SNAKES (*or* WORMS) IN THE UNDERWORLD. (2) He saith :—

"O Serpent! I am the flame which shineth upon the "Opener (?) of hundreds of thousands of years, and the "standard of the god Ṭenpu," or (as others say), "the "standard of young plants and flowers. Depart ye (3) "from me, for I am the divine Mafṭeṭ."[1]

[1] So far back as 1867 the late Dr. Birch identified the animal *mafṭet* with the lynx.

CHAPTER XXXV.

[From the Papyrus of Nu (Brit. Mus. No. 10,477, sheet 6).]

Vignette: This Chapter is without a vignette in the Papyrus of Nu, but in the Brocklehurst Papyrus three serpents form the vignette (see Naville, *op. cit.*, Bd. I. Bl. 48); in the Turin Papyrus (Lepsius, *op. cit.*, Bl. 17) the vignette shows the deceased in the act of spearing a serpent. See the vignette to Chapter XXXIII.

Text: (1) THE CHAPTER OF NOT [LETTING] NU, THE OVERSEER OF THE HOUSE OF THE OVERSEER OF THE SEAL, TRIUMPHANT, BE DEVOURED BY SERPENTS IN THE UNDERWORLD. He saith:—

"Hail, thou god Shu! (2) Behold Ṭaṭṭu! Behold "Shu! Hail Ṭaṭṭu! [Shu] hath the head-dress of the "goddess Hathor. They nurse Osiris. Behold the "two-fold being who is about to eat me! Alighting "from the boat I depart (?), (3) and the serpent-fiend "Seksek passeth me by. Behold *sām* and *àaqet* flowers "are kept under guard (?). This being is Osiris, and "he maketh entreaty for his tomb. (4) The eyes of "the divine prince are dropped, and he performeth the "reparation which is to be done for thee; [he] giveth "[unto thee thy] portion of right and truth according "to the decision concerning the states and conditions "[of men]."

CHAPTER XXXVI.

[From the Papyrus of Nu (Brit. Mus. No. 10,477, sheet 8).]

From the Papyrus of Nekhtu-Amen.

From the Papyrus of Nekht.

Vignette : This Chapter is without a vignette in the Papyrus of Nu, but in others containing the Theban Recension (see Naville, *op. cit.*, Bd. I. Bl. 49) the vignettes either show the deceased spearing a beetle, or standing, with a knife in one hand and a staff in the other, before a pedestal upon which stands the insect *Āpshait*, which has been identified with the cockroach. The *āpshait* is probably the beetle which is often found crushed between the bandages of poorly made mummies, or even inside the body itself, where it has forced its way in search of food.

Text : (1) THE CHAPTER OF DRIVING AWAY ĀPSHAIT. Osiris Nu, the overseer of the house of the overseer of the seal, triumphant, saith :—(2)

"Depart from me, O thou that hast lips which gnaw, "for I am Khnemu, the lord of Peshennu,[1] and [I]

[1] Read: "the lord of the city of Shennu," *i.e.*, of Kom Ombos.

"bring the words of the gods to Rā, and I report (3) "[my] message to the lord thereof."[1]

In the Papyrus of Nekht (Brit. Mus. No. 10,471, sheet 14) is a chapter entitled, "The Chapter of Repulsing the Pig," and the accompanying vignette represents the deceased piercing a pig with a spear, and at the same time holding with one hand the end of a rope by which a huge serpent is fettered. The text which follows the title of this chapter is that of Chapter XXXVI., and the only explanation of this unusual vignette is that the scribe confused the proper name Āpshait with the word for "pig," *shaā*  and wrote down the latter word. The artist, seeing the word for "pig" in the text, drew the picture of a pig in the vignette. The following is the vignette :—

[1] Or, "I report [my] message to Nebes" (or Nebses).

CHAPTER XXXVII.

[From the Papyrus of Nu (Brit. Mus. No. 10,477, sheet 8).]

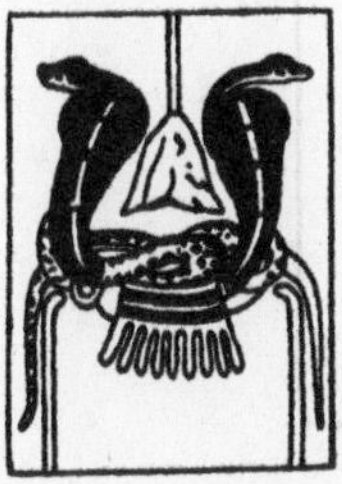

From the Papyrus of Åmen-ḥetep.

From the Papyrus of Nekht.

Vignette: Two uraei, with tails entwined, upon the emblem of gold (Naville, *op. cit.*, Bd. I. Bl. 50); or, the deceased threatening two serpents with a knife; in the vignette of this Chapter in the Turin Papyrus the deceased is seen spearing a serpent (Lepsius, *op. cit.*, Bl. 17).

Text: (1) THE CHAPTER OF DRIVING BACK THE TWO MERTI GODDESSES. Nu, the overseer of the house of the overseer of the seal, triumphant, saith:—

"Homage to you, ye two *Reḥt* goddesses,[1] ye two "Sisters, ye two *Mert* (2) goddesses, I bring a message "to you concerning my magical words. I shine from "the *Sektet* boat, I am Horus the son of Osiris, and I "have come to see (3) my father Osiris."

[1] The goddesses Isis and Nephthys.

CHAPTER XXXVIIIa.

[From the Papyrus of Nebseni (Brit. Mus. No. 9900, sheet 12).]

Vignette : The deceased holding a sail, symbolic of air.

Text : (1) The Chapter of living by air in the underworld. The scribe Nebseni, the lord to whom veneration is paid, saith :—

"[I am the god Tem], who cometh forth out of (2) "Nu into the watery abyss. I have received [my habi-"tation of Åmentet, and have given commands] with "my words to the [*Khus*] whose abiding places are "hidden (3), to the *Khus* and to the double Lion-god. I "have made journeys round about and I have sung "hymns of joy in the boat of Kheperà. I have eaten "therein, I have gained power (4) therein, and I live "therein through the breezes [which are there]. I am "the guide in the boat of Rā, and he openeth out for "me a path ; he maketh a passage for me through the "gates (5) of the god Seb. I have seized and carried "away those who live in the embrace of the god Ur "(*i.e.*, Mighty One); I am the guide of those who live "in their shrines, the two brother-gods Horus and Set; "and I bring the (6) noble ones with me. I enter in "and I come forth, and my throat is not slit; I go into "the boat of Maāt, and I pass in among (7) those who "live in the *Āṭet* boat, and who are in the following of "Rā, and are nigh unto him in his horizon. I live "after my death day by day, and I am strong even as "is the double Lion-god. (8) I live, and I am delivered "after my death, I, the scribe Nebseni, the lord of "piety, who fill the earth and come forth like the lily "of mother-of-emerald, of the god Ḥetep of the two "lands."

CHAPTER XXXVIIIB.

[From the Papyrus of Nu (Brit. Mus. No. 10,477, sheet 12).]

Vignette: The deceased, holding in his left hand a sail, symbolic of air, and attacking three serpents with a knife which he holds in his right hand (see Naville, *op. cit.*, Bd. I. Bl. 52) In the Turin Papyrus (Lepsius, *Todtenbuch*, Bl. 17) the deceased holds a sail in the left hand, and the symbol of life in the right.

Text: (1) THE CHAPTER OF LIVING BY AIR IN THE UNDERWORLD. Nu, the overseer of the house of the overseer of the seal, triumphant, the son of the overseer of the house of the overseer of the seal, Åmen-ḥetep, triumphant, saith:—(2)

"I am the double Lion-god, the first-born of Rā and "Tem of Aḥ-khebti,[1] [the gods] who dwell in their "divine chambers. Those who dwell (3) in their "divine abodes have become my guides, and they make "paths for me as they revolve in the watery abyss of "the sky by the side of the path of the boat of Tem. "(4) I stand upon the timbers (?) of the boat of Rā, and "I recite his ordinances to the beings who have know-"ledge, and I am the herald of his words to him whose "throat stinketh. (5) I set free my divine fathers at "eventide. I close the lips of my mouth, and I eat "like unto a living being. I have life (6) in Ṭaṭṭu, "and I live again after death like Rā day by day."

[1] *I.e.*, "the city of the papyrus swamps," alluding to the place in the Delta where Isis brought forth her son Horus after the death of Osiris.

CHAPTER XXXIX.

[From the Papyrus of Mes-em-neter (see Naville, *op. cit.*, Bd. I. Bl. 53).]

Vignette : The deceased spearing a serpent.

Text : (1) THE CHAPTER OF DRIVING BACK THE SERPENT REREK IN THE UNDERWORLD. Osiris Mes-em-neter saith:—

(2) "Get thee back, depart, retreat (?) from [me], O "Āāapef, withdraw, or thou shalt be drowned at the "Pool of Nu, at the place where thy father (3) hath "ordered that thy slaughter shall be performed. Depart "thou from the divine birthplace of Rā wherein is thy "terror. I am Rā who dwelleth in his terror. (4) Get "thee back, Fiend, before the darts of his beams. Rā "hath overthrown thy words, the gods have turned thy "face backwards, the Lynx hath (5) torn open thy breast,

"the Scorpion[1] hath cast fetters upon thee; and Maāt "hath sent forth thy destruction. Those who are in "(6) the ways have overthrown thee; fall down and "depart, O Āpep, thou Enemy of Rā! O thou that "passest over the region in the eastern part of heaven "with the sound of the roaring thunder-cloud, (7) O Rā "who openest the gates of the horizon straightway on thy "appearance, [Āpep] hath sunk helpless under [thy] "gashings. I have performed thy will, O Rā, I have per-"formed thy will; I have done that which is fair, I have "done that which is fair, I have laboured for the peace "of (8) Rā. [I] have made to advance thy fetters, O "Rā, and Āpep hath fallen through thy drawing them "tight. The gods of the south and of the north, of the "west and of the (9) east have fastened chains upon him, "and they have fettered him with fetters; the god Rekes "hath overthrown him and the god Ḥertit hath put him "in chains. Rā setteth, Rā setteth; Rā is strong at "[his] (10) setting. Āpep hath fallen, Āpep, the enemy "of Rā, departeth. Greater is the punishment [which "hath been inflicted on] thee than the sting (?) which "is in the Scorpion goddess, and mightily hath she, "whose course is everlasting, worked it upon thee and "with deadly effect. (11) Thou shalt never enjoy the "delights of love, thou shalt never fulfil thy desire, O "Āpep, thou Enemy of Rā! He maketh thee to go "back, O thou who art hateful to Rā; he looketh upon

[1] *I.e.*, the goddess Serqet or Selket.
[2] *I.e.*, the goddess of right and truth.

"thee, (12) get thee back! [He] pierceth [thy] head, "[he] cutteth through thy face, [he] divideth [thy] "head at the two sides of the ways, and it is crushed "in his land; thy bones are smashed in pieces, thy "members are hacked off thee, and the god [A]ker[1] hath "condemned (13) thee, O Apep, thou enemy of Rā! "Thy mariners are those who keep the reckoning for "thee, [O Rā, as thou] advancest, and thou restest "there wherein are the offerings made to thee. [As "thou] advancest, [as thou] advancest towards the "House (14) the advance which thou hast made towards "the House is a prosperous advance; let not any baleful "obstacle proceed from thy mouth against me when "thou workest on my behalf. I am Set who let loose "the storm-clouds and the (15) thunder in the horizon "of heaven even as [doth] the god Netcheb-ȧb-f."

"'Hail,' saith the god Tem, 'Make strong your faces, "O soldiers of Rā, for I have driven back the god "(16) Nentchā in the presence of the divine sovereign "princes.' 'Hail,' saith the god Seb, 'Make ye firm "those who are upon their seats which are in the boat "of Kheperȧ, (17) take ye your ways, [grasping] your "weapons of war in your hands.' 'Hail,' saith Hathor, "'Take ye your armour.' 'Hail,' saith Nut, 'Come "and repulse the god (18) Tchā who pursueth him that "dwelleth in his shrine and who setteth out on his way "alone, namely, Neb-er-tcher, who cannot be repulsed.'

[1] *I.e.*, the double Lion-god who presided over the sun's course in the night sky.

"'Hail,' say those gods who dwell in their (19) companies and who go round about the Turquoise Pool, "'Come, O mighty One, we praise and we will deliver "the Mighty One [who dwelleth in] the divine Shrine, "from whom proceeds the company of the gods, (20) let "commemorations be made for him, let praise be given "to him, let words [of praise] be recited before him by "you and by me.' 'Hail,' saith Nut to thy Sweet One. "'Hail,' say those who dwell among the gods, (21) 'He "cometh forth, he findeth [his] way, he maketh captives "among the gods, he hath taken possession of the "goddess Nut, and Seb standeth up.' Hail, thou "terrible one, the company of the gods is on (22) the "march. Hathor quaketh with terror, and Rā hath "triumphed over Āpep."

CHAPTER XL.

[From the Papyrus of Rā (see Naville, *op. cit.*, Bd. I. Bl. 54) and from the Papyrus of Nu (Brit. Mus. No. 10,477, sheet 8).]

Vignette : The deceased spearing a serpent which has sprung upon an ass and is biting into his back; see Brit. Mus. No. 10,471, sheet 21; and Naville, *op. cit.*, Bd. I. Bl. 54.

Text: (1) THE CHAPTER OF DRIVING BACK THE EATER OF THE ASS.[1] Osiris Rā, triumphant, saith:—

I. "Get thee back, (2) Hai, thou impure one, thou "abomination of Osiris! Thoth hath cut off thy head, "and I have performed upon thee all the things which "the company of the gods (3) ordered concerning thee "in the matter of the work of thy slaughter. Get thee "back, thou abomination of Osiris, from the *Neshmet* "boat .... which (4) advanceth with a fair wind. Ye "are holy, O all ye gods, and [ye] have cast down head-"long the enemies (5) of Osiris; the gods of Ta-ur "shout for joy. Get thee back, O thou Eater of the "(6) Ass, thou abomination of the god Ḥaās who "dwelleth in the underworld. I know thee, I know "thee, I know thee, I know thee. Who art thou? (7) "I am ...."

II. (2) "On thy face, [O fiend], and devour me not, "for I am pure, and I am with the time which cometh "of itself. Thou shalt not come to me, O thou that "comest[2] without being invoked, and whose [time of "coming] is unknown. I am the lord of thy mouth, "get thee back (3), thou and thy desires (?) Hail, "Ḥaās,[3] with his flint [knife] Horus hath cut asunder

[1] "Ass" is here a name of the Sun-god Rā, and the "Eater of the Ass" is a name of Set or of one of his fiends.

[2] These words are from the Papyrus of Rā.

[3] A god of whom little is known. He is called the "great god of the West," and is said to be the deity of the dwellers in the western desert and mountains; subsequently he was identified with a form of Osiris, and was especially worshipped in the sixth nome of Lower Egypt.

"thy members, and thou art destroyed within thy company, and thy bend (or dwelling-place) is destroyed "for thee by the company of thy gods who dwell in the "cities of Pe and (4) Ṭep. He that slayeth [thee] there "is in the form of the Eye of Horus, and I have driven "thee away as thou wast advancing, and I have van-"quished thee by the winds of my mouth. O thou "Eater (5) of those who commit sins, who dost plunder "and spoil, I have [committed] no sin; therefore let my "palette and the writings[1] with hostile charges [against "me upon them] be given unto me. I have done no "wrong in the presence of (6) the sovereign princes, "therefore shoot not thy [venom] at me. I give, do "thou take according to what I order; snatch me not "away, and eat me not, for I am the lord of life, the "Prince (Life, Health, Strength!) of the horizon."

[1] Apparently the palette upon which Thoth records the result of the weighing of the heart in the Hall of Osiris.

CHAPTER XLI.

[From the Papyrus of Nebseni, sheet 25.]

Vignette: The deceased armed with a knife and a short staff; see Naville, *op. cit.*, Bd. I. Bl. 55. In the Turin Papyrus the deceased is piercing a serpent which lies writhing on a barred instrument (see Lepsius, *op. cit.*, Bl. 19).

Text: (1) THE CHAPTER OF DRIVING AWAY THE SLAUGHTERINGS WHICH ARE PERFORMED IN THE UNDERWORLD. Nebseni, the scribe and designer in the Temples of Upper and Lower Egypt, he to whom fair veneration is paid, (2) the son of the scribe and artist Thena, triumphant, saith :—

"Hail, Tem, I have become glorious (*or* a *Khu*) in "the presence of the double Lion-god, the great (3) "god, therefore open thou unto me the gate of the god "Seb. I smell the earth (*i.e.*, I bow down so that "my nose toucheth the ground) of the great god who "dwelleth in the underworld, and I advance (4) into "the presence of the company of the gods who dwell "with the beings who are in the underworld. Hail, "thou guardian of the divine door of the city of Beta, "thou Neti[1] who dwellest in Ȧmentet, (5) I eat food, "and I have life through the air, and the god Āatch-ur "leadeth me with [him] to the mighty boat of (6) "Kheperȧ. I hold converse with the divine mariners "at eventide, I enter in, I go forth, (7) and I see the "being who is there; I lift him up, and I say that "which I have to say unto him whose throat stinketh "[for lack of air]. I have life, (8) and I am delivered, "having lain down in death. Hail, thou that bringest "offerings and oblations, bring forward thy mouth and "make to draw nigh the writings (9) (*or* lists) of offer-"ings and oblations. Set thou Right aud Truth firmly "upon their throne, make thou the writings to draw "nigh, and set thou up the goddesses (10) in the "presence of Osiris, the mighty god, the Prince of ever-"lastingness, who counteth his years, who hearkeneth "unto those who are in the islands (*or* pools), who "raiseth his (11) right shoulder, who judgeth the divine "princes, and who sendeth [the deceased] into the "presence of the great sovereign princes who live in "the underworld."

[1] *I.e.*, the "god of the double red crown."

CHAPTER XLII.

[From the Papyrus of Nu (Brit. Mus. No. 10,477, sheet 6).]

Vignette : The deceased standing before Osiris with his left hand raised to his mouth; or the deceased holding a serpent in his hands; or the deceased addressing a serpent which has its head turned away; or the deceased drawing a cord from round the top of a *tet* (?), emblem of stability.[1]

Text : (1) The Chapter of driving back the (2) slaughterings which are performed in Suten-ḥenen. Osiris Nu, triumphant, saith :—

"O thou land of the Sceptre (*literally*, wood) ! O "thou White Crown of the divine form ! O thou rest-"ing place of the boat ! I am the Child, (3) I am the "Child, I am the Child, I am the Child. Hail, Àbu-ur, "thou sayest day by day : 'The slaughter-block is made

[1] For these see Naville, *op. cit.*, Bd. I. Bl. 57.

"ready as thou knowest, and thou hast come to decay.' "I am (4) Rā, the stablisher of those who praise [him]. "I am the knot of the god within the *Åser* tree, the "doubly beautiful one, who is more splendid than "yesterday (say four times). I am Rā, the stablisher "of those who praise [him]. (5) I am the knot of the "god within the *Åser* tree, and my going forth is the "going forth [of Rā] on this day."

"My hair is the hair of Nu. My face is the face of "the Disk. My eyes are the eyes of (6) Hathor. My "ears are the ears of Åp-uat.[1] My nose is the nose of "Khenti-khas. My lips are the lips of Ånpu. My "teeth are the teeth of (7) Serqet.[2] My neck is the "neck of the divine goddess Isis. My hands are the "hands of Ba-neb-Ṭaṭṭu.[3] My fore-arms are the fore-"arms of Neith,[4] the Lady of Sais. My backbone is "(8) the backbone of Suti. My phallus is the phallus "of Osiris. My reins are the reins of the Lords of "Kher-āḥa. My chest is the chest of the Mighty one "of Terror. (9) My belly and back are the belly and "back of Sekhet. My buttocks are the buttocks of the "Eye of Horus. My hips and legs are the hips and "legs of Nut. My feet are the feet of (10) Ptaḥ. [My "fingers] and my leg-bones are the [fingers and] leg-

[1] *I.e.*, "the opener of the roads," a jackal-headed god who is sometimes identified with Osiris.

[2] The Scorpion goddess.

[3] *I.e.*, "Ram, Lord of Ṭaṭṭu," a name of Osiris.

[4] One of the oldest goddesses of Egypt. She was the goddess of hunting and weaving, but was identified with many other goddesses such as Isis, Meḥ-urt, and their attributes were assigned to her.

"bones of the Living Gods. There is no member of my "body which is not the member of some god. The god "Thoth shieldeth my body (11) altogether, and I am "Rā day by day. I shall not be dragged back by my "arms, and none shall lay violent hold upon my hands. "And shall do me hurt neither men, nor gods, (12) nor "the sainted dead, nor those who have perished, nor "any one of those of ancient times, nor any mortal, "nor any human being. I (13) am he who cometh "forth, advancing, whose name is unknown. I am "Yesterday, and Seer of millions of years is my name. "I pass along, I pass along the paths of the divine "celestial judges. (14) I am the lord of eternity, and "I decree and I judge like the god Kheperȧ. I am the "lord of the *Ureret* crown. I am he who dwelleth in "the *Utchat* [and in the Egg, in the *Utchat* and in the "Egg, and it is given unto me to live [with] them. I "am he that dwelleth in the *Utchat* when it closeth, "and I exist by the strength thereof. I come forth and "I shine; I enter in and I come to life. I am in the "*Utchat*],[1] my seat is (15) upon my throne, and I sit in "the abode of splendour (?) before it. I am Horus and "(I) traverse millions of years. I have given the "decree [for the stablishing of] my throne and I am the "ruler thereof; and in very truth, my mouth keepeth "an even balance both in speech (16) and in silence. "In very truth, my forms are inverted. I am Un-nefer,

[1] The words within brackets are supplied from the Papyrus of Mes-em-neter.

"from one season even unto another, and what I have "is within me; [I am] (17) the only One, who pro- "ceedeth from an only One who goeth round about in "his course. I am he who dwelleth in the *Utchat*, no "evil thing of any form or kind shall spring up against "me, and no baleful object, and no harmful thing, and "no disastrous thing shall happen unto (18) me. I "open the door in heaven, I govern my throne, and I "open up [the way] for the births [which take place] "on this day. I am (?) the child who marcheth along "the road of Yesterday. [I am] To-day for untold "nations and peoples. (19) I am he who protecteth "you for millions of years, and whether ye be denizens "of the heavens, or of the earth, or of the south, or of "the (20) north, or of the east, or of the west, the fear "of me is in your bodies. I am he whose being has "been moulded in his eye, and I shall not die again. "My moment is in your bodies, but my (21) forms are "in my place of habitation. I am he who cannot be "known, but the Red Ones have their faces directed "towards me. I am the unveiled one. The season "wherein [the god] created the heavens for me (22) and "enlarged the bounds of the earth and made great the "progeny thereof cannot be found out; but they fail "and are not united [again]. My name setteth itself "apart from all things [and from] the great evil [which "is in] the mouths [of men] by reason of the speech "which I address (23) unto you. I am he who riseth "and shineth, the wall which cometh out of a wall, an "only One who proceedeth from an only One. There "is never a day that passeth without (24) the things "which appertain unto him being therein; passing, "passing, passing, passing. Verily I say unto thee, I "am the Sprout which cometh forth from Nu, and my "Mother is Nut. Hail, O (25) my Creator, I am he "who hath no power to walk, the great Knot who is "within yesterday. The might of my strength is "within my hand. I myself am not known, but I am "he who knoweth thee. (26) I cannot be held with "the hand, but I am he who can hold thee in his hand. "Hail, O Egg! Hail, O Egg! I am Horus, he who "liveth for millions of years, whose flame shineth upon "you (27) and bringeth your hearts to me. I have the "command of my throne and I advance at this season, "I have opened a path, and I have delivered myself "from all evil things. (28) I am the dog-headed "ape of gold three palms and two fingers [high], "which hath neither arms nor legs and dwelleth "in Ḥet-ka-Ptaḥ (Memphis), and I go forth as "goeth forth the dog-headed ape that dwelleth in "Ḥet-ka-Ptaḥ."

In the Papyrus of Ani, sheet 32, only a portion of this Chapter is given, *i.e.*, the section which gives the names of the deities with whom the various members of the body of the deceased are identified. This section is arranged in tabular form, and carefully drawn vignettes giving pictures of the gods mentioned are added.

Nu. Rā. Hathor. Ȧp-uat. Anubis. Serqet. Isis.

Vignette: The god Nu.

Text: (1) The hair of Osiris Ani, triumphant, is the hair of Nu.

Vignette: Rā, hawk-headed, and wearing a disk.

Text: (2) The face of Osiris, the scribe Ani, triumphant, is the face of Rā.

Vignette: The goddess Hathor, with horns and a disk on her head.

Text: (3) The eyes of Osiris Ani, triumphant, are the eyes of Hathor.

Vignette: The god Ȧp-uat, jackal-headed, on a standard.

Text: (4) The ears of Osiris Ani, triumphant, are the ears of Ȧp-uat.

Vignette: The god Ȧnpu, jackal-headed.

Text: (5) The lips of Osiris Ani, triumphant, are the lips of Ȧnpu.

Vignette: The scorpion-goddess Serqet holding the emblems of life and eternity.

Text: (6) The teeth of Osiris Ani, triumphant, are the teeth of Serqet.

Vignette: The goddess Isis.

Text : (7) The neck of Osiris Ani, triumphant, is the neck of Isis.

Vignette : A ram-headed god, having a serpent between his horns.

Text : (8) The hands of Osiris Ani, triumphant, are the hands of Ba-neb-Ṭaṭṭu.

Vignette : The goddess Uatchet.

Text : (9) The shoulder of Osiris Ani, triumphant, is the shoulder of Uatchet.

Vignette : The goddess Mert standing on the symbol of gold; her hands are outstretched, and she has on her head a cluster of plants.

Text : (10) The throat of Osiris Ani, triumphant, is the throat of Mert.

Vignette : The goddess Neith.

Text : (11) The fore-arms of Osiris Ani, triumphant, are the fore-arms of the lady of Saïs.

Vignette : The god Set.

Text : (12) The backbone of Osiris Ani, triumphant, is the backbone of Set.

Vignette: A god.

Text: (13) The chest of Osiris Ani, triumphant, is the chest of the lords of Kherāḥa.

Vignette: A god.

Text: (14) The flesh of Osiris Ani, triumphant, is the flesh of the Mighty One of Terror.

Sekhet. Eye of Horus. Osiris. Nut. Ptaḥ. Orion. The Living Uraei.

Vignette: A goddess wearing the solar disk.

Text: (15) The reins and back of Osiris Ani, triumphant, are the reins and back of Sekhet.

Vignette: An *Utchat* upon a pylon.

Text: (16) The buttocks of Osiris Ani, triumphant, are the buttocks of the Eye of Horus.

Vignette: Osiris, wearing the *Atef* crown and holding the flail and crook.

Text: (17) The phallus of Osiris Ani, triumphant, is the phallus of Osiris.

Vignette: The goddess Nut.

Text: (18) The legs of Osiris Ani, triumphant, are the legs of Nut.

Vignette: The god Ptaḥ, standing on the pedestal of Maāt.

Text : (19) The feet of Osiris Ani, triumphant, are the feet of Ptaḥ.

Vignette : The star Orion.

Text : (20) The fingers of Osiris Ani, triumphant, are the fingers of Orion.

Vignette : Three uraei.

Text : (21) The leg-bones of Osiris Ani, triumphant, are the leg-bones of the living uraei.

In the Papyrus of Ani, following immediately after the tabulated form of Chapter XLII., is a vignette in which four dog-headed apes are seen seated each at a corner of the Lake of Fire. The text below it is in that of the Rubric which usually follows the last section of Chapter CXXV., though from its position in the papyrus it would seem to be connected in some way with Chapter XLII. The vignette is given below, but the translation of the text will be found at the end of Chapter CXXV.

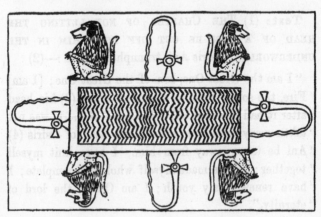

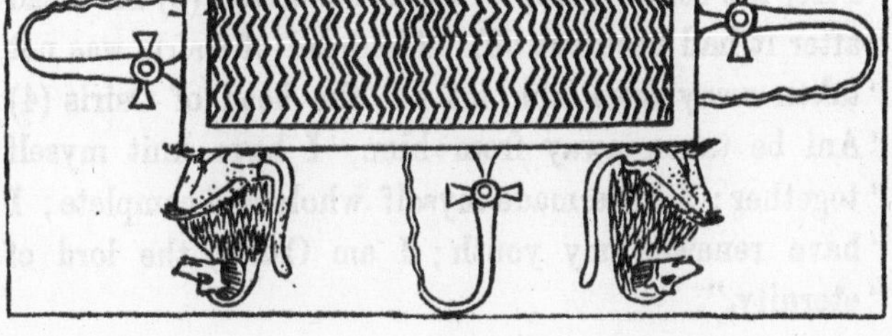

CHAPTER XLIII.

[From the Papyrus of Ani (Brit. Mus. No. 10,470, sheet 17).]

Vignette: The deceased adoring three gods, each of whom holds the emblem of life in his right hand and a sceptre in his left.

Text: (1) THE CHAPTER OF NOT LETTING THE HEAD OF A MAN BE CUT OFF FROM HIM IN THE UNDERWORLD. Osiris Ani, triumphant, saith :—(2)

"I am the Great One, son of the Great One; [I am] "Fire, the son of Fire, to whom was given (3) his head "after it had been cut off. The head of Osiris was not "taken away from him, let not the head of Osiris (4) "Ani be taken away from him. I have knit myself "together; I have made myself whole and complete; I "have renewed my youth; I am Osiris, the lord of "eternity."

CHAPTER XLIV.

[From the Papyrus of Ani (Brit. Mus. No. 10,470, sheet 16).]

Vignette : The scribe Ani, clothed in white and seated in a chair; he holds in the right hand the *kherp* sceptre, and in the left a long staff. Before him is a table. In the Turin Papyrus (Lepsius, *op. cit.*, Bl. 20) the deceased is seen standing before a funeral coffer or shrine.

Text : (1) THE CHAPTER OF NOT DYING A SECOND TIME IN THE UNDERWORLD. Osiris Ani, triumphant, saith :—

"My place of hiding is opened, my place of hiding is "revealed. The *Khus* have (2) fallen into the dark-"ness, but the Eye of Horus hath made me mighty "and the god Åp-uat hath nursed me like a babe. I "have hidden (3) myself with you, O ye stars that "never diminish! My brow is like unto that of Rā; "my face is open; (4) my heart is upon its throne; I "have power over the speech of my mouth; I have "knowledge; in very truth I am Rā himself. I am "not held to be a person of no account; (5) and "violence shall not be done unto me. Thy father "liveth for thee, O son of Nut; I am thy son, O Great "One, and I have seen the hidden things (6) which "belong unto thee. I am crowned king of the gods, I "shall not die a second time in the underworld."

CHAPTER XLV.

[From the Papyrus of Ani (Brit. Mus. No. 10,470, sheet 16).]

Vignette: The mummy of the scribe Ani being embraced by Anubis, jackal-headed, the god of the dead.

Text: (1) THE CHAPTER OF NOT SUFFERING CORRUPTION IN THE UNDERWORLD. Osiris Ani, triumphant, saith:—

"O thou who canst not move, like unto Osiris; O "thou who canst not move, like unto Osiris! (2) O "thou whose limbs cannot move, like unto [those of] "Osiris! Let not thy limbs be without movement; let "them not suffer corruption; let them not pass away; "let them not decay; and let them be fashioned (3) for "me as if I myself were Osiris."

RUBRIC: If [the deceased] know this chapter, he shall never suffer corruption in the underworld.

CHAPTER XLVI.

[From the Papyrus of Ani (Brit. Mus. No. 10,470, sheet 16).]

Vignette: The doorway of the tomb. By one post stands the soul of the scribe Ani in the form of a human-headed hawk, and by the other the *Bennu* bird.

Text: (1) THE CHAPTER OF NOT PERISHING AND OF BECOMING ALIVE IN THE UNDERWORLD. Osiris Ani saith:—

"Hail, (2) ye children of the god Shu! The Tuat

"(underworld) hath gained the mastery over his "diadem.[1] Like the *Hammemet*[2] beings may I arise, "even as Osiris doth arise and fare forth."

CHAPTER XLVII.

[From the Papyrus of Nu (Brit. Mus. No. 10,477, sheet 8).]

Vignette: In the Theban Recension this Chapter has no vignette; but in the Turin Papyrus (Lepsius, *op. cit.*, Bl. 20) a funeral shrine is depicted with the soul of the deceased on one side of it, and the *Bennu* bird on the other.

Text: (1) THE CHAPTER OF NOT ALLOWING THE SEAT AND THRONE OF NU, THE OVERSEER OF THE HOUSE OF THE OVERSEER OF THE SEAL, TO BE TAKEN

[1] The Papyrus of Nebseni reads:—"Each dawn gaineth the mastery over [his] diadem with rays of light; [your] hands rise up, [your] heads rise up each day."

[2] A class of celestial beings who either have been or may become men and women.

AWAY (2) FROM HIM IN THE UNDERWORLD. He saith:—

"O my Seat, O my Throne, come ye to me, and go "ye round about me. I am your lord, O ye gods, come "ye and take up your places in my train. (3) I am "the son of your lord, and ye belong to me through my "divine father who hath made you."

CHAPTER XLVII.

[From the Papyrus of Nebseni (Brit. Mus. No. 9,900, sheet 8).]

"O my Seat, O my Throne, come ye to me, and go ye "round about me, O ye gods. I am a spiritual body "(*sāḥ*), therefore let me rise up among those who follow "the great god. I am the son of Maāti, and that "which he abominateth is the speech of falsehood. I "am in triumph!"

CHAPTER XLVIII.

This Chapter is given twice in the Saïte Recension, once as Chapter X. and once as Chapter XLVIII.; for the translation of it as found in the Papyrus of Ani, sheet 18, see above, p. 58.

CHAPTER XLIX.

This Chapter is given twice in the Saïte Recension, once as Chapter XI. and once as Chapter XLIX.; for the translation of it as found in the Papyrus of Nu, sheet 21, see above, p. 59.

CHAPTER L. A.

[From the Papyrus of Nebseni (Brit. Mus. No. 9,900, sheet 12).]

Vignette: In the Papyrus of Ani, sheet 16, and in the Turin Papyrus (Lepsius, *op. cit.*, Bl. 21) the deceased is represented standing with his back to a gory knife which rests on its block.

Text: (1) THE CHAPTER OF (2) NOT ENTERING IN UNTO THE BLOCK OF THE GOD. Nebseni saith:—

"The four bones (*or* knots) of my neck and back have "been joined together for me by the (3) Guardian of "heaven, who stablished the knot for him who lay "helpless at the breasts [of his mother] on the day of "cutting off the hair. The bones of my neck and back "(4) have been knit together by the god Set and by the "company of the gods as strongly as they were in "the time that is past; may nothing happen to break "them apart! Make ye me strong! The goddess Nut "hath joined together the bones of my (5) neck and "back, [and they are] even as they were in the time "that is past, when I saw the true birth of the gods in "visible forms take place in its true and right order. I "am Peti, and I am in the presence of the great god."

CHAPTER L. B.

[From the Papyrus of Nu (Brit. Mus. No. 10,477, sheet 19).]

Vignette: This Chapter is without a vignette in the Theban Recension.

Text: (1) THE CHAPTER OF NOT ENTERING IN UNTO THE BLOCK. The overseer of the house of the overseer of the seal, triumphant, saith:—

"I have joined up my head and neck in heaven [and] "in earth. (2) Behold it is Rā who, day by day, "stablisheth the knot for him who stood helpless upon "his legs on the day of cutting off the hair. The god "Suti and the company of the gods have joined together "my (3) neck and my back strongly, and they are even "as they were in the time that is past; may nothing "happen to break them apart! Make ye me strong "against the slaughterer of my divine father. (4) I "have gotten power over my two hands. The goddess "Nut hath joined together the bones of my neck and "back, and I behold them as they were in the time "that is past, when as yet I had not seen Maāt, and "when the gods were not born (5) in visible forms. I "am Penti, and I am in the form of the destroyer of "the great gods."

CHAPTER LI.

[From the Papyrus of Nu (Brit. Mus. No. 10,477, sheet 8).]

Vignette: This Chapter is without a vignette in the Theban Recension; in the Turin Papyrus (Lepsius, *op. cit.*, Bl. 21) an upright figure of the deceased forms the vignette.

Text: (1) THE CHAPTER OF NOT MARCHING TO BE OVERTHROWN IN THE UNDERWORLD. The overseer of the palace, Nu, triumphant, saith :— (2)

"That which is an abomination unto me, that which "is an abomination unto me, let me not eat. That "which is an abomination unto me, that which is an "abomination unto me is filth; let me not eat it [in "the place of] the sepulchral cakes which are offered "unto the *Kas*.[1] (3) Let me not be destroyed thereby; "let me not be compelled to take it into my hands; "and let me not be compelled to walk thereon in my "sandals."

CHAPTER LII.

[From the Papyrus of Nu (Brit. Mus. No. 10,477, sheet 11).]

Vignette: This Chapter is without a vignette in the Theban Recension; in the Turin Papyrus (Lepsius, *op. cit.*, Bl. 21) the deceased is seated on a chair and his left hand is stretched out over a table.

[1] Or, "Let me not be compelled to eat it [in the absence of] the sepulchral cakes and provisions which shall be offered unto me."

Text: (1) THE CHAPTER OF NOT EATING FILTH IN THE UNDERWORLD. The overseer of the house of the overseer of the seal, Nu, triumphant, saith:—

"That which is an abomination unto me, that which "is an abomination unto me, let me not eat. That "which is an abomination unto me, (2) that which is "an abomination unto me is filth; let me not eat it [in "the place of] the sepulchral cakes [which are offered "unto] the *Kas*. Let it not light upon my body; let "me not be obliged to take it into my hands; and let "me not be obliged to (3) walk thereon in my sandals. "What, now, wilt thou live upon in the presence of "the gods? [Let food] come unto me from the place "whither thou wilt bring food (?), and let me live upon "the seven loaves of bread (4) which shall be brought as "food before Horus, and upon the bread which is "brought before Thoth. The gods shall say unto me: "'What manner of food wouldst thou have given unto "thee?' [And I reply:] Let me eat my food under "the sycamore tree (5) of my lady, the goddess Hathor, "and let my times be among the divine beings who "have alighted thereon. Let me have the power to "order my own fields in Ṭaṭṭu (Mendes) (6) and my "own growing crops in Ȧnnu (Heliopolis). Let me "live upon bread made of white barley, and let my "beer be [made] from red grain, and may the persons "of (7) my father and mother be given unto me as "guardians of my door and for the ordering of my "territory. Let me be sound and strong, let me have "a large room, and let me be able to sit wheresoever "I please."

CHAPTER LIII.

[From the Papyrus of Nu (Brit. Mus. No. 10,477, sheet 11).]

Vignette: This Chapter is without a vignette in the Theban Recension; in the Turin Papyrus (Lepsius, *op. cit.*, Bl. 22) the deceased is seated on a chair with a table of offerings before him, and his left hand, with a bowl therein, is stretched out over it. See the vignette to Chapter LII.

Text: (1) THE CHAPTER OF NOT EATING FILTH AND OF NOT DRINKING FOUL WATER IN THE UNDERWORLD. The overseer of the house of the overseer of the seal, Nu, triumphant, saith:—

"I am the Bull with two horns, and [I] lead (2) along "the heavens. [I am] the lord of the risings of the "heavens, the Great Illuminer who cometh forth out of "flame, the bestower of years, the far extending One, "the double Lion-god, and there hath been given to "me (3) the journey of the god of splendour (*Khu*).[1] "That which is an abomination unto me, that which is "an abomination unto me, let me not eat. [Let me not "eat] filth, and let me not drink foul water, and let me "not be tripped up and fall [in the underworld]. (4) I

[1] Var., Shu.

"am the lord of cakes in Ȧnnu, and my bread is in "heaven with Rā, and my cakes are on the earth with "the god Seb, for the *Sektet* boat and the *Āṭet* boat "have (5) brought them to me from the house of the "great god who is in Ȧnnu. I have put away from me "my associates, and I have united myself to the boat of "heaven. I eat of what they (*i.e.*, the gods, or the "divine boatmen) eat there; I live upon what (6) they "live upon there; and I eat of the cakes which are in "the hall of the lord of sepulchral offerings, I the over- "seer of the house of the overseer of the seal, Nu, "triumphant."[1]

[1] In the Leyden Papyrus of Rā the Chapter ends:—"triumphant before the great god, the lord of Ȧmentet, and before Ȧnpu"; in the Turin Papyrus (Lepsius, *op. cit.*, Bl. 22) it ends with the words:—"Filth is an abomination unto me, and I will not eat it."

CHAPTER LIV.

[From the Papyrus of Nu (Brit. Mus. No. 10,477, sheet 12).]

Vignette : The deceased arrayed in white and holding a sail, symbolic of air, in his left hand (see Papyrus of Ani, sheet 15).

Text : (1) THE CHAPTER OF GIVING AIR (2) TO THE OVERSEER OF THE HOUSE OF THE OVERSEER OF THE SEAL, NU, TRIUMPHANT, IN THE UNDERWORLD. He saith :—

"Hail, thou god Temu, grant unto me the sweet "breath which dwelleth in thy nostrils! I am the Egg "(3) which is in Ḳenḳenur (*i.e.*, the Great Cackler), "and I watch and guard that mighty thing which hath "come into being and with which the god Seb hath "opened the earth. I live; and it liveth; (4) I become "old, I live, and I snuff the air. I am the god Utchā-

"ãabet (*i.e.*, the god who trieth hostility), and I revolve "behind [to protect] his egg. I shine at the moment "(5) of Horus, the mighty god Suti, whose strength is "two-fold. Hail, thou who makest sweet the seasons "of the two earths, thou dweller among celestial food, "thou dweller in the cerulean heights of heaven,[1] keep "watch over the Babe that dwelleth in his (6) cot when "he cometh forth to you."

CHAPTER LV.

[From the Papyrus of Nu (Brit. Mus. No. 10,477, sheet 12).]

Vignette: The deceased holding a sail in each hand (see Naville, *op. cit.*, Bd. I. Bl. 67).

Text: (1) THE CHAPTER OF GIVING AIR IN THE UNDERWORLD. Saith Nu, triumphant:—(2)

"I am the Jackal of jackals, I am Shu, and [I] draw "air from the presence of the god of Light [*Khu*] to the "bounds of heaven, and to the bounds of (3) earth, and

[1] Literally, "Dweller in lapis-lazuli."

"to the bounds of the uttermost limits of the flight "(*literally* feather) of the *Nebeḥ* bird. May air be given "unto these young divine beings."[1]

CHAPTER LVI.

[From the Papyrus of Nu (Brit. Mus. No. 10,477, sheet 12).]

Vignette : The deceased holding in his hand a sail, symbolic of air.

Text : (1) THE CHAPTER OF SNUFFING THE AIR AMONG THE WATERS IN THE UNDERWORLD. The overseer of the house (2) of the overseer of the seal, Nu, triumphant, saith :—

"Hail, thou god Tem, grant thou unto me the sweet "breath which dwelleth in thy nostrils. I embrace "that great throne (3) which is in the city of Hermo- "polis, and I keep watch over the Egg of Ḳenḳen-ur "(*i.e.*, Great Cackler) ; I germinate as it germinateth ; "(4) I live as it liveth ; and [my] breath is [its] breath."

[1] A Papyrus at Leyden (see Naville, *op. cit.*, Bd. II. p. 125) adds : "My mouth is open, and I see with my two eyes."

CHAPTER LVII.

[From the Papyrus of Nu (Brit. Mus. No. 10,477, sheet 12).]

Vignette: The deceased standing in a stream of water, and holding a sail in his left hand (see Naville, *op. cit.*, Bd. I. Bl. 70).

Text: (1) THE CHAPTER OF SNUFFING THE AIR AND OF HAVING THE MASTERY OVER THE WATER IN THE UNDERWORLD. The overseer of the house of the overseer of the seal, Nu, triumphant, saith:—(2)

"Hail, Ḥāp-ur,[1] god of heaven, in thy name of "'Divider of heaven,' grant thou unto me that I may "have dominion over (3) the water, even as the goddess "Sekhet had power over Osiris on the night of the "storms and floods. Grant thou that I may have "power over the divine princes who have their habita- "tions in the place of (4) the god of the inundation, "even as they have power over their own holy god of

[1] *I.e.*, the "Great Ḥāpi," or the celestial Nile.

"whose name they are ignorant; and may they let me "have power even as [he hath let them have power]."

"My nostrils are (5) opened in Ṭaṭṭu," or (as others say), "My mouth and my nostrils are opened in "Ṭāṭāu, and I have my place of peace in Ȧnnu, which "is my house; it was built for me by the (6) goddess "Sesheta,[1] and the god Khnemu set it up for me upon "its walls. If to this heaven it cometh by the north, I "sit at the south; if to this heaven (7) it cometh by "the south, I sit at the north; if to this heaven it "cometh by the west, I sit at the east; and if to this "heaven it cometh by the east, (8) I sit at the west. I "draw the air of my nostrils, and I make my way into "every place in which I wish to sit."

In the Papyrus of Nefer-uben-f (see Naville, *op. cit.*, Bd. I. Bl. 70) this Chapter ends quite differently, and reads:—

"I am strong in my mouth and in my nostrils, for "behold Tem has stablished them; behold, O ye gods "and *Khus*. Rest thou, then, O Tem. Behold the "staff which blossometh, and which cometh forth when "a man crieth out in your names. Behold, I am Tem, "the tree (?) of the gods in [their] visible forms. Let "me not be turned back .... I am the *Ȧm-khent*, "Nefer-uben-f, triumphant. Let neither my flesh nor

[1] A goddess whose name was formerly read Sefek-āābui. She was a form of Hathor, and was the goddess of writing and of books; her worship goes back to the earliest dynasties.

"my members be gashed with knives, let me not be "wounded by knives by you. I have come, I have "been judged, I have come forth therein, [I] have "power with my father, the Old Man, Nu. He hath "granted that I may live, he hath given strength unto "me, and he hath provided me with the inheritance of "my father therein."

CHAPTER LVIII.

[From the Papyrus of Ani (Brit. Mus. No. 10,470, sheet 16).]

Vignette: Ani and his wife Thuthu standing in a pool of running water; each holds a sail, the symbol of air, in the left hand, and scoops up water to the mouth with the right hand. On the edges of the pool are palm trees, from the largest of which hang great clusters of dates.

Text: (1) THE CHAPTER OF BREATHING THE AIR

AND OF HAVING DOMINION OVER THE WATER IN THE UNDERWORLD. Osiris Ani saith:—

"Open to me." Who art thou? Whither goest thou? (2) What is thy name? "I am one of you."[1] Who are those with thee? "The two serpent goddesses "*Merti*. Separate thou from him, head from head, "when (3) [thou] goest into the divine *Mesqen* chamber. "He letteth me set out for the temple of the gods "who have found their faces. 'Assembler of Souls' "(4) is the name of my boat; 'Making the hair to "stand on end' is the name of the oars; 'Goad' is the "name of the (5) hold (?); 'Making straight for the "middle' is the name of the rudder; likewise [the "boat] is a type of my being borne onward (6) in the "pool. Let there be given unto me vessels of milk, "together with cakes, and loaves of bread, and cups of "drink, and flesh (7) in the Temple of Ȧnpu."

RUBRIC: If he (*i.e.*, the deceased) knoweth this chapter, he shall go into, after coming forth from, the underworld of the [beautiful Ȧmentet].

[1] *I.e.*, Isis and Nephthys.

CHAPTER LIX.

[From the Papyrus of Ani (Brit. Mus. No. 10,470, sheet 16).]

Vignette: Ani kneeling beside a pool of water, wherein grows a sycamore tree; in the tree appears the goddess Nut pouring out water for him from a vessel with the left hand, and giving him cakes with the right.

Text: (1) THE CHAPTER OF SNUFFING THE AIR, AND OF HAVING DOMINION OVER THE WATER IN THE UNDERWORLD. Osiris Ani saith:—

"Hail, thou sycamore tree of the goddess Nut! "Grant thou to me of [the water and of] the (2) air "which dwell in thee. I embrace the throne which is "in Unnu (Hermopolis), and I watch and guard (3) the "Egg of Neḳeḳ-ur (*i.e.*, the Great Cackler). It groweth, "I grow; it liveth, I live; (4) it snuffeth the air, I "snuff the air, I the Osiris Ani, in triumph."

CHAPTER LX.

[From Lepsius, *Todtenbuch*, Bl. 23.]

Vignette: The deceased holding in his left hand a lotus flower. In the Turin Papyrus the deceased holds a sail, symbolic of air.

Text: (1) ANOTHER CHAPTER. Osiris Áuf-ānkh, triumphant, saith :—

"Let the gates of heaven be opened for me by the "god [Thoth] and by Ḥāpi, and let me pass through "the doors of Ta-qebḥ[1] into the great heaven," or (as others say), "at the time," (2) [or (as others say)], "with the strength (?) of Rā. Grant ye, [O Thoth and "Ḥāpi,] that I may have power over the water, even as "Set had power over (3) his enemies on the day when "there were storms and rain upon the earth. Let me "have power over the divine beings who have (4) "mighty arms in their shoulders, even as the god who

[1] *I.e.*, the "land of cold and refreshing water."

"is apparelled in splendour and whose name is unknown
"had power over them; and may I have power over
"the beings whose arms are mighty."

CHAPTER LXI.

[From the Papyrus of Ani (Brit. Mus. No. 10,470, sheet 15).]

Vignette: The scribe Ani, clothed in white, clasping to his breast his soul, which is in the form of a human-headed hawk.

Text: (1) THE CHAPTER OF NOT LETTING THE SOUL OF A MAN BE TAKEN FROM HIM IN THE UNDERWORLD. Osiris, the scribe, Ani, saith:—

"I, even I, am he (2) who came forth from the water-
"flood which I make to overflow, and which becometh
"mighty as the river [Nile]."

CHAPTER LXII.

[From the Papyrus of Nebseni (Brit. Mus. No. 9900, sheet 4).]

Vignette: The deceased scooping up running water out of a stream into his mouth with both hands.

Text: (1) THE CHAPTER OF DRINKING WATER IN THE UNDERWORLD. (2) The scribe Nebseni .... saith:— (3)

"May be opened [to me] the mighty flood by Osiris, "and may the abyss of water be opened [to me] by "Teḥuti-Ḥāpi, (4) the lord of the horizon, in my name "of 'Opener.' May there be granted [to me] mastery "over the water-courses as over the members (5) of Set. "I go forth into heaven. I am the Lion-god Rā. I "am the Bull. (6) [I] have eaten the thigh, and I "have divided the carcase. I have gone round about "among the islands (*or* lakes) of Sekhet-(7)Åaru.[1] "Indefinite time, without beginning and without end, "hath been given to me; I inherit eternity, and ever-"lastingness hath been bestowed upon me."

[1] *I.e.*, a portion of the Elysian Fields (see Chapter CX.).

The last three Chapters, with a single vignette, are grouped in one in the Papyrus of Nefer-uben-f (see Naville, *op. cit.*, Bd. I. Bl. 72); but the order of them, as there given is 61, 60, 62. In the Turin Papyrus (Lepsius, *op. cit.*, Bl. 23) the vignette of each is the same, *i.e.*, the deceased holding a sail in his left hand.

CHAPTER LXIII.A.

[From the Papyrus of Nu (Brit. Mus. No. 10,477, sheet 7).]

Vignette: **The deceased drinking water from a running stream, or the deceased kneeling by the side of a pool of water and receiving water in a bowl, which he holds in his right hand, from a vessel which the goddess of the sycamore tree (Hathor) is emptying into it. In the Turin Papyrus (Lepsius, *op. cit.*, Bl. 23) the deceased is pouring out water from two vessels before the symbol of flame.**

Text: (1) THE CHAPTER OF DRINKING WATER AND OF NOT BEING BURNT (2) BY FIRE [IN THE UNDER-

WORLD. The overseer of the house of the overseer of the seal, Nu, triumphant, saith:—

"Hail, Bull of Åmentet! I am brought unto thee, "I am the oar of Rā (3) wherewith he ferried over the "divine aged ones; let me neither be burnt up nor "destroyed by fire. I am Bet,[1] the first-born son of "Osiris, who doth meet every god (4) within the temple "of his Eye in Ȧnnu. I am the divine Heir, the "exalted one (?), the Mighty One, the Resting One. I "have made my name to germinate, (5) I have delivered "[it], and thou shalt live through me day by day."

CHAPTER LXIIIB.

[From the Papyrus of Nu (Brit. Mus. No. 10,477, sheet 12).]

Vignette: The deceased standing before two symbols of fire, or the deceased sitting before a table of offerings and smelling a flower (Naville, *op. cit.*, Bd. I. Bl. 74).

[1] A better reading is Beb, .

Text: (1) THE CHAPTER OF NOT BEING SCALDED WITH WATER. The overseer of the palace, the overseer of the house of the overseer of the seal, Nu, triumphant, saith:—

"I am the oar made ready for rowing, (2) where-"with Rā transported the boat containing the divine "ancestors, and lifted up the moist emanations of Osiris "from the Lake of Fire, (3) and he was not burned. I "lie down like a divine Spirit, [and like] Khnemu who "dwelleth among lions. Come, break away (4) the "restraints from him that passeth by the side of this "path, and let me come forth by it."

CHAPTER LXIV.

The LXIVth Chapter is probably one of the oldest of all in the Book of the Dead, and two versions of it seem to have existed in the earliest times. The longer version is called the "Chapter of coming forth by day in the underworld," and the shorter the "Chapter of knowing the 'Chapters of coming forth by day' in a single Chapter." On a coffin of the XIth dynasty both versions occur. The rubric of one version says that it was discovered in the reign of Ḥesep-ti, *i.e.*, about B.C. 4266, while the rubric of the other attributes its discovery to the time of Menthu-ḥetep, which is clearly a mistake for Men-kau-Rā (Mycerinus). Thus in the XIth dynasty it was believed that the Chapter might even be as ancient as the time of the Ist dynasty. There is little doubt that the Chapter was looked upon as an abridgment of all the "Chapters of coming forth by day," and that it had a value which was equivalent to them all.

[From the Papyrus of Nebseni (Brit. Mus. No. 9900, sheets 23 and 24).]

Vignette : The deceased adoring the sun's disk, which rises above the top of a tree.

Text : (1) THE CHAPTER OF COMING FORTH BY DAY IN THE UNDERWORLD. Nebseni, the lord of reverence, saith :— (2)

"I am Yesterday, To-day, and To-morrow, [and I "have] the power (3) to be born a second time; [I am] "the divine hidden Soul who createth the gods, and "who giveth celestial meals unto the denizens of the "Ṭuat (underworld), Åmentet, and heaven. [I am] the "Rudder (4) of the East, the Possessor of two Divine

"Faces wherein his beams are seen. I am the Lord of "the men who are raised up; [the Lord] who cometh "forth from out of the darkness, and (5) whose forms "of existence are of the house wherein are the dead. "Hail, ye two Hawks who are perched upon your rest-"ing-places, who hearken unto (6) the things which are "said by him, who guide the bier to the hidden place, "who lead along Rā, and (7) who follow [him] into the "uppermost place of the shrine which is in the celestial "heights! [Hail,] Lord of the Shrine which standeth "in the middle of the earth. (8) He is I, and I am "he, and Ptaḥ hath covered his sky with crystal. "[Hail] Rā, thou who art content, thy heart (9) is "glad by reason of thy beautiful law of the day; thou "enterest in by Khemennu (?) and comest forth at the "east, and the divine (10) first-born beings who are in "[thy] presence cry out with gladness [unto thee]. "Make thou thy roads glad for me, and make broad for "me thy paths (11) when I shall set out from earth for "the life in the celestial regions. Send forth thy light "upon me, O Soul unknown, for I am [one] of those "who are about to enter in, and the divine speech is in "(12) [my] ears in the Ṭuat (underworld), and let no "defects of my mother be [imputed] unto me; let me "be delivered and let me be safe from (13) him whose "divine eyes sleep at eventide, when [he] gathereth "together and finisheth [the day] in night. I flood "[the land] with water and 'Qem-ur'[1] is (14) my name

[1] A name of Osiris.

"and the garment wherewith I am clothed is complete. "Hail, thou divine prince Åti-she-f,[1] cry out unto those "divine beings who dwell in their hair at the (15) "season when the god is [lifted upon] the shoulder, "saying: 'Come thou who [dwellest] above thy divine "abyss of water, for verily (16) the thigh [of the sacri-"fice] is tied to the neck, and the buttocks are [laid] "upon the head of Åmentet.' May the Ur-urti[2] god-"desses grant [such] gifts unto me when my tears start "from me as I see myself (17) journeying at the divine "festival of Ṭenȧ in Abydos, and the wooden fastenings "which fasten the four doors above thee are in thy "power (18) within thy garment. Thy face is like that "of a greyhound which scenteth with his nose the place "whither I go on my feet. The god (19) Åḳau[3] tran-"sporteth me to the chamber (?), and [my] nurse is the "divine double Lion-god himself. I am made strong "and I (20) come forth like him that forceth a way "through the gate, and the radiance which my heart "hath made is enduring; 'I know the abysses' is thy "name. I work for you, (21) O ye Spirits—four millions, "six hundred thousand, one thousand and two hundred "are they—concerning the things which are there. [I "am] over their affairs working (22) for hours and days "in setting straight the shoulders of the twelve Saḥ "gods, (23) and joining the hands of their company, "each to each; the sixth who is at the head of the

[1] *I.e.*, the "Boundless." [2] *I.e.*, Isis and Nephthys.
[3] A name of Anubis.

"abyss is the hour of the defeat of the Fiends. [I] "have come (24) there in triumph, and [I am] he who "is in the halls (*or* courtyards) of the underworld, and "I am he who is laid under tribute to (25) Shu. I rise "as the Lord of Life through the beautiful law of this "day, and it is their blood and the cool water of [their] "slaughter (26) which make the union of the earth to "blossom. I make a way among the horns of all those "who make themselves strong against me, and [among] "those who in secret (27) make themselves adversaries "unto me, and who are upon their bellies. I have "come as the envoy of my Lord (28) of lords to give "counsel [concerning] Osiris; the eye shall not absorb[1] "its tears. I am the divine envoy (?) of (29) the house "of him that dwelleth in his possessions, and I have "come from Sekhem to Ȧnnu[2] to make known to the "*Bennu* bird therein concerning the events of (30) the "Ṭuat (underworld). Hail, thou Ȧuḳert, (*i.e.*, under-"world) which hidest thy companion who is in thee, "thou creator of forms of existence like the god "Kheperȧ, grant thou that (31) Nebseni, the scribe and "designer to the temples of the South and of the North, "may come forth (32) to see the Disk, and that his "journeyings forth (?) may be in the presence of the "great god, that is to say, Shu, who dwelleth in ever-"lastingness. Let me journey on in peace; (33) let

[1] Literally, "eat."

[2] *I.e.*, I have come from Letopolis to Heliopolis; the *Bennu* bird in the latter city is, of course, Osiris (See Chapter XVII., line 25).

"me pass over the sky; let me adore the radiance of "the splendour [which is in] my sight; let me soar like "a bird to see (34) the companies (?) of the Spirits in "the presence of Rā day by day, who vivifieth every "human being (35) that walketh upon the regions "which are upon the earth. Hail, Hemti (*i.e.*, Runner), "hail, Hemti, who carriest away the shades of the "dead (36) and the Spirits from earth, grant thou unto "me a prosperous way to the Tuat (underworld), such "as is made for the favoured ones [of the god], "because (37) [I am] helpless to gather together the "emanations which come from me. Who art thou, "then, who consumest in its hidden place? (38) I am "the Chief in Re-stau, and 'He that goeth in in his "own name and cometh forth in that of Ḥeḥi (?), the "lord of millions of years, and of the earth,' is my "name. The pregnant goddess hath (39) deposited "[upon the earth] her load, and hath given birth to "Ḥit straightway; the closed door which is by the "wall is overthrown, (40) it is turned upside down and "I rejoice thereat. To the Mighty One hath his eye "been given, and it sendeth forth light from his face "when the earth becometh light (*or* at day-break). I "shall not become corrupt (41), but I shall come into "being in the form of the Lion-god and like the "blossoms of Shu;[1] I am the being who is never over-"whelmed in the waters. Happy, yea happy is he that

[1] The blossoms of Shu are the sun's rays.

"looked upon the funeral couch which hath come to its "place of rest, upon the happy day (42) of the god "whose heart resteth, who maketh his place of alight-"ing [thereon]. I am he who cometh forth by day; "the lord of the bier which giveth life in the presence "of Osiris. (43) In very truth the things which are "thine are stable each day, O scribe, artist, child of the "*Sesheț* chamber, Nebseni, lord of veneration. I clasp "the Sycamore tree, (44) I myself am joined unto the "Sycamore tree, and its arm[s] are opened unto me "graciously. I have come and I have clasped the "*Utchat*,[1] (45) and I have caused it to be seated in peace "upon its throne. I have come to see Rā when he "setteth, and I absorb into myself the winds [which "arise] (46) when he cometh forth, and both my hands "are clean to adore him. I have gathered together "[all my members], I have gathered together [all "my members]. I soar like a bird (47) and I descend "upon the earth, and mine eye maketh me to walk "thereon in my footsteps. I am the child of yesterday, "and the Akeru[2] (48) gods of the earth have made me "to come into being, and they have made me strong for "my moment [of coming forth]. I hide with the god "Āḥa-āāiu[3] who will walk (49) behind me, and my "members shall germinate, and my *khu* shall be as an "amulet for my body and as one who watcheth [to pro-

[1] *I.e.*, the Eye of Rā or Horus which was attacked by Set.
[2] *I.e.*, the two lion-gods who watch, one at each end, the path of the night sun.
[3] *I.e.*, "he who fights with both hands."

"tect] my soul (50) and to defend it and to converse "therewith; and the company of the gods shall hearken "unto my words."

RUBRIC: If this chapter be known [by the deceased] he shall be victorious both upon earth and in (51) the underworld. He shall do whatsoever a man doeth who is upon the earth, and he shall perform all the deeds which those do who are [alive]. Now it is a great protection [given] by the god. This chapter was found (52) in the city of Khemennu inscribed in letters of lapis-lazuli upon the block of iron which was under the feet of this god.

In the Rubric to this Chapter as found in the Papyrus of Mes-em-neter, the Chapter is said to have been "dis-"covered in the foundations of the shrine of the divine "Ḥennu[1] boat by the chief mason in the time of the "king of the North and of the South, Semti (or "Ḥesepti[2]), triumphant," and it is there directed that it "shall be recited by one who is ceremonially pure "and clean, and who hath not touched women, and who "hath not eaten flesh of animals or fish."

[1] See the note to Chapter I., p. 43.

[2] A king of the Ist dynasty. See also the rubric to the longer version of the 64th from the Papyrus of Nu, *infra*, p. 221.

CHAPTER LXIV. (Short Version).

[From the Papyrus of Nu (Brit. Mus. No. 10,477, sheet 13).]

Vignette: In the Papyrus of Nu this Chapter has no vignette.

Text: (1) The Chapter of knowing the "Chapters of coming forth by day" in a (2) single Chapter. The overseer of the house of the overseer of the seal, Osiris Nu, triumphant, begotten of the overseer of the house, Ȧmen-ḥetep, triumphant, saith:—

"I am Yesterday and To-day; and I have the power "to be born a second time. [I am] the divine hidden "(3) Soul, who createth the gods, and who giveth "celestial meals to the divine hidden beings [in the "Ṭuat (underworld)], in Ȧmenti, and in heaven. [I am] "the Rudder of the East, the Possessor of two Divine "Faces wherein his beams are seen. (4) I am the "Lord of those who are raised up from the dead, [the "Lord] who cometh forth from out of the darkness. "[Hail,] ye two divine Hawks who are perched upon "your resting-places, and who hearken unto the (5) "things which are said by him, the thigh [of the sacri-"fice] is tied to the neck, and the buttocks [are laid] upon "the head of Ȧmentet. May the Ur-urti[1] (6) goddesses "grant such gifts unto me when my tears start from me

[1] *I.e.*, Isis and Nephthys.

"as I look on. 'I know the abysses' is thy name. [I] "work for [you], O ye (7) Spirits, who are in number "[four] millions, [six] hundred and one thousand, and "two hundred, and they are [in height] twelve cubits. "[Ye] travel on joining the hands, each to each, but "the sixth [hour], (8) which belongeth at the head of "the Ṭuat (underworld), is the hour of the overthrow "of the Fiend. [I] have come there in triumph, and "[I am] he who is in the hall (*or* courtyard) of the "Ṭuat; (9) and the seven (?) come in his manifesta-"tions. The strength which protecteth me is that "which hath my Spirit under its protection, [that is] "the blood, and the cool water, and the slaughterings "which abound (?). I open [a way among] (10) the "horns of all those who would do harm unto me, who "keep themselves hidden, who make themselves adver-"saries unto me, and those who are upon (11) their "bellies. The Eye shall not eat (*or* absorb) the tears "of the goddess Åuḳert.[1] Hail, goddess Åuḳert, open "thou unto me the enclosed place, and (12) grant thou "unto me pleasant roads whereupon I may travel. "Who art thou, then, who consumest in the hidden "places? I am the chief in Re-stau, and [I] go in and "come forth (13) in my name of 'Ḥeḥi, the lord of "millions of years [and of] the earth'; [I am] the "maker of my name. The pregnant one hath deposited "[upon the earth] her load. The door by the wall is

[1] A name of the underworld.

"shut fast, and the (14) things of terror are overturned "and thrown down upon the backbone (?) of the *Bennu*[1] "bird by the two *Samait* goddesses.[2] To the Mighty "One hath his Eye been given, and his face emitteth "light when [he] (15) illumineth the earth, [my name "is his name].[3] I shall not become corrupt, but I "shall come into being in the form of the Lion-god; "the blossoms of Shu[4] shall be in me. I am he who "is never overwhelmed in the waters. Happy, yea "happy, is the funeral couch of the (16) Still-heart; he "maketh himself to alight upon the pool (?), and verily "he cometh forth [therefrom]. I am the lord of my "life. I have come to this [place], and I have come "forth from Re-āā-urt (17) the city of Osiris. Verily "the things which are thine are with the *Suriu* deities. "I have clasped the Sycamore tree and I have divided (?) "it (18); I have opened a way for myself [among] the "*Sekhiu* gods of the Ṭuat. I have come to see him "that dwelleth in his divine uraeus, face to face and "eye to (19) eye, and [I] draw to myself the winds "[which rise] when he cometh forth. My two eyes (?) "are weak in my face, O Lion[-god], Babe, who dwellest "in Utent. (20) Thou art in me and I am in thee; "and thy attributes are my attributes. I am the god "of the Inundation (*Bāḥ*), and 'Qem-ur-she' (21) is "my name. My forms are the forms of the god

[1] *I.e.*, Osiris. [2] *I.e.*, Isis and Nephthys.
[3] These words are added from the Papyrus of Nebseni.
[4] *I.e.*, the beams of the Sun-god.

"Ḳheperȧ, the hair of the earth of Tem, the hair of the "earth of Tem. (22) I have entered in as a man of no "understanding, and I shall come forth in the form of "a strong Spirit, and I shall look upon my form which "shall be that of men and women for ever and for ever."

RUBRIC[1]: I. [If this chapter be known] by a man he shall come forth by day, (23) and he shall not be repulsed at any gate of the Ṭuat (underworld), either in going in or in coming out. He shall perform [all] the transformations which his heart shall desire for him and he shall not die; (24) behold, the soul of [this] man shall flourish. And moreover, if [he] know this chapter he shall be victorious upon earth and in the underworld, and he shall perform every act of a living (25) human being. Now it is a great protection which [hath been given] by the god. This chapter was found in the foundations of the shrine of Ḥennu[2] by the chief mason during the reign of His Majesty, the King of the North and of the South, Semti (or Ḥesepti[3]), triumphant, who carried [it] away as a mysterious object which had never [before] been seen or looked upon. This chapter shall be recited by a man who is ceremonially clean and pure, who hath not eaten the flesh of animals or fish, and who hath not had intercourse with women.

RUBRIC[4]: II. (1) If this chapter be known [by the deceased] he shall be victorious both upon earth and in the underworld, and he shall perform every act of a living human (2) being. Now it is a great protection which [hath been given] by the god.

This chapter was found in the city of Khemennu upon a block of iron of the south, which had been inlaid [with letters] (3) of real lapis-lazuli, under the feet of the god during the reign of His Majesty, the King of the North and of the South, Men-kau-Rā (Mycerinus), triumphant,[5] by the royal son

[1] From the Papyrus of Nu, sheet 13.
[2] A name of Osiris.
[3] See above, p. 210.
[4] From the Papyrus of Nu, sheet 21.
[5] The builder of the third pyramid at Gîzeh.

Ḥeru-ṭā-ṭā-f,[1] triumphant; he found it (4) when he was journeying about to make an inspection of the temples. One Nekht (?) was with him who was diligent in making him to understand (?) it, and he brought it (5) to the king as a wonderful object when he saw that it was a thing of great mystery, which had never [before] been seen or looked upon.

This chapter (6) shall be recited by a man who is ceremonially clean and pure, who hath not eaten the flesh of animals or fish, and who hath not had intercourse with women. And behold, thou shalt make a scarab of green stone, with (7) a rim plated (?) with gold, which shall be placed in the heart of a man, and it shall perform for him the "opening of the mouth."[2] And thou shalt anoint it with *ānti* unguent, and thou shalt recite over it [these] enchantments:—[3]

[1] He was the son of Cheops, the builder of the Great Pyramid at Gîzeh.
[2] See Chapter XXIII.
[3] Here follows the text of Chapter XXXB. (see p. 149).

CHAPTER LXVA.

[From the Papyrus of Nu (Brit. Mus. No. 10,477, sheet 15).]

Vignette: The deceased kneeling in adoration before Râ, hawk-headed, and having a disk encircled by an uraeus on his head (see Naville, *op. cit.*, Bd. I. Bl. 77).

Text: (1) THE CHAPTER OF COMING FORTH BY DAY AND OF GAINING THE MASTERY OVER ENEMIES. The overseer of the house of the overseer of the seal, Nu, saith :— (2)

"Râ sitteth in his habitation of millions of years, "and he hath gathered together the company of the "gods, with those divine beings, whose faces are hidden, "who dwell in the Temple of Kheperȧ, who eat (3) the "god Bāḥ[1] and who drink the drink-offerings which "are brought into the celestial regions of light; and "conversely. Grant that I may take possession of the "captives (4) of Osiris, and never let me have my being "among the fiends of Suti! Hail, let me sit upon his "folds in the habitation of the god User-ba.[2] (5) "Grant thou that I may sit upon the throne of Rā, and "let me have possession of my body before the god Seb. "Grant thou that Osiris may come forth triumphant "over Suti [and over] the night-watchers (6) of Suti, "and over the night-watchers of the Crocodile, yea the "night-watchers of the Crocodile, whose faces are "hidden and who dwell in the divine Temple of the "King of the North in the apparel of the gods on the "sixth day of the festival, (7) whose snares are like "unto everlastingness and whose cords are like unto "eternity. I have seen the god Ȧbet-ka placing the "cord; the child is tied with (8) fetters, and the rope of "the god Ȧb-ka is drawn tight (?) . . . . . Behold me "I am born, and I come forth in the form of a living "*Khu*, (9) and the human beings who are upon the "earth ascribe praise [unto me]. Hail, Mer, who doest "these things for me, and who art put an end to by the "vigour of Rā, grant thou that I may see Rā; (10) "grant thou that I may come forth against my enemies; "and grant thou that I may be victorious over them in

[1] *I.e.*, "the Inundation of the Nile."
[2] *I.e.*, "he of the strong soul."

"the presence of the sovereign princes of the great god "who are in the presence of the great god. If, repuls "ing [me], thou dost not (11) allow me to come forth "against my Enemy and to be victorious over him "before the sovereign princes, then may Ḥāpi—who "liveth upon law and order—not come forth into "heaven—now he liveth by Maāt—(12) and may Rā— "who feedeth upon fish—not descend into the waters! "And then, verily shall Rā—who feedeth upon law "and order—come forth into heaven, and then, verily, "(13) shall Ḥāpi—who feedeth upon fish—descend "into the waters; and then, verily, the great day "upon the earth shall not be in its season. I have "come against my Enemy, (14) he hath been given "unto me, he hath come to an end, and I have gotten "possession [of him] before the sovereign princes."

CHAPTER LXV B.

[From Lepsius, *Todtenbuch*, Bl. 25.]

Vignette: The deceased standing up and holding a staff in his left hand.

Text: (1) THE CHAPTER OF COMING FORTH BY DAY AND OF GAINING THE MASTERY OVER ENEMIES.

"Hail, [thou] who shinest from the Moon and who "sendest forth light therefrom, thou comest forth "among thy multitudes, and thou goest round about, "let me rise," or (as others say), "let me be brought in "among the Spirits, and let the underworld be opened "[unto me]. (2) Behold, I have come forth on this "day, and I have become a *Khu* (*or* a shining being);

"therefore shall the *Khus* let me live, and they shall "cause my enemies to be brought to me in a state of "misery in the presence of the divine sovereign princes. "The divine *ka* (double) of my mother (3) shall rest in "peace because of this, and I shall stand upon my feet "and have a staff of gold," or (as others say), "a rod "of gold in my hand, wherewith I shall inflict cuts on "the limbs [of mine enemy] and shall live. The legs "of Sothis are stablished, and I am born in their state "of rest."

CHAPTER LXVI.

[From the Papyrus of Amen-em-ḥeb (Naville, *op. cit.*, Bd. I. Bl. 78).]

Vignette: In the only papyrus of the Theban period known to contain this Chapter it has no vignette. In the Turin Papyrus the vignette is the same as that of Chapter LXV.

Text: (1) THE CHAPTER OF COMING FORTH BY DAY. The scribe Māḥu saith:—

"I have knowledge. I was conceived by (2) the "goddess Sekhet, and the goddess Neith gave birth to "me. I am Horus, and [I have] (3) come forth from the "Eye of Horus. I am Uatchit who came forth from "Horus. I am Horus and I fly up (4) and perch "myself upon the forehead of Rā in the bows of his "boat which is in heaven."

CHAPTER LXVII.

[From the Papyrus of Nu (Brit. Mus. No. 10,477, sheet 15).]

Vignette: This Chapter is without a vignette in the Theban Recension, but in the Turin Papyrus the vignette is the same as that of Chapters LXV. and LXVI.

Text: (1) THE CHAPTER OF OPENING THE UNDERWORLD. The overseer of the house of the overseer of the seal, Nu, triumphant, saith:— (2)

"The chamber of those who dwell in Nu is opened, "and the footsteps of those who dwell with the god of "Light are set free. The chamber of Shu is opened, "and he cometh forth; and I shall come forth (3) "outside, and I shall advance from my territory(?), I "shall receive . . . . . and I shall lay firm hold upon "the tribute in the House of the Chief of his dead. "(4) I shall advance to my throne which is in the boat "of Rā. I shall not be molested, and I shall not suffer "shipwreck from my throne which is in the boat of Rā, "(5) the mighty one. Hail, thou that shinest and "givest light from Ḥent-she!"

CHAPTER LXVIII.

[From the Papyrus of Nu (Brit. Mus. No. 10,477, sheet 7).]

Vignette : The deceased kneeling before the goddess Hathor seated by a tree (see Naville, *op. cit.*, Bd. I. Bl. 80), or the deceased standing before a table of offerings and adoring a goddess who stands in a shrine (see Lepsius, *Todtenbuch*, Bl. 25).

Text : (1) THE CHAPTER OF COMING FORTH (2) BY DAY. The overseer of the house of the overseer of the seal, Nu, triumphant, saith :—

"The doors of heaven are opened for me, the doors "of earth are opened for me, the bars and bolts of Seb "are opened for me, (3) and the first temple hath been "unfastened for me by the god Petrá. Behold, I was "guarded and watched, [but now] I am released; "behold, his hand had tied cords round me and his "hand had darted upon me (4) in the earth. Re-ḥent[1] "hath been been opened for me and Re-ḥent hath been

[1] *I.e.*, the entrance to one of the great celestial canals.

"unfastened before me, Re-ḥent hath been given unto "me, and I shall come forth by day into whatsoever "place I please. I have gained the mastery over my "heart; (5) I have gained the mastery over my "breast (?); I have gained the mastery over my two "hands; I have gained the mastery over my two "feet; I have gained the mastery over my mouth; "I have gained (6) the mastery over my whole body; "I have gained the mastery over sepulchral offerings; "I have gained the mastery over the waters; I have "gained the mastery over the air; I have gained the "mastery (7) over the canal; I have gained the "mastery over the river and over the land; I have "gained the mastery over the furrows; I have gained "the mastery over the male workers for me; (8) I have "gained the mastery over the female workers for me in "the underworld; I have gained the mastery over [all] "the things which were ordered to be done for me "upon the earth, according to the entreaty which ye "spake for me (9) [saying], 'Behold, let him live upon "the bread of Seb.' That which is an abomination "unto me, I shall not eat, [nay] I shall live upon "cakes [made] of white grain, and my ale shall be "[made] of the red grain (10) of Ḥāpi.[1] In a clean "place shall I sit on the ground beneath the foliage of "the date palm of the goddess Hathor, who dwelleth in "the spacious Disk (11) as it advanceth to Ȧnnu

[1] *I.e.*, the Nile.

"(Heliopolis), having the books of the divine words "of the writings of the god Thoth. I have gained the "mastery over my heart; I have gained the mastery "over my heart's place (*or* breast) (12); I have gained "the mastery over my mouth; I have gained the "mastery over my two hands; I have gained the "mastery over the waters; I have gained the mastery "over the canal; I have gained the mastery over (13) "the river; I have gained the mastery over the "furrows; I have gained the mastery over the men "who work for me; I have gained the mastery over "the women who work (14) for me in the underworld; "I have gained the mastery over [all] the things which "were ordered to be done for me upon earth and in the "underworld. I shall lift myself up on my left side, "and I shall place myself on my right side; (15) I "shall lift myself up on my right side, and I shall "place myself [on my left side]. I shall sit down, I "shall stand up, and I shall place myself in [the path "of] the wind (16) like a guide who is well prepared."

RUBRIC: If this composition be known [by the deceased] he shall come forth by day, and he shall be in a position to journey about over the earth among the living, and he shall never suffer diminution, (17) never, never.

CHAPTER LXIX.

[From the Papyrus of Mes-em-neter (Naville, *op. cit.*, Bd. I. Bl. 81).]

Vignette: **This Chapter is without a vignette both in the Theban and Saïte Recensions of the Book of the Dead.**

Text: (1) ANOTHER (2) CHAPTER.

"I am the Fire-god, the divine brother of the Fire-"god, and [I am] Osiris the brother of Isis. My divine "son, together with his mother Isis, hath avenged me "on mine enemies. (3) My enemies have wrought "every [kind of] evil, therefore their arms, and hands, "and feet, have been fettered by reason of their wicked-"ness which they have wrought (4) upon me. I am "Osiris, the first-born of the divine womb, the first-"born of the gods, and the heir of my father Osiris-"Seb (?). I am Osiris, the lord of the heads (5) that "live, mighty of breast and powerful of back, with a "phallus which goeth to the remotest limits [where] "men and women [live]. I am Saḥ (Orion) who "travelleth over his domain and who journeyeth along "before (6) the stars of heaven, [which is] the belly of "my mother Nut; she conceived me through her love, "and she gave birth to me because it was her will so to "do. I am (7) Ánpu (Anubis) on the day of the god "Sepa.[1] I am the Bull at the head of the meadow. I,

[1] A name of Osiris.

"even I, am Osiris who imprisoned his father together "with his mother (8) on the day of making the great "slaughter; now, [his] father is Seb, and [his] mother "is Nut. I am Horus, the first-born of Rā of the "risings. I am Ȧnpu (Anubis) [on the day of] (9) "the god Sepa. I, even I, am the lord Tem. I am "Osiris. Hail, thou divine first-born, who dost enter "and dost speak before the divine Scribe and Door-"keeper of Osiris, grant that (10) I may come. I have "become a spirit, I have been judged, I have become a "divine being, I have come, and I have avenged mine "own body. I have taken up my seat by the divine "birth-chamber (11) of Osiris, and I have destroyed "the sickness and suffering which were there. I have "become mighty, and I have become a divine being "by the side of the birth-chamber of Osiris, I am "brought forth with him, I renew my youth, (12) I "renew my youth, I take possession of my two thighs "which are in the place where is Osiris, and I open "the mouth of the gods therewith, I take my seat by "his side, and Thoth cometh forth, (13) and [I am] "strengthened in heart with thousands of cakes upon "the altars (14) of my divine father, and with my "beasts, and with my cattle, and with my red feathered "fowl, (15) and with my oxen, and with my geese, and "with my ducks, for Horus my Chieftain, and with the "offerings which I make to Thoth, and with the sacri-"fices which I offer up to Ȧn-ḥeri-ertitsa."

CHAPTER LXX.

[From the Papyrus of Mes-em-neter (Naville, *op. cit.*, Bd. I. Bl. 82).]

Vignette: This Chapter is without a vignette both in the Theban and Saïte Recensions of the Book of the Dead.

Text: (1) ANOTHER CHAPTER.

"I have sacrificed unto Àn-ḥeri-ertitsa, and I am "decreed to be strengthened in heart, for I have made "offerings at the altars of my divine father (2) Osiris; "I rule in Ṭaṭṭu and I lift myself up over his land. "I sniff the wind of the east by its hair; I lay hold "upon the north wind by its (3) hair; I seize and hold "fast to the west wind by its body, and I go round "about heaven on its four sides; I lay hold upon the "south wind by (4) its eye, and I bestow air upon the "venerable beings [who are in the underworld] along "with the eating of cakes."

RUBRIC: If this composition be known [by the deceased] (5) upon earth he shall come forth by day, and he shall have the faculty of travelling about among the living, and his name shall never perish.

CHAPTER LXXI.

[From the Papyrus of Nebseni (Brit. Mus. No. 9900, sheet 16).]

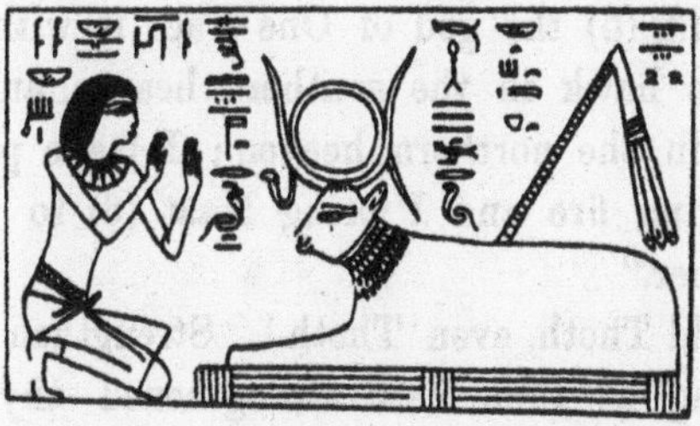

Vignette : The deceased kneeling, with both hands raised in adoration, before the goddess Meḥ-urt; the legend reads: "the homage of the scribe Nebseni to the goddess Meḥ-urt, lady of heaven, and mistress of earth." Elsewhere (Naville, *op. cit.*, Bd. I. Bl. 83) the deceased is seen adoring Rā alone, or Rā in the presence of Thoth and Osiris.

Text : (1) THE CHAPTER OF COMING FORTH BY DAY. The libationer, the lord of reverence, Nebseni, saith:—

"Hail, thou hawk who risest in heaven, thou lord of "the goddess Meḥ-urt! (2) Strengthen thou me ac-"cording as thou hast strengthened thyself, and show "thyself upon the earth, O thou that returnest and "withdrawest thyself, and let thy will be done."

"Behold the god of One Face (3) is with me. [I "am] the hawk which is within the shrine; and I open "that which is upon the hangings thereof. Behold "Horus, the son of Isis."

"[Behold] Horus the son of Isis! (4) Strengthen "thou me, according as thou hast strengthened thyself, "and show thyself upon earth, O thou that returnest "and withdrawest thyself, and let thy will be done."

"Behold, (5) the god of One Face is with me. [I "am] the hawk in the southern heaven, and [I am] "Thoth in the northern heaven; I make peace with "the raging fire and I bring Maāt (6) to him that "loveth her."

"Behold Thoth, even Thoth! Strengthen thou me "according as thou hast strengthened thyself, and "shew thyself upon earth, O thou that returnest and "(7) withdrawest thyself, and let thy will be done."

"Behold the god of One Face is with me. I am the "Plant (8) of the region where nothing sprouteth, and "the blossom of the hidden horizon."

"Behold Osiris, yea Osiris! Strengthen thou me "according as thou hast strengthened thyself, (9) and "show thyself upon earth, O thou that returnest and "withdrawest thyself, and let thy will be done."

"Behold, the god of One Face (10) is with me. "Hail, thou who [standest] upon thy legs, in thine "hour," or (as others say), "Hail, thou who art "victorious upon thy legs, in thine (11) hour, thou "lord of the divine Twin-gods,[1] who livest [in] the

[1] *I.e.*, the souls of Horus and Rā; see Chapter XVII., l. 110 ff.

"divine Twin-gods, strengthen thou me according as "thou hast strengthened thyself, and (12) show thyself "upon earth, O thou that returnest and withdrawest "thyself, and let thy will be done."

"Behold, the god of One Face is with me. (13) "Hail, thou Nekhen who art in thine egg, thou lord "of the goddess Meḥ-urt, strengthen thou me accord- "ing as thou hast strengthened thyself, (14) and show "thyself upon earth, O thou that returnest and with- "drawest thyself, and let thy will be done."

"Behold, the god of One Face is with (15) me. "The god Sebek hath stood up within his ground, "and the goddess Neith hath stood up within her "plantation, O thou that returnest and withdrawest "(16) thyself, show thyself upon earth and let thy "will be done."

"Behold, the god of One Face is with me. Hail, ye "Seven Beings[1] who make decrees, who (17) support "the Scales on the night of the judgment of the "*Utchat*, who cut off heads, who hack necks in "pieces, who take possession of hearts by violence "and rend the places (18) where hearts are fixed, "who make slaughterings in the Lake of Fire, I "know you and I know your names, therefore know "ye me even as (19) I know your names. I come "forth to you, therefore come ye forth to me, for ye

[1] These are the seven Spirits whose names are given in Chapter XVII., line 103 ff.; they are related in some way to the goddess Meḥ-urt, who is identified with the Eye of Rā, and some would see in them the Seven Stars of the constellation of the Great Bear.

"live in me and I would live in you. Make ye me to "be vigorous by means of that which is in your hands, "that is to say, by the rod of power which is (20) in "your hands. Decree ye for me life by [your] speech "year by year; give me multitudes of years over and "above my years of life, and multitudes of months over "and above my months (21) of life, and multitudes of "days over and above my days of life, and multitudes "of nights over and above my nights of life; and grant "that I may come forth and shine upon my statue; "and [grant me] (22) air for my nose, and let my eyes "have the power to see among those divine beings who "dwell in the horizon on the day when evil-doing and "wrong are justly assessed."

RUBRIC: If this chapter be recited for the deceased he shall be strong upon earth before Rā, and he shall have a comfortable burial (*or* tomb) with Osiris, and it shall be of great benefit to a man in the underworld. Sepulchral bread shall be given unto him, and he shall come forth into the presence [of Rā] day by day, and every day, regularly, and continually.[1]

[1] This Rubric is taken from the Papyrus of Thenna (see Naville, *op. cit.*, Bd. II. p. 153).

CHAPTER LXXII.

[From the Papyrus of Nebseni (Brit. Mus. No. 9900, sheet 3).]

From the Papyrus of Nebseni.

From the Brocklehurst Papyrus.

Vignette : The deceased standing and holding a staff in his left hand; or, the deceased standing before a funeral chest; or, the deceased kneeling in adoration before a ram-headed god; or, the deceased adoring three gods, who either sit on or stand in a shrine.

Text : (1) THE CHAPTER OF COMING FORTH BY DAY AND OF OPENING UP A WAY THROUGH THE ȦMEḤET.[1] Behold the scribe Nebseni, triumphant, who saith :—

"Homage to you, O ye lords of *Kas*, ye who are "without (2) sin and who live for the limitless and "infinite aeons of time which make up eternity, I "have opened up a way for myself to you! I have "become a spirit (3) in my forms, I have gained the "mastery over my enchantments, and I am decreed

[1] A section of the underworld, or of the tomb.

"to be a spirit; (4) therefore deliver ye me from the "crocodile [which liveth in] this country of right "and truth. Grant ye to me my mouth that I may "speak therewith, (5) and cause that my sepulchral "meals be placed in my hands in your presence, for I "know you, and I know (6) your names, and I know "also the name of the mighty god, before whose nose "ye set your celestial food; and his name is 'Tekem.' "(7) [When] he openeth up his path in the eastern "horizon of heaven, and [when] he fluttereth down in "the western horizon of heaven (8), may he carry me "along with him and may I be safe and sound! Let "not the *Mesqet*[1] make an end of me, let not the Fiend "gain the mastery (9) over me, let me not be turned "back at your portals, and (10) let not your doors be "shut in my face, because my cakes are in the city of "Pe and my ale is in (11) the city of Ṭep. And there, "in the celestial mansions of heaven which my divine "father Tem hath stablished, let my hands lay hold "(12) upon the wheat and the barley which shall be "given unto me therein in abundant measure, and may "the son of mine own body make [ready] for me my "food therein. And grant ye unto me therein sepul-"chral meals, and incense, and wax, and all the beau-"tiful and (13) pure things whereon the god liveth, in "very deed for ever in all (14) the transformations "which it pleaseth me [to perform]; and grant me

[1] A place where tortures are inflicted on the enemies of Rā.

"the power to float down and to sail up the stream "in Sekhet-Åarru [and may I reach Sekhet-ḥetep!] "(15) I am the double Lion-god."

RUBRIC[1]: (1) If (2) this chapter be known [by the deceased] upon earth, [or if it be done] in writing upon [his] coffin, he shall come forth by (3) day in all the forms which he is pleased [to take], and he shall enter in to [his] place and shall not be driven back. (4) And cakes, and ale, and joints of meat upon the altar of Osiris shall be given unto him; and he shall enter (5) in peace into Sekhet-åarru to know the decree of him who dwelleth in Ṭaṭṭu; (6) there shall wheat and barley be given unto him; there shall he flourish as he did (7) upon earth; and he shall do whatsoever it pleaseth him to do, even as the company of the gods which is in (8) the underworld, continually, and regularly, for millions of times.

CHAPTER LXXIII.

[See Chapter IX., Papyrus of Ani (Brit. Mus. No. 10,470, sheet 18).]

This Chapter is given twice in the Turin Papyrus (see Lepsius, *op. cit.*, Bll. 3 and 27); once with a vignette and once without; the vignette in the Theban Recension is quite different from that in the Saïte Recension, where the deceased is seen standing and holding a staff in his left hand.

[1] From the Papyrus of Ani (Brit. Mus. No. 10,470, sheet 6).

CHAPTER LXXIV.

[From the Papyrus of Nu (Brit. Mus. No. 10,477, sheet 6).]

Vignette: The deceased kneeling, with both hands raised in adoration, before the Ḥennu boat of the god Seker which is placed upon its sledge (Papyrus of Ani, sheet 18). In the Saïte Recension the deceased is standing near a two-legged serpent (Lepsius, *op. cit.*, Bl. 27).

Text: (1) THE CHAPTER OF LIFTING UP THE FEET AND OF COMING FORTH UPON THE EARTH. (2) The overseer of the house of the overseer of the seal, Nu, triumphant, saith :—

"Perform thy work, O Seker,[1] perform thy work, O "Seker, O thou [who dwellest in thy house], and who "[standest] on [thy] feet in the underworld! I am the "god who sendeth forth rays of light over the Thigh of

[1] A name of Osiris as the god who was "closed up" or "shut up" in his coffin.

"(3) heaven, and I come forth to heaven and I sit "myself down by the God of Light (*Khu*). Hail, I "have become helpless! Hail, I have become help-"less! but I go forward. I have become helpless, I "have become helpless (4) in the regions of those who "plunder in the underworld."

CHAPTER LXXV.

[From the Papyrus of Nu (Brit. Mus. No. 10,477, sheet 13).]

Vignette: In the Theban Recension the deceased, holding a staff, is seen standing before a pylon of a temple; but in the Saite Recension he is standing before the emblem of Annu (Heliopolis) (Lepsius, *op. cit.*, Bl. 28).

Text: (1) THE CHAPTER OF JOURNEYING TO ÅNNU (HELIOPOLIS) AND OF RECEIVING A THRONE THEREIN. The overseer of the house of the overseer of the seal, Nu, triumphant, saith:—(2)

"I have come forth from the uttermost parts of the

"earth, and [I have] received my apparel (?) at the "will (?) of the Ape. I penetrate into the holy habita- "tions of those who are in [their] shrines (*or* coffins), "(3) I force my way through the habitations of the god "Remrem, and I arrive in the habitations of the god "Åkhsesef, I travel on through the holy chambers, and "I pass into the Temple of the god (4) Kemkem. The "Buckle hath been given unto me, it [hath placed] its "hands upon me, it hath decreed [to my service] its "sister Khebent, and its mother Keḥkeḥet. It placeth "me (5) in [the eastern part of heaven wherein Rā "riseth and is exalted every day; and I rise therein "and travel onward, and I become a spiritual body "(*sāḥ*) like the god, and they set me][1] (6) on that "holy way on which Thoth journeyeth when he goeth "to make peace between the two Fighting-gods (*i.e.*, "Horus and Set). He journeyeth, he journeyeth to "the city of Pe, and he cometh to the city of Ṭepu."

[1] The words in brackets are supplied from Naville, *op. cit.*, Bd. II. p. 158.

CHAPTER LXXVI.

[From the Papyrus of Nu (Brit. Mus. No. 10,477, sheet 9).]

Vignette : This Chapter is without a vignette in the Theban Recension, but in the Saïte Recension a figure of the deceased is given above the Chapter (see Lepsius, *op. cit.*, Bl. 87).

Text : (1) THE CHAPTER OF A MAN TRANSFORMING HIMSELF INTO WHATEVER HE PLEASETH. (2) The overseer of the house of the overseer of the seal, Nu, triumphant, saith :—

"I have come into the House of the King by means "of the mantis[1] (*ābit*) which led me hither. Homage

[1] *I.e.*, the "praying μάντις," *i.e.*, "diviner," or "soothsayer" (*Mantis religiosa*), an insect of the Mantidae class. Its hips are greatly elongated, and the thigh bears on its curved underside a channel armed on each side by strong movable spines. Into this channel the stout shin bone is capable of closing like the blade of a pen-knife, its sharp serrated edges being able to cut and hold. With its head raised upon the much-elongated and semi-erect prothorax, and with the half-opened forelimbs held outwards in the characteristic devotional attitude, it rests motionless upon the four posterior limbs waiting for prey, or occasionally stalks it with slow and silent movements, finally seizing it with its knife blades and devouring it. This insect was greatly honoured in Egypt and Nubia, and the Greeks attributed to it supernatural powers; the Arabs, who call it "*marka'*" or "*masgad*," declare that it always prays with its head turned towards Mecca!

"to thee, (3) O thou who fliest into heaven, and dost "shine upon the son of the white crown, and dost "protect the white crown, let me have my existence "with thee! I have gathered together the great "god[s], I am mighty, I have made my way and I "have travelled along thereon."

CHAPTER LXXVII.

[From the Papyrus of Nu (Brit. Mus. No. 10,477, sheet 10).]

CHAPTER LXXVII.

[From the Papyrus of Nu (Brit. Mus. No. 10,477, sheet 10).]

CHAPTER LXXVII.

[From the Papyrus of Nu (Brit. Mus. No. 10,477, sheet 10).]

the house of the overseer of the seal, Nu, triumphant, saith :—(2)

"I have risen, I have risen like the mighty hawk [of "gold] that cometh forth from his egg; I fly (3) and I "alight like the hawk which hath a back four cubits "wide, and the wings of which are like unto the "mother-of-emerald of the south. (4) I have come "from the interior of the *Sektet* boat, and my heart "hath been brought unto me from the mountain of "the east. I have alighted (5) upon the *Āṭet* boat, "and those who were dwelling in their companies have "been brought unto me, and they bowed low in paying "(6) homage unto me and in saluting me with cries of "joy. I have risen, and I have gathered myself to-"gether like the beautiful hawk (7) of gold, which "hath the head of a *Bennu* bird, and Rā entereth in "day by day to hearken unto my words; I have taken "my seat among those (8) first-born gods of Nut. I "am stablished, and the divine Sekhet-ḥetep is before "(9) me, I have eaten therein, I have become a spirit "therein, I have an abundance therein—as much as I "desire—the god Neprȧ hath given to me my throat, "and I have gained the mastery over (10) that which "guardeth (*or* belongeth to) my head."

CHAPTER LXXVIII.

[From the Papyrus of Nu (Brit. Mus. No. 10,477, sheets 13 and 14).]

Vignette : A hawk, painted green, holding a flail, and standing upon a pylon-shaped pedestal (see Papyrus of Ani, sheet 25).

Text : (1) THE CHAPTER OF MAKING THE TRANSFORMATION INTO A DIVINE HAWK. The overseer of the house of the overseer of the seal, Nu, triumphant, saith :—

"Hail, Great God, come now (2) to Ṭaṭṭu! Make "thou smooth for me the ways and let me go round "about [to visit] my thrones; I have renewed (?) "myself, and I have raised myself up. O grant thou "that I may be feared, (3) and make thou me to be a "terror. Let the gods of the underworld be afraid of "me, and may they fight for me in their habitations "which are therein. (4) Let not him that would do "me harm draw nigh unto me, or injure (?) me, in the "House of Darkness, that is, he that clotheth and "covereth the feeble one, and whose [name] is "hidden; (5) and let not the gods act likewise "towards me. [Hail], ye gods, who hearken unto "[my] speech! Hail, ye rulers, who are among the "followers of Osiris! Be ye therefore silent, O ye "gods, (6) when one god speaketh unto another, for he "hearkeneth unto right and truth; and what I speak "unto [him] do thou also speak for me then, O Osiris. "Grant thou that I may journey round about [according to] that which cometh forth from my mouth "concerning me, (7) and grant that I may see thine "own Form (*or* forms), and the dispositions of thy "Souls. Grant thou that I may come forth, and that "I may have power over my legs, and that I may have "my existence there like (8) unto that of Neb-er-tcher "who is over [all]. May the gods of the underworld "fear me, and may they fight for me in their habitations. Grant thou that I may move along therein "(9) together with the divine beings who journey "onwards, and may I be stablished upon my resting-"place like the Lord of Life. May I be joined unto "Isis the divine lady, and may she protect me (10) "from him that would do an injury unto me; and let "not any one come to see the divine one naked and "helpless. May I journey on, may I come into the "uttermost (11) parts of heaven. I exchange speech "with the god Seb, I make supplication for divine "food from Neb-er-tcher; the gods of the underworld "have fear of me, and they (12) fight for me in their "habitations when they see that thou hast provided "me with food, both of the fowl of the air and of the "fish of the sea. I am one of those *Khus* who dwell "with (13) the divine *Khu*, and I have made my form "like unto his divine Form, when he cometh forth and "maketh himself manifest in Ṭaṭṭu. [I am] a spiritual "body (*sāḥ*) (14) and possess my soul, and will speak "unto thee the things which concern me. O grant "thou that I may be feared, and make thou me to be "a terror; let the gods of the underworld be afraid of "me, (15) and may they fight for me in their habita-"tions. I, even I, am the *Khu* who dwelleth with the "divine *Khu*, whom the god Tem himself hath created, "(16) and who hath come into being from the blossom, "(*i.e.*, the eyelashes) of his eye; he hath made to have "existence, and he hath made to be glorious (*i.e.*, to be "*Khus*), and he hath made mighty thereby those who "have their existence along with him. Behold, he is "the only One in Nu, (17) and they sing praises (*or* "do homage) unto him [when] he cometh forth from "the horizon, and the gods and the *Khus* who have "come into being along with him ascribe [the lordship "of] terror unto him."

"I am one of those worms (?) which the eye of the "Lord, the only One, (18) hath created. And behold, "when as yet Isis had not given birth to Horus, I had "germinated, and had flourished, and I had become "aged, (19) and I had become greater than those who "dwelt with the divine *Khu*, and who had come into "being along with him. And I had risen up like the "divine hawk, and Horus made for me a spiritual body "(20) containing his own soul, so that I might take "possession of all that belonged unto Osiris in the "underworld. The double Lion-god, the governor of "the things which belong to the Temple of the *nemmes* "crown, (21) who dwelleth in his secret abode, saith "[unto me]:—'Get thee back to the uttermost parts of "heaven, for behold, inasmuch as through thy form of "Horus thou hast become a spiritual body (*sāḥ*) the "*nemmes* crown is not for thee; but (22) behold, "thou hast the power of speech even to the uttermost "parts of heaven.' And I, the guardian, took posses-"sion of the things of Horus [which belonged] unto "Osiris in the underworld, and Horus told aloud unto "me (23) the things which his divine father Osiris "spake unto him in years [gone by] on the day of his "own burial. I have given unto thee[1] the *nemmes* "crown through the double Lion-god that thou mayest "pass onward (24) and mayest come to the heavenly "path, and that those who dwell in the uttermost "parts of the horizon may see thee, and that the "gods of the underworld may see thee and may fight "for thee (25) in their habitations. And of them is

[1] Literally, "Thou hast given unto me."

"Áaheṭ.[1] The gods, each and all of them, who are "the warders of the shrine of the Lord, the only one, "have fallen before my words."

"Hail! (26) He that is exalted upon his tomb is on "my side, and he hath bound [upon my head] the "*nemmes* crown, by the decree of the double Lion-god "on my behalf, and the god Áaheṭ hath prepared a "way for me. I, even I, am exalted (27) in my tomb, "and the double Lion-god hath bound the *nemmes* "crown upon my [head], and he hath also given unto "me the double hairy covering of my head. He hath "stablished my heart through his own backbone, he "hath stablished my heart through his own (28) great "and exceeding strength, and I shall not fall through "Shu. I make my peace with the beautiful divine "Brother, the lord of the two uraei, adored be he! "I, even I, am he who knoweth the roads through "the sky (29), and the wind thereof is in my body. "The bull which striketh terror [into men] shall not "drive me back, and I shall pass on to the place where "lieth the ship-wrecked mariner on the border of the "Sekhet-neḥeḥ (*i.e.*, Field of illimitable time), (30) "and I shall journey on to the night and sorrow of "the regions of Ámenti.

"O Osiris, I shall come each day into the House of "the double Lion-god, and I shall come forth there-

[1] The variants are Áahet Át, Áahet Áteḥ, and one papyrus gives the words: "I am the great god"; see Naville, *op. cit.*, Bd. II. p. 167.

"from into the House of (31) Isis, the divine lady. I "shall behold sacred things which are hidden, and I "shall be led on to the secret and holy things, even as "they have granted unto me (32) to see the birth of "the Great God. Horus hath made me to be a spiritual "body through his soul, [and I see what is therein. If "I speak near the mighty ones of Shu they repulse my "opportunity. I am the guardian and I] take posses-"sion of the things which Horus had from Osiris in "the underworld. I, even I, (33) am Horus who "dwelleth in the divine *Khu*. [I] have gained power "over his crown, I have gained power over his radiance, "and I have travelled over the remote, illimitable "parts of (34) heaven. Horus is upon his throne, "Horus is upon his royal seat. My face is like "unto that of the divine hawk, my strength is like "unto that of the divine hawk, and I am one who "hath been fully equipped by his divine Lord. I "shall come forth to Ṭaṭṭu, (35) I shall see Osiris, I "shall pay homage to him on the right hand and on "the left, I shall pay homage unto Nut, and she shall "look upon me, and the gods shall look upon me, "together with the Eye of Horus who (36) is without "sight (?) They (*i.e.*, the gods) shall make their arms "to come forth unto me. I rise up [as] a divine "Power, and [I] repulse him that would subject me to "restraint. They open unto me the holy paths, they "see (37) my form, and they hear that which I speak."

"[Down] upon your faces, ye gods of the Tuat

"(underworld), who would resist me with your faces "and oppose me with your powers, who lead along "the stars which never (38) rest, and who make the "holy paths unto the Ḥemati abode [where is] the "Lord of the exceedingly mighty and terrible Soul. "Horus hath commanded that ye lift up your faces "so that I may (39) look upon you. I have risen "up like the divine hawk, and Horus hath made for "me a spiritual body, through his own soul, to take "possession of that which belongeth to Osiris (40) in "the Ṭuat (underworld). I have bound up the gods "with divine tresses, and I have travelled on to those "who ward their Chambers, and who were on both "sides of me. I have made my roads and I have (41) "journeyed on and have reached those divine beings "who inhabit their secret dwellings, and who are "warders of the Temple of Osiris. I have spoken "unto them with strength, and have made them to "know (42) the most mighty power of him that is "provided with two horns [to fight] against Suti; "and I make them to know concerning him that hath "taken possession of the divine food, and who is pro-"vided with the Might of Tem. (43) May the gods of "the underworld [order] a prosperous journey for me!

"O ye gods who inhabit your secret dwellings, and "who are warders of the Temple of Osiris, and whose "numbers are great and multitudinous, grant ye (44) "that I may come unto you. I have bound up and I "have gathered together the powers of Kesemu-enenet," or (as others say), "Kesemiu-enenet; and I have made "holy (45) the Powers of the paths of those who watch "and ward the roads of the horizon, and who are the "guardians of the horizon of Ḥemati which is in "heaven. I have stablished habitations for Osiris, I "have made the ways holy (46) for him, I have done "that which hath been commanded, I have come forth "to Ṭaṭṭu, I have seen Osiris, I have spoken unto him "concerning the matters of his first-born son whom "(47) he loveth and concerning the wounding of the "heart of Suti, and I have seen the divine one who is "without life. Yea, I have made them to know con-"cerning the counsels of the gods which Horus carried "out (48) while his father Osiris was not [with him].

"Hail, Lord, thou most mighty and terrible Soul! "Verily I, even I, have come, look thou upon me, (49) "and do thou make me to be exalted. I have made my "way through thy Ṭuat (underworld), and I have "opened up the paths which belong to heaven and "also those which belong to earth, and I have suf-"fered no opposition therein. (50) Exalted [be thou] "upon thy throne, O Osiris! Thou hast heard fair "things, O Osiris! Thy strength is vigorous, O Osiris. "Thy head is fastened unto thee, O Osiris. Thy brow "is stablished, (51) O Osiris. Thy heart is glad, [O "Osiris]. Thy speech (?) is stablished, [O Osiris], and "thy princes rejoice. Thou art stablished like the "Bull of Åmentet. (52) Thy son Horus hath risen "like the sun upon thy throne, and all life is with "him. Millions of years minister unto him, and "millions of years hold him in fear; the company "of the gods are his servants, and the company of "the gods hold him in fear. The god Tem, (53) "the Governor and only One of the gods, hath "spoken [these things], and his word passeth not "away. Horus is both the divine food and the "sacrifice. [He] hath passed on (?) to gather to-"gether [the members of] his divine father (54); "Horus is [his] deliverer, Horus is [his] deliverer. "Horus hath sprung from the water of his divine "father and [from his] decay. He hath become the "Governor of Egypt. The gods labour for him, and "they toil for him for (55) millions of years; and he "hath made to live millions of years through his Eye, "the only One of its Lord (*or* Neb-s), Nebt-er-tcher."

CHAPTER LXXIX.

[From the Papyrus of Nu (Brit. Mus. No. 10,477, sheets 8 and 9).]

Vignette: The deceased, or his soul, in adoration before three gods (see Naville, *op. cit.*, Bd. I. Bl. 90).

Text: (1) THE CHAPTER OF BEING TRANSFORMED INTO THE GOVERNOR OF THE SOVEREIGN PRINCES. The overseer of the house of the overseer of the seal, Nu, triumphant, saith :— (2)

"I am the god Tem, the maker of heaven, the creator "of things which are, who cometh forth from the earth, "who maketh to come into being the seed which is "sown, the lord of things which shall be, who gave "birth to the gods; [I am] the great god who made "himself, (3) the lord of life, who maketh to flourish "the company of the gods. Homage to you, O ye "lords of divine things (*or* of creation), ye pure beings "whose abodes are hidden! Homage to you, O ye "everlasting lords, (4) whose forms are hidden and "whose shrines are hidden in places which are un-"known! Homage to you (5) O ye gods, who dwell "in the Tenait (?)! Homage to you, O ye gods of the "circuit of the flooded lands of Qebḥu! Homage to "you, O ye gods who live in Ȧmentet! (6) Homage "to you, O ye company of the gods who dwell in Nut! "Grant ye that I may come unto you, for I am pure, "(7) I am divine, I am a *khu*, I am strong, I am "endowed with a soul (*or* I am mighty), and I have "brought unto you incense, and sweet-smelling gums, "and natron; I have made an end of the spittle which "floweth (8) from your mouth upon me. I have come, "and I have made an end of the evil things which are "in your hearts, and I have removed the faults which "ye kept [laid up against me]. I have brought to you

"(9) the things which are good, and I make to come "into your presence Right and Truth. I, even I, know "you, and I know your names, and I know (10) your "forms, which are unknown, and I come into being "along with you. My coming is like unto that of the "god who eateth men and (11) who liveth upon the "gods. I am mighty with you like the god who is "exalted upon his resting-place; the gods come to me "in gladness, and goddesses make supplication (12) "unto me when they see me. I have come unto you, "and I have risen like your two divine daughters. I "have taken my seat in the (13) horizon, and I receive "my offerings upon my tables, and I drink drink-offer-"ings at eventide. My coming is [received] with (14) "shouts of joy, and the divine beings who dwell in the "horizon ascribe praises unto me, the divine spiritual "body (*Sāḥ*), the lord of divine beings (15). I am "exalted like the holy god who dwelleth in the Great "Temple, and the gods rejoice when they see me in "my beautiful coming forth from the body of Nut, "when my mother Nut giveth birth unto me."

CHAPTER LXXX.

[From the Papyrus of Ani (Brit. Mus. No. 10,470, sheet 28).]

Vignette: A god with the disk of the sun upon his head.

Text: (1) [THE CHAPTER OF] MAKING THE TRANSFORMATION INTO THE GOD WHO GIVETH LIGHT [IN] THE DARKNESS. Saith Osiris, the scribe Ani, triumphant:—

"I am (2) the girdle of the robe of the god Nu, "which shineth and sheddeth light upon that which "belongeth to his breast, which sendeth forth light "into the darkness, which uniteth the two fighting "deities (3) who dwell in my body through the mighty "spell of the words of my mouth, which raiseth up him "that hath fallen—(4) for he who was with him in the

"valley of Àbṭu (Abydos) hath fallen—and I rest. I "have remembered him. I have taken possession of "the god Ḥu in my city, for I found (5) him therein, "and I have led away captive the darkness by my "might. I have rescued the Eye [of the Sun] when "it waned at the coming of the festival of the fifteenth "day, (6) and I have weighed Sut in the celestial "houses against the Aged One who is with him. I "have endowed (7) Thoth [with what is needful] in the "Temple of the Moon-god for the coming of the fifteenth "day of the festival. I have taken possession of the "*Ureret* crown; Maāt (*i.e.*, right and truth) is in my "(8) body; its mouths are of turquoise and rock-"crystal. My homestead is among the furrows which "are [of the colour of] lapis-lazuli. I am (9) Ḥem-"Nu (?) who sheddeth light in the darkness. I "have come to give light in the darkness, which is "made light and bright [by me]. I have given light "in the darkness, (10) and I have overthrown the "destroying crocodiles. I have sung praises unto "those who dwell in the darkness, I have raised up "those who (11) wept, and who had hidden their faces "and had sunk down in wretchedness; and they did "look then upon me. [Hail, then,] ye beings, I am "Ḥem-Nu (?), and I will not let you hear concerning "the matter. [I] have opened [the way], I am Ḥem-"Nu (?), I have made light the darkness, I have come, "having made an end of the darkness, which hath "become light indeed."

CHAPTER LXXXIA.

[From the Papyrus of Nu (Brit. Mus. No. 10,477, sheet 11).]

Vignette: In the Papyrus of Nebseni (sheet 3) the vignette of this Chapter is simply a lotus flower in full bloom, but in the Papyrus of Ani (sheet 28) a human head is seen springing from the lotus which is growing in a pool of water. See also Lepsius, *op. cit.*, Bl. 31.

Text: (1) THE CHAPTER OF MAKING THE TRANSFORMATION INTO A LOTUS. The overseer of the house of the overseer of the seal, Nu, begotten by the overseer of the house of the overseer of the seal, Àmen-ḥetep, saith :— (2)

"I am the pure lotus which springeth "up from the divine splendour that be"longeth to the nostrils of Rā. I have "made [my way], and I follow on seek"ing for him who is Horus. I am the "pure one who cometh forth out of the "Field."

CHAPTER LXXXIB.

[From the Papyrus of Paqrer (see Naville, *op. cit.*, Bd. I. Bl. 93).]

Vignette: A human head springing from a lotus.

Text: (1) THE CHAPTER OF MAKING THE TRANSFORMATION INTO A LOTUS. Saith Osiris Paqrer :— (2) "Hail, thou lotus, thou type of the god Nefer-Temu! "I am the man that knoweth you, and (3) I know your "names among [those of] the gods, the lords of the "underworld, and I am one of (4) you. Grant ye that "[I] may see the gods who are the divine guides in the "Ṭuat (underworld), and grant ye unto me a place in "(5) the underworld near unto the lords of Amentet. "Let me arrive at a habitation in the land of Tchesert, "and receive me, O all ye gods, (6) in the presence of "the lords of eternity. Grant that my soul may come "forth whithersoever it pleaseth, and let it not be "driven away from the presence of the great company "of the gods."

CHAPTER LXXXII.

[From the Papyrus of Nu (Brit. Mus. No. 10,477, sheets 9 and 10).]

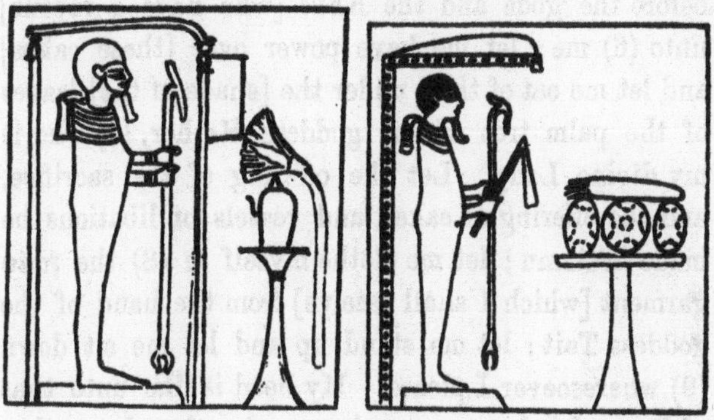

Vignette: The god Ptaḥ in a shrine, before which is a table of offerings.

Text: (1) THE CHAPTER OF MAKING THE TRANSFORMATION INTO PTAH, OF EATING CAKES, AND OF DRINKING ALE, AND OF UNFETTERING THE STEPS, AND OF BECOMING A LIVING BEING IN ÅNNU (Heliopolis).

The overseer of the house of the overseer of the seal, Nu, triumphant, saith :— (2)

"I fly like a hawk, I cackle like the *smen* goose, and "I perch (3) upon that abode of the underworld (*ȧat*) "on the festival of the great Being. That which is an "abomination unto me, that which is an abomination "unto me, I have not eaten; filth is an abomination "unto me and I have not eaten thereof, (4) and that "which is an abomination unto my *ka* hath not entered "into my belly. Let me, then, live upon that which "the gods and the *Khus* decree for me; (5) let me live "and let me have power over cakes; let me eat them "before the gods and the *Khus* [who have a favour] "unto (6) me; let me have power over [these cakes] "and let me eat of them under the [shade of the] leaves "of the palm tree of the goddess Hathor, (7) who is "my divine Lady. Let the offering of the sacrifice, "and the offering of cakes, and vessels of libations be "made in Ȧnnu; let me clothe myself in (8) the *ṭaȧu* "garment [which I shall receive] from the hand of the "goddess Tait; let me stand up and let me sit down "(9) wheresoever I please. My head is like unto that "of Rā, and [when my members are] gathered together "[I am] like unto Tem; the four [sides of the domain] "of Rā, (10) and the width of the earth four times. I "come forth. My tongue is like unto that of Ptaḥ, "and my throne is like unto that of the goddess "Hathor, and I make mention of the words of Tem, "my father, (11) with my mouth. He it is who con-

"straineth the handmaid, the wife of Seb, and before "him are bowed [all] heads, and there is fear of him. "Hymns of praise are repeated for [me] by reason of "[my] mighty acts, and I am decreed to be the divine "(12) Heir of Seb, the lord of the earth, and to be the "protector therein. The god Seb refresheth me, and "he maketh his risings to be mine. Those who dwell "in Ȧnnu (13) bow down their heads unto me, for I "am their lord and I am their bull. I am more power-"ful than the lord of time, and I shall enjoy the "pleasures of love, and shall gain the mastery over "millions of years."

CHAPTER LXXXIII.[1]

[From the Papyrus of Nu (Brit. Mus. No. 10,477, sheet 10).]

Vignette: A *Bennu* bird.

Text: (1) [THE CHAPTER OF MAKING THE TRANSFORMATION INTO (2) A BENNU BIRD.] The overseer of the house of the overseer of the seal, Nu, triumphant, saith:— (3)

"I came[2] into being from unformed matter. I came "into existence like the god Kheperá, I have ger"minated like the things which germinate (*i.e.*, plants),

[1] In the Papyrus of Nu the text which is given under the title of Chapter LXXXIII. is that of Chapter CXXIV.; Chapters LXXXIII. and LXXXIV. are given under the title of Chapter LXXXIV.

[2] Literally, "I flew."

"and I have dressed myself like the (4) tortoise.[1] I "am [of] the germs of every god. I am Yesterday of "the four [quarters of the world] and of those seven "Uraei which came into existence in Ȧmentet, that is to "say, [Horus, who emitteth light from his divine body. "(5) He is] the god [who] fought against Suti, but the "god Thoth cometh between them through the judg-"ment of him that dwelleth in (6) Sekhem, and of the "Souls who are in Ȧnnu, and there is a stream between "them. (7) I have come by day, and I have risen in "the footsteps of the gods. I am the god Khensu,[2] "who driveth back all that oppose him."

RUBRIC: [If] this chapter [be known by the deceased] he shall come forth pure by day after his death, and he shall perform whatsoever transformations his heart desireth. He shall be in the following of Un-nefer, and he shall be satisfied with the food of Osiris and with sepulchral meals. [He] shall see the disk, [he] shall be in good case upon earth before Rā, and he shall be triumphant before Osiris, and no evil thing whatsoever shall have dominion over him for ever and ever.

[1] I believe that "Turtle" is the correct translation.
[2] *I.e.*, the Moon-god.

CHAPTER LXXXIV.

[From the Papyrus of Nu (Brit. Mus. No. 10,477, sheet 10).]

Vignette : A heron.

Text : [THE CHAPTER OF MAKING THE TRANSFORMATION INTO A HERON. The overseer of the house of the overseer of the seal, Nu, triumphant, saith :—] (8)

"[I] have gotten dominion over the beasts that are "brought for sacrifice, with the knives which are "[held] at their heads, and at their hair, and at their "(9) . . . . [Hail], Aged ones [hail,] *Khus*, who "are provided with the opportunity, the overseer of the "house of the overseer of the seal, Nu, triumphant, "(10) is upon the earth, and what he hath slaughtered "is in heaven; and what he hath slaughtered is in

"heaven and he is upon the earth. Behold, I am "strong, and I work mighty deeds to the very heights of "heaven. (11) I have made myself pure, and [I] make "the breadth of heaven [a place for] my footsteps [as I "go] into the cities of Àuḳert; I advance, and I go "forward (12) into the city of Unnu (Hermopolis). I "have set the gods upon their paths, and I have "roused up the exalted ones who dwell in their "shrines. Do I not know Nu? (13) Do I not know "Ta-tunen? Do I not know the beings of the colour "of fire who thrust forward their horns? Do I not "know [every being having] incantations unto whose "words I listen? (14) I am the *Smam* bull [for "slaughter] which is written down in the books. "The gods crying out say: 'Let your faces be "gracious to him that cometh onward. The light (15) "is beyond your knowledge, and ye cannot fetter it; "and times and seasons are in my body. I do not "utter words to the god Ḥu,[1] [I do not utter words of] "wickedness instead of [words of] right and truth, (16) "and each day right and truth come upon my eyebrows. "At night taketh place the festival of him that is dead, "the Aged One, who is in ward [in] the earth."

[1] The god who provides celestial food for the beatified.

CHAPTER LXXXV.

[From the Papyrus of Nu (Brit. Mus. No. 10,477, sheet 9).]

From the Papyrus of Nebseni.

From the Papyrus of Ani.

Vignette: A soul, or a ram, the emblem of Osiris as Ba-Neb-Ṭaṭṭu, *i.e.*, the "Soul, Lord of Ṭaṭṭu."

Text: (1) THE CHAPTER OF MAKING THE TRANSFORMATION INTO A LIVING SOUL, AND OF NOT ENTERING

INTO THE CHAMBER OF TORTURE; whosoever knoweth [it] shall not see corruption. The overseer of the house of the overseer of the seal, Nu, triumphant, saith:—(2)

"I am the divine Soul of Rā proceeding from the "god Nu; that divine Soul which is God. [I am] "the creator of the divine food, and that which is an "abomination unto me is sin (3) whereon I look not. "I proclaim right and truth, and I live therein. I "am the divine food, which is not corrupted in my "name (4) of Soul; I gave birth unto myself together "with Nu in my name of Kheperȧ in whom I come "into being day by day. I am the lord of (5) light, "and that which is an abomination unto me is death; "let me not go into the chamber of torture which is in "the Ṭuat (underworld). I ascribe honour [unto] "Osiris, and I make to be at peace the heart[s] "of (6) those beings who dwell among the divine "things which [I] love. They cause the fear of me "[to abound], and they create awe of (7) me in those "beings who dwell in their divine territories. Behold, "I am exalted upon my standard (8), and upon my "seat, and upon the throne which is adjudged [to me]. "I am the god Nu, and the workers of iniquity shall "not destroy me (9). I am the first-born god of "primeval matter, that is to say, the divine Soul, "even the (10) Souls of the gods of everlastingness, "and my body is eternity. My Form is everlasting-"ness, and is the lord of years (11) and the prince of "eternity. [I am] the creator of the darkness who "maketh his habitation in the uttermost parts of the "sky, [which] I love, (12) and I arrive at the confines "thereof. I advance upon my feet, I become master "of (13) my vine, I sail over the sky which formeth "the division [betwixt heaven and earth], [I] destroy "the hidden (14) worms that travel nigh unto my foot-"steps which are towards the lord of the two hands "and arms. My soul is the Souls of the souls (15) of "everlastingness, and my body is eternity. I am the "divine exalted being who is the lord of the land of "Tebu. 'I am the Boy (16) in the city and the Young "man in the plain' is my name; 'he that never "suffereth corruption' is my name. I am the Soul, "the creator of the god Nu who maketh his habitation "in (17) the underworld: my place of incubation is "unseen and my egg is not cracked. I have done "away with all my iniquity, and I shall see my divine "Father, (18) the lord of eventide, whose body dwelleth "in Ȧnnu. I travel (?) to the god of night (?), who "dwelleth with the god of light, by the western region "of the Ibis (*i.e.*, Thoth)."

CHAPTER LXXXVI.

[From the Papyrus of Nu (Brit. Mus. No. 10,477, sheet 10).]

From the Papyrus of Nebseni.

From the Papyrus of Ani.

Vignette: A swallow perched upon either a rounded object or a tomb.

Text: (1) THE CHAPTER OF MAKING THE TRANSFORMATION INTO A SWALLOW. The overseer of the house of the overseer of the seal, Nu, triumphant, saith:— (2)

"I am a swallow, I am a swallow. I am the "Scorpion, the daughter of Rā. Hail, ye gods, whose "scent is sweet; hail, ye gods, whose scent is sweet!

"[Hail,] Flame, which cometh forth from the horizon! "Hail, thou who art in the city, I have brought (3) the "Warden of his Bight therein. O stretch out unto me "thy hand so that I may be able to pass my days in the "Pool of Double Fire, and (4) let me advance with my "message, for I have come with words to tell. O open "[thou] the doors to me and I will declare the things "which have been (5) seen by me. Horus hath become "the divine prince of the Boat of the Sun, and unto him "hath been given the throne of his divine father Osiris, "and (6) Set, that son of Nut, [lieth] under the fetters "which he had made for me. I have made a computa-"tion of what is in the city of Sekhem, (7) I have "stretched out both my hands and arms at the word (?) "of Osiris, I have passed on to judgment, and I have "come that [I] may (8) speak; grant that I may pass "on and declare my tidings. I enter in, [I am] judged, "and [I] come forth worthy at (9) the gate of Neb-er-"tcher. I am pure at the great place of the passage "of souls, I have done away with (10) my sins, I have "put away mine offences, and I have destroyed the evil "which appertained unto my members upon earth. "Hail, ye divine beings who guard the doors, make "ye for me (11) a way, for, behold, I am like unto "you. I have come forth by day, I have journeyed "on my legs, I have gained the mastery over my "footsteps [before] the God of Light, (12) I know "the hidden ways and the doors of the Sekhet-Åarru, "verily I, even I, have come, (13) I have overthrown "mine enemies upon earth, and yet my perishable "body is in the grave."

RUBRIC: If this chapter be known [by the deceased], he shall come forth by day, he shall not be turned back at (14) any gate in the underworld, and he shall make his transformation into a swallow regularly and continually.

CHAPTER LXXXVII.

[From the Papyrus of Nu (Brit. Mus. No. 10,477, sheet 11).]

Vignette: The serpent Sata with human legs.

Text: (1) THE CHAPTER OF MAKING THE TRANSFORMATION INTO THE SERPENT SATA. The overseer of the house of the overseer of the seal (2), Nu, triumphant, saith:— (3)

"I am the serpent Sata whose years are many.[1] I "die and I am born again each day. I am the serpent "Sata (4) which dwelleth in the uttermost parts of the "earth. I die, and I am born again, and I renew "myself, and I grow young (5) each day."

CHAPTER LXXXVIII.

[From the Papyrus of Nu (Brit. Mus. No. 10,477, sheet 11).]

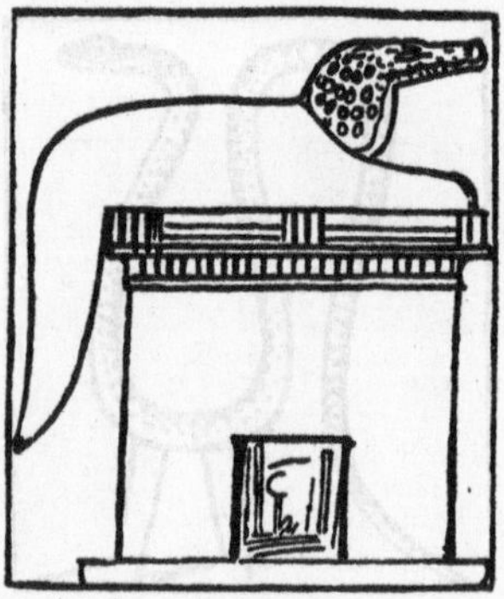

Vignette: A crocodile upon a pylon or gateway.

Text: (1) THE CHAPTER OF MAKING THE TRANSFORMATION INTO A CROCODILE. The overseer of the

[1] Literally, "dilated with years."

house of the overseer of the seal (2), Nu, triumphant, saith :—

"(3) I am the divine crocodile which dwelleth in his "terror, I am the divine crocodile, and I seize [my "prey] like (4) a ravening beast. I am the great "and mighty Fish which is in the city of Qem-ur. "I am (5) the lord to whom bowing and prostrations "are made in the city of Sekhem."

CHAPTER LXXXIX.

[From the Papyrus of Ani (Brit. Mus. No. 10,470, sheet 17).]

Vignette: The mummy of the deceased lying upon a bier; above is his soul in the form of a human-headed bird, holding *shen*, the emblem of eternity, in its claws.

Text: (1) THE CHAPTER OF CAUSING THE SOUL TO BE UNITED TO ITS BODY IN THE UNDERWORLD. The Osiris Ani, triumphant, saith :—

"Hail, thou god Anniu (*i.e.*, Bringer)! Hail, thou

"god Peḥrer (*i.e.*, Runner), (2) who dwellest in thy hall! "[Hail,] great God! Grant thou that my soul may "come unto me from wheresoever it may be. If [it] "would tarry, then let my soul be brought (3) unto me "from wheresoever it may be, for thou shalt find the "Eye of Horus standing by thee like unto those beings "who are like unto Osiris, and who never lie down in "death. Let not (4) the Osiris Ani, triumphant, lie "down in death among those who lie down in Ȧnnu, "the land wherein souls are joined unto their bodies "even in thousands. Let me have possession of my "*ba* (soul), and of my *khu*, and let me triumph (5) "therewith in every place wheresoever it may be. "[Observe these things which [I] speak, for it hath "staves with it][1]; observe then, O ye divine guar- "dians of heaven, my soul [wheresoever it may be].[1] "If it would (6) tarry, do thou make my soul to look "upon my body,[2] for thou shalt find the Eye of Horus "standing by thee (7) like those [beings who are like "unto Osiris].

"Hail, ye gods, who tow along the boat of the lord "of millions of years, who bring [it] (8) above the "underworld and who make it to travel over Nut, who "make souls to enter into [their] spiritual bodies, (9) "whose hands are filled with your ropes and who clutch "your weapons tight, destroy ye (10) the Enemy; thus

[1] Added from the Papyrus of Nebseni.
[2] The Papyrus of Nebseni has: "make thou me to see my soul and my shade."

"shall the boat of the sun be glad and the great God "shall set out on his journey in peace. And behold, "grant ye that the soul of Osiris Ani, (11) triumphant, "may come forth before the gods and that it may be "triumphant along with you in the eastern part of the "sky to follow unto the place where it was yesterday; "[and that it may have] peace, peace in Åmentet. (12) "May it look upon its material body, may it rest upon "its spiritual body; and may its body neither perish "nor suffer corruption for ever."

RUBRIC: [These] words are to be said over a soul of gold inlaid with precious stones and placed on the breast of Osiris.

CHAPTER XC.

[From the Papyrus of Nu (Brit. Mus. No. 10,477, sheet 8).]

Vignette: A jackal walking towards the funeral mountain (see Naville, *op. cit.*, Bd. I. Bl. 102), or the deceased standing upright in the presence of the god Thoth, who is about to give unto him a roll of papyrus (see Lepsius, *op. cit.*, Bl. 33).

Text: (1) THE CHAPTER OF DRIVING EVIL RECOLLECTIONS FROM THE MOUTH. The overseer of the house of the overseer of the seal, Nu, triumphant, the son of the overseer of the house of the overseer of the seal, Ȧmen-ḥetep, triumphant, saith:—(2)

"Hail, thou that cuttest off heads, and slittest brows, "thou being that puttest away the memory of evil "things from the mouth of the *Khus* by means of the "incantations which they have within them, look not "upon me with the [same] eyes (3) with which thou "lookest upon them. Go thou round about on thy "legs, and let thy face be [turned] behind thee so that "thou mayest be able to see the divine slaughterers of "the god Shu who are coming up (4) behind thee to "cut off thy head, and to slit thy brow by reason of the "message of violence [sent] by thy lord, and to see (?) "that which thou sayest. Work thou for me so that "the memory of evil things shall dart (5) from my "mouth; let not my head be cut off; let not my brow "be slit; and let not my mouth be shut fast by reason "of the incantations which thou hast within thee, "according to that which thou doest for the *Khus* "through (6) the incantations which they have within "themselves. Get thee back and depart at the [sound "of] the two speeches which the goddess Isis uttered, "when thou didst come to cast the recollection of evil "things into the mouth of Osiris (7) by the will of Suti "his enemy, saying, 'Let thy face be towards thy privy "parts, and look upon that face which cometh forth "from the flame of the Eye of Horus against thee from "within the Eye of Tem,' and the calamity (8) of that "night which shall consume thee. And Osiris went "back, for the abomination of thee was in him; and "thou didst go back, for the abomination of him is in "thee. I have gone back, for the abomination of "thee is in me; and thou shalt go back, for the abomi- "nation of me is in thee. (9) Thou wouldst come unto "me, but I say that thou shalt not advance to me so "that I come to an end, and [I] say then to the divine "slaughterers of the god Shu, 'Depart.'"

CHAPTER XCI.

[From the Papyrus of Nu (Brit. Mus. No. 10,477, sheet 6).]

Vignette: The soul of the deceased, in the form of a human-headed bird, standing in front of a door (see Papyrus of Ani, sheet 17).

Text: (1) THE CHAPTER OF NOT LETTING (2) THE SOUL OF NU, TRIUMPHANT, BE CAPTIVE IN THE UNDERWORLD. He saith :—

"Hail, thou who art exalted! [Hail,] thou who art "adored! O thou mighty one of Souls, thou divine "Soul, thou possessor of (3) terrible power, who dost "put the fear of thyself into the gods, thou who art "crowned upon thy throne of majesty, I pray thee to "make a way for the *ba* (soul), and for the *khu*, and "for the *khaibit* (shade) of the overseer of the house of "the overseer of the seal, Nu, triumphant (4) [and let "him be] provided therewith. I am a perfect *khu*, and "I have made [my] way unto the place wherein dwell "Rā and Hathor."

RUBRIC: If this chapter be known [by the deceased] he shall be able to transform himself into a *khu* provided [with his soul and with his shade] in the underworld, and he shall never be held captive at any door in Åmentet, in entering in or in coming out.[1]

[1] This Rubric is taken from the Papyrus of Ani, sheet 17.

CHAPTER XCII.

[From the Papyrus of Nebseni (Brit. Mus. No. 9900, sheet 6).]

From the Papyrus of Ani.

Vignette: The soul of the deceased, in the form of a human-headed bird, flying out from the doorway of the tomb. Variant vignettes represent the deceased as having opened the door of the tomb and having his soul by his side, or as standing before the open door with hands stretched out to embrace his soul. An interesting vignette represents the disk of the sun with rays shooting forth from it above the tomb, and the soul of the deceased hovering over his shade, drawn in solid black colour, which has just emerged therefrom (see Naville, *op. cit.*, Bd. I. Bl. 104).

Text: (1) THE CHAPTER OF OPENING THE TOMB TO THE SOUL [AND] TO THE SHADE OF OSIRIS the scribe Nebseni, the lord of reverence, born of the lady of the house Mut-resthà, triumphant, SO THAT

HE MAY COME FORTH BY DAY AND (2) HAVE DOMINION OVER HIS FEET. [He saith :—]

"That which was shut fast hath been opened, that is "to say, he that lay down in death [hath been unloosed]. "That which was open hath been shut to my soul "through the command of the Eye of Horus, (3) which "hath strengthened me and which maketh to stand "fast the beauties which are upon the forehead of Rā, "whose strides are long as [he] lifteth up [his] legs [in "journeying]. I have made for myself a way, my "members are mighty (4) and are strong. I am "Horus the avenger of his "divine father. I am he who "bringeth along his divine "father, and who bringeth "along his mother by means "of his sceptre (?). And the "way shall be opened unto him "who hath (5) gotten dominion "over his feet, and he shall "see the Great God in the Boat of Rā, [when] souls are "counted therein at the bows, (6) and when the years also "are counted up. Grant that the Eye of Horus, which "maketh the adornments of light to be firm upon the "(7) forehead of Rā, may deliver my soul for me, and "let there be darkness upon your faces, O ye who "would hold fast Osiris. O keep not captive my soul, "O keep not ward (8) over my shade, but let a way be "opened for my soul [and] for my shade, and let [them]

From the Papyrus of Khare.

"see the great God in the shrine (9) on the day of the "judgment of souls, and let [them] recite the utter- "ances of Osiris, whose habitations are hidden, to "those who guard the members of Osiris, and (10) "who keep ward over the Spirits, and who hold cap- "tive the shades of the dead who would work (11) "evil against me, so "that they shall "[not] work evil "against me. May "a way for thy "double (*ka*), along "with thee and "along with [thy] "soul, be prepared "by those who keep "ward over the "members of Osiris, and who hold captive (12) the "shades of the dead. Heaven shall [not] keep thee, "the earth shall [not] hold thee captive, thou shalt not "have thy being with the divine beings who make "slaughter, (13) but thou shalt have dominion over "thy legs, and thou shalt advance to thy body straight- "way in the earth [and to] those who belong to the "shrine and guard the members of Osiris."

From the Papyrus of Nefer-uben-f.

CHAPTER XCIII.

[From the Papyrus of Nu (Brit. Mus. No. 10,477, sheet 6).]

Vignette: A Buckle with human hands and arms which grasp the deceased by his left arm (see Naville, *op. cit.*, Bd. I. Bl. 105). In the Ani Papyrus (plate 17) and in the Saite Recension the vignette shows the deceased standing, with both hands raised in adoration, before a god who is seated in a boat and who has his head turned so that his face looks backwards (see Lepsius, *op. cit.*, Bl. 34).

Text: (1) THE CHAPTER OF NOT SAILING TO THE EAST IN THE UNDERWORLD. The overseer of the house of the overseer of the seal, Nu, triumphant, saith :— (2)

"Hail, phallus of Rā, who departest from thy "calamity [which ariseth] through opposition (?), the "cycles have been without movement for millions of "years. I am stronger (3) than the strong, I am "mightier than the mighty. If I sail away or if I "be snatched away to the east through the two horns,

(4) or (as others say), "if any evil and abominable thing "be done unto me at the feast of the devils, the phallus "of Rā shall be swallowed up, (5) [along with] the head "of Osiris. And behold me, for I journey along over "the fields wherein the gods mow down those who "make reply unto [their words]; now verily (6) the "two horns of the god Kheperå shall be thrust aside; "and verily pus shall spring into being in the eye of "Tem along with corruption if I be kept in restraint, "or if I have gone (7) towards the east, or if the feast "of devils be made in my presence, or if any malignant "wound be inflicted upon me."[1]

CHAPTER XCIV.

[From the Papyrus of Nu (Brit. Mus. No. 10,477, sheet 12).]

Vignette: The deceased seated with a table before him, on which rest an ink-pot and the palette of a scribe: in the Saïte Recension (see Lepsius, *op. cit.*, Bl. 34) the deceased is offering an ink-pot and a palette to the god Thoth.

[1] The Papyrus of Ani (see plates 16 and 17) contains what are, apparently, two versions of this Chapter.

Text: (1) THE CHAPTER OF (2) PRAYING FOR AN INK-POT AND FOR A PALETTE. The overseer of the house of the overseer of the seal, Nu, triumphant, saith:—

"Hail, aged god, who dost behold thy divine father "and who art the guardian of the book (3) of Thoth, "[behold I have come; I am endowed with glory, I am "endowed with strength, I am filled with might, and I "am supplied with the books of Thoth], and I have "brought [them to enable me] to pass through the god "Aker who dwelleth in Set. I have brought the ink-"pot and the palette as being the objects which are in "the hands (4) of Thoth; hidden is that which is in "them. Behold me in the character of a scribe! I "have brought the offal of Osiris, and I have written "thereon (5). I have made (*i.e.*, copied) the words of "the great and beautiful god each day fairly. O Ḥeru-"khuti, thou didst order me and I have made (*i.e.*, "copied) what is right and true, and I do bring it unto "thee each day."

CHAPTER XCV.

[From the Papyrus of Nu (Brit. Mus. No. 10,477, sheet 7).]

Vignette: The deceased standing before Thoth in adoration of the god. In the Papyrus of User-ḥāt (Brit. Mus. No. 10,009), which probably belongs to the period of the XVIIIth dynasty, the vignette is a goose, but this arises from the fact that the Chapter is there called "[The Chapter] of making the transformation into a goose."

Text: (1) THE CHAPTER OF BEING NIGH UNTO THOTH. The overseer of the house of the overseer of the seal, Nu, triumphant, saith:— (2)

"I am he who sendeth forth terror into the powers "of rain and thunder, and I ward off from the great "divine lady the attacks of violence. [I have smitten "like the god Shāṭ (*i.e.*, the god of slaughter), and I "have poured out libations of cool water like the god "Ashu, and I have worked for the great divine lady "[to ward off] the attacks of violence], I have made "to flourish [my] knife along with the knife (3) which "is in the hand of Thoth in the powers of rain and "thunder."

CHAPTERS XCVI. AND XCVII.

[From the Papyrus of Nu (Brit. Mus. No. 10,477, sheets 19 and 20.)]

Vignette: The deceased standing behind the god Thoth.

The vignette in which the deceased is seen kneeling in adoration before "Rā, the great god, the lord of the Semketet boat," really belongs to the second portion of the chapter.

Text: (1) THE CHAPTER OF BEING NIGH UNTO THOTH AND OF GIVING GLORY UNTO A MAN IN THE UNDERWORLD. The overseer of the house of the overseer of the seal, Nu, triumphant, saith:—

"I am the god Ḥer-àb-maat-f,[1] and I have come to "give (2) right and truth to Rā; I have made Suti to "be at peace with me by means of offerings made to

[1] *I.e.*, "he who dwelleth in his Eye."

"the god Aker and to the Ṭesheru deities,[1] and by "[making] reverence unto Seb."[2]

Vignette : **The Sun-god Rā seated in his boat. Before him stands Seb offering to the god the feather of Maāt; behind Seb is the sceptre of Anubis. The deceased kneels at the front of the boat.**

[The following] words are to be recited in the *Sektet* boat :—"[Hail,] (3) sceptre of Anubis, I have made the "four *Khus*[3] who are in the train of the lord of the "universe to be at peace with me, and I am the lord of "the fields through their decree. (4) I am the divine "father Bāḥ (*i.e.*, the god of the water-flood), and I "do away with the thirst of him that keepeth ward "over the Lakes. Behold ye me, then, O great (5) "gods of majesty who dwell among the Souls of Annu,

[1] *I.e.*, the red flames which appear in the sky at sunrise and sunset.

[2] The XCVIth Chapter ends here according to the Saïte Recension (see Lepsius, *op. cit.*, Bl. 34).

[3] The names of the four are Maa-ātep-f, Kheri-beq-f, Ḥeru-khenti-[ān]-maati, and Ānpu.

"for I am lifted up over you. I am the god Menkh "(*i.e.*, Gracious one), who dwelleth among you. (6) "Verily I have cleansed my soul, O great god of "majesty, set not before me the evil obstacles which "issue from thy mouth, (7) and let not destruction "come round about me, or upon me. I have made "myself clean in the Lake of Making to be at Peace, "[and in the Lake of] Weighing in the Balance, and I "have bathed myself in Netert-utchat, which is under "the holy Sycamore tree (8) of heaven. Behold [I "am] bathed, [and I have] triumphed [over] all [mine "enemies] straightway who come forth and rise up "against right and truth. I am right and true in the "earth. (9) I, even I, have spoken (?) with my mouth "[which is] the power of the Lord, the Only one, Rā "the mighty, who liveth upon right and truth. Let "not injury be inflicted upon me, [but let me be] "clothed on the day of those who go forward (?) (10) "to every [good] thing."

CHAPTER XCVIII.

[From the Papyrus of Nu (Brit. Mus. No. 10,477, sheet 9).]

Vignette: In the Theban Papyri this Chapter has no vignette; in the Saïte Recension (see Lepsius, *op. cit.*, Bl. 35) the vignette represents the deceased standing with his right hand outstretched in the act of addressing a god who is seated in a boat.

Text: (1) THE CHAPTER OF BRINGING ALONG A BOAT IN HEAVEN. The overseer of the house of the overseer of the seal, Nu, triumphant, saith:— (2)

"Hail to thee, O thou Thigh which dwellest in the "northern heaven in the Great Lake, which art seen "and which diest not. I have stood up over thee when "thou didst rise like a god. I have seen thee, (3) and "I have not lain down in death; I have stood over "thee, and I have risen like a god. I have cackled "like a goose, and I have alighted like the hawk (4) "by the divine clouds and by the great dew. I have "journeyed from the earth to heaven. The god Shu "hath [made] me to stand up, the god of Light (5) "hath made me to be vigorous by the two sides of the "Ladder,[1] and the stars which never "rest set [me] on [my] way and bring "[me] away from slaughter. I bring "along with me the things which drive "back (6) calamities as I advance over "the passage of the god Pen; thou "comest, how great art thou, O god "Pen! I have come from the Pool of (7) "Flame which is in the Sekhet-Sásȧ "(*i.e.*, the Field of Fire). Thou livest "in the Pool of Flame in Sekhet-Sásȧ, "and (8) I live upon the staff of the "holy [god]. Hail, thou god Kaa, who "dost bring those things which are "in the boats on the Lake of Hair. "May there be offerings of coolness [to "me as] (9) I stand up in the boat and "guide myself [over] the water; I have "stood up in the boat and the god hath "guided me. I have stood up. I have "spoken. [I am master of the] (10) "crops. I sail round about as I go "forward, and the gates which are in "Sekhem (Letopolis) are opened unto me, and fields

[1] A vignette of the Ladder is given in the Papyrus of Ani (2nd edit., plate 22) between Chapter CXXXIV. and the second copy of Chapter XVIII.; it is reproduced here.

"are awarded unto me in the city of Unnu (Her-"mopolis), (11) and labourers (?) are given unto me, "together with those of my own flesh and bone."

CHAPTER XCIX.

[From the Papyrus of Nu (Brit. Mus. No. 10,477, sheets 21 and 22).]

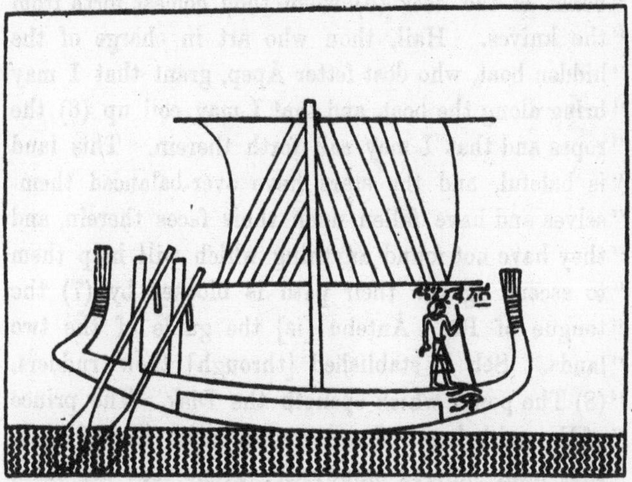

Vignette: The deceased in a boat, with or without a sail hoisted.

Text: (1) THE CHAPTER OF BRINGING ALONG A BOAT IN THE UNDERWORLD. (2) The overseer of the house of the overseer of the seal, Nu, triumphant, saith:—

"Hail, ye who bring along the boat over the evil "back [of Apepi], grant that I may bring the boat "along, and coil up (3) [its] ropes in peace, in peace. "Come, come, hasten, hasten, for I have come to see "my father Osiris, the lord of the *ȧnsi* garment, who "hath gained the mastery (4) with joy of heart. Hail, "lord of the rain-storm, thou Male, thou Sailor! Hail, "thou who dost sail over the evil back of Āpep! Hail, "thou that dost bind up heads and doth stablish the "bones of the neck (5) when thou comest forth from "the knives. Hail, thou who art in charge of the "hidden boat, who dost fetter Āpep, grant that I may "bring along the boat, and that I may coil up (6) the "ropes and that I may sail forth therein. This land "is baleful, and the stars have over-balanced them-"selves and have fallen upon their faces therein, and "they have not found anything which will help them "to ascend again: their path is blocked by (7) the "tongue of Rā. Ȧnṭebu [is] the guide of the two "lands. Seb is stablished [through] their rudders. "(8) The power which openeth the Disk. The prince "of the red beings. I am brought along like (9) him "that hath suffered shipwreck; grant that my *Khu*, "my brother, may come to me, and that [I] may set "out for the place whereof thou (10) knowest."

"Tell me my name," saith the Wood whereat I would anchor; "Lord of the two lands who dwellest in the "Shrine," is thy name.

"Tell me my name," (11) saith the Rudder; "Leg of "Ḥāpiu" is thy name.

"Tell me my name," saith the (12) Rope; "Hair "with which Ȧnpu (Anubis) finisheth the work of my "embalmment" (13) is thy name.

"Tell us our name," say the Oar-rests; "Pillars of "the underworld" is your name.

"Tell me (14) my name," saith the Hold; "Aker" is thy name.

"Tell me my name," saith the Mast; (15) "He who "bringeth back the great lady after she hath gone "away" is thy name.

"Tell me my name," saith the (16) Lower Deck; "Standard of Ȧp-uat" is thy name."

"Tell me my name," saith the Upper Post; (17) "Throat of Mesthȧ" is thy name.

"Tell me my name," saith the Sail; (18) "Nut" is thy name.

"Tell us our name," say the Pieces of Leather; "Ye "who are made from the hide (19) of the Mnevis Bull, "which was burned by Suti," is your name.

"Tell us our name," (20) say the Paddles; "Fingers "of Horus the first-born" is your name."

"Tell me (21) my name," saith the *Mātchabet;* "The "hand of Isis, which wipeth away the blood from the "(22) Eye of Horus," is thy name.

"Tell us our names," say the Planks which are in its (23) hulk; "Mesthi, Ḥāpi, Ṭuamāutef, Qebḥ-sennuf, (24) "Ḥaqau (*i.e.*, he who leadeth away captive), Thet-em-"āua (*i.e.*, he who seizeth by violence), Maa-án-tef (*i.e.*, "he who seeth what the father bringeth), and Ȧri-nef-"tchesef (*i.e.*, he who made himself)," are your names.

"Tell us our names," say the Bows; "He who is at "the head of his nomes" (25) is your name.

"Tell me my name," saith the Hull; "Mert" is thy name.

"Tell me my name," saith the Rudder; "Āqa" (*i.e.*, true one) is thy name, O thou who shinest from the water, (26) hidden beam (?) is thy name.

"Tell me my name," saith the Keel; "Thigh (*or* "Leg) of Isis, which Rā cut off with the knife (27) to "bring blood into the *Sektet* boat," is thy name.

"Tell me my name," saith the Sailor; "Traveller" is thy name.

"(28) Tell me my name," saith the Wind by which thou art borne along; "The North Wind which "cometh from Tem to the nostrils of Khenti-"Ȧmenti"[1] (29) is thy name.

"Tell me my name," saith the River, "if thou "wouldst travel upon me"; "Those which can be "seen" is thy name.

"Tell us our name," say the River Banks; "Des-"troyer of the god (30) Āu-ā (*i.e.*, he of the spacious "hand) in the water-house" is thy name.

[1] *I.e.*, the "Governor of Ȧmenti," or Osiris.

"Tell me my name," saith the Ground, "if thou "wouldst walk upon me"; "The Nose of heaven "which proceedeth from the god Utu, (31) who "dwelleth in the Sekhet-Åarru, and who cometh forth "with rejoicing therefrom," is thy name.

THEN SHALL BE RECITED BEFORE THEM THESE WORDS:—

"Hail to you, O ye divine beings with beautiful *Kas*, "ye divine lords (32) of things, who exist and who live "for ever, and [whose] double period of an illimitable "number of years is eternity, I have made a way unto "you, grant ye my food and sepulchral meals for my "mouth, [and grant that] I may speak (33) therewith, "and that the goddess Isis [may give me] loaves and "cakes in the presence of the great god. I know the "great god before whose nostrils ye place (34) celestial "food, and his name is Thekem; both when he maketh "his way from the eastern horizon of heaven and when "he journeyeth into the western horizon of heaven may "his journey be (35) my journey, and his going forth "my going forth. Let me not be destroyed at the "*Mesqet* chamber, and let not the devils gain dominion "over my members. I have my cakes (36) in the city "of Pe, and I have my ale in the city of Ṭepu, and let "the offerings [which are given unto you] be given "unto me this day. Let my offerings be wheat and "barley; let my offerings (37) be *ānti* unguent and "linen garments; let my offerings be for life, strength, "and health: let my offerings be a coming forth by "day in any form whatsoever (38) in which it may "please me to appear in Sekhet-Åarru."

RUBRIC: If this chapter be known [by the deceased] he shall come forth into Sekhet-Åarru, (39) and bread, and wine, and cakes shall be given unto him at the altar of the great god, and fields, and an estate [sown] with wheat and barley, which the followers of Horus shall (40) reap for him. And he shall eat of that wheat and barley, and his limbs shall be nourished therewith, and his body shall be like unto the bodies of the gods, and he shall come forth into (41) Sekhet-Åarru in any form whatsoever he pleaseth, and he shall appear therein regularly and continually.

CHAPTERS C. AND CXXIX.

[From the Papyrus of Nu (Brit. Mus. No. 10,477, sheets 27 and 28).]

Vignette: A boat, wherein stand the deities Isis, Thoth, Kheperà, and Shu, and the deceased sailing on a stream. The vignette in the Saite Recension (see Lepsius, *op. cit.*, Bl. 37) shows the deceased poling along a boat wherein are Ra and the *Bennu* bird, and in front of the boat stand the emblem of the

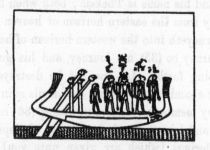

East, the god Osiris, and the *Ṭet, i.e.*, the emblem of Osiris and of stability. The four short lines of text written over the boat read:—The overseer of the house of the overseer of the seal, Nu, triumphant, raiseth up the *Ṭet,* and stablisheth the Buckle, and he saileth with Rā into any place that he pleaseth.

Text: (1) THE BOOK OF MAKING PERFECT THE *KHU* AND OF CAUSING HIM TO GO FORTH INTO THE BOAT OF RĀ ALONG WITH THOSE WHO ARE IN HIS FOLLOWING (?). (2) The overseer of the house of the overseer of the seal, Nu, triumphant, saith:—

"I have brought the divine *Bennu* to the east, and "Osiris to the city of Ṭaṭṭu. (3) I have opened the "treasure houses of the god Ḥāp, I have made clean "the roads of the Disk, and I have drawn the god "Sekeri[1] along (4) upon his sledge. The mighty and "divine Lady hath made me strong at her hour. I "have praised and glorified the Disk, (5) and I have "united myself unto the divine apes who sing at the "dawn, and I am a divine Being among them. I have "made myself a counterpart of the goddess Isis, (6) and "her power (*Khu*) hath made me strong. I have tied "up the rope, I have driven back Āpep, I have made "him to walk backwards. (7) Rā hath stretched out to "me both his hands, and his mariners have not repulsed "me; my strength is the strength of the Eye of Rā, "and the strength of the Eye of Rā is my strength. "(8) If the overseer of the house of the overseer of the "seal, Nu, triumphant, be separated [from the boat of

[1] *I.e.*, the god of the Hennu boat.

"Rā], then shall he (*i.e*, Rā) be separated (9) from the "Egg and from the *Ābṭu* fish."

RUBRIC: [This chapter] shall be recited over the design which hath been drawn above, and it shall be written upon papyrus (10) which hath not been written upon, with [ink made of] grains of green *ābut* mixed with *ānti* water, and the papyrus shall be placed on the breast (11) of the deceased; it shall not enter in to (*i.e.*, touch) his members. If this be done for any deceased person he shall go forth (12) into the boat of Rā in the course of the day every day, and the god Thoth shall take account of him as he cometh forth from (13) and goeth in the course of the day every day, regularly and continually, [into the boat of Rā] as a perfect *khu*, and he shall set up the *Ṭeṭ* and shall stablish the buckle, and shall sail about with Rā into any place he wisheth.

In the Saïte Recension Chapter C. is repeated as CXXIX, and both texts have the same vignette. The rubric of Chapter CXXIX. is, however, fuller than that of Chapter C., and it may conveniently be divided into two parts, the first of which refers to the picture which is ordered to be written upon a piece of new papyrus, and the second to the Chapter itself; the originals of both are to be found in the variant texts of the rubric of the Chapter published by Naville (*op. cit.* Bd. II. p. 236).

CHAPTER CI.

[From the Papyrus of Nu (Brit. Mus. No. 10,477, sheet 27).]

Vignette: In the Papyrus of Nu this Chapter has no vignette. In the Saite Recension the deceased is seen poling along a boat wherein are the god Ra and the *Bennu* bird (see Lepsius, *op. cit.*, Bl. 37).

Text: [THE CHAPTER OF PROTECTING THE BOAT OF RĀ.][1]

"(1) O thou that cleavest the water (2) as thou "comest forth from the stream and dost sit upon thy "place in thy boat, sit thou upon thy place in thy boat "as thou goest forth to thy station of yesterday, and "do thou join the Osiris, the (3) overseer of the house "of the overseer of the seal, Nu, triumphant, the perfect "*Khu*, unto thy mariners, and let thy strength be his "strength. Hail, Rā, in thy name of Rā, (4) if thou "dost pass by the eye of seven cubits, which hath a

[1] This title is taken from the Saïte Recension.

"pupil of three cubits, then verily do thou strengthen "the Osiris Nu, triumphant, the perfect *Khu*, [and let "him be among] thy mariners, and let thy (5) strength "be his strength. Hail, Rā, in thy name of Rā, if "thou dost pass by those who are overturned in death "then verily do thou make the Osiris (6) Nu, triumphant, the perfect soul, to stand up upon his feet, and "may thy strength be his strength. Hail, Rā, in thy "name of Rā, (7) if the hidden things of the underworld are opened unto thee and thou dost gratify (?) "the heart of the cycle of thy gods, then verily do thou "grant joy of heart unto the overseer of the house of "the overseer of the seal, Nu, triumphant, and let thy "strength be his (8) strength. Thy members, O Rā, "are established by (this) Chapter (?)."

RUBRIC: [This chapter] shall be recited over a bandlet of the fine linen of kings [upon which] it hath been written with *ānti*, which shall be laid upon the neck of the perfect *khu* (9) on the day of the burial. If this amulet be laid upon his neck he shall do everything which he desireth to do even like the gods; and he shall join himself unto the followers (10) of Horus; and he shall be stablished as a star face to face with Septet (Sothis); and his corruptible body shall be as a god along with his kinsfolk for ever; and the goddess (11) Menqet shall make plants to germinate upon his body; and the majesty of the god Thoth lovingly shall make the light to rest upon his corruptible body at will, even as he did for the majesty of the King of the North and of the South, the god Osiris, triumphant.

CHAPTER CII.

[From the Papyrus of Nu (Brit. Mus. No. 10,477, sheet 28).]

Vignette : The boat of Rā with the god seated therein and holding a paddle; before him kneels the goddess Isis (?), and behind him the deceased. Sometimes Rā is accompanied by the gods Thoth and Kheperà and sometimes by Anubis alone (see Naville, *op. cit.*, Bd. I. Bl. 114). In the Saïte Recension the deceased is kneeling before Rā at a table of offerings (see Lepsius, *op. cit.*, Bl. 38).

Text : (1) THE CHAPTER OF GOING INTO THE BOAT (2) OF RĀ. The overseer of the house of the overseer of the seal, Nu, triumphant, saith :—

"Hail, thou Great God who art in thy boat, bring "thou me into thy boat. [I have come forward to thy "steps], let me be the director (3) of thy journeyings "and let me be among those who belong to thee and "who are among the stars which never rest. The "things which are an abomination unto thee and the "things which are an abomination unto me I will not "eat, that which is an abomination unto me, (4) that "which is an abomination unto me is filth and I will "not eat thereof; but sepulchral offerings and holy "food [will I eat], and I shall not be overthrown "thereby. I will not draw nigh unto filth with my "hands, and I will not walk (5) thereon with my "sandals, because my bread [is made] of white barley, "and my ale [is made] of red barley; and behold, the "*Sektet* boat and the *Āṭet* boat have brought these "things (6) and have laid the gifts (?) of the lands "upon the altar of the Souls of Ȧnnu. Hymns of "praise be to thee, O Ur-ȧrit-s, as thou travellest "through heaven! Let there be food [for thee], O "dweller in the city of Teni,[1] (7) and when the dogs "gather together let me not suffer harm. I myself "have come, and I have delivered the god from the "things which have been inflicted upon him, and from "the grievous sickness of the body, (8) of the arm, and "of the leg. I have come and I have spit upon the "body, I have bound up the arm, and I have made the "leg to walk. (9) [I have] entered [the boat] and [I] "sail round about by the command of Rā."

[1] A city near the modern Abydos.

CHAPTER CIII.

[From the Papyrus of Nu (Brit. Mus. No. 10,477, sheet 8).]

Vignette: The goddess Hathor, having a disk and horns upon her head, and a sceptre in her left hand; behind her stands the deceased.

Text: (1) THE CHAPTER OF BEING WITH THE GODDESS HATHOR. The overseer of the house of the overseer of the seal, Nu, triumphant, saith:—

"I am the pure traveller. Behold, (2) O Àḥi, "behold, O Àḥi, let me be among those who follow "the goddess Hathor."

CHAPTER CIV.

[From the Papyrus of Nebseni (Brit. Mus. No, 9900, sheet 8).]

Vignette: Two "great gods" seated on thrones facing each other: on the ground between them sits the deceased. In the Saite Recension the deceased is seated on a low pedestal before three gods (see Lepsius, *op. cit.*, Bl. 38).

Text: (1) THE CHAPTER OF SITTING AMONG THE GREAT GODS. . . . . Behold Nebseni, (4) who saith :—

"I sit among the great gods, and I have made a way "for myself (5) through the house of the *Seḥeptet* boat; "and behold, the mantis[1] hath brought me to see the "great gods (6) who dwell in the underworld, and I "shall be triumphant before them, for I am pure."

[1] *Bebait* or *Abait*, *i.e.*, the "praying mantis," or *Mantis religiosa*; see the note to Chapter LXXVI.

CHAPTER CV.

[From the Papyrus of Nu (Brit. Mus. No. 10,477, sheet 7).]

Vignette: The deceased standing before a *ka* on a pedestal (𓂓); with his right hand he pours out a libation, and with his left he makes an offering of incense. In the Papyrus of Nebseni we have the deceased and his wife seated at a table of offerings, and their son pours out a libation and burns incense before them.

Text: (1) THE CHAPTER OF MAKING OFFERINGS TO THE *KA* IN THE UNDERWORLD. The overseer of the house of the overseer of the seal, Nu, triumphant, saith:— (2)

"Homage to thee, O my *ka*, who art my period of "life![1] Grant thou that I may come before thee, and "let me rise up [like the Sun], and let me be strong, "and let me have my soul, (3) and let me gain the "mastery [over mine enemies]. For I have brought to "thee an offering of incense, and I have made myself

[1] Or, "contemporary."

"pure therewith, and I will purify that which issueth "from thee therewith. (4) The evil things which I "have spoken, and the hateful transgressions which I "have committed lay thou not upon me, for I [have] "the mother-of-emerald amulet, which (5) belongeth "unto the neck of Rā, and which hath been placed "[there] by those who dwell in the double horizon (*i.e.*, "the eastern and western parts of the sky). Their "vigour is my vigour, their vigour is my vigour; my "*ka* is like unto their *kas*, and the celestial food of my "*ka* is like unto the celestial food of their *kas*. (6) O "thou who liftest up the Scales and who exaltest right "and truth to the nostrils of Rā this day, let not my "head fall away from me. (7) For, behold, am I not "the eye which looketh upon thee? And am I not the "ear which hearkeneth unto [thee]? For, behold, am "I not the bull of those who have fallen down in "death? And have not sepulchral meals [been made] "for me? (8) And are not those who live in the "heights," or according to another reading, "those "who are chiefs of Nut, for me? [Grant thou that] "I may go forward by thee, for I, even I, am pure, "and [I have] made Osiris to triumph over his "enemies."

CHAPTER CVI.

[From the Papyrus of Nu (Brit. Mus. No. 10,477, sheet 8).]

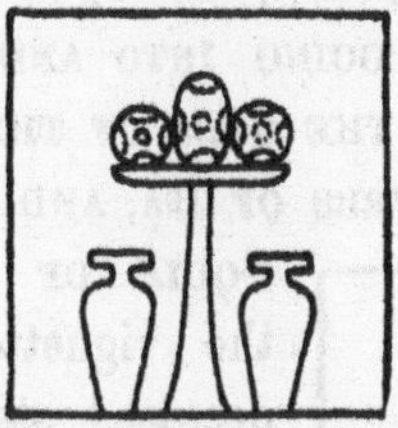

Vignette: A table of offerings. In the Saite Recension the deceased is making offerings to the god Ptaḥ (see Lepsius, *op. cit.*, Bl. 38).

Text: (1) THE CHAPTER OF GIVING SEPULCHRAL MEALS UNTO THE OSIRIS NU, TRIUMPHANT, IN ḤET-PTAḤ-KA (*i.e.*, MEMPHIS) IN THE UNDERWORLD. The overseer of the house of the overseer of the seal, Nu, triumphant, saith :— (2)

"Hail, Great God, thou lord of heavenly food! Hail, "Great God, thou prince of the celestial habitations "which supply bread for the god Ptaḥ! [Hail, Mighty "One who dwellest in the Great House!] Grant ye "unto me bread, grant ye (3) unto me ale, and let me "cleanse myself by means of the haunch and by the "offerings of cakes. Hail, thou divine boat of Sekhet-"Åarru, let these cakes be brought to me (4) by thy "stream, even as thy divine father, the mighty one, "passed thereon in the divine bark."

CHAPTER CVII.

There is no equivalent for this Chapter in the papyri containing the Theban Recension. In the Saïte Recension (see Lepsius, *op. cit.*, Bl. 39) this Chapter is called the "CHAPTER OF GOING INTO AND OF COMING OUT FROM THE GATE OF THE GODS OF THE WEST, OF BEING AMONG THE FOLLOWERS OF RĀ, AND OF KNOWING THE SOULS OF THE WEST," and the vignette represents the deceased standing, with both hands raised in adoration, before Rā, Sebek, Hathor, and a serpent, who rest on the slope of a mountain. The text is actually the first line and a half of Chapter CIX. which is entitled the "CHAPTER OF KNOWING THE SOULS OF THE EAST."

CHAPTER CVIII.

[From the Papyrus of Nu (Brit. Mus. No. 10,477, sheet 8).]

Vignette: The deities Temu, Sebek, lord of Bakhau, and Hathor, lady of Mäsheru, seated.

Text: (1) THE CHAPTER OF KNOWING (2) THE SOULS OF THE WEST. The overseer of the house of the overseer of the seal, Nu, triumphant, saith:—

"Now the Mountain of Bakhau,[1] whereupon this "heaven supports itself, (3) is situated in the eastern "part of heaven, and it hath dimensions of three hun-"dred *khet* (*i.e*, 30,000 cubits)[2] in length, and one "hundred and fifty *khet* (*i.e.*, 15,000 cubits) in breadth; "Sebek, the lord of Bakhau, (4) [dwelleth] to the east "of the Mountain, and his temple is on the earth there. "There is a serpent on the brow of that Mountain, and "he measureth thirty cubits in length; the first eight "cubits of his length are [covered] with (5) flints and "with shining metal plates. The Osiris Nu, triumphant, "knoweth the name of this serpent which [dwelleth] "on his hill, 'Dweller in his fire' (6) is his name. "Now after Rā hath stood still he inclineth his eyes "towards him and a stoppage of the boat [of Rā] taketh "place, and a mighty (7) sleep cometh upon him that is "in the boat, and he gulpeth down seven cubits of the "great waters. Thereby he maketh Suti to depart, "having the harpoon of iron (8) in him, and thereby "he is caused to throw up everything which he hath "eaten, and thereby is Set put into his place of re-"straint. And then [I] recite before him the enchant-

[1] *I.e.*, the mountain of the sunrise.

[2] The Papyrus of Nebseni reads:—"It is a cubit of seven and a half spans (*i.e.*, the width of 30 fingers) of the balance of the earth in its length, and 300 cubits in width, 200."

"ment, saying, (9) Get thee back to the sky, for that "which is in my hand is ready. I stand up in thy "place of restraint, the boat advanceth taking heed to "the way; (10) thy head is covered up while I sail on "and turn back [thy steps]. I am the Man who "covereth thy head and who poureth cold water upon "thy palm, I have strength and (11) I am strong, I "am the divine one who is mighty in enchantments, "namely, the son of Nut, and my splendour hath, "therefore, been delivered unto me. Who, then, is "this venerable *Khu* (12) who advanceth walking upon "his belly and upon his tail and upon the joints of his "back? Verily it is I myself who do walk over thee, "and thy strength is in my power. I am he who (13) "lifteth up strength, and I have come, and I have "become master of the serpents of Rā when he setteth "in my sight at eventide. (14) I go round about "heaven, but thou art fettered with fetters, which "thing was ordained for thee formerly when Rā set "in life in his horizon. I, even I, know (15) how to "guide the matters whereby the serpent Āpep is driven "back, and I know the divine Souls of the West, that "is to say, Tem, and Sebek, the lord of Bakhau, (16) "and Hathor, the lady of the evening."

CHAPTER CIX.

[From the Papyrus of Nu (Brit. Mus. No. 10,477, sheet 12).]

Vignette: The god Ḥeru-khuti (Harmachis) seated; before him is a spotted calf, behind which stands the deceased with both hands raised in adoration of the god; above is the Morning Star. Elsewhere the deceased is seen standing, with both hands raised in adoration, before three seated ibis-headed deities (see Naville, *op. cit.*, Bd. I. Bl. 120). In the Saite Recension (see Lepsius, *op. cit.*, Bl. 39) the vignette is quite different. The god Rā-Harmachis, hawk-headed and wearing a disk which is encircled by a serpent, is seated in a boat; above the disk is the emblem of air, and he holds on his knees the emblem of life. Before him in the boat is a calf, above which is a star, and behind him stands the deceased. The boat is about to sail between two sycamore trees, in front of which stands the deceased, with both hands raised in adoration.

Text: (1) THE CHAPTER OF KNOWING THE SOULS OF THE EAST. (2) The overseer of the house of the overseer of the seal, Nu, triumphant, saith :—

"I, even I, know the eastern gate of heaven—now "its southern part is at the Lake of Kharu (3) and its "northern part is at the canal of the geese—whereout "Rā cometh with winds which make him to advance. "I am he who is concerned with the tackle (?) (4) "[which is] in the divine bark, I am the sailor who "ceaseth not in the boat of Rā. I, even I, know the "two Sycamores (5) of turquoise between which Rā "showeth himself when he strideth forward over the "supports of Shu[1] towards the gate (6) of the lord of "the East through which Rā cometh forth. I, even I, "know the Sekhet-Áarru of (7) Rā, the walls of which "are of iron. The height of the wheat therein is five "cubits, of the ears thereof two cubits, and of the "stalks thereof three cubits. (8) The barley therein "is [in height] seven cubits, the ears thereof are three "cubits, and the stalks thereof are four cubits. And "behold, the *Khus*, each one of whom therein is nine "cubits in height, (9) reap it near the divine Souls of "the East. I, even I, know the divine Souls of the "East, that is to say, Ḥeru-khuti (Harmachis), and the "calf of the goddess Kherá, and (10) the Morning Star[2] "[daily. A divine city hath been built for me, I know "it, and I know the name thereof; 'Sekhet-Áarru' is "its name]."[3]

[1] *I.e.*, the four pillars at the South, North, West, and East of heaven upon which the heavens were believed to rest.

[2] In the Saïte Recension this Chapter is about twice as long as it is in the Theban Recension.

[3] The words in brackets are from the Papyrus of Nebseni.

CHAPTER CX.

[From the Papyrus of Nebseni (Brit. Mus. No. 9900, sheet 17).]

Sekhet-ḥetepet (Papyrus of Nebseni).

Vignette : The Sekhet-ḥetepet or "Fields of peace," commonly called the "Elysian Fields," surrounded and intersected by streams. The divisions contain the following :—(*a*) Nebseni, the scribe and artist of the Temple of Ptaḥ, with his arms hanging by his sides, entering the Elysian Fields. (*b*) The scribe Nebseni making an offering of incense to the "great company of the gods." (*c*) Nebseni seated in a boat paddling; above the boat are three symbols for "city." (*d*) The deceased addressing a bearded, mummied figure. (*e*) Three Pools or Lakes called Urti,[1] Ḥetep,[2] and Qeṭqeṭ respectively. (*f*) Nebseni reaping in Sekhet-ḥetepet. (*g*) Nebseni grasping the *Bennu* bird which is perched upon a stand; in front are three *kas* and three *khus*. (*h*) Nebseni seated and smelling a flower, the text reads: "Thousands of all good and pure things things to the *ka* of Nebseni." (*i*) A table of offerings. (*j*) Four Pools or Lakes called Neb-taui, Uakha, Kha (?), and Ḥetep. (*k*) Nebseni ploughing with oxen by the side of a stream which is one thousand [measures] in length, and the width of which cannot be said; in it there are neither fish nor worms. (*l*) Nebseni ploughing with oxen on an island "the length of which is the length of heaven." (*m*) A division shaped like a bowl in which is inscribed: "The birth-place of the god of the city, Qenqen[et nebt]." (*n*) An island whereon are four gods and a flight of steps; the legend reads: "The great company of the gods who are in Sekhet-ḥetep." (*o*) The boat Tcheṭetfet with eight oars, four at the bows and four at the stern, floating at the end of a canal; in it is a flight of steps. The place where it lies is called the "Domain of Neth." (*p*) Two Pools, the names of which are illegible.

In the Papyrus of Nebseni are two scenes, one on each side of "Sekhet-ḥetepet," or the Elysian Fields. In the first (*A*) Nebseni stands, with both hands raised, and adores the company of the gods who dwell in Sekhet-ḥetep, saying: "Homage "to you, O ye lords of food, I have come in peace to your Field "to receive heavenly food. Grant ye that I may come to the "Great God daily, and grant that I may attain to the offerings, "that is to say, to the cakes, and ale, and oxen, and ducks, and "bread, which are offered unto his *ka*." The three short lines of hieroglyphics (*B*) in front of Nebseni read:—"Nebseni, the "lord of reverence, the scribe and artist in the temples of the "South and of the North, ascribeth praise to the company of

[1] Var. Ḥemat. [2] Var. Ḥast.

"the gods and adoreth the great god." In the second scene Nebseni is standing upright and a youth is pouring a libation over him; at the same time another youth is bringing to him an offering of raiment. The text above him (*C*) reads:—"May "the god Osiris and all the company of the gods who dwell in "Sekhet-ḥetep grant offerings of cakes, and ale, and oxen, and "ducks, and bread, and all good things, and linen garments, "and incense each day, and an offering on the altar each day, "and the receiving of cakes of various kinds, and milk, and "wine, and heavenly food, and the following of the god at his "coming forth during his festivals of Re-stau along with the "favoured ones of the great god, to the *ka* of the scribe Neb-"seni," etc.

The vignette in the Papyrus of Ani (sheet 35) has some interesting variants, and may be thus described:—

(1) Ani making an offering before a hare-headed god, a snake-headed god, and a bull-headed god; behind him stands Thoth, holding his reed and palette. Ani paddling a boat, Ani addressing a hawk, before which are a table of offerings, a beatified being, three Lakes, and the legend "Being at peace in the Field [of Peace], and having air for the nostrils."

(2) Ani reaping corn, Ani driving the oxen which tread out the corn; Ani addressing (or adoring) a *Bennu* bird perched on a stand; Ani seated holding the *kherp* sceptre; a heap of red and a heap of white corn; three *kas* and three *khus*, which are perhaps to be read, "the food of the *khus*"; and three Lakes.

(3) Ani ploughing a field near a stream which contains neither fish nor serpents.

(4) The birthplace of the god of the city; an island on which is a flight of steps; a region called the place of the *khus* who are seven cubits high, the wheat is three cubits high and it is the *sāḥu* who have become perfect who reap it; the region Àshet, the god who dwelleth therein being Unnefer, a boat with eight oars, lying at the end of a canal; and a boat floating on a canal. The name of the first boat "Beḥuṭu-tcheser," and the name of the second, "Tchefau."

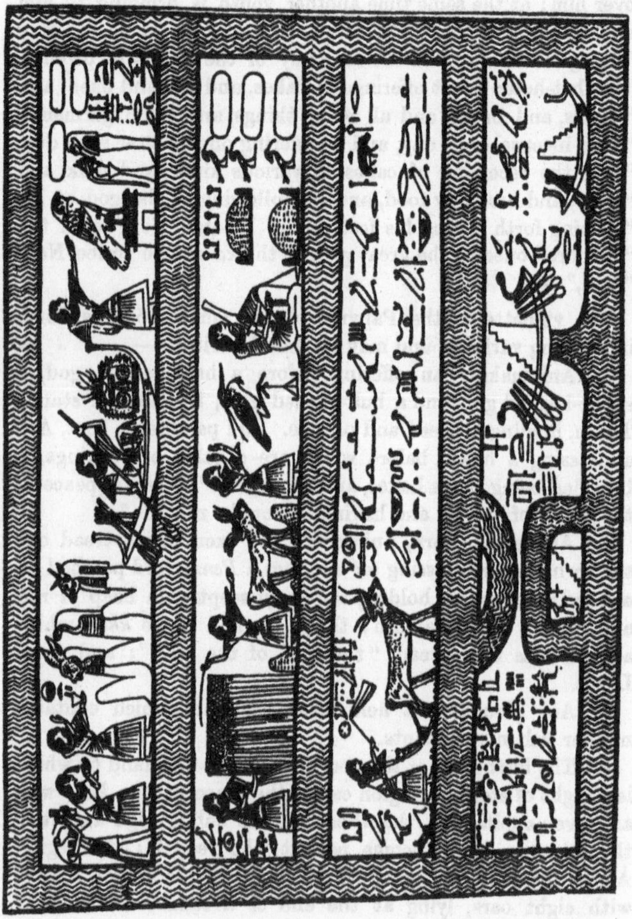

Sekhet-hetepet (Papyrus of Ani).

The vignette in the Papyrus of Ȧnhai (sheet 6) has some further interesting variants, and may be thus described :—

(1) Ȧnhai seated in a boat with her husband, who is rowing it towards two gods who probably represent her father and mother; the handles of the oars terminate in heads of hawks. Behind them stands the god Thoth, ibis-headed, who holds the symbol of life in his right hand, and a sceptre in his left; he is called the "lord of divine words" 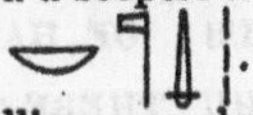. To the left is the lady Ȧnhai, with her hair falling over her face, bowing before two divine beings; one of these is "her mother Neferitu," , and the other is probably her father. Hence we may assume that the Egyptians expected to meet and to know their relatives in the world beyond the grave. Behind Ȧnhai is a male figure digging in a mound of earth; he is probably her husband. (2) The lady Ȧnhai, standing by the side of a table of offerings, with her hands raised in adoration before a seated god, who is here the representative of "the gods, the lords of the Ṭuat"; before him, on a table, are a libation vase and a lotus, and between the god and Ȧnhai stands the *bennu* bird on his accustomed perch. In the field close by are growing two kinds of cereals, i.e., red barley and wheat; Ȧnhai's husband is reaping the wheat, and Ȧnhai herself follows behind with what is, apparently, a rush basket or bag. (3) A field intersected by a portion of a stream, on each side of which Ȧnhai is seen ploughing with a yoke of oxen. In the text above the deceased says, "May I come therein, and "may my soul follow after me [and obtain] divine food. May "I plough therein and reap therein, even I, the singer of Ȧmen, "Ȧnhai, triumphant." (4) A field wherein are four lakes, the names of which are not given, two granaries, and two small islands. The upper island is the "birthplace of the god of the city," and the lower the abode of the company of the gods who are here represented by four of their number. On the bank of one canal stand two *bennu* birds, and at the end of an arm of the river is moored a boat wherein is a flight of steps; the boat is provided with four oars, two being placed at the bow and two at the stern.

Text: (1) HERE BEGIN THE CHAPTERS OF SEKHET-ḤETEPET, AND THE CHAPTERS OF COMING FORTH BY DAY; OF GOING INTO AND OF COMING OUT FROM THE UNDERWORLD; OF COMING TO SEKHET-ÅARU; OF BEING IN SEKHET-(2)ḤETEPET, THE MIGHTY CITY, THE LADY OF WINDS; OF HAVING POWER THERE; OF BECOMING A *KHU* THERE; OF PLOUGHING THERE; OF REAPING THERE; OF EATING THERE; OF DRINKING THERE; OF MAKING LOVE (3) THERE; AND OF DOING EVERYTHING EVEN AS A MAN DOETH UPON EARTH. Behold the scribe and artist of the Temple of Ptah, Nebseni, who (4) saith :—

"Set hath taken possession of Horus, who looked "with the two eyes upon the building (?) round Sekhet-"ḥetep, but I have unfettered Horus [and taken him "from] Set, and Set hath opened the ways of the two "eyes [which are] in heaven. (5) Set hath cast (?) his "moisture to the winds upon the soul [who hath] his "day (*or* his eye) and who dwelleth in the city of Mert, "and he hath delivered the interior of the body of Horus "from the Åkeru gods. Behold me (6) now, for I "make this mighty boat to travel over the Lake of "Ḥetep, and I brought it away with might from the "palace of Shu; the domain of his stars groweth young "and reneweth its former strength. I have brought the "boat (7) into the lakes thereof so that I may come "forth into the cities thereof, and I have sailed into "their divine city Ḥetep. And behold, it is because I, "even I, am at peace with his seasons, and with his

Sekhet-ḥetepet (Papyrus of Ȧnhai).

"guidance, and with his territory, and with the company of the gods who (8) are his firstborn. He maketh "the two divine fighters (*i.e.*, Horus and Set) to be at "peace with those who watch over the living ones whom "he hath created in fair form, and he bringeth peace "[with him]; he maketh the two divine fighters to be "at peace with those who watch over (9) them. He "cutteth off the hair from the divine fighters, he driveth "away storm from the helpless, and he keepeth away "harm from the *Khus.* (10) Let me gain dominion "within that Field, for I know it, and I have sailed "among its lakes so that I might come into its cities. "My mouth is strong; and I am equipped [with "weapons to use] against the *Khus*; let them not "have dominion over me. (11) Let me be rewarded "with thy fields, O thou god Ḥetep; that which is thy "wish shalt thou do, O lord of the winds. May I "become a *khu* therein, may I eat therein, may I drink "therein, (12) may I plough therein, may I reap therein, "may I fight therein, may I make love therein, may my "words be mighty therein, may I never be in a state of "servitude therein, (13) but may I be in authority "therein. Thou hast made strong (?) the mouth and "the throat (?) of the god Ḥetep; Qetetbu is its (?) "name. He is stablished upon the watery supports (?) "of the god Shu, and is linked unto the pleasant things "of Rā. (14) He is the divider of years, he is hidden "of mouth, his mouth is silent, that which he uttereth "is secret, he fulfilleth eternity and taketh possession of "everlastingness of existence as Ḥetep, the lord Ḥetep. "The god Horus (15) maketh himself to be strong like "unto the Hawk which is one thousand cubits in length "and two thousand [cubits in width] in life; he hath "equipments with him, and he journeyeth on and "cometh where the seat of his (16) heart wisheth in "the Pools thereof and in the cities thereof. He was "begotten in the birth-chamber of the god of the city, "he hath offerings [made unto him] of the food of the "god of the city, he performeth that which it is meet "to do therein, and the union thereof, in the matter of "everything of the birth-chamber (17) of the divine "city. When [he] setteth in life like crystal he per- "formeth everything therein, and these things are like "unto the things which are done in the Lake of double "Fire, wherein there is none that rejoiceth, and wherein "are all manner of (18) evil things. The god Ḥetep "goeth in, and cometh out, and goeth backwards [in] "that Field which gathered together all manner of "things for the birth-chamber of the god of the city. "When he setteth in life like (19) crystal he performeth "all manner of things therein which are like unto the "things which are done in the Lake of double Fire, "wherein there is none that rejoiceth, and wherein are "no evil things whatsoever. [Let me] live with the "god Ḥetep, (20) clothed and not despoiled by the lords "of the north (?), and may the lords of divine things "bring food unto me; may he make me to go forward "and may I come forth, and may he bring my power to

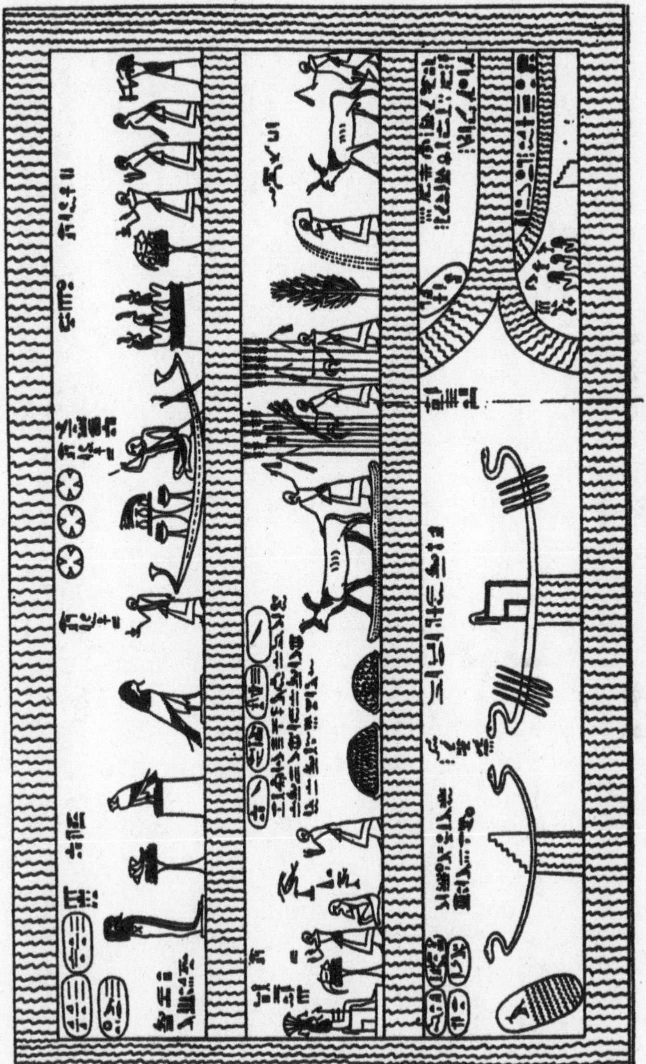

Sekhet-ḥetepet. (From the Turin Papyrus—Ptolemaic Period.)

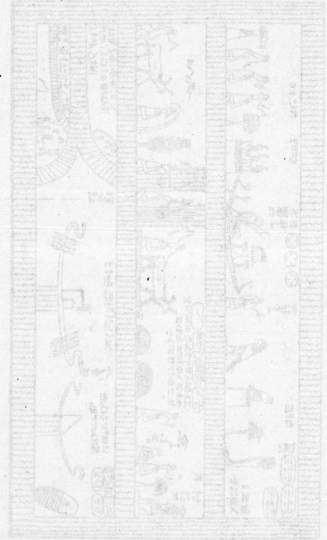

"me (21) there, and may I receive it, and may my "equipment be from the god Ḥetep. May I gain the "mastery over the great and mighty word which is in "my body in this my place, and by it I will (22) "remember and I will forget. Let me go forward "on my journey, "and let me "plough. I am "at peace in the "divine city,[1] "and I know the "waters, cities, "(23) nomes, and "lakes which are "in Sekhet-ḥe-

Khepera in his boat, by which stand Isis and Nephthys (Turin Papyrus).

"tep. I exist therein, I am strong therein, I become a "*khu* therein, I eat therein, I sow (24) seed therein, I "reap the harvest therein, I plough therein, I make "love therein, I am at peace with the god Ḥetep "therein. Behold (25) I scatter seed therein, I sail "about among its Lakes and I come forward to the "cities thereof, O divine Ḥetep. Behold, my mouth is "equipped with my horns [for teeth], grant me an over-"flowing supply of the food whereon the *kas* and *khus* "(26) [live]. I have passed the judgment of Shu upon "him that knoweth him, so that I may go forth to the "cities thereof, and may sail about among its lakes and "may walk about in Sekhet-ḥetep; (27) and behold, Rā

[1] Or, "I am at peace with the god of the city."

"is in heaven, and behold, the god Ḥetep is its double "offering. I have come onward to its land, I have put "on my girdle (?), I have come forth so that the gifts "which are about to be given unto me may be (28) "given, I have made gladness for myself. I have laid "hold upon my "strength which "the god Ḥetep "hath greatly in-"creased for me. "O Unen-em-"ḥetep,[1] I have "entered into "thee and my "soul (29) fol-

Deceased adoring Osiris (Turin Papyrus).

"loweth after me, and my divine food is upon both my "hands, O Lady of the two lands,[2] who stablishest my "word whereby I remember and forget; (30) I would "live without injury, without any injury [being done] "unto me, O grant to me, O do thou grant to me, joy "of heart. Make thou me to be at peace, bind thou up "my sinews and muscles, and make me to receive the "(31) air. O Un[en] em-ḥetep, thou Lady of the "winds, I have entered into thee and I have opened "(*i.e.*, shown) my head. Rā falleth asleep, but I am "awake, and there is the goddess Hast at the gate of

[1] *I.e.*, "Existence in Peace," the name of the first large section of the Elysian Fields.

[2] The name of a Pool in the second section of the Elysian Fields.

"heaven (32) by night. Obstacles have been set before "me, but I have gathered together what he hath "emitted. I am in my city. O Nut-urt,[1] I have "entered into thee, and I have counted my harvest, "(33) and I go forward to Uakh.[2] I am the Bull en-"veloped in tur-"quoise, the lord "of the Field of "the Bull, the "lord of the di-"vine speech of "the goddess "Septet (Sothis) "(34) at her "hours. O Uakh,

Deceased adoring two of the children of Horus (Turin Papyrus).

"I have entered into thee, I have eaten my bread, I "have gotten the mastery over choice pieces of the flesh "of oxen and of feathered fowl, and the birds of Shu "have been given unto (35) me; I follow after the "gods and [I come after] the divine *kas*. O Tchefet,[3] "I have entered into thee. I array myself in apparel "(36), and I gird myself with the *sa* garment of Rā; "now, behold, [he is] in heaven, and those who dwell "therein follow Rā, and [I] follow Rā in heaven. O "Unen-em-(37)ḥetep, lord of the two lands, I have "entered into thee, and I have plunged into the lakes

[1] The name of a Pool in the first section of the Elysian Fields.
[2] The name of a Pool in the second section of the Elysian Fields.
[3] The name of a district in the third section of the Elysian Fields.

"of Tchesert; behold me, for all filth hath departed "from me. The Great God (38) groweth therein, and "behold, I have found [food therein]; I have snared "feathered fowl "and I feed upon "the finest [of "them]. O Qen-"qentet,[1] (39) I "have entered "into thee, and "I have seen "the Osiris [my "father], and I have gazed upon my mother, and I "have made love. I have caught the worms and "serpents, and I am delivered. (40) And I know the "name of the god who is opposite to the goddess "Tchesert, and who hath straight hair and is equipped "with two horns; he reapeth, and I both plough (41) "and reap. O Ḥast, I have entered into thee, I have "driven back those who would come to the turquoise "[sky], and I have followed the winds of the company "of the gods. The Great God hath given my head "(42) unto me, and he who hath bound on me my head "is the Mighty one who hath turquoise (?) eyes, namely, "Åri-en-åb-f (*i.e.*, he doeth as he pleaseth). O Usert,[2] "I have come into thee at the head of the house wherein "(43) divine food is brought for me. O Smam,[2] I have

Deceased adoring two of the children of Horus (Turin Papyrus).

[1] The name of a Pool in the first section of the Elysian Fields.
[2] The name of a Pool in the third section of the Elysian Fields.

"come into thee. My heart watcheth, my head is "equipped with the white crown, I am led into "celestial regions, and I make to flourish (44) terres-"trial objects, and there is joy of heart for the Bull, "and for celestial beings, and for the company of the "gods. I am the god who is the Bull, the lord of the "gods, as he goeth forth from the turquoise [sky]. O "divine nome of wheat and barley, (45) I have come "into thee, I have come forward to thee, and I have "taken up that which followeth me, namely, the best of "the libations of the company of the gods. I have tied "up my boat in the celestial lakes, (46) I have lifted "up the post at which to anchor, I have recited the "prescribed words with my voice, and I have ascribed "praises unto the gods who dwell in Sekhet-ḥetep."

CHAPTER CXI.

In the Theban Recension this Chapter has not as yet been found. In the Saïte Recension it is called "The Chapter of knowing the Souls of Pe," but an examination of the text shows that it is identical with that of Chapter CVIII.; it has no vignette.

CHAPTER CXII.

[From the Papyrus of Nu (Brit. Mus. No. 10,477, sheet 18).]

Vignette: The gods Horus (hawk-headed), Mesthȧ, and Ḥāpi, seated.

Text: (1) ANOTHER CHAPTER OF KNOWING THE SOULS OF PE. The overseer of the house of the overseer of the seal, Nu, triumphant, saith:—

"[Hail,] Khaṭ, who dwellest in Khaṭ, in Ȧnpet,[1] and "in the nome of Khaṭ! [Hail,] ye goddesses of the "chase (2) who dwell in the city of Pe, ye celestial "lands (?), ye stars, and ye divine beings, who give "cakes and ale (?), do ye know (3) for what reason the "city of Pe hath been given unto Horus? I, even I, "know, though ye know it not. Behold, Rā gave the "city unto him in return for (4) the injury in his eye, "for which cause Rā said to Horus, 'Let me see what "is coming to pass in thine eye,' and forthwith he "looked thereat. Then Rā said (5) to Horus, 'Look

[1] A name of the city of Mendes, the metropolis of the sixteenth nome of Lower Egypt.

"at that black pig,' and he looked, and straightway an "injury was done unto his eye, [namely,] (6) a mighty "storm [took place]. Then said Horus unto Rā, "'Verily, my eye seems as if it were an eye upon "which Suti had inflicted a blow'; [and thus saying] "he ate (7) his heart.[1] Then said Rā to those gods, "'Place ye him in his chamber, and he shall do well.' "Now the black pig was Suti who had transformed "himself into a (8) black pig, and he it was who had "aimed the blow of fire which was in the eye of Horus. "Then said Rā unto those gods, 'The pig is an "abominable thing unto Horus; (9) O but he shall "do well although the pig is an abomination unto him.' "Then the company of the gods, who were among the "divine followers of Horus when he existed in the form of "his own child, said, (10) 'Let sacrifices be made [to "the gods] of his bulls, and of his goats, and of his pigs. "Now the father of Mesthi, Ḥāpi, Ṭuamāutef, (11) and "Qebḥsennuf is Horus, and their mother is Isis. Then "said Horus to Rā, 'Give me two divine brethren in "the city of Pe and two divine brethren in the city of "Nekhen, (12) who [have sprung] from my body and "who shall be with me in the guise of everlasting "judges, then shall the earth blossom and thunder-"clouds and rain be blotted out.' And the name of "Horus became 'Ḥer-uatch-f' (*i.e.*, Prince of his emerald "stone). I, even I, (13) know the Souls of Pe, namely, "Horus, Mesthi, and Ḥāpi."

[1] *I.e.*, he lost his temper and raged.

CHAPTER CXIII.

[From the Papyrus of Nu (Brit. Mus. No. 10,477, sheet 18).]

Vignette: The gods Horus, Tuamāutef and Qebhsennuf.

Text: (1) THE CHAPTER OF KNOWING THE SOULS OF NEKHEN. The overseer of the house of the overseer of the seal, Nu, triumphant, saith:— (2)

"I know the hidden things of the city of Nekhen, "that is to say, the things which the mother of Horus "did for him, and how she [made her voice to go forth] "over the waters, saying, 'Speak ye unto me concern-"ing the judgment which is upon me, [and show me] "the path behind you, and let me discover [it]'; and "how Rā said, 'This son of Isis hath perished'; and "what the mother of Horus did for him [when] she "cried out, saying, (3) 'Sebek, the lord of the papyrus "swamp, shall be brought to us.' [And Sebek] fished "for them and he found them, and the mother of Horus "made them to grow in the places to which they be-"longed. Then Sebek, the lord of his papyrus swamp, "said, 'I went and I found the place where they had "passed with my fingers on the edge of the waters, and "I enclosed them in [my] net: (4) and strong was that "net.' And Rā said, 'So, then, there are fish with the "god Sebek, and [he] hath found the hands and arms "of (5) Horus for him in the land of fish'; and [that] "land became the land of the city of Remu (*i.e.*, Fish). "And Rā said, 'A land of the pool, a land of the "pool to this net.' Then were the hands of Horus "brought to him (6) at the uncovering of his face at "the festivals of the month and half month in the "Land of Remu. And Rā said, 'I give the city of "Nekhen to Horus for the habitation of his two arms "and hands, and his face shall be uncovered (7) before "his two hands and arms in the city of Nekhen; and I "give into his power the slaughtered beings who are in "them at the festivals of the month and half month.' "Then Horus said, 'Let me carry off (8) Tuamāutet "and Qebḥsennuf, and let them watch over my body; "and if they are allowed to be there, then shall they "be subservient to the god of the city of Nekhen.' (9) "And Rā said, 'It shall be granted unto thee there and "in the city of Senket (*i.e.*, Sati), and there shall be "done for them what hath been done for those who "dwell in the city of Nekhen, and verily they shall be "with thee.' (10) And Horus said, 'They have been "with thee and [now] they shall be with me, and shall "hearken unto the god Suti when he calleth upon the "Souls of Nekhen.' Grant to me [that I, even I, may "pass on to the Souls of Nekhen, and that I may un-"loose the bonds of Horus]. I, even I, know the Souls "of Nekhen, namely, (11) Horus, Ṭuamāutef, and "Qebḥsennuf."

CHAPTER CXIV.

[From the Papyrus of Nebseni (Brit. Mus. No. 9900, sheet 7).]

Vignette: Three ibis-headed gods. In the Saïte Recension the deceased is standing, with both hands raised in adoration, before the gods Thoth, Sa, and Tem (see Lepsius, *op. cit.*, Bl. 43).

Text: (1) THE CHAPTER OF KNOWING THE SOULS OF KHEMENNU (Hermopolis).

"(2) The goddess Maāt is carried by the arm at the "shining of the goddess Neith in the city of Mentchat, "and at the shining (3) of the Eye when it is weighed. "I am carried over by it and I know what it bringeth "from the city of Kesi,[1] (4) and I will neither declare "it unto men nor tell it unto the gods. I have come,

[1] *I.e.*, Cusae, the metropolis of the fourteenth nome of Upper Egypt.

"being the envoy of Rā, to stablish (5) Maāt upon the "arm at the shining of Neith in the city of Mentchat "and to adjudge the eye to him that shall scrutinize it. "I have come as (6) a power through the knowledge of "the Souls of Khemennu (Hermopolis) who love to know "what ye love. I know Maāt, (7) which hath germi-"nated, and hath become strong, and hath been judged, "and I have joy in passing judgment upon the things "which are to be judged. Homage to you, O ye Souls "of Khemennu, I, even I, know (8) the things which "are unknown on the festivals of the month and half "month. Rā knoweth the hidden things of the night, "and know ye that it is Thoth who hath made me to "have knowledge. (9) Homage to you, O ye Souls of "Khemennu, since I know you each day."

CHAPTER CXV.

[From the Papyrus of Nu (Brit. Mus. No. 10,477, sheet 18).]

Vignette: In the Papyrus of Nu this Chapter has no vignette. In the Saïte Recension the deceased is standing, with both hands raised in adoration, before the gods Rā, Shu, and Tefnut (see Lepsius, *op. cit.*, Bl. 44).

Text: (1) THE CHAPTER OF COMING FORTH FROM HEAVEN, AND OF MAKING A WAY THROUGH THE ÅMME-ḤET, AND OF KNOWING THE SOULS OF ÅNNU (HELIOPOLIS). The overseer of the house of the overseer of the seal, Nu, triumphant, saith:—(2)

"I have passed the day since yesterday among the "great divine beings, and I have come into being along "with the god Kheperȧ. [My] face is uncovered before "the Eye, the only One, and the orbit of the night hath "been opened. (3) I am a divine being among you. I "know the Souls of Ånnu. Shall not the god Ur-ma "pass over it as [he] journeyeth (4) forward with "vigour? Have I not overcome (?), and have I not "spoken to the gods? Behold, he that is the heir of "Ånnu hath been destroyed. I, even I, know for what "reason was made the lock of hair of the (5) Man. Rā "spake unto the god Åmi-haf, and an injury was done "unto his mouth, that is to say, he was wounded in "[that] mouth. And Rā spake (6) unto the god Åmi-"haf, saying, 'O heir of men, receive [thy] harpoon'; "and the harpoon-house came into being. Behold, O "god Åmi-haf, two divine brethren have come into "being, [that is to say] (7) Senti-Rā came into being, "and Setem-ånsi-f came into being. And his hand "stayed not, and he made his form into that of a "woman with a lock of hair (8) which became the "divine lock in Ånnu, and which became the strong "and mighty one in this temple; and it became the "strong one of Ånnu, and it became the heir of (9) the "heir of Ur-maat-f (*i.e.*, the mighty one of the two "eyes), and it became before him the god Ur-ma of "Ȧnnu. I know the Souls of Ȧnnu, (10) namely, Rā, "Shu, and Tefnut."

CHAPTER CXVI.

[From the Papyrus of Nu (Brit. Mus. No. 10,477, sheet 18).]

Vignette: The deceased adoring three ibis-headed gods. In the Saïte Recension the deceased is standing, with both hands raised in adoration, before the gods Thoth, Sa, and Tem (see Lepsius, *op. cit.*, Bl. 44).

Text: (1) ANOTHER CHAPTER OF KNOWING THE SOULS OF KHEMENNU (HERMOPOLIS). The overseer of the house of the overseer of the seal, Nu, triumphant, saith:— (2)

"The goddess Neith shineth in Matchat, and the "goddess Maāt is carried by the arm of him who eateth "the Eye, and who is its divine judge, and the Sem "priest carrieth (3) me over upon it. I will not declare "it unto men, and I will not tell it unto the gods; I will "not declare it unto men, and I will not tell it unto the "gods. I have entered in being an ignorant man, and "I have seen the hidden things. (4) Homage to you, "O ye gods who dwell in Khemennu, ye know me even "as I know the goddess Neith, and [ye give] to the "Eye the growth which endureth. (5) There is joy [to "[me] at the judgment of the things which are to be "judged. I, even I, know the Souls of Ȧnnu; they "are great at the festival of the month, and are little "at the festival of the half month. They are Thoth "(6) the Hidden One, and Sa, and Tem."

RUBRIC: If this chapter be known [by the deceased] offal shall be an abomination unto him, and he shall not drink filthy water.

CHAPTER CXVII.

[From the Papyrus of Nu (Brit. Mus. No. 10,477, sheet 9).]

Vignette: The deceased, holding a staff in his left hand, about to walk up one side of a hill of the horizon. In the Saïte Recension the god Anubis is leading the deceased to a shrine which is set on a hill (see Lepsius, *op. cit.*, Bl. 44).

Text: (1) THE CHAPTER OF RECEIVING PATHS [WHEREON TO WALK] IN RE-STAU. The overseer of the house of the overseer of the seal, Nu, triumphant, saith :— (2)

"The paths which are above me [lead] to Re-stau. "I am he who is girt about with his girdle and who "cometh forth from the [goddess of] the *Ureret* crown. "I have come, and I have stablished things in Àbṭu "(Abydos), (3) and I have opened out paths in Re-stau. "The god Osiris hath eased my pains. I am he who "maketh the waters to come into being, and who "setteth his throne [thereon], and who maketh his "path through the funeral valley and through the "Great Lake. (4) I have made my path, and indeed "I am [Osiris].

"[Osiris was victorious over his enemies, and the "Osiris Nebqeṭ is victorious over his enemies. He "hath become as one of yourselves, [O ye gods], his "protector is the Lord of eternity, he walketh even as "ye walk, he standeth even as ye stand, he sitteth "even as ye sit, and he talketh even as ye talk in the "presence of the Great God, the Lord of Àmentet.]"[1]

[1] The words in brackets are from the Papyrus of Neb-qet (sheet 3).

CHAPTER CXVIII.

[From the Papyrus of Nu (Brit. Mus. No. 10,477, sheet 9).]

Vignette : The deceased holding a staff in his left hand. In the Saïte Recension this Chapter has no vignette.

Text : (1) THE CHAPTER OF COMING FORTH FROM RE-STAU. The overseer of the house of the overseer of the seal, Nu, triumphant, saith :—

"I was born in (2) Re-stau, and splendour hath been "given unto me by those who dwell in their spiritual "bodies (*sāḥu*) in the habitation where libations are "made unto Osiris. The divine ministers who are in "Re-stau shall receive [me] (3) when Osiris is led into "the twofold funeral region of Osiris; O let me be a "divine being whom they shall lead into the twofold "funeral region of Osiris."

CHAPTER CXIX.

[From the Papyrus of Nu (Brit. Mus. No. 10,477, sheet 9).]

Vignette: The deceased adoring the god Osiris who stands in a shrine. In the Saïte Recension the deceased is walking away from a shrine which is set upon a hill (see Lepsius, *op. cit.*, Bl. 44).

Text: (1) THE CHAPTER OF COMING FORTH FROM RE-STAU.[1] The overseer of the house of the overseer of the seal, Nu, triumphant, saith :— (2)

"I am the Great God who maketh his light. I have "come to thee, O Osiris, and I offer praise unto (3) "thee. [I am] pure from the issues which are carried "away from thee. Thy name is made in Re-stau, and "thy power is in Àbṭu (Abydos). Thou art raised up, "then, O Osiris, (4) and thou goest round about through

[1] A fuller title of this Chapter is, "The Chapter of knowing the name of Osiris, and of going into and of coming forth from Re-stau."

"heaven with Rā, and thou lookest upon the genera-"tions of men, O thou One who circlest, thou Rā. "Behold, verily I have said unto thee, O Osiris, 'I am "(5) the spiritual body of the God,' and I say, 'Let it "come to pass that I shall never be repulsed before "thee, O Osiris.'"

The following is the Chapter in a fuller form:—[1]

(1) THE CHAPTER OF KNOWING THE NAME OF OSIRIS AND OF ENTERING INTO AND OF GOING OUT FROM RE-STAU [IN ALL THE FORMS WHEREIN HE WILLETH TO COME FORTH].[2] The scribe, Mes-em-neter, triumphant, saith:— (2)

"I am the Great Name who maketh (3) his light. I "have come to thee, O Osiris, and I offer praise unto "thee. I am pure from the issues which are carried "away from thee. [Thy] name hath been made in Re-"stau when it hath fallen (4) therein. Homage to thee, "O Osiris, in thy strength and in thy power, thou hast "obtained the mastery in Re-stau. Thou art raised "up, O Osiris, in thy (5) might and in thy power, thou "art raised up, O Osiris, and thy might is in Re-stau, "and thy power is in Ȧbṭu (Abydos). Thou goest "round about through heaven, and (6) thou sailest "before Rā, and thou lookest upon the generations of "men, O thou Being who circlest, thou Rā. Behold, "verily I have said unto thee, O Osiris, 'I am the

[1] For the text see Naville, *op. cit.*, Bd. I. Bl. 130.
[2] The words in brackets are from the Papyrus of Ȧmen-em-ḥeb (see Naville, *op. cit.*, Bd. II. p. 267).

"spiritual body of the God,' and I say, 'Let it come
"to pass that I shall never be repulsed before thee, O
"Osiris.'"

CHAPTER CXX.

Vignette: **This Chapter is without a vignette both in the Theban and Saïte Recensions.**

Text: In the Saite Recension this Chapter is given twice; see Lepsius, *op. cit.*, Bll. 3 and 45, and *supra*, Chapter XII.

CHAPTER CXXI.

Vignette: **This Chapter is without a vignette both in the Theban and Saïte Recensions.**

Text: In the Saïte Recension this Chapter is given twice; see Lepsius, *op. cit.*, Bll. 4 and 45, and *supra* Chapter XIII.

CHAPTER CXXII.

[From the Papyrus of Nu (Brit. Mus. No. 10,477, sheet 9).]

Vignette: The Papyrus of Nu is the only document containing the Theban Recension which is known, at present, to give a text of this Chapter, but it is without a vignette. In the Saïte Recension the deceased is bowing before a shrine which is set upon a hill (see Lepsius, *op. cit.*, Bl. 45).

Text: (1) THE CHAPTER OF GOING IN AFTER COMING FORTH [FROM THE UNDERWORLD]. The overseer of the house of the overseer of the seal, Nu, triumphant, saith:— (2)

"Open unto me!" Who then art thou? Whither goest thou? What is thy name? "I am one of you, "'Assembler of Souls' is the name of my boat; (3) "'Making the hair to stand on end' is the name of the "oars; 'Watchful one' is the name of its bows; 'Evil "is it' is the name of the rudder; 'Steering straight "for the middle' is the name of (4) the Mātchabet; so "likewise [the boat] is a type of my sailing onward to "the pool. Let there be given unto me vessels of milk, "(5) together with cakes, and loaves of bread, and cups "of drink, and pieces of meat in the Temple of Ȧnpu," or (as others say), "Grant thou me [these things] "wholly. Let it be so done unto me that I may "enter in (6) like a hawk, and that I may come "forth like the *Bennu* bird, [and like] the Morning "Star. Let me make [my] path so that [I] may go in "peace into the beautiful Ȧmentet, and let the Lake "of Osiris be mine. (7) Let me make my path, and "let me enter in, and let me adore Osiris, the Lord of "life."[1]

CHAPTER CXXIII. OR CXXXIX.[2]

[From the Papyrus of Nu (Brit. Mus. No. 10,477, sheet 15).]

Vignette: The deceased, or his soul, standing before a palace or shrine; in the Saïte Recension this Chapter has no vignette.

[1] Several passages in this Chapter are also found in Chapter LVIII.

[2] This Chapter occurs twice in the Saïte Recension; see Lepsius, *op. cit.*, Bll. 45 and 57. As Chap. CXXIII. it is called "Another Chapter," but as Chap. CXXXIX. it is called "A hymn of praise to Tem."

Text: (1) The Chapter of entering into the Great House.[1] The overseer of the house of the overseer of the seal, Nu, triumphant, saith:—

"Homage to thee, O Thoth. I am Thoth, who have "weighed the two divine Fighters (*i.e.*, Horus and "Set), (2) I have destroyed their warfare and I have "diminished their wailings. I have delivered the *Àṭu* "fish in his turning back, and I have performed that "which thou didst order (3) concerning him, and after-"wards I lay down within my eye. [I am he who hath "been without opposition. I have come; do thou look "upon me in the Temple of Nem-ḥra (or Uḥem-ḥra).] "I give commands in the words of the divine aged ones, "and, moreover, I guide for thee the lesser deities."

[1] Two copies of this Chapter taken from royal tombs are given by Naville with Chapter CXXV. (Ueberschrift); see *Todtenbuch*, Bd. II., p. 335.

CHAPTER CXXIV.

[From the Papyrus of Nu (Brit. Mus. No. 10,477, sheet 10).]

Vignette: The deceased adoring Mesthȧ, Ḥāpi, Ṭuamāutef and Qebḥsennuf.[1]

Text: (1) THE CHAPTER OF GOING INTO THE PRESENCE OF THE DIVINE SOVEREIGN PRINCES OF OSIRIS. (2) The overseer of the house of the overseer of the seal, Nu, triumphant, saith:—

"My soul hath built for me a habitation in the city "of Ṭaṭṭu; I sow seed in the city of Pe, and (3) I "plough my field with my labourers (?), and for this "reason my palm tree is like Ȧmsu. That which is an "abomination unto me, that which is an abomination "unto me I shall not eat. (4) That which is an abo-"mination unto me, that which is an abomination unto "me is filth. I shall not eat thereof; by sepulchral

[1] In the Papyrus of Nu Chapter CXXIV. is given under the title, "Chapter of making the transformation into a *Bennu* bird," and the vignette above it is a *Bennu* bird. In the vignette here given the artist has omitted a god.

"meals and food I shall not be destroyed. [The abo-"minable thing] I shall not take into my hands, (5) I "shall not walk upon it in my sandals, because my "cakes are [made] of white grain, and my ale is [made] "of red grain, and behold, (6) the *Sektet* boat and the "*Māṭet* boat bring them to me, and I eat [thereof] "under the branches of [the trees], the beautiful arms "[of which] I know. O let (7) splendour be prepared "for me with the white crown which is lifted up upon "me by the uraei-goddesses. Hail, thou guardian of "the divine doors of the god Seḥetep-taui (*i.e.*, 'he who "maketh the world to be at peace'), bring thou (8) to "me that of which they make sepulchral meals; grant "thou that I may lift up the branches (?). (9) May the "god of light open to me his arms, and may the com-"pany of the gods keep silence whilst the denizens (10) "of heaven talk with the overseer of the house of the "overseer of the seal, Nu, triumphant. I am the leader "of the hearts of the gods who strengthen (11) me, "and I am a mighty one among the divine beings. If "any god or any goddess (12) shall come forth against "me he shall be judged by the ancestors of the year "who live upon hearts (13) and who make (?) cakes (?) "for me, and Osiris shall devour him at [his] coming "forth (14) from Ȧbṭu (Abydos). He shall be judged "by the ancestors of Rā, and he shall be judged by the "(15) God of Light who clotheth heaven among the "divine princes. I shall have bread in my mouth at "stated seasons, and I shall enter in before the gods

"Åḥiu. (16) He shall speak with me, and I shall "speak with the followers of the gods. I shall speak "with the Disk and I shall speak with the denizens of "heaven. (17) I shall put the terror of myself into "the blackness of night which is in the goddess Meḥ-"urt, [who is near] him that dwelleth in might. (18) "And behold, I shall be there with Osiris. My con-"dition of completeness shall be his condition of com-"pleteness among the divine princes. I shall speak "unto him [with] the words of (19) men, and he shall "repeat unto me the words of the gods. A *khu* who is "equipped [with power] shall come.[1] I am a *khu* who "is equipped [with power]; I am equipped [with the "power] of all the *khus*, [being the form of the *Sāḥu* "(*i.e.*, spiritual bodies) of Ånnu, Ṭaṭṭu, Suten-ḥenen, "Åbṭu, Åpu, and Sennu.[2] The Osiris Åuf-ānkh is "victorious over every god and every goddess who are "hidden in Neter-khertet]."[3]

CHAPTER CXXV.

The CXXVth Chapter consists of three parts: the Introduction, the Negative Confession, and a concluding text. The Introduction was said when the deceased arrived at the Hall of double Maāti; the Negative

[1] The Papyrus of Mes-em-neter adds, "bringing right unto thee the divine being who loveth her."

[2] *I.e.*, Heliopolis, Mendes or Busiris, Heracleopolis, Abydos, Panopolis, and Sennu (a city near Panopolis).

[3] The words in brackets are from the Saïte Recension (see Lepsius, *op. cit.*, Bl. 46).

Confession was recited by him before the forty-two gods who were in this Hall; and the concluding text when he came into the underworld.

I. The Introduction.

[From the Papyrus of Ani (Brit. Mus. No. 10,470, sheets 29 and 30).]

Vignette: The god Osiris, bearded and wearing the "white" crown, stands in a shrine, the roof of which is surmounted by a hawk's head and by uraei; he holds the usual emblems of sovereignty and dominion. Behind him is the goddess Isis, and before him, standing upon a lotus flower, are the four children of Horus, Mesthȧ, Ḥāpi, Ṭuamāutef, and Qebḥsennuf.

Text: (1) The Chapter of entering into the Hall of double Maāti; a hymn of praise to Osiris, the governor of Åmentet. Osiris, the scribe Ani, triumphant, saith:—

(2) "I have come, and [I] have drawn nigh to see "thy beauties; my hands [are raised] in adoration of "thy name 'Right and Truth.' I came and I drew "unto [the place where] the acacia tree groweth not, "where (3) the tree thick with leaves existeth not, and "where the ground yieldeth neither herb nor grass. "Then I entered into the hidden place, and I spake "with (4) the god Set, and my protector (?) advanced "to me, and his face was clothed (*or* covered), and [he] "fell upon the hidden things. He (5) entered into the "Temple of Osiris, and he looked upon the hidden "things which were therein; and the sovereign chiefs "of the pylons [were] in the form of *khus*. And the "god Ånpu (6) spake [to those who were on] both sides "of him with the speech of a man [as he] came from "Ta-merå;[1] he knoweth our paths and our cities. I "make offerings (?), (7) and I smell the odour of him "as if he were one among you, and I say unto him, I "am Osiris, the scribe Ani, triumphant in peace, trium-"phant! I have (8) come, and [I] have drawn nigh "to see the great gods, and I live upon the offerings "which are among their food. I have been to the "borders [of the territory of] (9) Ba-neb-Ṭeṭṭeṭ (*i.e.*, "the 'Soul, the lord of Ṭaṭṭu,' or Osiris), and he hath

[1] *I.e.*, the "Land of the inundation," a name of Egypt.

"caused me to come forth like a *Bennu* bird, and to "utter words. I have been in the water of the stream, "and (10) I have made offerings of incense. I have "guided myself to the *Shenṭet* tree of the [divine] "children. I have been in Ȧbu (or Ȧbu, *i.e.*, Ele- "phantine [?]) in the Temple of the goddess Satet. "(11) I have submerged the boat of mine enemies "[whilst] I myself have sailed over the Lake in the "*Neshmet* boat. I have seen the (12) *Sāḥu* (*i.e.*, the "spiritual bodies) [in] the city of Qem-ur. I have "been in the city of Ṭaṭṭu, and I have brought myself "to silence [therein]. I have caused the god to have "the mastery over his two feet. (13) I have been in "the Temple of Ṭep-ṭu-f (*i.e.*, 'he that is on his hill,' or "Anubis), and I have seen him that is lord of the "divine temple. I have entered into the Temple (14) "of Osiris, and I have arrayed myself in the apparel of "him that is therein. I have entered into Re-stau, "and I have seen the hidden things (15) which are "therein. I was shrouded [therein], but I found a "way for myself. I have gone into the city Ȧn-ȧarreṭ-f "(*i.e.*, the place where nothing groweth), and I covered "my nakedness with the garments (16) which were "therein. There was given unto me the *ānti* unguent "[such as] women [use], along with the powder of "human beings. Verily Sut (?) (17) hath spoken unto "me the things which concern himself, and I said, Let "thy weighing be in (?) us."

"The Majesty of the god Ȧnpu saith, (18) 'Knowest

"thou the name of this door so as to declare it unto "me?' And Osiris, the scribe Ani, triumphant in "peace, triumphant! saith, (19) 'Destróyer of the god "Shu' is the name (20) of this door. The Majesty of "the god Ȧnpu saith, (21) 'Knowest thou the name of "the upper (22) leaf and of the lower leaf?' 'Lord of "Maāt (23) upon his two feet' is the name of the upper "(24) leaf, and 'Lord of twofold strength, the subduer "of cattle,' (25) [is the name of the lower leaf. The "Majesty of the god Ȧnpu saith], 'Since thou knowest, "(26) pass on, O Osiris the scribe, the teller (27) of the "divine offeriugs of all the gods of Thebes, (28) Ani, "triumphant, the lord of reverence.'"

The Introduction.

[From the Papyrus of Nu (Brit. Mus. No. 10,477, sheet 22).]

Vignette: The deceased and his wife standing with hands raised in adoration.

Text: (1) [THE FOLLOWING] SHALL BE SAID WHEN THE OVERSEER OF THE HOUSE OF THE OVERSEER OF THE SEAL, NU, TRIUMPHANT, COMETH FORTH INTO THE HALL (2) OF DOUBLE MAĀTI[1] SO THAT HE MAY BE SEPARATED FROM EVERY SIN WHICH HE HATH DONE AND MAY BEHOLD THE FACES OF THE GODS. The Osiris Nu, triumphant, saith:— (3)

"Homage to thee, O Great God, thou Lord of double "Maāti, I have come to thee, O my Lord, and I have "brought myself hither that (4) I may behold thy "beauties. I know thee, and I know thy name, and "I know the name[s] of the two and forty gods who "exist with (5) thee in this Hall of double Maāti, who "live as warders of sinners and who feed upon their "blood (6) on the day when the lives of men are taken "into account in the presence of the god Un-nefer; in "truth 'Rekhti-merti-neb-Maāti' (*i.e.*, 'twin-sisters with "two eyes, ladies of double Maāti') is thy name. In "truth (7) I have come to thee, and I have brought "Maāt (*i.e.*, right and truth) to thee, and I have "destroyed wickedness for thee. [I have not done "evil to] mankind. I have not oppressed the members "of my family, (8) I have not wrought evil in the place "of right and truth. I have had no knowledge of "worthless men. I have not wrought evil. I have

[1] In other papyri this Chapter is called:—(1) "The Chapter of going into the Hall of double Maāti"; (2) "The Chapter of [the Hall of] double Maāti and of knowing what is therein"; and (3) "The Book of entering into the Hall of double Maāti"; see Naville, *op. cit.*, Bd. II, p. 275.

"not made to be the first [consideration] of each day "that excessive labour (9) should be performed for me. "[I have] not brought forward my name for [exaltation] "to honours. I have not ill-treated servants. [I have "not thought scorn of God.] I have not defrauded the "oppressed one of his property.[1] I have not done that "which is an abomination (10) unto the gods. I "have not caused harm to be done to the servant by "his chief. I have not caused pain. I have made no "man to suffer hunger. I have made no one to weep. "I have done no murder. (11) I have not given the "order for murder to be done for me. I have not "inflicted pain upon mankind. I have not defrauded "the temples of their oblations. I have not (12) pur-"loined the cakes of the gods. I have not carried off "the cakes offered to the *khus*. I have not committed "fornication. I have not polluted myself [in the holy "places of the god of my city],[2] nor diminished from "the bushel. (13) I have neither added to nor filched "away land. I have not encroached upon the fields [of "others]. I have not added to the weights of the "scales [to cheat the seller]. I have not mis-read "the pointer of the scales [to cheat the buyer]. (14) "I have not carried away the milk from the mouths of "children. I have not driven away the cattle which "were upon their pastures. I have not snared (15) the

[1] Variant, "I have not caused misery, I have not caused affliction."

[2] The words in brackets are added from the Papyrus of Ȧmen-neb (Brit. Mus. No. 9964); see Naville, *op. cit.*, Bd. II., p. 282.

"feathered fowl of the preserves of the gods. I have "not caught fish [with bait made of] fish of their kind. "I have not turned back the water at the time [when "it should flow]. I have not cut (16) a cutting in a "canal of running water. I have not extinguished a "fire (*or* light) when it should burn. I have not vio- "lated the times[1] [of offering] the chosen meat-offerings. "I have not driven off (17) the cattle from the property "of the gods. I have not repulsed God in his mani- "festations. I am pure. I am pure. I am pure. I "am pure. My purity is the purity of that (18) great "*Bennu* which is in the city of Suten-ḥenen (Hera- "cleopolis), for, behold, I am the nose of the God of "the winds, who maketh all mankind to live on (19) "the day when the Eye (Utchat) of Rā is full in Ȧnnu "(Heliopolis) at the end of the second month[2] of the "season Pert (*i.e.*, the season of growing) [in the "presence of the divine lord of this earth].[3] I have "seen the Eye of Rā when it was full in Ȧnnu, there- "fore let not evil befall me (20) in this land and in "this Hall of double Maāti, because I, even I, know "the name[s] of these gods who are therein [and who "are the followers of the great god]."[4]

[1] Variant, "I have not defrauded the gods of their chosen meat offerings."

[2] *I.e.*, the month called by the Copts Mekhir, the sixth month of the Egyptian year.

[3] These words are added from the Papyrus of Nebseni.

[4] These words are added from the Papyrus of Ani.

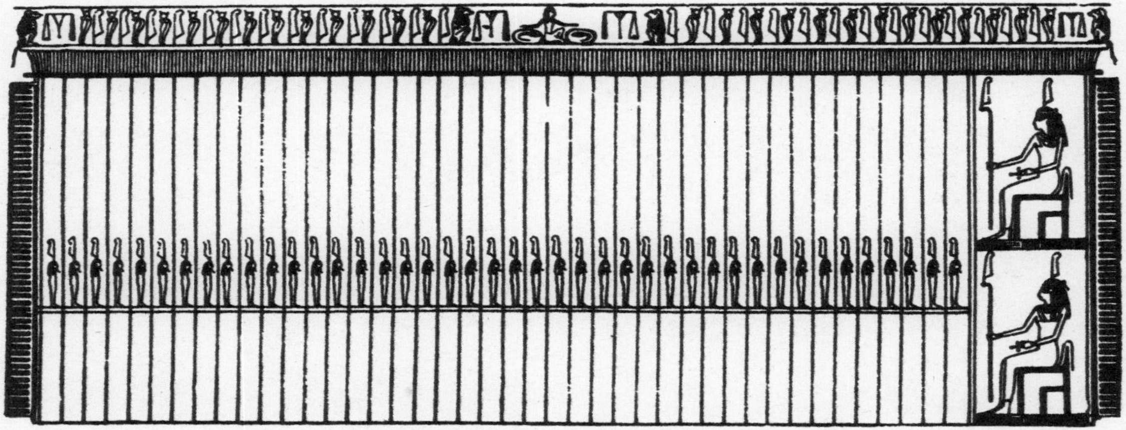

THE HALL OF DOUBLE MAĀTI. (From the Papyrus of Nebseni.)

Each of the forty-two gods wears the feather of Maāt on his head, and the Maāti goddesses are seated at the end of the Hall. Above each god is written the address of the deceased to him, and below him is the negative statement, but these texts have been omitted from the above plan to make clearer the general arrangement of the Hall according to the vignette.

The Negative Confession.

[From the Papyrus of Nebseni (Brit. Mus. No. 9900, sheet 30).]

Vignette :[1] The Hall of double Maāti, that is to say the Hall of the goddesses Isis and Nephthys who symbolize Right and Truth; herein are seated or stand forty-two gods, to each of whom the deceased must address a prescribed negative statement. At each end is one half of a folding door, one having the name of NEB-MAĀT-ḤERI-ṬEP-REṬUI-F and the other of NEB-PEḤTI-QESU-MENMENET.[2] On the centre of the roof, which has a cornice of uraei, typifying divinity, and feathers, symbolic of Maāt, is a

[1] The vignette here described is that of the Papyrus of Ani, sheet 31.

[2] See above, p. 359.

seated deity,[1] painted bluish-green, with hands extended, the right over the Eye of Horus, and the left over a pool. At the end of the Hall are four small vignettes, in which are depicted:—1. The Maāti goddesses, each seated upon a throne and holding a sceptre in her right hand, and the emblem of life in her left. 2. The deceased, arrayed in white, standing before the god Osiris with both hands raised in adoration. 3. A balance with the heart, symbolizing the conscience of the deceased, in one scale, and the feather, emblematic of Right and Truth, in the other. The god Anubis is testing the tongue of the balance, and close by stands the monster Ām-met. 4. Thoth, ibis-headed, seated upon a pylon-shaped pedestal, painting a large feather of Maāt. In the Papyrus of Ȧnhai the gods are seated in a double row; each has his characteristic head, and nearly all wear the feather of Maāt.

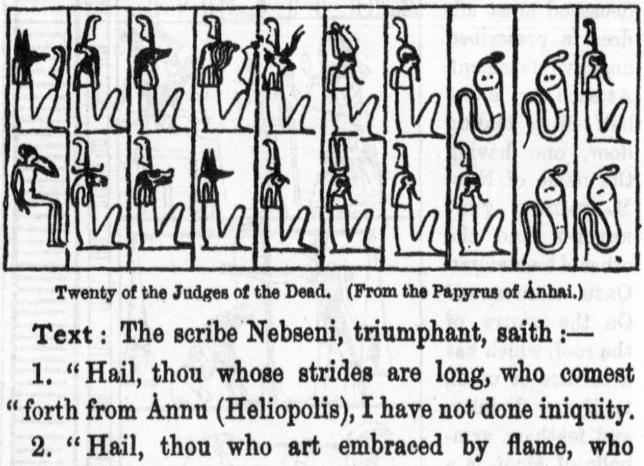

Twenty of the Judges of the Dead. (From the Papyrus of Ȧnhai.)

Text: The scribe Nebseni, triumphant, saith:—

1. "Hail, thou whose strides are long, who comest "forth from Ȧnnu (Heliopolis), I have not done iniquity.

2. "Hail, thou who art embraced by flame, who "comest forth from Kher-āḥa,[2] I have not robbed with "violence.

[1] In the XVIIth Chapter, line 46 (see above, p. 97) this god is called Ḥeḥ, *i.e.*, "Millions of years."

[2] A city near Memphis.

3. "Hail, thou divine Nose (Fenṭi), who comest "forth from Khemennu (Hermopolis), I have not done "violence [to any man].

4. "Hail, thou who eatest shades, who comest forth "from the place where the Nile riseth,[1] I have not "committed theft.

5. "Hail, Neḥa-ḥāu,[2] who comest forth from Re-stau, "I have not slain man or woman.

6. "Hail, thou double Lion-god, who comest forth "from heaven, I have not made light the bushel.

7. "Hail, thou whose two eyes are like flint,[3] who "comest forth from Sekhem (Letopolis), I have not "acted deceitfully.

8. "Hail, thou Flame, who comest forth as [thou] "goest back, I have not purloined the things which "belong unto God.

9. "Hail, thou Crusher of bones, who comest forth "from Suten-ḥenen (Heracleopolis), I have not uttered "falsehood.

10. "Hail, thou who makest the flame to wax strong, "who comest forth from Ḥet-ka-Ptaḥ (Memphis), I have "not carried away food.

11. "Hail, Qerti (*i.e.*, the two sources of the Nile), "who come forth from Àmentet, I have not uttered evil "words.

12. "Hail, thou whose teeth shine, who comest forth

[1] The *Qerti* or caverns out of which flowed the Nile were thought to be situated between Aswân and Philae.

[2] Variant, Neḥa-ḥrà.

[3] Variant, "like fire."

"from Ta-she (*i.e.*, the Fayyûm), I have attacked no "man.

13. "Hail, thou who dost consume blood, who "comest forth from the house of slaughter, I have "not killed the beasts [which are the property of "God].

14. "Hail, thou who dost consume the entrails, who "comest forth from the *mābet* chamber, I have not "acted deceitfully.

15. "Hail, thou god of Right and Truth, who comest "forth from the city of double Maāti, I have not laid "waste the lands which have been ploughed (?).

16. "Hail, thou who goest backwards, who comest "forth from the city of Bast (Bubastis), I have never "pried into matters [to make mischief].

17. "Hail, Āati, who comest forth from Ȧnnu "(Heliopolis), I have not set my mouth in motion "[against any man].

18. "Hail, thou who art doubly evil, who comest "forth from the nome of Āti,[1] I have not given way "to wrath concerning myself without a cause.

19. "Hail, thou serpent Uamenti, who comest forth "from the house of slaughter, I have not defiled the "wife of a man.

20. "Hail, thou who lookest upon what is brought "to him, who comest forth from the Temple of Ȧmsu, I "have not committed any sin against purity.

[1] *I.e.*, the ninth nome of Lower Egypt, the capital of which was Per-Ȧusȧr or Busiris.

Twenty-two of the Judges of the Dead. (From the Papyrus of Anhai.)

21. "Hail, Chief of the divine Princes, who comest "forth from the city of Nehatu,[1] I have not struck fear "[into any man].

22. "Hail, Khemi (*i.e.*, Destroyer), who comest "forth from the Lake of Ḳaui (Khas?), I have not en-"croached upon [sacred times and seasons].

23. "Hail, thou who orderest speech, who comest "forth from Urit, I have not been a man of anger.

24. "Hail, thou Child, who comest forth from the "Lake of Ḥeq-āṭ,[2] I have not made myself deaf to the "words of right and truth.

25. "Hail, thou disposer of speech, who comest forth "from the city of Unes,[3] I have not stirred up strife.

26. "Hail, Basti, who comest forth from the Secret "city, I have made no [man] to weep.

27. "Hail, thou whose face is [turned] backwards, "who comest forth from the Dwelling, I have not

[1] The "city of the sycamore"; a name of a city of Upper Egypt.
[2] The thirteenth nome of Lower Egypt.
[3] The metropolis of the nineteenth nome of Upper Egypt.

"committed acts of impurity, neither have I lain with "men.

28. "Hail, Leg of fire, who comest forth from "Àkhekhu, I have not eaten my heart.[1]

29. Hail, Kenemti, who comest forth from [the city "of] Kenemet, I have abused [no man].

30. "Hail, thou who bringest thine offering, who "comest forth from the city of Sau (Saïs), I have not "acted with violence.

31. "Hail, thou lord of faces, who comest forth from "the city of Tchefet, I have not judged hastily.

32. "Hail, thou who givest knowledge, who comest "forth from Unth, I have not . . . . , and I "have not taken vengeance upon the god.

33. "Hail, thou lord of two horns, who comest forth "from Satiu, I have not multiplied [my] speech over-"much.

34. "Hail, Nefer-Tem, who comest forth from Ḥet-"ka-Ptaḥ (Memphis), I have not acted with deceit, and "I have not worked wickedness.

35. "Hail, Tem-Sep, who comest forth from Ṭaṭṭu, "I have not uttered curses [on the king].

36. "Hail, thou whose heart doth labour, who comest "forth from the city of Ṭebti, I have not fouled (?) "water.

37. "Hail, Àḥi of the water, who comest forth from "Nu, I have not made haughty my voice.

[1] *I.e.*, "lost my temper and become angry."

38. "Hail, thou who givest commands to mankind, "who comest forth from [Sau (?)], I have not cursed "the god.

39. "Hail, Neḥeb-nefert, who comest forth from the "Lake of Nefer (?), I have not behaved with insolence.

40. "Hail, Neḥeb-kau, who comest forth from [thy] "city, I have not sought for distinctions.

41. "Hail, thou whose head is holy, who comest "forth from [thy] habitation, I have not increased "my wealth, except with such things as are [justly] "mine own possessions.

42. "Hail, thou who bringest thine own arm, who "comest forth from Ȧuḳert (underworld), I have not "thought scorn of the god who is in my city."

Address to the gods of the underworld.

[From the Papyrus of Nu (Brit. Mus. No. 10,477, sheet 24).]

Vignette: The deceased standing with both hands raised in adoration.

Text: [THEN SHALL THE HEART WHICH IS RIGHTEOUS AND SINLESS SAY][1]:—

(1) The overseer of the house of the overseer of the seal, Nu, triumphant, saith:—

"Homage to you, O ye gods who dwell in your Hall

[1] These words are added from Brit. Mus. No. 9905. Other papyri introduce the address with the words:—(1) "To be said when [the deceased] cometh forth victorious from the Hall of double Maāti"; (2) "To be said when he cometh forth to the gods of the underworld"; (3) "The words which [are to be said] after the Hall of double Maāti."

"of double Maāti, I, even I, know (2) you, and I know "your names. Let me not fall under your knives of "slaughter, and bring ye not forward my wickedness "unto the god in whose train ye are; (3) and let not "evil hap come upon me by your means. O declare "ye me right and true in the presence of Neb-er-tcher, "because I have done that which is right and true in "Ta-merà (Egypt). (4) I have not cursed God, and "let not evil hap come upon me through the king who "dwelleth in my day. Homage to you, O ye gods, who "dwell in your Hall of double Maāti, (5) who are without evil in your bodies, and who live upon right and "truth, and who feed yourselves upon right and truth "in the presence of the god Horus, who (6) dwelleth in "his divine Disk: deliver ye me from the god Baba "who liveth upon the entrails of the mighty ones "upon the day of the great judgment. (7) O grant "ye that I may come to you, for I have not committed "faults, I have not sinned, I have not done evil, I have "not borne false witness; (8) therefore let nothing [evil] "be done unto me. I live upon right and truth, and I "feed upon right and truth. I have performed the "commandments of men [as well as] the things whereat "are gratified the gods, (9) I have made the god to be "at peace [with me by doing] that which is his will. "I have given bread to the hungry man, and water to "the thirsty man, and apparel to the naked (10) man, "and a boat to the [shipwrecked] mariner. I have "made holy offerings to the gods, and sepulchral meals "to the *khus*. Be ye then my deliverers, (11) be ye "then my protectors, and make ye not accusation "against me in the presence of [the great god]. I "am clean of mouth and clean of hands; therefore "let it be said unto me by those who shall behold "me, 'Come in peace; come in peace,' (12) for I have "heard that mighty word which the spiritual bodies "(*sāḥu*)[1] spake unto the Cat (13) in the House of "Ḥapṭ-re. I have been made to give evidence before "the god Ḥrá-f-ḥa-f (*i.e.*, he whose face is behind him), "and he hath given a decision [concerning me]. I "have seen the things over which the persea tree "spreadeth [its branches] (14) within Re-stau. I am "he who hath offered up prayers to the gods and who "knoweth their persons. I have come and I have ad-"vanced to make the declaration of right and truth, "and to set the (15) balance upon what supporteth it "within the region of Åuḳert. Hail, thou who art "exalted upon thy standard, thou lord of the *Atefu* "crown, whose name is proclaimed as 'Lord of the "winds,' deliver thou me (16) from thy divine mes-"sengers who cause dire deeds to happen, and who "cause calamities to come into being, and (17) who "are without coverings for their faces, for I have "done that which is right and true for the Lord of "right and truth. I have purified myself and my "breast (18) with libations, and my hinder parts

[1] The ordinary reading is, "For I have heard the word which was spoken by the Ass with the Cat."

"with the things which make clean, and my inner "parts have been in the Pool of right and truth. "There is no single member of mine which lacketh "right and truth. (19) I have been purified in the "Pool of the south, and I have rested in the northern "city which is in the Field of the Grasshoppers, where- "in the divine sailors of Rā bathe at the (20) second "hour of the night and at the third hour of the day. "And the hearts of the gods are gratified (?) after they "have passed through it, whether it be by night, or "whether it be by day, and they say unto me, (21) "'Let thyself come forward.' And they say unto me, "'Who, then, art thou?' And they say unto me, "'What is thy name?' 'I am he who is equipped "under the flowers [and I am] the dweller in his olive "tree,' (22) is my name. And they say unto me straight- "way, 'Pass thou on'; and I passed on by the city to "the north of the olive tree. What, then, didst thou "see there? The leg and the thigh. What, then, (23) "didst thou say unto them? Let me see rejoicings "in those lands of the Fenkhu.[1] And what did they "give unto thee? A flame of (24) fire and a tablet (*or* "sceptre) of crystal. What, then, didst thou do there- "with? I buried them by the furrow of Mānāat as "'things for the night.' (25) What, then didst thou "find by the furrow of Māāat? A sceptre of flint, the "name of which is 'Giver of winds.' What, then,

[1] A people who dwelt, probably, on the north-east frontier of Egypt, and who have been by some identified with the Phœnicians.

"didst thou do to the flame of fire and the (26) tablet "(*or* sceptre) of crystal after thou hadst buried them? "I uttered words over them in the furrow, [and I dug "them out therefrom];[1] I extinguished the fire, and I "broke the tablet (*or* sceptre), and I created (27) a "pool of water. 'Come, then,' [they say,] 'and enter "in through the door of this Hall of double Maāti, for "thou knowest us.'"

"'We will not let thee enter in through us,' say the "bolts of (28) this door, 'unless thou tellest [us] our "names'; 'Tongue [of the Balance] of the place of "right and truth' is your name. 'I will not let thee "enter in by me,' saith the [right] lintel (29) of this "door, 'unless thou tellest [me] my name'; Balance of "the support of right and truth' is thy name. 'I will "not let thee enter in by me,' saith the [left] lintel of "this door, (30) 'unless thou tellest [me] my name'; "['Balance of wine' is thy name. 'I will not let thee "pass over me,' saith the threshold of this door, 'unless "thou tellest [me] my name'; 'Ox of the god Seb' is "thy name. 'I will not open unto thee,' saith the "fastening of this door, 'unless thou tellest [me] my "name'; 'Flesh of his mother' is thy name. 'I will "not open unto thee,' saith the socket of the fastening "of this door, 'unless thou tellest me my name';][1] "'Living eye of the god Sebek, the lord of Bakhau,' "is thy name. 'I will not open unto thee [and I will "not let thee enter in by me,' saith the guardian of the

[1] These words are added from the Papyrus of Nebseni.

"leaf of] this door, 'unless (31) thou tellest [me] my "name'; 'Elbow of the god Shu when he placeth him- "self to protect Osiris' is thy name. 'We will not let "thee enter in by us,' say the posts of this door, 'unless "thou tellest us our names'; (32) 'Children of the "uraei-goddesses' is your name.[1] 'Thou knowest us,' "[they say], (33) 'pass on, therefore, by us.'

"'I will not let thee tread upon me,' saith the floor "of (34) this Hall of double Maāti, 'because I am silent "and I am holy, and because I do not know the name[s] "of thy two feet wherewith thou wouldst walk (35) "upon me; therefore tell them to me.' 'Traveller (?) "of the god Khas' is the name of my right foot, and "'Staff of the goddess Hathor' is the name of my left "foot.' (36) 'Thou knowest me,' [it saith], 'pass on "therefore over me.'"

"'I will not make mention of thee,' saith the guardian "of the door of this Hall of double Maāti, 'unless thou "tellest [me] my name'; 'Discerner of (37) hearts and "searcher of the reins' is thy name. 'Now will I make "mention of thee [to the god]. But who is the god "that dwelleth in his hour? Speak thou it' (*i.e.*, his "name). Māau-Taui (*i.e.*, he who keepeth the record "of the two lands) [is his name]. 'Who then is (38) "Māau-Taui?' He is Thoth. 'Come,' saith Thoth. "'But why hast thou come?' I have come, and I press

[1] The Papyrus of Nu continues, "I will not open unto thee and I will not let thee pass by me,' saith the Guardian of this door, 'unless (33) thou tellest [me] my name'; 'Ox of Seb' is thy name." See above, l. 30.

"forward that I may be mentioned. What now (39) is "thy condition? I, even I, am purified from evil "things, and I am protected from the baleful deeds "of those who live in (40) their days; and I am not "among them. 'Now will I make mention of thee [to "the god].'[1] '[Tell me now], who is he[2] whose (44) "heaven is of fire, whose walls [are surmounted by] "living uraei, and the floor of whose house is a stream "of water? Who is he, I say?' It is (45) Osiris. "'Come forward, then: verily thou shalt be mentioned "[to him]. Thy cakes [shall come] from the Eye of "Rā, and thine ale [shall come] from (46) the Eye of "Rā, and the sepulchral meals which shall be brought "to thee upon earth [shall come] from the Eye of "Rā. This hath been decreed for the Osiris the over-"seer of the house of the overseer of the seal, Nu, "triumphant.'"

RUBRIC: (47) **The making of the representation of what shall happen in this Hall of double Maāti.** **This chapter shall be said [by the deceased] after he hath been cleansed and purified, and when he is arrayed in apparel, (48) and is shod with white leather sandals, and his eyes have been painted with antimony, and [his body] hath been anointed with unguent of *ānti*, and when he offereth oxen, and feathered fowl, and incense, and cakes, and ale, and (49) garden herbs. And, behold, thou shalt draw a representation of this in colour upon a new tile moulded from (50) earth upon which neither a pig nor other animals have trodden. And if [thou] doest this book upon it [in writing, the deceased] shall flourish, and his children (51) shall flourish, and [his name] shall never fall into**

[1] Here the Papyrus repeats a passage given above.
[2] The words *semā-kuā* are superfluous.

oblivion, and he shall be as one who filleth (*i.e.*, satisfieth) the heart of the king and of his princes. And bread, and cakes, and sweetmeats, (52) and wine, and pieces of flesh shall be given unto him upon the altar of the great god; and he shall not be turned back at any door in Åmentet, and he shall be (53) brought in along with the kings of Upper and Lower Egypt, and he shall be in the train of Osiris,[1] continually and regularly for ever.[2]

CHAPTER CXXVI.

[From the Papyrus of Nu (Brit. Mus. No. 10,477, sheet 24).]

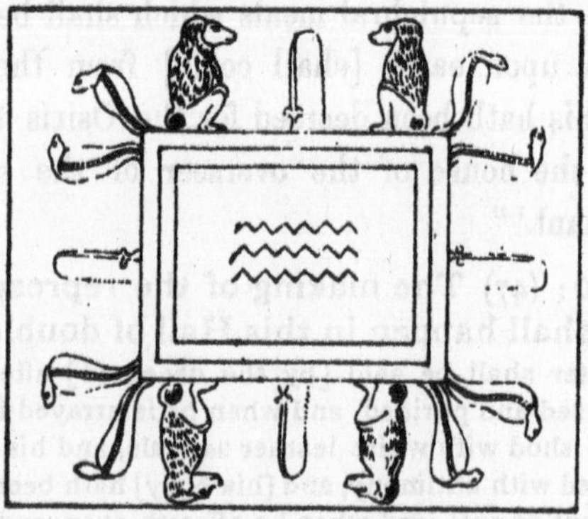

Vignette: A lake of fire, at each corner of which is seated a dog-headed ape.

[1] After "Osiris" a Paris papyrus adds, "He shall come forth in whatsoever form he is pleased to appear as a living soul for ever and ever."

[2] In the Papyrus of Ani (sheet 33) this Rubric comes after Chapter XLII., and is written below the vignette of Chapter CXXVI.

Text:[1] (1) The overseer of the house of the overseer of the seal, Nu, triumphant, the son of the overseer of the house of the overseer of the seal, Ȧmen-ḥetep, triumphant, saith:— (2)

"Hail, ye four apes who sit in the bows of the boat "of (3) Rā, who convey right and truth to Neb-er-tcher, "who sit in judgment (4) on my misery and on my "strength, who make the gods to rest contented by "means of the flame of (5) your mouths, who offer holy "offerings to the gods and sepulchral meals to the "*khus*, (6) who live upon right and truth, and who "feed upon (7) right and truth of heart, who are "without deceit and fraud, and to whom wickedness "is an abomination, (8) do ye away with my evil "deeds, and put ye away my sin [which deserved "stripes upon earth, and destroy ye any evil whatso-"ever that belongeth unto me],[2] and let there be no "obstacle whatsoever on my part (9) towards you. O "grant ye that I may make my way through the under-"world (*ämmeḥet*), let me enter into Re-stau, let me "pass through (10) the hidden pylons of Ȧmentet. O "grant that there may be given to me cakes, (11) and "ale, and sweetmeats (?), even as [they are given] to "the living *khus*, and grant that I may enter in (12) "and come forth from Re-stau."

"[The four apes make answer, saying], Come, then,

[1] This Chapter has no title either in the Theban or in the Saïte Recension.

[2] The words in brackets are added from Brit. Mus. No. 9913.

"for we have done away with thy wickedness, and we "have put away thy sin, along with the [sin deserving "of] stripes which thou [didst commit] upon earth, and "we have destroyed [all] the (13) evil which belonged "to thee upon the earth. Enter, therefore, into Re-"stau, and pass thou through the hidden pylons of "Åmentet, and there shall be given unto thee cakes, "(14) and ale, and sweetmeats (?), and thou shalt come "forth and thou shalt enter in at thy desire, even as "do those *khus* who are favoured [of the god], and "thou shalt be proclaimed (*or* called) each day in the "horizon."

CHAPTER CXXVIIA.

[From the Tomb of Rameses IV. (see Naville, *op. cit.*, Bd. I. Bl. 141; Lefébure, *Tombeau de Ramsès IV.*, Plate 18).]

Vignette: This version of the CXXVIIth Chapter has not yet been found in the papyri containing the Theban Recension. In the Saïte Recension (Lepsius, *op. cit.*, Bl. 51) the deceased stands, with both hands raised in adoration, before a table of offerings placed in the presence of six gods, three standing upright and three seated, each of whom holds in his hands a flail and a sceptre. The first god has the head of a bull, the second is jackal-headed, the third is snake-headed, the fourth is human-headed, the fifth is bull-headed, and the sixth is human-headed. The last three have feathers, emblematic of right and truth, on their heads.

Text: (1) THE BOOK OF THE PRAISE OF THE GODS OF THE QERTI[1] WHICH A MAN SHALL RECITE WHEN HE COMETH FORTH BEFORE THEM TO ENTER IN TO SEE THE GOD IN THE GREAT TEMPLE OF THE UNDERWORLD. And he shall say:—

"Homage to you, O ye gods of the *Qerti*, (2) ye "divine dwellers in Åmentet! Homage to you, O ye "guardians of the doors of the underworld, who keep "ward over the god, who bear and proclaim [the names "of those who come] into the presence of the god (3) "Osiris, and who hold yourselves ready, and who praise "[him], and who destroy the Enemies of Rā. O send "ye forth your light and scatter ye the darkness [which "is about] you, and behold ye the holy and divine (4) "Mighty One, O ye who live even as he liveth, and "call ye upon him that dwelleth within his divine "Disk. Lead ye the King of the North and of the "South, (Usr-Maāt-Rā-setep-en-Åmen), the son of the "Sun, (Rā-meses-meri-Åmen-Rā-ḥeq-Maāt), through "your doors, may his divine soul enter into your hidden "places, (5) [for] he is one among you, and he hath

[1] *I.e.*, districts or divisions of the underworld.

"shot forth calamities upon the serpent fiend Åpep, "and he hath beaten down the obstacles [which Åpep "set up] in Åmentet. Thy word hath prevailed mightily "over thine enemies, O great God, who livest in thy "divine Disk; thy word hath (6) prevailed mightily "over thine enemies, O Osiris, Governor of Åmentet; "thy word hath prevailed mightily over thine enemies "in heaven and in earth, O thou King of the North and "of the South, (Usr-Maāt-Rā-setep-en-Åmen), the son "of the Sun, (Rā-meses-meri-Åmen-Ra-ḥeq-Maāt), and "over the sovereign princes of every god and of every "goddess, (7) O Osiris, Governor of Åmentet; he hath "uttered words in the presence [of the god in] the "valley of the dead, and he hath gained the mastery "over the mighty sovereign princes. Hail, ye door-"keepers (?), hail, ye doorkeepers, who guard your "gates, who punish (8) souls, who devour the bodies "of the dead, who advance over them at their examina-"tion in the places of destruction, who give right and "truth to the soul and to the divine *khu*, the beneficent "one, (9) the mighty one, whose throne is holy in Åkert, "who is endowed with soul like Rā and who is praised "like Osiris, lead ye along the King of the North and "of the South, (Usr-Maāt-Rā-setep-en-Åmen), the son "of the Sun, (Rā-meses-meri-Åmen-Rā-ḥeq-Maāt), un-"bolt ye for him (10) the doors, and open [ye] the place "of his *Qerti* for him. Behold, make ye his word to

"triumph over his enemies, and indeed let meat-offer-
"ings and drink-offerings be made unto him by the god
"of the double door, and let him (11) put on the
"*nemmes* crown of him that dwelleth in the great
"and hidden shrine. Behold the image of Ḥeru-
"khuti (Harmachis), who is doubly true, and who is
"the divine Soul and the divine and (12) perfect Khu;
"he hath prevailed with his hands. The two great
"and mighty gods cry out to the King of the North
"and South (Usr-Maāt-Rā-setep-en-Åmen), the son
"of the Sun, (Rā-meses-meri-Åmen-Rā-ḥeq-Maāt), they
"rejoice in him, they sing praises to (13) him, [and
"clap] their hands, they accord him their protec-
"tion, and he liveth. The King of the North and
"South (Usr-Maāt-Rā-setep-en-Åmen), the son of
"the Sun, (Rā-meses-meri-Åmen-Rā-ḥeq-Maāt), riseth
"like a living soul in heaven. He hath been com-
"manded to (14) make his transformations, he hath
"made himself victorious before the divine sovereign
"chiefs, and he hath made his way through the
"gates of heaven, and of earth, and of the under-
"world, even as hath Rā. The King of the North
"and South, (Usr-Maāt-Rā-setep-en-Åmen), the son
"of the Sun, (Rā-meses-meri-Åmen-Rā-ḥeq-Maāt), (15)
"saith, 'Open unto me the gate[s] of heaven, and of
"earth, and of the underworld, for I am the divine soul

"of Osiris and I rest in him, and let me pass through "their halls. Let [the gods] sing praises unto me "[when] they see (16) me; let me enter and let favour "be shown unto me; let me come forth and let me be "beloved; and let me go forward, for no defect or fail-"ing hath been found clinging unto me.'"

CHAPTER CXXVIIB.

[From the Papyrus of Ptaḥ-mes (Naville, *op. cit.*, Bd. I. Bl. 142).]

Vignette: Sixteen gods in four groups, each containing two pairs; before each group is a table of offerings.

Text: (1) A CHAPTER TO BE RECITED ON COMING BEFORE THE DIVINE SOVEREIGN CHIEFS OF OSIRIS TO OFFER PRAISE UNTO THE GODS WHO ARE THE GUIDES OF THE UNDERWORLD. Osiris (2) the chief scribe and draughtsman, Ptaḥ-mes, triumphant, saith :—

"Homage to you, O ye gods who dwell in the *Qerti*,[1] "ye gods who dwell in Àmentet, (3) who keep ward "over the gates of the underworld and are the guardians "[thereof], who bear and proclaim [the names of those "who come] into the (4) presence of Osiris, who praise "him and who destroy the enemies of Rā. O send "forth your light and (5) scatter ye the darkness

[1] *I.e.*, divisions of the underworld.

"[which is about] you, and look upon the face of "Osiris, O ye who live even as he liveth, and praise "[ye] him (6) that dwelleth in his Disk, and lead [ye] "me away from your calamities. Let me come forth "and let me enter in through (7) your secret places, for "I am a mighty prince among you, for I have done "away with evil there, and I have beaten down the (8) "obstacles (?) [which have been set up] in Åmentet. "Thou hast been victorious over thine enemies, O thou "that dwellest in thy Disk; thou hast been victorious "over thine (9) enemies, O Thoth, who producest (?) "statutes; thou hast been victorious over thine enemies, "O Osiris, (10) the chief scribe and draughtsman, Ptaḥ-"mes, triumphant; thou hast been triumphant over "thine enemies, O Osiris, thou Governor of Åmentet, "in heaven and upon earth in the presence of the (11) "divine sovereign chiefs of every god and of every god-"dess; and the food (?) of Osiris, the Governor of "Åmentet, is in the presence of the god whose name "is hidden before (12) the great divine sovereign chiefs. "Hail, ye guardians of the doors, ye [gods] who keep "ward over their habitations (?), who keep the reckon-"ing, and who commit [souls] to (13) destruction, who "grant right and truth to the divine soul which is "stablished, who are without evil in the abode of "Åḳert, (14) who are endowed with soul even as is "Rā, and who are . . . . as is Osiris, guide ye "Osiris the chief scribe, the draughtsman, (15) Ptaḥ-"mes, triumphant, open ye unto him the gates of the "underworld, and the uppermost part of his estate and "his *Qert.* (16) Behold, make [ye him] to be victorious "over his enemies, provide [ye him] with the offerings "of the god of the underworld, make noble the divine "being who dwelleth in the *nemmes* (17) crown, the "lord of the knowledge of Åḳert. Behold, stablish ". . . . . this soul in right and truth, (18) [and let it "become] a perfect soul that hath gained the mastery "with its two hands. The great and mighty gods cry "out, 'He hath gotten the victory,' (19) and they "rejoice in him, and they ascribe praise unto him "with their hands, and they turn unto him their "faces. (20) The living one is triumphant, and is "even like a living soul dwelling in heaven, and he "hath been ordered to perform [his] transformations. "Osiris (21) triumphed over his enemies, and Osiris, "the chief scribe and draughtsman, Ptaḥ-mes, trium-"phant, hath gained the victory (22) over his enemies "in the presence of the great divine sovereign chiefs "who dwell in heaven, and in the presence of the great "divine sovereign chiefs who dwell upon the earth."

CHAPTER CXXVIII.

[From Lepsius, *Todtenbuch*, Bl. 51.]

Vignette: The deceased standing before a table of offerings, with both hands raised in adoration, in the presence of the gods Osiris, Isis, Horus the son of Isis, and Nephthys.

Text: A Hymn of praise to Osiris. (1) The Osiris, Àuf-ānkh, triumphant, saith:—

"Homage to thee, O Osiris Un-nefer, triumphant, "thou son of Nut, thou first-born son of Seb, thou "mighty one who comest forth from Nut, thou King "in the city of Nifu-ur,[1] thou Governor of Àmentet, "thou lord (2) of Àbṭu (Abydos), thou lord of souls, "thou mighty one of strength, thou lord of the *atef* "crown in Suten-ḥenen, thou lord of the divine form "in the city of Nifu-ur, thou lord of the tomb, thou "mighty one of souls in Ṭaṭṭu, thou lord of [sepulchral]

[1] A name of the city of Abydos.

"offerings, thou whose festivals are many in Ṭaṭṭu. (3) "The god Horus exalteth his father in every place (*or* "shrine), and he uniteth [himself] unto the goddess "Isis and unto her sister Nephthys; and the god "Thoth reciteth for him the mighty glorifyings which "are within him, [and which] come forth from his "mouth, and the heart of Horus is stronger than that "of all the gods. (4) Rise up, then, O Horus, thou son "of Isis, and avenge thy father Osiris. Hail, O Osiris, "I have come unto thee; I am Horus and I have "avenged thee, and I feed this day upon the sepulchral "meals of oxen, and feathered fowl, and upon all the "beautiful things [offered] unto Osiris. Rise up, then, "O Osiris, (5) for I have struck down for thee all thine "enemies, and I have taken vengeance upon them for "thee. I am Horus upon this beautiful day of thy "fair rising in thy Soul which exalteth thee along with "itself on this day before thy divine sovereign princes. "Hail, O Osiris, (6) thy *ka* hath come unto thee and "rests with thee, and thou restest therein in thy name "of Ka-Ḥetep. It maketh thee glorious in thy name of "Khu, and it maketh me like unto the Morning Star "in thy name of Peḥu, and it openeth for thee (7) the "ways in thy name of Ȧp-uat. Hail, O Osiris, I have "come unto thee and I have set thine enemies under "thee in every place, and thou art triumphant in "the presence of the company of the gods and of the "divine sovereign chiefs. Hail, O Osiris, thou hast "received thy sceptre and (8) the place whereon thou "art to rest, and thy steps are under thee. Thou "bringest food to the gods, and thou bringest sepul-"chral meals unto those who dwell in their tombs. "Thou hast given thy might unto the gods and thou "hast created the Great God; thou hast thy existence "with them in their spiritual bodies, thou gatherest "thyself unto (9) all the gods, and thou hearest the "word of right and truth on the day when offerings to "this god are ordered on the festivals of Uḳa."

CHAPTER CXXIX.

Vignette: This Chapter is without a vignette in the Theban Recension; in the Turin Papyrus we find the deceased poling along a boat wherein are Rā and the *Bennu* bird, and in front of the boat stand a table of offerings, the god Osiris, and the Teṭ.

Text: See Chapter C.

CHAPTER CXXX.

[From the Papyrus of Nu (Brit. Mus. No. 10,477, sheet 17).]

Vignette: The deceased standing between the two boats of the sun. In the Saïte Recension (see Lepsius, *op. cit.*, Bl. 52) the deceased is seen standing in the stern of a boat behind Ra and two other gods.

Text: (1) ANOTHER CHAPTER OF MAKING PERFECT THE *KHU*, WHICH IS [TO BE RECITED ON] THE BIRTH-DAY OF OSIRIS, AND OF MAKING TO LIVE THE SOUL FOR EVER.[1] (2) The overseer of the house of the overseer of the seal, Nu, triumphant, saith:—

"The heavens are opened, the earth is opened, the "West is opened, the East is opened, the southern half "of heaven is opened, the northern half of heaven is "opened, the doors are opened, and the (3) gates are "thrown wide open to Rā [as] he cometh forth from

[1] Variant, "The Book of making the soul to live for ever. [To be recited] on the day of embarking in the boat of Rā to pass over to the chiefs of flame." See Naville, *op. cit.*, Bd. II. p. 338.

"the horizon. The *Sektet* boat openeth for him the "double doors and the *Māṭet* boat bursteth open [for "him] the gates; he breatheth, and the god (4) Shu "[cometh into being], and he createth the goddess Tef-"nut. Those who are in the following of Osiris follow "in his train, and the overseer of the house of the "overseer of the seal, Nu, triumphant, (5) followeth "on in the train of Rā. He taketh his iron weapon "and he forceth open the shrine even as doth Horus, "and pressing onwards he advanceth unto the hidden "things of his habitations with the libations of (6) his "divine shrine; the messenger of the god that loveth "him. The Osiris Nu, the overseer of the house of "the overseer of the seal, triumphant, bringeth forth "the right and the truth, and he maketh to advance "the going forward[1] of (7) Osiris. The Osiris Nu, the "overseer of the house of the overseer of the seal, "triumphant, taketh in [his hand[s] the cordage and "he bindeth fast the shrine. Storms are the things "which he abominateth. (8) Let no water-flood be "nigh unto him, let not the Osiris Nu, the overseer "of the house of the overseer of the seal, trium-"phant, be repulsed before Rā, and let him not be "made to turn back; for, behold, the Eye is in his "two hands. (9) Let not the Osiris Nu, the overseer "of the house of the overseer of the seal, triumphant, "walk in the valley of darkness, let him not enter into "(10) the Lake of those who are evil, and let him have

[1] Or, "images."

"no existence among the damned, even for a moment. "Let not the Osiris Nu fall headlong (11) among those "who would lead him captive, and let not [his] soul go "in among them. Let his divine face take possession "of the place behind the block, the block of the god "Septu."

"Hymns of praise be unto you, O ye divine beings of "the Thigh, (12) the knives of God [work] in secret, "and the two arms and hands of God cause the light "to shine; it is doubly pleasant unto him to lead the "(13) old unto him along with the young at his season. "Now, behold, the god Thoth dwelleth within his "hidden places, and he performeth the ceremonies of "libation (14) unto the god who reckoneth millions of "years, and he maketh a way through the firmament, "and he doeth away with storms and whirlwinds from "his stronghold, and the Osiris Nu, the overseer "of the house of the overseer of the seal, triumphant, "arriveth in the places of his (15) habitations. [O ye "divine beings of the Thigh], do ye away with his "sorrow, and his suffering, and his pain, and may the "sorrow of the Osiris [Nu] be altogether put away. Let "the Osiris Nu, the overseer of the house of the over-"seer of the seal, triumphant, gratify (16) Rā, let him "make a way into the horizon of Rā, let his boat be "made ready for him, let him sail on happily, and let "Thoth put light into [his] heart; (17) then shall the "Osiris Nu, triumphant, praise and glorify Rā, and Rā "shall hearken unto his words, and he shall beat down "the obstacles which come from his enemies. I have "not been (18) shipwrecked, I have not been turned "back in the horizon, for I am Rā-Osiris, and the "Osiris Nu, the overseer of the house of the overseer "of the seal, shall not be shipwrecked (19) in the "Great Boat. Behold him whose face is in the god "of the Thigh, because the name of Rā is in the body "of the Osiris Nu, the overseer of the house of the "overseer of the seal, and his honour is in his mouth; "(20) he shall speak unto Rā, and Rā shall hearken "unto his words."

"Hymns of praise unto thee, O Rā, in the horizon, "and homage unto thee, O thou that purifiest with "light (21) the denizens of heaven, O thou who hast "sovereign power over heaven at that supreme moment "when the paddles of thine enemies move with thee! "The Osiris Nu, the overseer of the house of the overseer "of the seal, triumphant, (22) cometh with the ordering "of right and truth, for there is an iron firmament in "Ȧmentet which the fiend Ȧpep hath broken through "with his storms before the double Lion-god, (23) and "this will the Osiris Nu set in order; O hearken ye, "ye who dwell upon the top of the throne of majesty. "The Osiris Nu shall come in among thy divine sovereign chiefs, (24) and Rā shall deliver him from Ȧpep "each day so that he may not come nigh unto him, "and he shall make himself vigilant. The Osiris Nu "shall have power over the things which are written, "he shall receive (25) sepulchral meals, and the god

"Thoth shall provide him with the things which should "be prepared for him. The Osiris Nu maketh right "and truth to go round about the bows in the Great "Boat, (26) and hath triumph among the divine "sovereign chiefs, and he establisheth [it] for millions "of years. The divine chiefs guide him and give unto "him a passage in the boat (27) with joy and gladness; "the first ones among the company of the sailors of Rā "are behind him, and he is happy. Right and truth "are exalted, and they have come unto their divine "lord, and praises have been ascribed unto (28) the "god Neb-er-tcher. The Osiris Nu, the overseer of "the house of the overseer of the seal, triumphant, "hath taken in his hands the weapon and he hath "made his way through heaven therewith; the denizens "thereof have ascribed praises unto him as [unto] a "divine being who standeth up (29) and never sinketh "to rest. The god Rā exalteth him by reason of what "he hath done, and he causeth him to make of none "effect the whirlwind and the storm; he looketh (30) "upon his splendours, and he stablisheth his oars, and "the boat saileth round about in heaven, rising like "the sun in the darkness. Thoth, the mighty one, "leadeth the Osiris Nu (31) within his eye, and he "sitteth [upon his] thigh[s] in the mighty boat of "Kheperȧ; he cometh into being, and the things which "he saith come to pass. (32) The Osiris Nu ad-"vanceth, and he journeyeth round about heaven unto "Ȧmentet, the fiery deities stand up before him, and "the god Shu rejoiceth exceedingly, and they take in "their hands the bows [of the boat] of Rā along with "his divine mariners. (33) Rā goeth round about and "he looketh upon Osiris. The Osiris Nu is at peace, "the Osiris Nu is at peace. He hath not been driven "back, the flame of thy moment (34) hath not been "taken away from him, [O Rā,] the whirlwind and "storm of thy mouth have not come forth against "him, he hath not journeyed upon the path of the "crocodile—for he abominateth (35) the crocodile—"and it hath not drawn nigh unto him. The Osiris "Nu embarketh in thy boat, O Rā, (36) he is furnished "with thy throne, and he receiveth thy spiritual form. "The Osiris Nu travelleth over the paths of Rā at "daybreak to drive back the fiend Nebṭ; [he] cometh "(37) upon the flame of thy boat, [O Rā,] upon "that mighty Thigh. The Osiris Nu knoweth it, "and he attaineth unto thy boat, (38) and behold "he [sitteth] therein; and he maketh sepulchral "offerings."

RUBRIC: [This chapter shall be] recited over a boat of the god Rā which hath been painted (39) in colours in a pure place. And behold thou shalt place a figure of the deceased in the bows thereof, and thou shalt paint a Sektet boat upon the right side thereof, and an Āṭet boat upon the left side thereof, and there shall be made (40) unto them offerings of bread, and cakes, and wine, and oil, and every kind of fair offering upon the birthday of Osiris. If these ceremonies be performed his soul shall have existence, and shall live for ever, and shall not die (41) a second time.

The following is from the Rubric to this Chapter in the Saïte Recension (see Lepsius, *op. cit.*, Bl. 53) :—

"[He shall know] the hidden things of the under-"world, he shall penetrate the hidden things in Neter-"khertet (the underworld)."

"[This Chapter] was found in the large hall (?) of the "Temple under the reign of His Majesty Semti (Ḥesepti), "triumphant, and it was found in the cavern of the "mountain which Horus made for his father Osiris "Un-nefer, triumphant. Now since Rā looketh upon "this deceased in his own flesh, he shall look upon him "as the company of the gods. The fear of him shall "be great, and the awe of him shall be mighty in the "heart of men, and gods, and *Khus*, and the damned. "He shall be with his soul and shall live for ever; he "shall not die a second time in the underworld; and "on the day of weighing of words no evil hap shall "befall him. He shall be triumphant over his enemies, "and his sepulchral meals shall be upon the altar of "Rā in the course of each day, day by day."

CHAPTER CXXXI.

[From the Papyrus of Nu (Brit. Mus. No. 10,477, sheets 17 and 18).]

Vignette: This Chapter is without vignette, both in the Papyrus of Nu and in the Saïte Recension (see Lepsius, *op. cit.*, Bl. 54).

Text: (1) THE CHAPTER OF HAVING EXISTENCE NIGH UNTO RĀ.[1] The overseer of the house of the overseer of the seal, Nu, triumphant, saith:—

"I am that god Rā who shineth in the night. Every "(2) being who followeth in his train shall have life in "the following of the god Thoth, and he shall give "unto him the risings of Horus in the darkness. The "heart of Osiris Nu, the overseer of the house of the "overseer of the seal, triumphant, is glad (3) because "he is one of those beings, and his enemies have been "destroyed by the divine princes. I am a follower of "Rā, and [I have] received his iron weapon. (4) I "have come unto thee, O my father Rā, and I have "advanced to the god Shu. I have cried unto the "mighty goddess, I have equipped the god Ḥu, (5) and "I alone have removed the Nebṭ god from the path of "Rā. I am a Khu, and I have come to the divine "prince at the bounds of the horizon. I have met

[1] Or, "The Chapter of making the way into heaven nigh unto Rā."

"(6) and I have received the mighty goddess. I have "raised up thy soul in the following of thy strength, "and my soul [liveth] through thy victory and thy "mighty power; it is I who give commands (7) in "speech to Rā in heaven. Homage to thee, O great "god in the east of heaven, let me embark in thy boat, "O Rā, let me open myself out in the form of a divine "hawk, (8) let me give my commands in words, let me "do battle in my *Sekhem* (?), let me be master under "my vine. Let me embark in thy boat, O Rā, in "peace, (9) and let me sail in peace to the beautiful "Åmentet. Let the god Tem speak unto me, [saying], "'Wouldst [thou] enter therein?' The lady, the "goddess Meḥen, is a million of years, yea, two million "years in (10) duration, and dwelleth in the house of "Urt and Nif-urt [and in] the Lake of a million years; "the whole company of the gods move about among "those who are at the side of him who is the lord of "divisions of places (?). And I say, 'On every road "and among (11) these millions of years is Rā the lord, "and his path is in the fire; and they go round about "behind him, and they go round about behind him.'"

CHAPTER CXXXII.

[From the Papyrus of Ani (Brit. Mus. No. 10,470, sheet 18).]

Vignette: The deceased standing before a house and holding a long staff in his hand. In the Brocklehurst papyrus the soul of the deceased, in the form of a human-headed bird, is seen hovering over a house by the side of which is a tree (see Naville, *op. cit.*, Bd. I. Bl. 145).

Text: (1) THE CHAPTER OF CAUSING A MAN TO COME BACK TO SEE HIS HOUSE UPON EARTH.[1] The Osiris Ani saith:—

"I am the Lion-god (2) coming forth with extended "strides. I have shot arrows and I have wounded the "prey; I have shot arrows and I have wounded the "prey. I am the (3) Eye of Horus, and I pass through "the Eye of Horus at this season. I have arrived at "the furrows; let the Osiris Ani advance in peace."[2]

[1] In the Saïte Recension (see Lepsius, *op. cit.*, Bl. 54) the house is said to be "in the underworld."

[2] Another papyrus adds the words, "I have advanced, and behold, I have not been found light, and the Balance is empty of my affair."

CHAPTER CXXXIII.

[From the Papyrus of Nu (Brit. Mus. No. 10,477, sheet 16).]

Vignette: The god Rā, hawk-headed and having upon his head the sun's disk, seated upon the cubit of Maāt in a boat; before him he holds the emblem of "life." Above him is the legend, "Rā in his shrine." With him, in the boat, stands Ani, who "maketh adoration to Rā each day," with both hands raised in adoration.

Text: (1) THE BOOK OF MAKING PERFECT THE *KHU*, (2) WHICH IS TO BE RECITED ON THE DAY OF THE MONTH. The Osiris Nu, the overseer of the house of the overseer of the seal, triumphant, saith:—

"Rā riseth in his horizon, and his company of the "gods follow after him. The god cometh forth out of "his hidden (3) habitations, and food falleth out of the "eastern horizon of heaven at the word of the goddess "Nut who maketh plain the paths of Rā, whereupon "straightway the Prince goeth round about. (4) Lift "up then thyself, O thou Rā, who dwellest in thy "divine shrine, draw thou into thyself the winds, "inhale the north wind, swallow thou the skin (?) of "(5) thy net on the day wherein thou breathest right "and truth. Thou separatest the divine followers, and "thou sailest in [thy] boat to Nut; the divine princes "(6) march onwards at thy word. Thou takest count of "thy bones, thou gatherest together thy members, thou "settest thy face towards the beautiful Ȧmentet, and "thou comest, being renewed each day. Behold, "(7) thou art that Image of gold, and thou dost possess "the splendours of the disks of heaven and art terrible; "thou comest, being renewed each day. (8) Hail, the "horizon rejoiceth, and there are shouts of joy in the "rigging [of thy boat]; when the gods who dwell in "the heavens see the Osiris Nu, the overseer of the "house of the overseer of the seal, triumphant, (9) they "ascribe unto him as his due praises which are like "unto those ascribed unto Rā. The Osiris Nu, the "overseer of the house of the overseer of the seal, "triumphant, is a divine prince and he seeketh (?) the "*ureret* crown of Rā, (10) and he, the only one, is "strong in good fortune (?) in that supreme body which "is of those divine beings who are in the presence of "Rā. (11) The Osiris Nu is strong both upon earth "and in the underworld; and the Osiris Nu is strong "like unto Rā every day. (12) The Osiris Nu shall "not tarry, and he shall not lie without motion in this "land for ever. Being doubly beautiful [he] shall see "with his two eyes, and he shall hear (13) with his "two ears; rightly and truly, rightly and truly. The "Osiris Nu is like unto Rā, and he setteth in order the "oars [of his boat] among those who are in the train of "(14) Nu. He doth not tell that which he hath seen, "and he doth not repeat that which he hath heard in "the secret places. Hail, (15) let there be shouts of "joy to the Osiris Nu, who is of the divine body of Rā, "as he journeyeth over Nu, and who propitiateth the "KA of the god (16) with that which he loveth. The "Osiris Nu, the overseer of the house of the overseer of "the seal, is a hawk, the transformations of which are "mighty (*or* manifold)."[1]

RUBRIC: [This chapter shall be recited over a boat four[2] cubits in its length (17) and made of green porcelain [on which have been painted] the divine sovereign chiefs of the cities; and a heaven with its stars shall [also] be made, and this thou

shalt have made ceremonially pure by means of natron and incense. And, behold, (18) thou shalt make an image of Rā in yellow (?) colour upon a new plaque and set it at the bows of the boat. And behold, thou shalt make an image of the *khu*

[1] The Papyrus of Nebseni has, "The Osiris Nebseni is the lord of transformations in the presence of the hawk of gold."
[2] The Papyrus of Ani has "seven cubits."

(19) which thou dost wish to make perfect [and place it] in this boat, and thou shalt make it to travel about in the boat [which shall be made in the form of the boat] of Rā; and he shall see the god Rā (20) himself therein. Let not the eye of any man whatsoever look upon it with the exception of thine own self, or thy father,[1] or thy son, and guard [this] with great care.[2] [Now these things] shall make the *khu* perfect in the heart of Rā, and it shall give unto him power with the company of the gods; and the gods shall look upon him as a divine being like unto themselves; (21) and mankind and the dead shall look upon him and shall fall down upon their faces, and he shall be seen in the underworld in the form of the radiance of Rā.

CHAPTER CXXXIV.

[From the Papyrus of Nu (Brit. Mus. No. 10,477, sheet 17).]

Vignette:[3] The boat of the sun, before which stand the deceased and his daughter[4]; on the bows is perched the hawk of Horus with the crown of the South upon his head. In the boat are the gods Shu, Tefnut, Seb, Nut, Osiris, Isis, and Hathor, human-headed, and Horus, hawk-headed. In the Saïte Recension the gods in the boat are nine in number, and behind them is the disk of the sun (see Lepsius, *op. cit.*, Bl. 55).

[1] The words "or thy father" are from the Papyrus of Ani.

[2] These words are from the Brocklehurst papyrus (see Naville, *op. cit.*, Bd. II. p. 334). There are three copies of this rubric extant, and no one of them is complete!

[3] See the Papyrus of Nebseni, sheet 6.

[4] Called "Thent-Men-nefer."

Text: (1) ANOTHER CHAPTER OF MAKING PERFECT THE KHU.[1] The Osiris Nu, the overseer of the house of the overseer of the seal, triumphant, saith:—

"Homage to thee, O thou who art within thy divine "shrine, who shinest with rays of light (2) and sendest "forth radiance from thyself, who decreest joy for mil-"lions of years unto those who love him, who givest "their heart's desire unto mankind, thou god Khepera

"within thy boat who hast overthrown (3) Āpep. O "ye children of the god Seb, overthrow ye the enemies "of Osiris Nu, the overseer of the house of the overseer "of the seal, triumphant, and destroy ye them (4) from "the boat of Rā; and the god Horus shall cut off their "heads in heaven [where they are] in the form of "feathered fowl, and their hind parts shall be on the "earth in the form of animals and in the Lake in the "form of (5) fishes. Every male fiend and every female "fiend shall the Osiris Nu, the overseer of the house of

[1] In the Papyrus of Nebseni the title of this Chapter reads:— "The Chapter of embarking in the boat of Rā and of being with those who are in his following."

"the overseer of the seal, destroy, whether he descendeth "from the heaven, or whether he cometh forth from (6) "the earth, or whether they come upon the waters, or "whether they advance towards the stars, the god "Thoth, the son of Ȧner, coming forth from the Ȧnerti, "shall hack them in pieces. The Osiris (7) Nu is silent "and dumb (?); cause ye this god, the mighty one of "slaughter, the being greatly to be feared, to make "himself clean in your blood and to bathe (8) himself "in your gore, and ye shall certainly be destroyed by "him (9) from the boat of his father Rā. The Osiris "Nu is the god Horus to whom his mother the goddess "Isis hath given birth, (10) and whom the goddess "Nephthys hath nursed and dandled, even like Horus "when [he] repulsed the fiends of the god Suti; and "when they see the *ureret* crown stablished (11) upon "his head they fall down upon their faces and they "glorify [him]. Behold, when men, and gods, and "*Khus*, and the dead see the Osiris (12) Nu in the "form of Horus with the *ureret* crown stablished upon "his head, they fall down upon their faces. And the "Osiris Nu, the overseer of the house of the overseer "of the seal, (13) triumphant, is victorious over his "enemies in the heights of heaven, and in the depths "thereof, and before the divine sovereign chiefs of "every god and of every goddess."

RUBRIC: (14) [This Chapter] shall be recited over a hawk standing and having the white crown upon his head, [and over figures of] Tem, Shu, Tefnut, Seb, Nut, Osiris, Isis, Suti, and Nephthys painted in yellow colour (15) upon a new plaque, which

shall be placed in [a model of] the boat [of the sun], along with a figure of the deceased whom thou wouldst make perfect. These shalt thou anoint with cedar oil, and (16) incense shall be offered up to them on the fire, and feathered fowl shall be roasted. It is an act of praise to Rā as he journeyeth, and it shall cause a man to have his being (17) along with Rā day by day, whithersoever the god voyageth; and it shall destroy the enemies of Rā in very truth regularly and continually.

CHAPTER CXXXV.

[From Lepsius, *Todtenbuch*, Bl. 55.]

Vignette: This Chapter has no vignette.

Text: ANOTHER CHAPTER TO BE RECITED WHEN THE MOON RENEWETH ITSELF ON THE DAY OF THE MONTH. The Osiris Ȧuf-ānkh, triumphant, saith:—

"(1) Osiris unfettereth," or, as others say, "openeth "the storm cloud [in] the body of heaven, and is un-"fettered himself; Horus is made strong happily each "day. He whose transformations are great (*or* many) "hath offerings made unto him at the moment, (2) and "he hath made an end of the storm which is in the "face of the Osiris Ȧuf-ānkh, triumphant. Verily he "cometh, and he is Rā in [his] journeying, and he is the "four celestial gods in the heavens above. The Osiris "Ȧuf-ānkh, triumphant, cometh forth (3) in his day, "and he embarketh among the tackle of the boat."

RUBRIC: **If this chapter be known by the deceased he shall become a perfect *khu* in the underworld, and he shall not die therein a second time, and he shall eat his food side by side with Osiris. (4) If this chapter be known by him upon earth he shall be like unto Thoth, and he shall be adored by the living ones; he shall not fall headlong at the moment of royal flame of the goddess Bast, and the mighty princess shall make him to advance happily.**

THE BOOK OF THE DEAD

PART III

CHAPTER CXXXVIA. (I.)

[From the Papyrus of Nu (Brit. Mus. No. 10,477, sheet 28).]

Vignette: Three boats. In the first are Osiris, Horus (or, Râ), the deceased, and others; in the second and third are the two divine hawks on standards.

Text: (1) ANOTHER CHAPTER OF TRAVELLING IN THE GREAT BOAT OF RĀ. The Osiris Nu, the overseer of the house of the overseer of the seal, triumphant, saith:— (2)

"Behold now, O ye luminaries in Ȧnnu, ye people in

"Kherāḥa, the god Kha (?) hath been born; his cordage "(3) hath been completed, and the instrument where-"with he maketh his way hath [he] grasped firmly. I "have protected the implements of the gods, and I "delivered the boat Kha (?) for him. I have come "forth into heaven, and I have travelled therein with "Rā in the form of an ape, and have (4) turned "back the paths of Nut at the staircase of the god "Sebeḳ."

CHAPTER CXXXVIA. (II.)

[From the Papyrus of Nu (Brit. Mus. No. 10,477, sheet 16).]

Vignette: In the Theban Recension this Chapter has no vignette, but in the Saïte Recension the deceased stands in the boat of the god Rā who is seated therein (see Lepsius, *op. cit.*, Bl. 56).

Text: (1) ANOTHER CHAPTER OF MAKING PERFECT THE *KHU*; [it shall be recited] on the festival of Six. The Osiris Nu, the overseer of the house of the overseer of the seal, triumphant, saith :—

"Behold now, O ye luminaries in Ȧnnu (Heliopolis), "ye people in (2) Kher-āḥa, the god hath been born; "his cordage (?) hath been completed, and the instru-"ment wherewith he maketh his way he hath grasped "firmly; and the Osiris Nu is strong (3) with them to "direct the implement of the gods. The Osiris Nu hath "delivered the boat of the sun therewith . . . . . . , "and he cometh forth (4) into heaven. The Osiris Nu "saileth round about in heaven, he travelleth therein "unto Nut, he journeyeth along with Rā, and he "voyageth therein in the form of (5) apes; [he] "turneth back the water-flood which is over the "Thigh of the goddess Nut at the staircase of the "god Sebaḳu. (6) The hearts of Seb and Nut are "glad and repeat the name which is new. Un-neferu "reneweth [his] youth, Rā is in his splendours of light, "(7) Unti hath his speech, and lo, the god of the In-"undation is Prince among the gods. The taste of "sweetness hath forced a way into the heart of the "destitute one, and the lord of thy outcries (8) hath "been done away with, and the oars (?) of the com-"pany of the gods are in vigorous motion. Adored be "thou, O divine Soul, who art endowed more than the "gods of the South and North [in] their splendours! "Behold, (9) grant thou that the Osiris Nu may be "great in heaven even as thou art great among the "gods; deliver thou him from every evil and mur-"derous thing which may be wrought (10) upon him "by the Fiend, and fortify thou his heart. Grant "thou, moreover, that the Osiris Nu may be stronger "than all the gods, all the *Khus*, and all the dead. "(11) The Osiris Nu is strong and is the lord of "powers. The Osiris Nu is the lord of right and "truth (12) which the goddess Uatchit worketh. The "strength which protects the Osiris Nu is the strength "which protects the god Rā in heaven. O god Rā, "grant thou that the Osiris Nu may travel on (13) in "thy boat in peace, and do thou prepare a road where-"on [thy] boat may journey onwards; for the force "which protecteth (14) Osiris is the force which pro-"tecteth thee. The Osiris Nu driveth back the Croco-"dile from Rā day by day. (15) The Osiris Nu cometh "even as doth Horus in the splendours (?) of the horizon "of heaven, and he directeth (16) Rā through the "mansions of the sky; the gods rejoice greatly when "the Osiris Nu repulseth the Crocodile. The Osiris "Nu hath the amulet (?) of the god, and (17) the cloud "of Nebṭ shall not come nigh unto him, and the divine "guardians of the mansions of the sky shall not destroy "him. The Osiris Nu is a (18) divine being whose "face is hidden, and he dwelleth within the Great "House [as] the chief of the Shrine of the god. The "Osiris Nu carrieth the words of the god to Rā, (19) "and he cometh and maketh supplication unto the "divine lord with the words of his message. The "Osiris Nu is strong of heart, and he maketh his "offering at the moment (20) among those who perform "the ceremonies of sacrifice."

RUBRIC: [This chapter] shall be said over a figure of the deceased which shall be placed in [a model of] the boat of the sun, and behold, [he that reciteth it] shall be washed, and shall be ceremonially pure, (21) and he shall have burnt incense before Rā, and shall have offered wine, and cakes, and roasted fowl for the journey [of the deceased] in the boat of Rā. Now, every (22) *khu* for whom such things are done shall have an existence among the living ones, and he shall never perish, and he shall have a being like unto that of the holy God; no evil thing whatsoever shall attack him. (23) And he shall be like unto a happy *khu* in Åmentet, and he shall not die a second time. He shall eat and he shall drink in the presence of Osiris each day; he shall be borne along (24) with the kings of the North and of the South each and every day; he shall quaff water at the fountain-head; he shall come forth by day even as doth Horus; (25) he shall live and shall become like unto God; and he shall be hymned by the living ones, even as is Rā each and every day continually and regularly for ever.

CHAPTER CXXXVIB.

[From the Papyrus of Nu (Brit. Mus. No. 10,477, sheet 28).]

Vignette: A boat in which is the head of a hawk, emblematic of Rā, whereupon is a disk encircled by a serpent, sailing over a heaven of stars; over the bows and stern are *utchats*, or symbolic eyes.

Text: (1) THE CHAPTER OF SAILING IN THE GREAT BOAT OF RĀ TO PASS OVER (2) THE CIRCLE OF BRIGHT FLAME. The Osiris Nu, the overseer of the house of the overseer of the seal, triumphant, saith:—

"[Hail], ye bright and shining flames which keep "your place behind Rā, and which slay (3) behind him, "the boat of Rā is in fear of the whirlwind and the "storm; shine ye forth, then, and make [ye yourselves] "visible. I have come [daily] along with the god "Sek-ḥrȧ from the bight of his holy lake, (4) and I "have seen the Maāt [goddesses] pass along, and the "Lion-gods who belong unto them. Hail, thou that "dwellest in the coffer, who hast multitudes of plants (?), "I (5) have seen [what is] there. We rejoice, and "their princes rejoice greatly, and their lesser gods (?) "are glad. I have made a (6) way in front of the boat "of Rā, I have lifted myself up into his divine Disk, "I shine brightly through his splendours; he hath "furnished himself with the things which are his, "taking possession thereof as the lord of right and "truth. (7) And behold, O ye company of the gods, "and thou ancestor of the goddess Isis,[1] grant ye that "he may bear testimony to his father, the lord of those "who are therein. I have (8) weighed the . . . . . "in him [as] chief, and I have brought to him the "goddess Tefnut, and he liveth. Behold, come, come, "and declare before him the testimony (9) of right and "truth of the lord Tem. I cry out at eventide and at "his hour, saying;—Grant ye unto me (10) that I may "come. I have brought unto him the jaws of the

[1] Read "god Osiris"?

"passages of the tomb; I have brought unto him the "bones which are in Ȧnnu (Heliopolis); (11) I have "gathered together for him his manifold parts; I have "driven back for him the serpent fiend Āpep; I have "spit upon his gashes for him; I have made my road "and I have passed in (12) among you. I am he who "dwelleth among the gods, come, let [me] pass onwards "in the boat, the boat of the lord Sa. Behold, O "Ḥeru-ur, (13) there is a flame, but the fire hath been "extinguished. I have made [my] road, O ye divine "fathers and your divine apes! I have entered upon "the horizon, and I have passed on (14) to the side of "the divine princes, and I have borne testimony unto "him that dwelleth in his divine boat. I have gone "forward over the circle of bright (15) flame which is "behind the lord of the lock of hair which moveth "round about. Behold, ye who cry out over your-"selves, ye worms in [your] hidden places, grant ye "that I may pass onwards, (16) for I am the mighty "one, the lord of divine strength, and I am the spiritual "body (*sāḥ*) of the lord of divine right and truth made "by the goddess Uatchit. His strength which pro-"tecteth (17) is my strength which protecteth, which is "the strength which protecteth Rā. [Grant ye that I "may be in the following of Rā], and grant ye that I "may go round about with him in Sekhet-ḥetep [and "in] the two lands. (18) [I am] a great god, and [I "have been] judged by the company of his gods; grant "that divine, sepulchral meals may be given unto me."

CHAPTER CXXXVIIA.

[From the Papyrus of Nu (Brit. Mus. No. 10,477, sheet 26).]

Vignette : Four men, each holding a flame, standing in the presence of a god, before whom are four pools or lakes.

Text : (1) THE CHAPTER OF THE FOUR BLAZING FLAMES WHICH ARE MADE FOR THE KHU. Behold, thou shalt make four square troughs of clay, (2) whereon thou shalt scatter incense, and thou shalt fill them with the milk of a white cow, and by means of these thou shalt extinguish the flame. (3) The Osiris Nu, the overseer of the house of the overseer of the seal, triumphant, saith :—

"The fire cometh to thy KA, O Osiris, governor of "Åmenti; the fire (4) cometh to thy *Ka*, O Osiris Nu, "the overseer of the house of the overseer of the seal, "triumphant. He that ordereth the night cometh "after the day. (5) [The flame cometh to thy KA,

"O Osiris, governor of those in Åmenti][1] and the two "sisters (?) of Rā come likewise. Behold, [the flame] "riseth in Åbṭu (Abydos) and it cometh; and I cause it "to come [to] (6) the Eye of Horus. It is set in order "upon thy brow, O Osiris, governor of Åmenti,[2] and it "is (7) fixed within thy shrine and riseth upon thy "brow; it is set in order upon thy breast, O Osiris Nu, "(8) and it is fixed upon thy brow. The Eye of Horus "is protecting thee, O Osiris, governor of Åmenti, and "it keepeth thee (9) in safety; it casteth down headlong "all thine enemies for thee, and all thine enemies have "fallen headlong before thee. (10) O Osiris Nu, the "Eye of Horus protecteth thee, it keepeth thee in "safety, and it casteth down headlong (11) all thine "enemies. Thine enemies have fallen down headlong "before thy KA, O Osiris, governor of (12) Åmenti, the "Eye of Horus protecteth thee, it keepeth thee in "safety, and it hath cast down headlong all thine "enemies. (13) Thine enemies have fallen down head-"long before thy *Ka*, O Osiris Nu, the overseer of the "house of the overseer of the seal, triumphant, (14) the "Eye of Horus protecteth thee, it keepeth thee in "safety, it hath cast down headlong for thee all thine "enemies, and thine enemies have fallen down headlong "before thee. The Eye of Horus (15) cometh, it is "sound and well, and it sendeth forth rays like unto "Rā in the horizon; it covereth over with darkness the

[1] Added from the Papyrus of Nebseni.
[2] In the Papyrus of Nebseni the deceased is here addressed.

"powers of Suti, it taketh possession thereof, and it "bringeth its flame (16) against him upon [its] feet (?). "The Eye of Horus is sound and well, thou eatest the "flesh (?) of thy body by means thereof, and thou "givest praise (?) thereto. The four flames enter into "thy KA, O Osiris, governor of (17) Åmenti, the four "flames enter into thy *Ka*, O Osiris Nu, the overseer "of the house of the overseer of the seal, triumphant. "Hail, ye children of Horus, Mesthi, Ḥāpi, Ṭuamāutef, "(18) and Qebḥsennuf, ye have given your protection "unto your divine Father Osiris, the governor of "Åmenti, grant ye your protection to the Osiris Nu, "triumphant. (19) Now therefore, inasmuch as ye "have destroyed the opponent[s] of Osiris, the governor "of Åmenti, he liveth with the gods, and he hath "smitten Suti with his hand and arm since light "dawned upon the earth, and Horus hath gotten "power, (20) and he hath avenged his divine Father "Osiris himself; and inasmuch as your divine father "hath been made vigorous through the union which ye "have effected for him with the KA of Osiris, the "Governor of Åmenti—now the Eye of Horus (21) hath "avenged him, and it hath protected him, and it hath "cast down headlong for him all his enemies, and all "his enemies have fallen down before him—even so do "ye destroy the (22) opponent[s] of the Osiris Nu, the "overseer of the house of the overseer of the seal, "triumphant. Let him live with the gods, let him "smite down his enemy, let him destroy [him] (23) when "light dawneth upon the earth, let Horus gain power "and avenge the Osiris Nu, let the Osiris Nu have "vigour through the union which ye have effected for "him with his *Ka*. (24) O Osiris Nu, the Eye of Horus "hath avenged thee, it hath cast down headlong all "thine enemies for thee, and all thine enemies have "fallen down headlong before thee. Hail, Osiris, "(25) Governor of Ȧmenti, grant thou light and fire "to the happy soul which is in Suten-ḥenen (Hera-"cleopolis); and [O ye children of Horus] grant ye "power unto the living soul of the (26) Osiris Nu "within his flame. Let him not be repulsed and let "him not be driven back at the doors of Ȧmentet; O "let his offerings of bread and of linen garments be "brought unto him (27) among [those of] the lords of "funeral oblations, O offer ye praises as unto a god to "the Osiris Nu, destroyer of his opponent[s] in his "form of right and truth and in his (28) attributes of a "god of right and truth."

RUBRIC: [This chapter] shall be recited over four fires [made of] *ȧṭmȧ* cloth which hath been anointed with *ḥȧtet* unguent of Theḥennu, and they shall be placed in the hands of four men who shall have the names of the pillars of Horus written (29) upon their shoulders, and they shall burn the fires in the beautiful rays of Rā, and this shall confer power and might upon the *Khu* among the stars which never set. If this chapter be recited (30) for him he shall never, never fail, and he shall become a living soul for ever, and these fires shall make the *Khu* as vigorous as Osiris, (31) the Governor of Ȧmenti, regularly and continually for ever. It is a great struggle. Thou shalt not perform this ceremony before any human being except thine own self, or thy father,

(32) or thy son, because it is an exceedingly great mystery of Åmentet, and is a type of the hidden things of the underworld, for when [this ceremony hath been performed] the gods, and the *Khus*, and the dead shall see him (33) in the form of the Governor of Åmenti, and he shall have power and dominion like this god.

If thou shalt undertake to perform for him [what is ordered] in this "Chapter of the four blazing flames" each [day?] (34) thou shalt cause the form of the deceased to come forth from every hall [in the underworld] and from the seven halls of Osiris. And he shall have an existence in the form of the god, he shall have power and dominion corresponding to that of the gods and the *Khus* (35) for ever and ever; he shall enter in through the hidden pylons and shall not be turned back before the god Osiris. And it shall come to pass, if these things have been done for him, that he shall enter in and come forth, (36) he shall not be turned back, no limit [to his journeying] shall be set, and he shall not have sentence of evil passed upon him on the day of the weighing of words before the god Osiris for ever and ever.

And thou shalt perform [what is ordered in] this book for (37) the deceased, and he shall become perfect and pure, and [thou shalt] open his mouth with the iron instrument, and shalt write down these writings in accordance with the things which are found in the books of the royal son Ḥeru-ṭā-ṭā-f, (38) who discovered [them] in a hidden chest—now they were in the handwriting of the god himself—in the Temple of the goddess Unnut, the Lady of Unnu (Hermopolis), during his journey to make an inspection (39) of the temples, and of the lands, and of the funeral shrines of the gods. And these things shall be done secretly in the underworld, they are mysteries of the underworld, and they are (40) a type of the mysteries of Neter-khert.

And thou shalt say:—"[I] have come advancing "quickly and casting light upon [his] footsteps, and "hiding [myself] to cast light upon his hidden place (?). "I stand up behind the *Ṭeṭ*; I (41) stand up behind "the *Ṭeṭ* of Rā turning back the slaughter. I am "protecting thee, O Osiris."

RUBRIC: This chapter shall be recited over a *Ṭeṭ* of crystal which is set up upon a brick (42) made of green clay whereupon hath been inscribed this chapter. Then thou shalt make a cavity in the west wall, and, having [turned] the front of the *Ṭeṭ* towards the east [therein] thou shalt wall it up with earth moistened with (43) cedar juice (?). It will repulse the enemies of Osiris who set themselves at the east wall.

And thou shalt say:—"[I] have driven back [thy "foes, and I] have kept watch for thee; and he that is "upon his mountain (*i.e.*, Anubis) hath kept watch (44) "at thy moment, and hath repulsed [thy foes for thee]. "I have driven back the Crocodile [for thee] at thy "moment, and I am protecting thee, O Osiris Nu, the "overseer of the house of the overseer of the seal, "triumphant." (45)

RUBRIC: This chapter shall be recited over [a figure of] Anubis made of green clay kneaded (?) with incense and set up on a brick of green clay whereupon it hath been inscribed. (46) Then thou shalt make a cavity in the east wall, and having [turned] the face of Anubis towards the west [therein], thou shalt wall it up. [It will repulse the enemies of Osiris] who set themselves at the south (west ?) wall. (47)

And thou shalt say:—"I am the collar (*or* girdle) of "sand round the hidden coffer turning back the arm "from the blazing flame of the funeral mountain; I "have marched over the roads, and I am protecting the "Osiris (48) Nu, the overseer of the house of the over-"seer of the seal, triumphant."

RUBRIC: [This chapter] shall be recited over a brick of green clay whereupon it hath been inscribed; and thou shalt place incense (?) in the middle thereof, (49) and thou shalt smear it with pitch (*or* resin) and set light to it. Then thou shalt make a cavity in the south wall, and having [turned] the front of the brick towards the north [therein], thou shalt wall it up. [It will repulse the enemies of Osiris] who set themselves at the (50) north wall.

And thou shalt say:—"O thou that comest to make "a burning, I will not let thee do it; O thou that "comest to shoot forth [fire], I will not let thee do it. "I will burn thee, I will shoot forth [fire] (51) at thee, "for I am protecting the Osiris Nu, the overseer of the "house of the overseer of the seal, triumphant."

RUBRIC: [This chapter] shall be recited over a brick of green clay whereupon it hath been inscribed, along with a figure (?) of a (52) palm tree seven fingers in height; and thou shalt open its mouth. Then thou shalt make a cavity in the north wall, and having [turned] the face of the figure towards the south [therein], thou shalt wall it up [it will repulse the enemies of Osiris who set themselves at the south wall].

"And behold, these things shall be performed by a "man who is clean and is (53) ceremonially pure, "one who hath eaten neither meat nor fish, and who "hath not [recently] had intercourse with women; and "behold, thou shalt make offerings of cakes and ale, "and shalt burn incense on the fire of these gods. "(54) And every *Khu* for whom these things shall "be done shall become like a holy god in the under-"world; he shall not be turned back at any gate in "Åmentet, and he shall be in the following of (55)

"Osiris, wheresoever he goeth, regularly and con-"tinually."[1]

CHAPTER CXXXVIIb.

[From the Papyrus of Nebseni (Brit. Mus. No. 9900, sheet 6).]

Vignette: The goddess Âpi, the lady who giveth protection, in the form of a hippopotamus, setting light to a vessel of incense. In the Saite Recension the deceased is seen sitting upon a chair with two burning lamps on each side of him (see Lepsius, *Todtenbuch*, Bl. 56); there the Chapter is called, "Chapter of making the flame to burn up."

Text: (1) The Chapter of kindling a flame by Nebseni, the scribe and draughtsman in the Temple of Ptaḥ. [He saith]:—

"The white (*or*) shining Eye of Horus cometh. (2) "The brilliant Eye of Horus cometh. It cometh in

[1] The version of this Chapter found in the Papyrus of Nebseni (sheet 24) is much shorter than that here given, and that Papyrus omits all the supplementary Chapters and rubrics which are written in the Papyrus of Nu; a version much shorter still is given by Naville (*op. cit.*, Bd. II. p. 361) from the Papyrus of Nefer-uben-f in Paris.

"peace, it sendeth forth rays of light unto Rā in the "horizon, and it destroyeth the powers (3) of Set "according to the decree (?). It leadeth them on, "and it taketh possession [of him], and its flame is "kindled against him. [Its] flame cometh and goeth "about, and bringeth (4) adoration (?); [it] cometh and "goeth about heaven in the train of Rā upon the two "hands of thy two sisters, O Rā. The Eye of Horus "liveth, yea liveth within the great hall; the Eye of "Horus liveth, yea liveth, and is Ȧn-Māut-f."

CHAPTER CXXXVIII.

[From the Papyrus of Nu (Brit. Mus. No. 10,477, sheet 19).]

Vignette : The standard, emblematic of the nome of Teni, the capital of which was Abydos, surmounted by plumes and uraeus, etc., being set up by Isis and Osiris. On each side winged *utchats*, a fan or fly-flapper held upright by an emblem of life from which project human hands and arms, the hawk emblematic of Horus-Sept, a ram having plumes above his horns, and three gods standing upright. On one side are the

Souls of Pe, and the jackal, emblem of Ȧnpu (Anubis) or of Ȧp-uat; and on the other are the Souls of Ṭep and the jackal, emblem of Ȧp-uat or of Ȧnpu. Beneath the standard are the lion-gods of the horizon, one of whom is called "Yesterday" and the other "To-day."

Text: (1) THE CHAPTER OF ENTERING INTO ȦBTU, AND OF BEING IN THE FOLLOWING OF OSIRIS. The Osiris Nu, the overseer of the house of the overseer of the seal, triumphant, saith:— (2)

"Hail, ye gods who dwell in Ȧbtu (Abydos), ye "divine sovereign chiefs who are gathered together, "come ye forward with joy and gladness to (3) meet "me, and look ye upon my divine father Osiris. I "have been judged, and I have come forth from his "shrine. I am Horus, the lord of Qemt (Egypt), and "of the (4) red hilly desert; I have taken possession "thereof. There is none who hath power over him, "his Eye is mighty against his enemies, he hath "avenged his divine Father, he hath destroyed the "waterflood of his mother, he hath (5) crushed his "enemies, he hath put down violence mightily, and "hath stilled the strength of the god Nebṭ. The "divine prince of many peoples, the sovereign of the "two lands, hath taken possession of the house of his "divine Father (6) by means of the written decrees. I "have been tried in the Balance, my word is right and "true, I have gained the mastery over my enemies, and "bring to naught (?) the things (7) which they work "against me. I am strong in the strength which pro-

"tecteth me, I am the son of Osiris, and my divine "Father protecteth his body with strength and "might (?)."

CHAPTER CXXXIX.

[See Chapter CXXIII.]

CHAPTER CXL.

[From Lepsius, *Todtenbuch*, Bl. 57.]

Vignette : The deceased kneeling, with both hands raised in adoration, before the jackal of Anubis, which is couchant on a pylon, a kneeling figure having an *utchat* on his head, and the god Rā.

Text : THE BOOK WHICH IS TO BE RECITED ON THE LAST DAY OF THE SECOND MONTH OF THE SEASON

PERT[1] WHEN THE *UTCHAT* IS FULL IN THE SECOND MONTH OF THE SEASON *PERT*. (1) The Osiris Åuf-ānkh saith:—

"The divine Power hath risen and shineth [in] the "horizon, and the god Tem hath risen [out of] the "odour of that which floweth from him. The *Khus* "shine in heaven and Ḥet-benbenet (2) rejoiceth, for "there is among them a form which is like unto them-"selves; and there are shouts and cries of gladness "within the shrine, and the sounds of those who rejoice "go round about through the underworld, (3) and "homage [is paid] unto him at the decree of Tem "and Ḥeru-khuti (Harmachis). His Majesty ordereth "the company of the gods to follow in the train of his "Majesty; his Majesty ordereth the calling of the "*Utchat* with you [to] (4) my members. He hath "given strength to all my limbs, and hath made them "vigorous with that which cometh forth from the mouth "of His Majesty. His divine Eye resteth upon its seat "with His Majesty at that hour (5) of the night on the "day (?) of the fulfilment of the fourth hour (*or* four "hours) of the beautiful land (?), on the last day of the "second month of the season *pert*. The Majesty of the "*Utchat* is in the presence of the company of the gods, "and His Majesty shineth as he shone in the primeval "time, when the *Utchat* was [first] (6) upon his head. "Rā, Tem, Utchatet, Shu, Seb, Osiris, Suti, Horus,

[1] *I.e.*, the sixth month of the Egyptian year, which the Egyptian Christians or Copts call Mekhir ⲙϣⲓⲣ or ⲙⲉⲭⲓⲣ, Gr. Μεχίρ.

"Menth, Bāḥ, Rā-er-Neḥeḥ, Teḥuti, Nāȧm, (7) Tchetta, "Nut, Ȧsis, Nephthys, Hathor, Nekht, Mert (?), Maāt, "Ȧnpu, and Ta-mes-tchetta [are] the soul and body of "Rā. (8) The computation of the *Utchat* hath been "made in the presence of the divine lord of this earth; "it is full to the uttermost, and it resteth (*or* setteth). "And these gods are rejoicing on this day, and they "have their hands beneath (?) them, and the festival of "every god (9) having been celebrated, they say:— "Hail, praise be unto thee, O thou who art as Rā, "rejoice in him, for the mariners of [his] boat sail "round about, and [he] hath overthrown the fiend "Ȧpep. Hail, praise be unto thee, O thou who art "as Rā who maketh himself to come into being (10) in "the form of the god Kheperȧ. Hail, praise be unto "thee, O thou who art as Rā, for [he] hath destroyed "his enemies. Hail, praise be unto Rā, for he hath "crushed the heads of the children (11) of impotent "rebellion. And praise and rejoicing be unto the "Osiris Ȧuf-ānkh, triumphant."

RUBRIC: [This chapter] shall be recited over an *Utchat* of real lapis-lazuli or of *maḳ* stone plated with gold, before which shall be offered (12) every kind of fair and pure oblation when Rā showeth himself on the last day of the second month of the season *pert*. And thou shalt make another *Utchat* of jasper and place it upon such part of the dead man's body as thou pleasest, and when this chapter hath been recited (13) before the boat of Rā, the deceased shall be borne along with these gods, and he shall become one of them, and he shall be made to rise up in the underworld. And whilst this chapter is being recited, and likewise whilst the offerings are being made

(14) at the time when the *Utchat* is full, four altars shall be lighted for Rā-Tem, and four for the *Utchat*, and four for the gods who have been mentioned. And upon each one of them shall there be bread-cakes made of fine flour, and five white cakes, and plants (?), and five white cakes, and *shai*, and five *bȧaq*, and of incense one measure, and of *ṭeq* incense one measure, and one roasted joint of meat.

CHAPTERS CXLI. AND CXLII.

[From the Papyrus of Nu (Brit. Mus. No. 10,477, sheet 15).]

Vignette: The deceased, with hands raised in adoration, bowing before a table of offerings of every kind; or, the deceased standing and offering incense and pouring out a libation before Osiris; or, the god Osiris seated within a shrine on a throne, by the side of which stand Isis and Nephthys. On a lotus flower stand the four Children of Horus, and on a standard is a jackal, emblematic of Anubis. These vignettes are figured by Naville (*op. cit.*, Bd. I. Bl. 153), and differ entirely from the vignette which accompanies Chapter CXLII. in the Saïte Recension (see Lepsius, *op. cit.*, Bl. 59). Originally the text of Chapters CXLI. and CXLII. formed one composition, but it might readily be divided into two sections, viz., the list of the gods to whom a man was directed to make offerings for the benefit of his father and his son, and a list of the names of Osiris, and this is what the Editors of the Saïte Recension actually did, and they emphasized the division by giving to each section a distinct title.

Text: [HERE BEGINNETH] THE BOOK[1] [WHICH] A MAN SHALL RECITE FOR HIS FATHER OR FOR HIS SON DURING THE FESTIVALS OF ÅMENTET, WHEREBY HE SHALL MAKE HIM PERFECT WITH RĀ AND WITH THE GODS, AND WHEREBY HE SHALL HAVE HIS EXISTENCE WITH THEM; IT SHALL BE RECITED ON THE NINTH DAY OF THE FESTIVAL. Behold the Osiris Nu, the overseer of the house of the overseer of the seal, triumphant, maketh offerings of cakes, and ale, and oxen, and feathered fowl, and joints of roast meat; and he burneth incense

1. to Osiris, the governor of Åmenti,[2]
2. to Rā-Ḥeru-khuti (Rā-Harmachis),[3]
3. to Nu,[4]
4. to Maāt,
5. to the Boat of Rā,
6. to Temu,[5]
7. to the Great company of the gods,
8. to the Little company of the gods,
9. to Horus, the lord of the *ureret* crown,
10. to Shu,
11. to Tefnut,

[1] In the Saïte Recension the title of the first section runs:—"[HERE BEGINNETH] THE BOOK OF MAKING PERFECT THE DECEASED, "AND OF KNOWING THE NAMES OF THE GODS OF THE SOUTHERN "AND NORTHERN HEAVENS, AND OF THE GODS OF THE *QERTI*, AND "OF THE GODS WHO ARE THE GUIDES OF THE UNDERWORLD (*ṬUAT*). "IT SHALL BE RECITED BY A MAN FOR HIS FATHER OR FOR HIS "MOTHER," etc.

[2] The S. R. (*i.e.*, Saïte Recension) adds, "lord of the four districts of Åbṭu (Abydos)." [3] S. R., Ḥeru-khuti. [4] The S. R. adds, "Father of the gods." [5] S. R., Tem-Kheperå.

12. to Seb,[1]

13. to Nut,[1]

14. to Isis,

15. to Nephthys,[2]

16. to the Temple of the *Kas* of Nebt-er-tcher,

17. to the Raging-one-of-heaven-who-raiseth-up-the god,

18. to Åuḳert[3] -dwelling-in-her-place,

19. to the city of Meḥt-Khebitet, the *sāḥu* of the god,

20. to the Goddess-greatly-beloved-with-red-hair,

21. to the Goddess-joined-unto-life-with-flowing-hair,

22. to the Goddess-whose-name-is-mighty-in-her-works,

23. to the Bull, the husband of the divine Cow,[4]

24. to the beautiful Power of the beautiful Rudder of the northern heaven,[5]

25. to Him that revolveth, the guide of the two lands, the beautiful Rudder of the western heaven,[6]

26. to the God of light, who dwelleth in the Temple of the *āshemu*[7] beings, the beautiful Rudder of the eastern heaven,

27. to the Dweller in the Temple of the ruddy ones, the beautiful Rudder of the southern heaven,[8]

[1] In the S. R. Seb and Nut are mentioned together. [2] In the S. R. Osiris, Isis, and Nephthys are mentioned together. [3] In the S. R., Amenti. [4] In the S. R., "To the Bull of the Cows." [5] In the S. R., "To the beautiful Power, the Opener of the Disk. To the beautiful Rudder of the northern heaven." [6] In the S. R., "To Him that revolveth, the guide of the two lands. To the beautiful Rudder of the eastern heaven." [7] *I.e.*, the gods in material forms. [8] In the S. R. this paragraph is in two sections.

28. To Mesthi,
29. to Ḥāpi,
30. to Ṭuamāutef,
31. to Qebḥsennuf,[1]
32. to the *Ȧtert* of the South,
33. to the *Ȧtert* of the North,
34. to the *Sektet* boat,[2]
35. to the *Āṭet* boat,[3]
36. to Thoth,[4]
37. to the Gods of the South,
38. to the Gods of the North,[5]
39. to the Gods of the West,
40. to the Gods of the East,[6]
41. to the Gods of the Thigh,
42. to the Gods of the funeral offerings,[7]
43. to the Great House,
44. to the Temple of Flame,[8]
45. to the Gods of the places of the dead,
46. to the Gods of the horizon,[9]
47. to the Gods of the fields,
48. to the Gods of the divine *Perti*,[10]

[1] In the S. R. the four "children of Horus" are mentioned together. [2] In the S. R. the two boats of the Sun are mentioned together. [3] After "Āṭet boat," the S. R. adds, "to Hathor." [4] In the S. R., "To Thoth, the Bull of Maāt, to Thoth, the Weigher of the words of the Company of the gods, to Thoth, the Guide of the gods. [5] In the S. R. the gods of the South and North are mentioned together. [6] In the S. R. the gods of the West and East are mentioned together. [7] This line is omitted in the S. R. [8] In the S. R. the "Great Double-House," and the "Double-House of Flame" are mentioned together. [9] In the S. R. the gods of the cemeteries and of the horizon are mentioned together. [10] In the S. R. the gods of the fields and of the *Qerti* (not *Perti*) are mentioned together.

49. to the Gods of the divine *Nesti*,[1]

50. to the Roads of the South,

51. to the Roads of the North,[2]

52. to the Roads of the East,

53. to the Roads of the West,[3]

54. to the Doors of the Underworld,

55. to the Pylons of the Underworld,

56. to the Leaves of the hidden doors,

57. to the hidden doors,

58. to the Guardians of the leaves of the Doors of the *Ṭuat* (Underworld),[4]

59. to the Hidden Faces who guard the roads,

60. to the Guardians who give divine food (?),

61. to the Guardians of the funeral mountains who give happy faces (?),

62. to the Flaming Beings who give forth fire,

63. to the divine burning Altars,

64. to those who scatter and extinguish the flame of fire in Åmentet,[5]

[1] In the S. R., "little ones." [2] In the S. R. the gods of the *netches* and the southern and northern roads are mentioned together. [3] In the S. R. the roads of the West and East are mentioned together. [4] In the S. R. we have:—"To the Guide of the doors of the Ṭuat, to the Doorkeepers of the Ṭuat and of the pylons of the Ṭuat, to the hidden pylons of the Ṭuat, to the Doorkeepers of the pylons of the Ṭuat, to the hidden doors of the Ṭuat." [5] In the S. R. we have:—"To those that scatter and extinguish the fire, to the fire in Åmentet," and after these lines are added the following:—

"To Him that giveth triumph to the *Khu*,
"To the Perfect one in Åmentet,
"To the East (Åbtet) and to its *Ka*."

65. to Osiris-Un-nefer,[1]
66. to Osiris-Ȧnkhti,
67. to Osiris-lord-of-life,
68. to Osiris-lord-of-wholeness,
69. to Osiris-dweller-in-Peḳu (?),
70. to Osiris-Orion (*Saḥ*),
71. to Osiris-Saa,
72. to Osiris-dweller-in-temples,
73. to Osiris-in-Resenet,
74. to Osiris-in-Meḥenet,
75. to Osiris-golden-one-of-millions-of-years,
76. to Osiris-Bati-erpit,
77. to Osiris-Ptaḥ-lord-of-life,
78. to Osiris-dweller-in-Re-stau,
79. to Osiris-dweller-in-the-funeral-mountain,
80. to Osiris-in-Ati,
81. to Osiris-in-Seḥtet,
82. to Osiris-in-Netchefet,
83. to Osiris-in-Resu,
84. to Osiris-in-Pe,
85. to Osiris-in-Neteru,
86. to Osiris-in-Sau-the-Lower,
87. to Osiris-in-Bȧket,
88. to Osiris-in-Sunnu,
89. to Osiris-in-Reḥenenet,

[1] In the S. R. here begins Chapter CXLII. with the title, "The "Book of making perfect the deceased, and of making [him] to "advance with long strides, and to come forth by day in all the "transformations which he pleaseth, and to know the names of the "god Osiris in every place wherein he chooseth to be."

90. to Osiris-in-Åpen,
91. to Osiris-in-Qefennu,
92. to Osiris-Sekri-in-Peṭ-she,
93. to Osiris-dweller-in-his-city,
94. to Osiris-in-Pesḳ-re,
95. to Osiris-in-his-habitations-in-the-Land-of-the-North,
96. to Osiris-in-heaven,
97. to Osiris-in-his-habitations-in-Re-stau,
98. to Osiris-Netchesti,
99. to Osiris-Atef-ur,
100. to Osiris-Sekri,
101. to Osiris-governor-of-eternity,
102. to Osiris-the-begetter,
103. to Osiris-in-the-water (?),
104. to Osiris-in-battle (?),
105. to Osiris-lord-of-everlastingness,
106. to Osiris-Prince,
107. to Osiris-Taiti,
108. to Osiris-in-Re-stau,
109. to Osiris-upon-his-sand,
110. to Osiris-dweller-in-the-hall-of-the-Cow,
111. to Osiris-in-Tanenet,
112. to Osiris-in-Neṭebit,
113. to Osiris-in-Såa,
114. to Osiris-in-Beṭeshu,
115. to Osiris-in-Ṭepu,
116. to Osiris-in-Sau-the-Upper,
117. to Osiris-in-Nepert,

118. to Osiris-in-Shennu,
119. to Osiris-in-Ḥenket,
120. to Osiris-in-Ta-sekri,
121. to Osiris-in-Shau,
122. to Osiris-in-Fat-Ḥeru,
123. to Osiris-in-Maāti,
124. to Osiris-in-Henȧ.

In the Saïte Recension (see Lepsius, *op. cit.*, Bl. 59) Chapter CXLII. is much fuller than in the papyri extant which contain the Theban Recension; as there given it is in a tabular form and is divided into six sections each containing twenty-six lines. It runs:—

Text: The Book of making perfect the deceased and of making him to advance with long strides, and to come forth by day in all the transformations which please him, and to know the names of the god Osiris in every place wherein he chooseth to be. The Osiris Auf-ānkh, born of Sheret-Ȧmsu, triumphant, saith:—

I. (1) "Osiris-un-nefer, (2) Osiris-the-living-one, (3) "Osiris-lord-of-life, (4) Osiris-Neb-er-tcher, (5) Osiris-"opener-of-the-back-of-the-two-lands, (6) Osiris-dweller-"in-Un, (7) Osiris-dweller-in-corn, (8) Osiris-Saḥ "(Orion), (9) Osiris-holy-crown-of-the-Souls of-Ȧnnu "(Heliopolis), (10) Osiris-dweller-in-Thenenet, (11) "Osiris-in-Resenet, (12) Osiris-in-Meḥenet, (13) Osiris-"lord-of-millions-of-years, (14) Osiris-son-of-the-*Erpeti* "(*i.e.*, Isis and Nephthys), (15) Osiris-Ptaḥ-lord-of-life,

"(16) Osiris-dweller-in-Re-stau, (17) Osiris-governor-of-"the-world-dwelling-in-Ṭaṭṭu, (18) Osiris-dweller-in-"the-funeral-mountain, (19) Osiris-holy-Soul-in-Ṭaṭṭu, "(20) Osiris-in-Ati (?), (21) Osiris-in-Ḥeset," or as others say, "in Neter-seḥ, (22) Osiris-lord-of-Ta-ānkhtet "(*i.e.*, Land of Life), (23) Osiris-in-Sau (Saïs), (24) "Osiris-in-Netchet, (25) Osiris-in-the-South," or as others say, "among-the-divine-sovereign-chiefs, (26) "Osiris-in-Pe."

II. "(1) Osiris-in-Ṭept, (2) Osiris-in-Netrȧ, (3) "Osiris-in-Lower-Sau (Saïs), (4) Osiris-in-Upper-Sau "(Saïs), (5) Osiris-in-Ȧn-ruṭ-f, (6) Osiris-in-the-two-"hawk-gods, (7) Osiris-in-Sunnu, (8) Osiris-in-Renen, "(9) Osiris-in-Ȧper, (10) Osiris-in-Qenfennu, (11) "Osiris-in-Sekri, (12) Osiris-in-Peṭet, (13) Osiris-in-"his-temple-in-Re-stau, (14) Osiris-in-Nif-ur, (15) "Osiris in-Neṭit, (16) Osiris-dweller-in-his-city, (17) "Osiris-Ḥenti (*i.e.*, Osiris of the two crocodiles), (18) "Osiris-in-Peḳes, (19) Osiris-in-his-temple-in-the-Land-"of-the-South, (20) Osiris-in-his-temple-in-the-Land-of-"the-North, (21) Osiris-in-heaven, (22) Osiris-on-earth, "(23) Osiris-upon-[his-]throne, (24) Osiris-in-Atef-ur, "(25) Osiris-Seker-in-the-closed-chest, (26) Osiris-"prince-of-eternity-in-Ȧnnu."

III. (1) "Osiris-the-begetter, (2) Osiris-in-the-*Sek-*"*tet*-boat, (3) Osiris-in-Rertu-nifu, (4) Osiris-lord-of-"eternity, (5) Osiris-lord-of-everlastingness, (6) Osiris-"in-Ṭesher, (7) Osiris-in-Seshet, (8) Osiris-in-Ut-reset,

"(9) Osiris-in-Ut-meḥt, (10) Osiris-in-Åat-urt, (11) "Osiris-in-Āpert, (12) Osiris-in-Shennu, (13) Osiris-in-"Ḥe-kennut," or as others say, "in-Ḥesert, (14) Osiris-"in-Seker, (15) Osiris-in-Shau, (16) Osiris-fa-Ḥeru, "(17) Osiris-in-Uu-pek, (18) Osiris-in-Maāti, (19) "Osiris-in-Menȧ, (20) Osiris-Souls-of-his-father, (21) "Osiris-lord-of-the-world-king-of-the-gods, (22) Osiris-"in-Bener, (23) Osiris-Tai, (24) Osiris-on-his-sand, (25) "Osiris-dweller-in-the-hall-of-his-Cows, (26) Osiris-in-"Sȧ."

IV. (1) "Osiris-in-Sȧpti, (2) Osiris-in-Asher, (3) "Osiris-in-all-lands, (4) Osiris-dweller-in-the-pool-of-"the-Great-double-House, (5) Osiris-in-Ḥet-benbenet, "(6) Osiris-in-Ånnu, (7) Osiris-the-aged-Chief-in-Ånnu, "(8) Osiris-in-Ḥemaḳ, (9) Osiris-in-Ākesh, (10) Osiris-"in-Pe-of-Nu, (11) Osiris-in-the-Great-Temple, (12) "Osiris-lord-of-life-in-Åbṭu, (13) Osiris-lord-of-Ṭaṭṭu, "(14) Osiris-dweller-in-the-throne-of-his-habitations (?), "(15) Osiris-Prince-in-Åbṭu, (16) Osiris-Prince-in-the-"hidden-place, (17) Osiris-in-life-in-Ḥet-ka-Ptaḥ, (18) "Osiris-lord-of-might-destroyer-of-the-foe, (19) Osiris-"Bull-in-Qemt, (20) Osiris-ȧḥeti, (21) Osiris-seḥ, (22) "Osiris-Ḥeru-khuti, (23) Tem-Bull-of-the-body-of-the-"Great-Company-of-the-gods, (24) Opener-of-the-roads-"of-the-south-governor-of-the-two-lands, (25) Opener-"of-the-roads-of-the-north-governor-of-heaven, (26) "Ptaḥ-stablisher-of-the-holy-seat-of-Rā."

V. (1) "One-invoked (?)-in-Ḥet-benbenet, (2) Seb-

"prince-of-the-gods, (3) Ḥeru-ur, (4) Ḥeru-khentet-"ȧn-maati, (5) Ḥeru-sa-Ȧuset, (6) Ȧmsu-suten-Ḥeru-"nekht, (7) Ȧn-mut-f-āb-ur, (8) Ḱhnemu-Ḥeru-ḥetep, "(9) Ḥeru-sekhai, (10) Ḥeru-khent-Khaṭṭhi, (11) Ḥeru-"Teḥuti, (12) Ȧn-Ḥeru, (13) Ȧnpu-khent-neter-seḥ, "(14) Nut, (15) Isis-goddess-in-all-her-names, (16) Re-"sekhait, (17) Shenthit, (18) Ḥeqtit, (19) *Neshemet*-"Boat-lord-of-eternity, (20) Nit (Neith)-Serqet, (21) "Maāt, (22) Ahit, (23) The-four-birth-places-in-Ȧbṭu, "(24) Great-Meskhen, (25) Meskhen-Seqebet, (26) "Meskhen-Menkhet."

VI. (1) "Meskhen-nefert, (2) Ȧmseth, (3) Ḥāpi, (4) "Ṭuamāutef, (5) Qebḥsennuf, (6) Uraeus-within-the-"Divine-House, (7) Gods-guides-of-the-Ṭuat, (8) Gods-"of-the-Qerti, (9) Gods-goddess-within-Ȧbṭu, (10) "Shrines-North-South, (11) Devoted-ones-of-Osiris, "(12) Osiris-dweller-in-Ȧmentet, (13) Osiris-in-his-"every-place, (14) Osiris-in-his-place-in-the-Land-of-"the-South, (15) Osiris-in-his-place-in-the-Land-of-"the-North, (16) Osiris-in-every-place-where-his-KA-"wisheth-to-be, (17) Osiris-in-all-his-halls, (18) Osiris-"in-all-his-creations, (19) Osiris-in-all-his-names, (20) "Osiris-in-all-his-holdings, (21) Osiris-in-all-his-risings, "(22) Osiris-in-all-his-ornamentations, (23) Osiris-"in-all-his-stations, (24) Ḥeru-netch-tef-f-in-his-"every-name, (25) Ȧnpu-dweller-in-the-*seḥ*-hall-in-"his-every-name, (26) Ȧnpu-in-the-town-of-embalm-"ment . . . ."

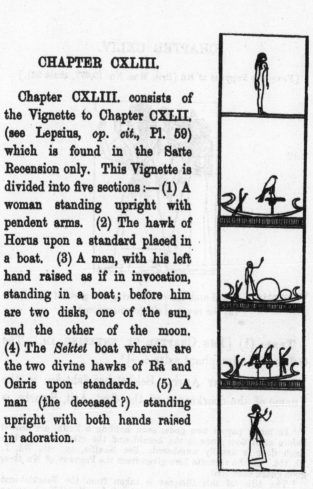

CHAPTER CXLIII.

Chapter CXLIII. consists of the Vignette to Chapter CXLII. (see Lepsius, *op. cit.*, Pl. 59) which is found in the Saïte Recension only. This Vignette is divided into five sections:—(1) A woman standing upright with pendent arms. (2) The hawk of Horus upon a standard placed in a boat. (3) A man, with his left hand raised as if in invocation, standing in a boat; before him are two disks, one of the sun, and the other of the moon. (4) The *Sektet* boat wherein are the two divine hawks of Rā and Osiris upon standards. (5) A man (the deceased?) standing upright with both hands raised in adoration.

CHAPTER CXLIV.

[From the Papyrus of Nu (Brit. Mus. No. 10,477, sheet 26).]

Vignette: (1) Ani and his wife adoring the gods of the *Ārits*; (2) the seven *Ārits* (or mansions).[1]

Text: (1) [THE CHAPTER OF ENTERING IN. The Osiris Nu, triumphant saith :—][2]

I. "THE FIRST ĀRIT. Sekhet-ḥrá-āsht-āru is the "name of the doorkeeper of the first Ārit, Semetu is

[1] In many papyri two gods, each holding a knife, are seated before each door; one is the herald and the other the watcher. Each door is usually numbered. See Naville, *op. cit.*, Bd. I. Bl. 154. In the vignette here given from the Papyrus of Nu *three* gods guard each *Ārit*.

[2] The title of this Chapter is taken from the Brocklehurst Papyrus (*ibid.*). In the Saïte Recension it is called "The knowing of the names of the *Ārits*."

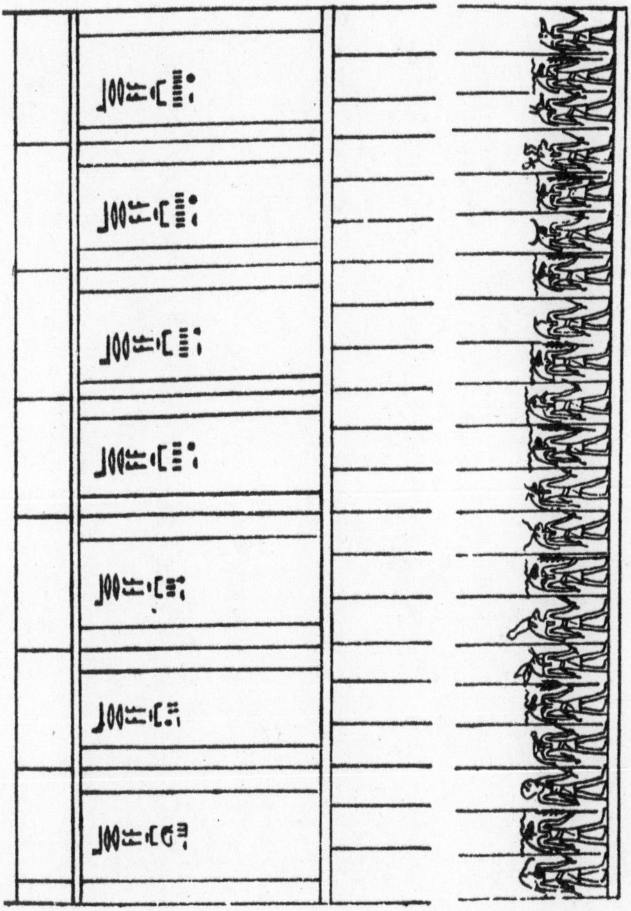

"the name of the watcher, and Hu-kheru is the name "of the herald thereof."

II. "The second Arit. Ṭun-ḥāt is the name of "the doorkeeper of the second Arit, Se-qeṭ-ḥrȧ is the "name of the watcher, and Sabes is the name of the "herald thereof."

III. "The third Ārit. Ȧm-ḥuat-ent-peḥ-fi is the "name of the doorkeeper of the third Arit, Res-ḥrȧ is "the name of the watcher, and Uāau is the name of the "herald thereof."

IV. "The fourth Ārit. Khesef-ḥrȧ-āsht-kheru is "the name of the doorkeeper of the fourth Arit, Res-ȧb "is the name of the watcher, and Neteḳa-ḥrȧ-khesef-aṭu "is the name of the herald thereof."

V. "The fifth Ārit. Ānkh-em-fentu is the name "of the doorkeeper of the fourth Arit, Ashebu is the "name of the watcher, and Ṭeb-ḥer-kehaat is the name "of the herald thereof."

VI. "The sixth Ārit. Ȧken-tau-k-ha-kheru is the "name of the doorkeeper of the sixth Ārit, Ȧn-ḥrȧ is "the name of the watcher, and Meṭes-ḥrȧ-ȧri-she is "the name of the herald thereof."

VII. "The seventh Ārit. Metes-sen is the name "of the doorkeeper of the seventh Ārit, Āāa-kheru is "the name of the watcher, and Khesef-ḥrȧ-khemiu is "the name of the herald thereof."

(1) "Hail,[1] ye Ārits! Hail, ye who make the Ārits

[1] A version of this portion of Chapter CXLIV. is found in Lepsius, *op. cit.*, Bll. 60, 61.

"for Osiris! Hail, ye who watch your Ārits! Hail, "ye who herald the affairs of the (2) two lands for the "god Osiris each day, the Osiris Nu, the overseer of "the house of the overseer of the seal, triumphant, "knoweth you, and he knoweth your names. The "Osiris Nu hath been born in Re-stau, (3) and every "glory of the horizon [and] every honour have been "given unto him. The Osiris Nu is in the city of "Pe like the pure being (?) Osiris. The Osiris Nu "hath received acclamations in Re-stau, and (4) the "gods lead [him] over the horizon along with the "divine princes who are behind Osiris. I am the "divine One among them, and [I am] their leader. "The Osiris Nu (5) is a *Khu*, the lord of the *Khus*, a "*Khu* [who] worketh. The Osiris Nu celebrateth the "monthly festival and he is the herald of the half-"monthly festival. Hail, thou that revolvest, the "Osiris Nu (6) is under the fiery Eye of Horus, and "he is under the hand of Thoth on the night when he "travelleth over heaven in triumph. The Osiris Nu "passeth onwards in peace, and he journeyeth (7) in "the boat of Rā. The strength which protecteth the "Osiris Nu is the strength which protecteth the boat "of Rā. The Osiris Nu (8) hath a name greater than "yours, and he is greater than ye are on the path of "Maāt; the Osiris abominateth defeat (?). The strength "which protecteth the Osiris Nu is (9) the strength "which protecteth Horus the first-born of Rā. [He] "hath made his heart, and the Osiris Nu shall not be "constrained and he shall not be repulsed at the Ārits "of the god Osiris. (10) The Osiris Nu hath been "provided [with all things] by the double Lion-god, "and the pure one (?) is in the following of Osiris, the "governor of Ȧmenti, throughout the course of each "day, daily. (11) His fields are in Sekhti-ḥetep with "the divine beings who know things, and with those "who perform things for the Osiris Nu (12) by the "hand of Thoth among those who make offerings of "propitiation. And Anubis hath commanded him that "dwelleth among offerings that the offerings of the "Osiris Nu shall be with him, and that they shall "not be taken away (13) from him by those divine "beings who dwell in fetters. The Osiris Nu, the "overseer of the house of the overseer of the seal, "triumphant, cometh like unto Horus in the splen-"dour of the horizon of heaven, and Rā hath set him "in order (14) for the Ārits of the horizon; the gods "rejoice in him when they meet him. The amulets (?) "of the god are for (15) the Osiris Nu, the god Nebṭ "shall not come to him, and the doorkeepers of the "Ārits shall not overthrow him. The Osiris Nu (16) "is hidden of face within the great celestial house "[which is] the shrine of the god, and he arriveth "there in the following of the pure one (?) Hathor. "The Osiris Nu (17) createth multitudes of human "beings, he maketh Maāt to advance to Rā, and he "destroyeth the twofold strength of Āpep. The Osiris "Nu (18) maketh a way through the firmament, he "driveth away the whirlwind and the storm, he maketh "the mariners of Rā to live, and he maketh offerings "to come unto the place where he (?) is. (19) The "Osiris Nu causeth a boat to be made, he travelleth "therein happily; the Osiris Nu maketh a way and he "advanceth thereon. The face of the Osiris Nu (20) "is like that of the god Ur-peḥi-f by reason of the "might (?), and the Osiris Nu is the lord of might. "The Osiris Nu is at rest in the horizon, and he is "(21) valiant to overthrow you, O ye *Nehesu* gods; "make a path, then, for your lord Osiris."

RUBRIC: This chapter shall be said over a drawing of the divine sovereign chiefs, which hath been done in yellow ink, (22) on the boat of Rā; and offerings and oblations shall be made unto them, and sacrifices of feathered fowl, and incense [shall be burnt] before them. These acts will make the deceased to live, and they will give him strength among (23) these gods, and he shall neither be repulsed nor turned back at the pylons of the underworld. And, moreover, thou shalt make a figure of the deceased in their presence, and thou shalt make it to come forth towards every one of (24) these gates which are painted [above]. And thou shalt recite this chapter at the door of each of the Ārits which are painted [above], and at each one of them thou shalt make offerings, viz., the thigh, the head, the heart, and the hoof of a red bull; (25) and four vessels of blood which hath not come from the breast; and amulets (?); and sixteen loaves of white bread, and eight *pasen (or persen)* loaves, and eight *shenen* loaves, and eight *khenfu* loaves, and eight *ḥebennu* loaves, and eight large vessels of beer, and (26) [eight] large vessels of grain; and four earthenware vessels filled with the milk of a white cow, and fresh herbs, and fresh olives, and unguent, and eye-paint, and *ḥātet* (27) unguent, and incense [to be burnt] on the fire, and [this chapter] shall be recited twice over each earthenware vessel, after the drawing *(or* image) hath been made, at the fourth

hour, going round about by day; (28) and take good heed to the time in the heavens. Now when thou doest [what is written in] this book do not allow any person whatsoever to see [thee]. [And this ceremony] shall make long the strides (29) of the deceased in heaven, and on earth, and in the underworld, and it shall benefit him in everything which he doeth, and he shall [possess] the things of the day regularly and continually.

CHAPTER CXLV.

[From Lepsius, *Todtenbuch*, Bll. 61—65.]

Chapter CXLV. and CXLVI. are two versions of one and the same text. Of these, Chapter CXLV. is the longer, and the two different forms of it—of each of which, unfortunately, only a single imperfect copy is extant—are described by Naville (*Einleitung*, pp. 111 and 173—176). Both are ancient, one appearing in the tomb of Seti II. Meri-en-Ptaḥ at Thebes, and the other in the papyrus of the royal military scribe Pa-ur (*Einleitung*, p. 104). A better general view of the contents of Chapter CXLV. will probably be obtained from the text as given in the Saïte Recension than from the mutilated ancient forms now known; it is, moreover, fuller than the others, and the following translation has been made from it.

Vignette: The twenty-one pylons of Sekhet-Ȧanre of the House of Osiris. In each section the deceased stands with hands raised in adoration before a god who stands by the side of a shrine.

Text: [HERE BEGIN THE CHAPTERS OF] THE PYLONS OF SEKHET-ÅANRE OF THE HOUSE OF OSIRIS. (1) The Osiris Åuf-ānkh, triumphant, saith :—

I. "Homage to thee, saith Horus, O thou first pylon "of the Still-Heart. I have made [my] way. I know "thee, and I know thy name,

"and I know (2) the name "of the god who guardeth "thee! 'Lady of trem-"blings, with lofty walls, "the sovereign lady, the "mistress of destruction, "who setteth in order the "words which drive back "the whirlwind and the storm, who delivereth from "destruction him that travelleth along the way,' is thy "name. (3) The name of the god who guardeth thee "is Nerāu. I have washed myself in the water wherein "the god Rā washeth himself when he leaveth the "eastern part of the sky. I have anointed myself "(4) with *ḥāti* unguent [made from] the cedar, I "have arrayed myself in apparel of *menkh*, and I "have with me my sceptre of *ḥeti* wood."

[Saith the pylon :—] "Pass on, then, thou art pure."

II. (5) "The Osiris Åuf-ānkh, triumphant, saith :—

"Homage to thee, saith Horus, O thou second pylon "of the Still-Heart. I have made [my] way. I know "thee, and I know thy name, and I know (6) the name "of the god who guardeth thee. 'Lady of heaven, the "mistress of the world, who terrifieth the earth from "the place of [thy] body,' is thy name. The name of "the god who guardeth thee "is Mes-Ptaḥ. I have washed "myself in the water wherein "the god Osiris (7) washeth "himself, to whom were given "the *Sektet* boat and the *Mā-* "*ṭet* boat when he came forth "over Ȧm-urt, and passed "through the pylons. I have "anointed myself with the unguent of the festivals, "(8) I have arrayed myself in apparel of *seshet*, and I "have with me my sceptre of *benben* wood."

[Saith the pylon :—] "Pass on, then, thou art pure."

III. (9) The Osiris Ȧuf-ānkh, triumphant, saith :—

"Homage to thee, saith Horus, O thou third pylon "of the Still-Heart. I have made [my] way. I know "thee, and I know thy "name, and I know the "name of the god (10) who "guardeth thee. 'Lady of "pylons, lady to whom "abundant offerings are "made, who giveth what- "soever is there, (?) the "guide of the offerings, "who gratifieth the gods, who giveth the day for the "sailing up of the boat *Neshemet* to Ȧbṭu (Abydos),' is

"thy name. (11) The name of the god who guardeth "thee is Beq. I have washed myself in the water "wherein the god Ptaḥ washeth when he saileth up "to carry away the god Ḥennu on the day of 'opening "the face.' I have anointed (12) myself with *ḥāti* "unguent [made] of *ḥekennu* unguent and of *tuḥennu* "unguent, I have arrayed myself in apparel of *shesa*, "and I have with me my sceptre of *ähen* (?) wood."

[Saith the pylon :—] "Pass on, then, thou art pure."

IV. (13) The Osiris Åuf-ānkh, triumphant, saith :—

"Homage to thee, saith Horus, O thou fourth pylon "of the Still-Heart. I have made [my] way. I know "thee, and I know thy "name, and I know the "name of the god (14) who "guardeth thee. 'She who "prevaileth with knives, the "mistress of the two lands, "who destroyeth the ene- "mies of the Still-Heart, "who maketh the decree "for the escape of the needy from evil hap,' is thy "name. The name of the god who guardeth thee is "Ḥu-tepa. (15) I have washed myself in the water "wherein the god Un-nefer, triumphant, washeth him- "self, when he hath had a dispute with Set, and when "victory is given unto him. I have anointed myself "(16) with *sunät* unguent and with *enen* unguent, I "am pure (?), I have arrayed myself in *shesä* apparel

"like unto that in which thy son [was arrayed], ". . . . . and I have with me my sceptre of *tau-* "*atutu* wood."

[Saith the pylon :]—"Pass on, then, thou art pure."

V. (17) The Osiris Åuf-ānkh, triumphant, saith :—

"Homage to thee, saith Horus, O thou fifth pylon of "the Still-Heart. I have made [my] way. I know "thee, and I know thy "name, I know the name "of the god who (18) "guardeth thee. 'Lady of "splendour, lady of praises, "lofty one, Neb-er-tchert, "the lady to whom suppli- "cations are made and "unto whom none en- "tereth . . . .' is thy name. The name of "the god who guardeth thee is Erṭā-ḥen-er-requa. "(19) I have washed myself in the water wherein "Horus washed himself when he made himself the "Chief Reader and Sa-mer-f for his father Osiris. I "have anointed myself with *åber* unguent [made] of "holy offerings, I have upon me the (20) skin of the "panther, and I have with me my sceptre wherewith "to smite those who are black of heart."

[Saith the pylon :—] "Pass on, then, thou art pure."

VI. (21) The Osiris Åuf-ānkh, triumphant, saith :—

"Homage to thee, saith Horus, O thou sixth pylon "of the Still-Heart. I have made [my] way. I know "thee, and I know thy name, and I know the name "of the god who guardeth thee (22) . . . ., 'lady "to whom abundant sup- "plication is made . . . . ; "the difference between "whose height and breadth "is unknown; the like of "whom for strength hath "not been overturned (?) "since the beginning; the "number of the serpents "which are there upon their bellies is unknown; the "divine image, the strengthener (23) out of the night, "being born in the presence of the Still-Heart,' is thy "name. The name of the god who guardeth thee is "Samti. I have washed myself in the water wherein "the god Thoth washed himself when he made himself "the *tchat* of Horus. (24) I have anointed myself with "*āḳa* unguent, I have arrayed myself in apparel of "*thesthes,* and I have with me my sceptre of *sept* "wood."

[Saith the pylon:—] "Pass on, then, thou art pure."

VII. (25) The Osiris Ȧuf-ānkh, triumphant, saith:—

"Homage to thee, saith Horus, O thou seventh "pylon of the Still-Heart. I have made [my] way. "I know thee, and I know thy name, and I know "the name of the god who guardeth thee. (26) "'Waterflood which clotheth the feeble one, weeper "for that which she loveth, shrouding the body,' is "thy name. The name of the god who guardeth "thee is Åm-Nit. I have washed myself in the water "wherein (27) the goddesses "Isis and Nephthys washed "themselves when they passed "the Crocodile with his croco- "diles on their way to the "opening of the place of "purity. I have anointed "myself with *ḥekennu* un- "guent, I have arrayed myself in (28) *unkh* apparel, "and I have with me my sceptre and [my] paddle."

[Saith the pylon :—] "Pass on, then, thou art pure."

VIII. (29) The Osiris Åuf-ānkh, triumphant, saith :—

"Homage to thee, saith Horus, O thou eighth pylon "of the Still-Heart. I have made [my] way. I know "thee, and I know thy name, and I know the name of "the god who guardeth thee (30). 'She that belongeth "to her lord, the mighty "goddess, the gracious one, "the lady who giveth birth "to the divine form of her "lord,'" or as others say, "'who passeth through and "traverseth [the land], the "head [of which] is millions "of cubits in depth and in "height,' is thy name. The name of the god who "guardeth thee is Netchses. I have washed myself

"in the water wherein (31) the god Anpu washed when "he had performed the office of embalmer and bandager," or as others say, "the Chief Reader of Osiris. (32) I "have anointed myself with *seft* unguent, I have arrayed "myself in apparel of *àṭmà*, and I have my garment (?) "of *enen* stuff," or as others say, "of cat's skin (?) with "me."

[Saith the pylon :—] "Pass on, then, thou art pure."

IX. (33) The Osiris Àuf-ānkh, triumphant, saith :—

"Homage to thee, saith Horus, O thou ninth pylon "of the Still-Heart. I have made [my] way. I know "thee, and I know thy name, "and I know the name of "the god who guardeth (34) "thee. 'Blazing flame of "Horus which cannot be "extinguished; which hav-"ing passed is followed by "another; which is pro-"vided with tongues of "flame that project to destroy; irresistible and im-"passable [by any] by reason of the injury which it "doeth,' is thy name. There is fear (35) through the "might of its roaring. The name of the god who "guardeth thee is Khau-tchet-f. I have washed my-"self in the water wherein the Ram, Lord of Ṭaṭṭu, "washed himself thoroughly from one end of his body "to the other. I have (36) anointed myself with *ānt* "unguent of the divine members, and with *ānkh*

"unguent, I have arrayed myself in a tunic of fair "white linen, and I have with me my sceptre of "*benen* wood."

[Saith the pylon :—] "Pass on, then, thou art pure."

X. (37) The Osiris Auf-ānkh, triumphant, saith :—

"Homage to thee, saith Horus, O thou tenth pylon "of the Still-Heart. I have made [my] way. I know "thee, and I know thy name "and I know the name of the "god who guardeth (38) thee. "'Lofty of gates, who raiseth "up those who cry (?), who "art terrible unto him that "would come unto thee,'" or as others say, "'She who "maketh one to make supplication, by reason of the "loudness of her voice; vanquisher of the foe who is "not constrained by that which is within her,' is thy "(39) name. The name of the god who watcheth thee "is Sekhen-ur. I have washed myself in the water "wherein the god Ȧsṭes washed himself when he "entered in to be an advocate for Set within the "hidden chamber. (40) I have anointed myself with "*ṭeshen* unguent, and I have with me a sceptre made "of the bone of the bird *ṭesher*, having a head like that "of a greyhound."

[Saith the pylon :—] "Pass on, then, thou art pure."

XI. (41) The Osiris Auf-ānkh, triumphant, saith :—

"Homage to thee, saith Horus, O thou eleventh

"pylon of the Still-Heart. I have made [my] way. I "know thee, and I know thy name, and (42) I know "the name of the being who is "within thee. 'She who repeateth slaughters, who burneth "up the Fiends, the mistress of "every pylon, the lady to whom "acclamation is made on the day "(43) of hearing iniquity' is thy "name. Thou hast the judgment "of the feeble bandaged one."

[Saith the pylon :—] "Pass on, then, thou art pure."

XII. (44) The Osiris Åuf-ānkh, triumphant, saith :—

"Homage to thee, saith Horus, O thou twelfth "pylon of the Still-Heart. I have made [my] way. "I know thee, and I know thy "name, and I know the (45) "name of the being who is with- "in thee. 'She who journeyeth "about in the two lands; who "destroyeth those who come with "flashings and with fire, the lady "of splendour; who hearkeneth "to the word of her lord every "day,' is thy name. Thou hast the (46) judgment of "the feeble bandaged one."

[Saith the pylon :—] "Pass on, then, thou art pure."

XIII. (47) The Osiris Åuf-ānkh, triumphant, saith :—

"Homage to thee, saith Horus, O thou thirteenth

"pylon of the Still-Heart. I have made [my] way. I "know thee, and I know (48) thy name, and I know "the name of the being who is "within thee. 'When the com- "pany of the gods is led along "their hands are [raised in] "adoration before her face, and "the watery abyss shineth with "light by reason of those who "are therein,' is thy name (49). "Thou hast the judgment of the feeble bandaged one."

[Saith the pylon :—] "Pass on, then, thou art pure."

XIV. (50) The Osiris Àuf-ānkh, triumphant, saith :—

"Homage to thee, saith Horus, O thou fourteenth "pylon of the Still-Heart. I have made [my] way. "I know thee, and I know thy "name, and I know (51) the "name of the being who is "within thee. 'Mighty one of "Souls, red of hair, Àakhabit, "who cometh forth by night; "who destroyeth the Fiends in "their created forms which their "hands give to the Still-Heart (52) in his hour; the "one who cometh and goeth,' is thy name. She hath "the judgment of the feeble bandaged one."

[Saith the pylon :—] "Pass on, then, thou art pure."

XV. (53) The Osiris Àuf-ānkh, triumphant, saith :—

"Homage to thee, saith Horus, O thou fifteenth

"pylon of the Still-Heart. I have made [my] way. "I know thee, and I know thy name, (54) and I "know the name of the being "who is within thee. 'Lady "of valour, destroyer of the "ruddy ones, who celebrateth "the Heker festivals (?) [when] "the fire is extinguished on "the day of hearing [cases of] "iniquity,' is thy name. (55) "She hath the judgment of the feeble bandaged one."

[Saith the pylon :—] "Pass on, then, thou art pure."

XVI. (56) The Osiris Åuf-ānkh, triumphant, saith :—

"Homage to thee, saith Horus, O thou sixteenth "pylon of the Still-Heart. I have made [my] way. "I know thee, and I know thy "name, and I know the name "of the being who is (57) within "thee. 'Lady of victory, whose "hand goeth after the Fiends, "who burneth with flames of "fire when she cometh forth, "creator of the mysteries of the "earth,' is thy name. She hath the judgment of the "(58) feeble bandaged one."

[Saith the pylon :—] "Pass on, then, thou art pure."

XVII. (59) The Osiris Åuf-ānkh, triumphant, saith :—

"Homage to thee, saith Horus, O thou seventeenth

"pylon of the Still-Heart. I have made [my] way. "I know thee, and I know thy name, and I know "(60) the name of the being "who is within thee. 'Mighty "one in the horizon, lady of the "ruddy ones, destroyer in blood, "Åakhabit, Power, lady of flame,' "is thy name. She hath the "judgment (61) of the feeble "bandaged one."

[Saith the pylon :—] "Pass on, then, thou art pure."

XVIII. (62) The Osiris Åuf-ānkh, triumphant, "saith :—

"Homage to thee, saith Horus, O thou eighteenth "pylon of the Still-Heart. I have made [my] way. "I know thee, and I know thy "name, and I know (63) the "name of the being who is "within thee. 'Lover of flame, "pure one, hearkening unto the ". . . . . . . behold, [she] loveth "to cut off the head[s] of the "venerated ones, lady of the "Great House, destroyer (64) of Fiends at eventide,' "[is thy name]. She hath the judgment of the feeble "bandaged one."

[Saith the pylon :—] "Pass on, then, thou art pure."

XIX. (65) The Osiris Åuf-ānkh, triumphant, saith :—

"Homage to thee, saith Horus, O thou nineteenth

"pylon of the Still-Heart. I have made [my] way. "I know thee, and I know thy. name, and I know "(66) the name of the being who "is within thee. 'Dispenser of "strength,'" or as others say, "'of "light, of the palace (?), the mighty "one of the flame, the lady of the "strength and of the writings of "Ptaḥ himself,' is thy name. "She hath the judgment of the "(67) feeble bandaged one."

[Saith the pylon :—] "Pass on, then, thou art pure."

XX. (68) The Osiris Ȧuf-ānkh, triumphant, saith :— "Homage to thee, saith Horus, O thou twentieth "pylon of the Still-Heart. I know thee, and I know "thy name, and (69) I know the "name of the being who is within "thee. 'Stone (?) of her lord, "field with a serpent (?), Clother, "what she createth she hideth, "taking possession of hearts, "opener of herself,' is thy name. "She hath the (70) judgment of "the feeble bandaged one."

[Saith the pylon :—] "Pass on, then, thou art pure."

XXI. (71) The Osiris Ȧuf-ānkh, triumphant, saith :— "Homage to thee, saith Horus, O thou twenty-first "pylon of the Still-Heart. I have made [my] way. "I know thee, and I know thy name, (72), and I know "the name of the god who guardeth thee. 'Sword that "smiteth at the utterance of its own name, goddess with "face turned backwards, "the unknown one, over- "thrower of him that "draweth nigh to her "flame,' is thy name. "Thou keepest the secret "things of the avenger of "the god who guardeth "thee, and his name is "(73) Āmām. He maketh it to come to pass that "the cedar trees grow not, that the acacia trees bring "not forth, and that copper is not begotten in the "mountain. The divine sovereign chiefs of this pylon "are as seven gods. Tchen or Āṭ is the name of the "(74) one at the door; Ḥetep-mes is the name of the "second; Mes-sep is the name of the third; Utch-re "is the name of the fourth; Ȧp-uat is the name of the "fifth; Beq is the name of the sixth; and Ȧnpu is the "name of the seventh."

(75) "I have made [my] way. I am Ȧmsu-Ḥeru, "the avenger of his father, the heir of his father "Un-nefer. I have come, and I have caused to be "overthrown all the enemies of my father Osiris. I "have come day by day with victory, doing myself the "worship of the god (76) in the house of his father "Tem, the lord of Ȧnnu. The Osiris Ȧuf-ānkh, "triumphant, is in the southern heaven. I have

"done what is right and true for him that made "right and truth; I have celebrated the Haker "festivals for the lord thereof; I have led the way "in the festival; I have given cakes unto the lords "of the altar; (77) and I have brought offerings and "oblations, and cakes, and ale, and oxen, and ducks, to "my father Osiris Un-nefer. I have my being in a "body which hath a soul, and I make the *Bennu* "bird to come forth at [my] words. I have come daily "into the house of the god to make offerings of incense. "I have brought (78) garments of byssus, and I have "sailed on the [sacred] lake in the *Neshem* boat. I have "made Osiris, the Governor of Åmentet, to be triumphant over his enemies; I have carried away all his "foes to the place of slaughter in the East; and they "shall never come forth from the durance of the god "(79) Seb therein. I stand up for him [along with] "the divine Kefaui of Rā, and I make [him] to be "triumphant (?). I have come even as a scribe and I "have made all things plain. I have made the god to "have power over his legs. I have come into the "house of 'him that is upon his hill' (*i.e.*, Anubis), "and I have seen him that is ruler in the divine hall "(*i.e.*, Anubis). (80) I have entered into Re-stau; I "have hidden myself, and I have found out the way: "I have travelled unto Ån-rutf-f. I have clothed him "that was naked, (81) I have sailed up to Åbṭu "(Abydos), I have praised the gods Ḥu and Sau. I "have entered into the house of Åsṭes, and I have "made supplication to the (82) Khati gods and to "Sekhet in the Temple of Neith," or as others say, "to the princes. I have entered into Re-stau; I have "hidden myself, and I have found out the way; I have "travelled (83) unto Ån-ruṭ-f. I have clothed him "who was naked. I have sailed up to Åbṭu; I have "praised Ḥu and Sa. I have received my (84) "crown (?) at my rising, and I have crowned myself "upon my throne in the habitation of my father and "of the first company of the gods. I have worshipped "[in my] birthplace of Ta-tchesertet, and my mouth "is filled (?) with (85) right and truth. I have drowned "the serpent Åkhkha. I have come into the Great "House which giveth vigour unto the limbs; and it "hath been granted unto me to sail about in the Boat "of Ḥai. The fragrance of *ānt* unguent ariseth from "(86) the hair of the beings who have knowledge. I "have entered into the house of Åsṭes, and I have "made supplication unto the Khati gods and unto "Sekhet in the Temple of the (87) Prince."

[Saith the pylon:—] "Thou hast come being a "favoured one in Ṭaṭṭu, O Osiris Åuf-ānkh, trium-"phant, son of Sheret-Åmsu, triumphant."

CHAPTER CXLVI.

[From the Papyrus of Nu (Brit. Mus. No. 10,477, sheet 25).]

Vignettes: (1) Ani and his wife adoring the gods; (2) Ten pylons.

Text: (1) [Here begin] The Chapters of Entering in at the Secret Pylons of the House of Osiris in Sekhet-(2) Åanreru I. The Osiris Nu, the overseer of the house of the overseer of the seal, triumphant, when he cometh to the first pylon (3) of Osiris, saith:—

"I have made [my] way. I know you, and I know "your name, and I know (4) "the name of the god who "guardeth you. 'Lady of "tremblings, with lofty walls, "the sovereign (5) lady, the "mistress of destruction, who "setteth in order the words "which drive back the whirl-"wind and the storm, who "delivereth from destruction "him that travelleth along "the way,' (6) is thy name. "The name of thy doorkeeper "is Neri."

II. The Osiris Nu, (7) when he cometh to the second pylon of Osiris, saith:—

"I have made [my] way. I "know you, and I know (8) "your name, and I know the "name of the god who guardeth "you. 'Lady of heaven, the "mistress of the world, who "devoureth with fire, the "lady of (9) mortals, who "knoweth mankind,' is thy "name. The name of thy "doorkeeper is Mes-Peḥ" (*or* "Mes-Ptaḥ).

III. The Osiris Nu, (10) when he cometh to the third pylon of Osiris, saith :—

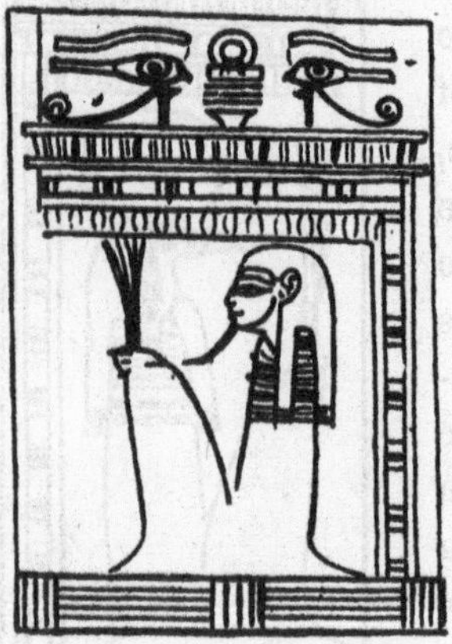

"I have made [my] way. "I know (11) you, and I "know your name, and I "know the name of the "god who guardeth you. "'Lady of the (12) altar, "the lady to whom abun-"dant offerings are made, "in whom every god re-"joiceth on the day of "sailing up to Abṭu (Aby-"dos),' is thy name. The "name of thy doorkeeper is Erṭāt-(13)Sebanqa."

IV. The Osiris Nu, (14) when he cometh to the fourth pylon of Osiris, saith :—

"I have made [my] way. I "know you, and I know (15) "your name, and I know the "name of the god who guardeth "you. 'She who prevaileth "with knives, the mistress of "the world, (16) destroyer of the "foes of the Still-Heart, who "maketh the decree for the escape "of the needy from (17) evil hap,' "is thy name. The name of thy "doorkeeper is Neḳau."

V. The Osiris Nu, (18) when he cometh to the fifth pylon of Osiris, saith :—

"I have made [my] way. "I know you, and I know "(19) your name, and I know "the name of the god who "guardeth you. 'Fire, the "lady of flames, who inhaleth "(20) the supplications which "are made to her, who per-"mitteth not the . . . . . "to enter in,' is thy name. "The name of thy doorkeeper "is Ḥenti-Requ."

VI. (21) The Osiris Nu, when he cometh to the sixth pylon of Osiris, saith :—

"I have made [my] way. I "know (22) you, and I know "your name, and I know the "name of the god who guardeth "you. (23) 'Lady of light, the "lady to whom abundant sup-"plication is made; the differ-"ence between her height and "her breadth is unknown; the "like of her hath never been "found (24) since the begin-"ning. There is a serpent "thereupon whose size is not known; it was born (25)

"in the presence of the Still-heart,' is thy name. The "name of the doorkeeper is Semamti."

VII. (26) The Osiris Nu, when he cometh to the seventh pylon of Osiris, saith :—

"I have made [my] way. (27) "I know you, and I know your "name, and I know the name (28) "of the god who guardeth you. "'Robe which doth clothe the "divine feeble one, weeping (29) "for what it loveth and shrouding "the body,' is thy name. The name "of the doorkeeper is Åkenti."

VIII. (30) The Osiris Nu, when he cometh to the eighth pylon of Osiris, saith :—

"I have made [my] (31) "way. I know you, and I "know your name, and I "know the name of the "god (32) who guardeth "you. 'Blazing fire, the "flame whereof [cannot] be "quenched, provided with "tongues of flame (33) "which reach afar, the "slaughtering one, the irre-"sistible one, through whom "a man may not pass by reason of the hurt which she "doeth,' is thy name. (34) The name of the doorkeeper "is Khu-tchet-f."

IX. (35) The Osiris Nu, when he cometh to the ninth "pylon of Osiris, saith :—

"I have made [my] way. (36) I "know you, and I know your name, "and I know the name of the god "(37) who guardeth you. 'She who "is in the front, the lady of strength, "quiet of heart, who giveth birth "to her lord; whose girth is three "hundred and fifty measures; (38) "who sendeth forth rays like the "*uatch* stone of the south; who "raiseth up the divine form and "clotheth the feeble one; who giveth [offerings] to (39) "her lord every day,' is thy name. The name of the "doorkeeper is Tchesef."

X. (40) The Osiris Nu, when he cometh to the tenth pylon of Osiris, saith :—

"I have made [my] way. (41) "I know you, and I know your "name, and I know the name of "the god who guardeth you. "(42) 'Thou who art loud of "voice, who raisest up those "who cry and who make sup- "plication unto her, whose voice "is loud, the terrible one, (43) the lady who is to be "feared, who destroyeth not that which is in her,' is thy "name. The name of the doorkeeper is Sekhen-ur."[1]

XI. (44) The Osiris Nu, when he cometh to the eleventh pylon of Osiris, saith:—

"I have made [my] way. I know (45) you, and I "know your name, and I know the name of her who "is within thee. 'She who slaughtereth always, (46) "the burner up of fiends, mistress of every pylon, the "lady to whom acclamation is made on the (47) day of "darkness,' is thy name. She hath the judgment of "the feeble bandaged one."

XII. (48) The Osiris Nu, when he cometh to the twelfth pylon of Osiris, saith:—

"I have made [my] way. I know you, (49) and I "know your name, and I know the name of her who is "within thee. 'Thou who invokest thy two lands, "(50) who destroyest those who come with flashings "and with fire, the lady of splendour, who hearkeneth "unto the speech (51) of her lord,' is thy name. She "hath the judgment of the feeble bandaged one."

XIII. (52) The Osiris Nu, when he cometh to the thirteenth pylon of Osiris, saith:—

"I have made [my] way. I know (53) you, and I "know your name, and I know the name of her who is

[1] In the Papyrus of Ani ten pylons only are enumerated. In the version of this Chapter published by Naville (*Todtenbuch*, Bd. I. Bll. 160—162) there are *twenty* vignettes, and each represents a god seated in a chamber. The Turin Papyrus gives *fifteen* vignettes.

"within thee. 'Osiris bringeth (54) his two hands over "her and maketh the god Ḥāpi (*i.e.*, the Nile) to send "forth splendour out of his hidden places,' is thy name. "(55) She hath the judgment of the feeble bandaged "one."

XIV. (56) The Osiris Nu, when he cometh to the fourteenth pylon of Osiris, saith:—

"I have made [my] way. (57) I know you, and I "know your name, and I know the name of her who is "within thee. (58) Lady of might, who danceth on the "blood-red ones, who keepeth the festival of Haker on "the day of the hearing (59) of faults,' is thy name. "She hath the judgment of the feeble bandaged one."

XV. The fifteenth pylon. The Osiris Ḥeru-em-khebit, triumphant, saith when he cometh to this pylon:—(38) "'The Fiend, red of hair and eyes, who cometh forth "by night, (39) and doth fetter the fiend in his lair; "may her hands be given to the Still-Heart (40) in his "hour, and may [she] advance and go forward,' [is thy "name]. She hath the judgment of the feeble (41) "bandaged one."

XVI. The sixteenth pylon. The Osiris Ḥeru-em-khebit, triumphant, saith (42) when he cometh forth to this pylon:—"'Terrible one, the lady of the rain-"storm, who planteth ruin (?) in the (43) souls of men, "the devourer of the dead bodies of mankind, the "orderer, and producer, and (44) creator of slaughter,' "[is thy name]. She hath the judgment of the feeble "bandaged one." (45)

XVII. The seventeenth pylon. [The Osiris Ḥeru-em-khebit, triumphant, saith when he cometh forth to "this pylon :—] "'Hewer-in-pieces in blood, Åḥabit (?), "lady of (46) hair,' [is thy name]. She hath the judg-"ment of the feeble bandaged one."

XVIII. The eighteenth pylon. The Osiris Ḥeru-em-khebit, triumphant, (47) saith when he cometh to this pylon :—"'Lover (48) of the fire, pure of slaughterings "which she loveth, cutter off of heads, (49) venerated "one (?), lady of the Great House, destroyer of fiends "at eventide,' [is thy name] (50). She hath the judg-"ment of the feeble bandaged one."

XIX. The nineteenth pylon. (51) The Osiris Ḥeru-em-khebit, triumphant, saith when he cometh to this "pylon :—"'Dispenser of light during her period (52) "of life, watcher of flames, the lady of the strength "and of the writings of the god Ptaḥ himself,' [is thy "name]. She hath the judgment (53) of the bandages "of Per-ån" (*or* Per-ḥetch).

XX. The twentieth pylon. The Osiris Ḥeru-em-khebit, triumphant, saith when he cometh to this pylon :—(54) "'She who dwelleth within the cavern "of her lord, Clother is her name, (55) she hideth what "she hath created, she taketh possession of hearts, she "swalloweth (?),' [is thy name]. She hath (56) the "judgment of the bandages of Per-ån" (*or* Per-ḥetch).

XXI. The twenty-first pylon. The Osiris Ḥeru-em-khebit, triumphant, saith when he cometh to this pylon :—(57) "'Knife which cutteth, when [its name] "is uttered, (58) and, slayeth those who advance "towards its flames,' [is thy name]. She hath (59) "secret plots and counsels."

CHAPTER CXLVII.

[From the Papyrus of Ani (Brit. Mus. No. 10,470, sheets 11 and 12).]

The First Ārit.

Vignette: Ani and his wife Thuthu approaching the first Ārit, at the entrance of which sit three gods, having the head of a hare, of a serpent, and of a crocodile respectively.

Text: (1) The name of the doorkeeper is Sekheṭ-ḥrá-āsht-àru; the name of the (2) watcher is [Se]metti; the name of the herald is Ha-kheru. The Osiris Ani, (3) triumphant, shall say when he cometh unto the first Ārit:—"I am the mighty "one who createth his own "light. (4) I have come "unto thee, O Osiris, and, "purified from that which "defileth thee, I adore thee. "Lead on: (5) name not the "name of Re-stau unto me. "Homage to thee, O Osiris,

"in thy might and in thy strength (6) in Re-stau. "Rise up and conquer, O Osiris, in Ábṭu. Thou "goest round about heaven, thou sailest in the "presence of Rā, (7) thou lookest upon all the "beings who have knowledge. Hail, Rā, thou who "circlest in the sky! Verily I say, O Osiris, I am "the spiritual body (*sāḥ*) (8) of the god, and I say, "(9) let me not be driven (10) hence, nor upon (11) "the wall of (12) burning coals. (13) Open the way "in (14) Re-stau, (15) ease the (16) pain of Osiris, "(17) embrace that which the balance hath weighed; "make a path for him in the great valley, make "light to be on the way to Osiris."

The Second Ārit.

Vignette: An Ārit guarded by three gods having the head of a lion, of a man, and of a dog respectively.

Text: (1) The name of the (2) doorkeeper is Un-ḥāt; (3) the name of the watcher is Seqeṭ-(4)ḥrā; the name of the herald (5) is Uset. The Osiris Ani, triumphant, shall say when he cometh (6) to this Ārit:—"He sitteth to do his heart's "desire, and he weigheth (7) "words as the second of Thoth. "The strength which protecteth "Thoth humbleth the hidden "Maāt gods (?) (8) who feed

"upon Maāt throughout the years [of their lives]. I "make offerings (9) at the moment when he maketh his "way; I pass on and enter upon the way. Grant thou "that I may pass onwards and that I may gain sight "of Rā together with those who make offerings."

THE THIRD ÅRIT.

Vignette: An Årit guarded by three gods having the head of a jackal, of a dog, and of a serpent respectively.

Text: (1) The name of the (2) doorkeeper is Åm-ḥauatu(3)-ent-peḥui; the name of the watcher (4) is Seres-(5)ḥrå; the name of the herald is Åa. The Osiris Ani, triumphant, shall say [when he cometh to this Årit:]—"I am "the hidden one (6) [in] the "great deep, [I am] the judge "of the Reḥui. I have come "and I have done away with "the offensive thing which was "upon Osiris. I am fastening "the place whereon he shall "stand (7) which projecteth from the *Ureret* crown. I "have perfected matters in Åbṭu, I have opened the "way in Re-stau, I have eased (8) the pain which was "in Osiris. I have made straight his standing place, "and I have made [his] path. He shineth in Re-stau."

The Fourth Ārit.

Vignette: An Ārit guarded by three gods having the head of a man, of a hawk, and of a lion respectively.

Text: (1) The name of (2) the doorkeeper is Khesef-ḥrà-āsht-(3)kheru; the name of the (4) watcher is Seres-ṭepu; (5) the name of the herald is (6) Khesef-aṭ. The Osiris Ani, triumphant, shall say [when he cometh to this Ārit]:—"I am the Bull, (7) the son of "the ancestress of Osiris. O "grant ye that his father, the "lord of his godlike (8) com-"panions, may bear witness for "him. I have weighed the guilty "in judgment. I have brought unto (9) his nostrils "the life which is everlasting. I am the son of Osiris, "I have made the way. I have passed thereover into "Neter-khert."

The Fifth Ārit.

Vignette: An Ārit guarded by three gods having the head of a hawk, of a man, and of a snake respectively.

Text: (1) The name (2) of the doorkeeper is Ānkh-f-em-fenṭ; (3) the name of the watcher is (4) Shabu; the name of (5) the herald is Ṭeb-ḥrà-(6)ha-kheft. The Osiris Ani, triumphant, shall say [when he cometh to this Ārit]:—"I have brought [unto thee] the bones "of thy (7) jaws in Re-stau, I have brought thee thy "backbone in Ȧnnu (Heliopolis), "gathering together its manifold "parts (8) therein. I have driven "back Āpep for thee, I have spit "upon the wounds [which are in "him], I have made a path among "you. I am (9) the Ancient One "among the gods. I have made "the offering of Osiris, I have "avenged (?) him in triumph, "gathering his bones and bringing together all his "limbs."

The Sixth Ārit.

Vignette: An Ārit guarded by three gods, the first having the head of a jackal, and the second and third the head of a dog.

Text: (1) The name (2) of the doorkeeper is Ȧtek-tau-kehaq-(3)kheru; the name of the (4) watcher is Ȧn-ḥrȧ; (5) the name of the herald is (6) Aṭes-ḥrȧ-[ȧri]-she. The Osiris Ani, triumphant, shall say [when he cometh to this Ārit]:—"I have come (7) daily, "I have come daily. I have "made [my] way; I have passed

"along that which was created by Ánpu (Anubis). I "am the lord of the *Ureret* crown, (8) possessing words "of magical power, the avenger of Maāt. I have "avenged his Eye, I have delivered (9) Osiris, and "I have made the way; the Osiris Ani passeth along "with you in [triumph]."

The Seventh Ārit.

Vignette: An Ārit guarded by three gods having the head of a hare, of a lion, and of a man respectively.

Text: (1) The name (2) of the doorkeeper is Sekhemet-em-ṭesu-(3)sen; the name of the (4) watcher is Āa-maā-kheru; (5) the name of the herald is Khesef-khemi. The Osiris Ani, triumphant, (6) shall say [when he cometh to this Ārit]:—"I have come unto "thee, O Osiris, who art cleansed "of [thine] impurities. Thou "goest round about heaven, thou "seest Rā, thou seest the beings "who have knowledge. (7) [Hail,] "Only One! behold, thou art in "the *Sektet* boat [as] it goeth round about the horizon "of heaven. I speak what I will unto his spiritual "body (*sāḥ*); (8) it waxeth strong and it cometh into "being, even as he spake. Thou meetest his face.

"Prosper thou for me all the ways [which lead] unto "thee."[1]

[1] In the Papyrus of Thenna the scribe the following words are added:—"If [these] words be recited by the deceased when he "cometh to the seven Ārits and entereth into the pylons he shall "neither be turned back nor repulsed before Osiris, and he shall "be made to have his being among the blessed *Khus* and to have "dominion among the principal followers of Horus. If these "things shall be done for any deceased person he shall have his "being there like a lord of eternity in one body along with Osiris, "and at no place shall any great fight be made [concerning him]."

CHAPTER CXLVIII.

[From the Papyrus of Nu (Brit. Mus. No. 10,477, sheet 11).]

Vignette : A hall, or shrine, within which, on the left, Ani stands before two tables of offerings adoring Rā (or Osiris), hawk-headed. Next are ranged seven kine and a bull, each animal having offerings before it. Behind are four rudders, emblematic of the cardinal points, and on the extreme right are four triads of gods. The speech of Ani reads:—"Homage "to thee, O thou lord, thou lord of right and truth, the only "One, the lord of eternity and creator of everlastingness, I "have come unto thee, O my lord Rā. I have made offerings "of herbs unto the seven kine and unto their bull. O ye who "give cakes and ale unto the *Khus*, grant ye to my soul to be "with you. May Osiris Ani be born upon your thighs; may he "be like unto one of you for ever and for ever; and may he "become a *Khu* in the beautiful Åmenti."

Text: (1) THE CHAPTER OF PROVIDING THE DECEASED WITH FOOD [IN THE UNDERWORLD]. The Osiris Nu, the overseer of the house of the overseer of the seal, triumphant, the son of the overseer of the house of the overseer of the seal, Åmen-ḥetep, triumphant, saith:—

(2) "Homage to thee, O thou who shinest from thy "Disk, thou living [Soul] who comest forth from the "horizon, the Osiris Nu knoweth thee, and he knoweth "thy name, and he knoweth the name of (3) thy seven "kine and of the bull that belongeth unto them. Hail, "ye who give cakes, and ale, and splendour to the souls "who are provided with food in the underworld, (4) "grant ye cakes and ale unto the Osiris Nu; provide "ye him with food, let him be in your following, and "let him be born upon your thighs."

[Here follow the names of the seven kine and of their bull, with the address to them by the deceased.]

(1) Ḥet-kau-Nebt-er-tcher. (2) Åḳert-khentet-åuset-s. (3) Meḥ-khebitet-sāḥ-neter. (4) Ur-mertu-s-ṭeshert-

sheni. (5) Khenemet-em-ānkh-ȧnnuit. (6) Sekhemet-ren-s-em-ābet-s. (7) Shenȧt-pet-utheset-neter. (8) Ka-tchai-kauit.[1]

"[Hail, ye cows and bull,] grant ye cakes, and ale, "and offerings of food, to the Osiris Nu, and supply ye "him with food, (8) and make him to be a perfect *Khu* "in the underworld."

[Here follow the addresses to the four rudders by the deceased.]

(1) "Hail, thou beautiful Power, thou beautiful "rudder of the northern heaven;

(2) "Hail, thou who revolvest, thou pilot of the two "lands, thou beautiful rudder of the western heaven;

[1] *I.e.*, "Bull, making the kine to be fruitful."

(3) "Hail, thou shining one, who dwellest in the "Temple wherein are the gods in visible forms, thou "beautiful rudder of the eastern heaven;

(4) "Hail, thou who dwellest within the Temple of "the ruddy beings, thou beautiful rudder of the "southern heaven;

"grant ye cakes, and ale, and offerings of food, and "splendour to the *Khu* of the Osiris Nu. (11) Grant "ye unto him life, and strength, and health, and abiding joy of heart upon earth, and grant ye unto him "[triumph] in the horizon of Ȧnnu, and in heaven, and "upon earth, and in the underworld[1] . . . . . .

[Here follow the addresses to the four triads.]

[1] Reading *maākheru em khut Ȧnnu pet ta ṭuat.*

(12) "Hail, ye fathers of the gods, hail, ye mothers "of the gods, ye who are above the earth and who "dwell in the underworld, deliver ye the Osiris Nu "(13) from every obstacle of evil [from every attack of "evil], from the cruel snare, and [from] the slaughter-"ing knives, and from every wicked and evil thing "whatsoever (which) ye could order to be done unto "him (14) by men, and by gods, and by the *Khus*, and "by the dead on this day, or on this night, or in this "month, or in this half-monthly festival, or (15) in this "year, or in any of the seasons thereof whatsoever."

RUBRIC: [These words] shall be said when Rā appeareth over [figures] of the gods written (*or* painted) in colour upon a board (?), and thou shalt place offerings and (16) *tchefau* food before them, cakes, ale, flesh, feathered fowl, and incense, and they shall cause the deceased to possess sepulchral meals with Rā, and shall give him (17) an abundance of food in the under-world, and shall deliver him from every evil thing whatsoever. And thou shalt not recite this book of Un-nefer in the presence of (18) any person except thine own self. And if this be done for the deceased Rā shall be a rudder for him and shall be a strength protecting him, and he shall make an end of all (19) his enemies for him in the underworld, and in heaven, and upon earth, and in every place wheresoever he may enter, and he shall have abundance of food regularly and continually for ever.

CHAPTER CXLIX.

[From the Papyrus of Nu (Brit. Mus. No. 10,477, sheets 28, 29, 30).]

The Fourteen Åats, or divisions of Sekhet-Åanru.

I. Vignette: The first Åat.

Text: (1) The first Åat [which is to be painted] green. The Osiris Nu, the overseer of the house of the overseer of the seal, triumphant, saith:— (2)

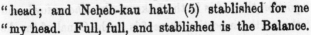

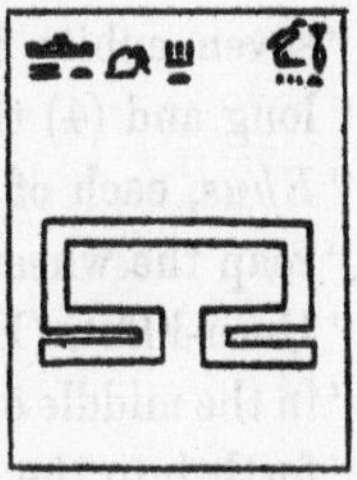

"Hail, thou Åat of Åmentet, wherein a man liveth "upon cakes and ale,[1] remove thy wigs (3) when I come "towards thee. And behold, the "Mighty god who dwelleth in thee "hath bound up my bones, and he "hath stablished my members; (4) "and the *Åḥi*, the lord of hearts, "hath gathered (?) together my "bones, and hath stablished the "*Ureret* crown of Tem [upon my "head; and Neḥeb-kau hath (5) stablished for me "my head. Full, full, and stablished is the Balance. "Thou shalt have dominion among the gods, O "Åmsu-qeṭ."

[1] Or, "upon bread [made of] the finest grain."

II. **Vignette** : The second Åat. The horizon.

Text : (1) The second Åat [which is painted] green. "The god therein is Rā-Ḥeru-khuti." The Osiris Nu saith:—

"I am the mighty one of possessions in Sekhet-"Åarru. Hail, thou Sekhet-(2)Åarru, the walls of "which are of "iron! The "height of the "wheat thereof "is five cubits, "the ears (3) "thereof being "two cubits long "and the stalks three cubits; the barley thereof is "seven cubits in height, the ears being three cubits "long and (4) the stalks four cubits. And behold, the "*Khus*, each of whom therein is nine cubits in height, "reap the wheat and the barley (5) side by side with "Ḥeru-khuti (Harmachis). I know the door which is "in the middle of Sekhet-Åarru wherefrom (6) Rā cometh "forth into the eastern part of heaven; the southern "portion thereof is in the Lake of the *Kharu* fowl, and "the northern portion thereof is in the Canal of the *Re* "fowl, (7) in the place wherein Rā saileth round about "by means of the winds which bear him along. I am "he who watcheth the leathers in (8) the divine boat, "I am in the boat, and I am he who doth navigate it

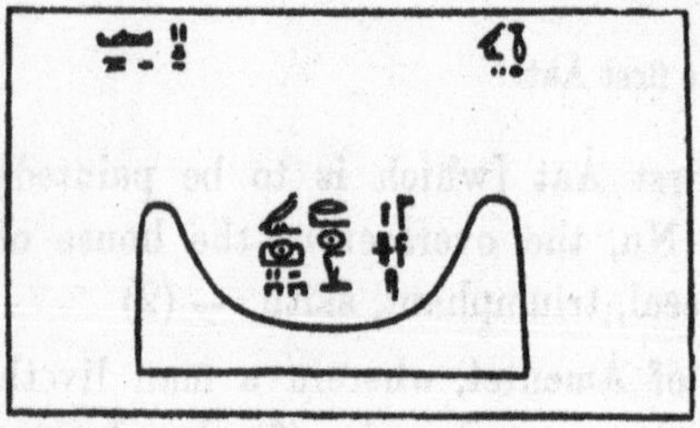

"without ceasing. I know (9) the two sycamore trees "of turquoise, from between which the god Rā doth "emerge when he setteth out upon his journey (10) "over the pillars of Shu towards the door of the lord "of the East, wherefrom Rā cometh forth. I (11) "know the Sekhet-Åarru of Rā. The wheat therein "is (12) five cubits in height, the ears being two cubits "long, and the stalks three cubits; the barley thereof "is seven cubits in height, (13) the ears being three "cubits long and the stalks four cubits. And behold, "the *Khus* therein, who are nine cubits in height, (14) "reap the wheat and the barley, side by side with the "divine Souls of the East."

III. **Vignette**: The third Åat, which is called "the Åat of the *Khus*."

Text: (1) The third Åat [which is to be painted] green. The Osiris Nu, triumphant, saith:—

"Hail, thou Åat of the *Khus*, whereover none can "sail (2) and wherein are the *Khus*; the fire thereof "is blazing with flame. Hail, thou "Åat of (3) the *Khus*! Your faces "are in the land (?) [make clear your "ways], and purify ye your Åats, and "what hath been decreed by Osiris do "ye for me (4) for ever. I am the "mighty one of the *Ṭeshert* crown "which is on the brow of the god "of Light, and which maintaineth in life the two lands

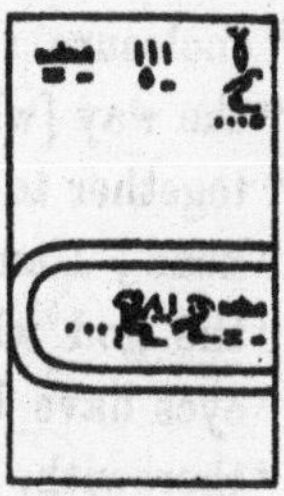

"and the men and women thereof (5) by means of the "flame of its mouth. The god Rā hath been delivered "from the Fiend Åpep."

IV. **Vignette**: The fourth Åat, wherein is inscribed "the double mountain, doubly high, and doubly great."

Text: (1) The fourth Åat [which is to be painted] green. The Osiris Nu, triumphant, saith :— (2)

"Hail, thou who art chief of the hidden Åat. Hail, "thou One who art lofty and great, who dwellest in the "underworld, over whom the "heaven spreadeth itself. (3) "Thou art three hundred "measures in length, and "two hundred and thirty "measures in width, and "thou hast over thee a ser-"pent the name of which is "Sati-ṭemui[1] (?); (4) he is seventy cubits in length, "and he liveth by slaughtering the *Khus* and the dead "who are in the underworld. I stand up in thy "enclosure, (5) O Maā, I sail round about, and I see "the way [which leadeth] unto thee. I gather myself "together to thee. I am the Man, and I clothe (6) thy "head; I am strong and I have become strong. I am "the god who is mighty in enchantments; my two "eyes have been given to me, and I am glorious (7) "therewith. Who art thou, O *Khu* that goest upon

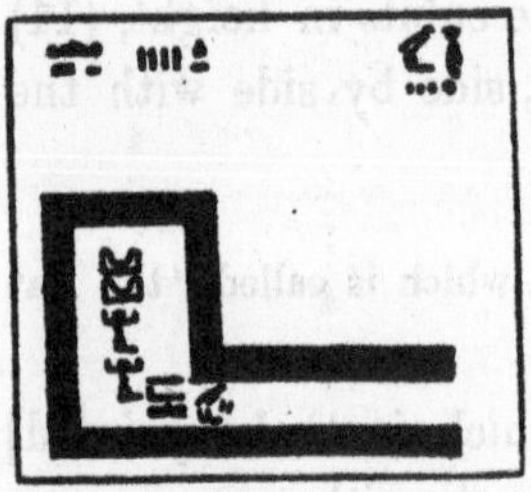

[1] *I.e.*, Sati of the two knives.

"thy belly, and whose two-fold strength is upon thy "mountain? Grant thou unto me (8) that I may go "unto thee, and that thy two-fold strength may be "with me. I lift up myself by [thy] two-fold strength, "I have come, (9) and I have vanquished the *Akriu* "serpent of Rā. His peace is to me at eventide; I "revolve in (10) the heavens and thou art in the "mountain valley. A decree [hath been made] concerning thee upon earth."

V. **Vignette**: The fifth Åat.

Text: (1) The fifth Åat [which is to be painted] green. The Osiris Nu, triumphant, saith:—

"Hail, thou Åat of the *Khus*, whereover none may "pass. (2) The *Khus* who are therein have thighs "seven cubits long, and they live "upon the shades of the weak and "helpless. (3) Hail, thou Åat of "the *Khus*, open ye unto me your "ways so that I may pass by you "and may go on (4) to the beautiful "Åmentet, according to that which "Osiris, the *Khu*, the lord of *Khus*, "hath decreed. I live by reason of my splendour, (5) "I perform every festival of the month, and I observe "rightly the festival of the half month. I revolve, "and the Eye of Horus is under my hand in the (6) "following of Thoth. The mouth of every god and

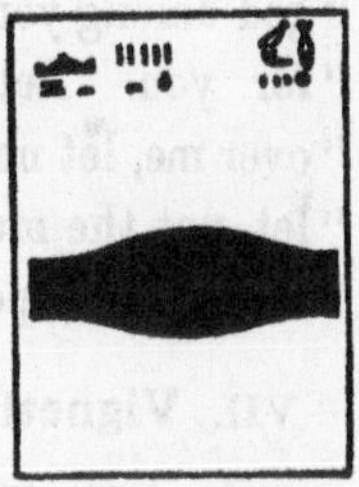

"of every dead person devoureth mine enemy this day, "and he falleth down at the block of slaughter."

VI. **Vignette :** The sixth Åat, with a fish inside it.

Text : (1) The sixth Åat [which is to be painted] green. The Osiris Nu, triumphant, saith :—

"Hail, thou Åmmeḥet which art holy unto the gods, "and art hidden unto the *Khus*, (2) and art baleful "unto the dead; the name of the "god who dwelleth therein is Sekher-"Åṭ (?). Homage to thee, O Åmme-"ḥet, I have come (3) to see the "gods who dwell in thee. Uncover "your faces and lay down your "head-dresses when ye meet me, "(4) for, behold, I am a mighty "god among you, and I have come to prepare provisions "for you. Let not (5) Sekher-Åṭ (?) have dominion "over me, let not the divine slaughterers come after me, "let not the murderous fiends come (6) after me, but "let me live upon sepulchral offerings among you."

VII. **Vignette :** The seventh Åat.

Text : (1) The seventh Åat [which is to be painted] green. The Osiris Nu, triumphant, saith :— (2)

"Hail, thou city of Åses, which art remote from "sight, and the fire of which is in flame. There is a "serpent within thee (3) and his name is Rerek; the "length of his backbone is seven cubits, and he liveth "upon the *Khus*, and he annihilateth (4) their glorious "strength. Get thee back, O Rerek, who dwellest in "the city of Åses, who devourest "with thy mouth, and from whose "eyes (5) evil looks pour forth. "Let thy bones be broken, and let "thy emissions be impotent. Come "thou not against me, and let not "thy emissions (6) come upon me; "let thy poison fall and lie dead "upon the earth, and let thy two lips be in [thy] den. "(7) The *Ka* of the serpent hath fallen, and, conversely, "I have gained glorious strength. The Maftet (*i.e.*, "Lynx), hath cut off thy head."

VIII. **Vignette**: The eighth Åat.

Text: (1) The eighth Åat [which is to be painted] green. The Osiris Nu, triumphant, saith:— (2)

"Hail, Ha-ḥetep, great and mighty one of the canal! "None can obtain the mastery over the water which is "therein. (3) It is mightily to be "feared, and the roarings which are "therein are mighty. The (4) name "of the god therein is Qa-ha-ḥetep, "and he guardeth it gladly so that "none may enter. I am the *Ennur* "bird which is (5) above the thigh "of the god (?) Ån-ker-s, and I have "brought the possessions of the earth to the god Tem,

"and [I] make strong and fortify the mariners [of Rā], "(6) I have set the terror of myself in the divine lords "of the shrine, and I have set the awe of me in the "divine lords (7) of things; therefore I shall not be "carried off to the slaughter block of those who would "willingly destroy me. (8) I am the guide of the "northern horizon [and I know the god who is "therein]."

IX. Vignette: The ninth Ȧat. A crocodile thrusting his snout into a vase (?) called Ȧkesi.

Text: (1) The ninth Ȧat [which is to be painted] yellow. The Osiris Nu, triumphant, saith:—

"Hail, thou city Ȧkesi, which art hidden (2) from "the gods, the *Khus* know the name of which the gods "are afraid. None can enter "therein, and none can come "forth therefrom except that "holy god (3) who dwelleth "in his egg, and who putteth "his fear into the gods and "the terror of himself into "the *Khus*. (4) The opening "[into the city] is of fire, and the winds thereof destroy "both nostrils and mouths, and the god hath made it "for those who follow willingly (5) in his train; none "can breathe the winds [thereof] except that holy god "who dwelleth in (6) his egg. He hath made the city "so that he may dwell therein at will, and none can

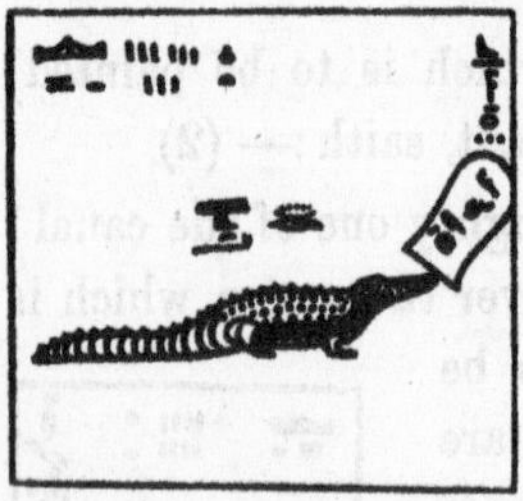

"enter therein except on the day of great (7) trans-"formations. Homage to thee, O thou holy god who "dwellest in thine egg, I have come unto thee (8) that "I may be among those who follow thee; let me come "forth from the city of Åkesi, let me enter therein, let "the gates thereof be opened unto me, let me breathe "the air (9) which is therein, and let me have posses-"sion of the offerings thereof."

X. Vignette: **The tenth Åat. A man holding a knife in each hand; above him is a serpent.**

Text: (1) The tenth Aat [which is to be painted] yellow. The Osiris Nu, triumphant, saith :— (2)

"Hail, thou city of the gods *Qaḥu*, who take pos-"session of *Khus* and gain the mastery over the shades "(*khaibit*), who devour vigorous "strength (3) and consume (?) filth "when their eyes see, and who "guard not the earth. (4) Hail, "ye who dwell in your Åats, cast "yourselves upon your bellies when "I pass by you. My glorious "strength shall not be taken away,

"(5) and none shall gain the mastery over my shade, "for I am a divine hawk. Offerings of *ānti* unguent "have been made ready by me, incense hath been "offered by me, [animals have] been slaughtered (6) "by me, Isis hath made offerings to my head, Nephthys "is behind me, and a road hath been made clear for "me. [Hail,] serpent (7) Nāu, Bull of Nut, Neḥeb-"kau, I have come unto you, O gods, deliver ye me, "and grant ye unto me my glorious strength for ever."

XI. **Vignette** : The eleventh Åat, wherein stands a jackal-headed god holding a knife.

Text : (1) The eleventh Åat [which is to be painted] green. The Osiris Nu, triumphant, saith :—

"Hail, thou city which art in (2) the underworld "(Neter-khert), which coverest over the body and "gainest the mastery "over the *Khus*. None "can come forth there-"from and none can "enter therein (3) by "reason of fear of "the opposing power "which is therein— "now the gods who "are therein look upon it in iron (?) and (4) the dead "who are therein look upon it in his slaughterings— "except the gods who live therein in his mystery (5) of "the *Khus*. Hail, thou city of Åtu, grant thou unto "me that I may pass on, for I am the god who is "mighty of enchantments by reason of the knife which "came forth from the god Suti. (6) I have my feet "and legs for ever. I rise like Rā, I am strong "through the Eye of Horus, my heart is lifted up "(7) after it was brought low, [I am] glorious in

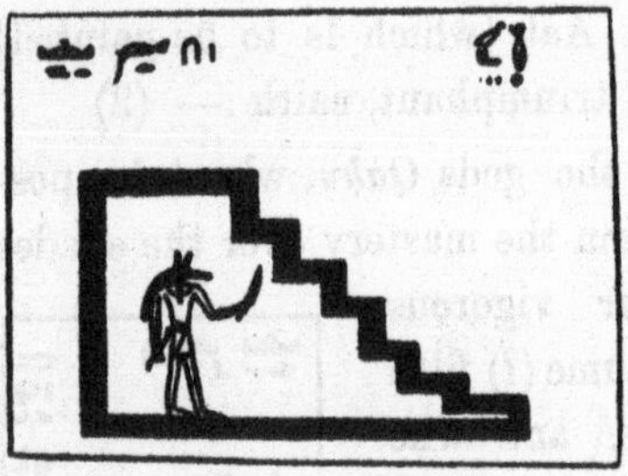

"heaven, and [I am] mighty upon earth. I fly like "a hawk, (8) and I cackle like the *smen* goose, and it "hath been given to me to alight at the 'Thigh of the "Lake.' I stand up upon it, I sit down (9) upon it, "I rise up like a god, I eat of the food of Sekhti-ḥetep, "and I go onwards to the (10) domain of the starry "gods. The double doors of Maāt are opened unto me, "and the double doors of the land of the great deep "(11) are unbolted before me. I set up a ladder to "heaven among the gods, and I am a divine being "among them. I speak with the voice of (12) the "*smen* goose to which the gods listen, and my speech "and my voice are those of the star Sepṭ (Sothis)."

XII. **Vignette**: The twelfth Åat, called "Åstcheṭet em Åment."

Text: (1) The twelfth Åat [which is to be painted] green. The Osiris Nu, triumphant, saith :— (2)

"Hail, thou Åat of the city of Unt (?) at the head of "Re-stau, the flame of which is a blazing fire, the gods "are unable to approach thee (3) and "the *Khus* are unable to gather to-"gether therein by reason of the uraei "which (4) would blot out their names. "Hail, thou Åat of Unt, I am in the "form of the mighty god who dwelleth "among the *Khus* and who dwelleth "in thee. (5) I am among the stars "that never fail within thee; I shall never fail,

"and my name shall never fail. (6) 'Hail, odour "of the god,' say they, the gods who dwell in the "Åat of Unt; [I shall be with you, I shall live with "you, O ye gods who dwell in the Åat of Unt;] love "ye me more than your own gods, (7) for I shall be "with you for ever [in the presence of the followers of "the great god]."

XIII. Vignette: The thirteenth Åat, called "Uart ent mu." Behind it stands the hippopotamus Ḥebeṭ-re-f, with the right fore paw resting on a beetle.

Text: (1) The thirteenth Åat [which is to be painted] green. The Osiris Nu, triumphant, saith:—

"Hail, thou Åat wherein the *Khus* gain (2) no "mastery. Thy waters are of fire, and the streams "which are in thee "burn with fire, and "(3) thy flame is a "blazing fire, those "who are there and "who wish to drink "thy waters to "quench (4) their "thirst cannot do "so by reason of the mighty dread which possesseth "them and by reason of the great terror which it causeth "them to have. The gods and the *Khus* (5) look "upon the waters thereof and retreat without having "quenched their thirst, and their hearts are not (6)

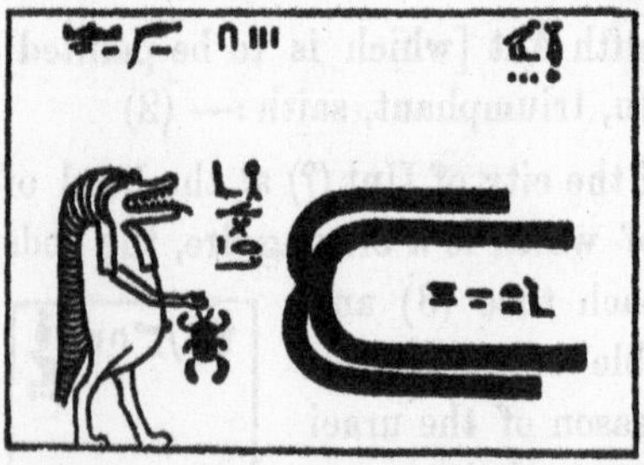

"set at rest; and though they wish to enter into them "they cannot do so. The stream is filled with reeds, "even as the stream (7) which floweth from the issues "which come forth from Osiris. I have gained the "mastery over the waters [thereof], I have drunk "from the canal [thereof] (8) like the god who dwelleth "in the Åat of the waters, and who is the guardian "thereof. The gods are more afraid to drink (9) the "waters thereof than are the *Khus*, and they retreat[1] "therefrom. Homage to thee, O thou god who dwellest "in the Åat of the waters, (10) I have come unto thee, "grant thou that I may gain power over the waters "[thereof], and that I may drink from the canal "thereof, (11) even as thou dost allow to drink the "great god from whom cometh Ḥāp (*i.e.*, the Nile), "who maketh green things to come into being, (12) "who maketh to grow the things which grow, who "maketh vigorous young plants and herbs, and who "also giveth to the gods gifts which proceed from him "and offerings (?). And grant thou that I may come "to Ḥāp, (13) and that I may gain power over young "plants and herbs, for I am the son of thy body for "ever."

XIV. **Vignette**: The fourteenth Åat. A range of mountains called "Field of Kher-āḥa," a man holding a libation vase, the god Anubis, a hawk with a disk, a lion-god, a man setting the *tesher* crown upon a god, a hippopotamus, a crocodile, and a worm.

[1] Or, "they are terrified thereat."

Text: (1) The fourteenth Åat [which is to be painted] yellow. The Osiris Nu, triumphant, saith:— (2) "Hail, thou Åat of Kher-āḥa, which turneth back "Ḥāp at Ṭaṭṭu, grant thou that Ḥāp may come (3) "abundant in grain as "he advanceth for the "mouth of those who "eat, and giving divine "offerings to the gods, "and (4) sepulchral meals "to the *Khus*. There is "a serpent in the double "*qerti* of Åbu (Elephan-"tine) at the mouth of (5) Ḥāp, and he cometh with "water and he standeth up upon the Thigh of Kher-āḥa "with his divine sovereign princes (6) at the head of "the canal, and he seeth in his hour, which is the silence "of the night. Hail, ye gods of (7) Kher-āḥa, and ye "sovereign princes at the head of the canal [thereof], "let your pools be opened to me, let your streams be "opened (8) to me, let me gain power over the water, "let me rest on the canal, let me eat grain, (9) let me "be satisfied with your food, let me lift myself up, let "my heart be great, even as [is that of] (10) the god "who dwelleth in Kher-āḥa, let offerings like unto "yours be made to me, let me not be destroyed by the "(11) issues which come forth from Osiris, and let me "not be withdrawn therefrom for ever."

CHAPTER CL.[1]

[From the Papyrus of Nu (Brit. Mus. No. 10,477, sheet 30).]

Vignette : I. Four serpents, emblematic probably of the cardinal points, and fifteen Åats:—

I. "Sekhet-Åarru; "the god wherein is "Rā-Ḥeru-Khuti (Rā-"Harmachis)."

II. "The brow of "fire; the god where-"in is Fa-ākh (Bearer "of altars)."

III. "Mountain, exceedingly high."

IV. "Åat of the "*Khus*."

V. "Åmmeḥet; the "god wherein is Sekh-"er-remu (Over-"thrower of fish)."

VI. "Åsset."

VII. "Ha-sert, the "god wherein is Fa-

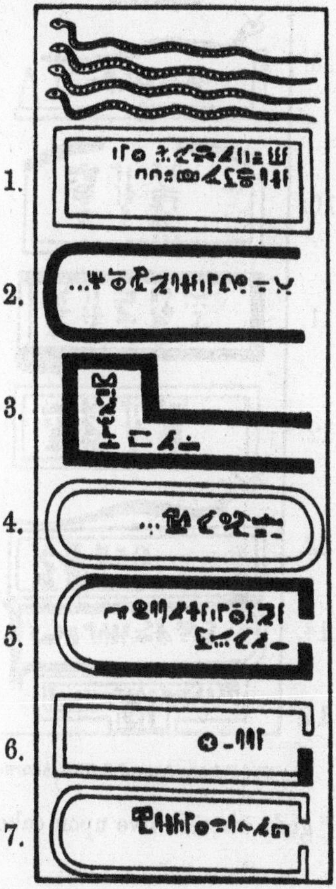

The Fifteen Åats of Sekhet-Åanru.

[1] The Papyrus of Nu ends with this Chapter.

"pet (Bearer of "Heaven."

VIII. "The brow of "the god Qaḥu."

IX. "Åṭu; the god "wherein is Sepṭ "(Sothis)."

X. "Unt; the god "wherein is Ḥetemet-"baiu (Destroyer of "souls)."

XI. "The brow of "the waters; the god "wherein is Åā-sekh-"emu."

XII. "Åat of Kher-"āḥa; the god where-"in is Ḥāp (Nile)."

XIII. "Stream of "the Lake of flame "which is in the fire."

XIV. "Åkesi, the "god wherein is Maa-"Thet-f."

XV. "The beauti-"ful Åmentet; the "gods wherein live upon cakes and ale (?)."

8. 9. 10. 11. 12. 13. 14. 15.

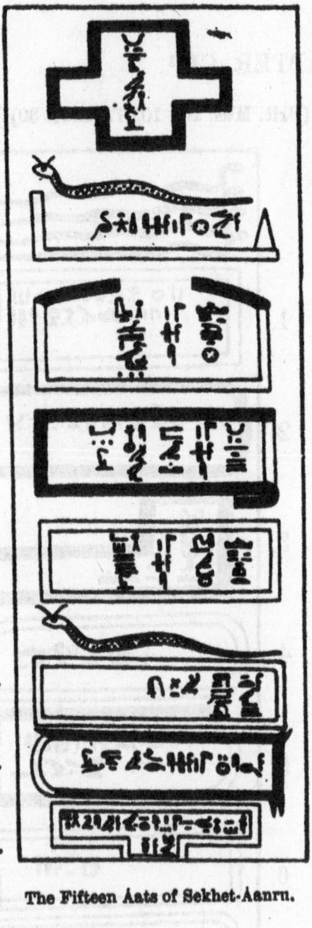

The Fifteen Åats of Sekhet-Åanru.

Here endeth the book in peace.

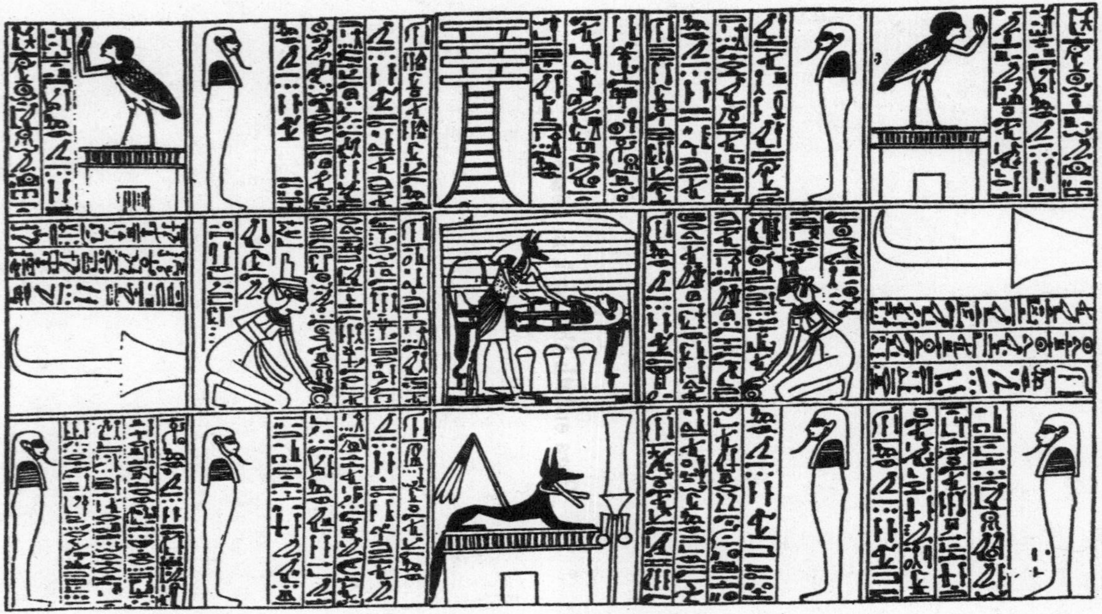

The Mummy Chamber (Papyrus of Ani).

CHAPTER CLIA.

[From the Papyrus of Mut-ḥetep (Brit. Mus. No. 10,010, sheet 5).]

Vignette: The mummy chamber. In the centre, upon a bier, lies the mummy of the deceased; the god Anubis, jackal-headed, stands by the side bending over the mummy. At the head of the bier kneels Nephthys, and at the foot Isis. The walls, which are here depicted as lying flat on the ground, are ornamented with emblems and texts, and at each corner stands one of the gods of the cardinal points. Two *ushabtiu* figures, two souls, two flames, a *Ṭeṭ*, and Anubis on his pylon, fill up the remaining spaces.

Text: (1) "Thy right eye is like the *Sektet* boat; "thy left (2) eye is like the *Āṭet* boat; thine eyebrows "are like (3) Ȧnpu; thy fingers are like Thoth: (4) "thy hair is like Ptaḥ-Seker; (5) they make a fair "way for thee, and they smite down (6) for thee the "fiends of Set."[1]

I. Isis saith:—(7) "I have come to protect thee, O "Osiris, (8) with the north wind which cometh forth "from Tem; I have (9) strengthened for thee thy "throat; I have caused thee (10) to be with (11) the "god; and I have placed all thine enemies (12) under "thy feet."

II. Nephthys saith:—(1) "I go round about behind "my sister Osiris Mut-ḥetep. I have come that (2) I "may protect thee, and my strength which protecteth

[1] This text is a part of the speech of Ȧnpu; see *infra*, p. 507.

"shall be behind thee for (3) ever and ever. The god "(4) Rā hearkeneth unto thy cry; (5) thou, O daughter "of Hathor, art made to triumph, thy head shall never "be taken away from thee, and thou shalt be made to "rise up in peace."

III. A deity (?) saith:—"(1) If any would come to "fetter thee I will not allow him to do so; (2) if any "would come to hurl missiles at thee I will not allow "him to do so. But I will (3) fetter thee, and I will "hurl missiles at thee; and I am (4) protecting thee, "O Mut-ḥetep, triumphant."

IV. The *Ṭeṭ* saith:—(1) "O thou that comest "quickly, I turn back thy steps, (2) O Kep-ḥrà, and "I illumine thy hidden (3) place. I stand behind the "*Ṭeṭ* on the day (4) of turning back slaughters, (5) "and I am protecting thee, O Mut-ḥetep, (6) trium-"phant, before Osiris."

V. The flame saith:—(1) "I surround with sand "the hidden tomb, (2) and drive away him that would "attack it. I lighten the funeral mountain, I cast "light (3) thereon. I traverse the way, and I protect "(4) Mut-ḥetep, triumphant."

VI. (1) Anubis, (2) who is at the head of the divine hall and who [dwelleth] upon his mountain, (3) the lord of Ta-tchesert, saith:—"I have come (4) to pro-"tect Osiris Mut-ḥetep, triumphant."

VII. (1) The living soul of Mut-(2)ḥetep saith:—"Let (3) Rā be adored in heaven, and when (4) he "setteth on the western horizon of heaven."

VIII. (1) The living soul and the perfect *Khu* of Mut-ḥetep, (2) triumphant (3) before Osiris, say:— [" Adored be Rā when he riseth in the eastern horizon "of heaven."] [1]

IX. *a* and *b*. (1) The lady of the house Mut-ḥetep, saith:—" Hail, *shabti* figure, if I be condemned (2) or "if there be allotted to me any work to do in the "underworld—behold, let (3) opposition be set aside "—such as is done by a man in his turn, namely, "sowing (4) the fields, and filling the channels with "water, and bringing the (5) sand of the west to the "east, O be thou present when I call unto thee."

X. (1) Mesthȧ saith:— "I am thy daughter, O "Mut-ḥetep, and I have come (2) to protect thee; I "make thy house to germinate and to be stablished "firmly (3) according to what Ptaḥ hath commanded "and according to what Rā hath commanded."

XI. (1) Ḥāpi saith:—"I have come to protect thee, "O (2) Osiris Mut-ḥetep; I bind up for thee thy head "and thy members, I smite down thine enemies (3) for "thee beneath thee, and I give thee thy head for ever."

XII. (1) Ṭua-māut-ef saith:—"I am thy daughter "who loveth thee, O Mut-ḥetep, triumphant for ever; "(2) I have come and I have avenged [thee, O] my "father Osiris, [upon him that] did [evil] unto thee "and I have brought (3) him under thy feet."

XIII. (1) Qebḥ-sennu-f saith:— "I am Qebḥ-sennuf,

[1] Added from the Papyrus of Qenna at Leyden, ed. Leemans, Plate xviii.

"and I have come (2) that I may protect Mut-ḥetep; I "have collected into a whole body for thee thy bones, "I have gathered (3) together for thee thy members, I "have brought thy heart and I do set it upon its seat "within thy body, and I make thy house to germinate "after thee."

CHAPTER CLIB.[1]

Vignette: The god Anpu (Anubis) standing by the mummy of the deceased which lies on a bier.

Text: (1) The god Ȧnpu, who dwelleth in the [city of] embalmment, the governor of the divine house, placeth his two hands upon the lord of life[2] (2) of Nebseni, the scribe and draughtsman of the Temple of Ptaḥ, the lord of piety, the son of the scribe and

[1] A shortened form of this Chapter also occurs in the Papyrus of Nebseni (sheet 21); it has for a vignette a male head, and is entitled, "The Chapter of a head of secret things."

[2] *I.e.*, the dead body of Nebseni.

designer Thena, triumphant, born of the lady of the house Mut-resth, triumphant, (3) and he furnisheth him with the things which belong to him. "Homage "to thee, O happy one, divine lord, who art endowed "with the sight of the *Utchat* (?), (4) Ptaḥ-Seker hath "bound thee up, Ånpu hath exalted thee, and Shu hath "caused thee to be lifted up, O (5) Face of beauty, "thou divine prince of eternity. Thou hast thine eye, "O scribe Nebseni, thou lord of piety, and beautiful it "is. Thy right eye is (6) in the *Sektet* boat, and thy "left eye is in the *Āṭet* boat; and thine eyebrows are "of fair appearance in the presence of the (7) company "of the gods. Thy brow is in the protection of "Ånpu; and the back of thy head, O beautiful one, (8) "is before the holy Hawk. Thy fingers are stablished "with written works in the presence of the lord of "Khemennu, Thoth, (9) who hath given to me the "speech of the sacred books. Thy hair is beautiful "before Ptaḥ-Seker, and thou, O scribe Nebseni, thou "lord of piety, art beautiful before (10) the great "company of the gods. The great god looketh upon "thee, and he leadeth thee along the path of happi-"ness, and sepulchral meals are bestowed upon thee; "he overthroweth for thee [all] thine enemies, (11) "and setteth them under thee in the presence of the "great company of the gods who dwell in the mighty "House of the Aged One which is in Ånnu (Helio-"polis)."

CHAPTER CLII.

[From the Papyrus of Nu (Brit. Mus. No. 10,477, sheet 13).]

Vignette : The deceased standing before a house.[1]

Text : (1) THE CHAPTER OF BUILDING A HOUSE UPON THE EARTH. The overseer of the house of the overseer of the seal, Nu, triumphant, saith :— (2)

"Hail ! Seb rejoiceth, for the Osiris Nu standeth "up over his body, [and he goeth round about among "those who follow Rā]. To men [and to the gods] "who have given birth to their own fathers (3) I have "ascribed praise ; and they have sight. The goddess "Sesheta hath brought the god Nebṭ, and Ȧnpu "(Anubis) hath called unto the Osiris Nu (4) to "build a house on the earth. Its foundation is in "Ȧnnu (Heliopolis), and the circuit thereof [reacheth] "to Kherāḥa, the shrine (?) is [like that of] the god

[1] In the Saïte Recension (see Lepsius, *op. cit.*, Bl. 74) the vignette represents the deceased seated in a chair holding out his hands to receive the bread and water which the kneeling goddess of the sycamore tree is about to give him.

"Sekhem, who dwelleth in (5) Sekhem, according to "that which I have written for the renewal (?) thereof, "and men and women bring offerings, and libations, "and ministrants (?). And Osiris saith unto (6) the "gods who are in [his] following and who journey "along, 'Behold ye the house which hath been built "for a *Khu* who is provided (7) with [all his attributes], "who cometh daily to renew himself among you. O "hold ye him in awe, and ascribe ye unto him praises, "and let him be a favoured being with you; look "ye (8) to what I have done and to what I have said.' "And Osiris saith concerning the god, 'Let him come "daily to renew himself among you. And let beasts "[for sacrifice] be brought unto him (9) by the south "wind, and let grain be brought unto him by the north "wind, and let barley be brought unto him from the "ends of the earth'; the mouth of Osiris hath ordered "[this] for me. Drawing onward may he (10) go round "about on his left hand, may he place himself on his "right hand, and may he see men, and the gods, and "the *Khus*, and the dead drawing him along with "praises and cries of joy, (11) and may he be a "favoured being with them."[1]

[1] In the Saïte Recension these words are followed by a speech of the deceased, a speech of the "lady of the sycamores," and a prayer to her on behalf of the deceased.

CHAPTER CLIIIA.

[From the Papyrus of Nu (Brit. Mus. No. 10,477, sheet 20).]

Vignette: A net fastened at one end to ground below or near water by means of a stake driven through a coil of rope which is drawn tight by the deceased.

Text: (1) THE CHAPTER OF COMING FORTH FROM THE NET. The Osiris Nu, the overseer of the house of the overseer of the seal, triumphant, saith:—

"Hail, thou 'god who lookest behind thee,' thou "'god who hast gained the mastery (2) over thine "heart,' I go a-fishing with the cordage of the 'uniter "of the earth,' and of him that maketh a way through "the earth. Hail, ye fishers who have given birth to "your own fathers, (3) who lay snares with your nets, "and who go round about in the chambers of the "waters, take ye not me (4) in the net wherewith ye "ensnared the helpless fiends, and rope me not in with "the rope (5) wherewith ye roped in the abominable "earth-followers, which had its wooden frame (?) [reach-

"ing] unto heaven, and its weighted parts upon the "earth. Let me come forth (*i.e.*, escape) from the "pegs (?) thereof, let me rejoice along with (6) the "god of the Ḥennu boat, let me come forth from its "bars (?), let me rise up like the god Sebek, and let me "make a flight to you away from the snare of the "fowler (7) whose fingers are hidden. I know the pole "with curved ends which is in it; 'Mighty finger of "Sekri' [is its name]. I know the *mekhes* which is "in it; (8) 'Thigh of the god Nemu' [is its name]. I "know the piece of wood which openeth in it; 'Hand "of Isis' [is its name]. I know the knife of slaughter "(9) which is in it; 'Slaughtering knife wherewith "Isis cut off a piece of flesh from Horus' [is its name]. "I know the names of the frame (?) and weights which "are in it; 'Leg and Thigh (10) of the double Lion-"god' [are their names]. I know the name of the "cordage wherewith it snareth [living things]; 'Vigour "of Tem' [is its name]. (11) I know the name of the "snarers who lay snares therewith; 'Akeru gods, an-"cestors of Akhabiu gods' [are their names]. (12) I "know the names of its hands; 'Two hands of the "great god, the lord who heareth speech in Ȧnnu "(Heliopolis) on the night of the festival of the half-"month in the Temple of the Moon-god'. . . (13) [are "their names]. I know the name of the Thigh which "surroundeth it at its upper part; 'Thigh of iron "whereupon the gods stand' [is its name]. I know "(14) the name of the superintendent who receiveth "the fish therefrom; 'Knife and vessel of the superin-"tendent of the god' [is his name]. I know the name "of the table (15) whereat he placeth himself; 'Table "of Horus [whereat he] sitteth in solitude in the dark-"ness and is not seen, the abjects fear him and those "therein ascribe unto him (16) praises,' [is its name]."

"I have come, and I am crowned (*or* have risen) like "the Mighty god who leadeth along the earth, and I "have gone down to the earth in the two great (17) "boats; and behold, the mighty one hath placed me "within the Temple of the Mighty god. I have come "along with the snarer, my wooden tools (*ārit*) are "with me, my knife is with me, (18) and my hacking "knife is with me; I come forth and I go round about, "and I snare (?) with the Net."

"I know the name of the pole with curved ends; "'*Temen reu* flowing (19) from the great finger of "Osiris,' [is its name]. I know the name of the two "pieces of wood which hold fast: 'Hooks of the "ancestors of Rā' [is the name of one], and 'Hook "of the ancestor of Hathor' [is the name of the other]. "(20) I, even I, know the cords which are on the pole "with curved ends: 'Cords (?) of the lord of mankind' "[is their name]. I know (21) the name of the table; "'Hand of Isis' [is its name]. I know the name of "its ropes (?); 'Rope of the god, the firstborn' [is their "name]. (22) I know the name of the cordage (?); "'Cordage of the day' [is its name]. I know the "names of the fowlers and of the fishermen; (23)

"'*Akeru* gods, ancestors of Rā' [is their name]. I "know the names of the *tememu;* 'Ancestors of Seb' "[is their name]."

(24) "I have brought unto thee that which thou "eatest, and I have brought that which I eat; and "thou eatest that which Seb eateth with Osiris. Hail, "thou 'god whose face is behind him,' (25) thou 'god "who hast gained the mastery over his heart,' thou "fisher and fowler of the opener of the earth! Hail, "ye fishers who have given birth to your own fathers, "(26) and who lay snares within the city of Nefer-sent, "take ye me not into your net, and snare ye me not "with the (27) snares wherewith ye ensnared the help-"less fiends and wherewith ye caught the abominable "earth-followers; for I know the Net. (28) I know "the upper framework (?) and the lower heavy parts "thereof. Behold me, then, for I have come. I have "my pole with curved ends with me, I have my *mekhes* "with me, (29) I have my table with me, and I have "my slaughtering knife with me. I have come, and I "have entered in, and I have myself pressed forward (?). "Know ye that I, even (30) I, know the name of the "snarer of (*or* that which snareth) fowl [in] his place? "I have smitten [it], I have opened [it] out, I have "struck [it], and I have set it upon its seat. Now the "*mekhes* which is with me is (31) the 'Thigh of the "god Nemu'; and the pole with curved ends which is "with me is the 'Finger of Sekeri'; and the table "which is with me is the 'Hand of Isis'; (32) and the

"slaughtering knife which is with me is the 'Slaughter-"ing knife of the god Nemu.' O grant that I may "come; O grant, then, that I may sit (33) in the boat "of Rā; let me sail forth on the Lake of Testes (?) "towards the northern heaven; let me do as do they "who sing when they sing praises (34) of my *ka*; and "let me live as do they there. The Osiris Nu, trium-"phant, cometh forth upon your ladder which Rā hath "made for him, (35) and Horus and Suti hold him fast "by the hand."

In the Saïte Recension (see Lepsius, *op. cit.*, Bl. 74), the following rubric is added to this Chapter:

[This chapter] shall be recited over a figure of the deceased which shall be put in a boat. And behold, thou shalt make a *sektet* boat on his right side, and a *māṭet* boat on his left, and let them bring offerings of cakes, and of ale, and of all kinds of fair things on the day of the birth of Osiris. The soul of him to whom these things have been given shall live for ever, and he shall not die a second time.

CHAPTER CLIIIB.

[From the Papyrus of Nu (Brit. Mus. No. 10,477, sheet 20).]

Vignette : A net full of fish being drawn together by three dog-headed apes.

Text : (1) THE CHAPTER OF COMING FORTH FROM THE CATCHER OF THE FISH. The Osiris Nu, the overseer of the house of the overseer of the seal, triumphant, saith :— (2)

"Hail, ye who lay snares (?), and ye who work the "nets, and ye who are fishers; hail, ye who have given "birth to your own fathers, know ye (3) that I know "the name of the great and mighty net? 'Ȧnqet' "(*i.e.*, Clincher) is its name. Know ye that I know "(4) the name of its cordage? '*Ruṭ* (*i.e.*, Vigour) of "Isis' [is its name]. Know ye that I know the name "of the (5) *meḥes?* 'Thigh of Tem' [is its name]. "Know ye that I know the name of its pole with "curved ends? 'Finger of Nemu' [is its name]. (6)

"Know ye that I know the name of its table? 'Hook "of Ptaḥ' [is its name]. Know ye that I know (7) "the name of its slaughtering knife? 'Chopper of "Isis' [is its name]. Know ye that I know the "name of its weights? 'Iron (8) in heaven' [is their "name]. Know ye that I know the name of [its] "rushes? 'Feathers (*or* hair) of the Hawk' [is their "name]. Know ye (9) that I know the name of the "fishers? 'Ape' [is their name]. Know ye (10) that "I know the name of the Thigh? ['Thigh] whereon "standeth the Temple of the Moon' is its name. Know "ye that (11) I know the name of the fowler? 'Prince, "mighty one who sitteth on the eastern side of heaven' "[is his name]. I have not eaten, O great divine one. "(12) Behold, the great divine one hath given me "drink; I have not seated myself upon [my] thighs "[in] the waters, but I eat and I satisfy myself with "food before him. (13) The seeds of death are in my "body. I am Nekh, I am Rā, coming forth from Nu, "the divine soul of the god. I create the god (14) "Ḥu; and wrong is the thing which I abominate. I "am Osiris, the maker of Maāt whereon Rā doth live "each and every day. (15) I am invoked [by the name "of] 'Bull,' and I am addressed among the company of "the gods by the name of 'Neḥ.' I create mine own "self along with Nu in my name (16) of Kheperȧ, "whereby I create myself each and every day. I am "the god of divine splendour, and I rise up as Rā, the "lord of the East; life is given unto me through his

"(17) comings forth therefrom. I have come into "heaven, and I embrace my seat which is in the East "with the children of the princes who dwell (18) in "[their] fields, and I have delivered her that brought "me forth in peace. I eat like the god Shu, I satisfy "myself with food like the god Shu, (19) I ease myself "like the god Shu. The divine kings of the North "and South are with me, the god Khensu is with me, "and those who bind up their heads are with me; "embrace ye, then, (20) the flame in the land of the "multitude."

CHAPTER CLIV.

[From the Papyrus of Nu (Brit. Mus. No. 10,477, sheet 18).]

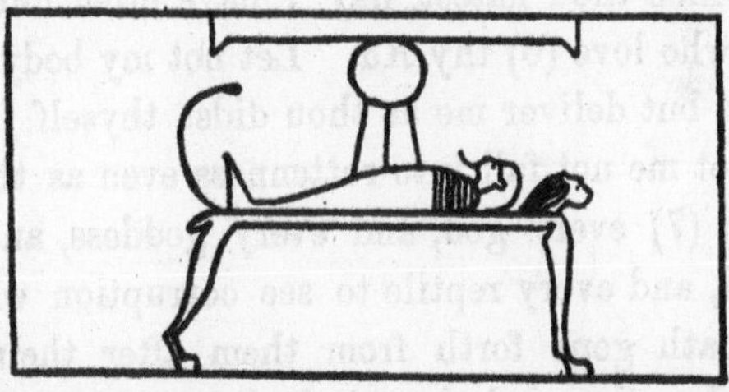

Vignette: This Chapter has no vignette in the Theban Recension; in the Saite Recension (see Lepsius, *op. cit.*, Bl. 75) the mummy of the deceased is seen lying upon a bier with the sun shining upon it.

Text: (1) THE CHAPTER OF NOT LETTING THE BODY PERISH. The Osiris Nu, the overseer of the house of the overseer of the seal, triumphant, saith:— (2)

"Homage to thee, O my divine father Osiris. I "came to embalm thee, do thou embalm these my "members, for I would not perish and come to an "end (3) [but would be] even like unto my divine "father Kheperå, the divine type of him that never "saw corruption. Come, then, make strong my breath, "then, O lord of the winds, (4) who dost magnify those "divine beings who are like unto himself. Stablish "me doubly, then, and fashion me strongly, O lord of "the funeral chest. Grant thou that I may enter into "the land of everlastingness, according to that which "was done for thee (5) along with thy father Tem, "whose body never saw corruption, and who is the "being who never saw corruption. I have never done "that which thou hatest, nay, I have cried out among "those who love (6) thy *Ka*. Let not my body become "worms, but deliver me as thou didst thyself. I pray "thee, let me not fall into rottenness even as thou dost "permit (7) every god, and every goddess, and every "animal, and every reptile to see corruption when the "soul hath gone forth from them after their death. "And when the soul departeth (*or* perisheth), a man "seeth corruption and the bones (8) of his body rot "and become wholly stinkingness, the members decay "piecemeal, the bones crumble into a helpless mass, "and the flesh becometh foetid liquid, (9) and he "becometh a brother unto the decay which cometh "upon him, and he turneth into multitudes of worms, "and he becometh altogether worms, and an end is "made of him, and he perisheth in the sight of the "god Shu even as doth every god, and every goddess "(10) and every feathered fowl, and every fish, and "every creeping thing, and every reptile . . . . "and every animal, and every thing whatsoever. There-"fore shall they [fall] on (11) their bellies [when] they "recognize me, and behold, the fear of me shall terrify "them; and thus likewise shall it be with every being "after death, whether it be animal, (12) or bird, or "fish, or worm, or reptile. Let life [come] from its "death,[1] and let not decay caused by any reptile make "an end [of me], and let them not come against (13) "me in their [various] forms. Do not thou give me "over unto that slaughterer who dwelleth in his "torture-chamber (?), who (14) killeth the members "and maketh them rot, being [himself] hidden—who "worketh destruction upon many dead bodies and "liveth by slaughter. Let me live and perform his "message, and let me do that which (15) is com-"manded by him. Give me not over unto his fingers, "let him not gain the mastery over me, for I am under "thy command, O lord of the gods."

"Homage to thee, O my divine father Osiris, thou "hast thy being with thy members. (16) Thou didst

[1] *I.e.*, the death of the body.

"not decay, thou didst not become worms, thou didst "not diminish, thou didst not become corruption, thou "didst not putrefy, and thou didst not turn into worms. "I am the god Kheperȧ, and my members shall have "an everlasting existence. (17) I shall not decay, I "shall not rot, I shall not putrefy, I shall not turn into "worms, and I shall not see corruption before the eye "of the god Shu. I shall have my being; I shall have "my being; (18) I shall live, I shall live; I shall ger- "minate, I shall germinate, I shall germinate; I shall "wake up in peace; I shall not putrefy; my intes- "tines (?) shall not perish; I shall not suffer injury; "(19) mine eye shall not decay; the form of my "visage (?) shall not disappear; mine ear shall not "become deaf; my head shall not be separated from "my neck; my tongue shall not be carried away; my "hair shall not (20) be cut off; mine eyebrows shall "not be shaved off; and no baleful injury shall come "upon me. My body shall be stablished, and it shall "neither fall into ruin (21) nor be destroyed on this "earth."

CHAPTER CLV.

[From the Papyrus of Nu (Brit. Mus. No. 10,477, sheet 27).]

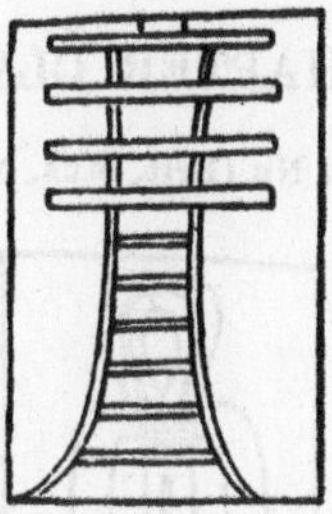

Vignette: A *Ṭeṭ*.

Text: (1) THE CHAPTER OF A ṬEṬ OF GOLD. The Osiris Nu, the overseer of the house of the overseer of the seal, saith:— (2)

"Rise up thou, O Osiris. [Thou hast thy backbone, "O Still-Heart, thou hast the ligatures of thy neck and "back, O Still-Heart].[1] Place thou thyself upon thy "base. I put water beneath thee, and I bring unto "thee a *Ṭeṭ* of gold that thou mayest rejoice therein."

RUBRIC: [This chapter] shall be recited over a *Ṭeṭ* of gold set in (3) a plinth (?) of sycamore wood which hath been steeped in water of *ānkham* flowers, and it shall be placed at the neck of the deceased on the day of the funeral. If this amulet be placed at his neck, he shall become a perfect (4) *khu*

[1] Added from the Papyrus of Nebseni, sheet 10.

in the underworld, and at the new year [festivals he shall be] like those who are in the following of Osiris continually and for ever.[1]

CHAPTER CLVI.

[From the Papyrus of Nu (Brit. Mus. No. 10,477, sheet 27).]

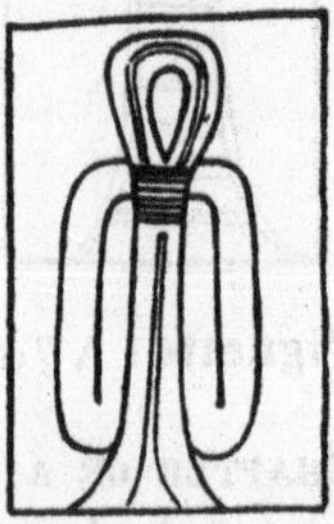

Vignette: A Buckle.

Text: (1) THE CHAPTER OF A BUCKLE OF CARNELIAN. The Osiris Nu, the overseer of the house of the overseer of the seal, saith:—

"May the blood of Isis, and the powers of Isis, and "the enchantments of Isis be powers to protect (2) "this mighty one and to guard him from him that "would do unto him anything which he abominateth."

[1] The Rubric in the Saïte Recension (see Lepsius, *op. cit.*, Bl. 75) adds:—"He shall not be thrust back at the doors of Åmentet; cakes, and ale, and meat-offerings shall be offered unto him upon the altars of Rā, or (as some say) of Osiris Un-nefer; and he shall triumph over his foes in the underworld for ever and for ever."

RUBRIC: [This chapter] shall be said over a buckle of carnelian, which hath been steeped in water of *ānkhami* flowers, and set (3) in a plinth of sycamore wood, and it shall be placed at the neck of the deceased on the day of the funeral. If these things be done for him the powers of Isis (4) shall protect his limbs, and Horus the son of Isis shall rejoice in him, when he seeth him; and there shall be no hidden places on his path, and one hand shall be towards heaven, and one hand shall be towards earth, regularly and continually. (5) Thou shalt not let any person who is with thee see it. . . . .[1]

CHAPTER CLVII.

[From Lepsius, *Todtenbuch*, Bl. 76.]

Vignette: A vulture with outstretched wings holding the symbol of life in each talon.

[1] The Rubric in the Saïte Recension (see Lepsius, *op. cit.*, Bl. 75) adds:—"If this Chapter be known [by the deceased] he shall be among those who follow Osiris Un-nefer, triumphant. The gates of the underworld shall be opened unto him, and a homestead shall be given unto him, together with wheat and barley, in the Sekhet-Aaru; and the followers of Horus who reap therein shall proclaim his name as one of the gods who are therein."

Text: (1) THE CHAPTER OF THE VULTURE OF GOLD WHICH IS TO BE PLACED AT THE NECK OF THE DECEASED. (2) The Osiris Àuf-ānkh, triumphant, saith:—

"Isis cometh and hovereth over the city, and she "goeth about seeking the secret habitations of Horus "as he emergeth from his papyrus swamps, and she "lifteth up his shoulder which is in evil case. He is "made one (3) of the company in the divine boat, and "the sovereignty of the whole world is decreed for him. "He hath warred mightily, and he maketh [his] deeds "to be remembered; he hath made fear of him to exist, "and awe [of him] to have its being. His mother, the "mighty lady, protecteth him, and she hath (4) trans-"ferred her power to Horus."

RUBRIC: **[This chapter] shall be said over a vulture of gold whereupon it hath been inscribed, and thou shalt place the vulture on the neck to protect the perfect deceased one on the day of the funeral continually and regularly.**

CHAPTER CLVIII.

[From Lepsius, *Todtenbuch*, Bl. 76.]

Vignette: A collar.

Text: (1) THE CHAPTER OF A COLLAR OF GOLD which shall be placed at the neck of the deceased. (2) The Osiris Åuf-ānkh, triumphant, saith:—

"O my father, my brother, my mother Isis, I am "unswathed, and I see. I am one of those who are "unswathed and who see the god Seb."

RUBRIC: [This chapter] shall be said over a collar of gold whereon it hath been engraved, and the collar shall be placed on the neck of the deceased on the day of the funeral.

CHAPTER CLIX.

[From Lepsius, *Todtenbuch*, Bl. 76.]

Vignette: The *Uatch* amulet.

Text: (1) THE CHAPTER OF THE UATCH AMULET [MADE OF] MOTHER-OF-EMERALD which shall be placed at the neck of the deceased. (2) The Osiris Ȧuf-ānkh, triumphant, saith:—

"Hail, thou who comest forth daily from the Temple "of the god. The mighty lady speaketh and she goeth "round about in the gate of the double house, and she "taketh possession of the might of her father, that is "to say, the *Sāḥu* (3) [who is] the bull of the goddess

"Renenet. She taketh those who are in her following, "and she maketh an opportunity for those, the oppor- "tunity of the door (?)."

RUBRIC: [This chapter] shall be said over an *Uatch* of mother-of-emerald whereupon it hath been inscribed, and the *Uatch* shall be placed on the neck of the deceased.

CHAPTER CLX.

[From the Papyrus of Nebseni (Brit. Mus. No. 9900, sheet 10).]

Vignette: Thoth, the great god, giving an *Uatch* amulet of mother-of-emerald to the deceased.

Text: [THE CHAPTER OF] GIVING AN *UATCH* OF MOTHER-OF-EMERALD to the scribe Nebseni, triumphant [who saith]:—

"I am the *Uatch* of mother-of emerald which "cannot be injured (?), and which the hand of Thoth "adoreth; injury is a thing which I abominate. It "is in sound state and I am in sound state; it is "not injured and I am not injured; it is not [worn "away] and I am not worn away. The words of "Thoth [are at] thy back, O thou who comest in "peace, O divine Prince of Ȧnnu (Heliopolis), thou "mighty god who dwellest in the city of Pe. The "god Shu advanceth to him and findeth him in the "city of Shenmu in his name 'Neshem' (*i.e.*, mother-"of-emerald); he maketh his place in the fortress of "the mighty god. The god Tem resteth upon his eye, "and his members shall not suffer injury."[1]

[1] In the Saïte Recension (see Lepsius, *op. cit.*, Bl. 76) this Chapter has a rubric which reads:—"[This Chapter] shall be "recited over an *Uatch* of mother-of-emerald whereupon it hath "been inscribed, and the *Uatch* shall be placed on the neck of the "deceased."

CHAPTER CLXI.

[From the Papyrus of Nefer-uben-f (see Naville, *op. cit.*, Bl. 184).]

Vignette: The god Thoth opening the doors of the four winds.

Text: (1) THE CHAPTER OF FORCING AN ENTRANCE INTO HEAVEN. [This] Thoth doeth to make felicitous [the way for him that] would enter into the Disk.

I. [To the Door of the west wind.] (2) "Rā "liveth, the Tortoise[1] "dieth. Pure is the "body in the earth, "and pure are the "bones of Osiris the "*àm-khent*,[2] Nefer-"uben-f, triumphant."

II. [To the Door of the east wind.] (3) "Rā liveth, "the Tortoise dieth. Sound is he who is in the chest,

[1] Turtle (?). [2] A priestly title.

"who is in the chest, Osiris Nefer-uben-f, triumphant."

III. [To the Door of the north wind.] (4) "Rā "liveth, the Tortoise dieth. The Osiris Nefer-uben-f, "triumphant, is strong in his members, Qebḥ-sennuf "guardeth them."

IV. [To the Door of the south wind.] (5) "Rā "liveth, the Tortoise dieth. The bolts (?) are drawn and "they pass through his foundation."

RUBRIC:[1] **(1) Every** ***sāḥu*** **for whom these divine figures have been painted upon his coffin shall make his way through these (2) four entrances into heaven. That of the north wind belongeth to Osiris; that of the south wind to Rā; (3) that of the west wind to Isis; and that of the east wind to Nephthys. Each one of these winds (4) shall breathe into his nostrils as he entereth in his daily course. Let none who is outside know [this chapter]; (5) it is a great mystery, and those who dwell in the swamps (*i.e.*, the ignorant) know it not. Thou shalt not do this in the presence of any person (6) except thy father or thy son, or thyself alone; for it is, indeed, an exceedingly (7) great mystery which no man whatsoever knoweth.**

[1] This Rubric is added from the Saïte Recension (see Lepsius, *op. cit.*, Bl. 76).

CHAPTER CLXII.

[From Lepsius, *Todtenbuch*, Bl. 77.]

Vignette: A cow having the disk with plumes between her horns, and wearing the collar, from which is suspended the emblem of "life" round her neck.

Text: THE CHAPTER OF MAKING HEAT TO BE UNDER THE HEAD OF THE DECEASED. (1) To be recited:—"Homage to thee, O thou god Par, thou "mighty one, whose plumes are lofty, thou lord of the "*Urevet* crown, who rulest with the whip; thou art the "lord of the phallus, thou growest as thou shinest with "rays of light, (2) and thy shining is to the uttermost "parts [of earth and sky]. Thou art the lord of trans-"formations, and hast manifold skins, which thou hidest "in the *Utchat* at its birth. Thou art the mighty one "of names (?) among (3) the gods, the mighty runner "whose strides are mighty; thou art the god the "mighty one who comest and rescuest the needy one "and the afflicted from him that oppresseth him; give "heed to my cry. I am the Cow, (4) and thy divine "name is in my mouth, and I will utter it; 'Haqa-"haḳaḥer' is thy name; 'Àuràuàa qersaànqrebathi' "(5) is thy name; 'Kherserâu' is thy name; 'Khar-"sathá' is thy name. I praise thy name. I am the "Cow that hearkeneth unto the petition on the day "wherein (6) thou placest heat under the head of Rā. "O place it for him in the divine gate[1] in Ànnu "(Heliopolis), and thou shalt make him to become "even like him that is upon the earth; he is thy soul ". . . . O be gracious unto Osiris Àuf-ānkh, trium-"phant, (7) and cause thou heat to exist under his "head, for, indeed, he is the soul of the great divine "Body which resteth in Ànnu, Khu-kheper-uru' (?) is "his name; 'Barekathàtchaua' is his name. Be gra-"cious, then, (8) and grant that he may become like "unto one of those who are in thy following, for he is "even as art thou."

RUBRIC: [This chapter] shall be recited over the image of a cow which hath been made in fine gold and placed at the neck of the deceased, and it shall be written upon (9) new papyrus and placed under his head, then shall abundant warmth be in him throughout even like that which was in him when he was upon earth. This hath exceedingly great protective power, for it was made by the cow for her son Rā when he was setting and when (10) his habitation was surrounded by a company of beings of fire. And the deceased shall become divine in the underworld, and he shall never be turned back at any of the gates thereof. (11)

And thou shalt say when thou placest [the image of] this

[1] Or "underworld."

goddess at the neck of the deceased:—"O Âmen, O Âmen, "who art in heaven, turn thy face upon the dead body of thy "son and make him sound and strong in the underworld." (12) This is a composition of exceedingly great mystery. Let not the eye of any man whatsoever see it, for it is an abominable thing for [every man] to know it; therefore hide it. "Book of the mistress of the hidden temple" is its name.

Here endeth the Book.[1]

[1] The document from which the scribe of the Turin Papyrus copied this Chapter probably ended with it.

CHAPTER CLXIII.

[From Lepsius, *Todtenbuch*, Bl. 77.]

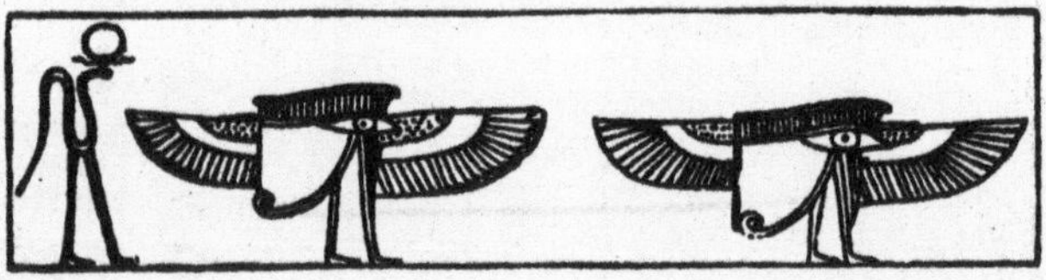

Vignette: Two winged *Utchats* on legs, and a serpent also upon legs, with a disk and horns upon his head.

Text: The Chapters which are taken from another work and are here added to the "Book of coming forth by day."

THE CHAPTER OF NOT ALLOWING THE BODY OF A MAN TO MOULDER AWAY IN THE UNDERWORLD, AND

OF DELIVERING HIM FROM THOSE WHO DEVOUR THE SOULS THAT ARE SHUT IN IN THE UNDERWORLD, AND OF NOT ALLOWING TO RISE UP AGAINST HIM THE THINGS WHICH HE ABOMINATETH UPON EARTH, AND OF MAKING SOUND AND STRONG HIS LIMBS AND BONES AGAINST WORMS AND AGAINST EVERY GOD WHO WOULD ATTACK HIM IN THE UNDERWORLD, AND OF CAUSING HIM TO COME FORTH AND TO GO IN AS HE PLEASETH AND TO DO WHATSOEVER HE HATH IN HIS HEART TO DO WITHOUT HINDRANCE. (1) The Osiris Ȧuf-ānkh, triumphant, saith:—

"I am the divine soul of the great divine body which "is laid to rest in Ȧthabu, which protecteth the body "of (2) Ḥarethi, the . . : . which resteth in the marshes "of Senhaqareha. O divine soul which hath no languor "of heart either in rising (3) or setting, and which "resteth within his divine body which is laid to rest "in Senhapareḳana, grant thou to Osiris Ȧuf-ānkh, "triumphant, that he may deliver himself (4) from the "souls of the god-of-the-savage-face, who gaineth the "mastery over hearts and taketh possession of limbs, "and from whose mouths fire cometh forth to devour "souls. Hail, thou who art lying prostrate within thy "body, whose flame (5) cometh into being from out of "the fire which blazeth within the sea (*or* water) in "such wise that the sea (*or* water) is raised up on high "out of the fire thereof, grant thou that the flame (6) "may leave the fire, wherever it may be, to raise up "the hand of Osiris Ȧuf-ānkh, triumphant, and to make "him to have an existence for ever and for ever. Verily, "let his period of existence be as the period of existence "(7) of heaven in the limitless boundaries thereof. "Heaven holdeth thy soul, O Osiris Àuf-ānkh, and "earth holdeth thy form. O deliver thou Osiris Àuf-"ānkh, triumphant, and let him not be [consumed] by "the *kaus* (8) who devour the souls of those who have "raised up evil (?). Let his soul have its being within "his body, and let his body have its being with his "soul; and let him be hidden within the pupil of the "*Utchat* of the god whose name is Sharei-sharei-shapu-"neter-àri(9)-ka, who reposeth at the northwest of the "brow of the Àpt of the land of Kenset (Nubia), and "journeyeth not to the east. Hail, god Àmen, thou "divine Bull-Scarab, (10) thou lord of the divine "*Utchats*! God-the-pupil-of-whose-eye-is-terrible is "thy name, the Osiris Àuf-ānkh, triumphant, born of "Sheret-Àmsu, triumphant, is the emanation of thy "two Eyes, the name of one of which is Share-share-"khet, and (11) Shapu-neter-àri-ka of the other, though "'Shaka-Àmen-Shakanasa at the brow of Tem who illu-"mineth the two lands' (12) is his name in very truth. "Grant that Osiris Àuf-ānkh, triumphant, may be of "this land of Maāt, let him not be left in his solitude, "for he is of this earth wherein he will no [more] "appear, and 'Àn' (13) is his name. O let him be "with a perfect *Khu*, or (as others say), a strong Khu, "and let him be the soul of the mighty body which is "in Sau (Saïs), the city of Neith."

RUBRIC: [This chapter] is to be recited over a serpent having legs and wearing (14) a disk and two horns, and over two *Utchats* having both eyes and wings. In the pupil of one of the *Utchats* there shall be a figure of the god-of-the-lifted-hand with the face of the divine soul, and having plumes and a back (15) like a hawk; and in the pupil of the other there shall be a figure of the god-of-the-lifted-hand with the face of the goddess Neith, and having plumes and a back like a hawk. And this chapter shall be written with *ānti* either upon a *meh* stone . . . . or upon mother-of-emerald (16) of the south and [dipped] in water of the western lake of Qemt (Egypt) or upon a bandage of *uatchet* linen wherewith a man should swathe every limb. And the deceased shall not be turned back at any gate of the underworld; he shall eat (17) and drink and ease himself even as he did when he was upon earth; and none shall rise up to cry out against him; and he shall be protected from the hands of the enemy for ever and ever. If this book be recited for him upon earth he shall not be seized (18) by the messengers of attack who work evil in all the earth; he shall not have gashes inflicted upon him; he shall not die through the slaughter of Set; and he shall not be carried off to any place of restraint whatsoever; but he shall go in unto the *qenbet*, and he shall come forth with triumph, (19) and he shall go out to terrify the evil-doers who exist in all the earth.

CHAPTER CLXIV.

[From Lepsius, *Todtenbuch*, Bl. 78.]

Vignette : A goddess, with a head of a woman and two heads of a vulture, standing with outstretched wings. On each side of her is a dwarf with two heads, one of a man and one of a hawk; each dwarf has a disk and plumes upon his head.

Text : ANOTHER CHAPTER.

(1) "Homage to thee, O Sekhet-Bast-Rā, thou "mistress of the gods, thou bearer of wings, lady "of the *Ȧnes* bandlet, queen of the crowns of the "South and of the North, only One, sovereign of her "father, superior to whom the gods cannot be, thou "mighty one of enchantments (2) in the Boat of "Millions of Years, thou who art pre-eminent, who "risest in the seat of silence, mother of Pashakasa, "royal wife of Parehaqa-Kheperu, (3) mistress and "lady of the tomb, mother in the horizon of heaven, "gracious one, beloved, destroyer of rebellion, offerings "are in thy grasp, and thou art standing in the bows "of the boat of thy divine father (4) to overthrow the

"Fiend. Thou hast placed Maāt in the bows of his "boat. Thou art the fire goddess Åmit, whose oppor-"tunity escapeth her not; thy name is Tekaharesa-"pusaremkakaremet. (5) Thou art like unto the mighty "flame of Saqenaqat which is in the bows of the boat "of thy father Ḥarepuḳaka-share-sha-baiu, (6) for be-"hold, thus is [the name uttered] in the speech of the "Negroes, and of the Ånti, and of people of Ta-Kensetet "(Nubia). Praise be to thee, O lady, who art mightier "than the gods, and words of adoration rise to thee "from the Eight gods. The living souls who are in "their chests (7) praise thy mystery. O thou who art "their mother, thou source from whom they sprang, "[who] makest for them a place of repose in the hidden "underworld, [who] makest sound their bones and "preservest them from terror, (8) who makest them "strong (?) in the abode of everlastingness, who pre-"servest them from the evil chamber of the souls of "the god-of-the-terrible-face [who is] among the com-"pany of the gods. 'Babe that comest forth from the "god-of-the-terrible-face who keepeth his body hidden' "is thy name. (9) 'Åtare-åm-tcher-qemtu-rennu-par-"sheta' is the name of one divine son, 'Pa-nemmå' [is "the name] of the other. 'Utchat of Sekhet, mighty "lady, (10) mistress of the gods' is thy name. 'Eman-"ation of . . . . .' is the name of Mut, who maketh "souls strong (?) and who maketh sound bodies, and "who delivereth them from the abode of the fiends "which is in the evil chamber. (11) The goddess "saith with her own mouth, 'They shall never be "fettered, and I will do according to what ye say, O "ye *Tchaui* of the divine son, for whom they per-"formed the funeral rites.'"

RUBRIC: (12) [This chapter] shall be recited over [a figure of] Mut which hath three heads; the first shall be like unto that of Pekhat, and shall have [upon it] plumes; the second shall be like unto that of a man and shall have [upon it] the crowns of the South and North; and the third shall be like unto that of a vulture and shall have [upon it] plumes. And the figure shall have a phallus (13), and a pair of wings, and the claws of a lion, and it shall be painted with *ānṭ* and powder (?) of *uatch* mixed (?) with yellow colour (?) upon a bandage of *ȧnes* linen. In front of it shall stand one dwarf, and behind it [another]; and (14) [each] shall have upon him plumes, and [one] hand and arm shall be raised, and [each] shall have two faces, one of a hawk and one of a man, and the body of each shall be fat. [Then shall the deceased] be divine along with the gods in the underworld; (15) he shall never, never be turned back; his flesh and his bones shall be like those of one who hath never been dead; he shall drink water at the source of the stream; a homestead shall be given unto him in Sekhet-ȧanre; (16) he shall become a star of heaven; he shall set out against the serpent-fiend Nekȧu and against Tar, who are in the underworld; he shall not be shut in along with the souls which are fettered; he shall deliver himself wherever he may be; and worms shall not devour him.

CHAPTER CLXV

[From Lepsius, *Todtenbuch*, Bl. 79.]

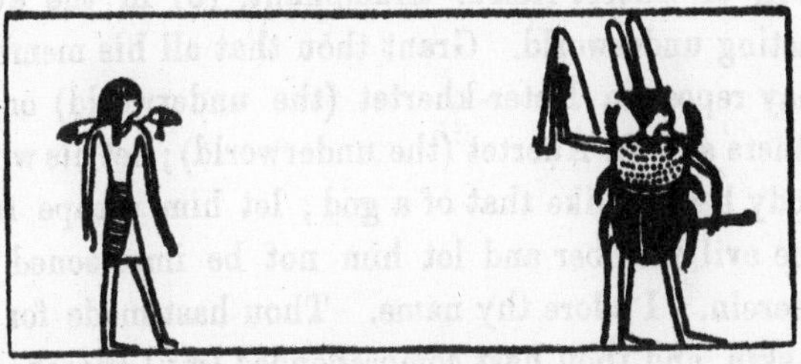

Vignette: An ithyphallic god with the body of a beetle; on his head are plumes, and his right hand and arm are raised. Behind him is a man who has a ram's head on each shoulder.

Text: THE CHAPTER OF ARRIVING IN PORT ..... To make the body germinate, and to drink water, and not to disappear recite the following:—

(1) "Hail, O Bekhennu, Bekhennu; O Prince, "Prince; O Åmen, Åmen; O Re-Iukasa; O god, "Prince of the gods of the eastern part (2) of "heaven, O Åmen-Nathekerethi-Åmen. O thou whose "skin is hidden, whose form is secret, thou lord of the "two horns, ... of Nut, thy name is Na-(3)åri-k, "or (as others say) 'Ka-åri-ka.' 'Kasaika' is thy "name. 'Arethikasathika' is thy name. 'Åmen-na-"ån-ka-entek-share,' (4) or (as others say), Thekshare-

"Ȧmen-Rerethi' is thy name. O Amen, let me make "supplication unto thee, I, even I, know thy name. "Thy transformations (5) are in my mouth, thy skin "is before my eyes. Come, I pray thee, and place thou "thy heir and thy image, Osiris Ȧuf-ānkh, triumphant, "born of Sheret-Ȧmsu, triumphant, (6) in the ever-"lasting underworld. Grant thou that all his members "may repose in Neter-khertet (the underworld) or (as "others say) in Ȧḳertet (the underworld); let his whole "body become like that of a god; let him escape from "the evil chamber and let him not be imprisoned (7) "therein. I adore thy name. Thou hast made for me "a skin, and thou hast comprehended [my] speech, and "thou knowest it exceedingly well. 'Ȧmen' is thy "name. O Retasashaka, (8) I have made for thee a "skin, [namely] a divine soul. 'Ireqai' is thy name; "'Mārqatha' is thy name; 'Rerei' is thy name; "'Nasaqbubu' (9) is thy name; 'Thȧnasa-Thȧnasa' is "thy name; 'Shareshathȧkathȧ' is thy name. O "Ȧmen, O Ȧmen, O God, O God, O Ȧmen, (10) I "adore thy name, grant thou to me that I may com-"prehend thee; grant thou that I may have peace in the "Ṭuat (underworld) and may possess all my members "[therein]. And the divine Soul which is in Nut (11) "saith:—'I will make my divine strength to protect "thee, and I will perform everything which thou hast "said.'"

RUBRIC: [This chapter] shall be recited over [a figure of] the god-of-the-lifted-hand which shall have plumes upon its head; the legs thereof shall be wide apart, and the middle portion of it shall be in the form of (12) a beetle, and it shall be painted blue with lapis-lazuli mixed with *qamài* water. And [it shall be recited over] a figure with a head like unto that of a man, and the hands and arms thereof shall be stretched (13) away [from its body]; above its right shoulder shall there be the head of a ram, and above its left shoulder shall there be the head of a ram. And thou shalt paint upon a piece of linen a figure of the god-of-the-lifted-hand (14) immediately over his heart, and thou shalt paint the [other] figure over the breasts. Let not the god Sukati (15) who is in the underworld know it. Then shall the deceased drink water from the source of the stream, and he shall shine like the stars in the heavens above.

CHAPTER CLXVI.

[From the Papyrus of Nebseni (Brit. Mus. No. 9900, sheet 21).

Vignette : A head-rest.

Text : (1) THE CHAPTER OF THE PILLOW.

"Thou art lifted up, O sick one that liest prostrate, "(2) O scribe Nebseni. (3) They lift up thy head to "the horizon, thou art raised up, and dost triumph by "reason of what hath been done for thee. Ptaḥ hath "overthrown (4) thine enemies [according to what] was "ordered to be done for thee. Thou art Horus, the "son of Hathor, Nesert, Nesertet, who giveth [back] "the head (5) after the slaughter. Thy head shall not "be carried away from thee after [the slaughter], thy "head shall never, never be carried away from thee."

CHAPTER CLXVII.

[From the Papyrus of Nebseni (Brit. Mus. No. 9900, sheet 22).]

Vignette : An *Utchat* resting upon the emblem of gold (?).

Text : (1) THE CHAPTER OF BRINGING THE UTCHAT. (2) Nebseni, the scribe, saith:—(3)

"The god Thoth hath brought the Utchat, (4) and "he hath made it to rest (*or* to be at peace) after it "departed, [O] (5) Rā. It was grievously afflicted by "storm, but Thoth (6) made it to be at rest after it "had departed from the storm. I am sound, (7) and it "is sound; I am sound, and it is sound; and Nebseni, "the lord of piety, is sound."

CHAPTER CLXVIII.

[From the Papyrus of Mut-ḥetep (Brit. Mus. No. 10,010, sheet 2).]

Vignette: (*a*) A stream upon which sail three boats. The first contains Khnemu, the second Kheperȧ, and the third Rā; each god is seated in a shrine. Harpocrates occupies the place of look-out in the boats of Khnemu and Rā. Behind the boats Rā is seated on a throne which rests on the water; two hands and arms stretch down from heaven and enshrine him. (*b*) A man-headed sphinx on a bier. A god with a serpent on his head. Two gods lying on biers with a serpent between. Anubis. A goddess

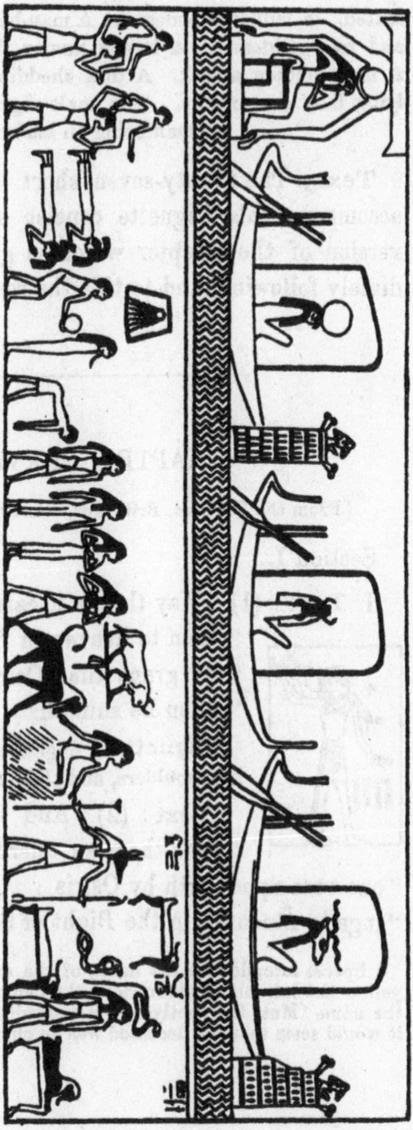

seated. A bull on a pedestal. A man-headed lion. Two gods and two goddesses. A bowed human figure and a mummy. A man holding a disk. A disk shedding light. Two women lying face downwards. Two male figures, each carrying a human being on his head.

Text: The twenty-seven short lines of text which accompany this Vignette consist of extracts from a version of the Chapter which is given in full immediately following, and to this the reader is referred.

CHAPTER CLXVIII.

[From the Papyrus, Brit. Mus. No. 10,478, sheets 2—7.]

Section I.

1. **Text**: (1) "May they who carry the burden above "them to heaven in front of the boat of "Rā grant that Osiris . . .[1] may see Rā "when he shineth."

Vignette: A god carrying a child upon his shoulders, and the number four, IIII.

Text: (2) "And there shall be made "unto them an offering of a libation of "one vase upon earth by Osiris . . . the lord of offer-"ings in Åmentet, in the Bight of Sekhet-ḥetep."

[1] Spaces intended for the name of the deceased are painted in yellow but left blank throughout the papyrus; from the fact that the name 'Mut' frequently occurs immediately following a space, it would seem that the deceased was an official of this goddess.

2. **Text**: (1) "May they who carry the burden "above them to heaven in front of the "boat of Rā grant that Osiris . . . . "may see Rā when he shineth."

Vignette: A god carrying a child upon his shoulders, and IIII.

Text: (2) "And there shall be made "unto them an offering of a libation of "one vase upon earth by Osiris . . . the follower of "the great god, the lord of the beautiful Ȧmentet."

---

3. **Text**: (1) "May they who smite Rā grant that "cakes shall come unto Osiris ". . . . as to the followers of Rā "[when] he setteth."

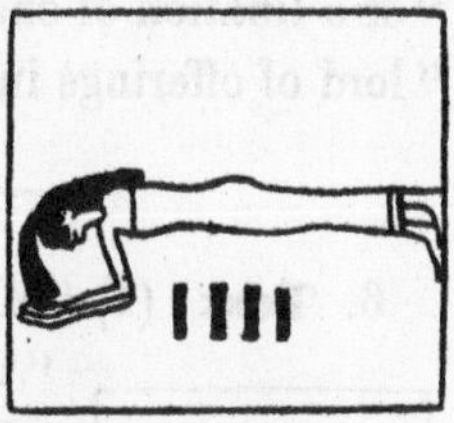

Vignette: A woman lying face downwards, and IIII.

Text: (2) "And there shall "be made unto them an offering "of a libation of one vase upon earth by Osiris . . . "when Horus, the lord of Ṭehent, cometh."

---

4. **Text**: (1) "May they who possess offerings grant "that Osiris . . . . shall exist, "even as do those who are in "the underworld."

Vignette: A woman lying face downwards, and IIII.

Text: (2) "And there shall be "made unto them an offering of a "libation of one vase upon earth by Osiris . . . . who "shall come forth and go in along with Rā for ever."

---

5. **Text**: (1) "May those who build up grant that "Osiris . . . . shall arrive happily in the Hall of Double "Truth."

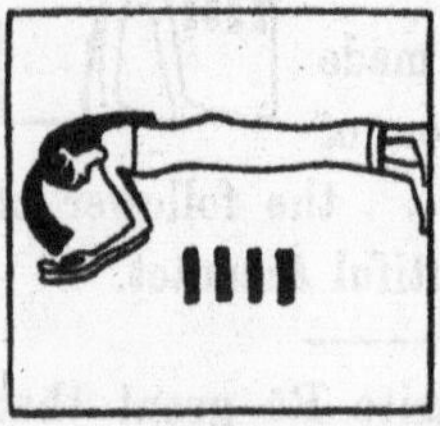

Vignette: A woman lying face downwards, and IIII.

Text: (2) "And there shall "be made unto them an offering "of a libation of one vase upon earth by Osiris . . . as "lord of offerings in the beautiful Åmentet."

---

6. **Text**: (1) "May those who make adorations grant "that Osiris . . . . shall follow after "Rā in his boat."

Vignette: A god bowing to the ground, and IIII.

Text: (2) "And there shall be "made unto them an offering of a "libation of one vase upon earth by "Osiris . . . . who shall walk with long strides with "the gods of the underworld."

---

7. **Text**: (1) "May those who have offerings, and

"who make sacrificial meals for the gods, grant obla-
"tions of *tchefau* food to Osiris . . . .
"in the underworld.

Vignette: A god holding upright a conical object ▽.

Text: (2) "And there shall be made "unto them an offering of a libation of "one vase upon earth by Osiris . . . . "along with them, whose souls shall stand up at the "pylon."

Section II. The gods of the eighth Qerert in the underworld, whose attributes are hidden, and who . . . . winds.

1. **Text**: (1) "May the gods who dwell in their "shrines, the princes of Nu, grant that "Osiris . . . . shall drink water."

Vignette: A god in a shrine, with three serpents in front of him and three behind him; at the entrance to the shrine is the number fourteen ∩ IIII.

Text: (2) "And there shall be "made unto them an offering of a "libation of one vase upon earth by Osiris . . . .; may "his soul live and his body be preserved in the under-"world."

2. Text: (1) "May the gods who are in the follow-"ing of Osiris grant that the body "of Osiris . . . . shall rest along "with his *sāḥ*."

Vignette: A woman, and a god, and the number fourteen ∩IIII.

Text: (2) "And there shall be "made unto them an offering of a "libation of one vase upon earth by Osiris . . . . by the "side of the great god within his boat."

---

3. Text: (1) "May Āḥā (*i.e.*, He who standeth) "make Osiris . . . . to praise Rā when he "riseth."

Vignette: A god, standing, holding a sceptre.

Text: (2) "And there shall be made "unto them an offering of a libation of "one vase upon earth by Osiris . . . . , "triumphant, who shall be with those who are over "[their] altars."

---

4. Text: (1) "May Āmen (*i.e.*, the Hidden one) "give power unto Osiris . . . . in "the Hall of Seb."

Vignette: A cow on a standard.

Text: (2) "And there shall be "made unto them an offering of a "libation of one vase upon earth by

"Osiris . . . . triumphant, who knoweth all the mysteries "of the Ṭuat."

---

5. **Text**: (1) "May Sheta (*i.e.*, the Secret one), "make the body of Osiris . . . . to grow "and to be sound upon earth and in the "underworld."

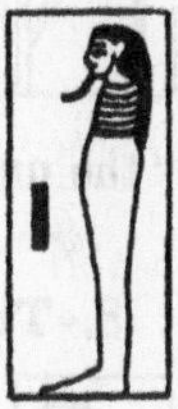

Vignette: A god standing upright.

Text: (2) "And there shall be made unto "them an offering of a libation of one vase "by Osiris . . . . as the lord of strides in "the underworld and in Re-stau."

---

6. **Text**: (1) "May Seṭeḳ give cakes and ale to "Osiris . . . . along with you in the "House of Osiris."

Vignette: A star and a god, standing, with a platform upon his head, whereon are a cow and an uraeus.

Text: (2) "And there shall be "made unto them an offering of a "libation of one vase upon earth by Osiris . . . . who "hath entered into all the secret places of the Ṭuat."

---

7. **Text**: (1) "May Sesheta Ȧusȧr (*i.e.*, he who "maketh Osiris to be secret) grant that Osiris . . . .

"may be a lord of stride[s] in the habitation of "Tchesert."

Vignette: A cow standing on a platform, and uraeus.

Text: (2) "And there shall be made "unto them an offering of a libation "of one vase upon earth when he "becometh the lord of an abode in "the underworld."

---

8. **Text**: (1) "May Sherem not allow any evil "thing to come to Osiris . . . . in the "underworld."

Vignette: A god standing upright.

Text: (2) "And there shall be made "unto them an offering of a libation of one "vase upon earth by Osiris . . . . the soul "that hearkeneth unto the words of the gods."

---

9. **Text**: (1) "May Sta (*i.e.*, the leader) grant that "Osiris . . . . may see Rā when he "riseth and when he setteth."

Vignette: A cow and uraeus upon a standard.

Text: (2) "And there shall be made "unto them an offering of a libation of "one vase upon earth by Osiris . . . .; "may his limbs live and may his limbs be sound for "ever."

10. **Text** : (1) "May Senk (*i.e.*, splendour), give "glory to Osiris . . . . upon earth, and "make him strong in Ȧmentet."

Vignette : A god standing upright.

Text : (2) "And there shall be made "unto them an offering of a libation of one "vase upon earth by Osiris . . . .; may "his legs have power as the lord of an "abode in Ȧmentet."

---

11. **Text** : (1) "May He-who-liveth-in-darkness "(*i.e.*, Horus) grant that Osiris . . . . "shall be among those who are over "their altars."

Vignette : A crocodile-headed god standing upright.

Text : (2) "And there shall be made "unto them an offering of a libation of "one vase upon earth by Osiris . . . . who is in the "everlasting Ṭuat."

---

12. **Text** : (1) "May the . . . . of Osiris . . . . "grant that he shall be near the great "god, the lord of Ȧmentet."

Vignette : A god standing upright, and the number four, IIII.

Text : (2) "And there shall be made "unto them an offering of a libation of "one vase upon earth by Osiris . . . .;

"may he become the lord of [his] hands and have power "over [his] heart in the underworld."

13. Text: (1) "May those whose hands hide grant "that Osiris . . . . shall be along with "them in the underworld."

Vignette: A goddess standing upright, and hiding something with her hands.

Text: (2) "And there shall be made "unto them an offering of a libation of "one vase upon earth by Osiris . . . . ; "may they bring me to the throne of Osiris."

14. Text: (1) "May those whose hands hide grant "that Osiris . . . shall be sound, and that "offerings shall be before him continually."

Vignette: [As in No. 13, but with IIII.]

Text: (2) "And there shall be made "unto them an offering of a libation of "one vase upon earth by Osiris . . . who "shall be [a lord of] horns and shall listen "unto the words of the gods."

15. Text: (1) "May He whose limbs are hidden "give right and truth to Osiris before "Rā, and in the company of his gods."

Vignette: A god standing upright.

Text: (2) "And there shall be made "unto them an offering of a libation of "one vase upon earth by Osiris . . . .

"as lord of the phallus and ravisher of women for "ever."

---

16. **Text**: (1) "May the souls who come forth open "the mouth of Osiris . . . . among "the gods who are along with them."

Vignette: A bird on a tree, and the number four, IIII.

Text: (2) "And there shall be "made unto them an offering of a "libation of one vase upon earth by "Osiris . . . . among the living ones, the lords of "eternity."

---

17. **Text**: (1) "May those who belong to their ". . . . grant that Osiris . . . . may "have power over his offerings upon "earth, even as have the gods, the lords "of [offerings]."

Vignette: A god standing upright, and the number four, IIII.

Text: (2) "And there shall be made "unto them an offering of a libation of one vase upon "earth by Osiris . . . . who shall be endowed abun- "dantly with *tchefau* food in the underworld."

---

18. **Text**: (1) "May those who receive grant that

"Osiris . . . . shall enter in over all the secret "places of the Ṭuat."

Vignette: A god bowing to the ground, and a star.

Text: (2) "And there shall be made "unto them an offering of a libation of "one vase upon earth by Osiris . . . "who shall have power over offerings "upon earth, and be the lord of altars."

---

19. **Text**: (1) "May the Ȧnenit (*i.e.*, Widows (?)) "grant that Osiris . . . shall be with "the great god as possessor of a "phallus before . . ."

Vignette: A woman kneeling on a couch.

Text: (2) "And there shall be "made unto them an offering of a "libation of one vase upon earth by Osiris . . . who "shall be ordered to dwell in the secret place in the "darkness."

---

20. **Text**: (1) "May Osiris-Anubis grant that "Osiris . . . may be a possessor of a "seat in Ta-tchesertet."

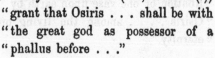

Vignette: Anubis holding a hawk-headed sceptre in each hand.

Text: (2) "And there shall be made "unto them an offering of a libation "of one vase upon earth by Osiris

"... . who shall go in and pass through the pylon of Osiris."

Section III.

THE GODS OF THE [TENTH] QERERT IN THE ṬUAT WHO ARE TO BE PRAISED AND WHOSE MYSTERIES ARE HOLY.

1. **Text**: (1) "May those who are denizens of light "grant that Osiris . . . shall shine in "the darkness."

Vignette: A god standing upright, and the number eight, IIII IIII.

Text: (2) "And there shall be made "unto them an offering of a libation of "one vase upon earth by Osiris . . . who "praiseth the great god in his abode day by day."

---

2. **Text**: (1) "May the Smiters grant that Osiris ". . . may be among those who sing "praises."

Vignette: A goddess standing upright holding in her upraised hand a hatchet dripping with blood, and the number eight, IIII IIII.

Text: (2) "And there shall be "made unto them an offering of a libation of one vase "upon earth by Osiris . . . . on the day when he "repulseth the serpent fiend Bi, the mighty one of "iniquity."

---

3. **Text**: (1) "May the company of the gods who "guard those who are in [the "Tuat], ... give the breaths "of life to Osiris upon earth and "in the underworld."

Vignette: A god lying on a bier, and the number nine, ||| |||.

Text: (2) "And there shall "be made unto them an offering of a libation of one "vase upon earth by Osiris . . . ., who shooteth forth "[his] hand, and repulseth him that cometh."

---

4. **Text**: (1) "May the company of the gods of the "hidden hand give glory unto Osiris ". . . . as unto the perfect *Khus*."

Vignette: A god standing upright, and the number nine, ||| |||.

Text: (2) "And there shall be made "unto them an offering of a libation "of one vase upon earth by Osisis . . . ., "who shall be sound upon earth and in the under-"world."

---

5. **Text**: (1) "May the Hidden goddess grant that

"the soul of Osiris . . . may grow, and that his "body may be preserved even as are "those of the gods who dwell in the "Tuat."

Vignette: A woman standing before an *Utchat*.

Text: (2) "And there shall be "made unto them an offering of a "libation of one vase upon earth by Osiris . . ., whose "soul shall rest upon whatever seat he pleaseth.

---

6. **Text**: (1) "May the souls of the gods who have "come into being in the members "of Osiris . . . grant that he "shall have peace."

Vignette: A woman lying upon her back, and the number twenty-one, ∩I∩.

Text: (2) "And there shall be "made unto them an offering of a libation of one vase "upon earth by Osiris . . ., who shall receive his place "in the land of the underworld."

---

7. **Text**: (1) "May those who praise Rā not turn "Osiris . . . back at the pylons of the "Tuat."

Vignette: A god standing upright, and the number four, IIII.

Text: (2) "And there shall be made unto "them an offering of a libation of one vase "upon earth by Osiris . . ., who shall come "forth by day and shall refresh himself in the place of "coolness."

---

8. **Text**: (1) "May the beings of warlike face grant "coolness unto Osiris . . . in the place of "flame."

Vignette: A woman standing upright, and the number four, IIII.

Text: (2) "And there shall be made "unto them an offering of a libation of one "vase upon earth by Osiris . . ., who shall "sit in the shrine with the great god."

Section IV.

THE GODS OF THE ELEVENTH QERERET [OF THE ṬUAT] . . . .

1. **Text**: (1) "May the goddess Àmemet grant that "Osiris . . . shall be strong before "the great god in the Ṭuat."

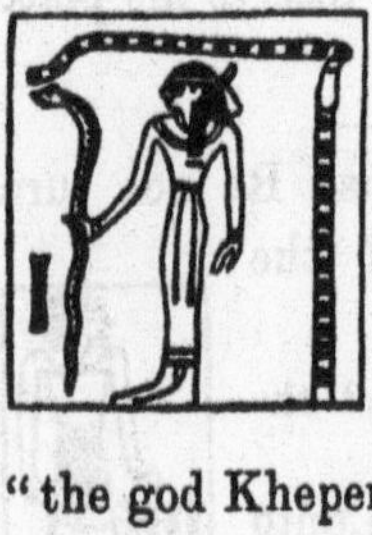

Vignette: A woman in a shrine.

Text: (2) "And there shall be "made unto them an offering of a "libation of one vase upon earth by "Osiris . . ., who shall become like "the god Kheperà in Àmentet."

---

2 **Text**: (1) "May the Soul of Àment grant sepul-

"chral meals unto Osiris . . . upon earth and in the "underworld.

Vignette: A god standing upright.

Text: (2) "And there shall be made "unto them an offering of a libation of "one vase upon earth by Osiris . . ., the "lord of the abode of peace in the moun-"tain of the underworld."

---

3. **Text**: (1) "May the Soul of the Earth make "Osiris . . . . to triumph over his ene-"mies in heaven and upon earth."

Vignette: A god standing upright, with drooping hands, and the number four, IIII.

Text: (2) "And there shall be made "unto them an offering of a libation of "one vase upon earth by Osiris . . . ., "whose body shall be concealed from any that would "look upon him."

---

4. **Text**: (1) "May those who sing praises grant that "Osiris . . . shall be like the divine "mariners who are in heaven."

Vignette: A god standing upright with his hands raised, and the number IIII.

Text: (2) "And there shall be "made unto them an offering of a "libation of one vase upon earth by

"Osiris . . . when he entereth through the hidden "pylons."

---

5. **Text**: (1) "May the company of the gods who "rule over Ament grant that Osiris ". . . . shall go in through the "secret door of the House of "Osiris."

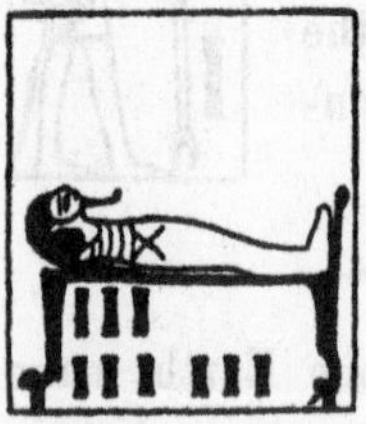

Vignette: A god lying upon a bier, and the number nine, III III III.

Text: (2) "And there shall be "made unto them an offering of a libation of one vase "upon earth by Osiris . . ., who shall walk with long "strides among the lords of the Ṭuat."

---

6. **Text**: (1) "May the company of the gods who "are in the following of Osiris "grant that Osiris . . . shall "have power over his enemies."

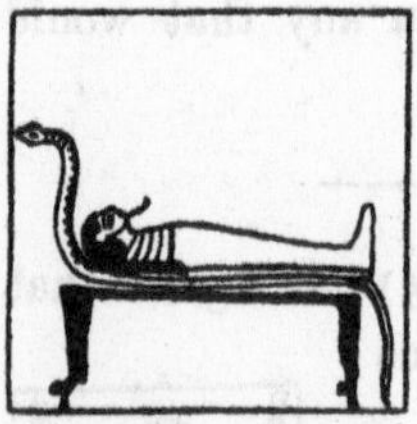

Vignette: A god lying upon, or by the side of, a serpent on a bier.

Text: (2) "And there shall be "made unto them an offering of "a libation of one vase upon earth by Osiris . . . when "he becometh a perfect soul day by day (?)."

---

7. **Text**: (1) "May Åqeh grant that Osiris shall be

"with Rā, and that he shall walk over heaven for "ever."

Vignette: A god standing upright and holding a sceptre.

Text: (2) "And there shall be made "unto them an offering of a libation of "one vase upon earth by Osiris . . . when "he is in the following of him that "dwelleth in the city of embalmment (*i.e.*, Anubis), the "lord of Ta-tchesert."

---

8. **Text**: (1) "May those who . . . . Osiris grant "that the soul of Osiris . . . . may live, and "that it may never die a second time."

Vignette: A god standing upright, and the number four, IIII.

Text: (2) "And there shall be made "unto them an offering of a libation of one "vase upon earth by Osiris . . ., for whom "lamentation shall be decreed as for his god."

---

9. **Text**: (1) "May the Nine Watchers grant that "Osiris . . . may wake up and that "he may never be destroyed."

Vignette: Anubis on a standard, and the number nine, III III III.

Text: (2) "And there shall be "made unto them an offering of a "libation of one vase upon earth by Osiris . . ., trium-"phant before Osiris, the lord of the land of the Lake."

10. **Text**: (1) "May the Nine Mourners cause "mourning to be made for Osiris ". . . as was made for Osiris."

Vignette: A woman lying on the ground face downwards.

Text: (2) "And there shall be "made unto them an offering of a "libation of one vase upon earth "by Osiris . . . when his soul cometh forth with the "*Khu.*"

---

11. **Text**: (1) "May he that invoketh Rā invoke "Osiris . . . before Rā and before the "company of his gods."

Vignette: A god crying out to some one.

Text: (2) "And there shall be made "unto them an offering of a libation of "one vase upon earth by Osiris . . . "when his soul goeth into the hidden "place and cometh forth from earth."

---

12. **Text**: (1) "May Āqen drive away every evil "thing from Osiris . . . for ever."

Vignette: A god standing upright with hands hanging down.

Text: (2) "And there shall be made "unto them an offering of a libation of one "vase upon earth by Osiris . . . when he "cometh in peace and hath triumphed."

13. **Text**: (1) "May those who dwell with Ṭesert "grant that Osiris . . . . may go in "and come out with long strides like "the lords of the Ṭuat."

Vignette: A woman-headed serpent on a pylon.

Text: (2) "And there shall be "made unto them an offering of a "libation of one vase upon earth by Osiris . . ., who "shall go in and come forth through the door of the "Ṭuat."

---

14. **Text**: (1) "May the goddess Ṭesert grant that "Osiris . . . may have power over the "water."

Vignette: A god standing upright, and the number four, IIII.

Text: (2) "And there shall be made "unto them an offering of a libation of one "vase upon earth by Osiris . . . . when he "shall walk up the Great Staircase."

---

15. **Text**: (1) "May Meḥenit grant that Osiris . . . "may be a distinguished being in the "Ṭuat for ever."

Vignette: A serpent on a pylon.

Text: (2) "And there shall be made "unto them an offering of a libation of "one vase upon earth by Osiris . . . "as a perfect soul in his shrine."

16. **Text**: (1) "May those who dwell with Meḥenit "grant that Osiris . . . may walk with "long strides in the holy place."

Vignette: A woman standing upright, and the number four, IIII.

Text: (2) "And there shall be made unto "them an offering of a libation of one vase "upon earth by Osiris . . . . when he is "with the followers of Horus."

---

17. **Text**: (1) "May the company of the gods who "hide Osiris grant that Osiris . . . "shall sit upon the throne which he "loveth."

Vignette: A seated god, and the number nine, III III III.

Text: (2) "And there shall be made "unto them an offering of a libation "of one vase upon earth by Osiris . . ., who shall be "among the lords of Maāt."

---

18. **Text**: (1) "May he that destroyeth the face "open the face of Osiris . . and let him see "the *Khu*."

Vignette: A god standing upright.

Text: (2) "And there shall be made unto "them an offering of a libation of one vase "upon earth by Osiris . . ., who shall be in "the following of the goddess Meḥi of "Amentet."

Section V.

THE GODS OF THE TWELFTH QERERET IN THE ṬUAT . . . .

1. **Text**: (1) "May Maāt grant that Osiris . . . "be a lord of the Lake of Maāti."

Vignette: A god standing upright and holding a sceptre.

Text: (2) "And there shall be made "unto them an offering of a libation of "one vase upon earth by Osiris . . . as a "lord of offerings in Sekhet-Åaru."

---

2. "**Text**: (1) "May the gods who dwell in the land "of the Ṭuat grant justice unto Osiris . . . "in the Hall of Double Truth."

Vignette: A god standing upright and holding a sceptre.

Text: (2) "And there shall be made "unto them an offering of a libation of "one vase upon earth by Osiris . . ., "who shall plough in Sekhet-Ḥetep."

---

3. **Text**: (1) "May the gods who dwell with Meḥen "grant that Osiris . . . shall be "in whatsoever place his *ka* "wisheth to be."

Vignette: A god within the folds of a serpent.

Text: (2) "And there shall "be made unto them an offering "of a libation of one vase upon earth by Osiris . . ., "who shall come into being at the words of the "lord of Åmentet."

---

4. **Text**: (1) "May the gods who possess land grant "a lake unto Osiris . . . in Sekhet-"Åanru."

Vignette: A god standing upright, and the number four, IIII.

Text: (2) "And there shall be made "unto them an offering of a libation of "one vase upon earth by Osiris . . ., who "shall sit upon whatsoever place he would there."

---

5. **Text**: (1) "May Ḥer-ta (?) grant an estate unto "Osiris . . . in Sekhet-Ḥetep."

Vignette: A snake-headed god.

Text: (2) "And there shall be made "unto them an offering of a libation of "one vase upon earth by Osiris . . ., "who shall be protected by amulets (?) "like the lords of the Ṭuat."

---

6. **Text**: (1) "May the gods who dwell in the land

"grant offerings, and *tchefau* food, and joints of meat "to Osiris . . . in the underworld."

Vignette: A god standing upright with arms hanging down, and the number four, IIII.

Text: (2) "And there shall be made "unto them an offering of a libation of "one vase upon earth by Osiris . . . when "Rā sitteth in Manu."

---

7. **Text**: (1) "May the Chiefs of the secret things "who dwell in the land place their wall "behind Osiris . . . even as they do for "the Still-Heart."

Vignette: A ram-headed sceptre.

Text: (2) "And there shall be made unto "them an offering of a libation of one vase "upon earth by Osiris . . . when he cometh "forth and goeth into the underworld."

---

8. **Text**: (1) "May the gods who dwell in the folds "of the serpent goddess Meḥen "grant a sight of the Disk to "Osiris . . ."

Vignette: A god within the folds of a serpent.

Text: (2) "And there shall be "made unto them an offering of "a libation of one vase upon earth by Osiris . . .

"as a *khu* who hath gained power over fresh "water."

---

9. Text: (1) "May Àuu-ba (?) grant peace unto "Osiris . . . in Àmentet."

Vignette: A god bowing.

Text: (2) "And there shall be made "unto them an offering of a libation of one "vase upon earth by Osiris . . . in coming "out and going into Àment, along with "other folk [therein]."

CHAPTER CLXIX.

[From the Papyrus of Nefer-uben-f (see Naville, *op. cit.*, Bd. I. Bl. 190).]

Vignette: This Chapter is without vignette.

Text: The Chapter of making to stand up the Ḥenkit.[1] (1) The *Àm-kheut*, Osiris Nefer-uben-f, triumphant, saith:—

"Thou art the Lion god. Thou art the double Lion-"god. Thou art Horus, the avenger of his father "[Osiris]. Thou art Four, the four glorious gods.

[1] *I.e.*, the funeral bed.

"Acclamation is made [unto thee], along with cries "of delight (2) and sounds of joy, and the water from "their haunches and from their thighs I bring [unto "thee]. Thou art lifted up on thy right side, and thou "art lifted up on thy left side. The god Seb hath "opened for thee (3) thy two eyes which were blind, and "he hath given [thee] the power to stretch out thy legs "[in walking]. Hath been bound unto thee thy heart "(*ȧb*), [thy] mother, and thy heart (*ḥāt*) is in thy body. "Thy soul is in heaven, and thy body is under the "ground. There are cakes for thy body, and water for "thy throat, and sweet (4) breezes for thy nostrils, "and thou art satisfied with offerings. Those who "dwell in their shrines open their abodes (?) unto "thee, thou hast thy provisions (?), and thou journeyest "along. Thou art stablished upon that which ema-"nateth from thy existence, and thou comest forth "from heaven. The cord hath been coiled up for thee "(5) by the side of Rā, and thou snarest fish with the "net in the stream from which thou drinkest vessels of "water. Thou performest a journey on thy legs, and "in going forward thou dost not stumble (?); thou "comest forth (6) from over the earth, thou dost not "make thy appearance from below the walls [thereof]. "Thy walls are not thrown down, and what there is of "thine within hath been made for thee by the god of "thy city. Thou art pure, thou art pure. Thy fore "parts are washed by libations, and thy hinder parts "are cleansed (7) with resin and natron, and made cool "with incense. Thou art made clean with the milk of "the Ḥāp cow, and with the ale of the goddess Tenemit, "and with natron. All the evil which clung to thee "(8) hath been done away with, and Tefnet, the "daughter of Rā, hath made offerings on thy behalf "even as she did for her father Rā; and the funeral "valley which was the burial-place of her father Osiris "hath been set in order for thee. I make to eat of the "sweet things (9) which he giveth there the Osiris "Nefer-uben-f, triumphant, that is to say, the celestial "cakes which are before Rā, and the grain (?), and "drink, and the four terrestrial cakes which are before "the god Seb, and the grain [brought by] the citizens. "(10) I have brought unto thee Sekhet-ḥetep and the "gifts thereof are before thee. Thou comest forth as "Rā, thou hast gotten power as Rā, and thou hast "gotten power over thy legs; and thou, O Osiris "Nefer-uben-f, hast gotten power over thy legs at "every (11) season and at every hour. Thou hast "not been condemned in the judgment, thou hast not "been put under restraint, a guard hath not been set "over thee, thou hast not been imprisoned, and thou "hast not been given over to the chamber of the Fiends "(12) therein. The sand is gathered together before "thy face and guarded are the offerings which are for "thee; thy face is not suffered to be turned back, and "thou art guarded and dost not come forth. Thou "hast received thy tunic, and thy sandals, and thy "stick, (13) and thy garment, and thy weapons for "fighting of all kinds wherewith thou shalt cut off "heads; thou shalt turn back the necks of thy foes "whom thou shalt take captive, and thou shalt keep "away from thee death so that it shall not come nigh "unto thee. And the (14) Great God hath said concerning thee: 'Bring him [hither] on the day when "events take place.' The Hawk rejoiceth in thee, and "the *Smen* goose cackleth at thee. Rā openeth for "thee the doors of heaven, and Seb unbolteth for thee "the earth. (15) Thy *khu* is mighty, and it is perfect "knowing thy name; thy soul maketh a way through "Åment, and thy perfect soul, O Nefer-uben-f, triumphant, hath the power of speech. Thy form is within "Rā, (16) and it resteth within the divine sovereign "chiefs of him who uniteth the two paths; mankind "keepeth guard over it, and the double Lion-god guideth "it, to the place where thou, O Osiris Nefer-uben-f, "triumphant, makest thy *ka* to rest. And behold, the "two lands and mankind work (17) the snare for thee. "Thou livest, thy soul is strong, thy body is enduring "and great, thou hast sight of the fire, thou dost snuff "the breeze, thy face doth penetrate into the house of "darkness, (18) thou abidest at the Gap, thou dost not "see the whirlwind and the storm, thou followest in "the train of the prince of the two lands, and thou "refreshest thyself on the branch of *merit* tree on both "sides of the god Ur-ḥekau. The goddess Seshetet "sitteth (19) before thee, the god Sa protecteth thy "members, the steer and his cow give thee milk from "the breast [in] the following of Sekhat-Ḥeru. Thou "washest thyself at the mouth of the stream of Kher-"āḥa, (20) thou art in favour with the princes of the "cities of Pe and Ṭep, the god Thoth and thyself see "each other, and Rā in heaven holdeth converse with "thee, thou comest forth from and thou enterest into "the *ȧnit* chamber, and thou holdest converse with the "two divine combatants (*i.e.*, Horus and Set). (21) "Thy *ka* is with thee to make thee to rejoice, thy heart "is with thee to [give thee] thy transformations, happy ". . . keep watch over thee, the company of the gods "make thy heart glad, thou comest forth to four cakes "in the city of Sekhem, and four in (22) the city of "Ȧqennu, thou comest forth to four in the city of "Ȧnnu, upon the altar of the lady of the two lands. "The stars keep watch over thee by night, the lords "of Ȧnnu have a favour unto thee, the god Ḥu is in "thy mouth, thy feet are not (23) turned back, and thy "members have life. Thou graspest the *smȧ* in Ȧbṭu, "the sacrificial cakes of the divine chiefs and the liba-"tions of the celestial beings are brought forward to "thee, with the offerings in the festival (24) which are "due to Osiris on the morning of the Uaḳ festival for "hidden things (?). Thou art ornamented with objects "of gold, and thine apparel is interwoven (?) with "byssus. Ḥāpi (*i.e.*, the Nile) thrusteth himself upon "thy body (25), thou hast power over the tablet (?) "which is inscribed with [lists of] offerings, and thou "drinkest water on both sides of the Lake of Ṭesṭes (?).

"The gods who are there have a favour unto thee, "and thou comest forth from heaven along with the "gods (26) who make to advance the *maāt* of Rā, and "thou art led into the presence of the company of the "gods; and there is done for thee even as it is done "for one of them. Thou art the *Khart* bird of the "geese, and Ptaḥ of the Southern (27) Wall maketh "an offering unto Nefer-uben-f, triumphant."

CHAPTER CLXX.

[From the Papyrus of Nefer-uben-f (see Naville, *op. cit.*, Bd. I. Bl. 191).]

Vignette: This Chapter is without vignette.

Text: THE CHAPTER OF ARRANGING THE ḤENKIT.[1] (1) The Osiris Nefer-uben-f saith:—

"Thy flesh have I given unto thee. Thy bones have "I fastened together for thee. Thy members have I "collected for thee. The earth submitteth itself unto "thee. Thy limbs are guarded. Thou art the (2) "mighty one within the egg. Thou art set in order. "Thou seest the gods (?). Thou settest out on thy "way, and thy hand [reacheth] unto the horizon,

[1] *I.e.*, the funeral bed.

"and unto the holy place where thou wouldst be. "There is acclamation made unto thee, and there are "(3) shouts of joy raised to thee at thine appearances "at the altar. Horus maketh thee to stand up at his "risings, even as he did him who is in the chamber of "holiness. Hail, Osiris Nefer-uben-f, triumphant, the "goddess Ua (?) hath given thee birth, (4) and Ȧnpu "(Anubis), who dwelleth upon his hill, hath set thee "in order, and he hath fastened for thee thy swathings. "Hail, Nefer-uben-f, the god Ptaḥ-Sekri hath given "unto thee of the ornaments of the divine house which "he hath. (5) Hail, Nefer-uben-f, the god Thoth him-"self cometh unto thee with the books of holy words, "and he maketh thy hand [to reach] unto the horizon, "even unto the place [wherein] thy *ka* loveth to be; "and Osiris worketh [for thee on] the night of journey-"ing unto life. Thy white crown (6) is stablished on "thy brow. The god Nemu is with thee, and he giveth "unto thee fine feathered fowl. Hail, Osiris Nefer-"uben-f, triumphant, thou hast been set in order upon "thy funeral couch; thou comest forth, and Rā (7) "who is in the hidden horizon within his boat hath "set thee in order. Hail, Osiris Nefer-uben-f, trium-"phant, the god Tem, the father of the gods, hath "made for thee the things which are to endure for "ever. Hail, Osiris Nefer-uben-f, triumphant, (8) the "god Ȧmsu of Qebti hath set thee in order, and the "gods of the shrine praise thee. Hail, Osiris Nefer-"uben-f, with two-fold happiness thou settest out in "peace to thine everlasting habitation and to thine "abode of eternity. Homage is paid unto thee (9) in "the cities of Pe and Ṭepu in the shrine which thy *ka* "loveth and before thine abode, and thou art the "mighty one of souls, ... and hath "set thee in order, and the gods embrace thee. (10) "Thou art like a god, and thou hast been begotten for "transformations which are more numerous and with "a created form more perfect than those of the gods. "Thou hast more light (?) than the *Khus* and thou "art more mighty of souls than are those who are in "[them]. Hail, (11) Osiris Nefer-uben-f, Ptaḥ on his "Southern Wall hath set thee in order, and he hath "made to advance thine abode more than [that of] the "gods. Hail, Osiris, the *ȧm-khent*, Nefer-uben-f, thou "art Horus, the son of Isis, begotten of (12) Ptaḥ; "and Nut hath created [thee] a being of light like unto "Rā in the horizon when he illumineth the two lands "with his beauteous light. And the gods say unto "thee:—'Come forward, advance now and look thou "upon the things which are thine in thine (13) abode "of everlastingness.' The goddess Rennutet, the heir "and first-born of Tem, hath set thee in order in the "presence of the company of the gods (14) of Nut. I, "even I, am the heir of heaven, and the fellow of the "God who maketh his light. I have come forth from "the womb, and I shall grow young again even as doth "(15) my father, and I shall not be prevented from "making [my] answer in my season."

CHAPTER CLXXI.

[From the Papyrus of Àmen-ḥetep (see Mariette, *Papyrus de Boulaq*, Tom. III. Pl. 7).]

Vignette: This Chapter has no vignette.

Text: (1) THE CHAPTER OF TYING ON THE GARMENT OF PURITY (*āb*).

"O Tem, O Shu, O Tefnut, O Seb, O Nut, O Osiris, "O Isis, O Set, O Nephthys, (2) O Ḥeru-khuti (Har-"machis), O Hathor in the Great House, O Kheperȧ, "O Menthu, the lord of Thebes, O Àmen, the lord of "the thrones of the two lands, O Great Company of "the gods, O Little Company of the gods, O gods and "goddesses who dwell in (3) Nu, O Sebek of the two "*Meḥt*, O Sebek in all thy manifold names in thine "every place wherein thy *Ka* hath delight, O gods (4) "of the south, O gods of the north, O ye who are in "heaven, O ye who are upon earth, grant ye (5) this "garment of purity to the perfect *Khu* of Àmen-ḥetep. "Grant ye your strength [unto him], (6) and destroy "ye [all] the evil which belongeth unto Àmen-ḥetep by "means of this garment of purity. Hold [ye] him "guiltless, then, for ever and ever, and destroy ye [all] "the evil which belongeth unto him."

CHAPTER CLXXII.

[From the Papyrus of Nebseni (Brit. Mus. No. 9900, sheets 32, 33).]

Vignette: This Chapter has no vignette.

Text: (1) "THE FIRST OF THE CHAPTERS OF THE ARRANGEMENTS (OR PRAISINGS) WHICH ARE TO BE PERFORMED IN THE UNDERWORLD.

"[I snuff] the *bet* incense, I inhale the scent of "*ḥesmen* (natron) and (2) incense . . . ., I am pure "with the purity of . . . . ., [pure are] the praises "which come forth from my mouth, more pure than "*maāt* (?) itself (3) . . . . of the fish that are in "the river; to the statue of the Temple of *Ḥesmen* "(natron). Pure are the praises (4) of the scribe "Nebseni, the designer of the house of gold, begotten "of the scribe and designer Thena, triumphant, born "of the lady of the house Mut-resthȧ, triumphant. And "as for the scribe Nebseni, the lord of piety, who is "happy with a two-fold happiness, (5) Ptaḥ hath a "favour unto him, and He of the Southern Wall hath "a favour unto him, and every god hath a favour unto "him, and every goddess hath a favour unto him. "Thy beauties are a stream (6) [bearing] things which "cause rest and are like unto water which floweth "nearer (?); thy beauties are like a hall of festival "wherein each man may exalt his [own] god; thy "beauties are like unto the pillar of the god Ptaḥ "(7) and like the courtyard of incense (?) of Rā. Neb-"seni, the scribe and designer of the Temple of Ptaḥ, "hath been made a pillar of Ptaḥ, and the libation "vase of the god of the Southern Wall."

I. (8) "Hail, verily thou art invoked; hail, verily, "thou art invoked. Hail, verily thou art lamented. "Verily, thou art praised; verily, thou art exalted; "verily, thou art glorious; verily, thou art strong. "Hail, thou scribe Nebseni, thou who hast been raised "up, (9) thou art raised up by means of the ceremonies "which have been performed for thee. Thine enemies "have fallen and the god Ptaḥ hath thrown down head-"long (10) thy foes; thou hast triumphed over them "and thou hast gained power over them. They obey "thy words and they perform that which thou orderest "them [to do]; thou art raised up, and thy word is a "law unto the divine sovereign chiefs of every god, and "of every goddess." (11)

II. "Hail, verily thou art invoked; hail, verily thou "art invoked. Thy head, O my lord, is a standard "with locks of rippling hair like unto the hair of a "woman of Asia; thy face shineth more brightly than "the House (12) of the Moon-god; the upper part of "thy head is azure in colour; thy locks are blacker "than the doors of the underworld; thy hair is dark "as night; thy visage is decorated with an azure blue;

"(13) the rays of Rā are upon thy face; thy garments "are of gold which Horus hath deftly ornamented with "azure blue; thine eye-brows are the two sister god-"desses who are at peace with each other whom Horus "(14) hath deftly ornamented with azure blue; thy "nose snuffeth in and thy nostrils exhale as it were "the winds from heaven. Thine eyes look towards "(15) Mount Bakhau of the rising sun; thine eye-"lashes are fixed each day, and the upper eyelids to "which they belong are of veritable lapis-lazuli; the "apples of thine eyes are [as] offerings of peace (?); "and the lower eyelids are filled with (16) eye-paint of "*mestchem.* Thy two lips give unto thee law, they "repeat unto [thee] the law of Rā, and they make to "be at peace the hearts of the gods. Thy teeth are the "two heads (17) of the serpent goddess Meḥen which "sport (?) with the Horus gods; thy tongue is made "skilful; thy speech is more shrill than that of the "*tcheru* bird of the field; thy jawbones are starry "lamps; (18) thy breasts (?) are stablished upon their "seats; and they journey unto the funeral mountain "of Ȧmentet."

III. "[Hail, verily thou art invoked; hail, verily "thou art invoked.] Thy neck is decorated with gold, "and (19) it is girt about (?) with refined copper. Thy "gullet and throat are those of Ȧnpu; thy bones are "the bones of the two Uatch goddesses; thy backbone "is (20) studded with gold, and is girt about (?) with "refined copper; thy loins (?) are those of Nephthys;

"thy . . . is a Nile which is without water; thy "buttocks (21) are two crystal eggs; thy thighs are "strong for walking; thou sittest upon thy seat; and "the gods [give] (22) unto thee thine eyes, O scribe "Nebseni, thou lord of piety."

IV. "[Hail, verily thou art invoked; hail, verily "thou art invoked.] Thy throat is the throat of Ȧnpu; "thy members (23) are plated with gold; thy breasts "are two crystal eggs which Horus hath deftly orna-"mented with azure blue; thy shoulders are made like "unto crystal; thine arms (24) are stablished through "the strength which protecteth them; thy heart is "glad each day; thy breast is of the work of the two "divine Forms; thy person adoreth the starry deities "who dwell in the heights and depths of heaven; (25) "thy belly is, as it were, the heavens; thy navel is the "Ṭuat (*i.e.*, underworld) which is open, and which "ordereth the light in the darkness, and the offerings "of which are (26) *ānkhām* flowers. And Nebseni "praiseth the majesty of Thoth, the beloved one, "[saying]:—'May his beauties be in my tomb, and "may all the purity which he loveth (27) be there "even as my God hath commanded for me.'"

V. "Hail, verily thou art invoked; hail, verily thou "art invoked. Thy two hands are a pool of water in "the season of an abundant inundation, a pool of water "fringed about with the divine offering of the water-"god. Thy (28) thighs are encircled with gold; thy "knees are the plants of the waters which are the nests "of the birds; thy feet are stablished each day; thy "legs lead thee into a (29) path of happiness, O scribe "Nebseni, thou favoured one. Thy hands and arms "are pillars (?) [set] upon their pedestals; thy fingers "are strips (?) of gold, the nails of which are like sharp "flakes (30) of flint by reason of the works which they "perform for thee."

VI. "Hail, verily thou art invoked; hail, verily "thou art invoked. Thou clothest thyself with the "garment of purity (*ābu*), and behold, thou drawest off "from thyself the *umet* garment when (31) thou goest "up to stretch thyself upon the couch (?). Haunches "of meat are cut for thy *ka*, O scribe Nebseni, and a "breast (*or* heart) of the animal is offered unto thy "*sāḥu*. Thou receivest a garment of the finest linen "(32) from the hands of the ministrant (?) of Rā; thou "eatest the cakes upon the cloth which the goddess "Tait herself hath prepared; thou eatest the haunch "of the animal (33); thou takest boldly the joint which "Rā hath endowed with power in his holy place; thou "washest thy feet in the silver basins which the god "Seker, the artificer, hath wrought; and behold, (34) "thou eatest of the cake which appeareth on the altar "and which the two divine fathers have sanctified. "Thou eatest of the baked bread and of the hot meats "of the storehouse; thou (35) smellest the flowers; "thy heart feareth not [to advance] to the altar of the "offerings made to thee; and those who feed thee with "food make for thee the loaves and bread-cakes of the

"Souls of Ånnu (Heliopolis), (36) and they themselves "bear them unto thee. Thine offerings (?) are ordered "for thee, and thy ordinances are in the gates of the "Great House. Thou risest up like Saḥ (Orion); thou "arrivest like the star Bau; (37) and the goddess Nut "[stretcheth out] her hands unto thee. Saḥ (Orion), "the son of Rā, and Nut, who gave birth to the gods— "the two mighty gods in heaven—speak each to the "other, saying, (38) 'Take the scribe and draughtsman "Nebseni into thine arms, and I will take him into "mine on this day, and let us make happiness for him "when praises are sung to him and when mention is "made of him, and when [his name] is in the mouth "of all young men and maidens.' (39) Thou art raised "up, [O Nebseni,] and thou hearest the songs of com-"memoration through the door of thy house."

VII. "Hail, verily thou art invoked; hail, verily "thou art invoked. Anubis hath bestowed upon thee "thy winding-sheet, he hath (40) wrought [for thee] "according to his will, he hath provided thee with the "ornaments of his bandages, for he is the overseer of "the great god. Thou settest out on thy way and thou "hast been washed in the Lake of Perfection; thou "makest offerings in the celestial mansions, and thou "propitiatest (41) the lords of Ånnu (Heliopolis). The "water of Rā is presented unto thee in vessels, and "milk in large vases. Thou art raised up and thou "makest offerings upon the altar, thou washest thy "feet upon the stone of . . . . . (42) on the banks "of the Lake of God. Thou comest forth and thou "seest Rā upon the pillars which are the arms of "heaven, upon the head of Ȧn-mut-f and upon the "arms of Ȧp-uat; he openeth out for thee a way "(43) and thou seest the horizon wherein is the "place of purity which thou lovest."

VIII. "Hail, verily thou art invoked; hail, verily "thou art invoked. Offerings are allotted unto thee "in the presence of Rā, and according to that which "Horus and Thoth ordered for thee thou hast had a "beginning and aṇ end. (44) They invoke thee, O "scribe Nebseni, and see thy splendour there, causing "thee to come forth [as] a god (45) and to advance to "the Souls of Ȧnnu. Thou goest forth upon the great "roads in thy *Sāḥ*, who hast received the offerings of "thy father upon thy two hands; thou art furnished "with linen garments each day, at the beginning of "the journey of the god through the gates of the (46) "Great House."

IX. "Hail, verily thou art invoked; hail, verily "thou art invoked. The scribe Nebseni hath air for "his nose and breath for his nostrils, and one thousand "geese, and fifty baskets of pure and fair offerings. "Hail, Nebseni, thine enemies have fallen down head-"long and they shall nevermore exist."

CHAPTER CLXXIII.

[From the Papyrus of Nebseni (Brit. Mus. No. 9900, sheets 9 and 10).]

Vignette: "Osiris, the great god, the lord of Àbṭu, the lord of transformations, the prince of eternity," seated in a shrine; to the left of the text the deceased stands, with hands raised in adoration, before the god, and the ground between them is covered with the bodies of birds and beasts which have been prepared for sacrifice (see pp. 390, 391).

Text: The speeches of Horus to his divine father Osiris when he entereth in to see him, and when he cometh forth from near the great *Abt* chamber to look upon Rā as Un-nefer, the lord of Ta-tchesert; then doth each embrace the other at the pleasure of his *Khu*, there in the underworld. (1) A Hymn of Praise to Osiris, governor of those in the underworld, the great god, the lord of Abydos, the king of eternity, the prince of everlastingness, the holy god in Re-stau, (2) by the scribe Nebseni, who saith :— (3)

"I ascribe praise unto thee, O lord of the gods, thou "God One, who livest (4) upon right and truth, behold, "I thy son Horus come unto thee; (5) I have avenged "thee, and I have brought to thee *maāt*—even to the "place where is the company of thy gods. (6) Grant "thou that I may have my being among those who are "in thy following, for I have overthrown all thy (7) "foes, and I have stablished all those who are of thy "substance upon the earth for ever and ever."

[Here follow forty declarations, each of which is preceded by the words "Hail, Osiris, I am thy "son."]

(8) "I have come, and I have avenged [thee, O my "father Osiris].

(9) "I have come, and I have overthrown for thee "thine enemies.

(10) "I have come, and I have done away with every "evil thing which belcngeth unto thee.

(11) "I have come, and I have slain for thee him that "attacked thee.

(12) "I have come, and I have sent forth mine arm "against those who were hostile towards thee.

(13) "I have come, and I have brought unto thee "the fiends of Set with their fetters upon them.

(14) "I have come, and I have brought unto thee "the land of the South, and I have united unto thee "the land of the North.

(15) "I have come, and I have stablished for thee "divine offerings from the South and from the North.

(16) "I have come, and I have ploughed[1] for thee "the fields.

(17) "I have come, and I have filled for thee the "canals with water.

(18) "I have come, and I have hoed up for thee the "ground.

(19) "I have come, and I have built cisterns for thee.

(20) "I have come, and I have gone round about the "soil for thee.

(21) "I have come, and I have made sacrificial "victims of those who were hostile to thee.

[1] The text actually has, "I have overthrown."

(22) "I have come, and I have made sacrifices unto "thee of thine animals and victims for slaughter.

(23) "I have come, and I have supplied [thee] with "food in abundance [of the creatures which are upon "earth].

(24) "I have come, and I have brought unto thee ". . . . . . .

(25) "I have come, and I have slain for thee ". . . . .

(26) "I have come, and I have smitten for thee "emasculated beasts.

(27) "I have come, and I have netted for thee birds "and feathered fowl.

(28) "I have come, and I have taken captive for "thee thine enemies in their chains.

(29) "I have come, and I have fettered for thee thine "enemies with fetters.

(30) "I have come, and I have brought for thee cool "water from Ȧbu (Elephantine), wherewith thou "mayest refresh thine heart.

(31) "I have come, and I have brought unto thee "herbs of every kind.

(32) "I have come, and I have stablished for thee "those who are of thy substance daily.

(33) "I have come, and I have made thy cakes in "the city of Pe of the red barley.

(34) "I have come, and I have made thy ale in the "city of Ṭepu of the white grain.

(35) "I have come, and I have ploughed for thee "wheat and barley in Sekhet-Åaru.

(36) "I have come, and I have reaped it for thee "therein.

(37) "I have come, and I have glorified thee.

(38) "I have come, and I have given [to thee] thy "souls.

(39) "I have come, and I have given [to thee] thy "power.

(40) "I have come, and I have given [to thee thy] ". . . . .

(41) "I have come, and I have given [to thee thy] ". . . .

(42) "I have come, and I have given [to thee] thy "terror.

(43) "I have come, and I have given [to thee] thy "victory.

(44) "I have come, and I have given to thee thine "eyes, [which are] the plumes on thy head.

(45) "I have come, and I have given [to thee] Isis "and Nephthys that they may stablish thee.

(46) "I have come, and I have filled for thee the "Eye of Horus [with] oil (*or* unguent).

(47) "I have come, and I have brought unto thee the "Eye of Horus, whereby thy face shall be destroyed."

CHAPTER CLXXIV.

[From the Papyrus of Mut-ḥetep (Brit. Mus. No. 10,010, sheet 3).]

Vignette : The deceased standing with her back towards a door from which she has just come forth.

Text : (1) THE CHAPTER OF CAUSING THE *KHU* TO COME FORTH FROM THE GREAT DOOR.[1] Mut-ḥetepeth, triumphant, saith :—

"Thy son hath offered up for thee [a sacrifice], and "the divine mighty ones tremble (2) when they look "upon the slaughtering knife which is in thy hand "[when] thou comest forth from the Tuat. Homage "to thee, O god Saa, the god Seb hath created thee, "and the company of the gods have given birth unto "thee. (3) Horus resteth upon his Eye, and the god "Tem resteth upon his years, and the gods of the east

[1] For the original form of this Chapter as found in the Pyramid of Unás, see Maspero, *Recueil de Travaux*, tom. IV. p. 43, ll. 379—399.

"and of the west rest upon the mighty one who hath "come into existence within [thy] hand. (4) A god "hath been born [now that] I have been born; I see "and I have sight; I have my existence; I am lifted "up upon my place; [I have] done what hath been "decreed; (5) [I] hate slumber; I have endowed with "might the feeble one. He that dwelleth in the city "of Neṭet hath made cakes for me in the city of Pe, "and I have received [my form] in Ȧnnu, for it is "Horus who hath commanded (6) what shall be done "for his father the lord of winds (?), and the god Set "quaketh; he hath raised me up, and Tem hath raised "me up. O, I am the mighty one, (7) and I have come "forth from between the thighs of the company of the "gods. I have been conceived by Sekhet (8) and by "[Shes-]Khentet, and I have been brought forth at "the door of the star Sepṭ (Sothis), the foremost (?) one "who with long strides (9) bringeth along the celestial "path of Rā day by day. I have come to my habita-"tion (10) as prince of the North and South, and I rise "(*or* I am crowned) in the gate. Hail, thou of the (11) "double plumes who art called by the name of Mi-"shepes, I am the lotus (12) which shineth in the "Land of Purity and which hath received me and "which maketh my abode at the nostrils of the Great "Form, (13) I have come into the Lake of Flame, and "I have placed right and truth in the Place of Sin. "(14) I am the watcher of the *sesheru* garments, and "the watcher of the Uraeus on the night of the flood "of the Great one. (15) I rise like Nefer-Tem, who is "the lotus at the nostrils of Rā, when he cometh forth "from the horizon each day; and the gods are purified "at the (16) sight of the lady of the house Mut-"ḥetepeth, who is triumphant before the *Kas* and "who gathereth together hearts for Saau-ur, whom "(17) the god, Sȧa-Ȧmenti-Rā, holdeth (?). I have "come upon my seat before the *Kas*, and I have "gathered together hearts for Saa-urt, and I have "my being (18) as Sȧa whom Rā the god of Ȧmenti "holdeth (?); and the *tchetch* implement is with me. "I recite the mighty [words] which are in the heart "on the festival of the *Ȧnsi* garment, and I am Sa-"Ȧmenti(19)-Rā, the strong (?) of heart within the "hidden chamber of Nu."

CHAPTER CLXXV.

[From the Papyrus of Ani (Brit. Mus. No. 10,470, sheet 29).]

Vignette : The deceased and his wife standing, with hands raised in adoration, before the god Thoth, who is seated upon a pylon-shaped throne, and has the emblem of "life" upon his knees.

Text : (1) THE CHAPTER OF NOT DYING A SECOND TIME. Osiris, the scribe Ani, triumphant, saith :— (2) "Hail, Thoth! What is it that hath happened unto "the divine children of Nut? (3) They have done "battle, they have upheld strife, they have done evil, "(4) they have created the fiends, they have made "slaughter, they have caused (5) trouble ; in truth, in "all their doings the mighty have worked against the "weak. (6) Grant, O might of Thoth, that that which "the god Tem hath decreed [may be done]! And thou "regardest not evil, nor art thou (7) provoked to anger "when they bring their years to confusion and throng "in and push to disturb their months; for in all that "they have done (8) unto thee they have worked "iniquity in secret. I am thy writing palette, O "Thoth, and I have brought unto thee thine ink-jar. "I am not (9) of those who work iniquity in their "secret places; let not evil happen unto me."

Saith Osiris, the scribe Ani:—(10) "Hail, Tmu! "What manner [of land] is this into which I have "come? It hath not water, it hath not air; it is depth "unfathomable, (11) it is black as the blackest night, "and men wander helplessly therein. In it a man may "not live in quietness of heart; nor may the longings "of love be satisfied (12) therein. But let the state of "the shining ones be given unto me instead of water "and air and the satisfying of the longings of love, and "let quietness of heart be given unto me instead of "cakes (13) and ale. The god Tem hath decreed that "I shall see thy face, and that I shall not suffer from "the things which pain thee. May every god transmit "unto thee (14) his throne for millions of years. Thy "throne hath descended unto thy son Horus, and the "god Tem hath decreed that his course shall be among "the holy princes. (15) In truth, he shall rule over "thy throne, and he shall be heir of the throne of the "Dweller in the Lake of Double Fire. In truth, it "hath been decreed that in me he shall see his like-"ness, and that my face (16) shall look upon the face "of the lord Tem. How long then have I to live? It "is decreed that thou shalt live for millions of millions "of years, a life of millions of years. (17) May it be "granted unto me that I pass on unto the holy princes, "for indeed, I am doing away with all the wrong which "I did, from the time when this earth came into being "from Nu (18), when it sprang from the watery abyss "even as it was in the days of old. I am Fate (*or* "Time) and Osiris, and I have made my transforma-"tions into the likeness of divers (19) serpents. Man "knoweth not, and the gods cannot behold, the two-fold "beauty which I have made for Osiris, who is greater "than all the gods. I have given unto him (20) the "region of the dead. And verily, his son Horus is "seated upou the throne of the Dweller in the Lake of "Double Fire, as his heir. I have made him to have "his throne (21) in the boat of millions of years. "Horus is stablished upon his throne, [among his] "friends and all that belonged uuto him. Verily, the "soul of Set, which (22) is greater than all the gods, "hath departed. May it be granted that I bind his "soul in the divine boat (23) at my (?) will, and that "[he] may have fear of the divine body. O my father "Osiris, thou hast done for me that which thy father "Rā did for thee. May I abide upon the earth last-"ingly; (24) may I keep possession of my throne; may "my heir be strong; may my tomb and my friends who "are upon earth flourish; (25) may my enemies be "given over to destruction and to the shackles of the "goddess Serq. I am thy son, and Rā is my father. "(26) For me likewise thou hast made life, strength, "and health. Horus is established upon his throne. "Grant thou that the days of my life may come unto "worship and honour."

The remains of a much longer version of this Chapter have been found in the papyrus of "a scribe of the offerings of the King of the North and South," called Rā (see Lepsius, *op. cit.*, Bd. I. Bll. 198, 199), and from these we may see that the happiness of the deceased in the underworld was more fully described therein. No connected sense can, however, be given to this version, for the beginnings and ends of the lines of the text of the Chapter are wanting almost throughout. From the Rubric we learn that the Chapter was "to be recited over a figure of Horus made of lapis-lazuli which was to be laid upon the neck of the deceased," and that the performance of this ceremony was believed to be most efficacious in securing important benefits for the dead.

CHAPTER CLXXVI.

[From the Papyrus of Nu (Brit. Mus. No. 10,477, sheet 22).]

Vignette: This Chapter is without vignette.

Text: (1) THE CHAPTER OF NOT DYING A SECOND TIME. The Osiris Nu, the overseer of the house of the overseer of the seal, triumphant, saith :—

"That which I abominate is the land of the East. "Let me not enter into the torture chamber. Let "there not be done unto me any of those (2) things "which the gods hold in abomination, for behold [I] "have passed as a pure being through the *Mesqet* "chamber. And let the god Neb-er-tcher grant unto "me his glorious power on the day of burial (3) in the "presence of the Lord of Things."

RUBRIC: If [the deceased] know this chapter he shall become like a perfect *khu* in the underworld.

CHAPTER CLXXVII.

[From the Papyrus of Nebseni (Brit. Mus. No. 9900, sheet 18).]

Vignette: The deceased standing upright; pure water is being poured out before him, and offerings of linen garments are being made unto him.

Text: (1) THE CHAPTER OF RAISING UP THE *KHU* AND OF MAKING THE SOUL TO LIVE IN THE UNDERWORLD. The scribe Nebseni, the draughtsman of the Temple of Ptaḥ, the lord of piety who is in the favour of his god, saith:— (2)

"[Hail,] Nut,[1] Nut who castest thy father to earth "and settest (?) Horus behind him, his wings grow like "[those of] a hawk, and his plumes like (3) [those of] "him who seeth (?). His soul hath been brought unto "him, he is filled with words [of magical power], "and his place is decreed for him opposite to (4) the "stars of the heaven, for behold thou art a star of Nut "by thyself . . . Thou seest the scribe Nebseni, the "lord of piety, [in] happiness, (5) and giving his com-"mands unto the *Khus*; and behold, the divine Power "(*or* Prince) is not [among them], and thy . . . is not "among them, unless thou art among them. Thou "seest the chief Nebseni, the scribe (6) and draughts-

[1] For an original form of this text as found in the Pyramid of Unȧs, see Maspero, *Recueil de Travaux*, tom. IV. l. 361 ff.

"man of the Temple of Ptaḥ, in the form of a soul who "hath the horns of the cows Smamet and Ȧn-unser the "Black. [Hail,] children of Serȧt-Beqet, who have "sucked milk from (7) the four *Uaipu* cows (?), Horus "of the blue eyes cometh unto you; protect ye Horus "of the red eyes who is sick. Let not his soul be "turned back, (8) let his offerings be brought [unto "him], let the things which are for his benefit (?) be "carried to him; and let them come upon the shoulder "over the West. This only one advanceth to thee. "The God speaketh thy words . . . . . (9); the gods "make thy name to be triumphant before the gods, and "the company of the gods distinguish thee with their "hands. The God of the Field of the gods speaketh, "and thou gainest the power over the door of *Kas* in "their horizon; they unbolt (10) for thee their doors, "for they have a favour unto thee, and thou gainest "power over their shrines. The god [Seb and his "company of gods enter in], and they come forth "lifting on high (11) their faces, and they look "upon thee in the presence of the great god Ȧmsu ". . . . . . thy head . . . . thy head. I [make to] "stand up thy head [for thee], and thou hast power "thereover. His head diminisheth behind thee, but "thy head shall not diminish, and thou shalt not be "destroyed, and thou shalt do what thou hast to do "before men and before the gods."

CHAPTER CLXXVIII.

[From the Papyrus of Nebseni (Brit. Mus. No. 9900, sheet 19).]

Vignette: This Chapter has no vignette.

Text: (1) THE CHAPTER OF RAISING UP THE DEAD BODY, [OF GIVING SIGHT TO] THE EYES, OF GAINING POWER OVER THE EARS, OF STABLISHING (2) THE HEAD, AND OF PROVIDING THE FACE WITH THE POWER OF PROTECTION. The Osiris, the scribe Nebseni, the draughtsman of the Temple of Ptaḥ, the lord of piety, saith :—

"The Eye of Horus is presented unto thee, and it "feedeth thee with the food of offerings. Hail,[1] ye "who make the (3) labourers to rejoice and who raise "up the heart and purify the body, who have eaten the "Eye of Horus, thou Olive tree in Ȧnnu, (4) destroy ye "[what evil there is] in the body of [Osiris] Nebseni, "the scribe and draughtsman in the Temple of Ptaḥ. "O Osiris, let him not suffer thirst before his god, let "him suffer neither hunger nor thirst, and let the god "(5) Khas (?) carry them away, and let him do away "with his hunger, O thou that fillest, O thou that fillest "hearts. O chiefs who dispense cakes [and ale], O ye

[1] For a very ancient form of the text of this Chapter as found in the Pyramid of Unȧs, see Maspero, *Recueil de Travaux*, tome III. Unȧs, l. 166 ff.

"who have charge of (6) the water flood, command ye "that cakes and ale be given unto the Osiris Nebseni "even as Rā himself commanded this thing. And "moreover, Rā hath commanded those who are over "the abundance of the (7) year to take handfuls of "wheat and barley and to give them to him for his "cakes, for behold, he is a great bull; [these] shall ye "give to the Osiris Nebseni. O guardian of the five "cakes in (8) the divine house, three cakes are in "heaven before Rā, and two are upon earth before "the company of the gods; may he burst through "Nu, may he see, may he see! O Rā, be gracious "unto the scribe (9) Nebseni this day, be gracious. "The scribe Nebseni is as a lord of piety according "to the command of Shu and Isis, and he hath been "united (10) unto the piety of happiness before his "god. May [the gods] give cakes and ale unto the "scribe Nebseni, and may they prepare for him all "good and pure things (11) this happy day, things for "journeying and travelling, things of the Eye of Horus, "things of the boat (?), and all things which should "enter into the sight of the god. Thou shalt have "power over the water, and thou shalt advance to (12) "the table of offerings having cakes (?) and four "measures (?) of water. The Eye of Horus hath "ordered these things for the scribe Nebseni, and the "god Shu hath ordered the [means of] subsistence for "him, (13) [both] cakes and ale. Watch, O judges "of the form (?) of Thoth, watch him that lieth in "death. Wake up, O thou that dwellest in [Kenset]! "Grant thou offerings (14) in the presence of Thoth, "the mighty god, who cometh forth from Ḥāpi (*i.e.*, "the Nile), and of Ȧp-uat who cometh forth from "Ȧsert, for the mouth of Nebseni, the scribe and de- "signer of the (15) Temple of Ptaḥ, is pure. The "company of the gods offer incense to the scribe "Nebseni, and his mouth is pure, and his tongue "which is therein is right and true. That which "(16) the scribe Nebseni abominateth is filth, and he "hath freed himself therefrom even as Set freed him- "self [from it] in the city of Reḥiu, and he hath set "out [with] Thoth for heaven (17). O ye who have "delivered the scribe Nebseni along with yourselves, "let him eat of that whereof ye eat, let him drink of "that whereof ye drink, let him sit down upon that "whereon (18) ye sit, let him be strong in the strength "wherein ye are strong, let him sail about where ye "sail about; the scribe Nebseni hath drawn the net "together in the (19) region of Ȧaru, and he hath run- "ning water in Sekhet-ḥetep, and his offerings are "among [those of] the gods. The water of the scribe "Nebseni (20) is the wine of Rā, and Nebseni goeth "round about heaven and travelleth [therein] like unto "Thoth. It is an abomination unto the scribe Nebseni "to suffer hunger and not to eat, and it is an abomina- "tion unto him (21) to be thirsty [and not to drink]; "but sepulchral meals have been given unto him by "the lord of eternity, who hath ordered [these things] "for him. The scribe Nebseni was conceived in (22) "the night, and was brought forth in the daylight, and "those who are in the following of Rā, the divine an- "cestors, adore [him]. [The scribe Nebseni] was con- "ceived in Nu, and was brought forth in Nu, and he "hath come[1] and hath brought to you what he hath "(23) found of that which the Eye of Horus hath shed "upon the branches of the *Then* tree. The governor "of those in Àmenti cometh to him and bringeth to "him the divine food and offerings of Horus, (24) the "governor of Temples, and upon that whereon he doth "live the scribe Nebseni liveth also, and of that whereof "he drinketh doth the scribe Nebseni, the designer of "the (25) Temple of Ptaḥ, drink also, and facing his "offerings of cakes and ale is a haunch of meat "also. Osiris, the scribe Nebseni, is triumphant, and "he is favoured of Anubis (26) who is upon his "hill."

"Hail, scribe Nebseni, thou hast the form wherein "thou hadst thine existence upon earth, and thou livest "and renewest thy youth each day; thy face is un- "covered and thou seest (27) the lord of the horizon, "who giveth to thee sepulchral meals in thy hour and "in thy season of night. Horus hath avenged thee, "and he hath destroyed the jaw-bones (28) of thine "enemies; he hath shut in the doer of violence at the "mouth of his fortress."

[1] These words are added from the Pyramid of Unȧs, ll. 199, 200.

"Hail, scribe Nebseni, thou hast no enemies in Ḥet-"ur,[1] (29) and the scales balanced when thou wert "weighed therein, and the Hall wherein they were "belonged to Osiris, the lord of offerings of Åmentet. "And thou shalt enter in at will, and thou shalt see "(30) the Great God in his form, and life shall be given "to thy nostrils, and thou shalt triumph over thine "enemies."

"Hail, scribe Nebseni, what thou abominatest is (31) "iniquity. The divine lord of creation hath made "peace with thee on the night of silencing the weep-"ing. And sweet life, whereupon Thoth resteth, hath "been given unto thee from the mouth of the company "of the gods, (32) and thou dost triumph over thine "enemies, O scribe Nebseni. Thy mother Nut spreadeth "herself over thee[2] in her name of Shetet-pet, and she "maketh thee to be a follower (33) of the great god, "and to be without enemies, and she delivereth thee "from every evil thing in her name of Khnemet-urt, "the divine, mighty form who dwelleth among her (34) "children, O scribe Nebseni."

"Hail,[3] chief of the hours, ancestors of Rā, make ye "a way for the scribe Nebseni, the lord of piety, (35) "and let him pass within the circle of Osiris, the lord "of the life of the two lands, who liveth for ever. And

[1] *I.e.*, the "Great House," or the Hall of Judgment.

[2] This line is found on the cover of the wooden coffin of Men-kau-Rā (Mycerinus), Brit. Mus. No. 6647. See my *Papyrus of Ani*, p. xx.

[3] See the Pyramid of Unås, l. 399 f.

"let the scribe Nebseni, the draughtsman in the Temple "of Ptaḥ, the lord of piety, the happy one, (36) be in "the following of Nefer-Tem, the lotus at the nostrils "of Rā . . . . in the presence of the gods, and let "him see Rā for ever."

CHAPTER CLXXIX.

[From the Papyrus of Nu (Brit. Mus. No. 10,477, sheet 15).]

Vignette : This Chapter has no vignette.

Text : (1) THE CHAPTER OF ADVANCING FROM YESTERDAY AND OF COMING FORTH BY DAY; whereby he and his (2) members shall be provided with food. The overseer of the house of the overseer of the seal, Nu, triumphant, the son of the overseer of the house, Ȧmen-ḥetep, triumphant, saith:—

"Let my speech of yesterday be given [unto me]. I "come daily. I have come forth from the god of crea-"tion, (3) I am Sepes coming forth from his Tree, and "I am Nun coming forth from his might. I am the "lord of the *ureret* crown, and . . . . "the god Neḥeb-kau (4). I am Ṭesher who avengeth "his Eye. I died yesterday but I come to-day. The "mighty Lady who is the guardian of the door hath "made a way for me. I come forth (5) by day against "mine Enemy, and I have gained the mastery over "him; he hath been given over unto me, and he shall "not be delivered out of my hand. And he shall come "to an end before me in the presence of the [great] "divine sovereign chiefs [[1] who are in the underworld. "The first, great rank hath been given unto me by him, "along with the shade and form of the living gods; "and I have made [my] path . . . . . . Mine Enemy "hath been brought unto me, and he hath been given "unto me, and he shall not be delivered out of my "hand; the things which concern me have been ended "in the presence of the divine sovereign chiefs of] "Osiris (6) who is [clothed] in his apparel. And "behold, the governor of those in Ȧmenti . . . . . I "am the lord of redness on the day of transformations. "I am (7) the lord of knives, and injury shall not be "done unto me. I have made [my] path. I am the "scribe [who writeth down] the odorous things which "are in the sweet-smelling incense (?), and the things "which belong to the mighty Ruddy one have been "brought [to me], (8) and the mighty Ruddy one hath "been given to me. I have come forth by day against "my Enemy, I have brought him along, I have gained "the power over him; he hath been given unto me, "and he shall not be delivered (9) out of my hand. "He hath come to an end beneath me in the presence "of the divine sovereign chiefs, and I eat him in the

[1] The words in brackets are added from the Papyrus of Nebseni.

"great field on the altar of Uatchit; I have (10) "gained the mastery over him as Sekhet, the great "lady. I am the lord of transformations, for I have "the transformations of every god, and they go round "about in . . . me."

CHAPTER CLXXX.

[From a Papyrus at Paris (see Naville, *op. cit.*, Bd. I. Bl. 204).]

Vignette: The deceased kneeling in supplication before three gods.

Text: (1) THE CHAPTER OF COMING FORTH BY DAY, OF PRAISING RĀ IN ÅMENTET, OF ASCRIBING PRAISE UNTO THOSE WHO DWELL IN THE ṬUAT, OF OPENING UP A PATH FOR THE (2) PERFECT *KHU* IN THE UNDERWORLD, OF CAUSING HIM TO WALK, OF MAKING LONG HIS FOOTSTEPS, OF GOING IN AND COMING FORTH FROM THE UNDERWORLD, AND OF PERFORMING TRANSFORMA-

TIONS LIKE A LIVING SOUL. (3) The Osiris . . . . . triumphant, saith:—

"Rā setteth as Osiris with all the diadems (4) of the "divine *Khus*, and of the gods of Àmentet. He is the "One divine form, the hidden one of the Ṭuat, the "holy Soul at the head of Àmentet, Un-nefer, whose "duration of life (5) is for ever and for ever. Words "of praise are addressed to thee, [O Osiris,] in the "Ṭuat, and thy son Horus hath satisfaction in thee, "and he hath spoken [unto thee] the decree of words. "(6) Thou makest him to rise upon those who dwell in "the Ṭuat like a mighty divine Star, unto whom the "things which are his have been brought in the Ṭuat. "Thou travellest through it, O son of Rā, and comest "forth like Tem. (7) Words of praise are addressed "unto thee by those who dwell in the Ṭuat [which is] "the throne-chamber dear to thy Majesty, the King, "the Prince of Àuḳert, the mighty Ruler, [who is "crowned with] the *Ureret* crown, (8) the great God "whose seat is hidden, the Lord and Weigher of words, "and the Sovereign of his divine chiefs. And words "of praise are addressed unto thee by those who dwell "in the Ṭuat, and they have satisfaction [in] thee. "And words of praise are addressed (9) unto thee by "those who dwell in the Ṭuat, and the divine beings "who weep pluck out their hair for thee, and they "smite their hands together, and they praise thee, and "they cry out (10) before thee, and they weep for thee, "and they rejoice that thy soul hath glorified thy dead "body. The souls of Rā in Åmentet are exalted, and "in the zone (?) of the Ṭuat the souls . . . . (11) cry "out in their songs of exultation unto the souls of Rā "who dwelleth therein; the body and souls of the god "Tchentch dwell in the Ṭuat, and (12) his divine soul "resteth therein."

"Hail, Osiris, I am a servant of thy temple, and one "who dwelleth within thy divine house; and thou "utterest with command the words of the decree. "Grant thou that I may rise like a luminary among "the denizens (13) of the Ṭuat, and like a mighty star "unto whom in the Ṭuat the things which are his have "been brought. Let [me] journey through it [like] the "son of Rā, and let [me] come forth as Tem. Let me "have rest in the Ṭuat, (14) let me gain the mastery "over the darkness, let me enter therein, let me come "forth therefrom, let thy hands receive me, O Ta-tiunen, "(15) and let the Ḥetepu gods lift me up, O stretch ye "out your hands to me, for I, even I, [know your] "names. (16) Lead ye me along, praise ye me, O "Ḥetepu gods with your praises, for Rā rejoiceth over "the praises which are offered unto me (17) even as he "doth over those which are offered unto Osiris. I have "stablished for you your offerings, and ye have obtained "the mastery over your oblations, even as Rā hath com-"manded me [to do]. (18) I am the god Meḥiu and I "am his heir upon the earth, and I have made [my] "path. O ye Ḥetepu gods, grant ye that I may enter "into the Ṭuat, and let me make a way (19) into the "beautiful Àmentet. I have stablished the sceptre of "the god Saḥ and the *nemmes* crown for the god whose "name is hidden. Look ye, then, (20) O Ḥetepu gods, "and ye gods who are the guides of the Ṭuat, and grant "that I may receive my glorious might, and let me rise "like a luminary (21) above his hidden place, and "deliver ye me from the deadly stakes of those who "are chained thereunto. Chain ye me not unto your "(22) deadly stakes, and give ye me not over to the "habitation of the fiends who slay."

"I am the heir of Osiris, and I have received his "*nemmes* crown in the Ṭuat; (23) look ye upon me, then, "and let me rise like a luminary who hath come forth "from your members; and let me come into being like "my divine father (24) who is worshipped. Look ye "upon me, then, and rejoice ye in me, and grant that I "may rise up, (25) and that I may come into being like "him whose transformations were destroyed. Open ye "a way unto my divine soul, O ye who stand upon your "places. Grant ye that (26) I may rest in the beauti-"ful Àmentet, and decree ye for me a seat in front of "you. Open ye out to me your paths, and draw back "for me the bolts of your doors. (27) Behold, O Rā, "as thou art the guide of this earth, so let the divine "souls be [my] guides, and let [me] follow after the "gods. I am he who guardeth (28) his own pylon, and "[I am] led along by those who lead; I am he who "keepeth ward over his doors, and who setteth the gods "in their places; (29) I am he who dwelleth upon his "standard within the Ṭuat. I am the god Ḥenbi, the "guardian of the lands (?) of the gods; I am the "boundaries of the Ṭuat, (30) I am the god Ḥetepi "in Åuḳert. My offerings have been made in Åmentet "by the divine souls who dwell in the gods. (31) I "am the god Meḥ-ā-nuti-Rā. I am the hidden Bennu "bird; I enter in [as] he resteth in the Ṭuat, and [I] "come forth [as he] resteth (32) in the Ṭuat. I am "the lord of the celestial abodes and I journey through "the night sky after Rā. My offerings are in heaven "in the Field of (33) Rā, and my sepulchral meals are "on earth in the Field of Åaru. I travel through the "Ṭuat like the beings [who are with] Rā, and I weigh "(34) words like the god Thoth. I stretch myself at "my desire, I run forward with my strides in my spiritual form of (35) hidden qualities, and my transformations are those of the double god Horus-Set. I am "the president of the food of the gods of the Ṭuat, and "I give the sepulchral offerings (36) of the *Khus*. I "am the god of the Mighty Heart who smiteth his "enemies. Hail, ye gods and *Khus*, the ancestors (?) "of Rā, who follow after (37) the divine Soul which he "hath, lead ye me along as ye lead [him] along, and do "ye, who are the guides of Rā and who are leaders (38) "dwelling in the upper heaven, [guide me,] for I am "like unto the divine and holy Soul who is in Åmentet."

CHAPTER CLXXXI.

[From the Papyrus of Qenna (see Leemans, *Papyrus Égyptien*, T. 2, Pl. 16).]

Vignette : The deceased kneeling in adoration before three gods who are seated before a door; behind are a lion-headed and a vulture-headed god, each of whom has a serpent above his head.

Text : (1) THE CHAPTER OF ENTERING IN TO THE DIVINE SOVEREIGN CHIEFS OF OSIRIS, AND TO THE GODS WHO ARE GUIDES IN THE ṬUAT, (2) AND TO THOSE WHO KEEP WARD OVER THEIR GATES, AND TO THOSE WHO ARE HERALDS OF THEIR HALLS, (3) AND TO THOSE WHO ARE THE PORTERS OF THE DOORS AND PYLONS OF ÅMENTET; AND OF MAKING THE TRANSFORMATIONS LIKE (4) A LIVING SOUL; AND OF PRAISING OSIRIS AND OF BECOMING THE PRINCE OF THE DIVINE SOVEREIGN CHIEFS. The Osiris Qenna, triumphant, saith:—

"Homage to thee, O governor (5) of Åmentet, Un-"nefer, lord of Ta-tchesert, (6) O thou who art diademed "like Rā, verily I come to see thee and to rejoice (7) at "thy beauties. His disk is thy disk; his rays of light "are thy rays (8) of light; his *Ureret* crown is thy "*Ureret* crown; his majesty is thy majesty; his risings "are thy (9) risings; his beauties are thy beauties; the "terror which he inspireth is the terror which thou in-"spirest; his odour (10) is thy odour; his hall is thy "hall, his seat is thy seat; his throne is thy throne; "(11) his heir is thy heir; his ornaments are thy orna-"ments; (12) his decree is thy decree; his hidden "place is thy hidden place; his things are thy things; "(13) his knowledge (*or* powers) is thy knowledge; the "attributes of greatness which are his are thine; the "power (14) which protecteth him protecteth thee;[1] he "dieth not and thou diest not; he is not triumphed "over (15) by his enemies, and thou art not triumphed "over by thine enemies; no evil thing whatsoever hath "happened (16) unto him, and no evil thing whatsoever "shall happen unto thee for ever and for ever."

(17) "Homage to thee, O Osiris, son of Nut, lord of "the two horns, whose *Atef* crown is exalted, may the "*Ureret* crown be given unto him, along with sove-"reignty before the company of the gods. (18) May "the god Temu make terror of him to exist in the "hearts of men, and women, (19) and gods, and *Khus*, "and the dead. May dominion be given unto him in "Ȧnnu (Heliopolis); (20) may he be mighty of trans-"formations in Ṭaṭṭu (Mendes); may he be the lord

[1] Reading *măket-f măket-k*.

"greatly feared in the Ȧati; may he be mighty in "(21) victory in Re-stau; may he be the lord who is "remembered with gladness in the Great House; mȧy "he have manifold (22) risings like a luminary in Ȧbtu "(Abydos); may triumph be given unto him in the "presence of the company of the gods; (23) may he "gain the victory over the mighty Powers; may the "fear of him be made to go [throughout] the earth; "and may (1) the princes stand up[1] upon their sta-"tions before the sovereign of the gods of the Ṭuat, "(2) the mighty Form of heaven, the Prince of the "living ones, the King of those who are therein, and "the Glorifier of thousands in Kher-āḥa. The denizens "of heaven rejoice in him who is the (3) lord of the "chosen offerings in the mansions above; a meat "offering is made unto him in the city Ḥet-ka-Ptaḥ "(Memphis); and the 'things of the night' are pre-"pared for him in Sekhem (Letopolis). Behold, O "mighty god, thou great one of (4) two-fold strength, "thy son Horus avengeth thee. He doeth away with "every evil thing whatsoever that belongeth to thee, "he bindeth up in order for thee thy person, he "gathereth together for thee thy members, he col-"lecteth for thee thy bones, he bringeth to thee thy ". . . . . (5) . .; thou art raised up, then, O "Osiris, I have given unto thee thy hand, and I make "thee to stand up alive for ever and ever. The god

[1] What follows here is from the text given by Naville (*op. cit.*, Bd. I. Bl. 206).

"Seb directeth (?) thy mouth, the great company of the "gods protecteth thee, ... (6) . . . ., and they ac-"company thee unto the door of the gate of the Ṭuat. "Thy mother Nut placeth her hands behind thee, she "giveth thee strength, and she reneweth the power "which protecteth thee. (7) . . . . . births, thy two "sisters Isis and Nephthys come unto thee, and they "unite thee unto life, and strength, and health, and "thy heart rejoiceth before them; (8) . . . . . they ". . . in thee through love of thee, and they load thy "hands for thee with things of all kinds. All the gods "present unto thee provisions, and behold, (9) they "praise thee for ever. Happy art thou, O Osiris, for "thou art crowned, and art endowed with strength, and "art glorious; and thine attributes are stablished for "thee. Thy face is like that of Ȧnpu, (10) Rā re-"joiceth in thee, and he maketh himself to be a brother "to thy beautiful person. Thou sittest upon thy throne, "the god Seb maketh a libation for thee, and that which "thou wishest to receive is in thy hands in Ȧmentet. "(11) Thou sailest over the celestial regions each day, "thy mother Nut maketh thee to go forth on thy way, "and thou settest in life in Ȧmentet in the boat of Rā "each day, along with (12) Horus who loveth thee. "The protecting strength of Rā guardeth thee, the "words of might of Thoth are behind thee, and Isis "maketh strength to follow after thy person." (13)

"I have come to thee, O lord of Ta-tchesert, Osiris, "Governor of those who are in Ȧmentet, Un-nefer, "whose twofold existence is for ever and for ever. My "heart is right and true, my hands are pure, I have "brought (14) things unto their divine lord, and offer-"ings unto the god who made them. I have come and "I have advanced to your cities. I have done that "which was good upon earth, I have slain thine enemies "for thee like sacrificial oxen (15). I have slaughtered "for thee thy adversaries, and I have made them to fall "down [upon] their faces before thee. I am pure, even "as thou art pure; I have made pure for thee thy "festival; and I have . . . . . . (16) upon thine altar "to thy soul, and to thy Form, and to the gods, and to "the goddesses who are in thy train."

RUBRIC: (24) If this chapter be known [by the deceased] things of evil shall not gain the mastery over him, and he shall not be turned back from any of the doors of Åmentet; but he shall (25) go in and come out, and cakes, and ale, and all beautiful things shall be given unto him in the presence of those who dwell in the Ṭuat.

CHAPTER CLXXXII.

[From the Papyrus of Mut-ḥetep (Brit. Mus. No. 10,010, sheet 4).]

Vignette: The deceased lying upon a bier within a funeral chest or coffer; beneath the bier are three vases. At the foot stand Isis, Ḥāpi, and Ṭuamāutef, and at the head Nephthys, Mesthȧ, and Qebḥsennuf. In the upper and lower registers are a number of seated and standing man-headed and animal-headed deities who hold in their hands snakes, lizards, and knives.

Text: (1) THE BOOK OF STABLISHING OSIRIS FIRMLY, OF GIVING AIR TO THE STILL-HEART, WHILST THOTH REPULSETH THE FOES OF OSIRIS, who cometh there in his transformations, (2) and is protected, and made strong, and guarded in the underworld by the operation of the will of Thoth himself, and Shu setteth upon him each day. [Thoth saith :—]

"I am Thoth, the perfect scribe, (3) whose hands are "pure, the lord of the two horns, who maketh iniquity "[to be destroyed], the scribe of right and truth, who "abominateth sin. Behold, he is the writing-reed of "the god Neb-er-tcher, the lord of laws, (4) who giveth "forth the speech of wisdom and understanding, whose "words have dominion over the two lands. I am "[Thoth], the lord of right and truth, who trieth the "right and the truth for the gods, the judge of words "in their essence, whose words triumph over violence. "I have scattered (5) the darkness, I have driven away "the whirlwind and the storm, and I have given the "pleasant breeze of the north wind unto Osiris Un-"nefer as he came forth from (6) the womb of her who "gave him birth. I have made Rā to set as Osiris, "and Osiris setteth as Rā setteth. I have made him "to enter into the hidden habitation to vivify the (7) "heart of the Still-Heart, the holy Soul, who dwelleth "in Åmentet, and to shout cries of joy unto the Still-"Heart, Un-nefer, the son of Nut." (8)

"I am Thoth, the favoured one of Rā, the lord of "might, who bringeth to a prosperous end that which "he doeth, the mighty one of enchantments who is in "the boat of millions of years, the lord of laws, the "subduer of the two lands, (9) whose words of might "gave strength to her that gave him birth, whose word "doeth away with opposition and fighting, and who "performeth the will of Rā in his shrine."

"I am Thoth, who made Osiris to triumph (10) over "his enemies."

"I am Thoth who issueth the decree at dawn, whose "sight followeth on again after [his] overthrow at his "season, the guide of heaven, and earth, and the under-"world, (11) and the creator of the life of [all] nations "and peoples. I gave air unto him that was in the "hidden place by means of the might of the magical "words of my utterance, and Osiris triumphed over his "enemies. (12) I came unto thee, O lord of Ta-tcheser, "Osiris, Bull of Ȧment, and thou wert strengthened for "ever. I set everlastingness as a protection for thy "members, and I came [unto thee] having protection "(13) in my hand, and I guarded [thee] with strength "during the course of each and every day; protection "and life were behind this god, protection and life "were behind this god, and his *ka* was glorified with "power."

"The king of the Ṭuat, (14) the prince of Ȧmentet, "the victorious conqueror of heaven, hath the *Atef* "crown firmly stablished [upon him], he is diademed "with the white crown, and he graspeth the crook and "the whip; unto him, the great one of souls, the "mighty one of (15) the *Ureret* crown, every god is "gathered together, and love for him who is Un- "nefer, and whose existence is for everlasting and all "eternity, goeth through their bodies."

"Homage to thee, O Governor of those who are in "Åmenti, (16) who maketh mortals to be born again, "who renewest thy youth, thou comest who dwellest in "thy season, and who art more beautiful than . . . ., "thy son Horus (17) hath avenged thee; the rank (*or* "dignity) of Tem hath been conferred upon thee, O "Un-nefer. Thou art raised up, O Bull of Åmentet, "thou art stablished, yea stablished in the body of Nut, "who uniteth herself (18) unto thee, and who cometh "forth with thee. Thy heart is stablished upon that "which supporteth it, and thy breast is as it was "formerly; thy nose is firmly fixed with life and "power, thou livest, and thou art renewed, and thou "makest thyself (19) young like Rā each and every "day. Mighty, mighty is Osiris in victory, and he "is firmly stablished with life."

"I am Thoth, and I have pacified Horus, and I have "quieted the two (20) divine Combatants in their season "of storm. I have come and I have washed the Ruddy "one, I have quieted the Stormy one, and I have "filled (?) him with all manner of evil things." (21)

"I am Thoth, and I have made the 'things of the "night' in Sekhem (Letopolis)."

"I am Thoth, and I have come daily into the cities "of Pe and Ṭepu. I have led (22) along the offerings "and oblations, I have given cakes with lavish hand to "the *Khus*, I have protected the (23) shoulder of Osiris, "I have embalmed him, I have made sweet his odour, "even as is that of the beautiful god."

"I am Thoth, and I have come each day into the city "of (24) Kher-āḥa. I have tied the cordage and I have "set in good order the Măkhent boat, and I have "brought [it] [from] the East [to] the West. I am "more exalted upon my standard (25) than any god in "my name of 'He whose face is exalted.' I have "opened fair things in my name of Ȧp-uat (*i.e.*, Opener "of the road), and I have (26) ascribed praise and done "homage unto Osiris Un-nefer, whose existence is for "ever and for ever."

CHAPTER CLXXXIII.

[From the Papyrus of Hu-nefer (Brit. Mus., No. 9901, sheet 3).]

Vignette: (*a*) The deceased and his wife standing with hands raised in adoration; (*b*) Thoth, ibis-headed, standing upright and presenting symbols of "strength" and "life."

Text: (1) THE OSIRIS HU-NEFER, THE OVERSEER OF THE PALACE OF THE LORD OF THE TWO LANDS, TRIUMPHANT, PRAISETH OSIRIS AND ACCLAIMETH HIM, AND DOETH HOMAGE UNTO UN-NEFER, AND BOWETH

TO THE GROUND BEFORE THE LORD OF TA-TCHESERT, AND EXALTETH THOSE WHO ARE UPON HIS SAND, (2) saying :—

"I have come unto thee, (3) O son of Nut, Osiris, "Prince of everlastingness; I am in (4) the following "of the god Thoth, and I have rejoiced (5) at every "thing which he hath "done for thee. He "hath brought unto "thee sweet air (6) for "thy nose; and life and "strength to thy beau-"tiful face; and the "north wind which (7) "cometh forth from "Tem for thy nostrils, "O lord of (8) Ta-tche-"sert. He hath made "the god Shu to shine "upon thy body; (9) he hath illumined thy path with "rays of splendour; he hath destroyed (10) for thee "[all] the evil defects which belong to thy members by "(11) the magical power of the words of his utterance. "He hath made the two Horus brethren to be at peace "for thee; he hath destroyed the storm-wind and the "hurricane; he hath made the two Combatants to be "gracious unto thee and the two lands to be (12) at "peace before thee; he hath put away the wrath which "was in their hearts, and each hath become reconciled

"unto his brother. Thy son Horus is triumphant in "the presence (13) of the whole company of the gods, "the sovereignty over the world hath been given unto "him, and his dominion is in the uttermost parts of "the earth. The throne of the god Seb hath been "adjudged unto him, (14) along with the rank which "hath been founded by the god Temu, and which hath "been stablished by decrees in the Chamber of books, "and hath been inscribed upon an iron tablet according to the command (15) of thy father Ptaḥ-Tanen, "[when he sat upon] the great throne. He hath set "his brother upon that which the god Shu beareth up, "to stretch out the waters over the mountains, and to "make to spring up (16) that which groweth upon the "hills, and the grain (?) which shooteth upon the earth, "and he giveth increase by water and by land. Gods "celestial and gods terrestrial transfer themselves to "the service of thy son Horus, (17) and they follow "him into his hall, [where] a decree is passed that he "shall be lord over them, and they perform it straightway."

"Thy heart rejoiceth, O lord of the gods, thy heart "rejoiceth (18) greatly; Egypt and the Red Land are "at peace, and they serve humbly under thy sovereign "power. The temples are stablished upon their own "lands, cities and nomes (19) possess firmly the property which they have in their names, and we will "make to thee the divine offerings which we are bound "to make, and offer sacrifices in thy name for ever.

"(20) Acclamations are made in thy name, libations "are poured out to thy *ka*, sepulchral meals [are "brought unto thee] by the *khus* who are (21) in "their following, and water is sprinkled upon the "offerings (?) (22) upon both sides of the souls (23) "of the dead in this land; every (24) design which "hath been ordered for thee according to his (*i.e.*, Rā's) "commands in the beginning hath been perfected. (25) "Now, therefore, O son of Nut, thou art diademed as "(26) Neb-er-tcher is diademed at his rising. Thou "livest, (27) thou art stablished, thou renewest thy "youth, and thou art true and perfect; thy father Rā "maketh strong thy members, and the company of the "gods make acclamations unto thee. The goddess Isis "(28) is with thee and she never leaveth thee; [thou "art] not overthrown by thine enemies. The lords of "all lands praise thy beauties even as they praise Rā "when (29) he riseth at the beginning of each day. "Thou risest up like an exalted one upon thy standard, "thy beauties exalt the face [of man] and make long "[his] stride. (30) I have given unto thee the sove"reignty of thy father Seb, and the goddess Mut, thy "mother, who gave birth to the gods, brought thee "forth as the (31) firstborn of five gods, and created "thy beauties and fashioned thy members. Thou art "stablished as king, the white crown is upon thy head, "and thou hast grasped in thy hands the crook and "the whip; whilst thou wert in the womb, and hadst "not as yet come forth therefrom upon the earth, thou "wert (32) crowned lord of the two lands, and the *Atef* "crown of Rā was upon thy brow. The gods come "unto thee bowing low to the ground, and they hold "thee in fear; they retreat and depart when they (33) "see thee with the terror of Rā, and the victory of thy "Majesty is in their hearts. Life is with thee, and "offerings of meat and drink (34) follow thee, and that "which is thy due is offered up before thy face."

"Grant thou that I may follow in the train of thy "Majesty even as I did upon earth. Let my soul (35) "be called [into the presence], and let it be found by "the side of the lords of right and truth. I have come "into the City of God—the region [which existed] in "primeval time—with [my] soul, and with [my] double, "and with [my] *khu* to dwell in this land. (36) The "god thereof is the lord of right and truth, he is the "lord of the *tchefau* food of the gods, and he is most "holy. His land draweth unto itself every [other] "land; the South cometh sailing down the river "thereto, and the North, (37) steered thither by "winds, cometh daily to make festival therein ac-"cording to the command of the God thereof, who is "the lord of peace therein. And doth he not say, "'The happiness thereof (38) is a care unto me'? The "god who dwelleth therein worketh right and truth; "unto him that doeth these things he giveth old age, "and to him that followeth after them rank and honour, "and at length he attaineth unto (39) a happy funeral "and burial in Ta-tchesert."

"I have come unto thee, and my hands hold right "and truth, and my heart hath no crafty wickedness "therein. (40) I offer up before thee that which is "thy due, and I know that whereon thou livest. I "have not committed any sin in the land, and I have "defrauded no man of (41) that which is his."

"I am Thoth, the perfect scribe, whose hands are "pure. I am the lord of purity, the destroyer of evil, "the scribe of right and "truth, and that which I "abominate is (42) sin. "Behold me, for I am "the writing reed of the "god Neb-er-tcher, the "lord of laws, who giveth "forth the word of wis- "dom and understanding, "and whose speech hath "dominion over the two "lands. I am (43) Thoth, "the lord of right and "truth, who maketh the "feeble one to gain the "victory, and who aven- "geth the wretched and "the oppressed on him "that wrongeth him. I have scattered the darkness; "(44) I have driven away the storm, and I have "brought the wind to Un-nefer, the beautiful breeze

"of the north wind, even as it came forth from the "womb (45) of his mother. I have caused him to "enter into the hidden abode to vivify the heart of "the Still-Heart, Un-nefer, the son of Nut, Horus, "triumphant."

CHAPTER CLXXXIV.

[From the Papyrus of Uáa (see Naville, *op. cit.*, Bd. I. Bl. 210).]

Vignette: The deceased standing upright before Osiris, who wears the *Atef* crown, and holds in his hands the whip and crook, emblems of sovereignty and dominion.

Text: (1) The Chapter of being nigh unto Osiris.[1] [The Osiris Uáa, the overseer of the estates of Ȧmen, triumphant, saith :—]

[1] This Chapter contains about two short lines of text, of which only a few words have come down to us in a single copy; to make any connected sense of them is impossible.

CHAPTER CLXXXV.

[From the Papyrus of Sutimes (ed. Guieyesse and Lefébure, Paris, 1877, Pl. 1).]

Vignette: Osiris at the head of Àbṭu, the great god, Prince of eternity and Governor of Àmentet, enthroned within a shrine; he holds in his hands the whip and crook, emblems of sovereignty and dominion. Before the shrine, with hands raised in adoration, kneels the deceased, and on each side of it are two gods offering incense.

Text: (3) THE GIVING OF PRAISES UNTO OSIRIS, AND OF PAYING HOMAGE UNTO THE LORD OF ETERNITY, AND PROPITIATING THE GOD IN HIS WILL, AND DECLARING THE RIGHT AND TRUTH, THE LORD OF WHICH IS UNKNOWN. The Osiris Sutimes, the libationer and president of the altar chamber in the Àpts, the president of the scribes of the Temple of Åmen, triumphant, saith :—

"Homage to thee, O thou holy god, thou mighty "and beneficent being, thou Prince of eternity who "dwellest in thy abode in the *Sektet* boat, thou whose "risings are manifold in the *Ātet* boat, to thee are "praises rendered in heaven and upon earth. Peoples "and nations exalt thee, and the majesty of the terror "of him is in the hearts of men, and *khus*, and the "dead. Thy Soul is in Ṭeṭṭeṭ (Mendes) and the terror "of thee is in Suten-ḥenen; thou settest the visible "emblems of thyself in Ånnu and the greatness of thy "transformations in the double place of purification. I "have come unto thee, and my heart hath right and "truth therein, and there is neither craft nor guile in "my breast; grant thou that I may have my being "among the living, and that I may sail down and up "the river among those who are in thy following."

CHAPTER CLXXXVI.

[From the Papyrus of Ani (Brit. Mus. No. 10,470, sheet 37).]

Vignette : (1) Ani and his wife before a table of offerings adoring the god. (2) "Seker Osiris, the lord of the hidden place, the great god, the lord of the underworld," standing in a shrine. (3) The goddess Hathor, in the form of a hippopotamus, wearing upon her head a disk and horns; in her right hand she holds an unidentified object, and in her left the emblem of life. Before her are offerings, and behind her the cow Meḥ-urit, who may be identified with Hathor, looks forth from the funeral mountain. At the foot of the mountain is the tomb, and in the foreground grows a group of flowering plants.

Text : "Hathor, lady of Ȧmentet, mighty dweller in "the funeral mountain, lady of Ta-tchesert, daughter "(*or* eye) of Rā, dweller before him, beautiful of face in "the Boat of millions of years, the habitation (*or* seat) "of peace, creator of law in the boat (?) of the favoured "ones . . . .

In the versions of this Chapter given by Naville (*op. cit.*, Bd. I. Bl. 212) the deceased, sometimes accompanied by his wife, is seen standing in adoration before the hippopotamus and cow goddesses. The texts which occupy the upper portions of the scenes are longer than that given in the papyrus of Ani, part of which is manifestly corrupt, and though all of them are more or less fragmentary we learn from them that this Chapter is entitled, "The praise of Hathor, the mistress of Åmentet, and the paying of homage to Meḥurit." After reciting the titles of Hathor the deceased describes his devotion to the gods and the works which he did for them whilst he was upon earth, and having stated that he is innocent of offence, he entreats the goddess that he may have his existence among her divine followers, and that suitable offerings of all kinds may be made unto him in Åmentet.

Seker-Osiris. The hippopotamus of Hathor. Meḥ-urt, or Hathor, and the tomb in the funeral mountain.

CHAPTER CLXXXVII.

[From the Papyrus of Nu (Brit. Mus. No. 10,477, sheet 19).]

Vignette: This Chapter is without a vignette in the Papyrus of Nu.

Text: (1) THE CHAPTER OF ENTERING IN UNTO THE COMPANY OF THE GODS. The overseer of the house of the overseer of the seal, Nu, triumphant, saith:—

"Homage to you, O company of the gods of Rā, I "have come before you, I am in the following (2) of "Rā, I have made my way, and I have passed in among "you. Let not my hand be repulsed in whatsoever I "do this day."

CHAPTER CLXXXVIII.

[From the Papyrus of Nu (Brit. Mus. No. 10,477, sheet 19).]

Vignette: This Chapter is without a vignette in the Papyrus of Nu.

Text: (1) [THE CHAPTER OF] THE GOING IN OF THE SOUL TO BUILD AN ABODE AND TO COME FORTH BY DAY IN HUMAN FORM. (2) The overseer of the house of the overseer of the seal, Nu, triumphant, the son of the overseer of the house, Åmen-ḥetep, [triumphant,] saith :—

"[Come] in peace! Thou hast a *khu*. Enter [thou] "in peace into the divine Utchat! Behold, thou hast "a *khu*, together with a soul (*ba*) and a shade (*khaibit*), "to look (3) thereupon. May it behold [me], when I "am judged, in whatever place it may be, with my "attributes, and with my form, and with my faculties "(4) of mind, and with all my attributes ordered and "perfect, even as a soul which is provided [with all "things] and is divine. May I shine like Rā in his "divine splendour (5) in the temple of . . . . . and "may [my] soul and my shade come [to me] upon their "legs from the place where I am judged, and behold "me. (6) May I stand up, and sit down, and enter "into the house of his body, which, behold, hath "become one of the starry gods of Osiris (7) who "travel by day, and journey by night, and celebrate "the festivals."

CHAPTER CLXXXIX.

[From the Papyrus of Nu (Brit. Mus. No. 10,477, sheet 19).]

Vignette: This Chapter is without a vignette in the Papyrus of Nu.

Text: (1) THE CHAPTER OF NOT LETTING A MAN PERFORM A JOURNEY (2) BEING HUNGRY (?), AND OF NOT LETTING HIM EAT FILTH. The overseer of the house of the overseer of the seal, Nu, triumphant, the son of the overseer of the house, Ȧmen-ḥetep, triumphant, saith:—

"The things which are an abomination unto me, the "things which are an abomination unto me, I will not "eat. What I abominate (3) is filth, and I will not "eat thereof [in the place of] the sepulchral cakes "[which are offered unto] the *Kas*. Let [me] not be "thrown down upon it, let it not light upon my body, "let it not enter into my fingers, (4) and let it not "join itself unto my toes. Thou shalt live, then, upon "that which the gods and the Khus decree for me in "this place and upon that which is brought unto thee "there. Let me live upon the (5) seven cakes which "shall be brought unto me, four cakes before Horus, "and three cakes before Thoth. The gods and the "*Khus* shall say unto me, 'What manner of food "wouldst thou have given unto thee?' [And I reply,

"'Let me eat (6) my food beneath the sycamore tree of "the goddess Hathor, and let my times be among the "divine beings who have alighted thereon. Let me "have the power to order my own fields in Ṭaṭṭu and "[my own] growing crops (7) in Ȧnnu. Let me live "upon bread made of white barley, and let my beer be "[made] from red grain; and may the persons of my "father and mother be given unto me as (8) guardians "of my door and for the ordering of the divine terri-"tory. Let me be sound and strong, let me have a "large room, let me make a way, let me have my seat "wherever I please, like a living soul, (9) and let me "never be kept in restraint by mine enemy.'"

"That which is an abomination unto me is filth and "I will not eat thereof; let me never pass over filth "and offal in Annu, but let it depart from me. (10) I "am the Bull who ordereth his habitation. I fly like "the mighty one, I cackle like the *smen* goose, and I "alight upon the beautiful (11) sycamore which standeth "in the Lake of Aḳeb. I come forth and I alight upon "it; he who alighteth there in the form of the great "god shall not be driven away therefrom. The (12) "things which I abominate I will not eat; the things "which I abominate, the things which I abominate are "filth and offal, and I will not eat thereof. The things "which are an abomination unto my *ka* are filth and "offal; they shall never enter into my body, (13) they "shall never come into my hands, and I will never "tread upon them with my sandals. O send ye not "forth against me foul water, harm ye not me (14) "with the rod, give ye not unto [me] . . . . . ., snatch "ye me not away from the edge of your deep cisterns, "and let me not depart from you being (15) overthrown. "The divine *Åukhemu* beings of the god Pen-ḥeseb (?) "shall say [unto me], 'Upon what wilt thou live in "this land whither thou art going, and wherein thou "wouldst be glorious?' [And I reply], 'I will live "upon (16) the cakes [made] of black grain, and upon "ale [made] of white grain, and upon four cakes in "Sekhet Ḥetep, which is more than [the food] of any "(*or* every) god. Moreover, I have four loaves of bread "during the course (17) of each and every day, besides "four loaves in Ȧnnu, which is more than [the food] of "any (*or* every) god.' And the divine *Åukhemu* beings "of the god Pen-ḥeseb (?) shall say [unto me], 'What "hast thou brought to eat (18) in that holy furrow?' "on that day when I receive my offerings with *ānti* "unguent. [And I reply], 'I will not eat thereof, it "shall not come into (19) my hands, and I will not "tread thereon with my sandals.' And the divine "*Åukhemu* beings of the god Pen-ḥeseb (?) shall say "unto me, 'Upon what wilt thou live (20) in this land "whither thou art going, and wherein thou wouldst be "glorious?' [And I reply], 'I will live upon the seven "cakes which shall be brought, four in the Temple of "Horus, and three in the Temple of Thoth.' (21) And "the divine *Åukhemu* beings of the god Pen-ḥeseb (?) "shall say [unto me], 'Who, then, shall bring them "unto thee?' [And I reply], 'The divine associate of "the temples of the *Urḥetchati* goddesses of Ȧnnu.' "[And they say], (22) 'Where wilt thou eat them?' "[And I reply], 'Beneath the beams of the beautiful "ark to which hymns are sung as it is borne along; "thither shall I be taken.' And the divine *Aukhemu* "beings of the god Pen-ḥeseb (?) shall say [unto me], "(23) 'Wouldst thou live, then, upon the things [which "belong to] another every day?' And I reply, 'I will "myself plough the fields of [my] estate in Sekhet-"Ȧarru.' And the divine *Ȧukhemu* beings (24) of the "god Pen-ḥeseb shall say [unto me], 'Who will protect "them for thee?' And I reply, 'The two divine "daughters of the divine king of the North, besides "those who belong to them' (?). [And the divine *Ȧuk-"hemu* beings of the god Pen-ḥeseb (?) shall say unto "me,] 'Who will plough (25) them for thee?' [And "I reply], 'The divine chiefs who dwell among the "gods of heaven and the gods of earth. The treading "down [of the earth] shall be done for me by the cow-"goddess Ḥāpiu who dwelleth in the city of Sau, (26) "and the harvest shall be reaped for me by Suti, the "lord of heaven and of earth.' Hail, ye who turn "back (?) the blossoms upon yourselves, ye whose "transgressions are done away with, whose faces are "holy, (27) behold, I am with the divine beings of Set "at the mountain of Bakhau, and I sit down along "with the spiritual bodies who are perfect (28) on the "side of the Lake of Osiris to rejoice (?) [my] heart.

"Shall not I make the overseer of the house of the "overseer of the seal, Nu, triumphant, to know "life?"

CHAPTER CXC.[1]

[From the Papyrus of Nu (Brit. Mus. No. 10,477, sheet 16).]

Vignette: This Chapter is without a vignette in the Papyrus of Nu.

Text: (1) THE BOOK OF MAKING PERFECT THE *KHU* WITHIN RĀ, OF MAKING HIM TO GAIN THE MASTERY BEFORE TEM, OF MAGNIFYING HIM BEFORE OSIRIS, OF MAKING HIM (2) TO BE POWERFUL BEFORE THE GOVERNOR OF AMENTET, AND OF CAUSING HIM TO BE MIGHTY BEFORE THE COMPANY OF THE GODS.

RUBRIC: This book shall be recited on the [first] day of the month, on the festival of the six, on the festival of Uaḳ, on the festival of Thoth, (3) on the birthday of Osiris, on the festival of Sekri, and on the festival of the night of Haker. [It will enable a man to pass through] the hidden places of the Ṭuat, and to penetrate the secret habitations of Neter-khert, to break through (4) mountains, and to open up a way through the secret valleys which are unknown. This chapter shall preserve (*or* embalm) the khu, it shall make broad his steps, it shall give him [power to] walk, it shall destroy the (5) deaf-

[1] This Chapter may be merely the Rubric of the preceding Chapter in the Papyrus of Nu to which a title has been given; it is only printed here for the sake of convenience.

ness of his face, and it shall enable him to make a way for his face with the god. When thou recitest [this chapter] thou shalt not let any man whatsoever see thee except him that is indeed dear to thy heart and the priest who readeth the service (*kher heb*), (6) thou shalt not let any other person see [thee], and no servant shall come outside [the chamber wherein thou art]. Thou shalt recite [this chapter] inside a chamber [lined] with cloth decorated (*literally*, shot) with stars throughout. The soul of every khu (*i.e.*, the deceased) for (7) whom this book hath been recited shall come forth among the living, he himself shall come forth by day, and he shall gain the mastery among the gods and shall not be (8) repulsed by them. And these gods shall revolve round about him, and they shall acknowledge (*literally*, recognize) him, and indeed he shall be as the divine one among them. And he shall make thee to know the transformations which shall come to him in the light. (9) This book is indeed a very great mystery; and thou shalt never allow those who dwell in the papyrus swamps of the Delta (*i.e.*, ignorant folk) or any person whatsoever to see it.

APPENDIX.

A PRAYER FOR THE PRESERVATION OF A PYRAMID.

[From the Pyramid of Pepi II.]

663. O Temu-Kheperà, [when] thou hadst raised thyself on the *qaa* standard, and hadst shone as the "Great one in the place of shining" in Ḥet-ur in Ànnu, thou didst send forth water in the form of Shu, and didst spit in the form of Tefnut, and thou didst place thy hands behind them, and verily thy Ka existeth 664. in them. O Temu, place thou thy hands behind Pepi Nefer-ka-Rā, and verily the Ka of Pepi Nefer-ka-Rā [which is] in him shall flourish as long as eternity endureth.

O Temu, place thou thy protection over this Pepi Nefer-ka-Rā, [and] over this his pyramid, [and over] this work of 665. Pepi Nefer-ka-Rā, and guard thou it from every evil thing which might come to them for ever and for ever, in the same manner as thou throwest thy protection over Shu and Tefnut.

O Great Company of the Gods who dwell in Ànnu, Tem, Shu, Tefnut, Sab, Nut, Osiris, Isis, Set, and

Nephthys, ye children of Tem, 666. his heart (i.e., Tem's) was made large (or, was extended) when he brought you forth in your name of "Peṭ," and when his [number] "Nine" was on you. Now Temu shall protect this Pepi Nefer-ka-Rā, he shall protect this pyramid of Pepi Nefer-ka-Rā, he shall protect this work from all the gods, 667. and from all the dead (i.e., damned), and he shall guard them from every evil thing which might come to them for ever and ever.

O Horus, this Pepi Nefer-ka-Rā is Osiris, and this pyramid of Pepi Nefer-ka-Rā is Osiris, and this his work; behold thou, 668. let not be removed from him in his name of pyramid the long duration [which is] in thy name of "Ḥet-qem-ur," for Thoth hath put under thee the gods who go forth and who journey in the walled enclosure and in the "Fort of Horus," even as he did for thy father Osiris in his name of "Ḥet-ȧt," 669. for Horus hath given to thee the gods, and he hath led them for thee into the halls, and they shall illumine thy face for thee in the White Houses.

A PRAYER FOR THE PRESERVATION OF THE NAME.

[From the Pyramid of Pepi II.]

669. O Great Company of the Gods who dwell in Ȧnnu, grant ye that Pepi Nefer-ka-Rā may flourish. Grant ye that the pyramid of 670. Pepi Nefer-ka-Rā, this everlasting work, may flourish as flourisheth the name of Tem, the President of the Great Company of the Gods.

[As] the name of Shu, the Lord of the Upper Sanctuary, in Ȧnnu flourisheth, Pepi Nefer-ka-Rā shall flourish, and this his pyramid, this his work, 671. which is for ever and ever,[1] shall flourish.

[As] the name of Tefnut, the Lady of the Lower Sanctuary, in Ȧnnu endureth, the name of this Pepi Nefer-ka-Rā shall endure, and this his pyramid shall endure for ever and ever.

[As] the name of Sab flourisheth, the soul of the earth which is adored, the name of Pepi Nefer-ka-Rā shall flourish, 672. and this pyramid of Pepi Nefer-ka-Rā shall flourish, and this his work shall flourish for ever and ever.

[As] the name of Nut flourisheth in Ḥet-shenth (?)

1  = as long as eternity abideth.

in Ånnu, the name of this Pepi Nefer-ka-Rā shall flourish, and this his pyramid shall flourish, and this his work shall flourish 673. for ever and ever.

[As] the name of Osiris in Åbṭu (Abydos) flourisheth, the name of this Pepi Nefer-ka-Rā shall flourish, and this pyramid of Pepi Nefer-ka-Rā shall flourish, and this his work shall flourish for ever and ever.

[As] the name of Osiris Khenti-Åmenti flourisheth, 674. the name of this Pepi Nefer-ka-Rā shall flourish, and this pyramid of Pepi Nefer-ka-Rā shall flourish, and this his work shall flourish for ever and ever.

[As] the name of Set flourisheth in Nubt (Ombos), the name of this Pepi Nefer-ka-Rā shall flourish, and this pyramid of 675. Pepi Nefer-ka-Rā shall flourish, and this his work shall flourish for ever and ever.

[As] the name of Horus of Beḥuṭet flourisheth, the name of this Pepi Nefer-ka-Rā shall flourish, and this pyramid of Pepi Nefer-ka-Rā shall flourish, and this his work shall flourish for ever and ever. 676.

[As] the name of Rā of the horizon flourisheth, the name of this Pepi Nefer-ka-Rā shall flourish, and this pyramid of Pepi Nefer-ka-Rā shall flourish, and this his work shall flourish for ever.

[As] the name of Khenti-Maati of Sekhem endureth, the name of this Pepi Nefer-ka-Rā shall flourish, 677. and this his pyramid shall flourish, and this work of Pepi Nefer-ka-Rā shall flourish for ever and ever.

[As] the name of Uatchit in Ṭep flourisheth, the name of this Pepi Nefer-ka-Rā shall flourish, and this pyramid of Pepi Nefer-ka-Rā shall flourish, and this his **678.** work shall flourish.

Pepi Nefer-ka-Rā is Sab, the Erpā of the gods, and Tem, the President of the Nine gods, hath granted that the gods shall accede to (or, be at peace with) what he saith, and that the gods shall accede to all the things which this Pepi Nefer-ka-Rā hath said, **679.** which shall be good for him there [as long as] eternity endureth. Tem saith, "Pepi Nefer-ka-Rā is the Erpā of "those who dwell in Neṭu; he is the guardian of him "that goeth [and] of him that maketh an offering unto "him. O all ye gods, behold the gift cometh, the "offering cometh, even as these things **680.** which ye "have given and which ye have offered to Tem in "Ȧnnu. He crieth out to you, come ye and make "every good thing here for Pepi Nefer-ka-Rā for all "eternity. The king giveth a table of offerings to Sab, "who giveth a table of offerings of these chosen joints "of meat, and the things which appear at the word, "cakes, beer, and geese, **681.** to all the gods, that "they may grant that good things of every kind shall "be to Pepi Nefer-ka-Rā; that they may grant that "this pyramid of Pepi Nefer-ka-Rā shall flourish; that "they may grant that this work of Pepi Nefer-ka-Rā "shall flourish as long as he pleaseth, **682.** that is as "long as eternity endureth; that all the gods may "grant that this pyramid shall flourish greatly, and "this work of Pepi Nefer-ka-Rā; that they may be

"provided [with all things], and may have renown,
"and may have a soul, and may have a *Sekhem* (Power);
"**683.** that there may be given unto them a table of
"offerings [by] the king, bread, beer, oxen, geese,
"linen, and unguents; that they may receive their
"tables of offerings of the gods; that there may be
"chosen for them choice pieces of their oxen and
"geese; that their offerings may be made unto them;
"**684.** and that they may have possession of the *urert*
"crown with the Great and Little Companies of the
"Gods."

APPENDIX.

THE BOOK OF THE DEAD OF NESI-KHONSU, A PRIESTESS OF ÅMEN, ABOUT B.C. 1000.[1]

"This holy god, the lord of all the gods, Åmen-Rā, "the lord of the throne of the two lands, the governor "of Åpt; the holy soul who came into being in the "beginning; the great god who liveth by (*or* upon) "Maāt; the first divine matter which gave birth unto "subsequent divine matter![2] the being through whom "every [other] god hath existence; the One One who "hath made everything which hath come into exist-"ence since primeval times when the world was created; "the being whose births are hidden, whose evolutions "are manifold, and whose growths are unknown; the "holy Form, beloved, terrible, and mighty in his "risings; the lord of wealth, the power, Khepera "who createth every evolution of his existence, ex-

[1] A hieroglyphic transcript of the hieratic text of this remarkable document, together with a French translation, has been published by Maspero in *Les Momies Royales de Déir-el-bahari*, p. 594 f.

[2] Or, "the primeval *paut* which gave birth unto the [other] two *pautti*."

"cept whom at the beginning none other existed; "who at the dawn in the primeval time was Ȧtennu, "the prince of rays and beams of light; who having "made himself [to be seen, caused] all men to live; "who saileth over the celestial regions and faileth not, "for at dawn on the morrow his ordinances are made "permanent; who though an old man shineth in the "form of one that is young, and having brought (*or* "led) the uttermost parts of eternity goeth round about "the celestial regions and journeyeth through the Ṭuat "to illumine the two lands which he hath created; the "God who acteth as God, who moulded himself, who "made the heavens and the earth by his will (or heart)· "the greatest of the great, the mightiest of the mighty, "the prince who is mightier than the gods, the young "Bull with sharp horns, the protector of the two lands "in his mighty name of 'The everlasting one who "cometh and hath his might, who bringeth the re-"motest limit of eternity,' the god-prince who hath "been prince from the time that he came into being, "the conqueror of the two lands by reason of his "might, the terrible one of the double divine face, "the divine aged one, the divine form who dwelleth "in the forms of all the gods, the Lion-god with awe-"some eye, the sovereign who casteth forth the two "Eyes, the lord of flame [which goeth] against his "enemies; the god Nu, the prince who advanceth at "his hour to vivify that which cometh forth upon his "potter's wheel, the disk of the Moon-god who openeth "a way both in heaven and upon earth for the beau-"tiful form; the beneficent (or operative) god, who is "untiring, and who is vigorous of heart both in rising "and in setting, from whose divine eyes come forth "men and women; at whose utterance the gods come "into being, and food is created, and *tchefau* food is "made, and all things which are come into being; the "traverser of eternity, the old man who maketh himself "young [again], with myriads of pairs of eyes and "numberless pairs of ears, whose light is the guide "of the god of millions of years; the lord of life, who "giveth unto whom he pleaseth the circuit of the earth "along with the seat of his divine face, who setteth "out upon his journey and suffereth no mishap by the "way, whose work none can destroy; the lord of delight, "whose name is sweet and beloved, at dawn mankind "make supplication unto him the Mighty one of victory, "the Mighty one of twofold strength, the Possessor of "fear, the young Bull who maketh an end of the "hostile ones, the Mighty one who doeth battle with "his foes, through whose divine plans the earth came "into being; the Soul who giveth light from his two "Utchats (Eyes); the god Baiti who created the divine "transformations; the holy one who is unknown; the "king who maketh kings to rule, and who girdeth up "the earth in its courses, and to whose souls the gods "and the goddesses pay homage by reason of the might "of his terror; since he hath gone before that which "followeth endureth; the creator of the world by his "secret counsels; the god Kheperà who is unknown "and who is more hidden than the [other] gods, whose "substitute is the divine Disk; the unknown one who "hideth himself from that which cometh forth from "him; he is the flame which sendeth forth rays of "light with mighty splendour, but though he can be "seen in form and observation can be made of him at "his appearance yet he cannot be understood, and at "dawn mankind make supplication unto him; his "risings are of crystal among the company of the "gods, and he is the beloved object of every god; "the god Nu cometh forward with the north wind in "this god who is hidden; who maketh decrees for "millions of double millions of years, whose ordinances "are fixed and are not destroyed, whose utterances are "gracious, and whose statutes fail not in his appointed "time; who giveth duration of life and doubleth the "years of those unto whom he hath a favour; who "graciously protecteth him whom he hath set in his "heart; who hath formed eternity and everlastingness, "the king of the South and of the North, Àmen-Rā, "the king of the gods, the lord of heaven and of earth, "and of the deep, and of the two mountains, in whose "form the earth began to exist, he the mighty one, who "is more distinguished than all the gods of the first and "foremost company."

Àmen-Rā, the king of the gods, the great god, the beginning of what hath come into being, hath sent forth his great and holy edict for the deification of

Nesi-Khonsu, the daughter of Ta-ḥennu-Teḥuti, both in Åmentet and in Neter-khert . . . . . and he saith :—

"I deify Nesi-Khonsu, the daughter of Ta-ḥennu-"Teḥuti in Åmentet, and I deify her in Neter-khert; "I have granted that she shall receive water in Åmen-"tet and funeral offerings in Neter-khert. I deify her "soul and her body in Neter-khert, and I will not let "her soul be destroyed therein; nay, I deify her soul "in Neter-khert, [and I make it] like unto that of "every god and of every goddess who have been deified "therein, and like unto that of everything whatsoever "which hath been deified in Neter-khert. I have "granted that every god, and every goddess, and "every divine being, and every thing which hath been "deified shall receive her in Neter-khert; and I have "granted that all her kinsfolk (?) shall receive her "therein with a gracious reception; and I have "granted that every good thing, which cometh into "being with a man when he assumeth this form, "whether he be carried off into the underworld, or "whether he become deified, or whether every good "thing be wrought for him where he is, or whether he "be made to receive water and offerings, or whether he be "made to receive his cakes from those which those who "have been deified receive, or whether he be made to "receive his divine offerings from those which those "who have been deified receive, shall be done for her "so that it shall be with her."

Åmen-Rā, the king of the gods, the great god, the prince of that which hath come into being from the beginning, saith:—

"I cause Nesi-Khonsu, the daughter of Ta-ḥen-"Teḥuti-å, to make every kind of food and every kind "of drink which every god and every goddess who "have been deified in the underworld make; and I "cause her to make every good thing which is with "every god and every goddess who have been deified "in the underworld; and by means thereof I have "delivered my servant Pa-netchem from every evil "thing, and I will not let any of the calamities which "occur in the underworld fall upon Nesi-Khonsu to do "her harm; and I grant that her soul may come forth, "and that it may enter in according to its desire and "never be repulsed."

Åmen-Rā, the king of the gods, the great god, the prince of that which hath come into being from the beginning, saith:—

"I have gone round (*i.e.*, I have examined) the heart "of Nesi-Khonsu, the daughter of Ta-ḥen-Teḥuti-å, "and she hath done no evil thing against Pa-netchem, "the son of Åset-em-khebit. I have carefully exam-"ined her heart, and I have not let her attack his life, "and I have not allowed her to attack his life through "other folk. I have carefully examined her heart, and "I have not let her do any evil thing unto him such as "is done against a living man. I have carefully ex-"amined her heart, and I have not allowed her to do "by means of other folk any of the evil things which "are done against a living man."

Åmen-Rā, the king of the gods, the great god, the prince of that which hath come into being from the beginning, saith :—

"I have caused her not to seek to do any evil thing "which would cause death unto Pa-netchem, the son "of Åset-em-khebit. I have carefully examined her "heart and she hath done no evil thing unto him in "particular, nor any evil thing which could harm him "in general; she hath not worked against him by "means of any god or any goddess who has been "deified; nor by means of any male *khu* or of any "female *khu* who has been deified; and she hath not "worked against him by means of any kind of beings "whatsoever who work schemes and plans so that "beings of every kind may be obedient unto their "words. I have carefully examined her heart and "[see] that she hath sought that which was good for "him whilst he was upon earth; and I have caused "her to seek in every way to give him a long life upon "earth, and a life of health, and soundness, and power, "and strength, and might; and I have caused her in "every way to procure for him happiness wherever the "sound of his words was heard. I have caused her to "seek neither harm for him, nor anything which could "inflict an injury upon man, nor anything which could "cause evil to Pa-netchem, the son of Åset-em-khebit. "I have caused her not to seek any evil thing, or any "noxious thing which would induce death, or any "harmful thing like unto those things which make "the heart of man to tremble, or those which do "harm unto the men and women who were beloved "by Pa-netchem, nor unto him by making his heart "terrified at them by means of the evil words which "have been directed against them (the men and women). "I have caused all that concerneth the heart and soul "of Nesi-Khonsu to be in good case, that is to say, her "heart hath not been driven away from her soul; her "soul hath not been driven away from her heart; her "heart hath not been driven away from herself; Nesi-"Khonsu herself hath not been in any way driven back "with the repulse with which a being in her form—"that is to say a being who hath been deified in the "underworld, whatever its nature may be—is some-"times repulsed; and no evil thing whatsoever, such "as may be done unto the human being who is in a "state like unto hers, hath been done unto her. Nay, "but [I have given] all that could delight Nesi-Khonsu, "namely, that Pa-netchem might enjoy a very long life "along with might, and strength, and power; that his "life might not be cut short; that no evil thing of "any kind whatsoever, and none of the things which "do harm unto a man and strike terror into his heart "might come nigh him, or his wives, or his children, "or his brethren, or Ȧtaui, or Nesta-neb-ȧsher, or "Masahairthȧ, or Tchaui-nefer, the children of Nesi-"Khonsu, or the brethren of Nesi-Khonsu. And I "have caused that everything which would be of "advantage to Pa-netchem, and all that would be of "benefit to him in any way whatsoever and which "could happen to a man in his condition, and an "exceedingly long life for himself, and his wives, "and his children, and his brethren, may also come "to Nesi-Khonsu, and to her children, and to her "sisters."

Åmen-Rā, the king of the gods, the great god, the prince of that which hath come into being from the beginning, saith :—

"I grant that all things, of whatever kinds they "may be, which a man hath when he is in the state "in which Nesi-Khonsu is, and by which he is deified, "shall be possessed by her, and I grant that the "seventy addresses to Rā may be recited in my name, "so that her soul may not be destroyed in the under-"world."

Åmen-Rā, the king of the gods, the great god, the prince of that which hath come into being from the beginning, saith :—

"Every good word which can deify Nesi-Khonsu, "which will give her power to receive water and offer-"ings, and which shall be uttered or said before me by "any person whatsoever I will fulfil to the uttermost, "omitting nothing. Every good word which shall be "uttered before me on behalf of Nesi-Khonsu I will "fulfil at every season of the heavens when Shu "cometh forth, in such wise that none of the evil "things which can reach a person who is in the con-"dition in which she is shall touch her at any season "of the heavens, when Shu cometh forth from the "waters with his weapons and when day beginneth in "the sky. And I will utterly do away with the evil "effect of every word which may be spoken by any "person whatsoever of a being who is in the state in "which is Nesi-Khonsu, omitting nothing, at every "season of the heavens when Shu cometh forth from "the waters with his weapons and when day beginneth "in the sky."

Åmen-Rā, the king of the gods, the great god, the prince of that which hath come into being from the beginning, saith:—

"I have caused the seventy addresses to Rā to be "recited in my name, and I have not allowed any "single benefit which belongeth to a man who is in "the condition in which is Nesi-Khonsu to escape her. "And I have caused her to receive offerings, bread, "and ale, and unguents, and wine, and pomade, and "milk, and raisins (?); and I have caused her to re-"ceive all the benefits and all the good things which "a being who is in her condition and who is favoured "by me and who hath been deified can receive; and I "have caused her to share equally with every god and "every goddess every good thing whatsoever which "those who have been deified in the underworld re-"ceive; and I have caused her to receive her divine "offerings along with the gods."

Åmen-Rā, the king of the gods, the great god, the prince of that which hath come into being from the beginning, saith :—

"If the word by which the offering of Sekhet-Åaru "and of a field in Sekhet-Åaru is made is not one "which is good for the person who is in the condition "in which is Nesi-Khonsu, and it hath no effect, I my-"self will make unto her the offering of Sekhet-Åaru and "of a field in Sekhet-Åaru, when that which is beneficial "for her in this kind of offering shall come into being, "and it shall suffer no diminution thereof whatsoever."

Åmen-Rā, the king of the gods, the great god, the prince of that which hath come into being from the beginning, saith :—

"All good things which shall be spoken in my pre-"sence, saying, 'Let such and such things be done "for Nesi-Khonsu, the daughter of Ta-ḥennu-Teḥu-"ti-å,' I will perform for her, and they shall not be "lessened, and they shall not be abrogated, and nothing "therefrom shall be cut off at every season of the "heavens when Shu cometh forth. And, moreover, "she shall receive in abundance the choicest things "of all that is good for her, even as do every man "and every god who have been deified, and who go "forth and who come in, and who journey unto every "place as they please."

Åmen-Rā, the king of the gods, the great god, the prince of that which hath come into being from the beginning, saith :—

"As concerning all good things which have been "spoken in my presence, that is to say, 'Perform them "for Pa-netchem, the son of Åseṭ-em-khebit, my ser-"vant, and for his wives, and his children, and his "brethren, and his friends, and for those for whom "his heart is afraid lest evil come upon them': be-"hold, I will send forth my great and mighty and holy "word into every place that it may cause every good "thing to be with Pa-netchem, and his wives, and his "children, and his brethren, and all his friends, in "such wise that if any man shall omit to say, 'Let the "decree of Åmen-Rā, the king of the gods, the great "god, the prince of that which hath come into being "from the beginning, be performed,' I myself will "make that which the great god hath spoken to come "to pass."

BOOKS OF THE DEAD OF THE GRAECO-ROMAN PERIOD.

THE BOOK OF BREATHINGS.

PART I.

[From the Papyrus of Ḳerāsher (Brit. Mus. No. 9995, sheet 2).]

I. HERE BEGINNETH THE BOOK OF BREATHINGS.

(1) "Hail, Osiris Ḳerāsher, the son of Ṭashenȧtiṭ! "Thou art pure, and thy heart is pure. The fore-parts "of thee are pure, (2) thy hind-parts are cleansed, and "thy interior is made clean with *beṭ* incense and "natron; no member of thine hath any defect what-"soever. The Osiris Ḳerāsher, (3) the son of Ṭashen-"ȧtiṭ, hath been cleansed by means of the waters of "Sekhet-ḥetep (*i.e.*, Field of Peace) which is situated "to the north of Sekhet-Saneḥem (*i.e.*, Field of the "Grasshoppers). (4) The goddesses Uatchit and Nekh-"ebet make thee to be pure at the eighth hour of the "night and at the [eighth] hour of the day. Come, "then, O Osiris (5) Ḳerāsher, the son of Ṭashenȧtiṭ, "and enter into the Hall of Maāti. Thou art pure "from all offence and from (6) defect of every kind; "'Stone of Right and Truth' is thy name."

"Hail, [Osiris] Ḳerāsher, the son of Ṭashenātiṭ! Thou "enterest the Ṭuat (*i.e.*, underworld) (7) as one mighty "in purity. Thou art purified by the two Maāt god-"desses in the Great Hall. A libation hath been made "for thee in the Hall of Seb, and thy body hath been "made pure (8) in the Hall of Shu. Thou lookest "upon Rā when he setteth as Tem at eventide. Ȧmen "is nigh unto thee to give thee air, (9) and Ptaḥ like-"wise to mould into form thy members, thou enterest "the horizon along with Rā. They receive thy soul in "the Neshem boat of Osiris, (10) they make thy soul "divine in the House of Seb, and they make thee to "be triumphant for ever and for ever."

"[Hail] Osiris Ḳerāsher, the son of Ṭashenātiṭ! (11) "Thy name is made to endure, thy material body is "stablished, and thy spiritual body is made to ger-"minate; thou art turned back neither in heaven nor "upon earth. Thy face shineth before (12) Rā, thy "soul liveth before Ȧmen, and thy material body is "renewed before Osiris. Thou breathest for ever and "for ever, thy soul maketh offerings unto thee (13) "of cakes, and ale, and beasts, and feathered fowl, "and cool water in the course of each day; thou "comest, and it is triumphant. The flesh is upon "thy bones, (14) and thy form is even as it was upon "earth. Thou takest drink into thy body, thou eatest "with thy mouth, and thou receivest bread along with "the souls (15) of the gods. The god Anubis pro-"tecteth thee, and he maketh himself thy protector;

"thou art not turned away from the gates of the Ṭuat "(*i.e.*, underworld). Thoth, the most mighty (16) god, "the lord of Khemennu, cometh to thee, and he "writeth for thee the BOOK OF BREATHINGS with "his own fingers. [Then] doth thy soul breathe for "(17) ever and ever, and thy form is made anew with "life upon earth; (18) thou art made divine along with "the souls of the gods, thy heart is the heart of Rā, "and thy members (19) are the members of the great "god."

"Hail, Osiris Ḳerāsher, the son of Ṭashenȧtiṭ! "Ȧmen is nigh unto thee (20) to make thee to live "again. And the god Ȧp-uat (*i.e.*, the Opener of the "ways) hath opened up for thee a prosperous path. "Thou seest with thine eyes, thou hearest with thine "ears, thou speakest with thy mouth, (21) and thou "walkest with thy legs. Thy soul hath been made "divine in the Ṭuat so that it may make every trans-"formation; at thy will thou breathest with delight "[the odours] of (22) the holy Persea tree of Ȧnnu "(*i.e.*, Heliopolis). Thou wakest each day and seest "the rays of Rā. Ȧmen cometh to thee (23) having "the breath of life, and he causeth thee to draw thy "breath within thy funeral house. Thou appearest "upon the earth each day, and the BOOK OF BREATH-"INGS of Thoth (24) is a protection unto thee, for "thereby dost thou draw thy breath each day, and "thereby do thine eyes behold the beams of the divine "Disk. The goddess of Right and Truth maketh "speech on thy behalf before Osiris, (25) and her "writings are upon thy tongue. Horus, the avenger "of his father, protecteth thy body, he maketh thy soul "to be divine like those of all the gods."

II. (1) "The god Rā vivifieth thy soul, and the soul "of Shu uniteth the passages of thy nostrils."

"Hail, Osiris Ḳerāsher, (2) the son of Ṭashenȧtiṭ! "Thy soul draweth its breath in the place which thou "lovest. Thou art even as Osiris. Osiris the Governor "of those in Ȧmentet is thy name. (3) The water-flood "of the Prince cometh unto thee from Ābu (Elephan-"tine), and it filleth thy table of offerings with *tchefau* "food."

"[Hail] Osiris Ḳerāsher, (4) the son of Ṭashenȧtiṭ! "The gods of the South and of the North come unto "thee, and thou art led by them to the ends of the "countries of (5) millions of years. Thy soul liveth, "thou art in the following of Osiris, and thou drawest "thy breath in Re-stau; the strength which protecteth "thee (6) is hidden in the lord of Setet and [in] the "great god. Thy material body liveth in Ṭaṭṭu [and "in] Nif-urtet, and thy soul liveth in heaven (7) each "day."

"[Hail] Osiris Ḳerāsher, the son of Ṭashenȧtiṭ! the "goddess Sekhet hath gained the mastery over what "is baleful to thee, Ḥeru-āā-(8)ȧbu protecteth thee, "Ḥeru-sesheṭ-ḥrȧ maketh thy heart, and Ḥeru-maati "protecteth thy body," or as others say, (9) "thy "tongue. Thou art stablished with life, and strength, "and health, and thou art firmly seated upon thy "throne in Ta-tchesertet. Come, then, Osiris Ḳerāsher, "(10), the son of Ṭashenȧtiṭ, thou risest in thy form, "thou art arrayed in thine ornaments, thou hast firm "hold upon life, thou passest thy days (11) in health, "thou journeyest hither and thither, and thou drawest "thy breath in every place whatsoever. Rā riseth "upon thine abode even as Osiris; thou drawest thy "breath, (12) and thou livest through his rays. Ȧmen-"Rā-Ḥeru-khuti vivifieth thy *ka* (*i.e.*, double), and he "maketh thee to flourish by means of the Book of "Breathings. Thou (13) art in the following of "Osiris-Horus, the lord of the *Ḥennu* Boat; thou art "like the great god at the head of the gods. Thy face "liveth, O thou whose births are lovely; thy name "(14) blossometh each day. Thou goest into the most "mighty and divine Hall in Ṭaṭṭu; thou seest him "that is head of those in Ȧmentet during the Uḳa "festival. The odour of thee (15) is sweet like that of "the venerable ones [therein], and thy name is magni-"fied like those of the divine spiritual bodies."

"Hail, Osiris, Ḳerāsher, the son of (16) Ṭashenȧtiṭ! "Thy soul liveth through the Book of Breathings, "thou art united through the Book of Breathings, "(17) thou enterest into the Ṭuat and hast no enemy "therein. Thou art as a living soul in Ṭaṭṭu and "thou hast thine heart, which hath not departed "from thee. Thou hast (18) thine eyes, and they "open daily."

The gods who are in the train of Osiris speak unto Osiris Ḳerāsher, the son of Ṭashenātiṭ, (19) saying:—

"Thou followest Rā and thou followest Osiris, and "thy soul doth live for ever and ever."

The gods who dwell in the Ṭuat (20) of Osiris, the Governor of those in Āmentet, speak unto Osiris Ḳerāsher, the son of Ṭashenātiṭ, saying:—

"The gates of the Ṭuat are opened unto him, (21) "let him show himself in Neter-khertet. Verily, his "soul shall live for ever, he shall build habitations for "himself in (22) Neter-khertet, the god thereof shall "show favour unto his *ka*, and he shall receive the "BOOK OF BREATHINGS, and verily he shall (23) draw "his breath."

"May Osiris, the Governor of those in Āmentet, the "great god, the lord of Abydos, grant a royal oblation; "may he give offerings of cakes, (24) and ale, and oxen, "and wine, and *āqet* drink, and bread, and *tchefau* food, "and all beautiful things to the *ka* of Osiris Ḳerāsher, "(25) the son of Ṭashenātiṭ. Thy soul doth live, and "thy material body doth germinate by the command of "Rā himself; thou shalt never perish and thou shalt "never suffer diminution, III. (1) [but shalt be] like "Rā for ever and for ever."

"Hail, Usekh-nemtet, who comest forth from Ānnu, "the Osiris Ḳerāsher, the son of (2) Ṭashenātiṭ, hath "not committed sin."

"Hail, Ur-at, who comest forth from Kher-āḥa, the "Osiris Ḳerāsher, the son of Ṭashenàtiṭ, (3) hath not "done deeds of violence."

"Hail, Fenti, (4) who comest forth from Khemennu, "the Osiris Ḳerāsher, the son of Ṭashenàtiṭ, (5) hath "not committed slaughter (?)."

"Hail, Āmam-maat, who comest forth from the two "Qerti, the Osiris Ḳerāsher (6), the son of Ṭashenàtiṭ, "hath not plundered the possessions of the dead."

"Hail, Neḥa-ḥrà, (7) who comest forth from Re-stau, "the Osiris Ḳerāsher, the son of Ṭashenàtiṭ, (8) hath "not inflicted injury."

"Hail, Rereti, who comest forth from heaven, the "Osiris (9) Ḳerāsher, the son of Ṭashenàtiṭ, hath not "committed sins of . . . . of the heart."

"Hail, Maati-em-khet, (10) who comest forth from "Sekhem, the Osiris Ḳerāsher, the son of Ṭashenàtiṭ, "(11) hath not made revolt."

"Hail, ye gods who are in the Ṭuat, hearken ye "unto the voice of Osiris Ḳerāsher, the (12) son of "Ṭashenàtiṭ, and let him come before you, for there "is neither any evil whatsoever, nor any sin whatso- "ever (13) with him, and no accuser can stand [before "him]. He liveth upon Maāt, he feedeth upon Maāt, "and he hath satisfied (14) the heart of the gods by "all that he hath done. He hath given food to the "hungry, and water to the thirsty, and clothes (15) to "the naked. He hath made offerings to the gods, and "to the *Khus*, and no (16) report whatsoever hath been "made against him before the gods. O come, let him "enter the Ṭuat and not be repulsed; (17) come, let "him follow Osiris with the gods of the *Qerti*. Let "him be a favoured being among the favoured ones, "(18) and let him be divine among the perfect ones. "Come, let him live; come, let his soul live. Let his "soul (19) be received in whatsoever place it pleaseth, "and let him receive the BOOK OF BREATHINGS. (20) "Come, let him draw breath with his soul in the Ṭuat, "and let him perform (21) whatsoever transformations "he will along with those who are in Åmentet. Come, "let his soul go into every place where it would be, and "let it live upon earth for ever, and for ever, and for "ever."

THE BOOK OF BREATHINGS.

PART II.

[From a papyrus at Florence (Pellegrini, *Il libro secondo della respirazione*, Rome, 1904).]

I. 1. The Second BOOK OF BREATHINGS, which shall be placed under the head of the god, that it may be recited by the 2. Hathor Arisuiniat, whose word is *maāt*, the daughter of Tasheratetut, whose word is *maāt*.

I am Rā in his rising. I am **3.** Åtem in his setting. I am Osiris, governor of those who are in Åmentet by night and by day. Let your faces be turned towards me, O ye Gatekeepers of the Åmentiu gods, **4.** O ye Guardians of the Ṭuat, O ye Doorkeepers of Pa-Ḥennu. May Ånpu, the son of Osiris, [come] to me, **5.** the righteous Guardian of the Ṭuat.

Let your faces be turned towards me, O ye gods whose eyes are as sharp as knives, who are in the following of Osiris, **6.** ye gods who dwell in the Hall of the Maāti-gods, ye gods of the Hall of Sekhet-**7.** Åanru.

Let your faces be turned towards me, O Hathor, Mistress of those who are in Åmentet, and O Maāt, unto whom those who are in Åmentet make acclamations.

8. Let your faces be turned towards me, O all ye gods who are in the Ṭuat, ye gods who watch over Osiris.

I am your father Rā-Ḥeru-Khuti, **9.** from whom ye came forth in primaeval time.

I am Horus, the son of Isis, the son of Osiris, who is on his everlasting throne.

I am Horus the Great, **10.** the Lord of the South. Thoth hath the members of Rā to perform the act of union, and he hath placed Horus upon the throne of his father.

I am Horus of the Two Eyes, the Lord of the divine

staff, 11. whereby all the gods have been made to be victorious.

I am Horus, Lord of Sekhmit (Letopolis), Lord of . . . ., devourer of the enemies of 12. Ȧnnu (Heliopolis).

I am Thoth, the Lord of the words of the god, who giveth adoration to all the gods.

Let your faces be turned towards me, O ye Guardians of the Ṭuat, 13. I leave the desolation of the days and of the night; let, I pray, my soul come forth (or, appear) in the heavens with the divine Souls 14. of the great gods. Let me partake of the offerings with Ȧtem, and let me drink cool water from the river (?) in the House of the Prince 15. as doth the Aged Prince who is in Ȧnnu. Let me enter into Ȧnnu on the night of the offerings on the altar of the festival of the sixth day of the month, II. 1. with all the gods and goddesses of the South and of the North, and let me be like one of them. Let me enter 2. [before] Osiris Khenti-Ȧmentiu with the holy gods on the night of the festival of the divine Ḥennu Boat at the moment 3. of each day when my soul flieth upwards. Let me, I pray thee, enter in. Let me, I pray thee, come forth, [for] I am one of 4. them.

Hail, Thoth, let thy face be turned unto me. Make thou to be *maāt* my word against my enemies, just as thou didst make the word of Osiris to be *maāt* against 5. his enemies, in the presence of the great Tchatcha who dwell in Heliopolis, on that night of battle when the

6. Sebi fiend was slain, on the day wherein the enemies of Neb-er-tcher were destroyed; in the presence of the great Tchatcha who 7. dwell in Ṭeṭṭeṭ, on that night when the Ṭeṭ was set up in Ṭeṭṭeṭ; in the presence of the great Tchatcha who dwell in Sekhem, 8. on that night when the offerings were [placed] upon the altar in Sekhem; in the presence of the great Tchatcha who dwell in the city Pe-Ṭep, 9. on that night of the reception of Horus in the *Meskhent* of the gods, and of the stablishing Horus as heir 10. of the possessions of his father Osiris; in the presence of the great Tchatcha who dwell in the city of the Rekhti, on that night when Isis 11. lay down to watch and to weep for her brother Osiris; in the presence of the great Tchatcha who dwell in the ways of the 12. dead, on the night of making up the reckoning of those who are not to exist; in the presence of the great Tchatcha who dwell in Ȧn-ruṭ-f, on that night 13. of the Great Mystery of forms in Ḥet-Suten-ḥenen (Herakleopolis); in the presence of the great Tchatcha who dwell in Ṭeṭṭu, 14. on that night of the great festival of the ploughing up of the earth in Ṭeṭṭu; in the presence of the great Tchatcha who dwell in Re-stau, 15. on that night of the lying down of Ȧnep (Anubis) [with] his arms upon the things which were round about Osiris.

Hail, Lord of Splendour, Governor of the Great House, 16. let thy face be turned towards me. Give thou unto me my mouth that I may speak with it. Guide thou to me my heart at the moment of the Nebṭ

Fiend. Make thou for me my mouth that 17. I may speak with it . . . . . . with it in the presence of the Great God, the Lord of the Ṭuat, and let me not be turned back in heaven or upon earth III. 1. in the presence of the Tchatcha of every god and of every goddess.

I am the soul of Horus who quenched the fire when it came forth.

Hail, 2. Ptaḥ, father of the gods, let thy face be turned towards me. Open for me my mouth, open for me my two eyes, even as thou didst open the mouth and two eyes of Seker-Osiris 3. in the House of gold in the city of Ȧneb-ḥetch. Open for me my mouth with the iron instrument wherewith thou didst open the mouth of 4. the gods.

I am the son of Sekhet, the goddess who is seated at the western side of heaven. Make thou to flourish my name like [that of] Osiris, Governor 5. of Ȧmentet. Let me be distinguished at the head of the gods of the Two Companies of gods. Make thou to be for me my heart in the House of Hearts, and my heart-case in the House 6. of Heart-cases. Make thou my heart to rest for me upon its throne, and let my heart-case be stablished upon the things of power which protect it Give thou unto me my mouth that I may speak therewith, 7. and my legs that I may walk therewith, and my two arms that I may overthrow mine enemies. Let there be opened for me the doors of heaven and of earth, even as thou didst 8. open them for the gods and the goddesses. Grant that Ȧnep (Anubis) may open for me the pylons of the Ṭuat. Grant that I may be made 9. one of those who follow Osiris. Let the decrees which have been decreed concerning me [be found] in Ḥet-kau-Ptaḥ (Memphis) . . . . my body in Neter-Khertet. 10. Let it be granted unto me to do whatsoever my KA pleaseth in heaven and upon earth. Let it be granted to my soul to alight upon my body.

Hail, my heart, I am 11. thy lord; thou shalt not remove thyself from me any day; [this is] the decree of Tanenu, the Great. Hearken thou unto me, my own heart; thou shalt be in my body, and thou shalt not fall away (or, incline away) from me. 12. I am the being for whom were made the decrees in olden time (?) in Memphis whereby his heart was made to obey him, and the Two Divine Fighters (i.e., Horus and Set) in Ȧnnu shall not seize and 13. carry away my heart from me. I am that being for whom Ȧtem worked in olden time (?) under the holy Persea Tree in 14. Ȧnnu according to the decrees of Thoth himself. Let it be granted to me to have light within my eye, so that I may walk by night [as well as] by day, and let me see his radiance 15. every day.

O my heart, my divine mother! O my heart, my divine mother! O my heart-case, be stablished by the things which protect it. Let Ȧtem speak to me good [words]. Let my members be [made] anew, 16. and let Neḥebkamake them to be in a flourishing condition.

May he grant that I may travel over the earth [and] in the horizon of the sky, and may he grant that I shall never die in Neter-Khert.

IV. 1. He shall make my soul to be divine, he shall glorify my body (or, he shall make my body to be like that of a *khu*, i.e., spirit), and he shall revivify my members. The god Åtem shall place me on the 2. Boat of Rā, and he shall cause me to perform all the transformations which it shall please me [to make]. He shall give to me my mouth that I may speak therewith, and he shall make me to renew my life 3. like Rā every day. My health shall be the health of Rā, and the health of Rā shall be my health.

My hair is as the hair of Nu. My face is as the face of 4. Rā. My eyes are as the eyes of Hathor. My ears are as the ears of Åp-uat. My nose is as the nose of Ḥent-Sekhem. 5. My lips are as the lips of Ånep (Anubis). My teeth are as the teeth of Serqit. My neck is as the necks of Isis and Nephthys. My arms are as the arms of Ba-nebt-Ṭeṭṭu. 6. My body is as the body of Net, the Lady of Saïs. My backbone is as the backbone of the Lords of Kher-āḥa. 7. My body is as the body of Sekhit. My thigh is as the thigh of the Eye of Horus. My legs are as the legs of Nut. My feet are as the feet of Ptaḥ. 8. My toes are as the toes of the Living Uraei. There is no member in me which is without a god. Thoth maketh the passes of life over my members, and my flesh 9. is [filled] with life every day. I shall not be pinioned by my arms, and my hands shall not be put in restraint. My name shall endure for 10. millions of years, and I shall fly about in heaven and on the earth. The fear of me shall be in the body of the gods.

My father is Sebu, 11. and my mother is Nut. "Osiris, Governor of those in Åmentet," is my name. I am Horus, Governor of millions of festivals. 12. . . . . . . his secret place in every land.

I am the Great One, son of the Great One.

I am the Mighty One, son of the Mighty One.

I am Horus, the son of Rā.

I am 13. the Sekhem (Power) of my father Rā.

I am the Two Tchaui of Shu and Tefnut.

I am he who is born of Sebu and Nut.

I am the 14. Holy Soul who dwelleth in Thebes; Åmen is my name.

I am Thoth in every land.

I shall rise up like the king of the gods, and I shall never die in 15. Neter-Khertet.

Hail, all ye gods and all ye goddesses! let your faces be turned towards me. I am your lord, come ye therefore to me and be ye in my following. 16. I am your lord, and the son of your lord.

Let your faces be turned towards me. I am your father, I am in the following of Osiris. I shall stride over the heavens, 17. I shall open up a way for myself in the earth, I shall journey over the whole earth, and my steps shall be as the steps of the holy Spirits (KHU).

I am provided for millions of years, and "Rā-Ḥeru-khuti" is my name.

THE BOOK OF TRAVERSING ETERNITY.

[From a papyrus at Vienna (Bergmann, *Das Buch vom Durchwandeln der Ewigkeit*, Vienna, 1877).]

1. Hail, Osiris, divine father, prophet of Åmen-Rā, king of the gods, prophet of the goddess Bast, who dwelleth in Thebes, prophet of Khensu Pa-aru-sekheru in Thebes, the great one of the house (i.e., steward) of Khensu in Thebes Nefer-ḥetep, the fourth prophet of Åmen, who art over the secret of the god, libationer, MER-PER-PAUT-TAUI, the son of PASHEREĀSHKHET, divine father of Åmen-Rā, the king of the gods, born of TCHATHU, the lady of the house, the sistrum bearer
5. of Åmen-Rā! Thy soul liveth in heaven in the presence of Rā, thy *ka* (double) acquireth the divine nature with the gods, thy body remaineth permanent in the deep house in the presence of Osiris, and thy SĀḤU[1] becometh luminous among the Living. Thy

[1] The *sāḥu* was the luminous, translucent, transparent, and immaterial covering in which all the spiritual, intellectual, and mental members and faculties of a man arrayed themselves after the death of the material body; a useful rendering of the word is "spiritual body."

descendants flourish upon the earth in the presence of Sab, upon thy seat among those who live (on the earth), thy name is stablished (or, firm) in the utterance of those who have their being through the "Book of "traversing eternity." Thou comest forth by day, thou joinest thyself to the Disk **10.** (or, the god Åten) which floodeth thee with light, thy nostrils inhale the sweet breath of Shu, thy nose breatheth the full breath of the north wind, gentle breezes and zephyrs refresh thy throat, thou incorporatest life in thy body, thou openest thy mouth in speech to the Peḥti gods, thy words have power and vigour among the Spirits, thou eatest bread and thou imbibest ale, thy majesty maketh its appearance in the form **15.** of a Living Soul, thou openest thy two eyes and thou makest a passage through thy two ears, and thou seest and hearest with them, thy heart is stablished upon its seat, and the case of thy heart resteth upon its foundation, the organs in thy body are in the places where they should be, and the Divine Children (i.e., Ḳesthå, Ḥāpi, Ṭuamutef, and Qebḥsennuf) keep ward over them, thy two hands have power to grasp, and the soles of thy feet to walk, and thine arms are able to perform their work. Thou sailest easily through the air, thou hoverest in the **20.** shadow, and dost perform every act according to the dictates of thy heart. Thou risest in the sky and thy hand is not separated therefrom, thou descendest into the Ṭuat and art not repulsed therefrom. Thou treadest the way of the gods of the horizon, and thou makest thy seat with the divine beings of Åmenti. Thou journeyest round about the upper heaven in the following of the starry gods. Thou circlest about the night-sky face to face with their stars. Thou travellest therein under the 25. authority of the lords of the morning and evening horizons, and thou ministerest to those who are in the divine region of the earth. Thou unitest thyself to the god Ḥeḥ when he riseth in the early portion of the day, and to the god Tchetta when he entereth in at eventide, and thou passest [over] (or, on) this earth as a SÅḤU of air. Thou travellest on whatsoever way thou choosest, thou floatest down the river to Ṭaṭṭu, thou sailest up the river to Nifur, to the divine nomes which contain the burial [places] of Osiris. Thou embarkest in the Neshem Boat with the loyal and divine servants [of Osiris], advancing to thy seat in the Divine Boat, and thou 30. arrivest in port at the quay of the nome-city of Busiris. Thou journeyest about through the lands of the cities of Ḥapunebs, thou openest a passage on the road through the regions of the palace of Urtet, thy *ka* (double) passeth behind the doors of the upper heavens, thou marchest with long strides to the Lord of [the Land of] Silence, thou takest thy way to the Lord of the Land of Protection, thou liftest up thy legs in the Hall of Osiris, and thou goest about in the Hall of the Maāti, 35. thou approachest with the divine ministrants to see the Great God, the divine beings who lead thee along lead [thee] to the holy place, thou enterest into the Great House, thy feet not being turned back, and thou advancest to the Divine House without repulse. Thou drawest thy breath, O Osiris, in the double house of the Great One, in the [house of] gold, with those divine beings who dwell in Åmentet, and in the house of the lord of life, thou makest thy way through the doors of the gods of the QERTI, and thou becomest a companion of the divine beings who are at rest. The Master of the Throne (i.e., Anubis) saith, "Come! Come!" **40.** The Opener of the Books (i.e., Thoth) indicateth for thee a way, and the warders of the pylons say, "Put forth thy arm" (or, strengthen thy hand), and thou criest out to those who are over the Halls [of the Ṭuat]. Thou walkest over the domains of the House of twofold Stability, thou advancest over the land in the city of Ārq-ḥeḥ,[1] thou singest praises to Un-nefer, whose word is Maāt, in his hidden shrine, Fentch-f-ānkh-em-åbt-f,[2] and thou invokest Ṭeṭ of the city of Nifurtet in the body of his divine mother, the Holy Prince in Pa-år. **45.** Thou passest through the doors of the city of Uthesi-ḥeḥ, thou forcest a way for thyself on the roads in the Divine Ṭuat, thou lookest upon the KHU as he lieth upon his funeral couch, and the SĀḤU laid out upon his bier. Thou goest forth into the halls of the gods, and the princes, and the . . . . . . who are among the companies of the

[1] A shrine of Osiris at Abydos.

[2] The name of the shrine means, "His nose liveth in his dwelling."

gods, thou passest by the companies of the gods of the House of Sȧp, and the warders of the House of the Prince. **50.** There are given to thee life and power in Ḥet-Merithit, and the service book is recited for thee in the hidden house. Thy waking up (or, watch) is happy in Ḥet-Ȧsȧr of Ḥemaḳat, and thy body is in Ḥet-Ḥemaḳat. Thou makest thy appearance in the temple of the festival of the Great Ploughing of the earth, thou takest thy place at the pylon of the horizon, thou enterest the hall of Pa-shenthit, thou goest into Pa-ānkh-ȧrut in peace, thou seest the utterances **55.** which are demanded when a festival taketh place, thou watchest the ceremony of the work of the Ḥesep temple, unguent is given to thee on the hands of the god Nem in the shrine (?) of Neith in Ḥet-menennet, thou alightest upon the branches of the holy sycamore, and thou receivest the shadow [which falleth] from its leaves. Thou walkest through the central hall of the ancestor Seker when the god appeareth from his secret place, bandages are given to thee in the place of Ḥeb-ṭept, and the unguent *set-ḥeb* in **60.** Uatchit, and provisions are provided in abundance for thee in the house of books, and the things which are necessary for thee **61.** from the tree of the Double House of Life. Thou fliest into the shrines of the house of the gods **62.** of Ṭaṭṭu, thou wingest thy flight over the lands of Abydos, thou journeyest to the House of **63.** Horus-Set, thou smitest thine enemies in the House of Unnuitit, thou walkest **64.** to the Sanctuary of the Bull of the company of the gods, who performeth thy desire in the circle of his abode. **65.** Thine attributes are more remarkable than the pylon of Ḥet-ka-Ptaḥ (Memphis), thou walkest in the form of a soul (*ba*) in the House **66.** of the Ram-gods (Bau), thou travellest in the double Uarekh-Chamber in Ḥet- **67.** Mesnekht, thou enterest into the divine house of the Venerable Goddess, thou ascendest the staircase **68.** of Ḥet-Ḥebset, thy soul journeyeth into the Hall, **69.** are opened to thee the pylons of Tepḥut-Tchat, **70.** thou bowest thy head to the ground for the sake of the things of Khapkhap, the goddess Khenememtit giveth food in **71.** Åst-ḥeqet, the arms of the goddess Menqet [are stretched out] in Per-khut, thou sittest **72.** in the hall (?) of Ḥet-Ṭebutit with the Mābui gods, sealed up is the **73.** knife, the god Shai is vigorous in Ḥet-Meskhen-nekht **74.** by the side of the Åat gods, the writings are reckoned up, thou betakest thyself to walk outside the House **75.** of gold, thou unitest thyself to the earth at the seat of the holy house, thy duration of life is eternity, **76.** thy kingdom is everlastingness, thy *ḥenti* periods are unending, **77.** and thou renewest thyself for ever and for ever.

BOOKS OF THE DEAD OF THE ROMAN PERIOD.

FUNERAL TEXT OF HERTU.

[See Lepsius, *Denkmaler*, vi. 122, and Lieblein, *Que mon nom*, plate l. ff.]

I. 1. [This] concerneth the Osiris Hertu, whose word is law.

I am Rā in his rising. I am Åtem in his setting. I am Osiris Khenti-Åmenti by night 2. and by day. Let your faces be towards me, O ye doorkeepers of the Ṭuat, ye doorkeepers of Åmentet, ye doorkeepers of Per Ḥennu. 3. Let thy face be towards me, O Anubis, son of Osiris, thou just doorkeeper of the Ṭuat. Let your faces be towards me, O Hathor, Mistress of Åmentet, 4. and O Maāt, to those who rise up [before her] in Åmentet. Let your faces be towards me, O ye gods who dwell in the Hall of Sekhet-Åru. 5. Let your faces be towards me, O Hathor, Mistress of Åmentet, and O Maāt, to those who rise up [before her] in Åmentet. Let your faces be towards me, O ye gods of the Ṭuat, 6. all of you, [and] ye gods who keep watch over Osiris.

I am your father Ḥeru-khuti, from whom ye proceeded in primaeval time. I am 7. Horus, the son of Isis, the son of Osiris, who [sitteth] on the throne for ever. I am Ḥeru-uru (i.e., Horus the Elder), the Lord of the South, who gave pleasure to the members 8. of Rā, and who hath placed Horus upon the throne of his father. I am Horus of the Two Eyes, the giver of weapons (?), who made to be strong all the gods. I am 9. Horus, the Lord of Sekhem, the Lord of Per- . . . . . . [the destroyer of] the wicked in Ånnu.

I am Thoth, the Lord of divine words, who gave 10. a liturgy to every god. Let your faces be towards me, O ye guardians of the Ṭuat, and let me make to be empty things the hours of 11. the night.

Let, I pray, my soul fly upwards with the souls of the great gods. 12. Let me, I pray, gather together [my] things (i.e., offerings) with Åtem. Let me, I pray, enjoy cool drink offerings[1] in the House of the Prince, like the Aged 13. Prince in Ånnu. Let me, I pray, enter into Ånnu on the night [when] the offerings [are placed] on the altar, with 14. all the gods and the goddesses of the South and of the North, and let me be one of them. Let me, I pray, enter into Osiris Khenti-Åmenti, 15. with the holy gods on the night of the festival of the god of the Ḥennu Boat Let, I pray, my soul fly upwards daily. 16. Let me, I pray, enter in, and let [my soul] fly up as one of their souls.

O Thoth, let, I pray, tny face be towards me. Make

[1] Or, "Let me, I pray, cool myself in the Lake in the House of the Prince."

thou my word to be *maāt* against 17. my enemies, as thou didst make the word of Osiris to be *maāt* against his enemies, before the Sovereign Chiefs, who dwell in Ȧnnu, on the night of the fight to

II. 1. overthrow the Sebȧu fiend, on the day of the destruction of the enemies of Nebt-Tcher.

[O Thoth, let, I pray, thy face be towards me]. Make thou my word to be *maāt* against my enemies, 2. as thou didst make the word of Osiris to be *maāt* against his enemies, before the Great Sovereign Chiefs, who dwell in Ṭaṭṭu, on the night of setting upright the divine Ṭeṭ 3. in Ṭaṭṭu.

O Thoth, [let, I pray, thy face be towards me]. Make thou my word to be *maāt* against my enemies, as thou didst make the word of Osiris to be *maāt* against his enemies, before the Great Sovereign Chiefs, who dwell in 4. Sekhem, on the night of the offerings on the altar in Sekhem.

O Thoth, [let, I pray, thy face be towards me]. Make thou my word to be *maāt* against my enemies, as 5. thou didst make the word of Osiris to be *maāt* against his enemies, before the Great Sovereign Chiefs, who dwell in Pe and Ṭep, on the night of the conception of 6. Horus in the birth-place of the gods, and of the stablishing of the hands of Horus over the things of his father Osiris.

O Thoth, [let, I pray,] thy face be towards me. Make thou my word to be *maāt* against 7. my enemies, as thou didst make the word of Osiris to be *maāt* against his enemies, before the Great Sovereign Chiefs of the Lands of the Rekhti Goddesses, on the night of the 8. lying down of Isis, [and of her] watching her brother Osiris, and her weeping for him.

O Thoth, let, I pray, thy face be towards me. Make thou my word to be *maāt* against my enemies, 9. as thou didst make the word of Osiris to be *maāt* against his enemies, before the Great Sovereign Chiefs, who dwell in Ȧn-ruṭ-f upon his throne, on the night of the hidden 10. and great transformations (or, ceremonies) which are performed in Suten-ḥenen.

O Thoth, let, I pray, thy face be towards me. Make thou my word to be *maāt* against my enemies, as thou didst make the word of Osiris 11. to be *maāt* against his enemies, before the Great Sovereign Chiefs, who dwell in Ṭaṭṭu, on the night of the Great Festival of Ploughing in Ṭaṭṭu. 12.

O Thoth, let, I pray, thy face be towards me. Make thou my word to be *maāt* against my enemies, as thou didst make the word of Osiris to be *maāt* against his enemies, before the Great Sovereign Chiefs, 13. who dwell in Re-stau, on the night of the lying down of Anubis, [when] his hands were over the things [which were] behind Osiris.

O Lord of Light, 14. thou Occupant of the Great Throne, let thy face be towards me. Grant thou to me my mouth that I may speak therewith. Guide thou for me my heart at the moment [of wrath] of the Nebṭ Fiend, 15. and fashion thou for me my heart that I may speak therewith before the Great God of the Ṭuat. Let me not be driven forth from heaven and from earth in the presence of the Divine Sovereign Chiefs of every god 16. and every goddess.

I am Horus, who maketh to be extinguished the fire when it cometh forth.

O Ptaḥ, father of the gods, let thy face be towards me. Open thou for me my mouth,

III. 1. open thou it for me as thou didst make [to be opened the mouth of] Seker-Osiris in Ḥet-Nub (i.e., the House of Gold) in Ȧneb-ḥetch (Memphis).

I am the son of the goddess Sekhet, and I have my seat by the dweller in the Urtet region of the heavens. 2.

Make thou to flourish for me my name like the name of Osiris Khenti-Ȧmentiu, and distinguish thou me before the gods of the Divine Cycles. Make thou for me my heart in the house of hearts, and 3. my mind (?) in the house of minds. Make thou for me my heart to rest upon its throne, and let my mind (?) be stablished by means of its protective amulets. Give thou unto me my mouth for speech, 4. my legs for walking, and my hands to overthrow my enemies. Let there be opened for me the doors in the heavens and in the earth, even as thou hast done 5. for the gods and goddesses. Let, I pray, Anubis open for me the doors of the Ṭuat. Let me, I pray, be made one of the followers of Osiris, and let be written down 6. my commands in Ḥet-Ptaḥ-ka (Memphis). Let my Ka be in heaven and on the earth, and grant that my person (?) may alight on my body. I am the hearts of thy Lord (?); thou shalt not 7. depart from me any day, according to the decrees of Tanenu, the great god. Make thou for me my own heart. I am he for whom decrees are made in Ḥet-ka-Ptaḥ; 8. grant that they may be hearkened to by him that is in Neter-Khert. Let not my heart be carried away from me by the Fighter Gods (Āḥaiu) in Ȧnnu. I am he concerning whom Ȧtem maketh records 9. before him on the holy Acacia Tree which is in Ȧnnu in the writing of the god Thoth himself. Let light be placed in my two eyes that I may walk by night 10. [and] by day, and let me see his rays every day. My mind is stablished by means of (or, upon) its protective amulets.

O Ȧtem, declare unto me the beauty of my members a second time, and let Neḥebka 11. make them vigorous (or, fresh). May he grant that I may traverse the earth in the horizon of heaven. He will not permit me to die in Neter-Khert, he will make my soul to become like that of a god, he will make my body to become like that of a *khu*, 12. and he will vivify my members a second time.

Ȧtem hath granted me to be on the way of Rā, he hath granted that I shall make every transformation which I desire, he hath given me my mouth that I may speak with it, and he hath granted me to be 13. renewed like Rā every day. I am strong and Rā is strong; Rā is strong and I am strong.

My hair is of Nu. My face is of Rā. My eyes are of Hathor. 14. My ears are of Ȧp-uat. My nose is of Fent-Sekhem (or, Khent-Sekhem). My lips are of Ȧnpu. My teeth are of Serqet. My body resteth 15. upon its seat. My hands are of Ba-nebt-Ṭaṭṭu. My body is of Neith, Lady of Saïs. My backbone is of the Lords of Kher-Āḥau. 16. My belly is of Sekhet. My eyebrows are of the Eye of Horus. My thighs are of Nut. My legs are of Ptaḥ. The soles of my feet are of the Living Uraei.

IV. 1. There is not a member [of mine] without a god. Thoth protecteth my members, and my flesh possesseth perfect life. I come forth by day, 2. having been conceived by Sekhet and born of Nut. I am filled with [the strength of] the Utchat. I am the Ibis 3. which cometh forth from Ḥet-Ptaḥ-ka. Heaven is opened to me, and the earth is opened unto me. I have obtained the mastery over my heart. 4. I have obtained the mastery over my members. I have obtained the mastery over my mind. I have obtained the mastery over my hands (or, arms). I have obtained the mastery over my mouth. 5. I have obtained the mastery over my members and the things which belong to them. I have obtained the mastery over the things which appear at the word (i.e., offerings), [that is] beer, oxen, and geese. I have obtained the mastery over the water 6. from the depths of the river. I have obtained the mastery over my eyes on the earth. I have obtained the mastery over my eyes in Neter-

Khert. I live upon bread, **7.** and I have cool water to drink from Ḥāpi (the Nile). I stand up through bread. I sit down through milk. I drink wine. **8.** I create. I receive breath from the Erpuit goddesses.

I am the great god who cometh from Neter-Khert the rays of Rā, **9.** the breath of Åmen—I am they for ever. . . . . . Osiris, the Great God, the word Horus I-em-ḥetep, born of Mut-Menu (?). **10.**

O Rā, I am thy son. O Thoth, I am thine eyes. O Osiris, I am thy Power. O ye Lords of Khemennu (Hermopolis) I am thy heir, **11.** [and the heir] of Maāt.

O Horus, O Great Company of the Gods, O Little Company of the Gods, let, I pray, my name flourish in Thebes, as the **12.** name of Åtem, the Lord of Ånnu, flourisheth in Ånnu; as the name of Shu flourisheth in the Upper sanctuary in Ånnu; **13.** as the name of Tefnut flourisheth in the Lower sanctuary in Ånnu; as the name of Sab flourisheth in Ba-Shemaum; **14.** as the name of Nut flourisheth in Ḥet-Shennu; as the name of Osiris Khenti-Åmenti flourisheth in Abydos; **15.** as the name of Isis flourisheth in Nif-ur; as the name of Horus flourisheth in Pe; as the name of Uatchit flourisheth in **16.** Ṭep; and as the name of Nephthys flourisheth in Ånnu. Let me fly upwards, let fly upwards the soul of Osiris Hertu **17.** born of Mut-Menu, whose word is law, [and let him enjoy] breath for ever and for ever!

FUNERAL TEXT OF ÅNKH-F-EN-ḤETEMTI, AN UTCHEB PRIEST.

[From a papyrus in Cairo (Lieblein, *Que mon nom*, plate xvii. ff.).]

I. 1. [This] concerneth Osiris, the "divine father," the *utcheb* priest of the great god, Ånkh-f-en-ḥetemti, whose word is law, the son of Nes-Ptaḥ, 2. born of Thent-Ḥet.

I am Rā when he riseth. I am 3. Tem when he setteth. I am Osiris Khenti-Åmentiu by night, by day, 4. and during every hour of every day. I am the Ibis with the black head, the white belly (or, body), and the 5. lapis-lazuli (i.e., blue) back. I am he who maketh the book [to be] before him in the presence of 6. the Divine Lords of Ånnu.

Let your faces be towards me, O ye who are the doorkeepers of Åmentet, [and] ye 7. gods who guard the Ṭuat. I pray ye to let me go in, I pray ye to 8. let me come out, I pray ye to make me one of those who are with you.

Let thy face be towards me, O Ånpu, son of 9. Osiris, thou just doorkeeper of the Ṭuat. I pray thee to let me enter 10. into the Hall of Maāt, and I pray thee to make me one of those who are in the following of Seker. I am 11. as one of those with whom are "offerings the gift of the king." I am pure.

II. 1. Let thy face be towards me, O Hathor, Mistress of Åmentet, and thou goddess Maāt unto whom come those who are in Åmentet. I pray thee to let **2.** my soul fly into the region above, so that it may be face to face with the souls **3.** of the great gods, and also that it may descend and alight upon my body. I pray thee to let me have the cool waters **4.** from the Lake in the House of the Aged One, like the Great Aged One [who] is in Ånnu.

O Thoth, make thou my word to be *maāt*—let thy face be towards me—**5.** against my enemies, as thou didst make the word of Osiris to be *maāt* against his enemies before the great Tchatcha **6.** who dwell in Ånnu, on that night of weighing the . . . . . .; **7.** and before the great Sovereign Chiefs, who dwell in Ṭattu, on that night of the making to stand upright **8.** the divine Ṭeṭ in Ṭaṭṭu; and before the great Sovereign Chiefs, who dwell in Åbt (Abydos), on that night of **9.** the conception of Horus [in] the birth-place of the gods; and before the great Sovereign Chiefs, **10.** who dwell in the cities of Pe and Ṭep, on that night of making the word of Horus, the son of Isis, the son of Osiris, to be *maāt* **11.** against his enemies; and before the great Sovereign Chiefs, who are present at the great **III. 1.** festival of ploughing the earth in Abydos, on that night of the festival of Heker.

Let the **2.** hymns be repeated for Horus four times; let [the hymns] be repeated for Osiris Khenti-Åmenti (Un-Nefer), whose word is law, four times; **3.** let the hymns be repeated for my majesty four times.

O Thoth, turn thou thy face towards me! Let, I pray, 4. my name germinate (i.e., flourish) in Thebes, and in my own nome, for ever and ever, even as flourisheth the name of Åtem, 5. the Lord of Ånnu (Heliopolis) in Ånnu, and as flourisheth the name of Shu in Ment-ḥer[1] in Ånnu.

O Thoth, let, I pray, thy face be turned towards me! Let, I pray, my name flourish in Thebes, and in my own nome, for ever and ever,

6. even as flourisheth the name of Tefnut in Ment-kher[2] in Ånnu;

7. as flourisheth the name of Sabu (Ḳebu) in Shamauit;

8. as flourisheth the name of Osiris Khenti-Åmenti in Abydos;

9. as flourisheth the name of Isis in Nef-urti;

10. as flourisheth the name of Osiris, the Lord of Ṭaṭṭu and Lord of Åntchet, as [god of] the towns, and Sepṭ of the nomes;

11. as flourisheth the name of Horus in Ånnu;

12. as flourisheth the name of Uatchit in Ṭep;

13. as flourisheth the name of Nephthys in Ḥebt (Heliopolis);

14. as flourisheth the name of Isis in all the nomes;

15. as flourisheth the name of Ba-neb-Ṭaṭṭu; and

16. as flourisheth the name of Thoth, the Twice-

[1] I.e., the "Upper shrine."
[2] I.e., the "Lower shrine."

great, the great god, the Lord of Khemennu (Hermopolis).

IV. 1. Hail, Osiris, divine father, Utcheb priest of the great god, Ḥetemet, 2. whose word is law, the son of Nes-Ptaḥ, born of Thent-Ḥet!

Thy soul 3. liveth in heaven before Rā, and gifts are made unto thy Ka (Double) before the gods. 4. Thy Khu[1] and thy Sāḥu[2] are before the Beings of Light (Khu), and thy material body 5. is stablished in the Ṭuat before the Ka (Bull) of the Beings of Àmenti in thy beautiful name of . . . . . . The utterances of thy mouth 6. are thy hymns (?) . . . . . .[3] 7. . . . . . Behold, thou hast thy mourners. 8. . . . . 9. Thy life from the time when thou didst walk as a child [to the present], when these their offerings are made 10. to thy Ka, hath been defined by the Mistress of the Four Quarters of the Sky. Thy burial 11. is perfect, good, and permanent, and men make offerings to thy Ka at the west of Thebes 12. in the sight of thy city and of the Lady of the city. Thy sepulchre shall never be overthrown, 13. thy coffin shall never be broken to pieces, and thy body shall never be destroyed, 14. the worms shall never effect their work of destruction on thee, and thy sepulchre shall never be violated. [Thou] shalt find

V. 1. the entrance of the door of thy Great House

[1] I.e., the immortal soul.
[2] "Spiritual body."
[3] The text of lines 6–10 is corrupt.

in Åmentet (?). Thy soul shall receive offerings in accordance with the list thereof [made by] 2. the Royal Scribe, because the sepulchre of thy majesty is nigh unto his abode of light. Sennu cakes shall be 3. to thy Ka three times each day in accordance with the offerings [written down] on the tablet of the Ennu gods (i.e., Isis and Nephthys). 4. Their majesties shall come unto thee in the Divine Hall, and they shall applaud thy sepulture, 5. for thou hast been swathed (?) with understanding. [When thou] eatest there shall 6. take place in thee a transformation similar to that of the Bull with the two testicles.

Thy brother 7. is behind thee to perform ceremonies on behalf of thy soul, and thou shalt become glorious by reason of the beauty of thy face. 8. He shall provide offerings for thy majesty with the divine image of Rā 9. every tenth day. Thy hand shall not be repulsed when it entereth in to unite with the Land of Life, 10. to place things (i.e., offerings) and drink for its fathers and mothers. Thy nostrils 11. shall inhale breaths of wind with Khensu, and Shu, the great god in 12. Thebes, when he goeth up upon the water of Åat-Tchamutet regularly like Rā each day 13. bearing the daily food and the Sennu cakes of the Ḥetepti gods. Ḥeru-khuti shall illumine 14. thy face at his season every day. Thou shalt stand up in the funeral valley, 15. and thy hands shall [be raised] in praise of the Great Power, who is the Chief of all the gods. 16. The duration of thy life shall be for ever, and thy sovereignty shall be everlasting, and thy periods of one hundred and twenty years shall be endless.

FUNERAL TEXT OF TAKHERṬ-P-URU-ÅBT.

[From British Museum Papyrus No. 10,112.]

"Hail, Hathor Takherṭ-p-uru-åbt, triumphant, born "of Thent-nubt, triumphant. Thy soul liveth in "heaven before Rā, gifts are made unto thy *ka* before "the gods, thy spiritual body is glorious among the "Khus, thy name is stablished upon earth before Seb, "and thy body shall endure permanently in the Neter-"khert (underworld *or* tomb). Thy house is in the "possession of thy children and thy husband, who weep "as they follow thee when thou goest about therein "with thy children; and they are rewarded for what "they have done for thy *ka*. [They have given thee] "good and perfect burial, and they make offerings to "thy *ka* at the west of Thebes in the sight of the folk "of thy city and of the Lady of the Temples. The "beautiful Åmentet stretcheth out her hands to receive "thee according to the decree of the Lady of Abydos. "Thy tomb shall never be overthrown, thy swathings

[1] See Birch, *P.S.B.A.*, Vol. VII, p. 49; and Lieblein, *Que mon nom fleurisse*, p. 1.

"shall never be torn in pieces, and thy body shall never "be mutilated. The god Anubis hath received thee in "the land of the Hall of Double Maāt, and he hath "made thee to be one of those favoured and perfect "beings who are in the following of Seker. Thy soul "flieth up on high to meet the soul of the gods, and it "hovereth also over thy dead body which is in Àḳert. "Thou journeyest about upon the earth, thou seest all "that are therein, thou observest all the affairs of thy "house, and thou eatest bread, there having been per-"formed by thee transformations which are like unto "those of Baba. Thou goest to the city of Nif-urtet "at the festival of the altars on the night of the fes-"tival of Six, and at the festival of Ànep. Thou goest "into the city of Nif-urtet at the festival of the little "heat, and the festival of lifting up the sky. Thou "goest into the city of Ṭaṭṭu on the festival of Ka-ḥrá-"ka, on the day when the Ṭeṭ is set up. The breath "of the wind hath made thy throat to breathe with "Khensu and Shu, the mighty one, in Thebes; and "thou hast abundant offerings for thy *ka* every tenth "day with the living image of Rā in Thebes. Thy life "is for ever and ever, and thy sovereignty is for ever, "and thou shalt endure for an endless number of "periods of twice sixty years."

INDEX

INDEX

INDEX

INDEX

INDEX

INDEX

INDEX

PENGUIN CLASSICS

THE BOOK OF CHUANG ZHU
CHUANG ZHU

'Walk with Virtue and travel with the Tao, and you will reach the perfect end'

One of the great founders of Taoism, Chuang Tzu lived in the fourth century BC and is one of the most intriguing and entertaining of Chinese philosophers. He was firmly opposed to Confucian values of order, control and hierarchy, believing the perfect state to be one where primal, innate nature rules. *The Book of Chuang Tzu* perceives the Tao – the Way of Nature – not as a term to be explained but as a path to walk; a journey towards the edge of reality, and beyond to the world of nature. Radical and subversive, employing wit, humour and shock tactics, *The Book of Chuang Tzu* is concerned not with government but with life and growth of the individual spirit.

Martin Palmer's lyrical translation conveys the passion and tone of Chuang Tzu's writing, while his introduction places Chuang Tzu's ideas and terminology in context, and discusses his key themes. This edition also includes an Index to the text.

Translated by Martin Palmer with Elizabeth Breuilly
With an introduction by Martin Palmer

PENGUIN CLASSICS

THE EPIC OF GILGAMESH

'Surpassing all other kings, heroic in stature,
brave scion of Uruk, wild bull on the rampage!
Gilgamesh the tall, magnificent and terrible'

Miraculously preserved on clay tablets dating back as much as four thousand years, the poem of Gilgamesh, king of Uruk, is the world's oldest epic, predating Homer by many centuries. The story tells of Gilgamesh's adventures with the wild man Enkidu, and of his arduous journey to the ends of the earth in quest of the Babylonian Noah and the secret of immortality. Alongside its themes of family, friendship and the duties of kings, *The Epic of Gilgamesh* is, above all, about mankind's eternal struggle with the fear of death.

The Babylonian version has been known for over a century, but linguists are still deciphering new fragments in Akkadian and Sumerian. Andrew George's gripping translation brilliantly combines these into a fluent narrative and will long rank as the definitive English *Gilgamesh*.

'A masterly new verse translation' *The Times*

Translated with an introduction by Andrew George

read more

PENGUIN CLASSICS

THE ANALECTS
CONFUCIUS

'The Master said, "If a man sets his heart on benevolence, he will be free from evil" '

The Analects are a collection of Confucius' sayings brought together by his pupils shortly after his death in 497 BC. Together they express a philosophy, or a moral code, by which Confucius, one of the most humane thinkers of all time, believed everyone should live. Upholding the ideals of wisdom, self-knowledge, courage and love of one's fellow man, he argued that the pursuit of virtue should be every individual's supreme goal. And while following the Way, or the truth, might not result in immediate or material gain, Confucius showed that it could nevertheless bring its own powerful and lasting spiritual rewards.

This edition contains a detailed introduction exploring the concepts of the original work, a bibliography and glossary and appendices on Confucius himself, *The Analects* and the disciples who compiled them.

Translated with an introduction and notes by D. C. Lau

Penguin Classics

THE KORAN

'God is the light of the heavens and the earth …
God guides to His light whom he will'

The Koran is universally accepted by Muslims to be the infallible Word of God as first revealed to the Prophet Muhammad by the Angel Gabriel nearly fourteen hundred years ago. Its 114 chapters, or *surahs*, recount the narratives central to Muslim belief, and together they form one of the world's most influential prophetic works and a literary masterpiece in its own right. Above all, the Koran provides the rules of conduct that remain fundamental to the Muslim faith today: prayer, fasting, pilgrimage to Mecca and absolute faith in God.

N. J. Dawood's masterly translation is the result of his life-long study of the Koran's language and style, and presents the English reader with a fluent and authoritative rendering, while reflecting the flavour and rhythm of the original. This edition follows the traditional sequence of the Koranic *surahs*.

'Across the language barrier Dawood captures the thunder and poetry of the original' *The Times*

Over a million copies sold worldwide.

Revised translation with an introduction and notes by N. J. Dawood

PENGUIN CLASSICS

THE CONSOLATION OF PHILOSOPHY
BOETHIUS

'Why else does slippery Fortune change
So much, and punishment more fit
For crime oppress the innocent?'

Written in prison before his brutal execution in AD 524, Boethius's *The Consolation of Philosophy* is a conversation between the ailing prisoner and his 'nurse' Philosophy, whose instruction restores him to health and brings him to enlightenment. Boethius was an eminent public figure who had risen to great political heights in the court of King Theodoric when he was implicated in conspiracy and condemned to death. Although a Christian, it was to the pagan Greek philosophers that he turned for inspiration following his abrupt fall from grace. With great clarity of thought and philosophical brilliance, Boethius adopted the classical model of the dialogue to debate the vagaries of Fortune, and to explore the nature of happiness, good and evil, fate and free will.

Victor Watts's English translation makes *The Consolation of Philosophy* accessible to the modern reader while losing nothing of its poetic artistry and breadth of vision. This edition includes an introduction discussing Boethius's life and writings, a bibliography, glossary and notes.

Translated with an introduction by Victor Watts

THE STORY OF PENGUIN CLASSICS

Before 1946 … 'Classics' are mainly the domain of academics and students; readable editions for everyone else are almost unheard of. This all changes when a little-known classicist, E. V. Rieu, presents Penguin founder Allen Lane with the translation of Homer's *Odyssey* that he has been working on in his spare time.

1946 Penguin Classics debuts with *The Odyssey*, which promptly sells three million copies. Suddenly, classics are no longer for the privileged few.

1950s Rieu, now series editor, turns to professional writers for the best modern, readable translations, including Dorothy L. Sayers's *Inferno* and Robert Graves's unexpurgated *Twelve Caesars.*

1960s The Classics are given the distinctive black covers that have remained a constant throughout the life of the series. Rieu retires in 1964, hailing the Penguin Classics list as 'the greatest educative force of the twentieth century.'

1970s A new generation of translators swells the Penguin Classics ranks, introducing readers of English to classics of world literature from more than twenty languages. The list grows to encompass more history, philosophy, science, religion and politics.

1980s The Penguin American Library launches with titles such as *Uncle Tom's Cabin*, and joins forces with Penguin Classics to provide the most comprehensive library of world literature available from any paperback publisher.

1990s The launch of Penguin Audiobooks brings the classics to a listening audience for the first time, and in 1999 the worldwide launch of the Penguin Classics website extends their reach to the global online community.

The 21st Century Penguin Classics are completely redesigned for the first time in nearly twenty years. This world-famous series now consists of more than 1300 titles, making the widest range of the best books ever written available to millions – and constantly redefining what makes a 'classic'.

The Odyssey continues …